DISRUPTION, INNOVATION AND RE-ALIGNMENT IN UK CONSUMER LAW AND POLICY

This book sets out possible future directions for UK consumer law and policy.

After decades of EU-driven development, the continuous improvement of UK consumer law and policy has stalled since Brexit. Yet, there are major challenges, including the progressive digitalisation of the consumer environment, the need to reconcile sustainability with consumption, and the need for better crisis resilience, alongside more specific concerns such as better enforcement or subscription contracts. The disruption caused by Brexit demands a comprehensive solution to ensure that UK consumer law and policy remains current and robust rather than becoming moribund. It also presents an opportunity for realigning UK consumer law and policy towards more consumer-centric focus and to develop innovative solutions to contemporary consumer challenges.

With original contributions from leading consumer law scholars, the book shows how the UK could develop in response to both major and specific challenges. Topics include a historical perspective on consumer law, consumer law reform, the implications of Brexit, vulnerability, changing paradigms, challenges in the context of financial services and digital consumer law, and enforcement.

Disruption, Innovation and Re-alignment in UK Consumer Law and Policy

Edited by
Christian Twigg-Flesner
and
James Devenney

•HART•
OXFORD • LONDON • NEW YORK • NEW DELHI • SYDNEY

HART PUBLISHING

Bloomsbury Publishing Plc

Kemp House, Chawley Park, Cumnor Hill, Oxford, OX2 9PH, UK

1385 Broadway, New York, NY 10018, USA

Bloomsbury Publishing Ireland Limited, 29 Earlsfort Terrace, Dublin 2, D02 AY28, Ireland

HART PUBLISHING, the Hart/Stag logo, BLOOMSBURY and the Diana logo are trademarks of Bloomsbury Publishing Plc

First published in Great Britain 2026

A catalogue record for this book is available from the British Library.

A catalogue record for this book is available from the Library of Congress.

ISBN: HB: 978-1-50997-555-6
ePDF: 978-1-50997-557-0
ePub: 978-1-50997-556-3

Typeset by Compuscript Ltd, Shannon
Printed and bound in Great Britain

For product safety related questions contact productsafety@bloomsbury.com

To find out more about our authors and books visit www.hartpublishing.co.uk. Here you will find extracts, author information, details of forthcoming events and the option to sign up for our newsletters.

PREFACE

Consumer law in the UK is at a crossroads. For decades, the development of consumer law and policy in the UK was driven by European Union (EU) initiatives, often with the support of the UK Government. Following Brexit, this EU driver for advancing consumer law in the UK has diminished. Vague commitments to a 'high level of consumer protection' in the Trade and Co-operation Agreement aside,[1] the UK now is fully responsible for developing domestic consumer law. Already there are many challenges including digitalisation, sustainable consumption[2] and energy justice;[3] and there is also the need to learn from the implications of the COVID-19 pandemic. At the same time, new consumer issues might require further legislative, or non-legislative, action. After the UK's head-start in adopting legislation on digital content in the Consumer Rights Act 2015, the EU has not only caught up but rapidly overtaken the UK. This is in no small measure due to the fact that post-Brexit, the UK Government has failed to articulate a clear and comprehensive consumer policy.[4]

With all these challenges, and with no clear direction set by the Government, the purpose of this collection, which has emerged from a conference organised by the University of Warwick and the University of Reading, is to explore possible future directions for UK consumer law. Some of the chapters explore general themes whereas others explore more specific topics (such as the use of FinTech in the consumer field[5]), in order to chart possible future directions of consumer law. Yet, as Barnes and Wheeler[6] note in their chapter charting the social history of consumer law with particular reference to the role of academic scholarship, the future is, to some extent, influenced by the past. Moreover, as the unique insight provided by Goriely and Tyldesley demonstrates,[7] the path to new approaches can be long and often requires a 'coalition of allies'.

[1] The Preamble to the Agreement recognised the Parties' autonomy in respect of consumer protection generally but also noted a desire that the 'Agreement contributes to consumer welfare through policies ensuring a high level of consumer protection and economic well-being, as well as encouraging cooperation between relevant authorities'.

[2] Discussed by Vessio and Saintier in the context of the idea of the circular economy (ch 12).

[3] Discussed by Dodsworth and Saintier (ch 5).

[4] See G Howells and J Devenney, 'Developing product liability networks for AI systems in the medical context' (2025) 76 *Northern Ireland Legal Quarterly* 118, 120–21.

[5] See Hillman and Burgess (ch 9) and Miglionico (ch 8).

[6] ch 1.

[7] ch 2.

Contributors were asked to link their analysis to the (overlapping) themes of disruption, innovation and/or re-alignment. The term 'disruption' has, of course, been much-used (and sometimes over-used) in recent legal scholarship. Nevertheless, with some delineation, it can be a useful shorthand concept to assess the impact of a new development, or approach, on existing law and/or practice. Disruption might occur through developments in the marketplace such as, for example, the use of new technology for transacting;[8] and this may raise questions about the extent to which existing law can address the legal issues such developments might create. Importantly, not every such development necessarily entails *legal* disruption; rather, there has to be some feature of such a development which puts it beyond the limits of existing law. In order to establish such disruption, it is necessary to test novel legal issues against existing law (including by applying principles of statutory interpretation insofar as they can assist) to gauge whether there is a real gap. If this is established, then the conclusion that there has been a degree of legal disruption would be sound.

This then invites consideration of what needs to be done to respond:[9] adjustments to existing laws, or the development of entirely new, targeted laws. Roger Brownsword has developed two 'mindsets',[10] which he has labelled 'coherentism' and 'regulatory instrumentalism' respectively, to explain how we might think about the need to develop the law. Put in a simplified and binary way, a preference for adjusting existing laws essentially reflects a coherentist mindset, whereas the decision to develop laws that specifically address the new issues that have arisen, irrespective of their fit with existing laws, would reflect a regulatory-instrumentalist mindset.

Developing existing laws could entail amendments to legislation to broaden their scope as well as the creation of exceptions to established principles to better accommodate novel issues. In contrast, a decision to develop new laws would allow for a 'best solution' approach to providing clear laws for all of the novel issues which have been identified. If the latter approach is chosen, it would create new laws with a specific focus, but these may not be entirely isolated from existing laws. Consumer law as whole is an example of regulatory-instrumentalist thinking, with many targeted laws to tackle specific concerns arising in the context of consumer contracts – but consumer law and the common law of contract remain intertwined. A higher level of disruption[11] can occur in two ways: developing existing laws through permitting a new derogation (eg, departing from the strict offer-and-acceptance analysis for algorithmic contracts[12]) could eventually result in the derogation becoming the norm; alternatively, targeted laws might eventually be seen as the better solution beyond their intended target.

[8] See Twigg-Flesner (ch 10).

[9] See also Vessio and Saintier (ch 11).

[10] eg, R Brownsword, 'After Brexit: Regulatory-instrumentalism, Coherentism and the English Law of Contract' (2017) 34 *Journal of Contract Law* 139; Brownsword, *Law, Technology and Society* (Routledge, 2019) ch 8; and R Brownsword, 'Law Disrupted, Law Re-Imagined, Law Re-Invented' (2019) *Technology and Regulation* 10.

[11] C Twigg-Flesner, 'The Potential of the COVID-19 Crisis to Cause Legal "Disruption" to Contracts and Contract Law' in E Hondius et al (eds), *Coronavirus and the Law in Europe* (Intersentia, 2021).

[12] *cf* T Allen and R Widdison, 'Can computers make contracts?' (1996) 9 *Harvard Journal of Law & Technology* 26.

When we speak of 'disruption', we therefore mean more than simply the arrival of new development. That new development has, for example, to raise new legal questions/issues that cannot be resolved within existing laws. Yet, as Dodsworth and Saintier demonstrate,[13] *legal* disruption can also occur through reconceptualising legal doctrine (eg moving from a more instrumentalist[14] view of consumers to a more inclusive view of consumers).

Innovation, in its broadest sense, is a new idea or the introduction of something new. Innovation in law can be connected to the development of new, targeted, legal rules reflective of the regulatory-instrumentalist mindset. However, it can also be found where the existing approach of the law is overhauled to make the law work better, more efficiently, etc, in addressing familiar problems. For example, as Cartwright demonstrates,[15] some aspects of the enforcement powers in the Digital Markets, Competition and Consumers Act 2024 are genuinely innovative; although, as Cartwright as notes, it is too early to assess the real impact of this innovation. Innovation can therefore both be the creative response to tackling existing issues in a new (and arguably better) way or be prompted by the need to make new laws to address a novel issue.

Re-alignment can mean: (i) changing the way things are done already and to do them differently (in the same vein as a regulatory-instrumentalist response to novel issues and innovation); and/or (ii) changing or developing laws and policies to make them match those of somewhere else. A key example for re-alignment is the impact of 'Brexit' on consumer law. Here, re-alignment might drive a shift away from the way in which the EU continues to develop consumer law and set a new trajectory (with the eventual recalibration of the existing corpus of consumer law); and here Giliker[16] explores the emerging differences, despite their shared common law heritage, between the UK and Ireland post-Brexit. But it might also eventually lead to tracking EU developments more closely after the current period of aimlessness.[17] Further examples, and proposals, are discussed by Brown,[18] Lin,[19] Clubbs Coldron[20] and Flavian:[21] Brown explores the Financial Conduct Authority's (FCA) recent rebalancing of its approach to its objectives and the protection of the consumer; Lin continues the theme of regulatory re-alignment by the FCA, this time in the context of crowdfunding and financial consumers); Clubbs Coldron discusses re-alignment of consumer law with the United Nations Convention on the Rights of Persons with Disabilities (UNCRPD); whereas Flavian makes the case for aligning consumer collective actions to the collective action procedure under the Competition Appeal Tribunal in competition.

[13] c 12.

[14] On which see H Micklitz, 'The Consumer, Marketised, Fragmentised, Constitutionalised' in D Leczykiewicz, and S Weatherill (eds), *The Images of the Consumer in EU Law: Legislation, Free Movement and Competition Law* (Hart Publishing, 2016).

[15] ch 12.

[16] ch 4.

[17] See ch 3 by Geraint Howells, Chris Willett and James Devenney.

[18] ch 6.

[19] ch 7.

[20] ch 14.

[21] ch 13.

All in all, this collection of essays uncovers the multifaceted ways in which consumer law in the UK is dealing with disruption, innovation, and the need to re-align. We hope readers will find this collection insightful and thought-provoking.

We would like to thank Hart Publishing, and in particular Roberta Bassi and Verity Stuart, for all of their support, and patience, in seeing this project to completion. As always, we are indebted to the support of our partners, Paul and Claire, for their unfailing support.

Christian Twigg-Flesner and James Devenney
July 2025

CONTENTS

Preface .... *v*
Contributors .... *xi*

PART I
PAST DIRECTIONS OF CONSUMER LAW

1. *A Social History of Consumer Law, 1960–1980* *3*
   Victoria Barnes and Sally Wheeler

2. *Consumer Insurance Law Reform – Obstacles, Allies and Tactics* *17*
   Tammy Goriely and Peter J Tyldesley

PART II
FUTURE DIRECTIONS FOR CONSUMER LAW IN GENERAL

3. *The Acts and Scenes of the Brexit Consumer Law and Policy Melodrama* *43*
   James Devenney, Geraint Howells and Chris Willett

4. *Reforming Consumer Law in the Digital Market Post-Brexit: An EU–UK–Irish Divide?* *67*
   Paula Giliker

5. *Consumer Resilience and Vulnerable Energy Systems* *87*
   Timothy J Dodsworth and Séverine Saintier

PART III
FUTURE DIRECTIONS IN CONSUMER FINANCIAL SERVICES

6. *The New Consumer Duty in the Provision of Financial Services: A Re-alignment of the FCA's Approach to its Objectives and Protection of the Consumer?* *111*
   Sarah Brown

7. *Investment-Based Crowdfunding and Financial Consumers Protection: Realignment of FCA Financial Promotion Disclosure Rules* *131*
   Wangwei Lin

PART IV
FUTURE DIRECTIONS IN DIGITAL CONSUMER LAW

8. *The Quest for Protection of Vulnerable Consumers in Digital Financial Technologies*......145
Andrea Miglionico

9. *Cryptocurrencies and Consumer Protection:* Caveat Emptor......177
Henry Hillman and Thomas Burgess

10. *Digital Assistants and Consumer Law – Disruption or Innovation?*......197
Christian Twigg-Flesner

PART V
FUTURE DIRECTIONS IN OTHER AREAS OF CONSUMER LAW

11. *The (Servitised) Circular Economy: Are Consumers Truly Empowered?*......223
Monica Vessio and Séverine Saintier

12. *The 'Missing Link': Direct Enforcement, Monetary Penalties and Consumer Protection in the Digital Markets, Competition and Consumers Act 2024*......245
Peter Cartwright

13. *The Potential for the Expansion of the UK Collective Actions Regime at the Competition Appeal Tribunal to Consumer Claims*......271
Ariel Flavian

14. *Re-aligning Consumer Law with the Convention on the Rights of Persons with Disabilities: A Human Rights-Based Approach to Consumer Contracting*......287
Benjamin Clubbs Coldron

Index......315

CONTRIBUTORS

Victoria Barnes, Reader in Commercial Law, Queen's University, Belfast, UK.

Sarah Brown, Senior Visiting Research Fellow, School of Law, University of Reading, UK.

Thomas Burgess, School of Law and Politics, Cardiff University, UK.

Peter Cartwright, Professor of Consumer Protection Law, University of Nottingham, UK.

Benjamin Clubbs Coldron, Senior Research Assistant, Northumbria Law School, Northumbria University, UK.

James Devenney, Professor of Transnational Commercial Law, University of Reading, UK; Visiting Full Professor, University College Dublin, Ireland; Professor, Neapolis University of Pafos, Cyprus; and Visiting Professor, Dalian Maritime University, China.

Timothy J Dodsworth, Associate Professor of Contract Law, University of Reading, UK.

Ariel Flavian, External Lecturer, Haifa University.

Paula Giliker, Professor of Comparative Law, University of Bristol, UK.

Tammy Goriely, formerly the Commercial and Common Law Team Manager at the Law Commission and now a consultant for the Department for Transport, UK.

Henry Hillman, School of Law and Politics, Cardiff University, UK.

Geraint Howells, Established Professor, University of Galway, and Visiting Professor, University of Manchester, UK.

Wangwei Lin, Associate Professor in Company and Business Law, School of Business and Management, Queen Mary University London; Research Associate, Centre for Commercial Law and Financial Regulation, School of Law, University of Reading, UK.

Andrea Miglionico, School of Law, University of Reading, UK.

Séverine Saintier, Professor of Commercial Law, University of Exeter, UK.

Christian Twigg-Flesner, Professor of Contract and Consumer Law, Warwick Law School, University of Warwick, UK.

Peter J Tyldesley, formerly the lawyer responsible for the insurance law reform project at the Law Commission and now an Honorary Fellow in the School of Law at the University of Reading, UK.

Monica Vessio, Lecturer in Commercial and Banking Law, School of Law, University of Reading, UK.

Sally Wheeler, Birkbeck University of London, UK, and Honorary Professor of Law, Australian National University.

Chris Willett, Professor of Law, University of Essex, UK.

PART I

Past Directions of Consumer Law

1

A Social History of Consumer Law, 1960–1980

VICTORIA BARNES AND SALLY WHEELER

1.1. Introduction

The future directions of consumer law have in some way been set in the past. With the Consumer Rights Act 2015 (CRA 2015), consumers now have a firm set of have statutory rights to use in contractual disputes.[1] The principles behind the 2015 Act have a far longer history. They grew out of what was once known historically as mercantile law. Consumer law is now sufficiently established as a body of literature that scholars are looking back and constructing histories of it. The most recent can be found in *The Making of Consumer Law and Policy in Europe* edited by Hans-W Micklitz. Within this edited collection, there are a couple of chapters of note. Iain Ramsay's chapter book provides an excellent history of consumer law in the United Kingdom (UK).[2] It is written with detailed knowledge of consumer law and it provides the political context, which surrounded the law. Ramsay's own textbook on consumer law was published in 1989,[3] and it, of course, forms part of this history. Thomas Roethe's chapter in the same volume assesses the sociological underpinnings of consumer law. His focus is not on the UK, like Ramsay's, but instead looks outward to Europe.[4] The European Community then Union is his backdrop. Indeed, there are a number of other chapters in Micklitz's volume that see European thinking as the catalyst for legal change.[5] Historical analyses like these allow for greater understanding of past debates, but also allow us to theorise about

[1] James Devenney, 'The Legacy of the Cameron-Clegg Coalition Programme of Reform of the Law on the Supply of Goods, Digital Content and Services to Consumers' (2018) 6 *Journal of Business Law* 485.

[2] Iain Ramsay, 'Ordoliberalism and Opportunism? The Making of Consumer Law in the UK' in Hans-W Micklitz (ed), *The Making of Consumer Law and Policy in Europe* (Bloomsbury Publishing, 2021).

[3] Iain Ramsay, *Consumer Protection: Text and Materials* (Weidenfeld and Nicolson, 1989).

[4] Thomas Roethe, 'The Making of Consumer Law – A Sociological Critique' in Hans-W Micklitz (ed), *The Making of Consumer Law and Policy in Europe* (Bloomsbury Publishing, 2021).

[5] Ludwig Kraemer, 'The Origins of Consumer Law and Policy at the EU Level' in Hans-W Micklitz (ed), *The Making of Consumer Law and Policy in Europe* (Bloomsbury Publishing, 2021); Hans-W Micklitz, 'The Intellectual Community of Consumer Law and Policy in the EU' in Hans-W Micklitz (ed), *The Making of Consumer Law and Policy in Europe* (Bloomsbury Publishing, 2021).

consumer law and policy. It shows when and where the shifts in the market and/or regulatory aims took place.

This chapter does not focus on the political history of consumer law. This is because this has been already been done very well by Ramsay and Roethe. Rather, our chapter focuses on providing something new to this literature. It considers the social history of consumer law from its birth in 1960. Britain was then in the swinging sixties. It was a society with credit, consumer goods and full of joyful exuberance. Individuals stood amid a changing society, which sought to provide greater equality, justice and fairness for its collective members. We close our historical analysis in the 1980s. It stops then because the political and social landscape changed, quite dramatically. Then the contestation between individualism and collectivism had struck a new balance in the new era of economic thought in what became Thatcherite Britain. That said, these dynamics are visible in our analysis from the late 1970s onwards. Yet, they were not, at this point in time, quite yet part of the status quo and apparent formal apparatus of the Government – not until Thatcher became prime minister in 1979, anyway. Our aim here is to weave together the law with the context by examining the changing relationship between business and society, and the scholarly literature that prompted legal change. It does so by placing the theoretical foundations of English consumer law into their original context.

1.2. Consumer Law Emerges as a Field of Scholarly Inquiry

The first text in consumer law was almost certainly Gordon Borrie and Aubrey L Diamond's *The Consumer, Society and the Law*. It kick started a trend and a growing scholarly interest in consumer law. The book was published in 1964 by Penguin. Penguin was, no doubt, an interesting choice for a publishing house. It certainly would be an unusual choice for a publishing house for those writing about any area of law today. Borrie and Diamond's book had little in the way of ambition for popular readership. Consumer law, as exciting as it might be, was not going to be the next Agatha Christie.[6] Nor was it likely to create as much uproar as the publication of *Lady Chatterley's Lover*, a few years earlier.[7] Their book was not accessible to the lay reader by its juxtaposition of consumer statements nor was it orientated around solving issues in every day transactions.[8] The structure of this book was clearly and quite visibly legal. It replicated a textbook format by taking on doctrines or areas of law individually in each chapter. Those doctrines would come together to make up the wider field of consumer law. It was a methodical exposé of the field of consumer law. The book's purpose was,

[6] *A Caribbean Mystery* was published in 1964, although not by Penguin. There is more in the way of contract law in fiction than we might ordinarily think. Anat Rosenberg, *Liberalizing Contracts: Nineteenth Century Promises Through Literature, Law and History* (Routledge, 2017).

[7] Penguin published *Lady Chatterley's Lover* in full in 1960. Legal proceedings were brought against Penguin under the Obscene Publications Act 1959. For a historical treatment of this area of law, see AWB Simpson, 'Obscenity and the Law' (1982) 1 *Law and Philosophy* 239.

[8] See the discussion of Lowe and Woodroffe below.

however, far greater than simply educating would-be lawyers or those in practice as a textbook would.[9] The prose was written too crispy for that. The book's sentences were unlike those of the traditional lawyer and written in simple but effective manner. It was intended to have a wide general readership.

Borrie and Diamond explained what their book brought to its readers – and what it did that other books did not – in their introduction. They wrote:

> The militant march of the consumer has resulted in the publication of a number of books which attempt to guide the consumer in the many transactions into which he enters, to tell him what his legal rights are, and to advise him how to exercise them. This book is not another. There is, it must be admitted, a considerable amount of practical law in this book, and the consumer may find here guidance on particular problems. But our main purpose was not to write a legal textbook or a handbook of do's and don'ts for consumers. It was to describe how the law has evolved: how it became what it is today and how it might evolve in the future; and to try to evaluate how far it serves the ends of society, and in particular the consumer, in the second half of the twentieth century.[10]

Consumer law was, indeed, in its zenith in Britain at this point in time. It took off in the 1960s. This is in part due to the political mood and undercurrent of social change that swept through this decade. Two Conservative Party leaders, Harold Macmillan and Alec Douglas-Home, led the country for the first years of the 1960s. It was not until the 1964 general election that the Labour Party took power. Harold Wilson, leader of the Labour Party, served as prime minister from 1964 until 1970. Despite not being in power, the Labour movement was in full swing with issues of social mobility and social justice being at the forefront of social and political events before 1964. It had taken root following World War II. Welfare reforms were not only introduced but also felt to be needed after the devastating impact that war had had on society. The introduction of a National Health Service (NHS) 1948 is seen widely as synonymous with state welfare and one of Labour's crowning achievements.[11]

There were significant shifts that came in the 1960s in the corpus of British society, which followed the fall of the British Empire. There were winds of change in the British Empire with Somaliland, Cyprus and Nigeria becoming independent in 1960, and Sierra Leone, Kuwait and Tanganyika in 1961. Jamaica, Trinidad and Tobago, and Zanzibar followed suit in 1963. Kenya, Malawi, Malta and Zambia gained independence in 1964.[12] 1962 marked the end of free immigration from citizens of the Commonwealth.[13] These shifts in the British imperial mindset were not simply something that was observed overseas or in political circles. Perhaps the most celebrated event here is the Bristol Bus Boycott, where citizens of Bristol refused to use the Bristol Omnibus Company's service because it upheld a colour bar and would not employ

[9] David Sugarman, 'Legal Theory, the Common Law Mind and the Making of the Textbook Tradition' in William Twining (ed), *Legal theory and common law* (Blackwell, 1986).

[10] Gordon J Borrie and Aubrey L Diamond, *The Consumer, Society and the Law*, 2nd edn (MacGibbon & Kee, 1966) 10–11.

[11] John Stewart, 'Ideology and Process in the Creation of the British National Health Service' (2002) 14 *Journal of Policy History* 113.

[12] See the prime text: Nicholas White, *Decolonisation: The British Experience since 1945* (Routledge, 2013).

[13] Commonwealth Immigrations Act 1962.

persons of colour.[14] These celebrated stories did not result in simple triumph. Enoch Powell's criticisms of the Race Relations Act came in 1968 with his divisive 'Rivers of Blood' speech.[15] The Race Relations Act 1968 extended the probation of discrimination on the basis of race, ethnicity and nationality to employment and housing.

Race was a matter for social and political discussion, but so were class and gender. The Robbins Report came out in 1963. It recommended an immediate expansion of universities through an increase in student numbers and shifting the colleges of advanced technology into universities. One of those colleges later became Brunel University London. Another was the University of Warwick. The guiding principle here was that 'all young persons qualified by ability and attainment to pursue a full-time course in higher education should have the opportunity to do so'.[16] It was to train, educate and socialise: 'to promote the general powers of the mind. The aim should be to produce not mere specialists but rather cultivated men and women'[17] and 'the transmission of a common culture and common standards of citizenship'.[18] The value of a university education was well defined here as a social mission.[19] In the same year, Betty Friedan published *The Feminist Mystique*. Friedan, an American college-educated women, argued that women were unsatisfied with their feminine lives as housewives and sought more from their lives. While the text was American, the debate was also playing out in Great Britain around the same time. The 1960s are thought to mark the beginning of the modern era in women's lives because of the introduction of the pill and its availability on the NHS.[20]

With the focus on the changing structure of British society and the political will to, at least, reflect upon what it meant, it is no wonder that consumer law came into the fore when it did and in the way that it did. If political gaze was not on supporting the weakest in society, consumers, as a group, would not been conceptualised nor would a set of laws to uphold their rights been thought about. Although how and who should be supported remained contested issues by those in Britain society, there was clear political enthusiasm. The following section explains why consumers had become a weak and vulnerable social group in the mid-twentieth century rather than earlier.

1.3. Mercantile Society

Consumers, as we understand them today, were not common in the nineteenth century. Law did surround business to consumer transactions but it made for no or little distinction between business-to-business and business-to-consumer transactions. They were

[14] Madge Dresser, *Black and White on the Buses: The 1963 Colour Bar Dispute in Bristol* (Bristol Broadsides, 1986).

[15] Colin Holmes, *John Bull's Island: Immigration and British Society, 1871–1971* (Palgrave Macmillan, 1988).

[16] Committee on Higher Education, Higher Education Report of the Committee appointed by the Prime Minister under the Chairmanship of Lord Robbins (White Paper, Cm 2154, 1963), para 135.

[17] ibid para 26.

[18] ibid para 28.

[19] Alistair Ross, 'Higher Education and Social Access: To the Robbins Report' in Louise Archer, Merryn Hutchings and Alistair Ross (eds), *Higher Education and Social Class* (Routledge, 2005).

[20] Claire L Jones, 'Under the Covers? Commerce, Contraceptives and Consumers in England and Wales, 1880–1960' (2016) 29 *Social History of Medicine* 734.

treated alike. This is for good reason. Business-to-consumer transactions were, in truth, few and far between. The law here was known as mercantile law, reflecting the large numbers of merchants who traded with each other. It later became commercial law, out of which consumer law grew. That said, the key principles of English sales law were forged in the nineteenth century with growth of industry, trade and commerce in the Industrial Revolution. The socio-economic context at this time means that the law could hardly be described as 'consumer law', although Borrie and Diamond did, rightly, see a doctrinal lineage that could be traced. They cited cases such as *Chandelor v Lopus* (1606), *Gardiner v Gray* (1815) and *Jones v Bright* (1829) as examples.[21] These cases demonstrated the principle of *caveat emptor* and laissez-faire ideology, which would later come to be overturned. Yet, such an outlook was entirely fitting for English society, as it was at that time.

While regions, such as the Potteries in Staffordshire,[22] specialised in the manufacture of specific individual goods, the turnpikes then canals and later railways had enabled these regions of the UK to trade with each other. Goods moved freely around the regions thanks to good transportation links, strong mercantile networks and agency relationships. British businessmen also looked outwards to trade internationally. Even internationally, transactions were generally between a small, tightly knit group of merchants, industrialists and capitalists within the business community. Family firms and those bound together by values proved to be common.[23] While the term the 'political class' remains prevalent, those in business were in a group of their own. Those in finance or manufacturing had a distinctly different social status to those in the upper stratum of society, such as in politics, law and the landed gentry.[24] This group of merchants were of the middling sort – but upwardly mobile and large in number.[25] Owing to the make-up of English society and the large numbers of small and medium-sized enterprises, England was commonly referred to as 'a nation of shopkeepers'.[26]

Mechanisms for commercial regulation were largely internal, and efforts to push externally for new laws were self-organised. International trade was hampered by distance and different standards, weights and measures. So merchants came together to lobby to enact legislation that might standardise rules and make them clearer.[27] Disputes over remedies, although infrequent, were handled internally in this small group. It involved peer monitoring. As the group was so small and exchanged credit, the failure of one firm could lead to another. Bad actors were, therefore, excluded.[28] Chambers of

[21] Borrie and Diamond (n 10) 17–19.

[22] Andrew Popp, '"The True Potter": Identity and Entrepreneurship in the North Staffordshire Potteries in the Later Nineteenth Century' (2003) 29 *Journal of Historical Geography* 317.

[23] Mary B Rose, *Firms, Networks and Business Values: The British and American Cotton Industries Since 1750* (Cambridge University Press, 2000).

[24] WD Rubinstein, 'Wealth, Elites and the Class Structure of Modern Britain' (1977) 76 *Past & Present* 99.

[25] ibid.

[26] Andrew Alexander and Simon Phillips, '"Fair Play for the Small Man": Perspectives on the Contribution of the Independent Shopkeeper 1930–c.1945' (2006) 48 *Business History* 69.

[27] Annamaria Monti, 'Leone Levi (1821–1888) and the History of Comparative Commercial Law' in Ingrid Ivarsen et al (eds), *Common Law, Civil Law, and Colonial Law: Essays in Comparative Legal History from the Twelfth to the Twentieth Centuries* (Cambridge University Press, 2021).

[28] Francesca Carnevali, '"Crooks, Thieves, and Receivers": Transaction Costs in Nineteenth-Century Industrial Birmingham' (2004) 57 *The Economic History Review* 533.

Commerce and other forums were set up for dispute resolution.[29] Litigation over representations, and issues of business knowledge or skill in those representations, loomed larger. Arbitration over litigation was preferred because of the slow speed of judicial decision-making and costly nature of going to court.[30] To help arbitrators understand the law, reformers sought codification as opposed to judge-made law.[31] Once such codification came in 1893 with the Sale of Goods Act. The Act was not driven by entrepreneurs, but more by the internal logic of lawyers. Mackenzie Chalmers, the drafter of the legislation, was able to produce an Act of 60 sections that was able to state existing common law principles and still, as Bentham was so concerned to point out,[32] maintain sufficient flexibility to allow the judicial innovation of innominate terms without losing efficacy or requiring amendment.[33]

The structure of English society changed, however, in the late nineteenth to early twentieth century with the growth of big business. With merger and amalgamation movements,[34] small and medium-sized businesses were engulfed by larger-scale enterprises. Firms began to centralise with a London head office and so reaped the advantages of access to the capital markets,[35] but more so to scale and structure as they opened outlets across the country. Many sole traders and single-unit firms saw their occupation structure shift as they became employees and workers undertaking monotonous and repetitive tasks in a large firm.[36] Buyers no longer dealt with a shopkeeper, who they knew and lived locally, but a large-scale retailer. It was run by an individual that they would never meet and the owners so numerous, they could never be traced. It is at this moment that some, perhaps most notably, the legal scholar Patrick Atiyah, see the advent of consumerism. For Atiyah, what marked the change in industrial relations was the depersonalised relationship between buyer and seller. The rise of brands and depersonalised transactions made inroads into the more traditional principles of freedom of contract.[37] The 1893 legislation celebrated the impersonalisation of the market, by imposing a set of standardised implied terms. The growth of big business and large-scale manufacturers was one shift; another was in the availability of finance.

It was not until much later in the twentieth century that bankarisation, ie wide financial inclusion, took place. In the 1970s, the working classes, who had been excluded from the mercantile or business classes, were engaged fully in the market. There had been savings banks for the working classes since the nineteenth century, but these were

[29] Robert J Bennett, *Local Business Voice: The History of Chambers of Commerce in Britain, Ireland, and Revolutionary America, 1760-2011* (Oxford University Press, 2011).

[30] Monti (n 27).

[31] ibid.

[32] J Bentham, *General View of a Complete Code of Laws* (1802), oll.libertyfund.org/pages/bentham-toc.

[33] *Hongkong Fir Shipping Co Ltd v Kawasaki Kisen Kaisha Ltd* [1962] 2 QB 26 (CA) and more generally R Halson, 'A Common Lawyer's Perspective on Contract Codes' (2011) 15 *Jersey and Guernsey Law Review*.

[34] Leslie Hannah, *The Rise of the Corporate Economy*, 2nd edn (Methuen, 1983) ch 3.

[35] Victoria Barnes and Lucy Newton, 'Symbolism in Bank Marketing and Architecture: The Headquarters of National Provincial Bank of England' (2019) 14 *Management & Organizational History* 213.

[36] Peter Wardley, 'The Anatomy of Big Business: Aspects of Corporate Development in the Twentieth Century' (1991) 33 *Business History* 268, www.tandfonline.com/doi/abs/10.1080/00076799100000056; Peter Wardley, 'The Emergence of Big Business: The Largest Corporate Employers of Labour in the United Kingdom, Germany and the United States c. 1907 1' (1999) 41 *Business History* 88.

[37] PS Atiyah, *The Rise and Fall of Freedom of Contract* (Oxford University Press, 1979) 574. The 1893 Act is not discussed in much detail in this book.

not used for the receipt of the payment of wages, and the work of the bank did not extend to the provision of credit.[38] With the creation of the Girobank, working class customers were now part of the financial world.[39] Other high street banks, such Barclays and Lloyds, which had previously been seen as elitist, targeted the custom of those who were paid cash in hand. They offered credit facilities, like Barclaycards and Barclayloans.[40] The 'swinging sixties' were inspired by the white heat of technology, the rapid changes in industry and the widespread availability of consumer goods.[41] Marketers targeted consumers through mass advertising and, aided with finance and loans, now available to them, they began to purchase luxury goods.[42] A hire purchase market had begun. Consumers were pit against large-scale firms, first in the provision of credit, and then in the marketplace for the goods themselves.

The difference in bargaining power between the seller and buyer, once relatively equal, was now at an extreme. Hitherto, buyers were businesses or those involved in mercantile trade. They were essentially small or medium-sized firms. And so was the seller. The two were well known to each other, whether that be within the same industry or trading group, or the same regional community. Disputes, if they occurred, could be resolved quickly within that community, often without recourse to law and the use of expensive lawyers. The expansion in big business, however, meant that the seller was no longer small but a large-scale enterprise with huge resources and an in-house legal team. Armed with legal knowledge, sellers were well aware of their rights but also the ways in which they could avoid their contractual obligations. The gap between buyer and seller was furthered by size and location. To reach the centre of an organisation or the upper echelons of its management was now a task in itself. It was no longer as simple as reaching an individual, who was accessible, and well known in the local community. In short, the market had changed substantially. Developments in legal scholarship mapped this expansion of the market; they noted those changes and called for law to step in to redress the balance in bargaining power.

1.4. The Growing Network of Consumer Law Scholars and Scholarship

The Report of the Committee on Consumer Protection was published in 1962. It was dubbed the Molony Report after its chairman, Joseph Molony. Thought to be a fairly extensive and comprehensive report,[43] it considered a good number of legislative

[38] Victoria Barnes and Lucy Newton, 'Women, Uniforms and Brand Identity in Barclays Bank' (2022) 64 *Business History* 801.

[39] AE Booth and Mark Billings, 'Techno-Nationalism, the Post Office and the Creation of Britain's National Giro' in Bernardo Batiz-Lazo, J Carles Maixé-Altés and Paul Thomes (eds), *Technological Innovation in Retail Finance: International Historical Perspectives* (Routledge, 2011).

[40] Barnes and Newton (n 38).

[41] Dominic Sandbrook, *White Heat: A History of Britain in the Swinging Sixties* (Hachette UK, 2015).

[42] Peter Scott, *The Market Makers: Creating Mass Markets for Consumer Durables in Inter-War Britain* (Oxford University Press, 2017).

[43] *Hansard* HL Deb Vol 244 cols 653 (14 November 1962); JWA Thornely, 'Final Report of the Committee on Consumer Protection' (1963) 21 *The Cambridge Law Journal* 1, 6.

enactments, including the Hire Purchase Act 1938, the Merchandise Marks Act 1887, the Restrictive Trade Practices Act 1956 and the Sale of Goods Act 1893, for example. It recommended the formation of a Consumer Council, which did not regulate or provide enforcement, and instead collected information. Borrie and Diamond wrote their joint book in response to the Molony Report. Diamond was especially critical in his review of the report. He stated:

> If it had only displayed a keen and burning desire to protect the consuming public the Committee could have produced a milestone in the development of the law; we must hope that it will not prove to be a millstone round the neck of future generations of reformers.[44]

Borrie and Diamond did, indeed, see themselves as reformers.

Gordon Borrie (1931–2016) was a barrister before turning to work in higher education. He taught, for the most part, at the University of Birmingham. Before that, he worked at the College of Law.[45] He stood unsuccessfully for Labour in 1955 in his home town of Croydon, but became was appointed Baron Borrie, a Labour life peer, in 1995.[46] Aubrey Diamond (1923–2006) is probably best known among those in legal education today as a former director of the Institute of Advanced Legal Studies from 1976 until 1986.[47] His portrait sits alongside the portraits of the other past directors in what is now the Institute's Derek Roebuck Conference Room. Diamond spent most of his academic career in London. He also worked in the College of Law and what was then Queen Mary College. The College of Law traces its roots back to 1876 to a tutorial firm, Gibson and Weldon.[48] It was created in the 1960s by merging Gibson and Weldon to the Law Society's training facilities. It remained a college rather than a university until 2012, when it became the University of Law.[49] He was also a solicitor and became a Law Commissioner in 1971.[50] Both had roles outside of the legal world that had an impact on shaping the market. Diamond was president of the National Federation of Consumer Groups;[51] Borrie chaired the Advertising Standards Authority.[52] This brief overview of their lives tells us much about their scholarly aims and helps us to understand how they went about achieving them.

Borrie and Diamond wrote *The Consumer, Society and the Law* to promote legal change, but also change within society. Their aim was to sow the seeds for law reform. The book concluded, they said, with an 'attempt … to draw the threads together by

[44] Aubrey L Diamond, 'The Molony Committee Final Report of the Committee on Consumer Protection' (1963) 26 *Modern Law Review* 66, 75.

[45] Roger Cowe, 'Lord Borrie Obituary' *The Guardian* (23 October 2016), www.theguardian.com/business/2016/oct/23/lord-borrie-obituary.

[46] ibid.

[47] Anon, 'IALS – History of the Institute – Professor Aubrey Diamond: Director 1976-1986' (*IALS*, 4 October 2015), web.archive.org/web/20151004033748/http://ials.sas.ac.uk/about/IALS_History_Aubrey_Diamond.htm.

[48] Anon, 'University History and Heritage' (University of Law), www.law.ac.uk/about/history-and-heritage.

[49] ibid.

[50] Alison Green, 'Obituary – Professor Aubrey Diamond QC, 28 December 1923–6 July 2006, Former President of BILA, 1988–1990' (BILA), bila.org.uk/wp-content/uploads/old/4ff4163e7baea2.35452647.pdf.

[51] Anon, 'Professor Aubrey Diamond: Distinguished Lawyer, Teacher and Public Servant' *The Times* (20 July 2006), www.thetimes.com/article/professor-aubrey-diamond-zlm985rf7nc.

[52] Anon, 'Lord Borrie: Regulator Who Took a Cudgel to Anti-Competitive Practices across British Business' *The Times* (8 October 2006), www.thetimes.com/uk/article/lord-borrie-38vq2nj26.

putting forward the idea of a Consumers' Charter'.[53] They did not see new legislation as a simple solution to the problems they saw in the market.[54] 'Convinced as we are', they said, 'of the need and value of legislating for improvements in the law, we have to admit that "you cannot legislate for fools"'.[55] Consumers still had to become informed and this was not the job of lawyers, they argued. 'No legislation is going to change us overnight into a nation of knowledgeable, prudent, and discriminating shoppers. Law reform has to be accompanied by consumer education.'[56] Given that the two worked in fervently consumer rights organisations, it is perhaps unsurprising that they saw these groups as part of the solution. They argued for 'the work of the consumer organizations in this field [to be] supplemented not only by greater Press and Television coverage but also by the schools giving consumer matters a prominent place in their curricula'.[57] Borrie and Diamond led the scholarly response to the Moloney Report. A scholarly discourse in the UK known as 'consumer sales law' emerged in turn. The next pioneering legal text to be authored on consumer law was not published for another decade or so.

Ross Cranston's book, *Consumers and the Law*, was published in 1978 as part of Weidenfeld and Nicolson's Law in Context series.[58] Much like Borrie and Diamond's seminal book, its publisher was a generalist. It was not focused solely on legal or academic markets. Indeed, an academic reader today would find themselves perplexed by the book's scholarly apparatus. The references appear at the end of the text, which make for an amusing mode of flipping back and forth between the text and the end matter. The process often results in one losing their place and having to read it all over again. In the book itself, Cranston was not content to describe the law. Rather, he created a thoughtful dialogue with scholars about what the law should say and how it fitted society best.[59] Cranston's book engaged fervently with the scholarly agenda now emerging around the world. Although Cranston spent most of his life in the UK, he was born in Queensland, Australia. Cranston did not just look to the judgments of common lawyers outside of the UK as one might well expect. He also engaged keenly with the law and economics movement, which came from across the Atlantic. The mantra for this group of scholars was *deregulation*. The work here suggested that no regulation was, in fact, good regulation.[60] Cranston was not responding to Harold Wilson's era of politics, but instead to the growing right-wing neoliberal ideology. It would come to British economic policy with the appointment of Margaret Thatcher as prime minister a year later in 1979. Cranston was careful and thorough in his description of the aims of the Chicago School of Economics.[61] His work is sometimes so even-handed and factual that it is difficult to identify his critique, although this observation might well be expected for a monograph, where the argument is not contained in a few paragraphs,

[53] Borrie and Diamond (n 10) 11.
[54] See also Aubrey L Diamond, 'Codification of the Law of Contract' (1968) 31 *Modern Law Review* 361.
[55] Borrie and Diamond (n 10) 11.
[56] ibid.
[57] ibid.
[58] The third edition was published by Butterworths.
[59] Ross Cranston, *Consumers and the Law*, 1st edn (Weidenfeld and Nicolson, 1978) ch 1.
[60] Niklas Olsen, 'From Choice to Welfare: The Concept of the Consumer in the Chicago School of Economics' (2017) 14 *Modern Intellectual History* 507.
[61] Cranston (n 59) 18–28.

but evolves across chapters. For this reason, Cranston's book, now in its third edition, is a good primer on the subject of consumer law and makes for an excellent textbook. While a book in itself is rarely designed to be pithy, there were other types of publications, where Cranston did make his critique of law and economics. There, he made it in a rather decisive fashion.[62]

Cranston's politics are, in any event, clear. And patently so. He stood as a candidate for the Labour Party. He was elected as a Member of Parliament for Dudley North. He served in this role from 1997 until 2005. Dudley may not seem like the obvious place for Cranston, now a long-standing professor at the London School of Economics, nor is Dudley a natural home for a Labour politician. Dudley is a market town in the West Midlands, which was at the centre of the Industrial Revolution.[63] The iron and coal industries, while now long gone, remain at the centre of those from the Black Country's identity.[64] The industry there employed large numbers of individuals for numbers of generations to mine coal in the pits, smelt iron or dig transportation networks.[65] Working conditions, for large numbers of people, were, for a long period of time, notably tempestuous and difficult.[66] By the twentieth century, race was an issue here too: Wolverhampton South West was Enoch Powell's constituency from 1950 to 1974.[67] The West Midlands were an important place for Cranston. When Cranston wrote *Consumers and the Law* in 1976 and 1977,[68] he worked at the University of Warwick, one of the beneficiaries of the Robbins Report, in the city of Coventry. The touchstone there in this newly created law school was law in context.[69] Coventry is about 30 miles from Dudley. Cranson's politics can be seen through the choices he made in his career, which were informed by his location and the society that surrounded him. His political views can also be seen in the areas which he studied and captivated him. Consumer law is one such topic that has attracted the attention of more left-leaning scholars, such as Lord Borrie. The welfare state was another of Cranston's interests. He later published *Legal Foundations of the Welfare State*, again with Weidenfeld and Nicolson in their Law in Context book series, in 1985.

Another important book in consumer law was published in 1978. This was Bryan W Harvey's *The Law of Consumer Protection and Fair Trading*. It had a historical focus. The

[62] Ross Cranston, 'Consumer Protection and Economic Theory' in AJ Duggan and LW Darvall (eds), *Consumer protection law and theory* (Law Book, 1980).

[63] Neil Cossons and Barrie Stuart Trinder, *The Iron Bridge: Symbol of the Industrial Revolution* (Phillimore, 2002).

[64] See the assessment of the Black Country Living Museum in Simon Briercliffe, 'BCLM: Forging Ahead: Building a New Urban History of the Black Country' (2021) 48 *Urban History* 334; and the use of this identity as a tourist attraction in Sarah Watkins, Ahmed Hassanien and Crispin Dale, 'Exploring the Image of the Black Country as a Tourist Destination' (2006) 2 *Place Branding* 321.

[65] George J Barnsby, 'The Standard of Living in the Black Country during the Nineteenth Century' (1971) 24 *The Economic History Review* 220; Colin P Griffin, 'The Standard of Living in the Black Country in the Nineteenth Century: A Comment' (1973) 26 *The Economic History Review* 510.

[66] DC Woods, 'The Operation of the Master and Servants Act in the Black Country, 1858–1875' (1982) 7 *Midland History* 93; Eric Hopkins, 'Working Hours and Conditions during the Industrial Revolution: A Re-Appraisal' (1982) 35 *The Economic History Review* 52.

[67] Shirin Hirsch, *In the Shadow of Enoch Powell: Race, Locality and Resistance* (Manchester University Press, 2018) ch 2.

[68] Front matter and back matter.

[69] Ralph Folsom and Neal Roberts, 'Warwick Story: Being Led Down the Contextual Path of the Law' (1979) 30 *Journal of Legal Education* 166.

book started, not with an introduction, but with the history of consumer law.[70] Harvey focused there on the parish system and local governance,[71] not with case law and law's intellectual agenda. The book also rather literally started with history. The front cover was a scene from a sixteenth-century woodcut from the Radio Times Hulton Picture Library entitled 'Inspecting Weights and Measures'.[72] The inclusion of history was not a token gesture; it was a key part of what Harvey was trying to do. Although the book was published by Butterworths, a traditional legal publisher, it had a distinctly interdisciplinary feel. Economics too featured heavily here.[73] Harvey stated:

> A book which merely stated the current legal rules would have some difficulty in justifying its existence in so far as it purported to be useful for university degree work. I have therefore preceded the main part of the work with an economic and philosophical analysis of consumer protection laws. Many law students will not have studied economics before, and, with a few distinguished exceptions, authors of academic law books in England have given their readers little encouragement to think about the relationship between law and economics.[74]

Harvey was not critical of the economics movement in law as Cranston was. The first four chapters engaged in law and economics, although the remainder of the text focused on explaining the law. Harvey considered that there was a gap in the market that demanded such a textbook-like approach to consumer law. 'Although there have been excellent books or pamphlets dealing with the main principles of law involved', he said, 'these books have been aimed primarily at the layman.'[75] He saw law students as the target market audience. 'Apart from the legal encyclopaedias that exist on individual topics such as consumer credit, trade descriptions, food and drugs and weights and measures, at the present time no text book has been published in England.'[76] Harvey argued that there was not one that was 'suitable not only for the informed layman but also for students studying consumer protection law'.[77] He sought to provide materials for those 'at universities', 'polytechnics' and 'for the qualifying examinations for the legal profession, and those working in local authorities who take the Diploma in Consumer Affairs and the Diploma in Trading Standards'.[78] Much like Borrie and Diamond, Harvey saw those outside of the legal profession as being important in the application of consumer law. Harvey had much in common with them, professionally. Harvey, like Borrie, worked at the University of Birmingham. He was also a solicitor, like Diamond.

The next key text was written by Robert Lowe and Geoffrey Woodroffe. They published *Consumer Law and Practice* in 1980. It was unlike Cranston or Harvey's text, which were published a couple of years previously, for several reasons. First, and foremost, the law had changed, quite considerably. The Sale of Goods Act of 1979 had been passed and the book was the first to incorporate it and consider how it would change consumer law in practice. This consideration was evidence of the second

[70] Brian W Harvey, *The Law of Consumer Protection and Fair Trading*, 1st edn (Butterworths, 1978) 1–9.
[71] ibid.
[72] The image was replaced in the second edition by a photograph of a food market.
[73] Harvey (n 70) 1–9.
[74] ibid iv.
[75] ibid.
[76] ibid.
[77] ibid.
[78] ibid.

point of difference; the book embodied a very different stylistic and philosophical approach. Lowe and Woodroffe's approach was undeniably and overtly doctrinal but orientated very much towards consumer law as a practical application of contract law and for establishing rights and providing remedies. That is to say that the book had no theoretical or socio-legal agenda; it was focused exclusively on explaining the letter of the law, and considered what consumer law was and how it was enforced. It was 'written', so the preface said, 'primarily for law students and for those who are called upon to advise on consumer problems, whether legal or para-legal practitioners'.[79] The publisher was Sweet and Maxwell, a well-known and reputable legal publisher. Clearly, this was a choice well suited to Lowe and Woodroffe's aims. That said, Lowe and Woodroffe acknowledged that consumer law was not high law, but it focused on everyday problems. The front cover demonstrates this aptly.[80] It shows a car showroom with two cars in the windows. The one in view, which captivates the two men, presumably a consumer and sales man, closely resembles a Jaguar XJS. This was a luxury sports car manufactured from 1975 to 1996.[81] The showroom has a number of signs, which are the subject matter of typical problem questions, such as 'sorry no exchanges, refunds', 'conditions of sale', 'interest free credit', 'immaculate condition', and so on. Cars, of course, attracted a number of consumer disputes.[82] This is because they are high-value items and therefore worth suing over. The book is then structured by remedies and typical statements from consumers. One example is 'I can't remember what I signed'; another 'Can I get out of the agreement?'.[83] The text was intended to have 'practical' use with a 'basic approach' focused on narrow areas of law, which were commonly a matter of dispute.[84] Subjects, like housing, health services and so on, were excluded from Lowe and Woodroffe's gaze.

The two authors fitted well within the consumer law network. Their lives also mapped into the zeitgeist of the mid-twentieth century. Both were solicitors and worked at the College of Law, as had Audrey Diamond. Woodroffe moved from the College of Law to the newly created Brunel University, which was inspired by the Robbins Report, before the book's publication. It was at Brunel that Woodroffe taught, supervised and mentored today's consumer law scholars, most notably Geraint Howells, Chris Willett, Stephen Weatherall and Christine Riefa.[85] While consumer law was firmly on the legislative agenda in the UK, Lowe and Woodroffe's text inspired those in other common law jurisdictions to reflect on their blend of commercial and consumer law.[86] Ireland, for example, relied upon the 1893 Sales of Goods Act. It had not updated to the 1979 Act. The Sale of Goods Act 1893 was not inspired by a society that needed to worry about

[79] Geoffrey Woodroffe and Robert Lowe, *Consumer Law and Practice*, 1st edn (Sweet & Maxwell, 1980) v.
[80] It was dropped for the second and third edition.
[81] James Taylor, *Jaguar XJ-S: The Complete Story* (The Crowood Press, 2019).
[82] See *Van Gordon v Volkswagen Financial Services (UK) Ltd (ta Audi Finance)* [2019] 4 WLUK 476; *Bernstein v Pamson Motors (Golders Green) Ltd* [1987] 2 All ER 220; *Rogers v Parish* [1987] 2 WLR 353; *Lee v York Coach and Marine* [1977] RTR 35; *Crowther v Shannon Motor Co* [1975] All ER 139; *Barlett v Sidney Marcus Ltd* [1965] 1 WLR 1013.
[83] Woodroffe and Lowe (n 79) ix.
[84] ibid v.
[85] Geraint G Howells, 'Geoffrey Woodroffe 1934–2018: An Obituary to One of Consumer Law's Founding Fathers' (2018) 7 *Journal of European Consumer and Market Law*.
[86] AV Gill, 'Review of Consumer Law and Practice' (1983) 18 *Irish Jurist* (1966–) 375.

providing greater protection for buyers. Outside of the common law world, consumer law scholars had established strong links with those in Europe.

Ross Cranston, Brian W Harvey, Robert Lowe and Geoffrey Woodroffe were among the key proponents in this original debate about the scale and scope of consumer law in the UK. They advocated greater rights for consumers and better mediation between business and society. Geraint Howells and Stephen Weatherall inherited this body of scholarship and they too pushed for further policy change.[87] These were important first movers within these early academic circles – but also these were visible on the political scene. Their ideas were influential and perhaps most relevant in the Thatcher–Major era, where the political contestations between ideas of welfare and individualism became more protracted and the ideological divides became most clear. Although it is often overlooked within the wider context and when assessing legal change, the work of this group of academics remains important – and even central to understanding legal development.

1.5. Conclusion

This chapter has shone a light on the genesis of consumer law scholarship. It has showcased a history of consumer law. This is not *the* history, nor does it intend to be so. There are other ways to examine the way that this field has grown over time. Other different approaches to this subject are to be commended and encouraged. There are other works out there, which provide for a very different story to the one we map out here. Borrie and Diamond have in their founding text identified cases that come from the nineteenth century to represent the doctrines we now know.[88] We recognised them to be firmly within the mainstay of consumer law. Ramsay and Roethe have examined the political and conceptual backdrop to consumer law from the mid- to late-twentieth century.[89] These are all prominent examples of histories – in the plural – of consumer law. Ours quite deliberately takes a different approach to ones that have been proffered so far. Our focus has been on the social history of consumer law. We have shown the society in which consumer law, as a lens of legal inquiry, flourished. It has placed consumer law scholarship and the scholars, who gave rise to it, into that society. Overall, we have tried to place the first theorists in consumer law within their original social context. Reading them back provides some nostalgia, but, as readers, we benefit from hindsight.

A few of these pioneering ideas and predictions about the future did, indeed, come to pass. Some did not. Borrie and Diamond's call for a consumer charter took over 50 years to come to fruition. The CRA 2015 was a purpose-built statute that aimed to translate commercial law into ordinary parlance so the everyday person could understand it.[90] This consumer charter is what we now know to be the CRA 2015. While the CRA 2015 has reshaped consumer law, it is equally important to note that its

[87] Geraint G Howells and Stephen Weatherill, *Consumer Protection Law*, 1st edn (Ashgate, 1995).

[88] Borrie and Diamond (n 10) 17–19.

[89] Ramsay (n 2); Roethe (n 4).

[90] Kathy Conklin, Richard Hyde and Fabio Parente, 'Assessing Plain and Intelligible Language in the Consumer Rights Act: A Role for Reading Scores?' (2019) 39 *Legal Studies* 378.

substance is by no means brand new. The roots of consumer legislation can be understood by looking at old theory. Harvey believed in 1978 that consumer law was a distinct field of law, which could be divisible from commercial law and mercantile law. He said:

> There is a growing school of thought which holds that consumer protection law is at best only distantly related to commercial law, and it is legitimate as a separate exercise to focus on transactions between suppliers and the ultimate consumer.[91]

Today, this claim seems difficult to believe. Of the various syllabi in law schools today, consumer law is rarely a standalone module on its own. Rather, it sits (or, to be more accurate, elements of it sit) within commercial law or contract law. Of course, this may well not have been the case in 1978; as Harvey, states, consumer law might have been seen as a solid subject in its own right. This is one possibility. Harvey could also have engaged in what we might describe as wishful thinking. He was, after all, establishing a new scholarly discipline. His words here can be read here as potentially biased. He was perhaps intending to legitimise his scholarship and an emerging field. Consumer law was, certainly, a body of scholarship in its embryonic state that he and others were imagining and designing. It was a body of law that they sculpted together by using other discrete and more established areas of law. This project was successful in that consumer law has been taken up and studied by future generations. Harvey, when writing in 1978, did not know how this agenda would develop and whether consumer law would be a bit of a non-starter.

This chapter has shown that the scholars writing the first and foundational texts of consumer law were of a largely homogeneous socio-political group in alignment. One might note that they were all men but, alas, that was the state of legal education at the time.[92] Their views on how to fix the consumer market were not always so united. Borrie and Diamond pushed for further codification; Lowe and Woodroffe for greater education; Cranston on increasing the role of the state. That said, while there might have been minor quibbles about the solution, all agreed there was a problem within society to be fixed. Different solutions were proffered and they were, for the most part, complementary. These individuals were connected by a prevailing ideology, which was of class consciousness and an awareness of the different social groups. It was essentially left leaning, although not all had a critical approach to writing about law. They were also connected by institution. The College of Law was a fertile place for new thinking in commercial law, the environment there created a core group of scholars working on consumer law. Birmingham had key thinkers too. Brunel and Warwick served as initiatives of new higher education policy, which aimed to educate a wider social group. Consumer law as a topic, which focused on educating the everyday person, quite naturally, sat alongside the institution's aim for improving education. In other words, the intellectual agenda of these individuals fitted where they worked exceptionally well. There is no doubt that they were inspired by the social changes they saw through their roles in the new universities and the individuals they met there in the law faculty.

[91] Harvey (n 70) iii.

[92] See Fiona Cownie and Raymond Cocks, *A Great and Noble Occupation!': The History of the Society of Legal Scholars* (Hart Publishing, 2009).

2

Consumer Insurance Law Reform – Obstacles, Allies and Tactics

TAMMY GORIELY AND PETER J TYLDESLEY

2.1. Introduction: Getting Involved

This is the story of a collaboration to reform one small but vital aspect of consumer law, namely disclosure and representations in consumer insurance. It looks in detail at how the processes of disruption, innovation and re-alignment play out in practice, when people get together to effect change. It argues that reform does not just happen: it often takes a coalition of allies many years to overcome vested interests and government apathy, as they put the arguments for change and work together to devise solutions.

The law was eventually changed by the Consumer Insurance (Disclosure and Representations) Act 2012, which is based on a joint report of the Law Commissions for England and Wales and for Scotland. The two authors set up the underlying Law Commission project and saw the Bill through Parliament.

This is very much a personal account of what is involved in changing the law, and we tell it from our different perspectives.

Tammy joined the Law Commission in June 2002, to manage the commercial and common law team. [Tammy writes]: I recall seeing the advert for the job in a newspaper, discarded on a train. At the time I was an academic researcher, but I had worked for the National Consumer Council and was aware of the problems over consumer insurance. As my husband put it, 'this might be a chance to change that silly law that consumers have to tell the insurer anything they might want to know'. It sounded like an interesting thing to do for two to three years, before returning to an academic job. I had little idea that changing the disclosure rule for consumers would take 10 years.

Peter joined the Law Commission in May 2005, as the first lawyer with responsibility for the new project to reform insurance law. [Peter writes]: Before my appointment, the senior civil servant on my interview panel had stared rather sniffily at my CV and declared 'Mr Tyldesley, you have a most unusual career trajectory.' Yet an unorthodox career, spanning underwriting, complaints handling, insurance litigation and academia, proved crucial in getting the reforms through.

2.2. The Problem of Unfair Law

[Peter writes]: My concerns regarding insurance law had begun in the early 1980s, when I was working as a personal lines underwriter for an eccentrically managed insurer, the Western Australian Insurance Company.[1] One day a problem arose with a case, and the general manager handed me a half-leather-bound copy of *MacGillivray on Insurance Law* and told me to 'sort it out'. Although I already had a working understanding of the law, it was a surprise to read the details.

Insurance policies, including those effected by consumers, were contracts of the utmost good faith. This had been established in *Carter v Boehm*,[2] a case involving an attack by the French on Fort Marlborough on the Island of Sumatra in 1760. For a consumer, the practical implication was that pre-contractually they were obliged to make full disclosure of all material facts to their insurer, regardless of whether the insurer had asked any questions. The consumer was also required to refrain from misrepresenting such facts. As the rule had been codified within the Marine Insurance Act 1906, judges had little ability to change it.

In 1975, the resulting problems faced by consumers were recognised by Lord Justice Lawton in *Lambert v Co-operative Insurance*,[3] but he could offer no remedy:

> The present case shows the unsatisfactory state of the law. Mrs. Lambert is unlikely to have thought that it was necessary to disclose the distressing fact of her husband's recent conviction when she was renewing the policy on her little store of jewellery. She is not an underwriter and has presumably no experience in these matters. The defendant company would act decently if, having established the point of principle, they were to pay her. It might be thought a heartless thing if they did not, but that is their business, not mine.

Later, in 1994, *Pan Atlantic v Pine Top*[4] confirmed that a fact did not need to be decisive to be material: it just needed to have some effect on the decision-making of a hypothetical prudent insurer. If a non-disclosure or misrepresentation induced the contract, the insurer was entitled to set the policy aside from outset and decline to pay any claim.[5]

[Peter writes]: In 1997, as part of my research for an LLM dissertation at University College London, I wrote to Co-operative Insurance Society and asked whether it had heeded the words of Lord Justice Lawton and paid Mrs Lambert's claim. Somewhat to my surprise, I received a response. It provided an answer of sorts: 'The outcome of the Lambert case [is] now rather historical and we do not wish to comment.'[6]

A further demonstration of the impact of the law can be seen in the case of Mr and Mrs C, reported in April 2003 by the Financial Ombudsman Service. Mr C made a claim under a critical illness insurance policy after his wife died from leukaemia. The claim was rejected on the basis that the intermediary acting for Mrs C had failed to disclose

[1] A privately owned insurer, run by Martin Copley, Howard James and Colin Honey, and operating from locations in Wimbledon, notably The Alexandra, The Hand-in-Hand and San Lorenzo.

[2] *Carter v Boehm* (1766) 3 Burr 1905.

[3] *Lambert v Co-operative Insurance Society* [1975] 1 Lloyd's Rep 485 at 491.

[4] *Pan Atlantic Insurance Co Ltd v Pine Top Insurance Co Ltd* [1995] 1 AC 501.

[5] For an account of the law before reforms, see J Birds, 'The Current Law' in PJ Tyldesley (ed), *Consumer Insurance Law: Disclosure, Representations and Basis of the Contract Clauses* (Bloomsbury, 2013).

[6] Letter dated 29 May 1997.

that she suffered from mild hearing loss. The Ombudsman concluded that this error was probably inadvertent. Had the insurer been aware of the true position it would still have issued the policy, albeit with an exclusion relating to hearing. There was no connection between the hearing loss and leukaemia. Nevertheless, as a matter of strict law, the insurer was entitled to reject the claim.

It can be seen that the law had four key weaknesses:

(1) The materiality test required the consumer to look into the mind of a prudent underwriter to determine whether a fact was material – few had the expertise to do this.
(2) There was no obligation on the insurer to ask questions, encouraging poor underwriting practice. An unscrupulous insurer could limit the questions it asked when a policy was sold but, if a claim was made, it could search for a non-disclosure to escape liability.
(3) The degree of culpability of the consumer was irrelevant – even innocent non-disclosure or misrepresentation could lead to avoidance.
(4) When a policy was avoided, the consumer faced three consequences – loss of cover, loss of any claims and potentially serious difficulties in obtaining replacement cover at a manageable premium.

2.3. Failed Attempts at Reform

A succession of initiatives had attempted to ameliorate the position. However, these efforts were consistently undermined by vehement opposition from the insurance industry.

In 1957, the Law Reform Committee, predecessor to the Law Commission, considered insurance law. Its brief report suggested that 'no legal difficulties would arise' if certain changes were made, such as basing materiality on a 'reasonable insured test'. The insurance industry objected, and the report was never implemented.

In 1980, the Law Commission produced a report analysing many mischiefs in the law.[7] It firmly recommended moderate reforms such as requiring disclosure of material facts only where a 'reasonable man in the position of the applicant' would do so. Again, the insurance industry objected, and the report was not implemented. Instead, in 1986, the industry made limited improvements to two voluntary codes of practice which it maintained.[8]

In 1997 the National Consumer Council published a report authored by Professor John Birds which reviewed key aspects of insurance law. It concluded that there were areas 'where consumers are manifestly still at risk' and recommended a set of reforms.[9] Those recommendations were not implemented.

[7] *Insurance Law – Non-disclosure and Breach of Warranty* (Law Com No 104, 1980).

[8] The Statement of General Insurance Practice and, later, the Statement of Long-Term Insurance Practice. The origin of these codes was not altruistic – they had been introduced as part of a behind-the-scenes deal under which the industry gained an exemption from the Unfair Contract Terms Act 1977.

[9] National Consumer Council, *Insurance Law Reform: the consumer case for a review of insurance law* (May 1997).

2.4. Initiatives within the Industry

Not all insurers chose to rely on the harsh law. In 1980, the Guardian Royal Exchange circulated an internal memorandum stating that for consumer non-life insurance it would no longer rely on the duty of disclosure.[10] The move was driven by Mike Harris, Assistant General Manager, who explained his reasoning in a letter to the Post Magazine:

> You cannot import into the way we handle bulk insurance products now the close contractual relationship derived from the time a ship or cargo owner dealt directly with an underwriter in a coffee house 300 years ago and bargained over a single voyage … Defence of the traditional duty implies that although for many years we have handled hundreds of millions of transactions we still do not know all the right questions to ask. If this be so, then surely many of us should be seeking a living in some less demanding walk of life?[11]

Mike Harris was also the inspiration behind the Insurance Ombudsman Bureau (IOB), which opened in 1981 as the first private sector ombudsman scheme in the United Kingdom (UK). Harris's pride in his company's standards led him to propose that the ombudsman should be able to issue binding awards of up to £100,000 against those insurers which chose to join the voluntary scheme.[12]

2.5. The Ombudsman Provided Some Help, but was not a Full Answer

[Peter writes]: In 1989 I joined the IOB as an ombudsman's assistant. Later I continued as a consultant to the Ombudsman, Dr Julian Farrand QC, a former Law Commissioner. The work gave me invaluable insights into the real-life problems caused by the flawed law. Farrand decided that he would apply a proportionate approach in cases of non-fraudulent non-disclosure and in some cases award damages rather than avoidance for innocent misrepresentation. In 1994 Farrand also brought about an amendment to his terms of reference, allowing the ombudsman to decide cases on the basis of 'what solution would be fair and reasonable in all the circumstances'. Using this power, his successor, Laurie Slade, went further, suggesting that in the absence of clear questions at inception or renewal an insurer would be taken to have waived the requirement of disclosure. However, this was by no means a full solution to the flaws in the law – not least because membership of the IOB remained voluntary, and decisions were only binding on the cases in which they were made.

I left the IOB in 1994 to join the insurer Sun Alliance as its principal complaints adjudicator. This followed an approach by Ray Hunt, the complaints manager. Hunt's

[10] Internal memorandum, 3 December 1980.

[11] Letter to the Post Magazine, 14 May 1981.

[12] PJ Tyldesley, 'The Insurance Ombudsman Bureau – the early history' (2003) 39 *Journal of Insurance Research and Practice* 34.

high ethical standards were an example of the very best of the insurance industry.[13] His direction to me was clear: 'Change nothing about what you do – deal with cases as an Ombudsman would.' In my thinking about the need for insurance law reform, the strongest influences were Harris, Farrand and Hunt.

Sun Alliance merged with Royal Insurance in 1996. I left to undertake an LLM at University College London, qualified as a solicitor and began teaching part-time at London Guildhall University. Eventually I applied for a full-time academic post. Teaching on the MSc in Financial Regulation and Compliance Management in 2000, I introduced a new insurance law element which considered the effectiveness of voluntary codes. The first lecture slide contained two simple propositions:

(1) insurance law is unfairly weighted against the consumer;
(2) codes of practice are no substitute for reform of the law.

2.6. The Role of BILA

The British Insurance Law Association (BILA) is a highly influential organisation in its field because of the breadth of its membership – which includes solicitors, barristers, members of the judiciary and insurance practitioners.

[Peter writes]: In January 2001, BILA formed a sub-committee on Insurance Law Reform for which I was one of three academic advisers. Later that year, my university started to act as the secretariat for BILA. The sub-committee drew particular energy from Derrick Cole, a former insurance broker, who frequently visited me to discuss progress. On 1 September 2002 the sub-committee produced a report, addressed directly to the Law Commission. It recommended 'the speedy implementation of the recommendations of the 1980 Law Commission, which we believe to be non-controversial'.[14]

2.7. The Law Commission Sets Up a New Project

[Tammy writes]: In 2002, all seemed set for swift reform. The Law Commissioners agreed that reform was overdue. In October I noted that the Chairman, Sir Roger Toulson, 'was very keen', as was the Commissioner for Commercial and Common Law, Professor Hugh Beale. Our objective was to include insurance law in the Law Commission's next programme of law reform. The only snag was that this required government approval. Insurance was then the responsibility of HM Treasury, so we needed to persuade the Treasury that insurance reform was something that the Law Commission should at least look at. This was my first challenge.

In February 2003 I put together an internal paper, outlining the case for reviewing insurance law. It noted that the Law Commission had often considered returning to the

[13] In 1984 Sun Alliance & London had acquired the well-regarded Phoenix Assurance. Ray Hunt was not alone in continuing to describe himself post-acquisition as 'a Phoenix man'.

[14] BILA, *Insurance Contract Law Reform* (September 2002).

issue of insurance reform, but had been dissuaded by the Government's reluctance to legislate:

> Since 1985, we have reviewed the possibility of further work in this area periodically, including reviews in 1994, 1999, 2000 and 2001. Each time we have reviewed the issue, our conclusion has been the same. There seems little point in the Law Commission conducting further work unless we receive some indication from the Government that our recommendations would be implemented. And such indication has not been forthcoming. As the DTI put in it 1994 'there was no evidence that the ABI Statements of Practice and IOB were not working'. Or, as the Treasury repeated in 1999, it would need to be persuaded that the problems were having 'serious practical consequences'.[15]

We started negotiations with the Treasury on the possibility of a new project, but progress was slow. Rather than begin with a full review, we suggested a possible scoping study, asking whether there was a need for reform. The Treasury considered even this to be too radical, and proposed a small seminar to take informal soundings. The seminar, on 29 January 2004, supported the idea of reform, but one seminar was not enough. In this context, the conference at London Metropolitan University in May 2004 was particularly well-timed.

[Peter writes]: On 17 May 2004, I organised a full-day conference at London Metropolitan University entitled 'Protecting the consumer – is there a need for insurance law reform?'. The aim was to bring together the many different interests involved in this area, including the Association of British Insurers (ABI), the Financial Ombudsman Service and the Consumers' Association.[16] There was a good mixed audience, largely from the insurance industry. I had, of course, invited the Law Commission. Tammy attended, and this was the first time we met face-to-face.

The mood amongst both speakers and the audience was in favour of some measure of law reform, though the ABI maintained its opposition. Unfortunately, the Treasury seemed more attuned to the ABI than to broader views.

[Tammy writes]: Despite the success of the May conference, the Treasury remained cautious. In September 2004, officials indicated that they were still minded to reject a review of insurance law, mainly because there was little prospect of finding parliamentary time for it in the foreseeable future. They were not aware of any pressure for reform in this area, except from BILA. Furthermore, their internal soundings from industry and others did not suggest a need for change. The Treasury thought that those advocating change had underestimated the importance of forthcoming regulations from the Financial Services Authority (FSA).

We assured the Treasury that the project would be funded by the Law Commission, would consult carefully and would not produce legislation for five years. On this basis, the Treasury indicated, reluctantly, that it would not oppose insurance law reform from becoming part of the next Law Commission programme. Slowly, painfully slowly, the Law Commission's ninth programme of law reform was put together and

[15] Internal memorandum, 'Reforming Insurance Contract Law: a Draft Discussion Paper' (February 2003).

[16] The speakers were Mark Allen of the ABI, Reidy Flynn of the Financial Ombudsman Service, Alison Green the Vice President of BILA, Angela Darling of the then regulator GISC, John Birds of the University of Sheffield, Mick McAteer of the Consumers' Association, and myself.

approved. When it was published in March 2005, it included insurance contract law as a confirmed project. The programme stated:

> The current law is incoherent and arguably unfair to the insured. It is made tolerable only by codes of practice that in effect disapply parts of the law. The result is not comprehensible to the consumer, while businesses are not covered by the codes of practice. The law also contains uncertainties that encourage unnecessary litigation. It has been suggested that these defects are adversely affecting confidence in the UK market. This review will ensure the law reflects the need of modern insurance practice and allows both insured and insurer to know their rights and obligations.[17]

The project would cover both consumer and business insurance. It would be run jointly with the Scottish Law Commission, so that any changes could apply to England, Wales and Scotland, though only the London office would have dedicated staff. We were allocated the normal staff for Law Commission projects: one lawyer and one research assistant. It was a natural choice to employ Peter Tyldesley as the lawyer.

2.8. Learning the Lessons of the Past

The previous Law Commission project had ended in failure. The main trade body had opposed reform and their view had been repeated uncritically by successive governments. The name of the body had changed (from the British Insurance Association to Association of British Insurers).[18] Its views had not. Our first task was to understand why previous attempts at reform had failed, and how to avoid the mistakes of the past.

[Peter writes]: With convenient timing, the Freedom of Information Act 2000 was due to come into force on 1 January 2005. In late December 2004, I contacted the Department of Trade and Industry to ask if they held the papers relating to the 1980 Law Commission report. Eventually the papers were tracked down at the FSA, which in February 2005 sent me seven document wallets of photocopied documents. They made for fascinating and instructive reading.[19]

Although the 1980 report included a powerful analysis of the 'mischiefs' of the current law, its proposals for reform had failed to gather support. The Department of Trade (DoT) had been hoping for a detailed analysis of 'proportionate remedies', which were widely used in other European countries. The basic idea was that if an insurer would have increased the premium had it known the undisclosed information, the claim would be reduced proportionately. Such remedies were proposed in a draft European directive, to open up the insurance market across Europe. In 1977, the DoT viewed the idea favourably. They saw harmonisation of legal rules as leading to a potential increase in trade, and they thought that the industry would accept proportionate remedies. Yet, in 1979, the Law Commission's working paper dismissed the principle of proportionality,

[17] Law Commission, 9th Programme of Law Reform (March 2005) para 1.12.

[18] The Association of British Insurers was formed in 1985.

[19] For fuller details, see PJ Tyldesley, 'The reform of insurance contract law – why have consumers waited so long?' (2008) 2 *Journal of Insurance Research and Practice*.

suggesting that it 'would not be a desirable innovation in this country'.[20] DoT officials were dismayed. As one put it, 'if we flatly reject the essential points of the directive, there can be no further progress on this particular bit of harmonisation'.[21]

The British Insurance Association's reaction to the working paper was even more hostile. This extended over 15 pages and objected, sometimes in caustic terms, to almost every proposal made. DoT officials were sympathetic to some of the Association's arguments, but were still surprised by the tone of the document. The Assistant Secretary at the DoT, John Henes, wrote on the response that 'it seems at times to show the objective disinterestedness of a Millwall supporter'.

Consumer groups also argued against the proposed reforms. The 1980 report proposed a single 'reasonable insured' test for both business and consumer insurance. In February 1981 the National Consumer Council, the Consumers' Association and the National Federation of Consumer Groups all presented papers to the DoT arguing that this provided inadequate protection for consumers. Instead, different solutions were needed for consumer and business policyholders.

[Tammy writes]: When we started our new project, the 1980 report provided a helpful critique of the current law. However, it soon became clear that we should think again about the solutions. Genuine innovation (that is, developing new and better law) requires collaboration with others. We would need to take a different approach to engaging with industry and consumer groups. A major problem previously was that the Law Commission had only talked to trade bodies, which tend to be dominated by their most conservative members. Like convoys, they moved at the speed of the slowest. We would need to talk to individual insurance companies and engage with the most progressive and forward-thinking firms. And we could not just impose our own views on others. We would need to work towards finding some form of consensus, listening carefully to what others had to say. Much of 2005 was taken up in discussions – with academics, industry figures, consumer groups, brokers and insurance companies – to engage them in the project.

2.9. The Financial Ombudsman Service Survey

We needed to underpin our case for reform with empirical evidence of real problems. We therefore negotiated with IOB's successor, the Financial Ombudsman Service (FOS), to undertake a survey of their cases under a confidentiality agreement.[22] The FOS was able to identify 190 consumer cases involving these issues, plus 12 small business cases. We went to their offices at South Quay Plaza in January and February 2006 to read and classify the ombudsman's final decisions.[23]

[20] *Non-Disclosure and Breach of Warranty in Insurance Law* (Law Com Working Paper No 73) para 57.

[21] Memo from Michael Starforth, DoT's solicitor.

[22] The Chief Ombudsman, Walter Merricks, was supportive, as were the two ombudsmen, Peter Hinchliffe and Melissa Collett, who had developed the FOS approach to non-disclosure and misrepresentation.

[23] Much of the work was carried out by two research assistants, Saira Paruk and Laura Giachardi, with the results published as Appendix C to the first consultation paper: *Insurance Contract Law: Misrepresentation, Non-Disclosure and Breach of Warranty by the Insured* (LC CP 182; SLC DP134).

The survey showed the seriousness of the issues. Over half of all cases involved critical illness or permanent health cover, following an alleged discrepancy between the information disclosed and that in the full medical records. Almost two-thirds of consumers were seriously ill, and 16 had died before their cases reached a decision. Large sums could be at stake: in four cases, the amount in dispute exceeded the £100,000 limit, up to which ombudsman awards were binding on insurers, but the parties nevertheless asked the ombudsman to make a non-binding recommendation.

The survey also showed the strong influence exerted by the Marine Insurance Act 1906. The FOS declared that, unlike the legal position, it would place non-disclosures and misrepresentations into three categories: those that were deliberate or reckless (where the policy would be avoided); those that were 'inadvertent' (where proportionate remedies would be applied); and those which were 'innocent' (where the complaint would be upheld). Proportionate remedies were not part of English law, and in practice, ombudsmen were reluctant to use them. Only 14 cases were classified as inadvertent. The claim was reduced proportionally in five cases; and in eight cases, the FOS asked whether an exclusion would apply.[24]

These figures were useful, but we also learnt that if we were to capture audiences' imaginations we needed examples. The survey included cases where consumers had had their disability or critical illness claims declined because they had failed to mention a cold, a mole[25] or a negative MRI scan nine years earlier.[26] In renewing contents insurance, one policyholder had their policy avoided because they had failed to mention a county court judgment. Yet they had not been asked questions about judgments and few policyholders would realise it was relevant.[27] We used these case histories as often as we could.

2.10. Comparison with Other Common Law Jurisdictions

Another theme of the study was how far Britain had fallen behind other common law jurisdictions. In 1984 the Australians had introduced a new Insurance Contracts Act that reformed many of the issues we were considering, including non-disclosure and warranties. We needed to know more about how this worked in practice. We were therefore indebted to Professor Rob Merkin, who undertook both a legal and practical analysis of that 1984 Act. We published his paper on our website and referred to it often.[28]

2.11. Deciding Scope

In January 2006 we published a 'scoping study', for two reasons. First, we needed to show that a wide range of stakeholders supported the new project, to give us the

[24] ibid para C.78.
[25] ibid para C.40.
[26] ibid para C.42.
[27] ibid para C.29.
[28] Robert Merkin, *Reforming insurance law: is there a case for reverse transportation? A report for the English and Scottish law commissions on the Australian experience of insurance law reform* (2006).

legitimacy to continue. Secondly, we needed to make difficult decisions on what issues to tackle. The decision had already been taken to look at the law of non-disclosure (in both consumer and business insurance), together with breach of warranty. The paper asked about a range of other problems, including insurable interest, late payment, fraud, subrogation and broker's liability for marine premiums. It even asked whether the whole of insurance law should be rewritten into a single code.

The paper received 118 responses, far more than the 39 responses to the Law Commission's 1979 working paper. Importantly, we received responses from leading insurance companies (including Aviva, Royal Sun Alliance, Zurich and Munich Re). We were talking to the industry directly, rather than having their responses mediated through trade groups.

In August 2006, we published an analysis of responses and set out our decision on the scope of the project. The document concluded that the review should have a wide scope:

> As well as misrepresentation, non-disclosure and breach of warranty we will be looking at most of the other issues mentioned in the Scoping Paper … It follows that the project will cover the greater part of insurance contract law as it applies to insurance and reinsurance, life and general risks, business and consumer policyholders and international and domestic business.[29]

The decision reflected the approach of the Law Commissioner, Professor Hugh Beale. He believed strongly that law should be based on an overarching set of principles, as a seamless, coherent whole. Therefore, law reform should have a wide scope, rather than be targeted at the single presenting problem.

[Tammy writes]: Peter and I were unconvinced. By 2006, it was clear that even obvious and limited reform of non-disclosure would be difficult enough, without getting bogged down into the more obscure details of the Marine Insurance Act 1906. Internally, the most difficult discussions concerned whether to look separately at the needs for consumer and business policyholders. Peter and I both thought that we should start by looking at consumer insurance. The case for reform was stronger and less contentious. We could achieve a quick win, which would help our subsequent work. Professor Beale, however, followed the 1980 report, which argued against any fragmentation of legal principles. The following paragraph represented his views:

> We swiftly reached the view that it would be undesirable to divide the review by type of policyholder. Although we accept that the law should not necessarily be the same in every respect for, say, large businesses and consumers, any difference will need to be justified. In our view, proposed differences may most effectively be assessed if the impact of the law can be concurrently considered in respect of all types of policyholders.[30]

It was agreed, however, that we would look at one issue at a time, issuing a series of shorter 'issues papers' on individual subjects, rather than moving straight to a single heavy consultation paper (known internally, as a 'green brick'). Insurers were

[29] Law Commission and Scottish Law Commission, Insurance Contract Law: Analysis of Responses and Decisions on Scope (August 2006) para 1.5.

[30] ibid para 2.4.

accustomed to a similarly structured approach from the regulator.[31] We also took inspiration from the move towards serials rather than blockbusters. Like *The Wire*, producing regular 'episodes' might increase audience engagement and allow more complex plot lines.

2.12. Progress

For the next year, the Law Commission made brisk progress – publishing issues papers on misrepresentation and non-disclosure (September 2006), warranties (November 2006) and insurance intermediaries (March 2007).

[Peter writes]: Tammy and I retained our concerns about an approach that prioritised the coherence of the law over other values. In 2006, I carried out a series of speaking engagements around the country, and it was clear that there were far greater concerns about business reforms.[32] In September 2006, Beachcroft LLP agreed to host a working seminar at its offices to discuss the first issues paper. During a break in proceedings, the attendee from HM Treasury privately approached me and indicated that there was likely to be support for consumer reforms, but that business reforms were a rather different matter. Nothing was recorded or confirmed in writing, but a clear message had been delivered.

By the end of 2006, I wished to take a more partial role in promoting consumer law reform. I resigned from the Law Commission in February 2007, though I retained an involvement in the project during 2007 on a consultancy basis.

[Tammy writes]: In July 2007 we followed convention by producing a 'green brick': a 386 page consultation paper on 'Misrepresentation, Non-Disclosure and Breach of Warranty by the Insured'. It made an official, reasoned, in-depth case for reform.

Professor Beale's time at the Law Commission came to an end in the same month. He was replaced by David Hertzell, an insurance solicitor, who had been managing partner at the city law firm, DAC. Both Commissioners attended the launch of the consultation paper, and David became responsible for encouraging responses.

David Hertzell's arrival marked a difference of approach, with less emphasis on the overall coherence of insurance law, and much greater emphasis on persuasion. David was extremely well connected in the industry, and he understood people. His gift lay in listening to the stakeholders, understanding their concerns and obtaining their confidence. Over the next three months, he held more than 50 meetings and obtained 105 formal responses. The responses showed considerable support for a new statute on consumer insurance law – but a much more mixed picture on the law that should apply to businesses.

We took the decision to press ahead with legislation to reform the way the law treated non-disclosure by consumers. If we could achieve reform there, it would build credibility for the project and take people with us.

[31] The Financial Services Authority published Discussion Papers, Consultation Papers, and Policy Statements.

[32] I was rightly subjected to robust questioning by the industry – meetings in Liverpool and Leeds are particularly memorable in this regard! In every case, however, practitioners proved to be engaged, constructive and courteous once outside the bear pit of the formal event.

In May 2008 we published a summary of responses we had received to the July 2007 Consultation Paper, but limited to consumer insurance law. It explained that 'we are treating draft legislation to deal with pre-contract information from consumers as a priority'.[33] There was considerable support for this, not only from 'consumer groups, brokers and lawyers'. Importantly, 'of the 39 insurers and insurance organisations responding to our paper, only four argued against reform'. Many actively welcomed reform to make the law simpler and clearer.[34]

We then quoted a list of major insurers who supported new legislation, including Royal & Sun Alliance, Zurich and Aviva. The ABI, however, still opposed reform. As they put it:

> A sophisticated system of regulation exists via the FSA and any reform that might take place should not impinge on this system thereby creating duplication and uncertainty. There is no widespread evidence of consumer detriment in relation to the current legal position on non-disclosure and misrepresentation, and the need for reform is therefore not evident.[35]

The ABI was supported in this by Fortis Insurance and ACE European Group.

2.13. External Lobbying

Law Commission documents are influential, but they are not always sufficient on their own to bring about change. As Law Commission staff are civil servants, there are strict limits to how far they can engage in the rough and tumble of political debate. Sometimes a more partisan approach is needed.

[Peter writes]: Having left the Law Commission, I was free to engage in active lobbying for reform. Although I had no experience in such matters, it seemed clear that it would be helpful to engage in four activities:

(1) publishing informative articles, outlining the flaws in the existing law;
(2) bringing together organisations whose clients were affected by those flaws and who might add weight to calls for reform;
(3) raising the profile of the reform project within the media; and
(4) establishing contacts within Parliament, including through any relevant All-Party Parliamentary Groups.

In January 2008, I published the first in a series of articles. Entitled 'The reform of insurance contract law – why have consumers waited so long?',[36] it set out in detail the grim history of previous failed attempts at reform, and the unsatisfactory nature of alternatives such as industry codes. It was clear, however, that articles of this length would not function well as briefing papers for campaigning and that

[33] Law Commission and Scottish Law Commission, Reforming Insurance Contract Law: A Summary of Responses to Consultation (May 2008) para 1.5.
[34] ibid para 1.3.
[35] ibid para 2.9.
[36] Tyldesley (n 19).

publishing in peer-reviewed academic journals was in any event unlikely to be useful given the long lead times. Shorter articles in various legal periodicals were therefore to follow.[37]

We were fortunate also to gain the support of other commentators, including David Worsfold, the experienced and highly respected former editor of the leading trade publication, *Post Magazine*. David was now Group Editorial Services Director of Incisive Media which owned *Post Magazine* and provided the secretariat for the All-Party Parliamentary Group on Insurance and Financial Services. As will be seen, All-Party Parliamentary Groups were to play an important part in achieving reform.

2.14. The New 'Special Procedure'

[Tammy writes]: In 2008, the House of Lords agreed the trial of a new procedure for handling uncontroversial Law Commission bills. Under this special procedure, the Bill is introduced into the Lords. The second reading takes place 'off the floor of the house', in a rather grand committee room (the Moses Room). It then proceeds to a Special Public Bill Committee, which takes evidence and considers the Bill in depth. All the subsequent stages stay the same, but the hope is that they will take very little time, given the Committee's scrutiny.[38]

This procedure is not quick. In practice, it often takes nine months or more for the Bill to clear all its stages. But it removes some of the concern that governments so often express – that law reform takes up too much 'parliamentary time' – by which they mean time scheduled in the chamber. The procedure provides some reassurance to bill managers that fitting in some small but useful piece of law reform will not interfere with the Government's legislative programme.

Two pieces of legislation passed under the trial: the Perpetuities and Accumulations Act 2009; and the Third Parties (Rights Against Insurers) Act 2010. The 2010 Act gave us invaluable experience of the special procedure in operation, and demonstrated to insurers that Law Commission reports could bring about reforms. However, it made only small changes in the law. By contrast, any bill on consumer insurance law would represent a step change. On 7 October 2010, the House of Lords approved the Procedure Committee's report recommending that the special procedure should be permanently adopted.

There has never been any definition of 'uncontroversial' for the purposes of the special procedure. The House of Commons library merely cites Lord Newby in 2014, saying that there is 'no precise definition of what does and does not constitute

[37] PJ Tyldesley, 'Blowing their cover – looking forward to the reform of insurance contract law' (2009) 153 *Solicitors Journal* 11; PJ Tyldesley, 'Archaic, unclear and unfair' (2009) 159 *New Law Journal* 961 and 1358; PJ Tyldesley, 'Consumer insurance law – reform at last?' (2010a) 81 *Amicus Curiae* 1; PJ Tyldesley, 'Insurance Contract Law Reform: Bringing the Underpinning Law into the Twenty-First Century' (2010b) 47 *CII Thinkpiece* 1; PJ Tyldesley, 'Reform at last'(2011) 161 *New Law Journal* 843; PJ Tyldesley, 'Pearls of wisdom' (2011) 155 *Solicitors Journal* 10; PJ Tyldesley, 'Utmost Good Faith – Unintended Injustice?' (2011) 86 *Amicus Curiae* 1; PJ Tyldesley, 'Consumer insurance and the duty of disclosure' (2011) 123 *BILA Journal* 38.

[38] For an account of the special procedure, see Law Commission, *Inside Modern Law Reform* (2023) paras 8.22–8.35.

controversy for the purposes of a Law Commission Bill'.[39] We interpreted the word 'uncontroversial' as meaning 'will not create problems for the Government'. If any significant organisation lobbied against the Bill, it would be controversial. So if the ABI continued to oppose reform, it would be very unlikely to happen. Our efforts were therefore geared towards building sufficient pressure for reform from the public and the ABI's own members to prevent the ABI from campaigning against it.

2.15. Building Consensus

Many insurers supported new law on non-disclosure in consumer insurance. There was also agreement around the outline of a solution. Consumers should not be required to volunteer information to the insurer before taking out a policy. Instead, a consumer's duty would be to answer the questions the insurer asked, honestly and carefully. Consumers who acted reasonably should have their claim paid. However, if the consumer made a deliberate or reckless misrepresentation, the insurer should still be entitled to avoid the contract and refuse all claims. By contrast, if the misrepresentation was careless, proportionate remedies should apply. This means, for example, that if the insurer would have increased the premium had it known the undisclosed information, the claim would be reduced proportionately.

However, agreement around the basics did not mean that insurers supported each of our proposals. The most controversial area was what should happen if a broker or other intermediary put wrong information on the form. In law, the answer depends on whether the intermediary acts for the insurer or the consumer. If the intermediary acts for the insurer, the insurer is liable for their mistake and must take the consequences. But if the intermediary acts for the consumer, the consumer is responsible.

In the consultation paper, we had suggested that the intermediary should always be taken to act for the insurer, unless they conduct a fair analysis of the market. Most consultees disagreed.[40] The insurance intermediary market was changing quickly, with the increasing use of comparison sites and there was no other single test which would garner agreement. Instead, we produced an 'indicative and non-exhaustive list of the factors' relevant to the decision. If, for example, the agent had agreed to restrict the number of insurers they dealt with, that would indicate that they acted for the insurer.[41]

[Tammy writes]: These technical issues took time to negotiate, with constant back and forth. It would have been much easier to impose a simple test (such as basing the intermediary's status on whether they conducted a fair analysis). However, this would have shut out the industry's legitimate concerns. I reminded myself that innovation requires collaboration. An imposed test would have been more likely to have failed in practice and would have undermined the consensus we needed to get the legislation through.

[39] The Law Commission and Law Commission Bill Procedures, Standard Note: SN/PC/7156, March 2015. Lord Newby was talking to the House of Lords Special Public Bill Committee during the passage of the Insurance Bill.

[40] Of the 64 consultees who gave their views, on this issue, almost two thirds disagreed. See Law Commission and Scottish Law Commission (n 33) para 5.37.

[41] The list was first published in a policy statement, 'The Status of Intermediaries', in March 2009, and was revised before being set out in Sch 2 of the Insurance (Disclosure and Representations) Act 2012.

2.16. May 2009: The All-Party Parliamentary Group for Consumer Affairs and Trading Standards

[Peter writes]: By 2009, my efforts became more targeted, to prepare Parliament for a possible bill. While researching my January 2008 article, I encountered several critical comments on insurance law made in the early 1980s by the then Director General of Fair Trading, Gordon Borrie. In January 2009, I wrote to Lord Borrie seeking his assistance, and he invited me for tea at the House of Lords.[42]

This meeting led to me being invited to speak to the All-Party Parliamentary Group for Consumer Affairs and Trading Standards on 19 May 2009. The meeting was organised by the Trading Standards Institute (TSI) and attended by the Law Commission, the ABI, HM Treasury and the FOS. There was a febrile atmosphere in the House of Commons as the speaker, Michael Martin, had resigned earlier that day. Nevertheless, it was a useful meeting, and the start of a highly productive working relationship with the TSI – an organisation which contributed much to the reforms without ever demanding the limelight.

[Tammy writes]: During the meeting, the Treasury representative asked a key question. How long would the Bill be? I plucked a figure out of the air – '12 clauses'. This appeared to be the right answer and she nodded approvingly. This was sufficient endorsement to work with Parliamentary Counsel to draft a bill, circulating draft clauses to limited groups of people. When published, the Bill did indeed contain 12 clauses – together with two long and rather complex schedules. I discovered, however, that Parliament is not overly worried about schedules.

The May meeting was encouraging, but it was far from clear that the Bill would ever be introduced. It still faced two obstacles: indifference from politicians; and opposition from the ABI. The meeting minutes record the usual negative contribution from the ABI:

> By updating the law we will be locked into a legal framework that we will be unable to update and adapt to ongoing changes. There is consumer protection currently in place. We don't think the regulations proposed provide any more clarity or protection to the consumer. We would look to see some real evidence of the proposed Bill providing these things.[43]

2.17. Alerting Politicians

[Peter writes]: Following the meeting, one of my objectives was to ensure that the opportunity for reform was brought to politicians' attention. When the Government published its Draft Legislative Programme in June 2009, it did not include insurance law reform, although the draft Bill would be available later that year.[44] I drafted a letter to Harriet Harman, then Leader of the House of Commons, urging that the Queen's Speech should confirm the Government's intention to reform consumer insurance law.

[42] We met on 18 March 2009, following my letter of 14 January 2009.

[43] Minutes of the All-Party Parliamentary Group for Consumer Affairs and Trading Standards, Thirty-Second Meeting, 19 May 2009.

[44] Draft Legislative Programme for Consultation, 29 June 2009.

The letter was circulated to the leading UK insurance law academics, who all signed.[45] I copied the letter to Which?, asking if it might also write to Harman, and the Chief Executive, Peter Vicary-Smith did so on 28 July 2009.

The next step was to publish similar letters in newspapers. Again, the leading insurance law academics signed a letter published in the *Daily Telegraph* on 5 September 2009, urging the Government to include consumer insurance law reform in the Queen's Speech.[46]

I also started to put together a small informal action group to push the case for reform, representing organisations whose clients were affected by the flaws in the law. There was no funding for the group, but Belinda Crothers at the Institute of Advanced Legal Studies made its Council Room available free of charge for a first meeting on 27 August 2009. A list of agreed action points was circulated by Which?, which hosted a second meeting. Ultimately the group included representatives of Age UK, the British Heart Foundation, Consumer Focus, Macmillan Cancer Support, the MS Society, the Trading Standards Institute, UNLOCK and Which?. Together, they were a powerful consumer voice.

In October 2009, Jim Dobbin MP raised an Early Day Motion suggesting that the Government should give wider publicity to the risks involved with inaccurately answering questions in travel insurance applications. I wrote to Dobbin, pointing out that the problem was not limited to travel insurance and drawing his attention to the Law Commission's work. A few days later, on 11 November 2009, Dobbin asked a question at Prime Minister's Questions:

> Will the Prime Minister look at a report out soon by the Law Commission recommending reforms to the insurance industry across the insurance spectrum? They are providing a draft Bill, and it would be interesting if that were looked at in future legislation.[47]

In response, Gordon Brown stated that this was an 'important matter where a change of law is obviously needed' – the most positive comment yet made by a Government minister.

In November 2009, Which? called on MPs successful in the Private Members Bill ballot to adopt the forthcoming Bill. The call was backed by Macmillan Cancer Support, which put forward a helpful case study involving one of its contacts, Inga McVicar.[48] Interest in the need for insurance law reform was increasing, and on 7 December 2009, the topic gained mainstream coverage when Trevor McDonald explored some of the issues for *Tonight* on ITV.

2.18. A Bill is Published

[Tammy writes]: The draft Bill was published on 14 December 2009, and it was a tense time. We were all too conscious that, if the ABI continued to oppose reform, it would never become law. Would the ABI bow to the criticisms made externally by the media,

[45] Sent to Harman on 7 July 2009.

[46] John Birds, Malcolm Clarke, Richard Lewis, John Lowry, Andrew McGee, Robert Merkin, Philip Rawlings, Maggie Hemsworth, Ray Hodgin and Peter Tyldesley.

[47] *Hansard*, HC Deb Vol 499, cols 247–248 (11 November 2009).

[48] See 'Unfair insurance law may be overturned' *The Observer* (29 November 2009).

and internally by their more progressive firms? Or would they keep to the traditional line? In the event, we were kept guessing up until the last minute. I have an entry in my diary from the previous Saturday.

> At the very last minute, David phoned his new mate ... at the ABI and agreed a deal ... We have toned down the press release. We are no longer saying reform is needed to protect consumers against insurers. Instead, reform is needed to remove some confusion in the law. In return the ABI are saying they won't oppose reform.

On Monday morning, however, it was clear that the ABI had briefed against the Bill, and several journalists reported that our reforms would increase premiums. Fortunately, at the press conference itself, the ABI representative said 'we do support the reforms going forward and I don't think we will be opposing them'.

[Peter writes]: I had previously met the veteran legal journalist Joshua Rozenberg and briefly discussed the proposed reforms. On 14 December 2019, I emailed Rozenberg about the ambiguity of the ABI's position. I was very aware that a general election had to be held on or before 3 June 2010:

> Until last week the ABI was opposing reform, then it said that it was neutral – neither opposing or supporting change. I can't help wondering if it is trying to avoid criticism as the report is published but keep its options open in case there is a more sympathetic government in place post-June 2010.

Rozenberg kindly responded with a copy of the media release he had received from the ABI, signed by Nick Starling and carefully worded:

> We share the Law Commission's desire that customers should be treated fairly. The insurance industry is committed to ensuring that customers understand their rights and obligations, and have their genuine claims paid quickly. We are pleased that The Law Commission recognises that best practice throughout the industry, supplemented by FSA regulation and the approach of the Financial Ombudsman Service, already protects the consumer. The Commission's proposals give legal status to existing best practices, and brings them together in one place in a clear format.

The next day, Rozenberg sent me a link to his blog entry for *Standpoint* magazine which was scathing about the ABI's approach and concluded with a key message:

> What Starling didn't say was whether his association supported the proposals. It is time he did so.[49]

[Tammy writes]: In December 2009, we did not have unequivocal ABI support. However, it looked as if they would not actively oppose the reforms. That was all we needed: we could claim, after all, that the legislation would be 'uncontroversial'.

2.19. A General Election Intervenes

By early 2010, the talk was all about the likely date for the forthcoming general election. Increasingly, the view was that it would be held on 6 May 2010. Although this would not

[49] Joshua Rosenberg, 'Insuring Fair Play' Standpoint Blogs (15 December 2009).

be formally confirmed until 6 April 2010, *The Guardian* rightly called it 'the worst-kept secret in politics'.[50] The Law Commission's reform project had started under a Labour Government. With a high probability of a change of administration, we needed to consider how this would affect the Bill's chances of being enacted.

[Peter writes]: On 25 January 2010, Mark Hoban MP, Shadow Treasury Minister, spoke at a British Insurance Law Association seminar hosted at Lloyd's. He presented the Conservative Party's White Paper on 'Sound Banking', focusing on its relevance to insurance.[51] At the end of the talk, I secured the first question and used it to enquire about a different topic entirely: 'May I ask how quickly after 6 May the Conservative Government will implement the Law Commission's proposals for the reform of consumer insurance contract law?'. The response was polite but non-committal.[52]

Subsequently I contacted a special advisor, Sue Beeby, who was able to obtain a more promising statement from Henry Bellingham MP, the Shadow Justice Minister:

> We have looked at this and are supportive. We feel that these proposals will mean more certainty for both the consumer and the insurance industry.

My next article was therefore able to state that 'crucially there is agreement between the two main political parties'.[53] Regrettably, I was never able to obtain a response to the enquiries I directed to the Liberal Democrats.

[Tammy writes]: The election took place on 6 May 2010 and returned a hung Parliament, leading to a Conservative–Liberal Democrat coalition. The prospects for insurance reform looked good. We had met Mark Hoban before the election and he seemed sympathetic. The Bill was also on the civil service radar. The day before the election, I spoke to a colleague at the Cabinet Office, and made the following note in my diary:

> [X] … was very chatty when he rang yesterday. He explained proudly that he had written four Queen's speeches, based on the most likely results. He would go to bed early tonight so he could hand the most appropriate one to the PM tomorrow. Consumer insurance wasn't in any of them, but it was on the radar and he thought it had a good chance of being an 'also ran', ready for introduction in the Autumn.

We were hopeful that, only 104 years after the Marine Insurance Act 1906, the law was about to be changed.

2.20. 'One-In One-Out'

[Tammy writes]: At first, all went well. By September 2010 the Treasury was working with us to implement the Bill. However, it took another eight months before the Bill could be introduced into Parliament. The problem was that the new Conservative policy

[50] 'Gordon Brown confirms 6 May general election date' *The Guardian* (6 April 2010).

[51] Conservative Party, 'From Crisis to Confidence: Plan for Sound Banking' (20 July 2009).

[52] Mark Hoban took the diversion in good part, and was later kind enough to contribute a foreword to a book on the reforms: PJ Tyldesley (ed), *Consumer Insurance Law: Disclosure, Representations and Basis of the Contract Clauses* (Bloomsbury, 2013).

[53] Tyldesley (2010a) (n 37).

was committed to reducing regulatory burdens on business. They had a policy of 'one-in one-out'. Every potential burden on business had to be fully costed. No government department could introduce even £1 of additional burden unless they also removed a burden of an equivalent amount.

The Treasury was clear: the insurance reforms had to be shown to be 'burden neutral'. They would not remove any other burden to make way for our insurance reforms. So it was up to us to submit an impact assessment to the Regulatory Policy Committee (RPC) showing how much the reforms would cost insurers, and how these costs would be offset by benefits to them. The figures, however speculative, had to be approved by the RPC.

I spent the next few months trying to understand the arcane world of government impact assessments. It was irrelevant whether consumers would benefit: the 'one-in one-out' policy focused entirely on the costs and benefits *to business*. At first sight, it looked as if we had an insuperable problem. If consumers were paid more in claims, this would be a cost to insurers. I argued, however, that consumers would be happy to pay higher premiums for more reliable insurance. There is little point in buying insurance that fails when you most need it. Therefore, the cost of claims would be offset by the benefit of increased premiums. As far as claims and premium costs were concerned, the overall effect would be neutral. The main change would be to administrative costs, where the additional costs of training would be offset by a reduction in the cost of disputes. Furthermore, increased consumer confidence would grow the market for insurance, providing an overall benefit for insurers.

The committee was not wholly convinced by this reasoning. However, in February 2011, they gave the assessment an 'amber' rating, which was enough for the reforms to proceed.

2.21. Publicity

[Peter writes]: The delays were frustrating, and this seemed the right time to seek greater publicity through the media. I drafted two letters. The first, urging implementation of the forthcoming proposals, was published by the *Financial Times* on 2/3 October 2010. It was signed by those who had been active supporters of the informal action group, plus some other significant names – including Martin Lewis of MoneySavingExpert.com. I also sent a personal letter to *The Times*, which was published on 5 October 2010, leading to invitations for radio interviews.

2.22. The All-Party Parliamentary Group for Insurance and Financial Services

[Peter writes]: On 1 December 2010, I was invited to speak to a meeting of the All-Party Parliamentary Group for Insurance and Financial Services. At the time, I was working in Luton, and severe weather led to all trains into London being cancelled. A £60 taxi fare took me to a decidedly quiet House of Commons. Luckily, the Law Commission,

Which? and the ABI had been able to attend. During questioning, I pointed out that a difficulty in implementing the proposed reforms was that they did not appear to enjoy the support of the ABI. To my surprise, Kate Carr, an assistant director at the ABI, corrected me, stating that the ABI 'positively supported' the proposals. I asked the Chair, Jonathan Evans MP, if this could be confirmed in writing.[54] Carr agreed that this would be done. Later that week I wrote to Which?: 'I think we are tantalisingly close to achieving reform.'

2.23. The Bill in Parliament

On 16 May 2011, the Consumer Insurance (Disclosure and Representations) Bill was introduced into the House of Lords by Lord Sassoon under the special procedure for uncontroversial Law Commission Bills. There was a debate on the second reading in Committee on 13 June 2011. On 5 September 2011, a Special Public Bill Committee was constituted, with 11 members including Lord Borrie.[55]

Unlike many bill committee proceedings, special procedure bills cannot rely on the Government's majority to ram the legislation through. We needed to show that the Bill was actively welcomed, would help consumers and had no significant opposition. The Special Public Committee was keen to give real scrutiny to the Bill, taking both oral and written evidence.

[Peter writes]: James Whittle, the Clerk to the Committee, wrote to me on 21 September 2011, inviting me to submit written evidence. I drafted a Joint Position Statement, agreed by the action group on 10 October 2011. The first page was simply a list of the organisations that had worked within the action group, in each case with a colour logo. The aim was simple – maximum impact by showing the breadth of influential support for the Bill.

Oral evidence came from four witnesses: Lord Sassoon and David Hertzell on 11 October 2011; and Professor Malcolm Clarke and Lord Justice Longmore on 19 October 2011. Lord Hodgson was active in questioning the latter two witnesses, and the responses encouraged him to table some amendments. The first, for example, provided that 'it is the duty of the insurer to make it clear whether they comply with industry codes of practice'. This seemed both uncertain (what codes would be covered?) and unnecessary (the point of the Bill was to move away from reliance on codes).

[Tammy writes]: Special procedure bills can be amended, but amendments are problematic. Even if an amendment appears pro-consumer, it has the potential to upset the industry, and therefore disrupt the delicate consensus which caused the Bill to be deemed uncontroversial. It is important to keep good communication with both consumer and industry lobbies to ensure that any bill is not only uncontroversial when

[54] Jonathan Evans later recorded the importance of this meeting – see *Hansard*, HC Deb Vol 541, cols 789–790 (6 March 2012).

[55] The membership was: Chair: Lord Lloyd of Berwick; Conservative: Lord Sassoon, Lord De Mauley, Lord Hodgson of Astley Abbotts, Baroness O'Cathain; Liberal Democrat: Lord Goodhart, Baroness Kramer; Labour: Lord Eatwell, Baroness Wheeler, Lord Borrie, Lord Davies of Stamford.

it enters the procedure, but stays so until the end. Here Peter's work outside the Law Commission proved crucial.

[Peter writes]: I consulted with David Sanders of the TSI and we each wrote to James Whittle expressing concerns about the amendments. This produced a gratifying moment at Committee stage on 10 November 2011 when Lord Hodgson referred to the correspondence: 'I am sure the Minister will say, because he will also have received a copy of this letter, that we got a real savaging from Mr David Sanders, the principal trading standards officer from the Vale of Glamorgan. Rowing in behind him to give us an equally big beating is Peter Tyldesley.'[56] After some discussion, all three amendments were withdrawn.

2.24. The Bill Becomes Law

The Consumer Insurance (Disclosure and Representations) Act gained Royal Assent in March 2012 and entered into force on 6 April 2013. Consumer insurers were now obliged to ask questions: they carried out widespread reviews of application forms, to ask questions in the way that consumers could understand.

In 2006, we had looked to other common law jurisdictions to find the latest thinking on insurance contract law. Now other countries looked to the UK. The Law Reform Commission of Ireland, for example, said it paid 'particular attention' to these 'significant statutory reforms'.[57] Australia and New Zealand largely adopted the approach of the UK reforms by amendments to the Insurance Contracts Act 1984 and through the Contracts of Insurance Act 2024 respectively. Rob Merkin, who had been so helpful to us, played a significant role in the latter two developments.[58] Similar reforms have been suggested for Singapore,[59] and we are told that there have been early discussions in Hong Kong.

[Tammy writes:] It was over 10 years since I had first taken a job at the Law Commission. I had worked on many other projects while managing the team, including unfair contract terms and consumer rights, but insurance had been a dominant part of my work. The other reforms to insurance law took even longer. We eventually succeeded in changing the law of business non-disclosure and warranties in the Insurance Act 2015 and we changed the law of late payments in 2017.

It was now my turn for people to look askance at my CV. As my (new) boss explained, in few words, I could not be expected to be promoted within the Civil Service if I had stayed in the same job for 15 years. Instead, in 2018, I moved roles within the Law Commission to work on the legislation for self-driving cars – which took a mere six and a half years to gain Royal Assent.

[56] House of Lords Special Public Bill Committee, 10 November 2011.

[57] Report on Consumer Insurance Contracts (LRC 113-2015) 32.

[58] Rob Merkin wrote background papers on insurance law for the Australian Royal Commission which recommended the changes, and in New Zealand he was appointed early in 2019 as a consultant for insurance law reform by the Ministry of Business, Innovation and Employment.

[59] Singapore Academy of Law, Law Reform Committee, 'Report on Reforming Insurance Law in Singapore' (February 2020).

2.25. Conclusion

Commentators have identified two approaches to adapting laws to fit social and technological change: 'coherentism' and 'regulatory interventionism'.[60] As Roger Brownsword explains, coherentists prioritise 'the integrity and internal consistency of legal doctrine', believing that 'legal reasoning should be anchored to guiding general principles'. By contrast, regulatory interventionists are 'entirely focused on whether the law is instrumentally effective in serving specified regulatory purposes and policies'.[61] Their response to a problem is to fix it with a bespoke solution.

These approaches can be seen in the debates over adapting insurance law to the needs of a mass consumer market. Both the 1980 report and Professor Hugh Beale argued for 'coherentism', believing that the law should be consistent and governed by general principles. The 1980 report, for example, rejected separate rules for consumers on the grounds that 'a multiplication of legal categories would clearly be complex and undesirable'.[62] Professor Beale thought that any review should consider both, and should be wide-ranging, ensuring consistency with all the provisions of the Marine Insurance Act 1906. By contrast, HM Treasury were extreme 'regulatory interventionists'. Their initial view was that any problems could be fixed by regulation, and insurance regulation was the responsibility of the FSA. So why were we bothering them by talking about law reform? It took a great deal of effort to persuade civil servants that unfair law could not be fixed by the regulator's edict that insurers should treat their customers fairly.

The solution to the problem of non-disclosure in consumer insurance law lay between these two extremes. Reforming the whole of marine insurance law would have been beyond the abilities and capacity of the Law Commission. Law reform requires the attention of civil servants, ministers and Parliament. And this attention will only be forthcoming if law reformers can provide evidence of a clear and pressing problem. This is why the evidence produced by the FOS survey was so crucial. In other areas, such as insurable interest, it was not possible to present evidence of a pressing need for change, however incoherent the law. As a result, 19 years after the scoping study committed the Law Commission to review the law of insurable interest, no solution is in sight.[63]

On the other hand, simply adding one new fix after another can lead to a confusing hodge-podge of rules and regulations. The FOS survey showed that, among all the FSA rules, codes of practice and ombudsman guidance, insurers tended to default to what they knew best – the harsh rules set out in the Marine Insurance Act 1906. Where law has been codified, judges lose the ability to update the law to fit social, economic and technological changes. Parliament needs to step in to change the statute. But anyone

[60] See EL Rubin, 'From Coherence to Effectiveness' in R van Gestel, HW Micklitz and ELL Rubin (eds), *Rethinking Legal Scholarship* (Cambridge University Press, 2017) 310, 311. Brownsword develops this dichotomy in the context of technology regulation: see, for example, R Brownsword, 'Law Disrupted, Law Re-Imagined, Law Re-Invented' (2019) *Technology and Regulation* 10.

[61] Brownsword (n 60) 14.

[62] Law Com No 104 (n 7) para 4.38.

[63] Law Commission and Scottish Law Commission (n 29) para 3.8.

who wanted to bring about this change needed to be in it for the long haul. It is a long, slow, grinding business.

2.26. Lessons

So, what are the practical implications of this conclusion? What have we learnt about how to change an area of consumer law?

The first, and most crucial, lesson is that you have to involve people. No one has the expertise to provide solutions by themselves. Progress comes from talking, understanding the various points of view, looking to overseas experience and slowly finding consensus around solutions. The consumer insurance reforms were only possible because we worked with lawyers, consumer groups and the many progressive voices within the insurance industry itself. Never just talk to trade bodies – or (even worse) exchange bad-tempered memoranda with them. Trade bodies have a strong tendency to defend the status quo. Instead, you need to cultivate allies within the industry. The consumer insurance reforms were influenced by many people – and they were not politicians or 'big' public figures. Some were quite 'ordinary' individuals, who gave their time voluntarily to the cause. The list included academics, brokers, insurers, consumer advocates and ombudsmen staff.[64]

The second lesson is to focus on people's problems. In a political world dominated by the regulatory interventionist mindset, civil servants and politicians will not respond to dry arguments about incoherent law. You need case histories. Every change has to be explained to the media – think three-minute interview – so arguments need to be short and punchy. And do not try to do too much. We succeeded in getting the 2012 Act through because it was (reasonably) short: 12 clauses (albeit with two schedules). Replacing the 92 sections of the Marine Insurance Act 1906 was never a viable option.

Tactically, All-Party Parliamentary Groups are a useful resource. This is not because many parliamentarians attend – they do not – though the few who do can be important allies on subsequent bill committees. It is more that the gothic atmosphere of Westminster concentrates the minds of pressure groups and civil servants on the legislative process. In this story, crucial informal understandings took place around the meetings.

Finally, changing the law often requires people to work outside normal career structures. Civil servants who are committed to a particular change will need to stay in their posts for far longer than is compatible with career advancement – which is increasingly difficult now that consolidated salary increases are no longer awarded in-post.

[64] Any list risks offending by inadvertent omission, but we were particularly grateful for assistance from: Laurence Baxter, Lola Bello, John Birds, Lord Borrie of Abbotts Morton, Laura Burgoyne, Richard Buttle, Derrick Cole, Melissa Collett, Vera Cottrell, Belinda Crothers, Robert Cunnew, Teresa Fritz, Ron Gainsford, Alison Green, Julian Harris, Martin Hill, Peter Hinchliffe, Mike Hobday, Irja Howie, Phil Jones, Suzanne Kuyser, Geoffrey Lloyd, Rob Merkin, Lizi Piggins, Sylvia Rook, David Sanders, Christina Sparks, Christopher Stacey, Jessica Tangye, Elizabeth Waller, Laura Weir, Lucy Widenka and David Worsfold. Tom Williams and Susan Tyldesley demonstrated remarkable patience.

Academics will need to withstand pressures to publish in refereed journals with 18 month turnaround times – in favour of articles that are timely, short and accessible.

Legal innovation is not something that happens through abstract forces. Nor is it driven by remote politicians. It happens through the actions of ordinary people, acting together to put the arguments for change and to devise solutions. But it requires people skills, creativity and, above all, stamina.

PART II

Future Directions for Consumer Law in General

3

The Acts and Scenes of the Brexit Consumer Law and Policy Melodrama …

JAMES DEVENNEY, GERAINT HOWELLS AND CHRIS WILLETT

3.1. Introduction

Brexit was, in the words of Marcus Smith J., a truly 'seismic event',[1] the magnitude and consequences of which even unsettled some Brexiteers.[2] For some, Brexit promised a bonfire of European Union (EU) regulations, although the precise regulations remained largely unspecified;[3] and this would create opportunities for innovation and competitive advantage. Yet, despite, for example, the rhetoric around the (then) Retained EU Law (Revocation and Reform) Bill 2022, as well as much academic speculation on potentially affected areas, this bonfire has largely not materialised. This chapter, first, seeks to understand, in the context of consumer law, why this has been the case – a question which has simply not been addressed before. One reason, we will argue, has been the lack of a post-Brexit vision for consumer law in the United Kingdom (UK). Another reason is the previously nuanced relationship with EU consumer law in the UK; a relationship which, to some extent, already enabled the UK to develop a distinctive flavour or version of EU consumer law.

This chapter also charts the current degree of similarity and divergence between consumer law in the UK and the EU. In so doing it examines signs of a future degree of re-alignment with EU consumer law; a phenomenon which this chapter seeks to encourage. Our analysis takes into account a wide range of areas including unfair terms, unfair practices, digital content, digital services, product liability and safety, enforcement, and redress. By adopting such a pan-consumer-law viewpoint, which explores not only legislative provision, but also their application, this paper offers a unique insight into the *overall* effects of Brexit in this area, including the real degree of divergence and convergence between EU and UK consumer law. It also seeks to use this as a foundation to provoke debate about a post-Brexit vision of consumer law in the UK; central to

[1] *Canary Wharf (BP4) T1 Limited v European Medicines Agency* [2019] EWHC 335 (Ch) [241].

[2] See, for example, F O'Toole, 'Brexit and the politics of the fake orgasm' *Irish Times* (2 July 2016).

[3] See M. Kenny, 'The UK and the EU: The Whinge in (and out of) the Willows?' (2016) 27 *New Zealand Universities Law Review* 463, 470.

which, we shall argue, should be a degree of alignment or re-alignment. Yet alignment or re-alignment is not, in itself, sufficient; we shall argue, for example, that there also needs to be a re-establishment of consumer law co-operation frameworks between the UK and EU.

3.2. Prologue: Parody v Reality

The EU, of course, has had a significant impact on consumer law in the UK, particularly over the past 40 years or so.[4] At times this has also 'excited much [negative] feeling',[5] as in the so-called 'Metric Martyrs' cases, as well as giving rise to opportunities for parody.[6] Yet, as is so often the case, the reality is much more nuanced for a number of reasons. First, it seems there was not a great demand for a reduction in core consumer protection legislation;[7] for example one poll from IPSO Mori showed 79 per cent of young *leave* voters wanted to *maintain* or *even increase* EU-derived consumer protection laws.[8] Secondly, whilst it is clear that some aspects of core EU consumer law caused concern in the UK,[9] the UK, rather than begrudgingly transposing the letter of core consumer law directives, voluntarily went beyond the scope of relevant directives in a number of cases. One might, for example, point to the application, by the Consumer Rights Act 2015 (CRA 2015), of the unfair terms regime to negotiated terms,[10] or the voluntary extension of private rights of redress for unfair commercial practices by the Consumer Protection (Amendment) Regulations 2014.[11]

Thirdly, the way in which the UK often transposed EU core consumer law directives by, at least initially, merely copying them into primary or secondary legislation, with little attempt to integrate them into existing frameworks,[12] did little to aid the coherence of consumer law in the UK (such as with the previously overlapping, yet contrasting, provisions of the Unfair Contract Terms Act 1977 and the Unfair Terms in Consumer Contracts Regulations 1999).[13] Yet in more recent (pre-Brexit) years, driven

[4] See, for example, I. Ramsay, *Consumer Law and Policy*, 3rd edn (Hart Publishing, 2012) 5.1ff; and C Twigg-Flesner, 'United Kingdom: An Incomplete Transformation of Consumer Law' in HW Micklitz and C Twigg-Flesner (eds), *The Transformation of Consumer Law and Policy in Europe* (Bloomsbury, 2023) 325–46.

[5] *Thoburn v Sunderland City Council* [2002] EWHC 195 (Admin) [1] per Laws LJ.

[6] See, for example, R Sabey, 'IMPERIAL STRIKES BACK: pounds and ounces to be revived for Jubilee as UK ditches EU diktat' *The Sun* (online) (29 May 2022).

[7] See M Morris, 'Public attitudes to Brexit: The Referendum was more a vote for re-regulation than de-regulation' LSE, BPP Blog (2022).

[8] Unchecked UK, *Attitudes of younger Leave voters to regulation and deregulation: New findings on attitudes to regulation, deregulation and enforcement among younger Leave voters, from a poll by Ipsos MORI for Unchecked UK* (May 2020).

[9] See, for example, CRA 2015, s 71 and G Howells, 'The European Union's influence on English consumer contract law' (2017) *George Washington University Law Review* 1905.

[10] See CRA 2015, s 62. This was partly to remove the scope for 'sham negotiations' that sought to avoid application of the fairness test: see Law Commissions, *Unfair Terms in Contracts*, Law Com 292, Scot Law Comm 199, Cm 6464, 2005, 3.52, 3.156.

[11] See J Devenney, 'Private Redress Mechanisms in England and Wales for Unfair Commercial Practices' (2016) 5 *Journal of European Consumer and Markets Law* 100.

[12] See HM Treasury, *Davidson Review: Implementation of EU Legislation* (2006).

[13] See, for example, Law Commission (n 10) [3].

by the view that consumer law in the UK had become 'unnecessarily complex',[14] there was an attempt to better integrate core EU consumer law in the UK. Here one might point to the CRA 2015 with its much more integrated and coherent consumer remedies regime,[15] and its single unfair terms regime.[16]

Fourthly, despite the tide of EU consumer law, the UK was able to retain a distinctive UK flavour to core consumer law. This can be seen, for example, in the continuing imprint of the Sale of Goods Act 1979 on obligations and remedies in the CRA 2015; the recasting of (the pivotal) Article 4(2) of the Unfair Contract Terms Directive in the UK, first by *Office of Fair Trading v Abbey National Plc*[17] and then by the CRA 2015, section 64; and, whilst the implementation of the Unfair Commercial Practices Directive[18] brought the continental tradition of a general duty of fairness (drawing again on 'good faith' and 'professional diligence') – contrary to the less principled, piecemeal common law tradition[19] – its enforcement requirements were flexible enough to allow the UK to retain criminal law as a key tool, as it has done for almost 100 years in public consumer law enforcement.

Indeed, in some areas the UK had been afforded a notable degree of latitude to develop its own distinctive approach even when still a Member State. Thus, in the context of the Product Liability Directive,[20] the UK's existing contractual and non-contractual liability rules remained untouched by the maximum harmonisation approach as a result of Article 13. This contrasts with France, whose Civil Code rules were considered to have evolved into a system of strict producer liability which was not permitted to exist alongside the Directive's form of strict liability.[21] This freedom is explored further below in relation to case law.[22]

For present purposes the key point is that the Court of Justice of the European Union (CJEU) had been rather indulgent towards the UK's manner of implementing the Directive, dismissing an infringement action brought with respect to the scope of its development risks defence in section 4(1) Consumer Protection Act 1987 which had been forced though in a rush to enact the law before a general election.[23] That case related to the UK's transposition of the Directive which seemed to introduce a concept of expectancy of discovering a defect linked to the type of producer, whereas the Directive seems focused on objective discoverability. The UK, perhaps suspecting such a challenge lay ahead, had astutely, but unnecessarily, written into section 1 of the Act the obligation to construe the Act to comply with the Directive. The CJEU noted that there had not been any case law to establish the interpretation of the provision.[24] This seemed a little disingenuous as litigation on such a provision is always likely to be

[14] See Department for Business, Innovation and Skills, *Draft Consumer Rights Bill: Government Response to Consultations on Consumer Rights* (BIS/13/916, June 2013) 5.
[15] See, for example, CRA 2015, ss 19–24.
[16] CRA 2015, Pt 2.
[17] [2009] UKSC 6.
[18] Directive 2005/29/EC.
[19] See, for example, *Interfoto Picture Library v Stiletto Visual Programmes* [1988] 1 All ER 348.
[20] Directive 1985/374/EEC.
[21] Case C-52/00 *Commission v France* [2002] ECR I-3827.
[22] See pp 46–47.
[23] C-300/95 *Commission v UK* [1997] ECR I-2649.
[24] ibid [37].

limited due to the costs of litigating technical scientific evidence. In any event, defendants, particularly repeat players, are likely to settle cases that might have favourable facts for claimants and that risk an interpretation that narrows the defence.

Finally, the precise impact of EU consumer law in the UK was also affected by the way in which directives etc were approached and interpreted by the courts in the UK.[25] Take, for example, the case law in England and Wales on product liability and the swing between pro-claimant and pro-defendant approaches. *A v National Blood Authority*[26] marks a high point in the courts in England and Wales embracing a 'European approach' to strict product liability that produces a claimant-friendly outcome. In fact, the parties and judge in that case had agreed that the text of the Product Liability Directive should be used directly rather than the (implementing) Consumer Protection Act 1987. Burton J also reviewed the history and *travaux preparatoires* in seeking to interpret the Product Liability Directive in light of its policy rationale and the need to avoid imposing expensive litigation costs on the parties. The result was certainly pro-claimant even if, ultimately, much rested on the particular facts.

Yet subsequent High Court judgments, particularly involving litigation over artificial hips, have sought to distance themselves from the approach of Burton J.[27] They criticised his approach of starting by describing the harmful characteristic of the product, feeling that this leads almost automatically to finding causation and a finding of defectiveness.[28] They rejected 'legitimate expectations' as a yardstick of liability; for whilst, empirically, a risk might not be expected to occur, once it was disclosed it could not be expected never to materialise.[29] They thought a wide range of circumstances that Burton J had held to be irrelevant to be potentially relevant: avoidability; impossibility; cost of taking measures; benefit of utility (except perhaps with full information and proper knowledge); and information provided to learned intermediaries.[30]

Perhaps most significantly the judges in these cases (purportedly) used the CJEU jurisprudence emanating from *Boston Scientific v AOK Sachsen –Anhalt Gesundheitskasse*[31] to justify that restrictive interpretation. In fact, that decision had been very pro-claimant in holding pacemakers and defibrillators defective on the basis that they belonged to the same group, or formed part of the same production series, that had a potential defect. Yet the judges focused on the discussion about there being an 'abnormal potential for damage' in order to restrictively interpret defect.[32] Ironically, this had actually been used by the CJEU as a justification for taking the extra step of not needing identification of defect in products where similar products had been found to be defective! It is also worth noting that the restrictive approach of more recent courts

[25] *cf Freiburger Kommunalbauten GmbH Baugesellschaft & Co KG v. Ludger Hofstetter and Ulrike Hofstetter* [2004] ECR-I 3403.

[26] [2001] 3 All ER 289.

[27] *Wilkes v DePuy* [2016] EWHC 3096 (QB), [2017] 3 All ER 589 and *Gee v DePuy*, [2018] EWHC 1208. For a decision on the factual finding of non-defectiveness of an artificial hip see the Supreme Court decision in *Hastings v Finsbury Orthopaedics Ltd* [2022] UKSC 19.

[28] *Wilkes* (ibid) [58] and *Gee* (ibid) [106]–[108].

[29] *Wilkes* (ibid) [70]–[71] and *Gee* (ibid) [95].

[30] *Wilkes* (ibid) [76]–[108] and *Gee* (ibid) [139]–[178].

[31] C-503/13 *Boston Scientific v AOK Sachsen –Anhalt Gesundheitskasse* [2015] 3 CMLR 6.

[32] *Gee* (n 27) [127].

in England and Wales had not been challenged at the EU level. Indeed, it is often hard to detect non-compliance that is not blatant, and it is unclear how national application could be effectively controlled when applying an open textured norm.

3.3. Act One: The Referendum and the Promised Bonfire of Regulations …

Yet, as noted above and despite these nuances, one of the arguments advanced by supporters of Brexit was that Brexit would allow a bonfire of (unspecified) EU regulations.[33] Such an argument undoubtedly found popular support, no doubt fuelled for a number of years by sections of the media which, inter alia, generated some spectacular headlines.[34] Nevertheless, at an early stage the UK Government indicated that, at least in the short term, much of the *acquis* would be converted into domestic law. This was predominantly framed as a pragmatic solution for business;[35] but it might equally, in the current context and whilst recognising the complex nature of consumer decision-making,[36] have been framed around consumer confidence.[37] This was given effect to by, inter alia, the European Union (Withdrawal) Act 2018, which retained most pre-existing core consumer law of an EU origin in domestic law. There were, however, three notable areas where repeals were made in the current context.

First, Regulation (EU) No 524/2013 on consumer online dispute resolution (ODR)[38] was, perhaps inevitably, repealed in the UK.[39] That Regulation established a free multilingual European Online Dispute Resolution Platform. Whilst recognising the importance of effective dispute resolution for consumer rights and confidence,[40] Regulation (EU) No 524/2013 was not well used, with only approximately 200 cases across the EU enabled by it per year;[41] and has now also been repealed by the EU.[42]

[33] See J Devenney and M Kenny, 'The Post-Brexit Legacy of EU Consumer Law in the UK: Chronic Rejection or Continued Acceptance?' (2017) 1 *Journal of European Consumer and Markets Law* 1.

[34] ibid and M Kenny 'The UK and the EU: The Whinge in (and out of) the Willows?' (2016) 27 *New Zealand Universities Law Review* 463.

[35] See HM Government, *The United Kingdom's exit from and new partnership with the European Union* (2017), Cm 9417) para 1.1ff.

[36] See, for example, C Waddams Price and M Zhu, 'Empirical Evidence of Consumer Response in Regulated Markets' (2016) 12 *Journal of Competition Law & Economics* 113.

[37] On the impact of legal uncertainty see, for example, EU Commision, *Green Paper on policy options for progress towards a European Contract Law for consumers and businesses* (COM(2010)348 final) and C Willett, 'Re-Theorising Consumer Law' (2018) 77 *Cambridge Law Journal* 179, 181ff.

[38] Regulation (EU) No 524/2013 of the European Parliament and of the Council of 21 May 2013 on online dispute resolution for consumer disputes and amending Regulation (EC) No 2006/2004 and Directive 2009/22/EC.

[39] See Consumer Protection (Amendment etc) (EU Exit) Regulations 2018, reg 10.

[40] See, for example, OECD, Recommendation of the Council on Consumer Dispute Resolution and Redress (OECD/LEGAL/0356 (2024)).

[41] See Proposal for a REGULATION OF THE EUROPEAN PARLIAMENT AND OF THE COUNCIL repealing Regulation (EU) No 524/2013 and amending Regulations (EU) 2017/2394 and (EU) 2018/1724 with regards to the discontinuation of the European ODR Platform, 2023/0375(COD), Section 1 of Explanatory Memorandum.

[42] Regulation (EU) 2024/3228 of the European Parliament and of the Council of 19 December 2024 repealing Regulation (EU) No 524/2013, and amending Regulations (EU) 2017/2394 and (EU) 2018/1724 with regard to the discontinuation of the European Online Dispute Resolution Platform.

Secondly, whilst the Competition and Markets Authority (CMA) continues to have powers to seek undertakings and enforcement orders to prevent continued breaches that harm consumers collectively, the reach of those powers has been curtailed. It can, of course, continue to take action in the UK courts against UK businesses and businesses from EU countries where their activities harm UK consumers. However, post-Brexit the CMA can no longer take action against such businesses in their local courts.[43] This may mean UK consumers will sometimes go unprotected against activities that a business has been banned from continuing in their own country by a local court.

Finally, and also perhaps inevitably, the 2006[44] and the 2017[45] the Consumer Protection Cooperation (CPC) Regulations were repealed in the UK.[46] Given that many consumer issues, particularly in the digital market, transcend national boundaries, the 2006[47] and the 2017[48] CPC Regulations provided a general framework for pan-EU regulatory co-ordination. This creates a regime for EU cross-border consumer enforcement co-operation and assistance, providing reciprocal powers and duties for Member States' competent authorities to request and provide each other with assistance. For example, it allows relevant competent authorities to ask a cross-border authority for information on a business based in that authority's jurisdiction and to require it to take enforcement action against that local business to stop it committing infringements detrimental to consumers in the other Member State. The context for these Regulations can be found in Recitals (2) and (3) of Regulation (EC) No 2006/2004: some consumer issues transcend national borders and the inability to deal effectively with such issues undermines consumer confidence and distorts competition between domestic and cross-border traders. This intensified with the continued development of digital markets with the CPC Regulations being used in a number of high-profile areas: for example, to gain undertakings from Expedia,[49] Booking.com[50] and AirBnB[51] about the way they present deals; to gain transparency commitments from social media and search engine

[43] See amendments to Enterprise Act 2022, Pt 8 and CRA 2015, Sch 5 by the Consumer Protection (Enforcement) (Amendment etc) (EU Exit) Regulations 2018. See now Digital Markets, Competition and Consumers Act 2024 (DMCCA 2024), particularly s 173.

[44] Regulation (EC) No 2006/2004 of the European Parliament and of the Council on cooperation between national authorities responsible for the enforcement of consumer protection laws.

[45] Regulation (EU) 2017/2394 of the European Parliament and of the Council of 12 December 2017 on cooperation between national authorities responsible for the enforcement of consumer protection laws and repealing Regulation (EC) No 2006/2004. Regulation (EU) 2017/2394 was repealed by the Consumer Protection (Enforcement) (Amendment etc.) (EU Exit) Regulations 2020/1347, reg 3.

[46] Regulation (EC) No 2006/2004 was repealed by the Consumer Protection (Enforcement) (Amendment etc.) (EU Exit) Regulations 2019/203, Regulation 8. Regulation (EU) 2017/2394 was repealed by the Consumer Protection (Enforcement) (Amendment etc.) (EU Exit) Regulations 2020/1347, reg 3.

[47] Regulation (EC) No 2006/2004 of the European Parliament and of the Council on cooperation between national authorities responsible for the enforcement of consumer protection laws.

[48] Regulation (EU) 2017/2394 of the European Parliament and of the Council of 12 December 2017 on cooperation between national authorities responsible for the enforcement of consumer protection laws and repealing Regulation (EC) No 2006/2004.

[49] European Commission, *Expedia enforcement action Commitments obtained by the European Consumer Protection Cooperation (CPC) authorities* (December 2020).

[50] European Commission, *Booking.com enforcement action Commitments obtained by the European Consumer Protection Cooperation (CPC) authorities* (December 2020).

[51] European Commission, *AirBnB Enforcement Action* (July 2019).

providers such as WhatsApp,[52] Google,[53] Facebook[54] and TikTok;[55] and in respect of the consequences of the COVID-19 pandemic on air travel.[56] It has also been used to address 'dieselgate'[57] and issues of sustainable consumption[58] and/or 'greenwashing'.[59]

The CMA has said that it 'will seek to continue to work with EU enforcers as far as possible';[60] but, against the backdrop of increasingly strained relations between the UK and EU under the last UK Government, the fact that authorities in other countries no longer have a legal duty to co-operate with the CMA surely makes it harder to bring about necessary action against businesses, at least in relation to any detrimental impact they are having on UK consumers.[61]

3.4. Act Two: EU–UK Trade and Co-Operation Agreement (December 2020) ...

Subsequently, an EU–UK Trade and Co-Operation Agreement ('the Agreement') was finalised by negotiation teams from the EU and UK on 24 December 2020,[62] which, in the UK, was implemented by the European Union (Future Relationship) Act 2020. The Agreement covered a wide variety of issues including trade in goods and services, aviation and road transport, digital trade and energy. In respect of consumer protection, the Preamble to the Agreement recognised the parties' autonomy in respect of consumer protection generally,[63] but also noted a *desire* that the 'Agreement contributes to consumer welfare through policies ensuring a high level of consumer protection and economic well-being, as well as encouraging cooperation between relevant authorities'.[64]

[52] For background see BEUC, *Press release: Consumer groups file complaint against WhatsApp for unfairly pressuring users to accept its new policies*, BEUC-PR-2021-026 (12 July 2021).

[53] See European Commission, *Common position of national authorities of the CPC Network concerning the commercial practices and terms and conditions of Google.com* (26 January 2023).

[54] See European Commission, *Consumer Protection Cooperation Action on Facebook's Terms of Service* (April 2019).

[55] See European Commission, *List of commitments by TikTok to improve their practices* (21 June 2021).

[56] See, for example, European Commission, *Press Release: Consumer protection: Airlines reimburse over 500,000 flight vouchers as result of Commission and consumer authorities action in COVID-19 pandemic*, IP/22/4383 (8 July 2022).

[57] See European Commission, *Declaration of the Consumer Protection Cooperation (CPC) network on the use of defeat device software by the Volkswagen Aktiengesellschaft (VW)*, Ares(2021)4541653.

[58] European Commission, *Common position of national authorities of the CPC Network concerning the commercial practices of Nintendo of Europe GmbH* (4 April 2023).

[59] See: commission.europa.eu/live-work-travel-eu/consumer-rights-and-complaints/enforcement-consumer-protection/coordinated-actions/sustainable-consumption-actions_en.

[60] CMA, *Guidance on the Functions of the CMA after the Transition Period* (2020) 5.15.

[61] Note that Regulation (EU) 2017/2394, Art 32 provides: 'To the extent necessary to achieve the objective of this Regulation, the Union shall cooperate with third countries and with the competent international organisations in the areas covered by this Regulation in order to protect consumers' interests. The Union and the third countries concerned may conclude agreements setting out arrangements for cooperation, including the establishment of mutual assistance arrangements, the exchange of confidential information and exchange of staff programmes.'

[62] See commission.europa.eu/strategy-and-policy/relations-non-eu-countries/relations-united-kingdom/eu-uk-trade-and-cooperation-agreement_en.

[63] See also Art 123(2).

[64] See also Art 770.

The Preamble also noted the opportunities presented by digital trade and the issue of 'unjustified barriers' in that area.

Explicit consumer protection provisions in the Agreement include: marking or labelling of products;[65] co-operation on market surveillance and non-food product safety and compliance;[66] particular postal services;[67] promoting transparent and reasonable rates for international mobile roaming services;[68] safety of medicinal products;[69] and air travel.[70] There are also commitments around digital trade, particularly in respect of building consumer trust.[71] Interestingly, the Agreement also refers on numerous occasions to 'fair competition' or the equivalent.[72] This is significant given the link between competition law and consumer law, for instance the well-accepted idea that a lack of competition limits market discipline on traders, and may therefore necessitate stronger consumer protection laws.

3.5. Act Three: Brexit Freedoms Bill …

In January 2022 the then Prime Minister, Boris Johnson, against the backdrop of the Partygate scandal, announced an intention to introduce a 'Brexit Freedoms Bill'.[73] On 22 September 2022, the Retained EU Law (Revocation and Reform) Bill 2022 was introduced into Parliament, driven by prominent Brexiteer Jacob Rees-Mogg MP. This proposed to go even further than was suggested by the former Prime Minister's announcement. More specifically the Bill contained a 'sunset' provision for EU-derived subordinate legislation,[74] meaning that such legislation would be revoked at the end of 2023 unless saving regulations were made in respect of a particular piece (or pieces) of EU legislation. In relation to consumer law this caused concern, particularly around timeframes, for bodies such as the Consumers' Association,[75] the Chartered Institute of Trading Standards[76] and Consumer Scotland (the statutory body for consumers in Scotland).[77]

[65] Which, under Art 95(2)(a) 'shall only require information which is relevant for consumers or users of the product or information that indicates that the product conforms to the mandatory technical requirements'.

[66] Art 96.

[67] Art 162.

[68] Art 181.

[69] Annex 12.

[70] Under Art 438(2): 'the Parties shall ensure that effective and non-discriminatory measures are taken to protect the interests of consumers in air transport. Such measures shall include the appropriate access to information, assistance including for persons with disabilities and reduced mobility, reimbursement and, if applicable, compensation in case of denied boarding, cancellation or delays, and efficient complaint handling procedures.'

[71] See Art 208.

[72] See, for example, Arts 355 and 359.

[73] Prime Minister's Office, Press Release: Prime Minister pledges Brexit Freedoms Bill to cut EU red tape (31 January 2022).

[74] See cl 1–2.

[75] See: www.which.co.uk/news/article/consumer-rights-food-and-safety-laws-at-risk-of-being-scrapped-under-new-legislation-azzZF1N8tg2E.

[76] See Retained EU Law (Revocation and Reform) Bill, Written Evidence Submitted by the Chartered Trading Standards Institute (CTSI) (REULB31).

[77] See Retained EU Law (Revocation and Reform) Bill, Written Evidence Submitted by Consumer Scotland (REULB13).

Indeed, any major purge, particularly a hurried one, of core EU-derived consumer law (either subordinate legislation, as was the focus of the then Retained EU Law (Revocation and Reform) Bill 2022, or, more widely, primary legislation) would have been misplaced, for at least two reasons. First, the general view was that core EU-derived consumer law was broadly working well in the UK.[78] Secondly, on this basis, some continuity is desirable for business, and broad familiarity is important for consumer confidence.

Ultimately the Retained EU Law (Revocation and Reform) Act 2023 was much more modest than originally proposed.[79] Although it repealed, at the end of 2023, a significant amount of EU-derived subordinate legislation, it did not really affect core EU-derived consumer law which, along with other retained EU law, became known as assimilated law.[80] It also further prospectively modifies the European Union (Withdrawal) Act 2018, section 6 on the interpretation of assimilated law. The combined impact of the reforms to section 6 mean that the Supreme Court and, in certain instances, the High Court of Justiciary is not bound by assimilated EU case law;[81] and the Court of Appeal and Inner House of the Court of Session will not be bound by assimilated EU case law 'except so far as there is relevant domestic case law which modifies or applies the assimilated EU case law and is binding on the relevant appeal court'.[82]

The latter will raise some interesting 'heraldry' questions. For example, in relation to the Unfair Terms Directive the CJEU has said that 'plainness and intelligibility' goes beyond the term simply making grammatical sense to the average consumer. In addition, the language must enable the consumer 'to evaluate, on the basis of clear, intelligible criteria, the economic consequences for him/her which derive from it [the term]'; and the reason for the term and its relationship with other terms must be explained in a transparent manner.[83] The CJEU has also said that the term must enable the consumer 'to have to hand all the information which could have a bearing on the extent of his liability';[84] and, closely related to this, that where consumer obligations could change (eg, payments linked to an external index) that the term should set out the possible variations and risks.[85] We might call this the 'rigorous unpacking of risks' model of transparency.

[78] See Department for Business, Energy and Industrial Strategy, *Reforming Competition and Consumer Policy Driving growth and delivering competitive markets that work for consumers* (2021) 2.2: 'The consumer protection legal framework is essential to achieving this ambition. For example, the CRA 2015 consolidated in one place consumer rights covering contracts for goods, services, digital content and the law relating to unfair terms in consumer contracts, enabling consumers to buy and sell with confidence. It also gave the civil courts and public enforcers greater flexibility when dealing with breaches or potential breaches of consumer law. Overall, this legal framework is still working well: the UK has one of the world's strongest consumer protection regimes, with strong advocates for consumer interests and well-developed advice services working alongside a comprehensive package of statutory consumer rights.'

[79] Although note s 3(2): 'The principle of the supremacy of EU law is not part of domestic law. This applies after the end of 2023, in relation to any enactment or rule of law (whenever passed or made)'.

[80] See Retained EU Law (Revocation and Reform) Act 2023, s 5.

[81] See s 6(4)(a)–(b).

[82] See s 6(4)(ba).

[83] C-26/13 *Árpád Kásler and Hajnalka Káslerné Rábai v OTP Jelzálogbank Zrt* [2014] 2 All ER (Comm) 443; C-143/13 *Matei v SC Volksbank România* SA [2015] 1 WLR 2385 [73]–[77]; and C-96/14 *Jean-Claude Van Hove v CNP Assurances SA* [2015] 3 CMLR 31 [40]–[49].

[84] C488/17 *EOS KSI Slovensko Sro v Danko* [2019] 1 CMLR 22 [63].

[85] C51/17 *OTP Bank Nyrt v Ilyes* [2019] 1 CMLR 25 [75].

This is evidently a high standard of transparency, one which has been followed and unpacked further in CMA guidance.[86] It is especially important in the digital environment where so many transactions now take place and where there is so much scope for unfair terms, for example affecting privacy rights or excluding liability for lost data.[87] It is also important in promoting sustainability, which may be compromised by terms, for example, excluding liability for misleading environmental claims, or more generally excluding liability for misleading and aggressive practices inducing consumers to buy and consume what they do not need. However, this particular CJEU jurisprudence – the 'rigorous unpacking of risks' model of transparency – has never been expressly adopted by either the Court of Appeal or the Supreme Court, meaning that under the reformed section 6, the Court of Appeal would not be obliged to follow it going forward. It could, for instance, insist on no more than the basic language being linguistically clear and jargon-free, and that, where appropriate, certain terms should be more prominent than the others.[88]

In one sense, the common law tradition pulls in the direction of low standards of transparency. For example, the common law incorporation rules on standard terms generally[89] require only reasonable notice that terms exist, not that they are immediately available or are expressed in a transparent manner, far less anything approaching the sort of rigorous spelling out of risks in the CJEU approach.[90] However, consumer legislation has of course already moved to the plain language, intelligibility and prominence models of transparency, and there is little risk of backtracking from these at least. One compromise position might be for the CJEU 'rigorous unpacking of risks' model to be adopted in especially complex contracts such as financial services and the sort of digital situations mentioned above. This would reflect the pragmatic common law tradition which is uncomfortable with broad fairness principles applying across all contracting situations; but is more content to apply focused regulation to areas where the strongest need is well established. However, such an approach should not be left to the courts, but rather legislated for, in order to spell out precisely what is required. This seems particularly important when one bears in mind that the courts have not so far considered it important to adopt the CJEU approach, and generally have a record of setting relatively low fairness standards under the regime.[91]

[86] CMA, *Unfair Contract Terms Guidance* (2015) ch 2.

[87] See, eg, M Loos and J Luzak, 'Wanted: A Bigger Stick. On Unfair Terms in Consumer Contracts with Online Service Providers' (2016) 39 *Journal of Consumer Policy* 63; C Gardner, *Unfair Contract Terms on the Digital Age* (Elgar, 2022).

[88] This would follow the UK transparency and prominence approach in the CRA 2015, ss 64 and 68, and case law such as *Parking Eye v Beavis* [2015] UKSC 67 [108].

[89] Aside from special prominence rules in the case of the most extreme or unusual cases of substantive unfairness – *Interfoto Picture Library v Stiletto Visual Programmes* [1988] 1 All ER 348.

[90] *Parker v South Eastern Railway* (1877) 2 CPD 416.

[91] C Willett, 'General Clauses and the Competing Ethics of European Consumer Law in the UK' (2012) 71 *CLJ* 412; C Willett, 'Re-theorising consumer law' (2018) 77 179; C Mitchell, *Vanishing Contract Law* (Cambridge University Press, 2023) ch 5.

3.6. Act Four: Northern Ireland …

Northern Ireland posed a number of challenges for Brexit in general and for post-Brexit trade in particular;[92] and it has been the backdrop to some of the straining of the relationship between the UK and EU. It has also created difficulties for consumers in Northern Ireland with the Northern Ireland Consumer Council reporting,[93] for example, issues with the supply, availability, delivery times and costs of online shopping,[94] as well as Great Britain retailers no longer delivering to Northern Ireland.[95] Post-Brexit, the border between Northern Ireland and Ireland became a land border between the EU and the UK. One issue was how to protect trade between Ireland and the UK.[96] A related conundrum was how to ensure that goods crossing the border complied with relevant EU (or indeed UK) regulations without having a hard border on the island of Ireland (which was politically very sensitive[97]). This conundrum became embroiled in the issue of the so-called 'backstop'. Ultimately, the revised EU–UK Withdrawal Agreement,[98] with the Revised Protocol on Ireland/Northern Ireland, created, in effect, a border in the Irish Sea by, for example, creating checks on certain goods entering Northern Ireland from Great Britain. This was so even if the goods were to remain in Northern Ireland. This angered some communities in Northern Ireland[99] and was modified by the Windsor Agreement,[100] which created two lanes for goods coming into Northern Ireland from Great Britain: a green lane (for goods which would remain in Northern Ireland) and a red lane (for goods which would go on to the EU across the Northern Ireland/Ireland border).

Nevertheless, the Democratic Unionist Party (DUP), concerned about the potential detachment of Northern Ireland from the rest of the UK, refused to support the Windsor Framework and continued to boycott Stormont power-sharing until 30 January 2024 when it was widely reported that the DUP had endorsed a new trade deal for Northern Ireland proposed by the UK Government. More detail followed on 31 January 2024 with the publication of the *Safeguarding the Union*

[92] See, for example, the University of Strathclyde's Fraser of Allander Institute, *The New Northern Ireland Protocol: is Northern Ireland stuck in the middle?* (29 November 2021).

[93] Consumer Council, *Northern Ireland consumers and EU Exit: An overview of EU Exit experiences in 2023* (2023).

[94] ibid 12.7.

[95] ibid 12.6.

[96] See Department for Exiting the European Union, *The United Kingdom's exit from and new partnership with the European Union* (Cm 9417 (2017)) 4.3: 'Maintaining our strong and historic ties with Ireland will be an important priority for the UK in the talks ahead. This includes protecting the Common Travel Area (CTA) … The UK and Irish economies are deeply integrated, through trade and cross-border investments, as well as through the free flow of goods, utilities, services and people. Annual trade between the UK and Ireland stands at over £43 billion, while around 60 per cent of Northern Ireland's goods exports to the EU are to Ireland.'

[97] See, generally, F Cochrane, *Breaking Peace: Brexit and Northern Ireland* (Manchester University Press, 2020), esp ch 6. See also M Murphy, 'Northern Ireland and Brexit: where sovereignty and stability collide?' (2021) 29 *Journal of Contemporary European Studies* 405.

[98] See commission.europa.eu/strategy-and-policy/relations-non-eu-countries/relations-united-kingdom/eu-uk-withdrawal-agreement_en.

[99] See, for example, DUP, '7 Reasons the Irish Sea border must go' (14 January 2022).

[100] See HM Government, *The Windsor Framework: A New Way Forward* (CP 806 (2023)).

policy paper.[101] A key focus of the deal was strengthening the UK internal market[102] through, for example, replacing the green lane with an internal market system,[103] establishing a new body (IntertradeUK) to champion trade within the UK[104] and modifying the EU (Withdrawal) Act 2018 in connection with the Stormont Brake procedure set out in the Northern Ireland Protocol/Windsor Framework.[105] Significantly, as Northern Ireland remains subject to some EU laws (including consumer laws), there was to be a legal duty for ministers to consider whether Bills in the Houses of Parliament (which, for example, seek to move away from EU laws in England, Scotland and Wales) would affect trade between Northern Ireland and the rest of the UK;[106] and this was given effect to by a new section 13C in the European Union (Withdraw) Act 2018.[107] This was to be flanked by legislation which would prevent the UK Government making new agreements with the EU which would create new barriers to trade between Northern Ireland and the rest of the UK;[108] and this was given effect to by a new section 38A in the European Union (Withdrawal Agreement) Act 2020.[109] The overall result of the foregoing is that it is now harder for the rest of the UK to move away from those consumer-focused EU laws which bind Northern Ireland.

3.7. Act Five: The Digital Markets, Competition and Consumers Act 2024

The Digital Markets, Competition and Consumers Act 2024 (DMCCA 2024) contains a number of consumer protection provisions which were heralded by soundbites around the establishment of 'a more active pro-competition strategy to deliver more targeted and effective pro-competitive interventions'.[110] Yet, although the DMCCA 2024 does, for example, provide a (welcome)[111] sharpening of enforcement powers,[112] other changes are more modest. For example, it repeals[113] the Consumer Protection from Unfair Trading Regulations 2008 (CPUTR 2008), which transposed the EU Unfair Commercial Practices Directive (UCPD) only to resurrect them, with some tweaks, in the DMCCA 2024 itself![114] The DMCCA 2024 does make it clear that drip pricing is

[101] Northern Ireland Office, *Safeguarding the Union* (CP 1021 (2024)).
[102] See also the Windsor Framework (UK Internal Market and Unfettered Access) Regulations 2024.
[103] See Northern Ireland Office (n 101) [82]–[86].
[104] ibid[122]–[126].
[105] ibid [167]–[169].
[106] See ibid [145]–[146].
[107] Inserted by Windsor Framework (Constitutional Status of Northern Ireland) Regulations 2024, reg 3.
[108] See Northern Ireland Office (n 101) [69]–[71].
[109] Inserted by Windsor Framework (Constitutional Status of Northern Ireland) Regulations 2024, reg 2.
[110] Department for Business, Energy and Industrial Strategy, Reforming Competition and Consumer Policy Driving growth and delivering competitive markets that work for consumers (2021) 0.15.
[111] K Beioley, 'CMA chair Tyrie steps down early pointing to 'inherent limits' of role' *Financial Times* (online) 18 June 2020.
[112] See DMCCA 2024, Pt 3.
[113] See ibid s 251.
[114] See ibid Pt 4, Ch 1.

not allowed by requiring that the total price has to be provided or else there will be a material omission[115] This makes express what is implicit within the Unfair Commercial Practices Directive.[116] A similar pattern of modest change can also be seen in relation to ADR notification duties.[117]

The impact of these tweaks, in terms of levels of protection, is mixed. For example, under the CPUTR 2008, following the UCPD, it was provided that if traders could reasonably foresee that a group of consumers were vulnerable to a practice, then this vulnerability should be taken into account in assessing whether the practice had sufficient effect on consumers to count as misleading or aggressive.[118] This rule stays in place,[119] but as well as the criteria counting as vulnerability until now (age, physical or mental health and credulity) the DMCCA 2024 seems to have improved protection by including vulnerability to 'the product' and vulnerability based on 'the circumstances the. [consumers] are in'.[120] Vulnerability to 'the product' might allow account to be taken, for example, of whether addictive digital interfaces might be likely to pressurise consumers who would otherwise not be vulnerable. Vulnerability based on the consumer's 'circumstances' might, for example, allow consideration of financial difficulties, which might make some consumers more susceptible than others to being misled or pressured by online loan offers. So, in this respect, the law in the UK may now be more protective than the UCPD, which does not recognise these forms of vulnerability and, as it is a full harmonisation directive, does not allow for greater protection in the Member States than is provided for by the UCPD itself.[121]

In other respects, however, the DMCCA 2024 may reduce protection compared to the UCPD. For example, under the UCPD, and the CPUTR 2008, an aggressive practice could (and, in the case of the UCPD, still can) be established by *coercion*, *harassment* or *undue influence* significantly impairing 'freedom of choice' and being likely to cause a consumer transactional decision that would not otherwise be taken.[122] In the case of *undue influence*, this had to involve impairment of freedom of choice in the form of an *uninformed* decision.[123] However, the overarching freedom of choice concept (in the UCPD and under the CPUTR 2008) which is applicable to *coercion* and *harassment* is wider. It arguably includes situations where consumers have limited power/choice but do what the trader wants because, for example, of addictive interfaces or threats to take enforcement action for disputed debts.[124] Here the consumer will usually make a well-informed choice; indeed it is exactly *because* they understand their lack of practical substantive choice that they give in to the harassment or coercion!

[115] ibid s 230.
[116] See Guidance 4.2.8.
[117] See DMCCA 2024, Pt 4, Ch 4.
[118] Consumer Protection from Unfair Trading Regulations 2008, reg 2(5).
[119] DMCCA 2024, s 247.
[120] ibid s 247(3)–(4).
[121] Art 4.
[122] Unfair Commercial Practices Directive, Art 8 and Consumer Protection from Unfair Trading Regulations 2008, reg 7(1).
[123] Unfair Commercial Practices Directive, Art 2(j) and Consumer Protection from Unfair Trading Regulations 2008, reg 7(3)(b).
[124] See *OFT v Ashbourne Management Services* [2011] EWHC 1237 (Ch), where threatening to report a consumer to a credit reference agency for a disputed debt was an aggressive practice.

However, the DMCCA 2024 omits this broader overarching freedom of choice element. It refers solely to coercion, harassment or undue influence affecting transactional decision-making; while keeping the requirement that undue influence must involve uninformed decision-making.[125] This might lead regulators and courts to conclude that, as with undue influence, there can only be an aggressive practice in situations of coercion or harassment if the consumer's *informed* decision-making is impaired. So, if there is sufficient *transparency*, there can be no aggressive practice, even if the consumer has little power/choice. A consumer may, for example, make a purchase due to an addictive interface; yet there might be no unfair practice even though leaving the site is in practice very hard as long as it was made clear that the consumer could leave the site if they wished – the consumer has now made an informed decision to stay.

The Digital Markets, Competition and Consumer Bill (as it was then) also made a number of headlines when introduced, most notably around subscription contract traps[126] and the regulation of fake reviews.[127] Subscription traps are a typical online problem where consumers might believe they are making one-off payments, but later discover they are trapped into an expensive long-term contract. The DMCCA 2024 provisions on subscription contracts are complex,[128] but essentially provide for a 14-day cancellation period as well as detailed pre-contract and subsequent information/warnings. This broadly reflects EU enforcement action against subscription traps under the UCPD.[129]

In respect of fake reviews, and despite the headlines, there were actually no provisions on fake reviews in the original Bill and, in fact, fake reviews could have easily been dealt with under pre-existing legislation![130] Whilst the Bill was moving through Parliament the Government did consult on fake reviews[131] with the result that it was decided that there would be new banned practices[132] relating to fake reviews, but the liability would only be civil liability.[133] This broadly follows the Modernisation Directive (MD) provision[134] that it is a misleading omission (an unfair practice under the UCPD regime) if traders do not provide information about whether and how they ensure consumer reviews originate from those who have genuinely used the product.

[125] ss 228(1), 228(3)(b).

[126] J. Reilly, 'MONEY TRAPS Ministers set to crackdown on "subscription traps" costing Brits £1.6bn per year' *The Sun* (online) (22 April 2023).

[127] J Clark, 'CRACK DOWN Five new "laws" to stop Brits being ripped off including fake review fines and a subscription trap ban' *The Sun* (online) (19 July 2021).

[128] C Busch and C Twigg-Flesner, 'A roadmap for regulating subscriptions in the Digital Fairness Act' (2024) 13 *Journal of European Consumer and Markets Law* 234.

[129] European Commission, Study on Misleading 'free' trials and subscription traps for consumers in the EU (2017), op.europa.eu/en/publication-detail/-/publication/bf621260-9441-11e7-b92d-01aa75ed71a1; commission.europa.eu/live-work-travel-eu/consumer-rights-and-complaints/enforcement-consumer-protection/coordinated-actions/consumer-frequent-traps-and-scams_en and Guidance 2.96.

[130] *cf* CMA, 'Press release: CMA intervention leads to further Facebook action on fake reviews (9 April 2021).

[131] See Department for Business and Trade, *Smarter Regulation: Consultation on Improving Price Transparency and Product Information for Consumers* (September 2023).

[132] See now DMCCA 2024, Sch 20, para 13. Note also s 237(8) (breach of Sch 20, para 13 not a criminal offence).

[133] Department for Business and Trade, *Government response to consultation on 'Smarter Regulation: Improving consumer price transparency and product information for consumers'* (January 2024).

[134] Directive (EU) 2019/2161, Art 3(4)(c).

3.8. Act Six: EU Developments …

3.8.1. Representative Actions

In practical terms, one of the most significant illustrations to date of the impact on UK consumer law of Brexit is that the UK has not been required to introduce a representative action for consumers. The EU Representative Actions Directive[135] is based around the designation of qualified entities to bring actions to protect the collective consumer interest. Qualified entities can be public bodies or consumer organisations, so long as the latter meet specific criteria.[136] They are entitled to seek both injunctive and redress measures.[137] The effectiveness of these measures in providing consumer redress typically depends on whether they are opt-out regimes allowing the representative to claim for the harm caused to all affected consumers, and the relevant funding options available to finance the litigation. The Directive leaves it to Member States to determine whether the mechanism adopted for redress measures is an opt-in or opt-out regime.[138] Third-party funding is permitted, if allowed under national law, but there need to be controls to limit the influence of the funders.[139] So, the effectiveness of the regime will depend heavily on the choices made by Member States. The UK, by contrast, has no such general representative action procedure. It does have a collective redress procedure in the competition field,[140] which is very popular precisely because it allows opt-out claims that are financed by venture capital funds under damaged based fee agreements. The Government has decided that any extension of the collective procedure to other areas will be on an incremental basis after evaluating how collective redress in the competition field works in practice. There seems no appetite yet to extend the competition regime whose very dynamic use may indeed be a reason for hesitation in providing more collective redress mechanisms. In practice, many of the competition cases seem to be consumer cases where unfair terms are alleged to the result of abuse of a dominant position.

3.8.2. Product Safety

The EU General Product Safety Directive has now been replaced by the General Product Safety Regulation,[141] which modernises the law with respect to technology by taking into account factors such as the interconnectedness of products (internet of things),[142] and the evolving, learning and predictive functionalities of artificial intelligence (AI) products.[143]

[135] Directive (EU) 2020/1828.
[136] Art 4.
[137] Art 7(4).
[138] Recital 43.
[139] Art 10.
[140] G Howells, 'Class Actions in the UK and Ireland. A Tale of Two Common Laws Diverging Post-Brexit' (2024) *European Journal of Consumer Law* 277.
[141] Regulation (EU) 2023/988.
[142] Art 6(1)(b).
[143] Art 6(1)(h).

Although, on its face, the Regulation does not seem to cover independent software, the European Commission's view is that standalone software is covered as a product since it is an item.[144] It also extends the potentially responsible parties to fulfilment services providers and, in limited circumstances, online platforms. The information and communication mechanisms have been reformed. The new structure, now named Safety Gate, has three elements: (i) Safety Gate Rapid Alert System (rapid non-food information exchange between national authorities and Commission); (ii) Safety Gate Portal (complaints from the public); and (iii) Safety Business Gateway (for businesses to fulfil their obligations to inform national authorities).

The Labour Government has stressed the importance of product safety by introducing in its first legislative session a Product Regulation and Metrology Bill, now the Product Regulation and Metrology Act 2025. One senses that an important part of this was to give the Government the freedom to continue to align with the EU moving forward where it chooses to do so. However, one of the important themes in the earlier Product Safety Review was the desire to move to a more hazard-based regulation. This was clearly intended to signal a streamlined approach to regulation and be potentially deregulatory. How the tension between achieving a change in regulatory approach and seeking continued alignment with EU law works out will be an important touchstone for testing where the priorities lie going forward. Of course, it is possible that the EU would also be considering similar changes to promote its competitiveness, but unfortunately the UK is no longer able to directly influence these internal debates.

3.8.3. Product Liability[145]

The EU has adopted a new Product Liability Directive.[146] This brings software within the definition of a product;[147] introduces liability for substantially modified products;[148] extends the range of potential defendants to include authorised representatives, fulfilment service providers, online platforms (in some circumstances) and substantial modifiers;[149] ensures the features of AI, the internet of things and cybersecurity risks are included within the definition of defectiveness;[150] takes account of the ability to update and upgrade software when determining the time to assess defectiveness and the state of scientific and technical knowledge for the purpose of the development risks defence;[151] expands damages to include psychological harm and destruction or corruption of data;[152] extends the expiry (long-stop limitation) period to bring a case to 25 years in the case of latent personal injury;[153] and introduces access to justice reforms on disclosure

[144] European Commission, EU General Product Safety Regulation – Frequently Asked Questions para 2.9.
[145] See J Devenney and G Howells, 'Developing product liability networks for AI systems in the medical context' (2025) 76 *Northern Ireland Legal Quarterly* 118.
[146] Directive (EU) 2023/988.
[147] Art 4(1).
[148] Arts 4(18) and 8(2).
[149] Art 8.
[150] Art 7.
[151] Arts 7(2)(e)(e) and 11(1)(e).
[152] Art 6.
[153] Art 17.

of evidence and the burden of proof.[154] It is unclear how far the UK will follow these reforms. It seems, based on the *Smarter Regulation: UK Product Safety Review*,[155] that the Government will be open to including software within the strict product liability regime. However, it is not included in the Product Regulation and Metrology Act 2025.

3.8.4. Digital Content

Another key post-Brexit EU provision is the Digital Content and Services Directive 2019.[156] Digital content is data produced and supplied in digital form under a contract from a supplier to a consumer,[157] for example the download of films, apps, games etc. A digital service is one allowing 'the consumer to create, process, store or access [digital] data … or … allowing … sharing … or any other interaction with [digital] data uploaded or created by the consumer or other [service] user',[158] for example storage and sharing of consumer data in the cloud, on phones, social media etc, processing of consumer data in the provision of a money transfer or payment service etc. Since 2015, the UK, through the CRA 2015, has had similar rules for digital content, but digital services were not covered. Also, whereas the EU directive covered digital content and services supplied in return for data, in UK law there needs to be a price paid – although there is power to extend this to cover contracts made using data by ministerial order.[159]

Under the EU Directive both digital content and digital services must conform to the contract.[160] Conformity depends on express contractual provisions ('subjective' standards).[161] Crucially, it also includes non-excludable 'objective' requirements on fitness for purpose, quantity, accessories, instructions, compliance with trials, and reviews and updates; and on quality.[162] For breach of these conformity standards, consumers have the right to have the digital content or service brought into conformity, price reduction and/or termination.[163]

The EU seems to have benefited from the UK's experience to produce a more sophisticated set of rules. For example, when assessing conformity it made it clear that relevant factors include functionality, compatibility, security and integration instructions.[164] The EU Directive, unlike the UK Act, does not mention repair and replacement as specific remedies, but the recitals show the drafters were attuned to the digital context and cite issuing updates and providing a new copy as potential forms of cure.[165] The Directive also considers how data should be handled once the

[154] Arts 9–10.
[155] Department for Business and Trade and Office for Product Safety and Standards, 2023. The Law Commission has announced that it will be consulting on this area in 2026.
[156] Directive EU/2019/770.
[157] Art 2(1).
[158] Art 2(2); where the consumer is enabled to process data supplied by the trader – this seems to be both the supply of digital content and digital services.
[159] s 33(5).
[160] Art 6.
[161] Art 7, eg on description, quantity and quality, functionality, compatibility, interoperability, fitness for particular purpose, accessories, instructions and updates.
[162] Art 8.
[163] Arts 14–18.
[164] Art 8(1)(b).
[165] Recital 63.

contract has been brought to an end.[166] Obligations to update have been introduced by the EU[167] and these provide for an innovative potentially long-term post-contractual obligation.[168]

3.9. Epilogue: The Future …

3.9.1. UK Consumer Law Vision

At present a number of proposals for reform of core consumer law in the UK appear to have stalled. For example, the reforms to the law on the passing of property in goods proposed by the Law Commission[169] seems to have been indefinitely postponed.[170] Similarly, in 2021 the Law Commission tentatively suggested 'product liability and emerging technology' for its programme of Law Reform.[171] Yet in February 2023 the Law Commission concluded that the time was not right to establish a new programme of reform, noting that it had 'taken this decision in view of the Government's focus on priorities for the remainder of this Parliament'.[172] Subsequently, in a report mainly concerned with product safety reform, the Government has alluded briefly to the need for modernising product liability law, but concretely has only mentioned the possibility of extending the definition of product to include software and taking AI into account when assessing defectiveness.[173] The context, we would suggest, is a country hamstrung by Brexit, without, at least under the former Government, a real vision for the future of UK consumer law, nor for achieving the competitive advantages which Brexit promised to deliver.[174]

[166] Art 16.

[167] Arts 7–8.

[168] See L Nogler and U Reifner (eds), *Life Time Contracts: Social Longterm Contracts in Labour, Tenancy and Consumer Credit Law* (Eleven International Publishing, 2014).

[169] See Law Commission Consultation Paper, *Consumer Sales Contracts: Transfer of Ownership* (Law Com 398, (2021)). This was the culmination of much work at the Law Commission: see Law Commission, *Consumer Prepayments on Retailer Insolvency* (Consultation Paper No 221 (2015)), Law Commission, *Consumer Prepayments on Retailer Insolvency* (Law Com No 368 (2016)) and Law Commission Consultation Paper, *Consumer Sales Contracts: Transfer of Ownership* (Consultation Paper No 246 (2020)).

[170] See Law Commission Annual Report 2022–23 (Law Com, No 414) 54: 'However, any decision as to whether to implement the final draft Bill would need to balance a number of relevant considerations to ensure that the benefits justify the potential costs. In particular, during the course of our work, we identified a common practice among retailers of delaying the point at which the sales contract is formed until the goods are dispatched to the consumer. This would reduce the impact of our reforms which, like most consumer protections, depend on a sales contract being in place. The evidence we have received about the practice does not suggest that it causes consumer detriment in more general terms, but we think this, and the case for our reforms, should be kept under review …'.

[171] See: lawcom.gov.uk/14th-programme.

[172] See: lawcom.gov.uk/update-14th-programme-of-law-reform.

[173] Department for Business, Energy and Industrial Strategy, *Smarter Regulation: UK Product Safety Review* (August 2023) 42. See now the Product Regulation and Metrology Act 2025.

[174] *cf* general policy statements such as wanting 'a more active pro-competition strategy to deliver more targeted and effective pro-competitive interventions' (Department for Business, Energy and Industrial Strategy, *Reforming Competition and Consumer Policy Driving growth and delivering competitive markets that work for consumers* (2021) 0.15). See also the UK Government policy paper, *Establishing a pro-innovation approach to regulating AI* (CP 728, (2022)).

3.9.2. Economic Impact of Brexit

The precise economic impact of Brexit is, of course, keenly contested;[175] and this is not the place for a detailed rehearsal of that debate. However, in March 2022, the Office for Budget Responsibility found that *goods* exports to the EU fell by nine per cent in the fourth quarter of 2021 compared with 2019;[176] and this was not offset by exports to non-EU countries, which were down by 18 per cent in the same period.[177] Likewise, *goods* imported from the EU decreased by 18 per cent; whereas imports from non-EU countries increased by 10 per cent in the same period. Exports of services to the EU were down 5–10 per cent in the same period; whilst imports of services were down by about 30 per cent.[178] There was also evidence to suggest that the UK became a less trade-intensive economy.[179]

Some care needs to be taken with these figures given, for example, their proximity to the end of the transition period,[180] the delays in implementing full customs checks at the UK border[181] and the current degree of regulatory alignment between the UK and EU in certain sectors; as well as distorting global factors such as the COVID-19 pandemic and the war in Ukraine (which impacted prices for energy, which is largely imported from outside the EU[182]).[183] Nevertheless the Office of Budget Responsibility's more recent assessments[184] conclude that its 'assumptions about the impact of Brexit appear to be broadly on track'. Moreover, there is also evidence of emerging regulatory differences (and uncertainty about future directions[185]) impacting on UK businesses' trading (and possibly appetite for trading) in the EU[186]), as well as EU businesses' appetite to trade in the UK.[187]

[175] See, for example, R Freeman et al, 'UK trade in the Wake of Brexit' (Centre for Economic Performance Discussion Paper No 1847 (2022)).

[176] Office for Budget Responsibility, *The latest evidence on the impact of Brexit on UK trade* (March 2022). See also J Springford, *The Cost of Brexit* (Centre for European Reform, December 2021).

[177] ibid. In respect of services the Office for Budget Responsibility noted: 'UK services trade with the EU has fallen by more relative to 2019 levels than non-EU trade ... However, much of this decline is likely to reflect the impact of the pandemic, particularly in sectors such as travel and transport that accounted for a greater proportion of pre-pandemic EU services trade than non-EU. UK service exports to the EU and rest of the world have recovered to around 5 and 10 per cent below 2019 levels while imports of services from the EU are still down by over 30 per cent.'

[178] ibid.

[179] ibid.

[180] 31 December 2020.

[181] Discussed by K Forster-van Aerssen and T Spital, *The impact of Brexit on UK trade and labour markets* ECB Economic Bulletin (2023).

[182] Office for Budget Responsibility, *The latest evidence on the impact of Brexit on UK trade* (March 2022).

[183] ibid.

[184] Office for Budget Responsibility, *How are our Brexit trade forecast assumptions performing?* (March 2024). *cf* Office for Budget Responsibility, *Economic and Fiscal Outlook* (October 2024) 2.28.

[185] See Office for Budget Responsibility (March 2024) (n 184).

[186] See, for example, British Chamber of Commerce, *Brexit at Three: Fresh Trade Challenges Growing* (December 2023): 'Almost two thirds (60%) of firms trading with the EU say it is now more difficult to do so than it was a year ago ... Almost half (49%) of exporters disagree the Brexit deal is helping them grow sales ... Two fifths (41%) of firms exporting under the Brexit deal say they face difficulties adapting to its rules on buying and selling goods.'

[187] See, for example, KPMG and British Chamber of Commerce in Germany, *100 Days of Brexit – An Interim Conclusion* (2021). See also kpmg.com/de/en/home/media/press-releases/2024/04/brexit-continues-to-be-a-burden-for-companies.html.

Of course, some may not lament, for example, the decline of goods imports from the EU;[188] and there may be some advantages to a targeted reduction of certain imports.[189] On the other hand, the impact of Brexit on the overall economy does directly impact consumers. For example, there is evidence that Brexit significantly worsened the cost of living crisis in the UK[190] and that trade frictions often manifest in a negative impact for the price sensitivity of consumers.[191]

3.9.3. The Benefits of Trade for Consumers

Moreover, imports can contribute to competition and can help drive innovation,[192] and this resonates with the incoming Labour Government's election manifesto[193] which focused on the benefits of trade *for* consumers (as opposed to instrumentalising consumers in the development of the economy[194]):

> Openness to trade allows our firms to grow *and delivers greater choice and value for consumers*. Rather than prioritising insubstantial agreements which do not bring meaningful benefits to the UK, Labour will seek targeted trade agreements aligned with our industrial strategy and economic strengths, to bring prosperity to communities across England, Scotland, Wales, and Northern Ireland.[195]

Central to this manifesto objective was rebuilding the UK's relationship with the EU.[196] Nevertheless, Labour made it clear that this would not mean rejoining the EU, the single market or the customs union, nor a return the freedom of movement. However, it would 'mean tearing down unnecessary barriers to trade'.[197]

The incoming Labour Government's election manifesto[198] also contained general commitments (such as the Green Prosperity Plan[199]) which would benefit consumers as well as specific consumer law commitments in relation to energy market regulation[200] and ticket touting.[201] The subsequent King's Speech contained a number of Bills

[188] C MacKinlay, 'The EU restricted cheap food imports but now we can scrap their measures' *The Express* (online) 4 April 2022.

[189] *cf* Department for Environment, Food and Rural Affairs, *A Blueprint to Grow the UK Fruit and Vegetable Sector* (14 May 2024) in respect of food security and environment impacts.

[190] See, for example, JD Bakker et al, *Brexit and consumer food prices: 2023 update* (Centre for Economic Performance, Brexit Analysis No 18 (2023)).

[191] See, for example, Freeman et al (n 175).

[192] See also J Jessop, *The Importance of Imports* (IEA Current Controversies No 82, July 2021).

[193] Labour Party Manifesto, *Change* (June 2024).

[194] *cf* B Heiderhoff and M Kenny, 'The Commission's 2007 Green Paper on the Consumer Acquis: deliberate deliberation?' (2007) 32 *European Law Review* 740.

[195] Labour Party Manifesto (n 194) 121 (emphasis added). See also 32: 'Labour will ensure economic regulation supports growth and investment, promotes competition, *works for* consumers, and enables innovation' (emphasis added).

[196] ibid 117.

[197] ibid 118.

[198] Labour Party Manifesto (n 194).

[199] ibid 50.

[200] ibid 54.

[201] ibid 87.

which might impact generally on consumers (such as a then Passenger Railway Services (Public Ownership) Bill, a Better Buses Bill and a Water (Special Measures) Bill) as well as more specific consumer measures in a Product Safety and Metrology Bill (now the Product Regulation and Metrology Act 2025).

3.9.4. Voluntary Alignment

Given the evidence that emerging regulatory differences (and uncertainty about future directions[202]) are impacting UK business' trading (and possibly appetite for trading) in the EU,[203] as well as EU business' appetite to trade in the UK,[204] we would encourage a reset in the current context. A reset from a culture of difference ('Brexit means Brexit') to one where voluntary, targeted and distinct alignment is seen both as an autonomous sovereign choice and as a strength for the UK economy. Nevertheless, despite the controversy generated by the May Government's common rulebook proposal,[205] in some areas the UK has in fact decided, without a fanfare, to broadly voluntarily align with the EU. We have already discussed aspects of the DMCCA 2024. Another example relates to the EU's Circular Economy Plan. Here EU initiatives have been followed in the Eco-design for Energy Related Products and Energy Information Regulations 2021, which in addition to covering design and labelling requirements introduces a right to repair by requiring manufacturers of certain products to make spare parts and information on repairs available to professional repairers.[206]

The Product Regulation and Metrology Act 2025 may mark an important step in voluntary alignment in the consumer protection arena.[207] Here the UK had already taken a step in that direction by not requiring the UKCA mark to be used for many products if the CE marking was used.[208] The Act provides enabling powers that would allow the UK to align with developing EU rules. It even gives an express power to adopt EU regulations making provision, in relation to the marketing or use of products in the UK, which corresponds with, or is similar to, a provision of relevant EU law for the purpose of reducing or mitigating the environmental impact of products.[209] It also moves UK law into line with the EU's Digital Services Act by

[202] See Office for Budget Responsibility (March 2024) (n 184).

[203] See, for example, British Chamber of Commerce, *Brexit at Three: Fresh Trade Challenges Growing* (December 2023): 'Almost two thirds (60%) of firms trading with the EU say it is now more difficult to do so than it was a year ago ... most half (49%) of exporters disagree the Brexit deal is helping them grow sales ... Two fifths (41%) of firms exporting under the Brexit deal say they face difficulties adapting to its rules on buying and selling goods.'

[204] See, for example, KPMG and British Chamber of Commerce in Germany (n 188). See also kpmg.com/de/en/home/media/press-releases/2024/04/brexit-continues-to-be-a-burden-for-companies.html.

[205] See HM Government, *The Future Relationship between the United Kingdom and the European Union*, Cm 9593 (July 2018) esp [11].

[206] See, for example, Sch 13.

[207] Even in the King's Speech there was a suggestion of voluntary alignment in respect of the then proposed Product Safety and Metrology Bill: see Prime Minister's Office, *The King's Speech 2024: background briefing notes* (17 July 2024) 37. This is now the Product Regulation and Metrology Act 2025.

[208] The Product Safety and Metrology etc (Amendment) Regulations 2024.

[209] See cl 1(2).

allowing enforcement action in relation to unsafe goods to be taken against online marketplaces.[210]

3.9.5. Re-establishing Co-Operation Frameworks with the EU

Given the way in which consumer markets transcend national borders, as well as the new Labour Government's emphasis on the importance of trade *for* consumers, international co-operation is crucial for the effectiveness of both aligned and non-aligned core consumer laws. Indeed, this had previously been stressed by the Department for Business, Innovation and Skills,[211] and also chimes with the EU–UK Trade and Co-Operation Agreement ('the Agreement'), the Preamble to which highlighted 'encouraging cooperation between relevant authorities'.[212]

In some areas a co-operation framework has been maintained. For example, the importance of exchange of information about *safety risks* was signified by the UK's continued cooperation in this area being provided by the Agreement. If one was going to be critical about that aspect of the Agreement, one might note that the Agreement was only framed in terms of the exchange of 'selected' information between the UK and EU databases rather than more widely.[213] The Agreement also provided for the possible exchange of information on measures taken in relation to product safety not covered by the EU Rapid Exchange of Information System (RAPEX).[214] There are wide-ranging powers to co-operate and exchange information on areas including market surveillance, enforcement activities and measures, risk assessment methods and product testing, coordinated product recalls or other similar actions, scientific, technical and regulatory matters in order to improve non-food product safety and compliance, emerging issues of significant health and safety relevance, standardisation-related activities, and exchanges of officials.[215] This co-ordination in the area of product safety is, of course, linked to the challenge of avoiding a hard border on the island of Ireland. It is also important to note that the UK can also stay in the Prosafe network as that is open to it as member of the Council of Europe.

On the other hand, more general co-operation frameworks, such as the CPC Regulations, have, for the reasons outlined above, been a regrettable loss, particularly against the backdrop of increasingly strained relations between the UK and EU;[216] and

[210] See, for example, cl 2–3.

[211] Department for Business, Innovation and Skills, *The Review of the EU Regulation on Consumer Protection Cooperation* (BIS/16/176, May 2016). See also Department for Business, Energy and Industrial Strategy, *Reforming Competition and Consumer Policy Driving growth and delivering competitive markets that work for consumers* (2021) 3.120: 'Now that we have left the EU, there is an opportunity to put in place a new set of cooperation arrangements compatible with our new global perspective to improve our ability to cooperate on consumer protection matters with our international partners.' See also, for example, OECD, Recommendation of the Council on Consumer Dispute Resolution and Redress (OECD/LEGAL/0356 (2024)).

[212] See also Art 770.

[213] Art 96(4).

[214] Art 96(5). Now named Safety Gate.

[215] Art 96(3).

[216] Note that Regulation (EU) 2017/2394, Art 32 provides: 'The Union and the third countries concerned may conclude agreements setting out arrangements for cooperation, including the establishment of mutual assistance arrangements, the exchange of confidential information and exchange of staff programmes.'

the rebuilding of such frameworks should feature in the UK's future consumer law strategies.

3.10. Conclusion

This chapter has sought to understand an unexplained aspect of Brexit: *why* it did not result, as some suggested at the time of the referendum, in a bonfire of pre-existing consumer laws of EU origin. We have argued that one reason has been the lack of a post-Brexit vision for consumer law in the UK. We have also argued that another reason is the previously nuanced relationship with EU consumer law in the UK; a relationship which, to some extent, already enabled the UK to develop a distinctive flavour or version of EU consumer law. The chapter has also charted the ongoing degree of similarity and divergence between consumer law in the UK and EU consumer law. in so doing it adopted a novel pan-consumer law viewpoint, looking across a wide range of areas including unfair terms, unfair practices, digital content, digital services, product liability and safety, enforcement, and redress. By adopting such a pan-consumer-law viewpoint, which has explored not only legislative provision, but also their application, we have been able to provide a unique insight into the *overall* effects of Brexit in this area, including the real degree of divergence and convergence between EU and UK consumer law. As such, this chapter provides a platform for debate about a post-Brexit vision of consumer law in the UK; central to which, we would argue, should be a degree of alignment or re-alignment in both consumer law and practice with developments in the EU.

4

Reforming Consumer Law in the Digital Market Post-Brexit: An EU–UK–Irish Divide?

PAULA GILIKER*

4.1. Introduction

In this chapter, I examine significant changes to European Union (EU) consumer law post-Brexit, focusing on three directives which recently came into force in Member States: the EU's Omnibus Directive[1] (implementing the EU's New Deal for Consumers[2]); the Digital Content and Services Directive (2019/770/EU);[3] and the Sale of Goods Directive (2019/771/EU)[4] ('the 2019 Directives'). These directives form part of a major overhaul of EU law that seeks to embrace the way in which digital technologies are transforming our world with the aim to produce 'a Europe fit for the digital age'.[5] Directive 1999/44/EC on Consumer Sales and Guarantees is repealed.[6] Key EU directives are amended.[7] Micklitz and Twigg-Flesner argue that the 2019 Directives represent much-needed adaptations of EU consumer law to respond to the progressive

* I would like to thank the editors, Christian Twigg-Flesner and James Devenney, for their helpful comments on an earlier draft.

[1] Directive (EU) 2019/2161 of the European Parliament and of the Council of 27 November 2019 amending Council Directive 93/13/EEC and Directives 98/6/EC, 2005/29/EC and 2011/83/EU of the European Parliament and of the Council as regards the better enforcement and modernisation of Union consumer protection rules, [2019] OJ L 328/7 (the Omnibus Directive).

[2] European Commission, 'Review of EU consumer law', commission.europa.eu/law/law-topic/consumer-protection-law/review-eu-consumer-law_en.

[3] Directive (EU) 2019/770 of the European Parliament and of the Council of 20 May 2019 on certain aspects concerning contracts for the supply of digital content and digital services, OJ L 136, 22.5.2019, pp.1–27.

[4] Directive (EU) 2019/771 of the European Parliament and of the Council of 20 May 2019 on certain aspects concerning contracts for the sale of goods, [2019] OJ L 136/28.

[5] European Commission, 'A Europe fit for the digital age', commission.europa.eu/strategy-and-policy/priorities-2019-2024/europe-fit-digital-age_en.

[6] Directive (EU) 2019/771, Art 23 repeals Directive 1999/44/EC with effect from 1 January 2022.

[7] The Omnibus Directive, for example, amends Council Directive 93/13/EEC (Unfair Contract Terms Directive) and Directives 98/6/EC (Price Indication Directive), 2005/29/EC (Unfair Commercial Practices Directive) and 2011/83/EU (Consumer Rights Directive).

digitalisation of the economy and society, although they argue that more needs to be done.[8] In 2021, the European Commission presented a vision and avenues for Europe's digital transformation by 2030 in which it proposed a digital decade that will evolve around four cardinal points: digital skills; digital transformation of businesses; secure and sustainable digital infrastructures; and the digitalisation of public services.[9] It is unsurprising that directives focusing on the digitalisation of consumer markets form part of this transformation. The twenty-first century has seen a move to online markets, accelerated by the COVID-19 pandemic, which has dramatically changed how consumers engage in transactions.[10] For example, in 2022, United Kingdom (UK) consumers spent £224 billion in online retail markets, almost double that spent in 2015 (£115 billion).[11] The 2019 Directives were required to be brought into force in Member States in 2022.

Following the Brexit referendum in 2016 and subsequent UK legislation,[12] there was no obligation to bring the 2019 Directives into UK law, and they are indeed not part of UK law. This chapter will address the potentially 'disruptive' effect of Brexit on European consumer law from the perspective of two fellow common law jurisdictions: England and Wales; and Ireland. It will examine to what extent these new developments will disrupt the traditional ties that have existed between these two jurisdictions and raise the question whether the UK needs to engage in legal change. These ties run deep, not least the retention of the 1893 Sale of Goods Act (SGA 1893) in Ireland post-independence. English law is still regarded as persuasive authority in the Irish courts and UK legislation seen as a potentially helpful guide to drafting. Commentators in the past have argued that given similarities in their sale of goods law, English law provides Irish courts 'with access to a significant pool of case law … This is vital in an Irish context where relevant modern case law is a scarce commodity'.[13] Post-Brexit, however, Ireland has implemented the 2019 Directives in its 2022 Consumer Rights Act. The UK has not.

What does this mean, then, for UK consumer law? This chapter will compare reforms in the Irish Consumer Rights Act 2022 with the pre-Brexit UK Consumer Rights Act 2015 (CRA 2015) and post-Brexit Digital Markets, Competition and Consumers Act 2024 (DMCC 2024). Will Brexit, combined with reforms to EU consumer law, disrupt the close relationship that previously existed between Irish and UK sale of goods law, symbolised by the shared SGA 1893? Or will a mutual desire to ensure that businesses and consumers benefit from the digital market mean that, regardless of the politics of Brexit, UK law will need to change?

[8] H-W Micklitz and C Twigg-Flesner (eds), *The Transformation of Consumer Law and Policy in Europe* (Hart, 2023) 7. It may be debated, however, to what extent the EU continues to utilise traditional models of contracting rather than embracing fully the changes of digitalisation: G Howells, C Twigg-Flesner and T Wilhelmsson, *Rethinking EU Consumer Law* (Routledge, 2018) 334–35.

[9] European Commission, Europe's digital decade: 2030 targets', commission.europa.eu/strategy-and-policy/priorities-2019-2024/europe-fit-digital-age/europes-digital-decade-digital-targets-2030_en.

[10] See, for example, V Mak, 'A primavera for European consumer Law: Re-birth of the consumer image in the light of digitalisation and sustainability' (2022) 11 *Journal of European Consumer and Market Law* 77.

[11] Statista, 'Online retail spending in the United Kingdom (UK) from 2011 to 2023', www.statista.com/statistics/285374/online-retail-spending-in-the-united-kingdom-uk.

[12] EU (Withdrawal) Act 2018; EU (Withdrawal Agreement) Act 2020 (which implements the Withdrawal Agreement, as agreed between the UK and the EU)).

[13] F White, 'Sale of Goods law reform: An Irish perspective' (2013) 42 *Common Law World Review* 172, 184.

4.2. The 2019 Directives

The 2019 Directives make significant changes to EU consumer law.[14] The Consumer Sales Directive 1999/44/EC is repealed and earlier consumer directives updated. Notably, new measures are introduced to deal with online transactions. Directive 2019/771/EU (SGD) puts in place a new sale of goods regime which covers all sales channels, including online sales, and renders the seller liable to the consumer for any lack of conformity which exists at the time when the goods were delivered, and which becomes apparent within two years of that time. By replacing a minimum harmonisation directive (Directive 1999/44/EC) with one of maximum harmonisation, it seeks to offer EU consumers the same remedies throughout the EU and requires that goods must be in conformity both with what is agreed and with what the consumer could reasonably expect.

Directive 2019/770/EU (DCSD) on contracts for the supply of digital content and digital services is the most innovative of the 2019 directives. For the first time across the EU, a specific regime is created for digital contracts, giving consumers the right to a remedy when digital content or a digital service is faulty. The DCSD seeks to extend EU consumer protection beyond tangible goods and deal with the fact that, in many cases, the consumer will not pay money to access digital content or services, but simply provide personal data instead. Remedies include asking the trader to fix the problem and, if the problem persists, obtaining a price reduction or terminating the contract to get a refund.

Finally, the Omnibus Directive 2019/2161/EU modifies earlier consumer directives dealing with unfair contract terms, price indication, unfair commercial practices and the 2011 Consumer Rights Directive (CRD). The aim is to protect e-commerce consumers and update EU consumer protection laws to respond to new market developments. Traditional consumer rights are therefore extended to digital transactions, for example, to include the right to withdraw from the transaction within 14 days, and the right to receive vital pre-contractual information. Modern digital issues such as fake online reviews are addressed; the Directive seeking to enhance online marketplace transparency. The CRD now covers contracts under which the trader supplies or undertakes to supply a digital service to the consumer, and the consumer provides or undertakes to provide personal data. Additional guidance is provided concerning unfair commercial practices in digital markets such as data-driven personalisation, dark patterns, influencer marketing and consumer reviews, as well as on the obligations of online platforms and marketplaces.

While the merits of the 2019 Directives have inevitably been debated,[15] they do represent an attempt to modernise EU consumer law in the light of the digitalisation

[14] C Kelly, 'The digital single market for consumers: Mapping reforms of European Union consumer law' (2018) 25 *Commercial Law Practitioner* 148.

[15] See, eg, JM Carvalho, 'Sale of goods and supply of digital content and digital services – Overview of Directives 2019/770 and 2019/771' (2019) 8 *Journal of European Consumer and Market Law* 194; D Staudenmacher, 'The directives on digital contracts: First steps towards the private law of the digital economy' (2020) 28 *European Review of Private Law* 219; J Vanherpe, 'White smoke, but smoke nonetheless: some (burning) questions regarding the Directives on sale of goods and supply of digital content' (2020) 28 *European Review of Private Law* 251.

of the consumer market, whilst also marking a move to a maximum harmonisation approach.[16] The aim of these Directives, states the Commission, is to

> harmonise key consumer contract law rules across the EU. This will ensure a high level of consumer protection and increase legal certainty for both consumers and traders in millions of everyday transactions concerning goods, smart goods, digital content and digital services.[17]

4.3. The Irish Consumer Rights Act 2022

4.3.1. The Background to the Act

On 29 November 2022,[18] the Irish Consumer Rights Act 2022 came into force. It implements the 2019 Directives with only a slight delay with respect to the deadlines set by the EU Directives.[19] The Act, however, goes beyond implementation of the 2019 Directives and involves a major consolidation and amendment of Irish consumer law.[20] It represents 'the biggest overhaul of consumer rights law in 40 years'.[21] On its passing, the relevant Minister of State, Dara Calleary, welcomed the Act, arguing that 'By strengthening protections for consumers and creating clearer rules for businesses, this legislation will ensure the market works fairly and effectively for everyone.'[22] Calleary also noted that there had been cross-party support and constructive engagement with the Bill's provisions in the Oireachtas, which indicated recognition of the importance of the Act to Ireland, its consumers and businesses.

Indeed, there was an undoubted need for change in Ireland. Prior to the Act, the last major legislative reform to the law relating to goods and services had been the Sale of Goods and Supply of Services Act 1980.[23] While the main purpose of the 1980 Act was to strengthen the protections available to consumers, this had been achieved by means of additions and amendments to the Sale of Goods Act 1893 rather than its repeal and replacement. Subsequent EU consumer directives had been transposed by means

[16] SGD, Art 4; DCSD, Art 4.

[17] European Commission, 'Digital contract rules', commission.europa.eu/business-economy-euro/doing-business-eu/contract-rules/digital-contracts/digital-contract-rules_en#:~:text=For%20a%20real%20digital%20single%20market%20to%20take,embrace%20the%20benefits%20of%20the%20digital%20single%20market.

[18] Consumer Rights Act 2022 (Commencement) Order 2022 (SI 2022 No 596) Art 2 (except s 161). See www.irishstatutebook.ie/eli/2022/act/37/enacted/en/html and consumer-rights-bill-2022-explanatory-memorandum.pdf.

[19] For Directives (EU) 2019/770 and 771: 1 January 2022. For Directive (EU) 2019/2161: 28 May 2022.

[20] New rules also give the Irish Competition and Consumer Protection Commission (CCPC) stronger powers to uphold consumer rights.

[21] Robert Troy TD, Minister of State with responsibility for Consumer Protection legislation: Department of Tourism, Enterprise and Employment, Government approves new law strengthening consumer rights' enterprise.gov.ie/en/news-and-events/department-news/2022/february/20220222.html.

[22] 'Minister Calleary welcomes Oireachtas approval of the Consumer Rights Bill 2022' Press release (26 October 2022, www.gov.ie/en/department-of-enterprise-tourism-and-employment/press-releases/minister-calleary-welcomes-oireachtas-approval-of-the-consumer-rights-bill-2022.

[23] Hence the reference by Robert Troy TD earlier to 40 years. See R Clark, *Contract Law in Ireland*, 9th edn (Round Hall, 2022) ch 8 on consumer protection.

of numerous free-standing regulations and not integrated into core legislation.[24] This piecemeal approach resulted in a complex law, leading to calls for reform. In 2008, the Irish Government established an expert group to advise on reform to the law of sale of goods and related transactions. The Sales Law Review Group reported back in 2011 with over 120 recommendations for change,[25] including the introduction of a new Consumer Contract Rights Act that would incorporate the core statutory provisions applicable to consumer contracts and the provisions of the Consumer Rights and Unfair Contract Terms Directives. The aim was to provide Ireland with a dedicated piece of consumer legislation (the 1893 and 1980 Acts covering both commercial and consumer contracts).

In May 2015, the Irish Department of Jobs, Enterprise and Innovation published a Consumer Rights Bill. This was heavily influenced by the (then) recent UK CRA 2015. However, with the publication of two draft maximum harmonisation EU directives on contracts for the sale of goods and supply of digital content in December 2015,[26] the Irish Government halted the prospective legislation.

Given these delays, there was a clear appetite for reform of Irish consumer law. The challenges for the 2022 Act were three-fold: (i) to update and consolidate Irish consumer law; (ii) to integrate the 2019 Directives into Irish law; and (iii) to integrate pre-existing EU consumer law into the Act which had previously been implemented through free-standing regulations. Given the calls for reform since 2011, expectations were high.

The resulting Consumer Rights Act 2022 (CRA 2022) has 176 sections, 14 Parts and six Schedules, and amends a number of existing Irish statutes such as the Consumer Credit Act 1995 and Consumer Protection Act 2007, while repealing other statutory provisions (Schedule 1). It is a long and complex statute. It also involves a mixture of domestic reforms, consolidation of existing EU law and implementation of the 2019 Directives.

In the next section, I will examine key sections of the 2022 Act and the extent to which we see a move away from the position in the UK. It must be recalled that the UK *did* introduce reforms via its own Consumer Rights Act in 2015.[27] As with Ireland, this included domestic law, existing EU law measures and, innovative for the time, specific provision for the regulation of contracts for the supply of digital content (Part 1, Chapter 3).[28] The UK Act updates the law on services,[29] but no specific provision is

[24] See eg the European Communities (Unfair Terms in Consumer Contracts) Regulations 1995 (SI 1995 No 27) and European Communities (Unfair Terms in Consumer Contracts) (Amendment) Regulations 2000 (SI 2000 No 307) transposing the Unfair Contract Terms Directive (UCTD); the European Communities (Certain Aspects of the Sale of Consumer Goods and Associated Guarantees) Regulations 2003 (SI 2003 No 11) transposing the Consumer Sales Directive; and the European Union (Consumer Information, Cancellation and Other Rights) Regulations 2013 (SI 2013 No 484) transposing the Consumer Rights Directive. All these Regulations have been repealed by the 2022 Act: Sch 1, Pt 2.

[25] Sales Law Review Group, *Report on the Legislation Governing the Sale of Goods and Supply of Services* (Stationery Office, 2011), Annex I.

[26] These ultimately became Directives 2019/770/EU and 2019/771/EU.

[27] For an overview of the key reforms of the CRA 2015, see A Samuels, 'The Consumer Rights Act 2015' [2016] *Journal of Business Law* 159.

[28] For an overview of the differences between the CRA 2015 and Directive 2019/770/EU, see P Giliker, 'Regulation of contracts for the supply of digital content: the EU and UK response' in T Synodinou et al, *EU Internet Law* (Springer, 2017).

[29] Pt 1, Ch 4 (ss 48–57), replacing earlier provision in the Supply of Goods and Services Act 1982. Consumer contracts are now excluded from the 1982 Act: s 12(1) of the 1982 Act.

made for digital services. Both statutes therefore seek to consolidate consumer law in response to criticisms that it had previously been unnecessarily complex, fragmented and had failed to keep up with technological change. Given these common goals, to what extent do we see division between the UK and Ireland?

4.3.2. Tracing Disruption: Key Changes to Irish Consumer Law in Comparison with UK Law

Under the 2022 Act, consumer rights will now extend to anything streamed or downloaded, and cloud products, as Ireland fulfils its obligations to implement the DCSD, SGD and Omnibus Directive. Below I will identify three key characteristics of the Act. In so doing, I will address two key questions which lie at the heart of the chapter: To what extent do these provisions distance Irish law from UK consumer law? *and* Do such reforms indicate that change is needed to UK law?

4.3.2.1. A Modernised Sale of Goods Regime with Key Definitions Tied to the EU Standard

The sale of goods regime is set out in Part 2 of the 2022 Act.[30] It is divided primarily into: (1) Interpretation and application (sections 10–13); (2) Consumer rights in sales contracts (sections 14–22); (3) Consumer remedies (sections 23–34); (4) Other rules, eg, passing of risk and exclusion/limitation of liability (sections 35–39).[31]

4.3.2.1.1. Key Definitions: Consumer; Trader; Goods

Section 2(1) of the 2022 Act defines 'consumer' as an individual acting for purposes that are wholly or mainly outside that individual's trade, business, craft or profession. This is identical to wording of the UK statute.[32] The definition of 'trader' is, in contrast, more detailed:

> (a) a natural person, or
> (b) a legal person, whether –
>
> (i) privately owned,
> (ii) publicly owned, or
> (iii) partly privately owned and partly publicly owned,
>
> who is acting for purposes relating to the person's trade, business, craft or profession, and includes any person acting in the name, or on behalf, of the trader.

[30] See C Kelly, 'Au revoir to merchantable quality for consumers – The New Consumer Sales Law in the Consumer Rights Act 2022' (2023) 30 *Commercial Law Practitioner* 32; G Howells and F White, 'Ireland' in A De Franceschi and R Schulze, *Harmonizing Digital Contract Law: The Impact of EU Directives 2019/770 and 2019/771 and the Regulation of Online Platforms* (Nomos, 2023).

[31] Pt 2, Ch 5 deals with commercial guarantees and Ch 6 domestic issues involving third party rights (protection for consumers that receive defective goods as a gift and rights of users of defective motor vehicles). See, further, Howells and White (n 30) paras 27–29, 65–71.

[32] CRA 2015, s 2(3).

The UK statute has a similar definition.[33]

'Goods' has an equally elaborate definition following the example of the SGD and in contrast to its UK counterpart.[34] Section 2(1) defines them as

> any tangible movable items (other than money and any item sold by way of execution or otherwise by authority of law) and includes—
>
> (a) tangible movable items that incorporate, or are inter-connected with, digital content or a digital service in such a way that the absence of that digital content or digital service would prevent the goods from performing their functions, and
>
> (b) water, gas and electricity where they are supplied in a limited volume or set quantity.

A number of drafting choices may be identified here. 'Consumer' does not include legal persons,[35] but is wider than the Directive to include dual purpose contracts.[36] 'Trader' includes legal persons partly privately owned and partly publicly owned, not found in the Article 2(3) SGD. The 'goods' definition, in contrast, is very close to the wording of Article 2(5) SGD and expressly includes those with a digital element.[37] The Act, however, in common with the UK prefers the term 'trader' to that of 'seller' found in the SGD. This is inevitable given that both the UK and Irish statutes deal with a variety of consumer transactions extending beyond the seller of goods.

4.3.2.1.2. Conformity

A key element of the 2019 Directives is an updated definition of 'conformity',[38] and indeed this took some time to finesse. Article 5 SGD indicates that goods must meet subjective and objective conformity requirements, as set out in Articles 6–8 SGD. These replace Article 2 of the Consumer Sales Directive (now repealed). Sections 15–19 set out the new test for conformity.[39] The Act retains the device of the implied term (in common with UK law). Section 14[40] and sections 16–19 are implied into every sales contract[41] and shall have effect as if they were terms of such a contract: section 20.

[33] CRA 2015, s 2(2): 'a person acting for purposes relating to that person's trade, business, craft or profession, whether acting personally or through another person acting in the trader's name or on the trader's behalf'. A 'person' here is not just a natural person, but can also include companies, charities and arms of government.

[34] CRA 2015, s 2(8): 'any tangible moveable items, but that includes water, gas and electricity if and only if they are put up for supply in a limited volume or set quantity'.

[35] There was an option to include legal persons such as non-governmental organisations, start-ups or small and medium-sized enterprises; see SGD, Recital 21.

[36] See SGD, Art 2(2): any natural person who, in relation to contracts covered by this Directive, is acting for purposes which are outside that person's trade, business, craft or profession. This is permitted: see Recital 22.

[37] A good, however, that is itself a tangible medium that serves exclusively as a carrier for digital content, eg a CD falls within Pt 3 (Digital content contracts and digital service contracts) apart from issues dealing with the passage of risk and delay (see Pt 2, Ch 4). In keeping with the pre-existing position, the option was not taken to exclude second hand goods sold at auction or living animals: Howells and White (n 30) para 8.

[38] See C Twigg-Flesner, 'Conformity of Goods and Digital Content/Digital Services' in E Arroyo Amayuelas and S Camara Lapuente (eds), *El Derecho Privado en el Nuevo Paradigma Digital* (Marcial Pons, 2020).

[39] s 15(1): Where a sales contract is concluded between a trader and a consumer, the trader shall deliver goods to the consumer that are in conformity with the sales contract at the relevant time. The relevant time is defined at s 15(4).

[40] Right to terminate sales contract where trader has no right to sell.

[41] Defined in s 11. See also s 12.

Section 17 CRA 2022 outlines the subjective[42] requirements for conformity which specifically include elements directed at goods with digital elements.[43] Section 17, however, goes further than the SGD to integrate reference to information requirements for distance and off-premises contracts (found in Part 5 of the Act)[44] and to spare parts and after-sales services offered by the trader. Section 18 (objective requirements for conformity) makes explicit reference to technical and sector-specific industry standards, accessories the consumer may reasonably expect to receive and features such as durability,[45] functionality, compatibility and security normal for goods of the same type. Specific provision is again made for goods with digital elements: section 18(4)–(7).[46] The trader shall be liable to the consumer for any lack of conformity of the goods with the sales contract which exists at the relevant time: section 21. The burden of proof (section 22), as per Article 11 SGD, is presumed to be on the trader where it becomes apparent during the period of 12 months[47] that goods supplied under a sales contract are not in conformity with the sales contract unless such a presumption is incompatible with the nature of the goods or with the nature of the lack of conformity.

This detailed framework contrasts with the more traditional content of the UK CRA 2015.[48] The UK Act remains influenced by domestic law, as revised to comply with the 1999 Consumer Sales Directive.

4.3.2.1.3. Remedies

Breach of the conformity standard leads to remedies in Chapter 3, giving rise to the right to exercise the short-term right to terminate (section 24)[49] and the right to have the goods brought into conformity with the contract through repair or replacement (section 25, subject to section 23(2)–(3)) with the default of a proportionate reduction in price or final termination of the contract (sections 26–28). Specific provision is again made for contracts that also provide for the supply of digital content (section 29).

Given that the SGD provides an updated and revised version of the basic framework of the earlier Consumer Sales Directive,[50] the differences between Irish and UK law are not as profound as might be expected. What the 2022 Act gives Ireland, ahead

[42] Requirements *agreed* between the trader and the consumer in the sales contract.

[43] eg s 17(1)(a) requires that they be of the description, type, quantity and quality, and possess the functionality, compatibility, interoperability and other features, specified in the sales contract and s 17(1)(c) that they be supplied with all accessories and instructions, including on installation of the goods, specified in the sales contract.

[44] Consumer information, cancellation and other rights (ss 96–125).

[45] Defined in s 18(2).

[46] s 13 provides for the Minister for Enterprise, Trade and Employment by regulations to apply Pt 1 provisions to contracts for the sale of goods with digital elements where the consumer instead of paying provides or undertakes to provide personal data to the trader. At present, therefore, such contracts are *not* covered by Pt 1. Note equivalent power under s 76 (services).

[47] *cf* s 19(14) CRA 2015 (six months as per Art 5 CSD).

[48] See CRA 2015, Pt 1, Ch 2.

[49] We can draw analogies between s 24, and ss 20 and 22 CRA 2015. Recital 19, SGD provides that Member States retain the freedom to allow consumers to reject goods with a defect and to treat the contract as repudiated or ask for immediate replacement, within a specific short period of time after the delivery of the goods, which should not exceed 30 days.

[50] Note also similarities in terms of the core definitions of 'consumer' and 'trader'.

of the UK, however, are provisions that address conformity in far more detail and, in particular, address the issue of goods with digital elements. In contrast, conformity under the UK Act still adheres to traditional ideas of 'satisfactory quality' and 'fitness for purpose'. It therefore lacks the sophistication and detail of the Irish Act and notably does not give specific guidance to matters that are particularly relevant to consumers in the digital market.

4.3.2.2. A New Regime for Contracts for the Supply of Digital Content and Digital Services: Part 3 CRA 2022

Here the divide between UK and Irish law broadens. Part 1, Chapter 3 of the UK statute indeed deals with contracts for a trader to supply digital content to a consumer, if it is supplied or to be supplied *for a price* paid by the consumer: section 33(1).[51] Digital content is defined narrowly (and somewhat unhelpfully) as 'data which are produced and supplied in digital form' (section 2(9)). The CRA 2015 establishes a regime by which the digital content must be of satisfactory quality (section 34), fit for a particular purpose (section 35), as described (section 36), with a right to supply (section 41).[52] Specific provision is made for the supply by transmission and facilities for continued transmission (section 39), but generally the provisions for contracts for the supply of digital content mirror those of Part 1 Chapter 2 (goods) whenever possible.

The result is a far less ambitious piece of legislation tied to traditional sale of goods law that is far less innovative than the DCSD. There is further no provision for digital *services*, which means that consumer concerns related to cloud computing and social media contracts are not addressed in the UK Act. It may be possible to argue that section 16, which deals with goods with digital content, should be interpreted generously to include smart goods and thus make available in this context the full suite of goods remedies (including the short-term right to reject).[53] There is a limit, however, to how much can be legitimately read into the UK Act.

Remedies in the UK Act are again modelled on the CSD except termination is not permitted: section 42(8). This represents a contrast with the DCSD and hence the Irish statute. The drafters of the UK Act took the view that in most cases,[54] digital content cannot be returned in any meaningful sense and so a remedy of termination would be inappropriate.[55]

[51] s 33(5): The Secretary of State may by order provide for this Chapter to apply to contracts in return for personal data if the Secretary of State is satisfied that it is appropriate to do so because of significant detriment caused to consumers under contracts of the kind to which the order relates. However, the wording 'significant detriment' indicates an obvious reluctance to utilise this power.

[52] s 37 also makes a cross-reference to pre-contractual information requirements under the Consumer Rights Directive 2011 to be found in the Consumer Contracts (Information, Cancellation and Additional Charges) Regulations 2013 (SI 2013 No 3134).

[53] The Explanatory Notes to CRA 2015 indicate that such goods include digital content supplied on a disk (para 79) and digital content preloaded on a device or embedded within other goods such as a washing machine which relies on software for its programming (para 192). I am grateful to C Twigg-Flesner for raising this argument.

[54] s 16 provides the digital content that can be returned (digital content sold on a tangible medium) will be subject to the ordinary goods remedies.

[55] Explanatory Notes to CRA 2015 para 205. Contrast remedies for sale of goods: s 19.

Examining the Irish legislation, we can see that, implementing the DCSD, the Act covers both digital content and digital services, defined in section 2.[56] The definition of 'digital content' goes beyond that stated in the DCSD; the Irish drafters believing that given the novelty of these terms, consumers would need practical examples to assist in understanding the scope of the legislation. It is defined as 'data which are produced and supplied in digital form, including in particular computer programs, applications, video files, audio files, music files, digital games, e-books and other e-publications'.[57]

Digital services are also broadly defined:

> (a) a service that allows a consumer to create, process, store or access data in digital form, or
> (b) a service that allows the sharing of or any other interaction with data in digital form uploaded or created by a consumer or other users of that service, and includes in particular video and audio sharing and other file hosting, social media, and word processing and games offered in the cloud computing environment.[58]

Key provisions of Part 3 of the Act include specific duties and rights relating to the supply of digital content or digital services.[59] The failure of traders to supply the digital content or service to the consumer (or delaying doing so) was seen as a specific issue that the Commission believed the Directive needed to address. Significantly, digital content and digital services contracts include consumers paying a price or *providing or undertaking to provide personal data to the trader*.[60] This broader view of consideration follows the Directive's intention to provide law attuned to the digital market. We see this further in the conformity standard for digital content and services which raises matters such as compatibility, interoperability, accessibility, continuity and security. Other matters that are important to digital consumers are also addressed, eg availability of updates, accessories and instructions, notably on the installation or integration of the digital content or digital service, and customer assistance as specified in the digital content contract or digital service contract: sections 52–55. Objective conformity requirements such as compliance with any trial version or preview of the digital content or digital service that the trader made available to the consumer before the conclusion of the digital content contract or digital service contract[61] again highlight the differences between the UK general 'satisfactory quality' or 'fitness for purpose' standards and measures that seek to deal head-on with the concerns of digital consumers.

Remedies are similar to those applicable to goods including right to terminate (sections 60, 62, 66–67),[62] right to have digital content or digital service brought into

[56] Non-digital services are dealt with at Pt 4 (ss 74–95) which update and modify previous provisions found in the Irish Sale of Goods and Supply of Services Act 1980 (ss 39–42).

[57] Contrast the less detailed DCSD Art 2(1): data which are produced and supplied in digital form.

[58] Contrast the less detailed DCSD Art 2(2).

[59] The Act provides for a duty on the trader, except where the parties have agreed otherwise, to supply the digital content or the digital service to the consumer without undue delay after the conclusion of the contract: s 51. There is also a right to terminate for breach of the s 50 right to supply the digital content or service: ss 66, 67.

[60] Other than where the personal data are processed by the trader only for the purpose of supplying the digital content or service in accordance with the Act or complying with any other legal requirement to which the trader is subject: s 2(1).

[61] s 54(1)(b). See also s 55 (Incorrect integration of the digital content or digital service into the consumer's digital environment treated as lack of conformity) and s 58(2).

[62] Note distinction with UK law raised above in relation to digital content.

conformity with contract (section 61), and right to proportionate reduction in price (sections 62–63). The burden of proof similarly will be on the trader for 12 months beginning with the supply of the digital content or digital service (section 59).

Certain core common law characteristics do, however, remain. The Act continues to use the mechanism of implied terms (see sections 50, 53–55) and the limitation period adheres to national standard (six years).[63] The Act also takes up freedoms permitted by the DCSD, eg to make provision for the right to terminate mixed contracts (section 65)[64] and the right to withhold payment of any outstanding part of the price until the trader has fulfilled the trader's obligations (section 69).[65]

The Irish statute thus generally represents a faithful reproduction of the DCSD,[66] albeit explained in far more detail. The 26 sections of Part 3 highlight, however, a key characteristic of the CRA 2022: complexity. In seeking to make the provisions easier to understand, the drafters have decided to expand the concise Articles of the Directive by, for example, integrating material from its recitals and/or adding examples. The aim is to bring together relevant information to provide a one-stop shop for consumers. However, this drafting choice, while well intentioned, has perhaps inevitably resulted in a statute that is difficult to navigate and at times far too technical for the average consumer to use.

The Act also reproduces a drafting weakness in the Directive. It envisages a clear division between goods with digital elements, and goods which serve exclusively as a carrier of digital content. However, as commentators have pointed out, this rather clumsy division is far from clear to all consumers.[67] Inevitably this weakness has been transposed into national law. Section 49 of the Irish Act thus faithfully replicates the EU stance that the latter is treated as digital content and the former (digital content/service incorporated in or inter-connected with goods with digital elements and supplied with the goods under a sales contract) covered by the sale of goods provisions.

4.3.2.3. *Modernisation of Existing Law Following the Omnibus Directive*

The 2019 Omnibus Directive also introduces measures that increase the divide between UK and EU consumer law post-Brexit. The Directive revises and updates key consumer directives that exist in their pre-reform state as retained (or, to use the new term, 'assimilated') law in the UK. Specific provision is made in the Irish CRA 2022 for changes to the Unfair Contract Terms Directive (Part 6) and Consumer Rights Directive (Part 5). The Act, however, goes beyond merely transposing the Omnibus Directive but seeks to consolidate the general provisions of these earlier Directives into the Act.[68] Part 9,

[63] s 58 (see also s 21(5) goods). *cf* Art 11 DCSD: not be less than two years from the time of supply.

[64] See SGD recital 60.

[65] DCSD recital 15.

[66] See s 48(3)–(4).

[67] See R Barcelo Compte and G Rubio Gimeno, 'Supply of goods with digital elements: a new challenge for European Contract Law' (2022) 11 *Journal of European Consumer and Market Law* 81.

[68] These had previously been transposed into Irish law via Regulations. See C Walsh and L Lambe, 'The Irish Consumer Rights Bill 2022: paving a path to 21st century consumer protection' (2022) 11 *Compliance & Risk* 2.

however, merely amends the Irish Consumer Protection Act 2007, which was enacted to give effect to the Unfair Commercial Practices Directive. New rules, introduced by the Omnibus Directive, deal with the online environment, including the regulation of online marketplaces (such as eBay), online searches (such as price comparison sites) and online reviews.[69]

Given the breadth of the Omnibus Directive, this section will focus on one issue considered by the Commission to be of particular importance to consumers engaging in online transactions: fake online reviews.[70] Research indicates that this is a significant problem and, of course, not one confined to the EU. UK consumer body Which? has identified that fake reviews make consumers more than twice as likely to choose poor-quality products.[71] A 2023 Department of Business and Trade report[72] found that 11–15 per cent of all reviews on e-commerce platforms for three common product categories (consumer electronics, home and kitchen, sports and outdoors) are likely fake, and that fake review text on products alone causes an estimated £50 million to £312 million in total yearly harm to UK consumers alone.[73] In addressing how EU and UK legislators have responded to an unfair commercial practice affecting consumers in the digital market, we can gain a clearer insight into the willingness of the UK legislator to intervene, and the extent to which Brexit raises a barrier to the UK intervening in a manner similar to its European counterpart.

Article 3 of the Omnibus Directive introduces measures to force traders to take greater steps to ensure online reviews are genuine, and to provide greater transparency for consumers. It provides that:

> (4)
>
> …
>
> (c) Where a trader provides access to consumer reviews of products, information about whether and how the trader ensures that the published reviews originate from consumers who have actually used or purchased the product shall be regarded as material.[74]
>
> …
>
> (7) Annex I [the blacklist] is amended as follows:
>
> …

[69] B Duivenvoorde, 'The Upcoming Changes in the Unfair Commercial Practice Directive: A Better Deal for Consumers' (2019) 8 *Journal of European Consumer and Market Law* 219.

[70] See eg M Narciso, 'The regulation of online reviews in European consumer law' (2019) 27 *European Review of Private Law* 557, who argues that this priority is consistent with the fact that the regulation of contractual information has been one of the EU's main concerns in consumer law.

[71] 'Fake reviews make consumers more than twice as likely to choose poor-quality products' Which? (29 May 2020), www.which.co.uk/news/article/the-real-impact-of-fake-reviews-aqg3x3G8bPpE.

[72] 'Investigating the prevalence and impact of fake review' GOV.UK (25 April 2023), www.gov.uk/government/publications/investigating-the-prevalence-and-impact-of-fake-reviews.

[73] This estimate does not include the impact of fake reviews on consumers who purchase services, on future consumer behaviour or the separate impact of inflated star ratings (which often accompany fake reviews). As a result, this is a conservative estimate and the true consumer detriment arising from fake reviews is likely to be higher.

[74] It is an unfair commercial practice to omit material information that the average consumer needs to take an informed transactional decision and that causes or is likely to cause them to take a transactional decision they would not otherwise have taken.

(b) the following points are inserted:

...

'23b: Stating that reviews of a product are submitted by consumers who have actually used or purchased the product without taking reasonable and proportionate steps to check that they originate from such consumers.

23c: Submitting or commissioning another legal or natural person to submit false consumer reviews or endorsements, or misrepresenting consumer reviews or social endorsements, in order to promote products.'

These measures are implemented in Ireland by sections 155 and 157 of the 2022 Act, which amend section 46 (Misleading commercial practices) and section 55 (List of prohibited commercial practices) of the Consumer Protection Act 2007 respectively. To section 46 is now added by section 155:

(3B) Where a trader provides access to reviews by consumers of products, information in relation to whether and how the trader ensures that the published reviews originate from consumers who have actually used or purchased the products shall be treated as material information for the purposes of this section.

Section 55 of the 2007 Act lists specific commercial practices that are prohibited regardless of their effect on the transactional decisions of the average consumer. This is based on the 'blacklist' at Annex I, UCPD. To section 55(1) is now added:

(za) stating that reviews of a product are submitted by consumers who have actually used or purchased the product without taking reasonable and proportionate steps to check that the reviews originate from such consumers;

(zb) submitting or commissioning a person to submit false reviews or endorsements by consumers, or misrepresenting reviews or social endorsements by consumers, in order to promote products.

Parallel to such developments, in the UK, the Competition and Markets Authority in 2019 launched a programme of work aimed at tackling fake and misleading online reviews.[75] By 2023, the UK Government had stated that it intended to deal with online fake reviews in its forthcoming Digital Markets, Competition and Consumers Bill.[76] Brexit thus has not prevented items on the European Commission's agenda being raised in the UK. Given global recognition of the problem of fake online reviews, it is not surprising that some consumer issues surpass Brexit concerns.

However, what one notices is a different process to that found in the EU. First of all, the UCPD, as assimilated law, has been redrafted and placed in a new UK statute. The Consumer Protection from Unfair Trading Regulations 2008,[77] which implemented the UCPD, are therefore replaced by Chapter 1 of Part 4 of the DMCC which recreates the legal effect (with minor amendments) of the 2008 Regulations. More generally, DMCC, Part 4 (Consumer Rights and Disputes) takes on the task of

[75] 'Fake and misleading online reviews trading' GOV.UK (21 June 2019), www.gov.uk/cma-cases/fake-and-misleading-online-reviews.

[76] Government clampdown on fake reviews and hidden fees to help customers cut the costs of living' GOV.UK (4 September 2023), www.gov.uk/government/news/government-clampdown-on-fake-reviews-and-hidden-fees-to-help-customers-cut-the-costs-of-living.

[77] SI 2008 No 1277.

dealing with selected abuses of the digital market that affect consumers. The aim of Part 4 does, however, have similarities to that of the Commission in that it, in the words of the Government, seeks 'to ensure businesses and consumers are protected from rip-offs and can reap the full benefits of the digital economy with confidence'.[78]

However, rather than engaging in direct reform (as seen in the Omnibus Directive and Irish legislation), the UK Government's initial approach in April 2023 was to delay dealing with what it termed 'emerging harms' such as fake online reviews and provide in the Act merely a power to deal with this issue via secondary legislation. On this basis, fake online reviews were not placed on the blacklist of prohibited unfair commercial practices which are in all circumstances considered unfair, but were subject to a power granted to the Secretary of State to add them to this list at a later date. This led to an outcry from consumer groups, and the Government committed in September 2023 to a consultation whether fake reviews should be added to the blacklist.[79] Given clear evidence of the negative impact of fake online reviews on consumer choice, it is hard to understand why the Government needed to be persuaded to come to this view. Its hesitancy can most likely be attributed to concerns as to the impact of regulation on businesses, given its recognition that online businesses often depend on reviews to attract custom,[80] and that it would be undesirable to over-burden small businesses.[81] We also know that the Government was subject to pressure from tech companies in the passing of the Bill.[82] Intervention, the Government argued, must be proportionate: acting against fake reviews that give rogue businesses an illegitimate advantage must be balanced against allowing businesses to incentivise legitimate customers to review their products. Finally, in the face of pressure, the Government introduced an amendment in the House of Lords in March 2024 which added various activities relating to online fake reviews directed at consumers to the list of banned commercial practices (now Schedule 20).[83] Such measures are not, however, subject to criminal sanctions which the consumer lobbyists had requested.[84]

[78] 'New Bill to crack down on rip offs, protect consumer cash online and boost competition in digital markets' GOV.UK (25 April 2023), www.gov.uk/government/news/new-bill-to-crack-down-on-rip-offs-protect-consumer-cash-onlineand-boost-competition-in-digital-markets.

[79] See Department for Business and Trade, Consultation on improving price transparency and product information for consumers' (4 September 2023), assets.publishing.service.gov.uk/government/uploads/system/uploads/attachment_data/file/1182962/consultation-on-improving-price-transparency-and-product-information-for-consumers.pdf. In December 2023 it was still considering its response: 'Enhancing consumer rights: policy summary briefing' GOV.UK (21 December 2023), www.gov.uk/government/publications/digital-markets-competition-and-consumers-bill-supporting-documentation/enhancing-consumer-rights-policy-summary-brief.

[80] See eg 'Measures to Address Fake Online Reviews – impact assessment' (1 September 2023), assets.publishing.service.gov.uk/media/650c015c52e73c000d9425b6/fake-reviews-consultation-impact-assessment.pdf.

[81] ibid paras 29, 36, 63.

[82] It was noted in the House of Lords that the Government had been subject to heavy lobbying and intense pressure from big tech during the passage of the Bill: *Hansard* HL Deb Vol 836, cols 1814–1816 (11 March 2024).

[83] For an overview see House of Commons Library 'Research Briefing: Digital Markets, Competition and Consumers Bill: Lords stages and amendments' (April 2024), researchbriefings.files.parliament.uk/documents/CBP-10008/CBP-10008.pdf. s 225 DMCC prohibits unfair commercial practices including (s 225(4)(c)) those listed in Sch 20 of the Act, which are in all circumstances considered unfair.

[84] s 237(7), (8)(b).

Given this somewhat tortuous process, it is of interest to compare the UK provisions with the earlier measures brought in by the EU. Similarities abound. The 2024 Act specifically prohibits the submitting and commissioning of online fake reviews. Article 3(7)(b) blacklists 'submitting or commissioning another legal or natural person to submit false consumer reviews'. A person 'submits' a review or information if they supply it with a view to publication, while 'commissioning' includes incentivising by any means (a very ill-defined phrase).

The Act also requires traders to take 'reasonable and proportionate steps' to prevent their publication. This is more onerous than Article 3(7)(b), which is confined to taking reasonable and proportionate steps to check reviews that are stated to originate from consumers who have used or purchased the product.

Schedule 20, paragraph 13 DMCC thus lists as a prohibited unfair commercial practice:

> (1) Submitting, or commissioning another person to submit or write—
>
> (a) a fake consumer review,[85] or
> (b) a consumer review[86] that conceals the fact it has been incentivised.[87]
>
> (2) Publishing consumer reviews, or consumer review information, in a misleading way.
> (3) Publishing consumer reviews, or consumer review information, without taking such reasonable and proportionate steps as are necessary for the purposes of—
>
> (a) preventing the publication of—
>
> (i) fake consumer reviews,
> (ii) consumer reviews that conceal the fact they have been incentivised, or
> (iii) consumer review information that is false or misleading, and
>
> (b) removing any such reviews or information from publication.
>
> (4) Offering services to traders—
>
> (a) for the doing of anything covered by sub-paragraph (1) or (2);
> (b) for the facilitating of anything covered by sub-paragraph (1) or (2) to be done.

Guidance is given as to the meaning of publishing in a 'misleading way' (paragraph 13(2)) which includes: failing to publish, or removing from publication, negative consumer reviews whilst publishing positive ones (or vice versa; giving greater prominence to positive consumer reviews over negative ones (or vice versa); and omitting information that is relevant to the circumstances in which a consumer review has been written (including that a person has been commissioned to write the review). Again, comparisons can be made with Article 3(7)(b), which provides for 'misrepresenting consumer reviews or social endorsements, in order to promote products'. 'Reasonable and proportionate steps' under paragraph 13(3) are not defined, although guidance to enable

[85] Defined at para 13(5)(b) as: a consumer review that purports to be, but is not, based on a person's genuine experience.

[86] Defined at para 13(5)(a) as: a review of a product, a trader or any other matter relevant to a transactional decision.

[87] Para 13(5)(c) provides that a consumer review conceals the fact it has been incentivised if: (i) a person has been commissioned to submit or write the review, and (ii) that fact is not made apparent (whether through the contents of the review or otherwise).

businesses to understand the scope of their obligations under these rules was provided by the Competition and Markets Authority (CMA) in April 2025.[88] While the precise steps which are required will depend on the circumstances of the case, the Guidance sets out a non-exhaustive list of examples of specific steps which, depending on the circumstances, might be required to comply with the law (with an explanation of what is reasonable and proportionate in a given context at paragraphs 8.28–8.32).

Despite the different wording, what we see are measures that approximate those of the EU. The key elements of Article 3(7)(b) – taking reasonable and proportionate steps to check the origins of consumer reviews/submitting or commissioning false consumer reviews/misrepresenting consumer reviews – are present. The UK Government has not, however, proposed an equivalent provision to Article 3(4)(c) Omnibus Directive.

This indicates that, despite Brexit, consumer concerns in the digital market will arise in both the EU and UK, and the UK Government will need to consider whether to introduce legislation to meet these concerns. The process described above, however, was less than smooth, with considerable lobbying needed by consumer groups and in the House of Lords for the Government to agree finally to the measures that now form part of the 2024 Act.[89] While the provisions may be similar, this was for a long time far from certain and subject to parliamentary debate. Equally, similar, but not identical, measures do nevertheless increase costs for businesses, giving rise to more, not less, 'red tape' as they identify their legal obligations to UK and EU visitors to their websites. We can be in no doubt that businesses are now actively comparing their obligations under the DMCC with those imposed under the Omnibus Directive to decide whether any material differences exist.

4.4. Reflecting on Disruption: The 2019 Directives, UK Consumer Law Post-Brexit and the Irish Consumer Rights Act 2022

This chapter has compared changes to consumer law in Ireland in the light of the 2019 Directives with measures introduced in the UK in the CRA 2015 and the DMCC 2024. The 2019 Directives form part of the EU Digital Market strategy and seek to modernise EU consumer law to respond to the needs of digital consumers. The EU Directives seek to address the concerns of digital consumers head-on, whether it be regulating fake reviews that undermine consumer choice, reconfiguring 'conformity' to apply to digital goods and services, or providing remedies that better meet the specific characteristics of digital content and digital services. The approach of the UK's CRA 2015 (making minor adjustments to deal with digital content while largely following the traditional sale of goods law model) seems unambitious and outdated by comparison. Further, the failure of the 2015 Act to address digital services at all, and its refusal to regulate digital content

[88] CMA, 'Fake Reviews: Guidance on the prohibition under paragraph 13 of Schedule 20 to the Digital Markets, Competition and Consumers Act 2024'(CMA, 2025), www.gov.uk/cma.

[89] The measures also nearly fell with the declaration of a general election with Royal Assent taking place just in time on 24 May 2024.

contracts based on the provision of personal data seems backward-looking. Revisions to directives such as the Unfair Contract Terms Directive, Consumer Rights Directive and Unfair Commercial Practices Directive further highlight that EU regulation is an ongoing process, and assimilated EU law in the UK will increasingly be based on pre-digitalisation versions of EU directives.

What conclusions can we draw, then, from this study, bar the fact that differences between EU and UK consumer law now exist and are likely to continue in the future? The first, and most obvious, is that Ireland's continued membership of the EU is likely to mean that sales of goods law in Ireland and England and Wales will now diverge. Clark, in his leading Irish contract law textbook, commented that this 2019 'trio of EU Directives will transform the Irish consumer law landscape relating to goods, services and digital contracts of all kinds'.[90] The status of the 2019 Directives as maximum harmonisation directives specifically ties Ireland to an 'EU', rather than common law, path of legal development, although certain characteristics, such as use of implied terms, persist. Cherednychenko argues that maximum harmonisation EU regulatory private law rules, which substitute EU law for national private law norms, will inevitably change the core values of national law, tilting it decisively in favour of the EU's instrumentalist discourse.[91] Kelly warns that, in contrast to the past, reference to English law will now prove of little assistance:

> The increasing impact of the EU, and in particular of the civil law tradition within the Union, … affect not merely the substance of the right in question, but also the architecture of statutes and categorization of consumer rights, the language and conceptual tools used, and how rights are interpreted by the courts.[92]

Clark also suggests that while the reforms will prove a hard learning curve for Irish businesses, once learnt, they are likely to affect contract law generally. He suggests that it is likely that even business-to-business and consumer-to-consumer contracts, not regulated currently by the EU, will change.[93] The differences between Irish and UK contract law therefore go beyond the provisions of the 2019 Directives themselves, but will affect the language, structure and policy of Irish contract law.

A second conclusion is that the differences identified in this chapter raise a dilemma for UK lawyers. Legislation such as the CRA 2015, which includes assimilated EU law, now looks dated in comparison to the willingness of the EU to embrace the digital market. At the same time, the UK Government has clearly expressed its desire that UK businesses take advantage of the digital market, while consumer groups are highlighting the vulnerability of many consumers in a high-tech market and demanding intervention. The digital market, further, is not static, but by its very nature innovative and evolutionary. New threats (and business opportunities) are therefore likely to arise in future years, as recognised by the European Commission in its mission to update its consumer law. One option is for the UK Government to introduce its own legislation such as the DMCC. Another is for the courts to try to adapt existing law to reflect the

[90] Clark (n 23) 314.
[91] OO Cherednychenko, 'Islands and the Ocean: Three Models of the Relationship between EU Market Regulation and National Private Law' (2021) 84 *Modern Law Review* 1294, 1328–29.
[92] C Kelly, 'Consumer reform in Ireland and the UK: Regulatory divergence before, after, and without Brexit' (2018) 47 *Common Law World Review* 53, 54.
[93] Clark (n 23) 314.

needs of the digital market. This chapter has identified a number of areas where change to UK consumer law would be desirable, with the 2019 Directives highlighting that a response to the new digital market must go beyond traditional ideas of sale of goods. The three most important are set out below.

4.4.1. Updating the Definition of 'Conformity'

The UK retains the basic definition of 'conformity' stated in the 1999 Consumer Sales Directive. Despite the CRA 2015 making specific provision for digital content contracts (Chapter 1, Part 3), the measures bear a distinct resemblance to their goods counterparts (Chapter 1, Part 2). On this basis, the digital content must be 'of satisfactory quality' (section 34); 'fit for particular purpose' (section 35); 'as described' (section 36), and so on. There is an obvious contrast with the more detailed and technically sophisticated provisions of the 2019 Directives and now, Irish law. One argument might be that this can be fixed without legislation if we rely on the courts to interpret these provisions in a way that meets the needs of the digital market. This assumes, of course, a 'digitally savvy' judiciary and of course a sufficient volume of reported cases to guide the parties involved. From a consumer perspective, the Irish/EU provisions are more likely to induce the courts to engage with the needs of the digital consumer. On this basis, the CRA 2015 would benefit from a revision of the conformity provisions in relation to digital content. The UK Act lacks the sophistication and detail of the Irish Act, notably in relation to matters such as updates, accessories and matters such as functionality and interoperability. At present, UK law is reliant on courts to take on this revising role. At the very least, government guidance on this point would be helpful.

4.4.2. Including Contracts for Digital Content or Services to be Supplied in Return for Personal Data

This was explicitly rejected by the UK Government in drafting the CRA 2015, bar a power to revise this decision in the face of proof of significant detriment to consumers. This is, however, a key part of the new EU framework. It must be questioned whether this places UK consumers in a particularly vulnerable position, in contrast to their EU counterparts, given that personal data is commonly used in the marketplace. Can the UK persist in its refusal not to regulate this part of the market? Again, there seems to be a degree of path dependency that adheres to traditional contract law concepts such as consideration. Will it be left again to the courts to rethink what 'consideration' means in this context?

4.4.3. Regulating Digital Services

With the benefit of hindsight, it is hard to understand why the UK CRA 2015 would regulate digital content and not digital services. This now seems to be an obvious omission. Most of us use digital services daily (this chapter has been saved on the Cloud!)

and to focus on digital content without addressing digital services seems outdated and again derivative of reasoning that focuses on viewing contracts for digital content as a variant of contracts for the sale of goods, rather than a distinct transactional model in its own right. It is hard to see how the courts alone could bring change here, and it would require a statutory intervention.

My final conclusion is that the 'fake online review' example discussed in this chapter highlights the fact that, regardless of Brexit, the nature of the digital market will lead to calls for regulation not only in Brussels and Dublin, but in the UK as well. Digital contracts and services expose a common problem: they create a power imbalance between trader and consumer because of the technical ignorance of many consumers in the face of new and innovative technologies ('digital vulnerability'). Helberger et al have shown that, in digital marketplaces, most, if not all, consumers are potentially vulnerable to (the exploitation of) power imbalances that are the result of increasing automation of commerce, datafied consumer–seller relations, and the very architecture of digital marketplaces.[94] Liu argues that we need to rethink what we mean by 'vulnerability' and recognise that power imbalances can arise regardless of the age or intelligence of the consumer.[95] Digitalisation, in other words, threatens the autonomy of consumer choice, and consumers will have understandable concerns about fraud, data security and access to updates that ensure the ongoing functionality and reliability of the item/service purchased. Traditional sale of goods law offers little practical assistance for these consumers. In this light, while Brexit gives rise to formal divergence, the realities of the market and consumer lobbying will lead to pressure for informal convergence, at least in relation to certain key issues. The fake online review example shows that Brexit does not necessarily mean that new measures at EU level will not be matched by changes in UK law, but that similar measures are likely to be introduced more slowly and with differently weighted policy debates (in the UK case, greater weight seems to have been given to the impact on businesses). The DMCC equally has underlined the importance of enforcement, increasing, for example, the powers of the CMA to directly enforce consumer protection law to enable consumers to avoid the need to go through the expensive and slow court system.[96]

Will, then, the EU–UK–Ireland divide be bridged by UK measures that respond to key consumer law concerns? Much depends on the willingness of the UK Government to monitor EU change and contemplate measures that are, at the very least, similar to EU regulatory intervention. There are some signs that the current Labour Government

[94] See N Helberger et al, 'Choice Architectures in the Digital Economy: Towards a New Understanding of Digital Vulnerability' (2022) 45 *Journal of Consumer Policy* 175. See also OECD, *Challenges to Consumer Policy in the Digital Age* (2019). H-W Micklitz et al, 'Towards Digital Fairness' (2024) 13 *Journal of European Consumer and Market Law* 24 argue in support of a new EU Digital Fairness Act to meet the specific vulnerabilities of digital consumers.

[95] M Liu, 'Digital Vulnerability: Rethinking Power Imbalances in the Digital Age' (2024) 32 *European Review of Private Law* 827.

[96] See C Cullen and H Homewood, 'Digital Markets, Competition and Consumers Bill – Bolstering consumer protection and sharper teeth for the CMA' (2023) 34 *Entertainment Law Review* 178. The Act grants the CMA the ability to make determinations on whether breaches of consumer law have occurred, to impose monetary penalties directly and also empower consumers to resolve disputes directly with businesses through the introduction of alternative dispute resolution (ADR) provisions.

may be more willing to intervene than its predecessor.[97] Doherty comments that 'it appears that the [Labour] government is at the very least contemplating a world where a greater degree of regulatory alignment in terms of product liability may be desirable'.[98] However, convergence will require more than ad hoc legislation dealing with specific areas of law such as product safety. What is needed is a move away from the hesitancy of the previous Government, which confined itself to a 'proportionate' response that would not overburden (small) businesses. The Labour Government will too face potential tension between consumer and business interests. In relation to product safety, for example, it has expressed its intention to deliver more protection for consumers by maintaining high product standards, while, at the same time, providing regulatory stability and supporting businesses consistent with its targets for economic growth.[99]

In sum, while the 2019 Directives give rise to a growing gap between the protection awarded to digital consumers in the UK and the EU, they also raise the key question: how will the UK legislator react? This chapter has indicated that some reaction is needed – the changes in the digital market require a response if UK businesses are not to stagnate in a competitive market and UK consumers suffer. The DMCC is clearly a positive step forward, but it is important also to recognise its limitations. Part 4 DMCC focuses on protection from unfair trading (including new rules on fake reviews and drip pricing), subscription contracts, consumer savings schemes and alternative dispute resolution for consumer contract disputes, but there are clearly more issues that concern consumers. Consumer measures are further placed at the end of a much longer statute that is primarily concerned with expanding the powers of the CMA in relation to digital markets and competition. Nevertheless, I would argue that there are practical reasons to be optimistic about informal convergence in consumer law. Despite Brexit, pressure from UK businesses (and consumers) are likely to lead to measures that bear some functional equivalence to EU measures.

In conclusion, Brexit does indicate that there will be an EU/Ireland and UK divide in consumer sales and services law, but this does not prevent convergence. However, this will only occur if there is ongoing pressure from consumer organisations and businesses for change, and a government willing to set aside the political 'message' of Brexit and focus on the needs of the digitally vulnerable consumer.

[97] See, for example, Labour's Product Regulation and Metrology Act 2025, which seeks to ensure that the law can be updated to allow recognition of new or updated EU product requirements, with the intention of preventing additional costs for businesses and providing regulatory stability: Explanatory Notes to Act, para 3. It adds, however, that it can end such recognition if this is the right decision for the UK. Note also commitments in the EU–UK Trade and Co-operation Agreement 2021 such as Art 208 (Enhancing online consumer trust), discussed in C Twigg-Flesner, 'Who knows what the future holds? The fate of the EU's acquis in English Contract Law' (2022) 21 *Nederlands Tijdschrift voor Burgerlijk Recht* 160, 166.

[98] J Doherty, 'Product Safety in the Digital Age' (2024) 174 *New Law Journal* 11, 12.

[99] Explanatory Notes to the Product Regulation and Metrology Act 2025, para 3.

5

Consumer Resilience and Vulnerable Energy Systems

TIMOTHY J DODSWORTH AND SÉVERINE SAINTIER

5.1. Introduction

Consumer law as a discipline is at a crossroad. Following Brexit, the United Kingdom (UK) is no longer bound by European Union (EU) developments in the field, although provisions based on EU law continue to exist. Yet, the negative effects of the 'instrumentalisation of consumer law'[1] on vulnerable consumers cast a long shadow and are still being felt. Such negative effects are well known, and consumer weakness was viewed primarily through a transactional lens, ie transactional weakness and information assymetry. The consumer was viewed homogeneically, as the average consumer. This homogeneity allowed for a one-size-fits-all approach lending itself to an easily applicable form of protection – categorical protection[2] – itself leading to the adoption of a narrow concept of vulnerability.

Although efficient, this limited form of protection nevertheless created a perfect storm for vulnerable consumers. Never designed to protect actual vulnerability, this one-size-fits-all failed to offer any kind of protection 'based on any substantive consideration of whether [the consumer] is in actual need of protection in the context at hand'.[3] The consequences of focusing on the transactional element to the detriment of the other facets of the consumers 'as a citizen and a human being'[4] are particularly stark in the context of essential services, especially in energy, where vulnerable consumers are no longer those just unable to understand the terms of their contract (transactional vulnerability), but those unable to keep their home warm and their appliances switched on, ie 'energy poverty' (social vulnerability).

[1] H Micklitz, 'The Consumer, Marketised, Fragmentised, Constitutionalised' in D Leczykiewicz and S Weatherill (eds) *The Images of the Consumer in EU Law: Legislation, Free Movement and Competition Law* (Hart Publishing, 2016) 21–41.

[2] M Hesselink, *Justifying Contract in Europe: Political Philosophies of European Contract Law* (Oxford University Press, 2021) 273.

[3] ibid.

[4] G Davies, 'The Consumer, the Citizen and the Human Being' in D Leczykiewicz and S Weatherill (eds), *The Images of the Consumer in EU Law: Legislation, Free Movement and Competition Law* (Hart Publishing, 2016) 326.

Still in the context of the essential service of energy, the complexity of this social vulnerability is further exacerbated when seen through the lens of climate change where, in that context, alongside 'energy poverty' are also distributive and generational issues linked to access to clean and renewable energy. The climate change lens, and its associated need for more sustainable consumption, is crucial since it helps to articulate how the consumer is also 'a citizen and a human being', and as such forms a crucial part of this chapter. This lack of substantive protection, to be widely understood, is further compounded by a systemic vulnerability,[5] ie that vulnerable consumers do not have the processes by which to seek protection from their transactional and social vulnerabilities.

The need to consider this wider dimension of the consumer is clear, but nevertheless challenging and as such creates a disruptive influence on consumer law in the context of this edited collection. This challenge is not unsurmountable, and the main aim of this chapter is therefore to find ways to solve this disruption through a realignment of the manner in which consumer law views consumers and consumer contracts.

To do so is necessary since, as highlighted above, the current state of play is unsatisfactory: consumer law does not provide the protection that consumers of essential services actually need because of lack of coherence and inclusion. This disruptive influence on consumer law is, regrettably, not new; the need to go beyond this narrow transactional view and protect real vulnerability in order to reflect the complex 'images'[6] of consumers' needs has been discussed for a while in academic circles.[7] Although the requirement to act and protect vulnerable consumers not only transactionally but socially has been acknowledged in policy circles,[8] real action never materialised. This lack of action is perhaps not surprising given the daunting complexity of the task at hand. But the problems have not gone away – far from it, in fact, especially through the lens of the wider context of climate change which has been made sharper under the light of the cost of living crisis. The need to act is as pressing as ever and the first aim of this chapter is to provide a way forward to solve this disruption.

What is needed is to 'rethink consumer law in an inclusive way'[9] by providing a coherent and inclusive approach which protects the consumer in all their guises. To do so requires two steps. First, to enquire as to the nature of the needs of the consumer. Only by understanding those needs can we provide a coherent and inclusive system which puts values protecting the weaker members of society at its core.[10]

[5] C Riefa and S Saintier, 'The way forward: for an inclusive access to justice to protect vulnerable consumers' in C Riefa and S Saintier (eds), *Vulnerable Consumers and the Law: Consumer Protection and Access to Justice* (Routledge, 2020) 244, 248–49.

[6] Expression borrowed from the title of D Leczykiewicz and S Weatherill (eds), *The Images of the Consumer in EU Law: Legislation, Free Movement and Competition Law* (Hart Publishing, 2016).

[7] For a non-exhaustive list, see C Riefa and S Saintier (eds), *Vulnerable Consumers and the Law: Consumer Protection and Access to Justice* (Routledge, 2020); C Willett, 'Retheorising consumer law' (2018) 77 *Cambridge Law Journal*, 179, 179–210; P Siciliani, C Riefa and H Gamper, *Consumer Theories of Harm* (Hart, 2018); C Twigg-Flesner, G Howell and T Wilhelmsson, *Rethinking Consumer Law* (Routledge, 2018).

[8] See The Department for Business, Energy and Industrial Strategy (BEIS), *Modernising Consumer Markets, Consumer Green Paper* (Cmd 9595, 2017).

[9] Riefa and Saintier (n 5) 257; See also Willett (n 7); Siciliani, Riefa and Gamper (n 7); Twigg-Flesner, Howell and Wilhelmsson (n 7).

[10] Willett (n 7) 179.

The recognition of the need to protect vulnerable consumers not only transactionally but socially was an important step towards understanding of the consumer in all their facets and as 'a citizen and a human being'.[11] However, that enquiry alone, which focused on the substantive needs of the consumer, was not sufficient to provide a view of the whole system. To do so a second step is needed: to formally acknowledge the existence of the systemic vulnerability in and of itself as well as its impact on transactional and social vulnerabilities. To do so is crucial since those vulnerabilities are interlinked – the transactional and social vulnerabilities are also a symptom of the wider context of 'systemic vulnerability'.[12] Understanding the interaction is therefore crucial to capture social vulnerability in all its aspects of dimensions and is the key to a coherent and inclusive approach (a whole-system approach) to allow consumers to be resilient to those vulnerabilities. To provide that second step is the second the aim of this chapter.

To do so, however, requires us to go beyond consumer law and consider the question of vulnerable consumers 'as citizens and human beings' in the essential service of energy through a sustainable lens by asking how a sustainable shift will (and should) disrupt consumer contracts. To do so, this chapter looks to a distinct, yet, connected debate: that of a just energy transition and energy democracy which considers the very needs of the consumer in their guise as a citizen and a human being. Looking at those debates will demonstrate how to embed a wider (social) context of transactions. But more importantly, it will show the interaction between the substantive vulnerability and the systemic vulnerability.

In those debates, it is recognised that achieving a just energy transition (outcome dimension) can only be done through energy democracy (process dimension). Importing this wider outlook is particularly important in the context of essential services where the essential nature of the product/service creates a human-like dependency of consumer on supplier, supplier on state and state on supplier, highlighting that a systemic view is needed to allow consumers to be resilient. Resilience is usually provided by the system so when the system itself contributes to the vulnerability, the way consumers' resilience is considered must also change by assessing what kind of resilience is needed, as well as defining exactly to whom the system is intending to provide such assets. To do this, a different framework is needed, which this chapter argues can be built by viewing essential services contracts as relational.

This chapter connects disparate debates of energy justice and relational contract theory, to the issue of vulnerable consumers to propose a path which recognises vulnerability in all its dimensions, and consequently embeds solutions to build consumer resilience. This chapter will begin by suggesting a framework which facilitates a systemic view of energy contracts as an essential service. Section 5.2 underlines the requirement to which energy contracts can only be correctly seen as relational in nature. Section 5.3 focuses on the structure of the energy system and the impact on vulnerability and equality. Section 5.4 offers a solution for capturing, defining and importing the requirements of energy justice in consumer contracts.

[11] Davies (n 4) 326.
[12] Riefa and Saintier (n 5) 244.

5.2. Essential Services Contract as Relational Contracts: The Framework to Facilitate a Systemic View

Consumer law as it stands does not have the right tools to provide the necessary protection for consumers to be resilient to their vulnerability because the current view of vulnerable consumers is too narrow (see section 5.2.1 below). Looking at the debate in the context of the energy transition highights the need to understand vulnerability using a wider lens to take account of external factors surrounding the transaction of the purchase of energy and to have a systemic approach (see section 5.2.2 below). Adopting a systemic approach is needed in consumer law to give consumers the tools to be resilient to their vulnerability. To do so requires the right framework, which is through relational contract theory. As will be demonstrated, this allows the placing of the transaction in its wider social setting through the recognition of wider norms beyond the pure transactional, and permits consideration of the obligations that must necessarily be implied in the context of the energy transition (see section 5.2.3 below).

5.2.1. Consumer Law and Vulnerable Energy Consumers: A Difficult Relationship in Need of a Coherent View

The consequences of focusing on the transactional element to the detriment of the other facets of consumers 'as a citizen and a human being'[13] are particularly stark in the context of essential services, and even more so through the lens of energy services and the energy market. Focusing on energy is important because energy, as an essential service, is not confined to consumer law and as such lends itself very well to a discussion beyond consumer law. Indeed, energy forms a crucial part of 'the basic structure of society'.[14] As such, its essential nature, its critical place in the fabric of society and its social value are widely legally recognised at domestic,[15] European[16] and international levels.[17] Although recognised domestically as a service of social significance,[18] following the liberalisation of public services markets, energy nevertheless comes within the private sector, and for consumers, consumer law, which, as mentioned, categorises and separates the 'economic' transaction from the 'social' context in which it takes place.[19] The energy market might be more efficient,[20] but as the rise in inequality and

[13] Davies (n 4) 326.

[14] J Rawls, *A Theory of Justice* (Oxford University Press, 1973) 7.

[15] Energy, together with water and telecommunication, is accepted as an essential service in the UK. But as highlighted by the pandemic, it is clear that this list should be expanded to contextually defined essential services such as groceries, educational services, medical supply contracts, etc.

[16] The Treaty of Amsterdam formally recognises energy as a 'service of economic general interest' which access is protected by the Charter of Fundamental Rights (Art 36).

[17] At the global level, the 7th UN Sustainable Development Goal aims to 'ensure acess to affordable, reliable, sustainable and modern energy for all'. See https://sdgs.un.org/goals/goal7.

[18] T Prosser, *The Limits of Competition Law, Market and Public Services* (Oxford University Press, 2005) ch 4.

[19] Against this, K Polanyi, *The Great Transformation: The Political and Economic Origins of Our Time*, 2nd edn (Beacon Press, 2001).

[20] Prosser (n 18) 21.

fuel poverty highlights, the energy market is certainly not fairer, and 'tensions between market, rights and social solidarity'[21] perdure.

Consumer law is definitely the correct arena to protect vulnerable consumers in their relations with energy suppliers. But are those relations of a contractual nature? The question is important since in *Norweb v Dixon*,[22] the court held that given the nature of the obligations of the public electricity supplier, the supply of electricity between a customer and a public electricity supplier is not contractual. This decision is important since it acknowledges the distinct nature of the supply of energy and the relation that it gives rise to. We nevertheless contend that the energy market has changed considerably since this decision. Looking at more recent legislation and the language used in that context seems to clearly indicate that there is a contract.[23] It is therefore possible to use relational contract theory as a basis for what follows.

As mentioned in the introduction, the facets of the consumer as a human being and a citizen must be considered. To do so is important not only to protect vulnerable consumers, but also because, in the context of climate change, that notion of the vulnerable consumer is changing. To understand all these other facets of the consumer as well as the notion of vulnerability, it is necessary to turn to another debate, that of energy justice and energy transition, which also enquires about the need to protect the more vulnerable members of society, but primarily in terms of protecting the citizen and the human being. That debate is highly relevant as it mirrors the debate in consumer law calling for a wider view of consumers. Indeed, seen from a different angle, the debate nevertheless also highlights tensions between 'market, rights and social solidarity' by highlighting 'a worldwide inequality not only in terms of "income, wealth and resource ownership" but also in terms of "access to safe and affordable energy" and distribution'.[24] Linking the two will therefore contribute to a coherent and inclusive approach.

The idea of a fair and just transition links the idea of energy justice[25] with that of energy democratisation.[26] In that debate, it is recognised that to achieve a just energy transition, (outcome dimension), individuals must also have access to the way structures facilitating this are created, and notion of energy democracy (process dimension).

[21] ibid.

[22] [1995] 3 All ER 952.

[23] See esp the the language of Sch 2b, para 8(1) Gas Act 1986 and Sch 6 Electricity Act 1989 on 'deemed contracts'.

[24] MA Heldeweg and S Saintier, 'Renewable Energy Communities as 'Socio-Legal Institutions': A Normative Frame for Energy Decentralisation?' (2020) 119 *Renewable and Sustainable Energy Reviews* 1, 3, www.sciencedirect.com/science/article/pii/S1364032119307269.

[25] The debate on energy justice is not very old. For a non-exhaustive list of publications, see K Bickerstaff, G Walker and G Bulkeley (eds), *Energy Justice in a Changing Climate: Social Equity and Low Carbon Energy* (Zed Books, 2014); D McCauley et al, 'Advancing Energy Justice: the Triumvirates of Tenets' (2013) 32 *International Energy Law Review* 107, 107–10; K Jenkins et al, 'Energy Justice: A Conceptual Review' (2016) *Energy Research and Social Science* 174; BK Sovacool, R Sidortsov and B Jones, *Energy Secutrity Equality and Justice* (Routledge, 2013); BK Sovacool and MH Dworkin, 'Energy justice: conceptual insights and practical applicaitons' (2015) 142 *Applied Energy* 435.

[26] Although the debates are distinct, they are nevertheless interrelated. The link avoids dilution of the concepts and uncertainty: R Fleming, K Huhta and L Reins, 'What is Sustainable Energy Democracy in Law?' in R Fleming, K Huhta and L Reins (eds), *Sustainable Energy and the Law* (Brill Nihoff, 2021) 20; To link them is also important since it helps to emphasise the role of social, economic and political power in energy transition: B Van Veelen, 'Negotiating Energy Democracy in Practice: Governance Processes in Community Energy Projects' (2018) *Environmental Politics* 644, 644.

This requires consideration of the (energy) system as a whole, adopting a whole-system approach.[27] This whole-system approach needs a framework upon which to sit, and this is where energy justice comes in.

Energy justice as a concept is particularly crucial to the quest for a more contextualised view of consumers since 'it is suited to interdisciplinary engagement with energy systems and their social, cultural and political embeddedness'.[28] Although energy is acknowledged as an 'essential service' and therefore forms part of a different category of contracts, that category does not really help vulnerable consumers. As just mentioned, this is because the wider context of energy provision is not taken into consideration. It is still based on the sameness (one-size-fits-all) approach. In other words, economic relations are not embedded in the social ones[29] and the real needs of the consumer are not covered. To do so is not only important for vulnerable consumers, but is also important in terms of autonomy (see section 5.2.3). This is where the energy justice debate is important since it starts from a needs basis[30] and calls for a whole-system view.

As a concept, energy justice has been given several definitions,[31] the most popular of which is based on three tenets: distributional; procedural; and recognition.[32] Each tenet serves a particular purpose, but also interacts with the others. Energy justice allows us to understand the interaction between the source of injustice (distributional justice), who this injustice affects (justice as recognition), and through which processes (procedural justice).[33] All provide an understanding of the complexities of inequalities, ie needs which must be acknowledged in order to have a 'just (energy) system' and not simply an efficient one. The concept is therefore entirely based on a needs basis across the entire system, linking production to consumption. This is what is particularly interesting for this chapter: consumer law only considers vulnerability on the consumption side and does not link it to the production side. This is regrettable since 'production, consumption and population are not independent variables … issues of production are inextricably connected to consumption when considering energy justice in the distribution of energy services'.[34] The main advantage of a whole-system view (and the three tenets above) is that it provides the context needed to understand justice in all its dimensions. Much more than a 'goal-centred definition of energy justice',[35] it gives a

[27] D McCauley et al, 'Advancing Energy Justice: the Triumvirates of Tenets' (2013) 32 *International Energy Law Review* 107, 109.

[28] ibid 110.

[29] On this, see Polanyi (n 19); His work 'emphasises the interconnection between economy and society by perceiving economic relations as embedded in social ones'. B Lange and F Haines, 'Regulatory transformations: an introduction' in B Lange, F Haines and D Thomas (eds), *Regulatory Transformations – Rethinking Economy- Society interactions* (Bloomsbury, 2017) 11.

[30] This is important from a goverenance viewpoint since 'by bringing greater awareness of human needs and actions it is possible to improve the system overall': Jenkins et al (n 25) 174, citing M Bevier, *Key Concepts in Governance* (Sage Publishing, 2009) 202.

[31] Fleming, Huhta and Reins (n 26) 10.

[32] Jenkins et al (n 25) 107–10. For an update of this article where Heffron adds two more tenets, namely restorative justice and cosmopolitan justice: R Heffron 'Energy justice – the triumvirate revisited and revised' (2023) 32 *Journal of Energy and Natural Resouces Law*, doi.org/10.1080/02646811.2023.2256593. The add-on does not change the premise of our argument.

[33] Jenkins et al (n 25) 174.

[34] S Hall, 'Energy Justice and Ethical Consumption' (2013) 18 *Local Environment* 422, 424.

[35] A Mejia Montero and K Jenkins, 'Whole-Systems Energy Justice' in S Bouzarovski, S Fuller and T Reames (eds) *Handbook on Energy Justice* (Edward Elgar, 2023) ch 1.

contextualisation of the extent of the injustice, including the systemic injustice. This is a disruptive view since it challenges the status quo, and will require realignment, but that realignment is necessary.

Energy justice as a concept is constantly evolving, and can be refined and modified. This versatility is an asset.[36] There are three aspects of the definition which link to the energy system and energy supply chain.[37] At its heart, energy justice seeks to highlight distributional procedural and recognition injustices in order to tackle them.

'Distributional justice' refers to the sources of injustice. As such it has to be understood widely so as to include its 'spatial, temporal and societal'[38] dimensions. It is therefore important to understand, in those terms, the inequity not only in terms of environmental benefits and ills, but also in terms of unequal distribution of risk and responsibilities such as exposure to risk.[39] Given that in the UK poorer and less powerful social groups tend to be disproportionately affected,[40] it is important, for instance, to consider how the 'siting of energy infrastructure' can lead to distributional injustices.[41]

Linked to this is procedural justice, which seeks to assess how these injustices impact the various stakeholders. Considering the highly centralised nature of energy systems, and the limited role for consumers, this requires impartiality and full information disclosure by government and industry.[42] In light of the global nature of energy markets, due process does not stop at the domestic level; it is therefore also required at every level 'of energy decision-making at local, provincial, national and global'.[43] Tools have certainly improved, with for example, the possibility for anyone to make a freedom of information request under the Freedom of Information Act 2000. However, such tools are still by their nature reactionary and rely on a definition of vulnerability which is limited in scope.[44]

Finally, recognition justice seeks to consider who is affected by the injustices. This is particularly important here for 'vulnerable consumers' and the bluntness of the tool that categorical protection provides. Justice as recognition therefore calls 'to recognise the divergent persepctives rooted in social, cultural, ethnic, racial and gender differences'.[45]

This rapid view of energy justice has shown that 'injustice' comes in many guises and forms and, although difficult to define precisely, nevertheless has clear contours, one of which is to fight the injustice created by the system itself, which is still 'a predominantly centralised (hierarchical and exclusive) view of energy systems'.[46] In such a light, consumers are 'completely detached from energy in terms of both technologies and

[36] Some have referred to the notion as 'pluralist'; Jenkins et al (n 25) 180.

[37] RJ Heffron, D McCauley and BK Sovacool, 'Resolving Society's Energy Trilemma through the Energy Justice Metric' (2015) 87 *Energy Policy* 168.

[38] ibid 168, 169.

[39] G Walker, 'Beyond Distribution and Proximity: Exploring the Multiple Spatialities of Environmental Justice' (2009) 41 *Antipode* 614.

[40] H Todd and C Zografos, 'Justice for the Environment: Eeveloping a Set of Indicators of Environmental Justice for Scotland' (2005) *Environmental Values* 483, 487.

[41] Heffron, McCauley and Sovacool (n 37) 169.

[42] Walker (n 39) as cited by Heffron, McCauley and Sovacool (n 37) 170.

[43] ibid 170.

[44] Definitions of vulnerability will be covered in section 3 of this chapter.

[45] Heffron, McCauley and Sovacool (n 37) 170.

[46] Heldeweg and Saintier (n 24) 3.

framework of governance'.[47] This makes both procedural and recognition justice difficult to achieve given that the current legal and governance tools have been created to serve this centralised system. This systemic injustice exacerbates the injustice/vulnerability of consumers and other stakeholders of the energy system.

The holistic, whole-system view that energy justice requires calls for a radical paradigm shift in terms of governance and tools to assist in the quest. To counter this highly centralised nature of the energy system, a more radical solution is required which is where energy decentralisation and energy democratisation – two distinct, yet connected concepts[48] – come in. These are important as 'two intertwined means to an end, ie a just energy transition'.[49]

The concepts of energy democratisation and energy decentralisation are premised on the idea that aside from being 'energy consumers' we are also 'energy citizens'.[50] At the heart of this bottom-up approach[51] is the delivery of a more democratic and inclusive just energy transition. To do so, however, requires 'the need to change the socio-economic relations embedded in the energy system by encouraging greater public involvement and control'.[52] A more inclusive and participatory energy system was supported at EU level through the Renewable Energy Directive RED-II which aimed in part at stimulating the formation of renewable energy communities in all Member States.[53] Post-Brexit, the issue remained topical following a governmental consultation on the topic of community energy projects.[54] Where the Government will take this is unknown, and is beyond the scope of this chapter.

This section has shown how the debate for a more democratic and inclusive just energy transition calls for a more coherent and inclusive system to protect the more vulnerable members of our society and shows a way forward. For some, this 'echoes Hirst's associative democracy principles which proposed to recast the relations between the market and civil society to enable "market economies to work better"'.[55] More importantly for the purpose of this chapter, the just energy transition debate mirrors the consumer law academic debate calling for the need to recognise the various images of the consumer 'as a citizen and a human being', and to embed the economic relations within the social ones.[56] Although no proposal was ever put forward as to how to do so,

[47] I Soutar and C Mitchell, 'Towards Pragmatic Narratives of Societal Engagement in the UK Energy System' (2018) *Energy and Social Sciences* 132, 134.

[48] ibid 136.

[49] Heldeweg and Saintier (n 24) 3.

[50] P Devine-Wright, 'Energy Citizenship: Psychological Aspects of Evolution in Sustainable Energy Technologies' in J Murphy (ed), *Governing technology for sustainability* (Earthscan, 2007) 67.

[51] Expression borrowed from M Peeters and T Schomerus, *Renewable Energy Law and the EU: Legal Perspectives on Bottom-up Approaches* (Edward Elgar, 2014).

[52] B Van Veelen and D Van der Horst, 'What is Energy Democracy? Connecting Social Science Energy Research and Political Theory' (2018) 46 *Energy Research & Social Science* 19, 25.

[53] Directive 2018/2001 of the EP and the Council on the promotion of the use of energy from renewable sources, OJ L382/82.

[54] Department for Energy Security and Net Zero, *Barriers to Community Energy Projects* (launched April 2024), assets.publishing.service.gov.uk/media/660ec2099f92ac001a516cee/barriers-to-community-energy-projects-call-for-evidence.pdf.

[55] Heldeweg and Saintier (n 24) 2 referring to P Hirst, *Associative Democracy: New Forms of Economic and Social Governance* (Polity Press, 1993).

[56] Davies (n 4) 325.

the problems have not disappeared. This chapter proposes a solution which embodies a wider view of needs supported through vulnerability into the framework of relational contracts. The juridical basis for importing such obligations arises from the definition of the essential services contract as relational.

5.2.2. A Relational View of Essential Services Contracts

As aptly summarised by LJ Leggatt, 'relational contracts as a term' was coined by Ian MacNeil, a Scottish American scholar who developed his 'relational contract theory in a series of publications between the late 1960s and early 1980s'.[57] The notion has developed in English law in the context of commercial contracts,[58] following Leggat J's now famous decision of *Yam Seng v ITC Ltd*.[59] But relational contract theory can also apply to consumer contracts.[60] In fact, it is argued that this sociological tool is even better suited to consumer contracts since relationalists apply contract law in a manner which is more sensitive to broader concerns of public policy and social solidarity.[61] Not only is relational contract theory accepted in principle as a category, but it was widened by Fraser J in *Bates v PO Ltd* in terms of the consequences that flow (implied duty of good faith in law rather than simply in fact). Naturally, the theory remains in a developmental stage, with the fringes being tested and reshaped. Yet, resorting to it is not a red herring since clear contours are emerging 'as the law on this subject gets worked out'.[62]

The considerable appeal of seeing essential services contracts through a relational lens is the recognition that contracts, as all economic relations, are deeply embedded into social ones and as such are 'framed by social norms, practices, actors and institutions'.[63] Indeed, relational contract theory formally recognises those norms and practices as being part of the contractual adventure. The recognition of these wider norms is particularly important in guiding consumer law to look beyond the transactional dimension and to bring in the missing dimension in the debate: the fact that consumers are also citizens and human beings. In other words, that consumer law needs to incorporate wider societal norms. In doing so, it helps to provide an inclusive and

[57] G Leggatt, 'The Emerging Concept of a Relational Contract in English law' in M Heidemann (ed), *The Transformation of Private Law, Principles of Contract and Tort as European and International Law* (Springer, 2024) 456.

[58] Professor Collins makes a convincing argument that within this category, employment contracts are relational: H Collins, 'Employment as a relational contract' (2021) 137 *Law Quarterly Review* 426.

[59] *Yam Seng v ITC Ltd* [2013] EWHC 111 (QB), [2013] 1 All ER (Comm) 1321.

[60] Professor Leib commented that 'Macaulay's early work laid the groundwork for a relational law of consumer form contract': E Leib, 'What is the Relational Theory of Consumer Form Contract?' in J Braucher, J Kidwell and WC Whitford (eds), *Revisiting the Contract Scholarship of Stewart Macaulay* (Hart, 2013) 262. For an opposite opinion, see Collins (n 58) 436, who argues that for weaker parties, the protection is left to Parliament.

[61] Collins (n 58) 429. These norms are already articulated through measures such as the Universal Services Obligation. This therefore reinforces the point made by T Dodsworth, '*The Underlying Values of German and English Contract Law*' (Cambridge University Press, forthcoming) 3–8 that these values underlie these doctrines which are not articulated. The aim of this chapter is to offer a way for consumer contracts in general to take into account these norms more openly. For similar views, see n 7.

[62] Leggatt (n 57) 479.

[63] B Lange and F Haines, 'Regulatory Transformations: an Introduction' in B Lange, F Haines and D Thomas (eds), *Regulatory Transformations – Rethinking Economy – Society Interactions* (Bloomsbury, 2017) 4.

coherent system of protection since it allows the economic transaction to be embedded in its social context, which in turn allows for terms to be implied into the contract that take into account those wider needs. The substance of these implied terms will be covered in section 5.2.4 below.

But, for the moment, for relational contract theory to have any impact, it must first be constructed as a workable paradigm from which clear legal consequences can flow.[64] This is done by adapting Collins' paradigm.[65] For Collins, the main components of a relational contract are:

(1) A long-term business relationship *that will provide sufficient pay-offs to both parties* to continue with the relationship even through periods of considerable adversity.
(2) *Obtaining the benefits of the business relationship* will require adaptation, co-operation, and evolution of performance obligations, so *that indeterminate implicit obligations of this kind must be central to the deal.*
(3) These implicit indeterminate obligations must be understood as arising not from general moral standards or norms of reciprocity such as honesty, *but will be tailored to achieve what is necessary to secure the success of the venture*. Business necessity in this context requires *acceptance of obligations derived from the general concepts of cooperation and loyalty or commitment to the project.*[66]

In italics are what is considered as the most important elements of Collins' analysis. Although distilled from a narrow basis of 'the trilogy of relational contracts',[67] they have nevertheless been jurisprudentially validated further. Of particular importance is the fact that by recognising the category in *Bates v PO Ltd*, Fraser J states that the implication of a duty of good faith is in law rather than in fact as envisaged by Leggatt J in *Yam Seng*. The validation of the concept as a paradigm together with the legal consequences that flow highlight that a contract is not 'solely an adversarial process',[68] but it is also 'a cooperative endeavour'.[69] Articulating what the latter part entails is crucial to understanding the core of relational contract theory[70] and goes to the core of our enquiry to find a model that supports the needs of vulnerable consumers. These elements help 'to reconcile the individual interest of the parties with the wider purpose of the contract'.[71] This wider social purpose, the implicit dimension, currently not recognised is particularly important for this chapter's aim since it is what sets essential services contracts apart. The focus should be on the

[64] H Collins, 'Is a relational contract a legal concept?' in S Degeling, J Edelman and J Goudkamp (eds), *Contract in Commercial Law* (Thomson Reuters, 2016) 38–39.

[65] Later, Collins refines those criteria, but this does not impact the analysis here. Collins (n 58) 429.

[66] ibid 55. Emphasis added.

[67] ibid 39.

[68] Z Gounari, 'Developing a relational law of contracts: striking a balance between abstraction and contextualism' (2021) 41 *Legal Studies* 177, 182.

[69] P Finn, 'Contract and the Fiduciary Principle' (1989) 12 *The University of new South Wales Law Journal* 76.

[70] Professor Collins refines the features of a relational contract as containing 'an implicit expectation of cooperation and loyalty that shape performance obligations to give business efficacy to the project'; Collins (n 64) 429.

[71] D Christie, S Saintier and J Viven-Wilksch, 'Industry Led Standards, Relational Contracts and Good Faith: Are the UK and Australia Setting the Pace in (Construction) Contract Law?' (2022) 43 *Liverpool Law Review* 287.

relation and the behaviour that allows the exchange/transaction to take place, and not the other way around.[72]

5.2.2.1. Common Aim of an Essential Services Contract; a Contract with a Social Purpose

Contracts are relational, as understood here, when the parties enter into a contract with a particular aim in mind, which both parties aim to share the benefits of achieving. Although Collins ranks this in second place, it is clearly what drives the parties to contract with each other – 'the common aim'[73] – the first criteria from which everything flows.[74] This common aim is the core of the contract and what makes the contract relational. It is the element that shapes the implicit obligations that will be tailored to ensuring the success of the venture.

For commercial contracts, this common aim is usually financial. For essential services contracts this aim is necessarily different. Indeed, essential services contracts have internally generated norms, ie the transaction of providing the service. But, crucially for our purpose, they also have an externally generated norm, ie the recognition of the wider social context and the fact that they serve the public interest (eg sustainable/continuous supply of the service avoiding socially unwanted results and furthering of the network). Consumer law only focuses on the internally generated norm and therefore fails to protect the vulnerable. To remedy this lacuna, the externally generated norm must be recognised and given effect.[75] This can be achieved by the common interest, ie the social purpose of essential services contracts. This recognises the fact that all contracts are embedded in 'social practices and norms'.[76] The common interest, as a norm, a standard, 'guides the behaviour of the parties far more … than the exclusive focus on the express terms of the contract'.[77]

Although this wider social purpose is already clearly acknowledged through measures such as universal service obligations (USOs) or, in the context of energy, the price cap, the protection provided by the price cap does not provide the protection actually needed. This is because it focuses too much on the transaction alone. As much is expressed by Fraser J in *Bates v Post Office Ltd* when he states that 'the spirits and objectives of [their venture] may not be capable of being expressed exhaustively in a written contract'.[78] A stronger basis of protection is therefore necessary to give effect to these

[72] J Rochfeld, 'Les modes temporels d'exécution du contrat' (2004) *Revue des Contrats* 47, para 25. This is again in line with Polanyi's embedding of the economic relation into social ones.

[73] Also referred to as 'the common interest' by Rochfeld, ibid; The centrality is also clear in Collins's later piece when he reasserts that relational contracts are indeterminate by design and 'because of this indeterminacy, such contracts are accompanied by cooperation (mutual expectations of) to bring a successful outcome'. Collins (n 64) 429, fn 2.

[74] This has been described as adopting a project-centric approach, see Christie, Saintier and Viven-Wilksch, (n 71).

[75] In line with Polanyi's claim that 'social norms, practice, actors and institutions frame economic transactions', B Lange, F Haines and D Thomas (eds), *Regulatory Transformations – Rethinking Economy- Society interactions* (Bloomsbury, 2017) 11.

[76] S Macaulay, 'Non-Contractual Relations in Business' (1963) 28 *American Sociological Review* 45, as quoted by Collins (n 58) 433.

[77] Collins, ibid.

[78] *Bates v Post Office Ltd* [2019] EWHC (606) QB [725].

wider expectations of achieving certain social standards. Relational contracts would allow this. To do so is not dissimilar to what the courts have done by using implied terms on the quality of the goods, to 'ensure that certain quality standards are maintained and promoted in society'.[79]

5.2.2.2. A Long-Term Relationship with Sufficient Pay-Offs to Both Parties

The contract need not be long term to be characterised as relational since, as seen, the relationality comes not from the length of the contract, but from its social purpose; this characteristic therefore also needs adapting. This adaptation is not too problematic since 'in the social science literature, length is neither necessary nor sufficient for a relational contract'.[80] Collins himself softened the feature by referring to 'an expectation of a longer-term relation'.[81] LJ Leggatt, upon reviewing cases, states that contracts of very short durations can be relational.[82] This is important for the energy context since it does not prevent consumers from changing suppliers when there is a better deal. The relational element of essential services contracts can therefore be recognised from day one, in the same manner that USOs apply regardless of the length of the contract. This is not to say that length is unimportant; arguably, the longer the contract is, the more important it is for the supplier to co-operate (more on this in in the next section). Renewal is another issue since once the contract outlives the original term and the supplier places the consumer on a standard variable tariff. This is where the issue of pay-offs for both parties also needs to be adapted and understood in the context of contracts to protect vulnerable consumers. This contextual understanding is at the core of relational contract theory[83] and is one of the main justifications for using it.

5.2.2.3. Adaptation, Cooperation and Evolution of Performance Obligations to Protect the Common Aim

Given the aforementioned social element of essential services contracts, the aim of the contract may be considered to be nothing more than the right to access a continuous and resilient supply of a product (eg energy, mobile phone coverage), which includes protection from disconnection (but as the British Gas scandal shows, this does not work). However, that can only be half the picture. The good/service that is being provided is so essential that it has been likened to a human right.[84] The question of access to basic

[79] R. Beheshti, 'The circular economy and the implied terms of contract in English sales law' (2020) *Journal of Property Planning and Environmental Law* 4.

[80] Collins (n 58) 53.

[81] Collins (n 64) 429.

[82] Leggatt (n 57) 457.

[83] Collins states that when interpretating relational contracts, 'the central point for the court is to examine the social and economic context of the purpose of the transaction in order to understand the reasonable expectations and implicit understanding of the parties'. Collins (n 64) 437.

[84] M Hesselman, A Hallo de Wolf and B Toebes, 'Common challenges for socio-economic human rights and essential public service provisions' in M Hesselman, A Hallo de Wolf and B Toebes (eds), *Socio-economic rights in essential public services provisions* (Routledge, 2020) 3.

services is therefore also relevant. The greater risk is that of social exclusion, which in the context of energy poverty, as seen, is particularly serious, and in the context of the energy transition translates as access to clean and renewable energy. The need to adapt and to co-operate arises from the expectation of vulnerability. This is where relational contract theory is particularly helpful as it recognises that it is not 'solely an adversarial process',[85] but also a 'a cooperative endeavour'.[86]

The above has shown that the view of essential services contracts as relational is not optional but necessary since consumer law does not 'see the wider picture ie the way it fits with the lives of individuals'.[87] Reich summarised the situation particularly well:

> [T]he improved information and market transparency are of little help to vulnerable consumers when the goal is to enable them to lead self-determined lives. It is rather the targeted improvement of infrastructure and intelligent realistic schemes of providing advice, that enable consumers, including vulnerable consumers, to participate independently in economic and social life.[88]

To live independently, and to be given effect to all their facets, as human beings and citizens, consumers must be provided with the tools to be resilient to their vulnerability. But that can only be done if the true extent of their vulnerability is acknowledged and part of the contracting process. Relational contract theory – which aims to recognise the aforementioned wider norms than those internally generated by the contract as relevant to 'how the contractual relations should be understood, the obligations derived and interpreted and the disputes resolved'[89] – is therefore particularly important as it places the transaction in its wider social setting through the recognition that the individual contract for energy must be impacted by (and itself impacts) wider social and societal norms – beyond the basic economic transaction – and allows consideration of obligations that must necessarily be implied in order to capture the context of the energy transition.

The argument has been made elsewhere that the combination of relational contract theory and vulnerability theory places obligations on suppliers to reduce the dependency of the consumer on the supplier.[90] In order to capture the dependency, whether collective or individual, requires a fresh look at the assumptions that underlie the system of energy. There are two reasons for this. First, a just energy transition cannot take place within a system that perpetuates inequality (what might be meant by inequality will be explored shortly) and, second, an obligation to reduce dependency requires a framework in which the dependency can be sufficiently recognised.

Let us now turn to the other side of the discussion; that of the manner in which we also need to consider inequality and vulnerability, which goes towards considering the regulatory vulnerability itself.

[85] Gounari (n 68) 182.
[86] Finn (n 79).
[87] Riefa and Saintier (n 5) 245.
[88] N Reich, 'Vulnerable Consumers in EU Law' in D Leczykiewicz and S Weatherill (eds), *The Images of the Consumer in EU Law: Legislation, Free Movement and Competition Law* (Hart Publishing, 2016) 150.
[89] C Mitchell, *Contract Law and Contract Practice, Bridging the Gap between Legal Reasoning and Contract Expectation* (Bloomsbury, 2013) 238; see also Collins (n 58) 239.
[90] T Dodsworth and S Saintier, 'Relational Contracts: A new Theory for (Consumer) Contracts for Essential Services' presented at the Consumer law conference held at the University of Reading in July 2021. Paper with the authors.

5.3. Inequality, Vulnerability and Intervention

The focus in the first part of this chapter has been on recognising that the structure of a future energy system, and therefore the energy transition, is driven by specific conceptions of justice. The broad assumption underlying systems of justice is that they must hinge on something that frames what is required for justice. Here, that is the idea of equality. The starting point for this section is therefore to build a picture of the current framework of equality in the energy system and how the origins of the energy system provide an understanding of how certain inequalities became embedded.

The distribution of energy as a business commodity (eg to power factories) provided the foundation for conceptualising energy as a unit which could be sold for profit. However, the distribution of energy through publicly owned channels naturally requires some form of state intervention. The role of energy in society has changed significantly from business commodity to essential requirement. Whilst the state takes a role in the distribution of energy (through the national grid), the allocation of energy to citizens is based on equal unit price (with some exceptions through Universal Credit). Equality in this context is based on the unit price (and daily connectivity rate) being the same for every citizen. The role of the state is consequently seen to be limited to the maintenance of the distribution system and equal (as defined above) access for all citizens.

This approach to equality entrenches the view of the neoliberal, rational individual within the energy system which provides the structural backbone to privatisation of the energy market. It assumes therefore that sufficient and clear information provides the antidote to non-engagement which consequently justifies the operation of a privatised market. However, it has become apparent that even with sufficient information and knowledge, many consumers considered to be in vulnerable circumstances will not engage in the market.[91] It has been argued elsewhere that this is because of the limited understanding of vulnerability as being rooted in capacity (either to understand or get access to information).[92] Autonomy in these circumstances is rooted in having access to information which it is assumed will lead to rational decision-making. The equality propounded when information and knowledge become the core of defining vulnerability is that it focuses on sameness of treatment. In other words, if the information is provided, the individual is assumed to be making decisions to maximise their own autonomy.[93] Equality is grounded in the 'sameness' of information both of all users and between the contracting parties. However, this alone has been accepted in the most basic format as not being sufficient to provide equality because the capacity to understand the provided information is a significant second branch of the autonomous being envisaged by law. Hence, externally identifiable features assume a reduction in autonomy which must be addressed to provide the desired equality/sameness of treatment.

[91] T Dodsworth, 'Vulnerability in the UK Energy Market' in C Riefa and S Saintier (eds), *Vulnerable Consumers and the Law – Consumer Protection and Access to Justice* (Routledge, 2021) 110.

[92] Dodsworth and Saintier (n 90) 44.

[93] See the forthcoming chapter: R Mullender, 'Negligent Misstatement, Antifragility and the State' in T Dodsworth, M Hemsworth and S Saintier (eds), *The Future of Contract Law: Global Challenges and Disruptions* (Edward Elgar, 2026) 20–21.

This sameness of treatment is achieved through identifying groups as inherently vulnerable.[94] For example, age might be considered an externality which indicates that the individual is vulnerable. Similarly, not reaching a certain age would mean that the individual is not vulnerable. In this context vulnerability is construed as a feature which identifies the group (and individual) as weak or in need of help even though equality in terms of information has already been achieved. This is a step in the right direction, but too crude an understanding of vulnerability.

The importance of what has so far been discussed is that:

(1) The system which governs the allocation of energy has itself subscribed to a certain model of equality based on individual autonomy – same price for everyone.
(2) That there is an underlying asymmetry of power with regard to information which requires adjustment to ensure equality between the contracting parties by providing information.
(3) That equality between users requires intervention based on external features (eg age) described as vulnerabilities.

The system is thereby subscribed to a model of equality which is not a 'natural' state, but is derived from a construction of equality based on autonomy which can (and should) be questioned, and there is an acknowledgement that there is a need for intervention to mediate a 'pure' approach to equality.

The suggestion that the system (here both the energy system and the legal system) has adopted a form of equality requires an investigation into the effect of results of that choice. First, the effect of identifying groups as vulnerable has a stigmatising effect which means that even though individuals might be vulnerable, they do not identify as such. Whilst the stigmatisation itself adds to the vulnerability it also points to the broader issue of vulnerability being enmeshed with identity. Instead, Martha Fineman offers a definition of vulnerability in post-identity terms which takes a systemic view of privilege and consequently detriment.[95] In other words, the system of energy distribution (ultimately controlled by the state) must be viewed as perpetuating existing privilege to the detriment of others. Further examination of vulnerability is therefore required.

Before further examination of the concept of vulnerability, it is important to acknowledge that both the intervention by law and the absence of intervention, both in the energy system and in the energy transition, impact the actual and perceived level of vulnerability of groups and individuals. The law's role in society is broadly to ensure equality and social justice. As such, 'Legal norms … generate an a priori sense of legitimacy of the decisions they entrench. Reconciling different interests in society, they balance a power that becomes normalised'.[96] The history of the distribution of energy therefore entrenches, through law, conceptions of vulnerability which need to be continuously questioned. Law (in contrast to policy) has, both at national and European level, entrenched an understanding of vulnerability and of the balance of power which

[94] M Fineman, 'The Vulnerable Subject: Anchoring Equality in the Human Condition' (2008) *Yale Journal of Law and Feminism* 1, 1.
[95] ibid 1.
[96] V Moreno-Lax and N Vavoula, 'Vulnerability's Legal Life: An Ambivalent Force of Migration Governance' (2024) *International Jounral of Law in Context* 1, 5.

places the self-interested individual at the centre of the system without questioning the role of the state or energy. It has done so by beginning the discussion from a position of the rational individual whose weaknesses most often relate to an understanding of the terms or their inequality of bargaining power. In contracts for essential services, such as energy, the 'solution' to vulnerability is therefore 'the clear provision of core terms and/or the creation of competitive markets'.[97]

Similarly, where the law has intervened to address perceived injustices (eg by imposing a price cap or offering 'warm home' discounts) it entrenches ideals of vulnerabilities. Legally, relevant vulnerabilities entitle individuals to protection, but also exclude others from the same treatment. In short, the systems as they exist today entrench vulnerabilities (whether by action or inaction)[98] which justify calls for continuous review and thereby form the very basis of the legitimacy to question prevailing structures without the need to reference prior structures. In other words, there would not normally be the need to prove that the review of the current energy system equality (set out above) requires review because of the system assumption. Instead, the fact that the system creates (whether by action or inaction) vulnerabilities should itself be sufficient to justify review. As seen above, the debate on energy justice highlights precisely how and in what way the system creates and exacerbates vulnerabilities.

Learning from other areas of law:

> Putting the 'vulnerable subject' at the centre of legal institutional responses, taking account of the political structures that allow to impede individuals from leading a dignified, rights-enjoying life, invites consideration of the factors that effect available options and sustain existing barriers to substantive equality.[99]

Fineman's argument begins by reasoning from the human condition rather than from the hypothetical *homo economicus*.[100] The human condition presupposes that vulnerability is constant and ever-present whilst also fluctuating. What at first seems like a contradiction needs to be viewed through the definition of vulnerability: the ever-present possibility of injury and dependency. Viewed as such, vulnerability remains ever-present whilst fluctuating as the possibility of harm/dependency also fluctuates. Vulnerability is unavoidably part of the human condition as it arises from the very nature of being human and therefore must be constant and universal. The possibility of harm can nevertheless be more or less remote depending on the context. The contextualisation occurs by acknowledging the vulnerable subject's lived environments which either provide or remove resilience assets.[101] Once vulnerability is conceptualised in this way, it is hard to justify the system of energy distribution as it stands today.

The first reason why it is hard to justify is the reliance on the current understanding of equality, which assumes that the individual at the heart of the system is at all stages rational and autonomous. The argument at the beginning of this section was that the

[97] Beyond consumer law there are more specific support mechanisms (eg social care and limited legislative initiatives). However, these remain disconnected from the transaction and thereby ignore an obvious point of intervention.

[98] Fineman (n 94) 1.

[99] Moreno-Lax and Vavoula (n 96) 5.

[100] Fineman (n 94) 1.

[101] P Kirby, *Vulnerability and Violence. The Impact of Globalization* (Pluto Press, 2006) 55–72.

system is reliant on a system of equality which is not merely a natural state but rather a creation. It might be argued that the 'vulnerable subject' is a form of legal fiction, but the fact that this subject is grounded in the human condition means that it relies on traits of reality.

There are some arguments to address before moving to an assessment of the energy transition. The first argument is that if everyone is always vulnerable then it normalises vulnerability and so in reality nobody is considered vulnerable.[102] A similar argument is that the vague nature of defining vulnerability as 'universal' undermines the system's ability to react to specific instances of vulnerability. In other words, it is easier to categorise vulnerability (eg using age) than it is to work with a general concept. Both arguments miss the purpose of the definition of vulnerability in this instance. The first reason for using vulnerability theory (in the energy context) is to interrogate the allocation of resilience assets through what is represented as a neutral system.[103] Parallels can be drawn to arguments in the energy justice debate, mentioned above, where the system of allowing individuals to transition to renewable energy through their own means distorts who actually has access to clean energy. The second reason is to question the moral and political basis upon which the system has entrenched structures of privilege. Most legal measures that are aimed at addressing privilege are aimed at removing discrimination.[104] Vulnerability theory goes further and identifies that structures/systems were built on and sustain privilege without falling into the legal discrimination realm.[105] This is also where the debate connects with energy justice and in particular energy democratisation. Where the transition is built on existing structures, or even where they are reasoned from those existing structures, they will need to be questioned. However, before bringing together these strands, the role of autonomy must first be addressed.

The argument put forward here is not about eliminating autonomy or creating barriers to individual autonomy. In fact, autonomy is a source of resilience (resilience is a topic which will be addressed later). Moreno-Lax and Vavoula suggest that 'To be vulnerable is to be susceptible to harmful wrongs, abuse, and threats to one's own autonomy (by others). Under this optic, autonomy and vulnerability are co-constituted and dialectically entwined.'[106] Consequently, autonomy-promoting measures which attempt to build equality by adjusting power and influence still align with a vulnerability theory approach.

The difference, though, is that the starting point cannot be the assumption of an autonomous individual. Therefore, the aim is not to remove exchange or autonomy.[107] The aim is to embed these principles in a broader balance of values[108] which takes

[102] See further on this, D Schroeder and E Gerfanas, 'Vulnerability: Too Vague and Too Broad' (2009) 18 *Cambridge Quarterly of Healthcare Ethics* 113, 113.

[103] Dodsworth and Saintier (n 90) 44.

[104] M Fineman, 'Beyond Identities: The Limits of an Antidiscrimination Approach to Equality' (2012) 92 *Boston University Law Review* 1713.

[105] M Fineman, 'Vulnerability and Inevitable Inequality' (2017) 4 *Oslo Law Review* 133.

[106] Moreno-Lax and Vavoula (n 96) 4.

[107] On autonomy see also P Formosa, 'The Role of Vulnerability in Kantian Ethics' in C MacKenzie, W Rogers and S Dodds (eds), *Vulnerability: Essays in Ethics and Feminist Philosophy* (Oxford University Press, 2013) 94.

[108] Dodsworth (n 61) 14–18.

account of and begins reasoning from the vulnerable subject. This means that the inherent vulnerability can (and should) be assumed to form the basis of any transaction involving essential services.[109] The aim of the essential services contract is not to assume autonomy, but instead to be providing resilience which in the context of the energy transition will also include the building of autonomy. This is a fundamental shift in the understanding of the purpose of the contract and contractual venture moving the goal from an assumption of autonomy to the development of autonomy.

The final element to consider from the vulnerability theory perspective is the notion of resilience. As mentioned above, the system would need to be evaluated in light of how it (re)distributes resilience assets. Resilience assets mitigate the dependency and also thereby link to building autonomy. The exposition of energy justice above mentioned the need to consider how the system design allocates resources, yet this is not mirrored in contract or consumer law. Rather than questioning whether the law is treating energy consumers equally, the starting point must be to identify what harms are generated or even aggravated through law and often through law's commitment to the entrenched commitment to 'equality'. This broader analysis of how the system redistributes resilience assets throughout the system invites a further obligation to the contract. The contractual venture is no longer limited to the individual (and their own resilience), but must also consider the systemic impact of how privilege (and resilience assets) are perpetuated through the compounding effect of transaction of this type. This wider aspect can, as shown, be integrated through relational contract theory.

The shift, for contract law, to move from a focus on autonomy to a more pluralistic view of the values that should underlie the assessment of contracts is legitimised, on a doctrinal assessment, by identifying that the nature of the contract is relational. Nevertheless, it is worth exploring further avenues which legitimise this new approach.

5.4. Legitimising a Different Approach

The call here is not to amend the entire basis of contract law for every exchange. This chapter is limited to contracts for energy and specifically for energy as an essential good/service. However, reviewing existing structures through the vulnerability lens does not require justification from those pre-existing structures because in most instances the system itself is self-justificatory and therefore commits to a certain understanding of equality, as was discussed above.[110] Nevertheless, in this instance the system itself provides the possibility to justify a different approach by the very nature of the subject matter of the contract being 'essential'. The ability to freely opt out of the market, as would normally be the economic threshold for participation, does not (realistically) exist. The elements of this argument are best highlighted through an example: for many participants the engagement in the market itself provides autonomy, but engagement

[109] Dodsworth and Saintier (n 90) 46–49.

[110] M Fineman, 'Reasoning from the Body: Universal Vulnerability and Social Justice' *Emory Legal Studies Research Paper 22-18* (2022) 1, 5.

(and the mechanisms to engagement) does not necessarily lead to autonomy. This is also true where there is an element of monopoly or dependence.

In the energy context, the cost of energy is not the same to everyone. What one might normally expect in an open market is the ability not to purchase. The core tenet of a neoliberal and competitive market, and surely also of freedom of contract, is the option not to contract. Whilst in the abstract this might be a possibility, living off-grid or in self-sufficient eco-homes is, in practical terms, not available to the public at large. Alternatives, where they are available, are not themselves taking into account the entire cost nor the relative ability to engage with the system requirements. There is therefore an underlying dependency on what is being provided. Whilst it has generally been professed that information is the key for consumers to engage with and benefit from a competitive market, it is clear that even with the relevant information individuals have different thresholds to engagement.

There are a number of elements to draw from this illustration. First, engagement with/in the market can be a source of resilience.[111] However, the need to engage can also be a form of harm in that it neglects those that are unable (or unwilling) to engage. Second, there is an inherent dependency on the product of energy by the very nature of being essential and monopolised – further complicated when seen in the context of the energy transition. The system is inherently dependent on engagement and on the energy supply itself. This final point brings with it a certain dichotomy: the system gains resilience if users produce their own electricity, but requires sufficient usage and also requires consumers to engage with the system in order for it to function. Third, as with resilience, engagement is not singular. Engagement by comparing energy prices (within the Ofgem framework) is different to engagement in community energy projects. Whilst both can likely result in some resilience for the engaged, these are different in the results they produce. Fourth, if the resilience differs depending on particular groups in society, then they need to be reviewed because they are (re-)distributing resilience. In other words, if the structure of the system favours a particular group in society by providing more/less resilience assets this should provide sufficient legitimacy to amend the system. Climate change and the need to look for more sustainable sources of energy complicate this assessment further; for example, if the market offers reduced rates for consumers who have solar panels, then the system is providing more resilience assets to home-owners than renters.

In summary, the current energy system's (largely) transactional approach has been justified by reference to the individual's autonomy. Although the system is self-referential in legitimising this current approach, there are sufficient arguments, even within the system, to legitimise the new approach suggested in this chapter.

5.5. Conclusion

The aim of this chapter was to show that consumer law can provide the protection that vulnerable consumers need by providing a coherent and inclusive system of protection which shows that consumer law can 'see the wider picture ie the way it

[111] Exemplified through Target 7.1 of the United Nations Sustainable Development Goals: to ensure universal access to affordable, reliable and modern energy services.

fits with the lives of individuals'.[112] This has been done by bringing together energy justice arguments, vulnerability theory and consumer law approaches to more accurately articulate the various facets of 'the energy consumer'. The importance of consumer law's understanding and acknowledgement of the interplay of these different elements is underscored by energy's crucial role as 'the basic structure of society'.[113]

This chapter has suggested that the energy justice and vulnerability debate are fundamental to understanding the shifting nature of consumer law. The energy justice debate calls for a whole-system view of energy which involves taking into consideration the impact of the energy transition, which is naturally the environment of the future consumer. This whole-system view is necessary for law to consider the consumer in their guise as citizen and human being. However, this alone is not sufficient for consumer law to capture the realities of systemic inequality. Rather, vulnerability theory demands a view of the energy system which takes into account how the individual interacts with the system in the redistribution of resilience assets (and the system's underlying decision making process).

This is a particularly relevant consideration for future consumer law. Resilience is provided by the system, so rather than thinking of consumers as inherently resilient this chapter considers how and to whom the system provides resilience assets. With this in mind, the current reductive view of consumer law to either view the consumer contract for the purchase/sale of energy as a singular, disconnected transaction, or to view consumers as economic, independent actors is untenable. The various iterations of relative inequality question the system of consumer contracts in the field of energy and particularly in the shifting world of the energy transition.

Bearing in mind the energy context and the overarching aim, the question this chapter set out to answer was how a sustainable shift will (and should) disrupt consumer contracts. The starting point and premise of the argument lies in the call in the energy justice debate for a holistic and contextual view of energy consumption. This means that consumer law also requires a holistic and contextual view of energy contracts for consumers. The juridical vehicle for achieving this aim is that essential services contracts are by their nature relational contracts. The reason for viewing essential services contracts as relational is, first, that terms must be implied into the contract which support the shared endeavour and, second, that it allows for an alternative view of vulnerability. The need for a broader view of vulnerability arises from consumer law's continued focus on transactional vulnerability and which ignores the other facets of the consumers 'as a citizen and a human being'.[114] Working on the premise of the relational energy contract then requires the implication of terms which further the cooperative endeavour of the contract.

Having established that a term must be implied into the contract, this chapter turned to the substance of such an implied term. If the aim of the contract is no longer just the supply of energy and actually a step towards a just energy transition, then it must also take into account principles of energy justice. The energy justice debate suggests three

[112] C Riefa and S Saintier, (n 5), 245.
[113] J Rawls, *Justice as Fairness, A Restatement* (Belknap Press, 2001) 10.
[114] Davies (n 4) 326.

lenses of justice through which energy should be viewed: distributional; procedural; and recognition. These lenses define the co-operative aim of the contractual venture, far beyond a simple transaction of money for energy. This chapter then identified that in order to define the substance of the term, the system must set out the relative equality that the system should be aiming to achieve and for which vulnerability theory provided the most appropriate insight.

Vulnerability theory provided the input for identifying that the very foundation of the energy system and the way that the state interacts with it is not neutral. The system itself creates inequality (particularly through inaction by the state) and entrenches vulnerabilities. As the terms in the contract must build towards the aim of building resilience, the system itself must be understood as self-legitimising. This legitimacy is premised on a specific, neoliberal framework which will justify the view of energy contracts as individual, disconnected transactions. Whilst there might justifiably be calls for the system as it stands to be overhauled, the legitimacy argument is relevant to the extent that it justifies a departure from the inaction as neutral perspective. In other words, vulnerability theory counters the systemic assumptions of equality to justify intervention.

Returning to the substance of the implied terms, the energy contract is premised on the need to respond to dependencies which arise not just from the contract itself but from the system and the structure of the system. These dependencies permeate and perpetuate existing inequalities even through the energy transition. It is inevitable that energy justice will disrupt consumer law and that the implied term to reduce dependency, requiring positive action in an unequal system, will lie at its heart.

PART III

Future Directions in Consumer Financial Services

6

The New Consumer Duty in the Provision of Financial Services: A Re-alignment of the FCA's Approach to its Objectives and Protection of the Consumer?

SARAH BROWN

6.1. Introduction

The Financial Conduct Authority (FCA) regulates the conduct of financial services 'firms'[1] in the United Kingdom (UK). As part of this function, it issues rules of conduct, underpinned by a set of fundamental obligations, framed as High Level Principles. In the latest drive for higher consumer protection in financial markets, the FCA has introduced a new Principle as part of a 'Consumer Duty' ('the Duty') whereby firms must act to deliver good outcomes for retail consumers. The Duty came into force through phased introduction from 31 July 2023.[2]

The FCA's powers are seated in the Financial Services and Markets Act 2000 (FSMA),[3] which sets out the general functions of the regulator together with a number of objectives to which it must adhere, 'as far as is reasonably possible'. These objectives consist of the strategic objective, three operational objectives and a secondary objective, the latter being introduced by the Financial Services and Markets Act 2023. The operational objectives consist of the consumer protection objective, the integrity objective and the competition objective. The secondary objective is the 'international' competitiveness and growth objective. The FCA has stated this new objective will not apply to individual enforcement decisions and that it will not dilute the focus on consumer protection – whilst still acknowledged as a focus, consumer protection does not take centre stage.[4]

[1] If authorised under the Financial Services and Markets Act 2000 (FSMA 2000) (has permission to carry out regulated activities under the statutory scheme). The FCA also has prudential responsibilities in relation to certain financial institutions.

[2] www.fca.org.uk/publications/policy-statements/ps22-9-new-consumer-duty.

[3] As amended by the Financial Services Act 2012 (FSA 2012).

[4] FCA, 'Secondary international competitiveness and growth objective' (14 July 2023) 2, www.fca.org.uk/publication/corporate/secondary-international-competitiveness-growth-objective-statement.pdf.

The FCA has consistently maintained its commitment to competition in the interests of consumers and the importance of consumer responsibility, reflecting the influence, as required by the objectives, of the competitive market. As noted by Eilis Ferran, there is the risk of a tension between the consumer protection and competition objectives.[5] There is a difficult balance to be made,[6] and the extent to which this has been successful is debatable. There are complaints that consumer protection has been sacrificed for the ultimate goal of competition;[7] and policy in protecting consumer interests has been contextualised within the importance of the competitive market. Problems for consumers continue – commission payments in the motor industry being a case in point.[8] The FCA is coming under increasing pressure in terms of how it protects consumers who engage in the financial services market. The Duty is a response to the challenges it faces and suggests a more robust approach to consumer protection and a potential shift in the weight given to these 'competing' objectives.

A useful means of exploring the potential impact of the Duty is through the lens of disruption, innovation and re-alignment. The Duty may not be disruptive in a legal sense.[9] However what *is* clear is that an attempt is being made to change the way things are done, both by the regulator and service providers. This is not only in the re-alignment of the emphasis given to the FCA objectives (by approaching the objectives differently), but also the vehicle through which this re-alignment takes place, ie the Duty. It is also a development which brings FCA supervision and regulation closer to a recognition of the 'open-textured' aspects of consumer law, with specific use of the common law principle of good faith as a means of advancing higher standards. The FCA's intentional incorporation of common law principles as a means of creating a more protective market culture may even prompt other consumer protection agencies to consider the emphasis of their own approach.

The objective is the result of a wider review of financial services regulation post-Brexit under the Future Regulatory Framework Review; see HM Treasury, 'Building a Smarter Financial Services Regulatory Framework for the UK, Policy Statement' (December 2022) para 2.12, www.gov.uk/government/publications/building-a-smarter-financial-services-framework-for-the-uk. This new objective is 'facilitating, subject to aligning with relevant international standards – (a) the international competitiveness of the economy of the United Kingdom (including in particular the financial services sector), and (b) its growth in the medium to long term.' FSMA 2000, s 1EB. The objective is secondary so will not be advanced on its own but will 'shape' how the FCA advances the primary objectives.

[5] E Ferran, 'The New Mandate for the Supervision of Financial Services Conduct' (2012) 65 *Current Legal Problems* 411, 412, 440. Ferran discusses the Financial Services Bill which became the FSA 2012, amending FSMA 2000, creating the FCA.

[6] ibid 416, 441.

[7] See eg *Hansard* HL (series 6) Vol 811, col 858 (24 March 2021).

[8] eg the recent Court of Appeal decision in *Johnson v Firstrand Bank Ltd (t/a MotoNovo Finance)* [2024] EWCA Civ 1282. The Court held in the consumers' favour, deciding that when arranging car finance the dealer acted as credit broker, owing a duty to give disinterested advice and a fiduciary duty. Breach of these duties through payment of a non-disclosed or non-disclosed ('secret' or 'half secret') commission exposed the lender to liability. This, however, was overturned by the Supreme Court, although the related question of an unfair relationship in Johnson's case was upheld. *Hopcraft v Close Brothers Ltd* [2025] UKSC 33. See also FCA, 'Motor finance discretionary commission models and consumer credit commission disclosure – feedback on CP19/28 and final rules' (PS20/8), www.fca.org.uk/publication/policy/ps20-8.pdf.

[9] As discussed in C Twigg-Flesner, 'The potential of the covid-19 crisis to cause legal "disruption" to contracts and contract law' in E Hondius et al (eds), *Coronavirus and the Law in Europe* (Intersentia, 2021).

This chapter considers the Duty with these themes in mind, in particular the extent to which, whilst not truly innovative,[10] it provides a degree of innovation which in turn delivers a re-alignment in approach to FCA objectives. The examination begins with a brief overview of the statutory basis and framework within and upon which the FCA operates, followed by an explanation of the concept and introduction of the Duty. It will then go on to consider whether the introduction of the Duty reflects a true realignment in the FCA's approach to its statutory objectives, and if this will further advance effective consumer protection in the financial services market.

6.2. The Creation and Operational Framework of the FCA

As is well known, the FCA replaced the Financial Services Authority (FSA) in 2013, also taking over from the Office of Fair Trading in relation to consumer credit in 2014. The rationale behind the establishment of this new regulatory body was to rebuild trust and confidence in the financial system after the financial crisis.[11] One element of the rationale behind reform was to put 'appropriate consumer outcomes at the centre of the regulatory process' as a means of rebuilding this trust and confidence.[12] The new regulatory body was to be a 'consumer champion', although this came with the caveat of proportionality and consumer responsibility.[13] The subsequent inclusion of consumer credit within the FCA's remit was to provide 'stronger protections for consumers', but also to 'remove unnecessary regulatory duplication and burdens for business' with a 'flexible and proportionate' regime 'reflecting the diverse nature of the sector'.[14]

The FCA's purpose is to regulate and supervise financial markets and services that are within its regulatory purview, FSMA being its primary reference point.[15] This legislation sets out the FCA's 'general functions' of rulemaking, preparation and issue of codes, general guidance and determination of general policy and principles. In essence there are three elements to the FCA's control over the financial services sector. The first is the FCA's 'statutory mandate'[16] which consists of the objectives referred to above – in effect a set of statutorily imposed aims. The second element is the mechanism for achieving these objectives, namely the regulatory framework, and supervision and enforcement by the regulator. The third is policy, which informs and influences how the FCA interprets its objectives and how it employs the regulatory and supervisory mechanism to achieve these aims.

[10] ibid.

[11] For a critique of this approach see eg Ferran (n 5) 412–16; E Ferran 'The Break-up of the Financial Services Authority' (2011) 31 *OJLS* 455.

[12] HM Treasury, 'A new approach to financial regulation: building a stronger system' (Cm 8012, 2011) para 1.13, assets.publishing.service.gov.uk/media/5a78da20ed915d07d35b2ee7/consult_newfinancial_regulation170211.pdf.

[13] ibid para 4.9.

[14] HM Treasury and Department for Business Innovation and Skills, 'A new approach to financial regulation: consultation on reforming the consumer credit regime' (December 2010) 3, assets.publishing.service.gov.uk/media/5a78a00a40f0b62b22cbb7c5/consult_consumer_credit211210.pdf.

[15] The FCA has functions under other legislation and secondary regulation as a 'regulator' and 'enforcer' in specific contexts, eg by virtue of FSMA 2000, s 234J; Consumer Rights Act 2015, Sch 3.

[16] For a detailed discussion of this see the extensive analysis in Ferran (n 5).

6.2.1. The Objectives

The FCA's objectives set out the basis upon which the FCA performs its role and discharges its general functions:[17]

> In discharging its general functions the FCA must, so far as is reasonably possible, act in a way which—
>
> (a) is compatible with its strategic objective, and
>
> (b) advances one or more of its operational objectives.[18]

The FCA's strategic objective is ensuring that the relevant markets function well.[19] Its operational objectives consist of the consumer protection objective,[20] the integrity objective[21] and the competition objective,[22] plus the secondary objective of competitiveness and growth. In addition, the FCA must 'discharge its general functions in a way which promotes effective competition in the interests of consumers', as long as this is 'compatible with acting in a way which advances the consumer protection objective or the integrity objective'.[23] Dissecting this a little further, the consumer protection objective requires the FCA to secure 'an appropriate degree of protection for consumers'.[24] In doing this the FCA must consider a number of issues. These include a risk analysis on behalf of consumers in relation to 'different kinds of investment or other transaction' and the varying expectations and needs of consumers in relation to accurate and timely information and advice.[25] This is, together with the principle that consumers should receive 'an appropriate level of care', again based in risk analysis in the context of varying consumer capability, although tempered with the general principle that 'consumers should take responsibility for their decisions'.[26] The competition objective is 'promoting effective competition in the interests of consumers in the [relevant] markets'.[27] In contrast, salient factors here are framed in looser terms in that they are factors to which, unlike the consumer protection objective, the FCA 'may' rather than 'must' have regard.[28] These include consideration of differing consumer needs and accessibility, not only to products but also to information 'that enables … informed choices'.[29] Additionally, the FCA should have regard to ease of entry into markets and innovation.[30]

[17] eg rulemaking, preparing and issuing codes and general guidance and determining the general policy and principles by reference to which it performs these functions FSMA 2000, s1B (6).

[18] FSMA 2000, s 1B(1). For a detailed examination of the purpose and wording of this section see Ferran (n 5) 426–29.

[19] FSMA 2000, s 1B(2).

[20] ibid s 1C.

[21] ibid s 1D.

[22] ibid s 1E.

[23] S Brown, *The Regulation of Consumer Credit A Transatlantic Approach* (Edward Elgar, 2019) 84–85. FSMA 2000, s 1B(4).

[24] FSMA 2000, s 1C(1).

[25] FSMA 2000, s 1C(2)(a)(c)(f).

[26] FSMA 2000, s 1C(2)(b)(d)(e).

[27] FSMA 2000, s 1E.

[28] Ferran sees the 'have regard' approach as potentially leading to uncertainty, as effective competition is not 'exhaustively defined' Ferran (n 5) 432.

[29] FSMA 2000, s 1E(2).

[30] FSMA 2000, s 1E(2)(d)–(e).

At first glance it seems there is an emphasis on consumer protection. Indeed, Ferran suggested the framing of the competition objective is 'a mandate to pursue a consumer welfare version of competition policy',[31] and this is to some extent supported by the policy documents leading up to the FCA's introduction.[32] However, whilst the FCA *must* promote competition and advance the consumer protection objective (within the context of effective competition) there is flexibility in terms of how the FCA interprets its functions: in relation to the consumer, it is seated in what the FCA deems 'appropriate';[33] in relation to competition, the extent to which the FCA considers various factors.[34] This is further facilitated by the caveats of 'reasonable possibility'[35] and a proportionate approach, evident in the FCA's regularly stated *modus operandi*.[36] The result, in effect, is FCA discretion in how it proceeds and how it responds to its objectives. Ferran observes that regulatory reform can be influenced by political pressure and public demand, and that contemporary market failures can influence how this plays out,[37] with potential for consumer protection 'give[ing] way to a competition-promoting business-friendly agenda' and lighter regulation.[38] Regardless of any judgment as to whether this has come true, there can be little doubt a competitive market was the ultimate driver behind the envisaged approach of the FCA.[39]

6.2.2. Regulatory and Supervisory Framework

The regulatory framework within which the FCA operates is principles and outcomes-based, moving away from, for example, the original rules-based approach to the regulation of consumer credit.[40] The FCA Handbook sets out what is expected of firms regulated by the FCA via a set of High Level 'Principles' (PRIN), based in integrity, skill, care and diligence, adequate and responsible administrative procedures and adequate financial resources. These Principles are supported by business standards (Rules) within its various conduct of business source books – the Rules are

[31] Ferran (n 5) 431.
[32] eg HM Treasury and Department for Business Innovation and Skills (n 12) para 1.13.
[33] Responsibility for decision-making should not be abrogated by the consumer and placed 'wholesale' upon the supplier, ibid para 4.17.
[34] ie 'may' rather than 'must'; FSMA 2000, s 1E(2).
[35] FSMA 2000, s 1B(1).
[36] See the language of FCA policy documents and publications, eg FCA 'Our Strategy 2022–25' 26, www.fca.org.uk/publication/corporate/our-strategy-2022-25.pdf; and those of Government – see eg HM Treasury and Department for Business Innovation and Skills (n 14) 6, ch 3.
[37] Ferran (n 5) 416.
[38] ibid 452. For similar concerns around regulatory capture and the FCA's approach to innovation see IH-Y Chiu, 'A Rational Regulatory Strategy for Governing Financial Innovation' (2017) 8 *European Journal of Risk Regulation* 743.
[39] Explanatory notes to the FSA 2012 note – in discharging its general functions 'the effect of this duty is that where the FCA decides to act in pursuance of an operational objective and has the choice between two options, one of which would have a negative impact on competition (option 1), the other which would have a positive impact on competition (option 2), the FCA must choose option 2 unless this would be incompatible with its objectives.'
[40] Principles-based is a set of general standards with some flexibility in how these standards are met; rules-based is a set of 'hard and fast' obligations, outcomes- based sets targets to be achieved.

interpreted in accordance with the underlying Principles and published Guidance.[41] Beyond observing these standards, firms' behaviour towards their customers should include treating them fairly based on a set of six outcomes, adopted from the FSA's Treating Customers Fairly Initiative (TFI).[42] It perhaps goes without saying that the firm must co-operate with the regulator in the exercise of its supervisory and enforcement functions.[43]

The FCA envisages supervisory practices and the employment of wide-ranging enforcement measures as the way forward in delivering heightened protection.[44] The FCA has numerous powers which include issuing warnings, revoking authorisation, issuing fines, applying to the court for injunctive relief or restitution orders, etc. Consumers also have avenues of complaint to the regulator. Breach of the FCA rules allows a private cause of action for the affected consumer(s) as a breach of statutory duty under s 150. Where there has been breach of a Principle, remedies fall to the regulator, and can include disciplinary action (such as fines) and criminal sanctions for unauthorised activity.

6.2.3. Policy

How the FCA conducts itself in terms of supervision and enforcement, together with its rulemaking powers is informed by policy. The FCA uses a number of policy tools, for example commissioned research/empirical studies, with a number of 'Occasional Papers' being published every year.[45] There has been some recent focus on behavioural economics, employed to analyse consumer errors in decision-making and predict/assess how firms respond and how this may impact negatively on consumer interests and competition.[46] Firms themselves are expected to take into account consumers' motivations and are urged to consider behavioural factors that may affect the consumer's decision-making process.[47] Thrust of reform comes from the FCA agenda, driven by 'thematic review'. This has resulted in, for example, research and a report into retirement financial advice and responsible lending.[48]

[41] Specific sourcebooks cover specific provision eg CONC (consumer credit) ICOBS (insurance), BCOBS (banking).

[42] This covers consumer confidence in fair treatment being central to corporate culture, products designed to meet consumer needs, provision of clear information, suitable advice, products and services to perform as expected, no unreasonable post-sale barriers in relation to switching, claims or complaints. See further www.fca.org.uk/firms/fair-treatment-customers.

[43] PRIN 11.

[44] FCA (n 36) 21.

[45] See, as a recent example, FCA, I Chak et al, 'Robo-Advice for Borrower Repayment Decisions' (Occasional Paper 61, August 2022), www.fca.org.uk/publication/occasional-papers/occasional-paper-61.pdf.

[46] Crises have allowed behavioural economics to develop as a potential policy benchmark; Ferran (n 5) 419. See also FSA, 'Journey to the FCA' (October 2012) 44, www.fca.org.uk/publication/corporate/fsa-journey-to-the-fca.pdf.

[47] FCA, 'Final non-Handbook Guidance for firms on the Consumer Duty' (FG22/5, July 2022) para 4.22, www.fca.org.uk/publication/finalised-guidance/fg22-5.pdf.

[48] FCA, 'Retirement income advice thematic review' (TR24/1, March 2024), www.fca.org.uk/publication/thematic-reviews/tr24-1.pdf; FCA, 'Embedding the Mortgage Market Review: Responsible Lending Review' (TR16/4, May 2016), www.fca.org.uk/publication/thematic-reviews/tr16-04.pdf.

The policy of the FCA, illustrated by its initiatives in terms of reform and research, has four essential elements: conduct; products; access; and cost. These are illustrated in its approach, for example, to the consumer credit market.[49] The main policy targets in terms of consumer protection more generally have been vulnerability, trust, financial capability and consumer empowerment.[50] Vulnerability was the central pillar of the FCA Business Plan 2017–18 and Mission Statement, and the FCA has recently published specific guidance for firms in their dealings with the vulnerable.[51] Trust, culture and governance are also a 'key priority'. The FCA has conducted thematic reviews into staff incentives, remuneration and performance management, and has strengthened the Senior Managers and Certification Regime (SM&CR).[52] In relation to the financial capability initiative, nudge techniques are seen as one way of delivering this policy agenda – the idea being to push people into better decision-making and removing sludge practices.[53] Vehicles for advice and help, whether pre-emptive or remedial, should also help with this. These are seen as tools for delivering consumer empowerment another policy target. Here the language has hardly changed over the last decade. Informed choice, more particularly in relation to communications with consumers is presented as enabling consumers to 'buy the products and services they need', with a 'good choice architecture', high-quality, good-value products and services, and appropriate protection.[54]

Here then we see a reflection in policy of the FCA responding to its consumer protection objective. However, the emphasis, as mentioned earlier, has been on a proportionate approach and there has been real concern that the FCA has not gone far enough. The possibly resultant slow responses to harmful innovations (particularly products) and economic impacts have called for greater consumer protection. This is what prompted the discussion and eventual introduction of the Duty.[55] The FCA now promotes itself as innovative, more assertive and more adaptive, and recognises needs to adapt to 'face threats and opportunities of constantly changing world'.[56] It considers the

[49] eg FCA, 'Rent-to-own price cap – feedback on CP18/35 and final rules Policy Statement' (PS19/6, March 2019), www.fca.org.uk/publication/policy/ps19-06.pdf. The price cap on payday lending was introduced under a legislative duty included in FSMA 2000, s 137C(1)(a)(ii)(b).

[50] Ferran highlights the importance of trust and confidence – regulation is needed to deliver boundaries of acceptable behaviour in the market. She warns however against blind faith in regulation here as 'a blunt instrument': Ferran (n 5) 413–15.

[51] FCA 'Guidance for firms on the fair treatment of vulnerable customers' (FG21/1, February 2021), www.fca.org.uk/publication/finalised-guidance/fg21-1.pdf.

[52] FCA, 'Staff incentives, remuneration and performance management in consumer credit – Feedback to CP17/20 and final rules Policy Statement' (PS18/7, March 2018), www.fca.org.uk/publication/policy/ps18-07.pdf. The SM&CR was introduced in 2016 as an accountability framework for senior management and is now subject to further review: www.fca.org.uk/firms/senior-managers-certification-regime.

[53] eg through 'rules of thumb'; see further Financial Advice Working Group (FAWG) for HM Treasury and the FCA, 'Rules of Thumb and Nudges: improving the financial wellbeing of UK consumers' (March 2017), www.fca.org.uk/publication/research/fawg-rules-of-thumb-nudges.pdf.

[54] Although it is recognised that information disclosure alone may not always be enough; 'FCA Mission: Our Future Approach to Consumers' 2017) 37, www.fca.org.uk/publication/corporate/our-future-approach-consumers.pdf.

[55] The continuing level of consumer harm was a reason for the FCA consultation into a duty of care; FCA, 'A duty of care and potential alternative approaches: summary of responses and next steps Feedback Statement' (FS19/2, April 2019) para 1.3, www.fca.org.uk/publication/feedback/fs19-02.pdf; IH-Y Chiu and AH Brener, 'Articulating the gaps in financial consumer protection and policy choices for the Financial Conduct Authority – moving beyond the question of imposing a duty of care' (2019) 14 *Capital Markets Law Journal* 217, 218–19.

[56] Echoing Ferran's comment about policy responses; Ferran (n 5) 416.

biggest cause of consumer harm to now come from online activity, and sees an ability to move at speed as crucial. Its aim is to set and test higher standards, requiring suppliers to consider the real impact of their products and services on consumers. The hope is that setting clearer standards, higher expectations of firms and a concentration on firms delivering on 'good' consumer outcomes will support future innovation and allow the FCA to move at speed to prevent harm, resulting in fewer rules/rule changes which should lower costs.[57] The Duty is seen as integral to this.

6.3. The Consumer Duty

6.3.1. Formulating the Duty

The FCA first considered a new duty in 2017 in response to stakeholder concerns that the regulatory framework, including the Principles, were insufficient and/or applied ineffectively to prevent harm to consumers and protect them appropriately. The FCA concluded that firms were not consistently and sufficiently prioritising good consumer outcomes, so causing consumer harm and eroding trust.[58] There was certainly political pressure for change.[59] Various options were considered: a statutory duty of care, a fiduciary duty of care, or a change to current FCA High Level Principles and Rules.

The imposition of a direct duty of care in legislation, or a widening of the consumer protection objective was rejected by the Government – it was felt that the FCA had adequate powers and was 'best placed to judge the merits of a duty of care for financial services providers'.[60] Nevertheless, in response to parliamentary concern about the pace and effectiveness of consumer protection measures, the Government legislated for FCA consultation on, and creation of, new rules. The ball was placed firmly in the FCA's court, leaving it to deal with the issue as it deemed appropriate,[61] whether based in a duty of care or other rules instead of, or in addition to an imposed duty.

The FCA therefore continued its consultations. In terms of a fiduciary duty, the FCA took the view that this being a difficult concept to define, and a negative obligation, went against the spirit of what it wanted to achieve, namely a positive approach to positive obligations. In any event the conflict of interest, one of the most relevant aspects of a fiduciary duty was/is already covered by the Principles.[62] The FCA was also of the view that creating a specific duty of care in legislation was not justified and that a statutory

[57] In terms of compliance for firms, FCA (n 36) 5, 11.

[58] FCA, 'A New Consumer Duty Consultation Paper' (CP21/13) (May 2021) para 1.8, ch 2, www.fca.org.uk/publication/consultation/cp21-13.pdf.

[59] see eg *Hansard* HL (Series 6) Vol 810 cols 115–117GC (22 February 2021); *Hansard* HC (Series 6) Vol 685 col 366 (3 December 2020).

[60] *Hansard* PBC Vol 685 col 371 (3 December 2020). For further discussion of why a duty of care is not the answer, see also Ferran (n 5) 448–49; Chiu and Brener (n 55) 219–26.

[61] Financial Services Act 2021, s 29.

[62] PRIN 8. See also Ferran's arguments against: Ferran (n 5) 448–49; The courts are of the view that, in the context of financial advice, a duty of loyalty will only arise on the facts *Bristol & West Building Society v Mothew* [1998] Ch 1; *McWilliam v Norton Finance (UK) Ltd (in liquidation)* [2015] EWCA Civ 186. In relation to motor finance and fiduciary duty see *Hopcraft* (n 8).

duty of care was already reflected in the Consumer Rights Act 2015 (CRA 2015).[63] The way forward was instead outcomes-based, through a new Principle with a complementary range of rules and guidance, ie the Duty.[64] The Duty was introduced in its final form in July 2023.

6.3.2. The Framework of the Duty

The Duty, upon its introduction, was described by the FCA, as a 'standard of care'. The Duty is designed to reinforce and complement what is already present in the FCA Handbook but, where it applies, also replaces PRIN 6 and 7 (that a firm must pay due regard to the interests of its customers and treat them fairly; a firm must pay due regard to the information needs of its clients, and communicate information to them in a way which is clear, fair and not misleading).[65] The aim underlying the imposition of the Duty is that firms must consider consumers' needs in everything they do – they are to be 'incentivised to compete in the interests of consumers'.[66]

The Duty applies to 'products and services offered to retail customers' and its reach is far. It applies to all firms authorised by FSMA, the Payment Services Regulations 2017[67] and/or the Electronic Money Regulations 2011,[68] and to firms even if they do not have a direct relationship with the client.[69] It can apply to unregulated activity in certain circumstances if connected to a regulated activity, for example a payment service. Retail customers include small businesses that come within the definition of small and medium-sized enterprise (SME).[70] However the Duty does not replace the general principle that consumers should take responsibility for their decisions or, according to the FCA, impose an open-ended duty that goes beyond the firm's ability to determine/influence consumer outcomes or protect consumers from potential harms.[71]

The Duty, as referred to above, consists of a new Principle, a set of cross-cutting rules and four outcomes. The Principle requires 'firms to act to deliver good outcomes for retail customers'. The four outcomes are seated in products and services, price and value, consumer understanding and consumer support.[72] The product and services outcome introduces a 'fitness for purpose' requirement and includes product design – firms will also need to identify groups of customers with characteristics of vulnerability in

[63] FCA (n 55) para 6.7; FCA (n 58) para 2.31.
[64] FCA (n 47) ch 1.
[65] PRIN 2A.1.3.
[66] FCA, 'A new Consumer Duty Feedback to CP21/13 and further consultation' (CP21/36, December 2021) para 1.4, www.fca.org.uk/publication/consultation/cp21-36.pd.
[67] SI 2017 No 752 provides a consistent set of rights and obligations for businesses and consumers making and receiving payments.
[68] SI 2011 No 99 establishes a new authorisation regime for certain issuers of electronic money who are not banks or building societies, plus conduct of business rules.
[69] Extends to manufacturers or suppliers of products; FCA (n 47) para 2.12. There are caveats in PRIN 3.1.
[70] SMEs are already covered by the FCA sourcebooks, eg BCOBS. It will not however cover lending to SMEs unless specifically covered already by the mortgage/consumer credit sourcebooks.
[71] FCA (n 47) para 4.11.
[72] PRIN 2A.3–2A.6.

their target market and take account of additional needs.[73] The price and value outcome concerns fair value. However, this is not just about low price – higher pricing may be justified, depending on the context/circumstances. The 'consumer understanding' outcome includes tailoring of communications to ensure they are understood by the consumer. Finally, the 'consumer support' outcome stipulates that firms should not create unreasonable barriers and should ensure consumers can use the relevant product as intended.[74]

There are rules that underpin each of these outcomes together with the three overarching 'cross-cutting rules' which are intended to 'articulate the conduct standards under the new Principle'.[75] These cross-cutting rules are that firms must act in good faith towards retail customers, must avoid foreseeable harm to retail customers, and enable and support retail customers to pursue their financial objectives.[76] Good faith is seen here as honest fair and open dealing, reflecting the reasonable expectation of customers, based in what is reasonable given the circumstances.[77] The foreseeability test in terms of harm includes omission, and reasonable predictions/expectation of harmful results. Such analyses fall to the firm, based on what it knows or could have reasonably expected to have known in connection with the product or service, as a prudent firm.[78] It seems then that firms' responsibility is based on an objective standard (although there has been some disquiet that in reality this will be a subjective test).[79]

In terms of use of the Duty to date, the FCA has used recent 'portfolio communications' (known as 'Dear CEO letters') to set out expectations and how the Duty may be enforced. Examples relate to lack of fair value in GAP insurance products,[80] and poor value/high risk in the wealth management and stock broking sector.[81] However, perhaps the greatest evidence of use of the Duty has been in complaints to the Financial Ombudsman Service (FOS). In 2024 the Duty featured in many complaints from across the market and has been instrumental in findings in favour of the consumer.[82]

[73] PRIN 2.A3. Separate requirements for manufacturers and distributors and firms will not be required to oversee other actors in the distribution chain although they may need to consider actions by others; FCA (n 47) paras 2.23–2.24.

[74] Prin 2A.4–2A.6; FCA (n 47) paras 7.2–7.4, 8.4, 9.3; FCA, 'A new Consumer Duty Feedback to CP21/36 and final rules' (July 2022) (PS 22/9), www.fca.org.uk/publication/policy/ps22-9.pdf, paras 6.1–6.2, 7.1–7.2, 8.1–8.2, 9.1–9.2.

[75] FCA (n 47) para 5.3.

[76] PRIN 2A.2.

[77] FCA (n 47) para 5.6.

[78] ibid paras 5.20–5.21.

[79] FCA (n 74) para 4.7. However, interestingly, the good faith element is seen as supporting the cross-cutting rules by focusing on the intent behind firms' actions or inactions. FCA (n 47) para 5.8.

[80] www.fca.org.uk/news/press-releases/gap-insurers-agree-suspend-sales-following-fca-concerns-over-fair-value.

[81] www.fca.org.uk/publication/correspondence/dear-ceo-letter-fca-expectations-wealth-management-stockbroking-firms.pdf.

[82] eg home insurance, non-refund of scam payments and the provision of misleading information; see eg DRN 4676986, DRN 4963953, DRN 4769758, www.financial-ombudsman.org.uk/decisions-case-studies/ombudsman-decisions. See also www.fca.org.uk/firms/consumer-duty/how-using-duty.

6.4. Re-alignment of FCA Approach

The internal management of a commercial relationship and the responsibilities that arise from it are seated primarily in the substance and construction of agreed terms. Contractual principles will be the starting point. However for business-to-consumer relationships it has been long recognised that something more is required – hence more generally the specific discipline of consumer law.[83] In regulation of financial services external management of these responsibilities by the regulator will also be a factor.[84] As part of the FCA's furthering of its objectives, the High Level Principles impose responsibilities on firms in terms of conduct, together with rules that also flesh out these responsibilities.[85] The Duty's four outcomes further frame these responsibilities and are seen as 'key elements' in the firm-consumer relationship.

However, the Duty changes the emphasis of the contractual obligations and responsibilities of the firm. The cross-cutting rules underline firms' responsibilities to consumers both before and when they become customers, and the FCA specifically references the need to act proactively.[86] The Duty potentially goes beyond an overall expectation that parties behave honestly whether substantively or procedurally in the specific moment before, at or after contracting, to seating obligations within the wider proactive context of how consumers are viewed and treated, whether as participants or *potential* participants, and whether individually, or as a community, within the financial services markets. In essence this is seen as a vehicle for creating a consumer-centric 'environment'.[87] Whilst this may seem to be in line, for example, with the prohibition of unfair commercial practices under the Digital Markets, Competition and Consumers Act 2024 (DMCCA) (replacing the Consumer Protection from Unfair Trading Regulations 2008 (CPUTR), which forbid practices that may influence the transactional behaviour of the average consumer,[88] the Duty goes beyond what firms should *not* do to what they *should*, creating a positive obligation, rather than a negative one. This reflects the need identified by Siciliani, Riefa and Gamper of a general duty to trade fairly in business to consumer contracts if the law is to properly protect consumers against unfairness and consumer detriment.[89] Indeed the Duty, whilst headlined in terms of achieving 'good outcomes' rather than fairness *per se*, looks very like the possible formulations of a general duty to trade fairly outlined by Bradgate, Brownsword and Twigg-Flesner, which, they suggested. might include inter alia requiring businesses to 'act in accordance with the principle of good faith and fair dealing' or 'trade fairly or in accordance with reasonable (consumer) expectations'.[90] To this extent, then, the Duty is innovative.

[83] I Ramsay and J Gardner, 'Key Themes in Landmark Consumer Law Cases' in I Ramsay and J Gardner (eds), *Landmark Cases in Consumer Law* (Hart, 2024) 2.
[84] Brown (n 23) 145.
[85] ibid 144.
[86] FCA (n 47) paras 4.3, 5.3, 5.22, 5.28, 5.38, 8.22, 9.51, 11.43.
[87] ibid paras 2.5, 2.8 (within the context of customer base/target markets).
[88] DMCCA, s 225; SI 2008 No 1277, regs 2, 3.
[89] The authors explore creation of a normative standard of professional diligence through the model of consumer theories of harm and economic theory; P Siciliani, C Riefa and H Gamper, *Consumer Theories of Harm An Economic Approach to Consumer Law Enforcement and Policy making* (Hart, 2021).
[90] R Bradgate, R Brownsword, and C Twigg-Flesner, 'The Impact of Adopting a Duty to Trade Fairly (Department of Trade and Industry, July 2003) para 1.7. See Siciliani et al (n 89) 188.

When considering consumer, as opposed to firms', responsibility in the context of financial services, the general principle is still that 'consumers should take responsibility for their decisions'.[91] As the consumer protection objective itself sets out, the FCA must have regard to this, also implied in other elements of the objective, with its reference to consumer capabilities, experience and expertise.[92] Whilst the intimation is that vulnerabilities should be accounted for, it is also implied that risk assessment can also allow for consumers, who have the ability, to make rational decisions, make their own choices, and therefore have a responsibility to take care in such choices. This is the empowered consumer described above in relation to general policy. Here too, however, the Duty may also indicate a subtle change. The responsibilities of the parties are now expressly linked through the Duty beyond the contractual terms of the relationship. Firms now have responsibility for creating optimum conditions (in terms of what is reasonable for consumers to expect) so consumers can meet their own responsibility for decision-making. This can be seen in the requirement to act in good faith and from a pre-contract perspective, for example in terms of product design or exploitation of behavioural biases.[93] How consumers respond to their own responsibility may therefore influence the likelihood of enforcement action against the firm where sub-optimal conditions can be linked to firms' and consequent consumers' behaviour.

So how does this all demonstrate 're-alignment' in the FCA's approach to its objectives? All firms now have the responsibility 'to deliver good outcomes for retail customers'.[94] At one level this is nothing new when considering the High Level Principles as they stood before the introduction of the Duty, and indeed with the introduction of the SM&CR.[95] However the good faith requirement is an attempt to emphasise the consumer interest and affirm a form of commercial morality and ethical behaviour in relation to firms; this in turn moves that behaviour from ethics based in consumer self-reliance to consumer protection, demonstrating a closer correlation with general consumer law.

The TFI, and Prin 6 and 7, already required firms to put fair treatment of customers at the heart of their culture, with products and services to be designed to meet the needs of identified consumer groups and meet consumers' expectations, the provision of clear information and suitable advice, and ensuring that consumers do not face unreasonable post-sale barriers. However, the Duty may represent an 'incremental' change, as outlined by Twigg-Flesner, which seeks to retain coherency and consistency within the current framework.[96] The Duty has 'overtaken' PRIN 6 and 7 with something the FCA believes presents a 'higher standard of care and expectation beyond [the] current set

[91] FSMA 2000, s 1C(2)(d).
[92] FSMA 2000, s 1C(2)(b)(e).
[93] FCA (n 47) para 5.9.
[94] ibid para 1.6.
[95] Now, however, it is clearly for the firm to assess whether they have met this responsibility; ibid.
[96] In relation to COVID-19 some of the FCA's mechanisms for dealing with the fall-out of the pandemic were what Twigg-Flesner terms transitional 'recovery arrangements'. Some of these have been kept in relation to consumer lending, demonstrating that they in effect redressed shortcomings in legal rules – see FCA, 'Policy Statement Strengthening protections for borrowers in financial difficulty: Consumer credit and mortgages Feedback to CP23/13 and final rules' (PS24/2, April 2024) www.fca.org.uk/publication/policy/ps24-2.pdf; Twigg-Flesner (n 9) 1103.

of Principles and Rules' with broader application.[97] The aim therefore is re-alignment building on what is already in place. Whilst the competitive market still features prominently in FCA language, there is a palpable change of emphasis. The Duty seems to demonstrate a clear move away from the standard of an 'average' or 'rational' consumer towards welfare enhancement of the consumer as benchmark for well-functioning market.

A re-alignment of approach, whilst relatively small, can also be seen in the persona of the consumer. The Duty has been introduced in the context of protecting consumers yet applies to SMEs in certain circumstances.[98] Again, in some respects this represents nothing new – the new Principle applies to SMEs in the same way current Rules and Principles apply. Yet here SMEs are explicitly drawn under the umbrella of consumer protection – they are expressed to be a 'consumer', as a retail customer, to whom the Duty applies. As we have seen, one particular aspect of the Duty is the good faith element. Business-to-consumer contracts are generally governed by consumer law and the legislation that underpins consumer protection, which includes good faith in the specific context of unfair terms under the CRA 2015 and professional diligence (procedure) under the CPUTR (now replaced with similar provisions by the DMCCA). The Duty therefore, by expressly including SMEs, extends good faith to commercial relationships, beyond current protection.[99]

This perhaps reflects a general movement towards good faith in commercial contexts. As has been well documented, the principle of good faith in this regard has been viewed with some suspicion.[100] Nevertheless in business-to-business contracts the implication that the parties should act in good faith has been recognised in the context of 'relational contracts' – essentially long-term agreements where the parties' contractual relationship develops over time and depends on mutual co-operation.[101] The usual financial services contract is unlikely to be seen as a relational contract, being more discrete in nature. However, bringing SMEs into the bracket of retail customer and the requirement they should be treated fairly and with good faith recognises the 'transactional risks' that SMEs also take when buying financial services.[102] Indeed, it takes the protection further –it has been said that a relational contract does not require 'a party to set another's interests above its own' – whilst the Duty may not go so far as putting the consumer interest above all else – it now prioritises it.[103] A seemingly simple shift

[97] FCA (n 58) para 2.32.

[98] FCA (n 47) para 2.4.

[99] The CPUTR (as amended), DMCCA 2024 and CRA 2015 define 'consumer' as an individual acting for purposes that are wholly *or mainly* (my emphasis) outside that individual's business.

[100] For a brief overview see H MacQueen and S O'Byrne, 'The Principle of Good Faith in Contractual Performance: A Scottish-Canadian Comparison' (2019) 23 *The Edinburgh Law Review* 301, 301–03; D Christie, S Saintier and J Viven-Wilksch, 'Industry-Led Standards, Relational Contracts and Good Faith: Are the UK and Australia Setting the Pace in (Construction) Contract Law?' (2022) 43 *Liverpool Law Review* 287, 290–91. There are some notable exceptions, ie insurance agency and partnerships.

[101] eg the maintenance contract in *Amey Birmingham Highways Ltd v Birmingham City Council* [2018] EWCA Civ 264. The requirements for a relational contract were set out by the court in *Bates v Post Office Ltd (No 3)* [2019] EWHC 606 (QB).

[102] For discussion of the relevance of relational contract theory to prescriptive standards in consumer protection see Siciliani et al (n 89) 184–86.

[103] MacQueen and O'Byrne (n 100) 303.

in language demonstrates a conceptual change with the consumer protection objective being directly linked to these types of customers. This is a welcome aspect to the Duty.[104]

These perceptible adjustments in emphasis described above demonstrate a realignment of approach of the FCA to its objectives where consumer protection now takes priority. It reflects the goal of 'general consumer law' which views the role and power of consumers as a collective vis-a-vis other economic agents.[105] FCA expectations, through the Duty, look not only to stamping out unfairness whether in substance or procedure, but also in encouraging and embedding a better market culture, with more emphasis on *ex ante* behaviour and the Duty's focus on product liability.[106] It shifts the balance between the parties in emphasising the firms' duty to engage in 'other regarding behaviour'.[107]

Whilst there may be some cynicism as to the extent real cultural change can be delivered in financial services, the Duty is more pro-active in 'structuring' and fostering the development of a consumer-oriented culture. It reflects the 'process-oriented approach' and a recalibration of 'internal governance arrangements' advocated by Awrey et al.[108] We see this for example in the requirement for a Duty champion within firms' governance frameworks.[109] The FCA must be careful, however – attempts to *impose* a culture are likely to fail.[110] At the very least, it has been argued that to engender cultural change, there needs to be an 'internalization of ethical norms' by managers.[111] In essence, FCA expectations have been ramped up – however, the change with potentially the biggest impact is how these expectations are met.

6.5. Will this Enhance Consumer Protection?

The FCA believes the Duty will advance the consumer protection objective – it will help ensure that the level of consumer protection is both appropriate for the

[104] Reflecting the definition of consumer put forward by T Bourgoignie, 'Characteristics of Consumer Law' (1992) 14 *Journal of Consumer Policy* 293, 298; see also eg S Brown, 'Protection of the Small Business as a Credit Consumer: Paying Lip Service to Protection of the Vulnerable or Providing a Real Service to the Struggling Entrepreneur?' (2012) 41 *Common Law World Review* 59.

[105] Bourgoignie (n 104) 299.

[106] Ferran's view was that how the FCA responded to product intervention would help predict to what extent it will favour consumer protection over competition; Ferran (n 5) 419, 441.

[107] This was already present to some extent in the TFI.

[108] D Awrey, W Blair and D Kershaw, 'Between Law and Markets: is there a role for culture and ethics in financial regulation?' (2013) 38 *Delaware Journal of Corporate Law* 191.

[109] FCA (n 47) para 10.10, although again this is nothing new – this was also encouraged in the TFI. FSA, 'Treating customers fairly – towards fair outcomes for consumers' (July 2006) para 3.3, www.fca.org.uk/publication/archive/fsa-tcf-towards.pdf. The requirement was dropped in February 2025 now the Duty is seen by the FCA as 'well-embedded': www.fca.org.uk/firms/consumer-duty-information-firms.

[110] Awrey, Blair and Kershaw (n 108) 220–21.

[111] J McGrath and C Walker, *New Accountability in Financial Services Changing Individual Behaviour and Culture* (Palgrave Macmillan, 2022) 4. There is a call for a 'professionalisation of banking' in J McGrath and C Walker, 'Regulatory Ethics in Financial Services: Engaging industry to achieve regulatory objectives' (2023) 17 *Regulation and Governance* 791, 803. *cf* Simon's conclusions in her research into the meta-regulation of the Australian retail energy sector which led her to conclude that 'objectively assigning moral values to business and their stakeholders is fraught with difficulty. Instead, the focus should be on regulation for responsive businesses and … compliance outcomes'. FC Simon, *Meta-regulation in Practice Beyond Normative Views of Morality and Rationality* (Routledge 2017) 223.

environment in which consumers transact, and supports more agile and assertive supervision. The FCA does not agree that it will have a negative effect on the competition objective; rather it sees the Duty as bringing the objectives together.[112] Competition can more effectively act in the interest of consumers where firms design products and services to meet consumer needs, and consumers are put in a position to make informed decisions and act in their interests. Nevertheless, there remains some emphasis, on a proportionate approach and, as has already been outlined, measurements of 'appropriate' consumer protection are qualified with the general principle that consumers should take responsibility for their decisions.

Whilst the FCA has at least embraced the idea of the need for protection of the vulnerable, ideas of self-help and self-reliance are still firmly engrained in the FCA approach – a recognition of consumer responsibility is still, in effect, 'a must', demonstrating Ramsay's argument of a 'responsibilisation' of the consumer, designed to support market competitiveness.[113] In other words, consumer protection supports competition rather than the other way round. Yet structures put in place to promote capability in the consumer, and therefore consumer responsibility, do not cope well with the nuances of consumer vulnerability.[114] The reality, as is well recognised by the FCA itself, is more complicated, and whilst competition has an element of consumer protection the contrasting needs of deep consumer protection and free competition create tension.[115] This has been highlighted by the vulnerability agenda,[116] and now the Duty initiative.

There are clearly problems with seating protection within the framework in empowerment and choice, where less than optimal choices by the consumer may signify the pressure of external factors. Views from welfare and behavioural economists argue that choices that result from unjust background conditions 'jeapordise' the goal of autonomy or empowerment and should not have overstated value.[117] Choices are a function of context – preferences that underlie choice may be the result of conditions that make them anything but autonomous.[118] Poverty, the cost of living crisis, and extraordinary events such as the COVID-19 pandemic, show respecting choice as the rationale for protection is flawed.

The Duty attempts to address this by imposing an express obligation to act in good faith. In terms of general consumer protection, this is nothing new. However, good faith is a requirement needing interpretation which inevitably raises concerns about uncertainty. Linking good faith with behaviours that are 'consistent with the reasonable expectations of retail consumers' has caused particular concerns around compliance

[112] FCA (n 74) para 15.7; FCA (n 66) para 2.20.

[113] I Ramsay, 'Consumer Law, Regulatory Capitalism and the New Learning in Regulation' (2006) 28 *Sydney Law Review* 9, 13; S Brown, 'Un-boxing vulnerability in protection of the credit consumer' (2019) *Journal of Business Law* 511, 518.

[114] For discussion of vulnerability descriptors and the significance of Fineman's vulnerability theory, see ibid 511.

[115] Ferran (n 5) 434–35, 440–41.

[116] FCA (n 58) paras 2.8–2.11. Relatively recent FCA work on vulnerability shows that one in seven adults have literary skills at or below those expected of a 9–11-year-old. FCA, 'Occasional Paper No 8 Consumer Vulnerability' (February 2015) 9, www.fca.org.uk/publication/occasional-papers/occasional-paper-8.pdf.

[117] RH Thaler and CR Sunstein, 'Libertarian Paternalism is not an Oxymoron' (2003) University of Chicago Public Law and Legal Theory Working Paper No 43, 9.

[118] C Sunstein, *Freemarkets and Social Justice* (Oxford University Press, 1997) 19, 26.

and, in effect, under the Duty, the FCA becomes an arbiter of good faith. Nevertheless whilst uncertainty brings its own problems there is accepted judicial interpretation from the House of Lords judgment in *Director General of Fair Trading v First National Bank Plc* to fall back on in the context of unfair terms where the consumer is the weaker party.[119] Here good faith is seen as fair and open dealing, and looks to good standards of commercial morality and practice.[120] The general principles underlined in the case of *Yam Seng Pte Ltd v International Trade Corp Ltd* may also be of assistance, where good faith in the context of relational contracts was seen broadly as an objective test, that whilst sensitive to the individual context, encompasses honesty, fair and open dealing, and adhering to accepted general standards of commercial conduct.[121]

The FCA hopes the Duty will increase consumer protection by imposing higher standards and underpin the requirement for firms to put their customers first. The FCA views firms' responsibility through the lens of accountability and liability for non-compliance.[122] This brings us to enforcement and how the FCA will use the Duty in its supervision and regulation of firms. There is no private right of action for breach of the Duty only the FCA will be able to take action on a breach. This has attracted criticism both politically and from consumer interest groups.[123] Strong enforcement is therefore key to the success of any regulatory framework, but so, again, is clarity for those subject to that framework. The Duty does suffer from some vagueness. The FCA calls for firms to put themselves 'in their customers' shoes'.[124] How can firms, as a legal corporate entity, really do this? What are the reasonable expectations of consumers? Firms have raised concerns over what compliance 'looks like' and the FCA has undertaken a programme of guidance, 'expectations', training seminars and exemplars to help alleviate this anxiety. The FCA has recently consulted on further transparency in enforcement measures as a means of encouraging compliance, including publishing details of ongoing investigations.[125] However, this has, in turn, drawn criticism as potentially disrupting market integrity.[126] Certainly, any success ultimately relies on good supervision and enforcement. As Di Lorenzo comments, 'legal compliance is less dependent on whether a framework is rules

[119] *Director General of Fair Trading v First National Bank Plc* [2001] UKHL 52, [2002] 1 AC 481 [17] per Lord Bingham of Cornhill. Good faith here was being measured in the context of the requirements in reg 5 of the now repealed Unfair Terms in Consumer Contracts Regulations 1999 (the provisions were effectively replaced by the Consumer Rights Act 2015).

[120] '[A] supplier should not, whether deliberately or unconsciously, take advantage of the consumer's necessity, indigence, lack of experience, unfamiliarity with the subject matter of the contract, weak bargaining position …' ibid.

[121] *Yam Seng Pte Ltd v International Trade Corp Ltd* [2013] EWHC 111 (QB), [2013] 1 All ER (Comm) 1321 [138]–[141]. Although it should be noted the subsequent case law has not come out fully in favour of the position of *Yam Seng*: ZX Tan, 'Keeping faith with good faith? The evolving trajectory post-Yam Seng and Bhasin' (2016) 5 *Journal of Business Law* 420, 429–33.

[122] Brown (n 24) 145, 151.

[123] FCA (n 74) para 1.26.

[124] FCA (n 47) para 8.9.

[125] Although Parker and Gilad's research suggests there is no failsafe way to ensure 'better' compliance: C Parker and S Gilad, 'Internal corporate compliance management systems: structure, culture and agency' in C Parker and VL Nielsen (eds), *Explaining compliance: business responses to regulation* (Edward Elgar, 2011) 190.

[126] See letter to FCA 18 April 2024: committees.parliament.uk/publications/44344/documents/220473/default.

based or principles based and more dependent on supervision record and policy'.[127] This is a statement with which most would agree.

The introduction of the Duty perhaps underlines Black's point about the paradox of principles-based regulation. One concern has centred around the fact general terms of principles may not be fully understood – certainty is sacrificed for flexibility. Another is that this type of regulation encourages a risk-based approach to compliance rather than balancing what is right and wrong, and that whilst it can give rise to trust, mutuality and responsibility, these need to already be in place for principles-based regulations to operate. The fact the new Duty needed to be introduced, followed by detailed guidance (on an ongoing basis),[128] suggests these concerns are well founded. Nevertheless, it may now be more difficult for a firm to complain that it does not understand what complying with the High Level Principles entails.

Yet this comes with a word of warning where the responsibility for interpreting compliance with 'flexible regulation' is placed with the regulated entities themselves. The Duty Rules require 'a firm's board, or equivalent governing body, [to] review and approve an assessment of whether the firm is delivering good outcomes for its customers which are consistent with the Duty, at least annually' and will need 'to be able to provide evidence of their monitoring and assessment of these outcomes and any resulting action'.[129] When the FSA introduced the TFI, senior managers were given responsibility for ensuring their firm treated customer's fairly and gave guidance to what managers should consider. This was against a background of an industry that already 'perceived their practices as fair'.[130] Research by Gilad into co-construction of regulation found that initially customer-facing practices only went through limited change, or firms relied on customer feedback based on satisfaction and loyalty rather than 'objective indicators' of fairness.[131] This was because, whilst the FSA saw the TFI as a cultural issue, firms saw it as simply a matter of providing evidence of compliance.[132] There followed a period of reaction and adjustment of messages, resulting in regulation and compliance that was 'shaped by regulators' and business professionals' interactive and iterative reframing of regulatory problems and solutions'.[133] As we have seen, however, this has not resulted in sound consumer protection. Furthermore, whilst initiatives such as the SM&CR introduced individual accountability which seemed to have some initial positive effect, similar problems of interpretation and compliance orientation rather than culture change can arise.[134] The FCA will therefore need to consider carefully the extent to which it endorses rather than challenges firms' response to and interpretation of the Duty.

[127] His discussion was in the context of the mortgage market; V Di Lorenzo, 'Barriers to Market Discipline: A Comparative Study of Mortgage Market Reform's (December 2011) St John's Legal Studies Research Paper No 1969405 52, dx.doi.org/10.2139/ssrn.1969405.

[128] eg see recently, www.fca.org.uk/publications/good-and-poor-practice/consumer-duty-implementation-good-practice-and-areas-improvement.

[129] FCA (n 47) paras 10.4, 11.16; PRIN 2A.8.4.

[130] S Gilad, 'Beyond Endogeneity: How Firms and Regulators Co-Construct the Meaning of Regulation' (2014) 36 *Law & Policy* 134, 142.

[131] Providing evidence of customers being satisfied is not the same as treating them fairly; ibid 153.

[132] ibid 151.

[133] ibid 155.

[134] In part due to complexity and requirements open to interpretation; McGrath and Walker (n 111) 4.

The Duty seats FCA regulation more clearly with the common law open-textured principle of good faith. Whilst already present in the context of consumer law, it is arguable that the explicit imposition of this obligation and strengthened outcomes-based approach may in time encourage such an approach in the strategy of other regulatory agencies that have consumer protection as their remit, in particular within the financial services 'regulatory family'.[135] The Competition and Markets Authority, already committed to alignment with the FCA through the 2019 Memorandum of Understanding,[136] has new powers to impose conduct requirements under the DMCCA.[137] This is only if it is proportionate to do so for the purposes of one or more objectives set out in the Act.[138] It will be interesting to see how this evolves.

6.6. Conclusion

The FCA objectives and how they operate have been described a 'mess'.[139] Whether or not you agree with this view, the FCA appear to have taken on board that the statutory mandate has not been working hard enough for consumer participants in the financial services market. It is clear from the FCA's own enquiry that firms have been 'bucking the system', and either 'playing the regulatory game' by finding loopholes and/or avoiding restrictions, or simply not engaging with it in a meaningful way.[140] For an industry that has been described as having 'a systemic tendency to malfeasance',[141] any meaningful change, particularly in terms of culture, will be an uphill struggle. It is a little depressing that the FCA has to articulate that firms should act with honesty and openness in their dealings with customers – after all, as Leggatt J said in *Yam Seng*, 'honesty is a paradigmatic norm'.[142] It is not all bad news: the FCA has been able to highlight some good practice, but clearly there is some way to go.[143]

Competition is still at the heart of financial regulation,[144] despite the FCA acknowledging competition 'was not working effectively' in the consumer interest, primarily due to detrimental firm behaviour.[145] Recent developments in the

[135] This is the 'Wider Implications Framework' – a formal agreement on collaboration of 'matters of common interest'. The members are the FOS, the FCA, the Financial Compensation Services Scheme, the Pensions Regulator and the Money and Pensions Service. FOS's use of the Duty is already in evidence; see text to n 82.

[136] www.fca.org.uk/publication/mou/fca-cma-consumer-protection-mou-2019.pdf.

[137] s 19, the CMA's digital markets competitive regime for firms with strategic market status. The CMA has set out how it intends to use these powers; factors include exploitation of consumers, fair treatment and reasonable terms. CMA, 'Guidance on the digital markets competition regime set out in the Digital Markets, Competition and Consumers Act 2024' (CMA194, December 2024) ch 3, assets.publishing.service.gov.uk/media/6762f4f6cdb5e64b69e307de/Digital_Markets_Competition_Regime_Guidance.pdf.

[138] Fair dealing, open choices, trust and transparency; DMCCA, s 19(5)–(8).

[139] *Hansard* HL (series 6) Vol 811, col 869 (24 March 2021).

[140] FCA (n 58) para 1.8.

[141] *Hansard* HL Vol 810 col GC 112 (22 February 2021).

[142] *Yam Seng* (n 121) [136].

[143] www.fca.org.uk/publications/good-and-poor-practice/consumer-duty-implementation-good-practice-and-areas-improvement.

[144] Ferran (n 5) 429.

[145] FCA (n 58) paras 2.9, 2.13.

FCA's regulatory approach to the digital market shows emphasis on proportionality has not gone away.[146] The Duty however has been billed as a paradigmatic shift in FCA expectations of firms and a 'reset' in its approach.[147] This does signify change of direction and more explicitly promotes the overall agenda of establishing trust and confidence through the good faith requirement. It moves firms' responsibility away from obligations within clearly stated parameters towards an 'open-textured' dynamic,[148] where there is a greater emphasis on 'principled' behaviour.[149] Saintier has described the articulated requirement of good faith as a control that happens where contractual discretion is used as an opportunity for exploitation[150] – the Duty is a good example. This has always been implied, of course, through the requirements of the High Level Principles, but the Duty now attempts to underline the message that tick box compliance is not enough.

The FCA frames the Duty as a vehicle for meeting the strategic objective and advancing its operational consumer and competition objectives. The underlying bases of the protection of both consumer and competitive market are intertwined in these objectives, including in how the FCA should generally discharge its functions. Yet, as discussed earlier, the overall legislative approach has until now encouraged the competitive.[151] The drive behind the Duty is stated to be consumer empowerment, not blanket protection.[152] This therefore still reflects a view of consumer law as a market behaviour law with adherence to view of attentive and self-responsible consumer.[153] However, what the Duty can do is change what is seen as appropriate in relation to degrees of protection and enforcement/intervention, and there is a real sense that the interests and welfare enhancement of consumer rather than business will now be the benchmark.[154]

In conclusion, the Duty does demonstrate a realignment of FCA approach even if, in essence, it is simply in giving the consumer protection objective greater weight. However, it is not just the relationship between the statutory objectives that is relevant

[146] See Department for Business & Trade, 'Smarter Regulation to Grow the Economy Policy Paper' (May 2023) 8, www.gov.uk/government/publications/smarter-regulation-to-grow-the-economy/smarter-regulation-to-grow-the-economy.

[147] FCA (n 58) para 2.36.

[148] For discussion of open-textured clauses in relation to unfairness, see C Willett, 'General clauses and the competing ethics of European consumer law in the UK' (2012) *CLJ* 71, 412. There was already some move towards this position; for example, in the consumer credit context with published FCA guidance around responsible lending, and the Supreme Court decision in *Plevin v Paragon Personal Finance Ltd* vis-a-vis unfair credit relationships. *Plevin v Paragon Personal Finance Ltd* [2014] UKSC 61, [2014] 1 WLR 4222.

[149] *cf* Simon (n 111) 223.

[150] S Saintier, 'The elusive notion of good faith in the performance of a contract, why still a bête noire for the civil and the common law?' (2017) 6 *Journal of Business Law* 441, 459.

[151] This was 'set' to be a/the 'defining feature' of the FCA's role; Ferran (n 5) 429.

[152] FCA (n 74) para 5.14.

[153] ie, the omnipotent market citizen as the dominating normative construct; HW Micklitz, 'Social justice and access justice in private law', EUI Working Papers Law (2011/022), papers.ssrn.com/sol3/papers.cfm?abstract_id=1824225, discussed in S Brown, 'Vulnerable consumers in financial services and access to justice. The regulatory response' in C Riefa and S Saintier (eds), *Vulnerable Consumers and the Law* (Routledge, 2021). This approach has been defended in that the line must be drawn somewhere, in the sense that consumers would otherwise be less cautious operating under a false sense of security; see Ferran (n 5) 448.

[154] Movement in this direction can be seen in earlier policy documents which recognised that a universal expectation of consumers is problematic due to any number of factors, both internal and external.

here, but also the relationship between market participants and protection of consumers. If the Duty delivers, it can change the regulatory background to consumer protection in financial services in a meaningful way – and the approach has potential to influence further afield. The journey will not, however, be an easy one. Accused of being 'slow and inadequate'[155] in relation to consumer protection, the FCA is now encouraged by the current Government to support economic growth through enabling informed and responsible risk-taking by authorised firms and customers.[156] Whether the Duty realises its potential therefore remains to be seen.

[155] All-Party Parliamentary Group on Investment Fraud and Fairer Financial Services 'Report on the Call for Evidence about The Financial Conduct Authority' (November 2024) 355, www.appgifffs.org/wp-content/uploads/2024/11/FINAL-Call-for-Evidence-Report-PUBLIC-1.pdf.

[156] HM Treasury letter to Nikhil Rathi (14 November 2024), www.gov.uk/government/publications/recommendations-for-the-financial-conduct-authority-november-2024/recommendations-for-the-financial-conduct-authority-html.

7

Investment-Based Crowdfunding and Financial Consumers Protection: Realignment of FCA Financial Promotion Disclosure Rules

WANGWEI LIN*

This chapter examines the Financial Conduct Authority's (FCA) regulatory realignment on the protection of investment-based crowdfunding (IBCF) financial consumers in the United Kingdom (UK). IBCF has become an essential financial innovation, revolutionising how start-ups and small businesses secure funding. By connecting entrepreneurs with a broad range of investors through online platforms, IBCF provides an alternative to traditional financing methods. However, this modern approach introduces unique regulatory challenges, particularly in protecting financial consumers while maintaining an innovative investment ecosystem. As the primary regulator of UK financial markets, the FCA faces the difficult task of realigning its rules with the rapidly expanding crowdfunding market. In this process, it addresses information gaps, reduces agency problems, and ensures transparency become key objectives.

This chapter explores the realignment of the FCA's regulations on financial promotions aimed at protecting financial consumers in the IBCF sector. It begins by discussing IBCF as an accessible financing option in the UK. The focus then shifts to the unique agency problems of IBCF, followed by an analysis of the FCA's regulatory realignment on financial promotion rules and disclosure requirements. Finally, it evaluates the balance between compliance costs and the benefits of transparency, offering policy recommendations for an effective regulatory framework.

* I thank Professor James Devenney and Professor Christian Twigg-Flesner for their invaluable feedback which has enriched the quality of this chapter. All remaining errors are my own.

7.1. IBCF as an Accessible Means of Finance in the UK

Crowdfunding over the internet, defined as an open call for the provision of financial resources to support initiatives for specific purposes,[1] has become an increasingly popular means of obtaining fintech finance for innovative entrepreneurial firms globally. Individuals invest in shares in private companies through digital IBCF platforms. In its Policy Statement 14/4 the FCA defines IBCF in the UK as firms that operate as 'platforms on which consumers can buy investments, such as equity or debt securities that are not listed or traded on a recognised exchange, or units in an unregulated collective investment scheme'.[2] The persons who use, have used or may use IBCF platforms are financial consumers according to section 1G of the Financial Services and Markets Act 2000 (FSMA).[3] For financial consumers, online investment platforms such as the IBCF platforms have made investing easier than ever, especially during the COVID-19 pandemic. Over one million UK adults increased or began holding high-risk financial products in the pandemic's first seven months.[4] Traditionally, those investment opportunities were mostly limited to institutional and high-net-worth individuals.

IBCF firms utilise digital platforms to connect startup firms with a wide base of potential investors/financial consumers. Conequently, traditional intermediaries such as banks or venture capital firms are often bypassed. It has emerged as a transformative mechanism for startup firms to obtain access to external funding, especially for companies that encounter securing funding through traditional means of financial channels.

For startup firms, IBCF is a more accessible means of finance when compared to initial public offerings (IPOs). The compliance costs and entry requirements for issuers are lower. The IPO process is expensive and highly resource-intensive. It requires significant financial commitments for regulatory compliance and disclosure. These fixed costs often make IPOs unsuitable for most early-stage entrepreneurial ventures. This distinction highlights the growing relevance of IBCF as a viable and inclusive funding option for entrepreneurs.[5] In the UK, entrepreneurs and financial consumers are further incentivised by the Enterprise Investment Scheme (EIS), along with the Seed Enterprise Investment Scheme (SEIS) to use IBCF, which are the two government tax incentives aiming to stimulate early-stage investments for individual investors. In 2014

[1] P Belleflamme, T Lambert and A Schwienbacher, 'Crowdfunding: Tapping the Right Crowd' (2014) 29 *Journal of Business Venturing* 592; A Schwienbacher and B Larralde, 'Crowdfunding of Small Entrepreneurial Ventures' in D. Cumming (ed), *Handbook of Entrepreneurial Finance* (Oxford University Press, 2010).

[2] FCA, 'PS14/4: The FCA's Regulatory Approach to Crowdfunding over the Internet, and the Promotion of Non-readily Realisable Securities by other Media' (2014) 5, www.fca.org.uk/publications/policy-statements/ps14-4-fca%E2%80%99s-regulatory-approach-crowdfunding-over-internet-and.

[3] Financial consumers are persons who use, have used or may use regulated financial services according to the Financial Services and Markets Act 2000 (FSMA), s 1G (affirmed by Financial Services Act 2021, s 29(5)). In the UK, the IBCFs are regulated under the FSMA.

[4] FCA, 'Beyond Disclosure: High-Risk Investments – Slow Down and Think' (2024), www.fca.org.uk/publications/research/beyond-disclosure-high-risk-investments-slow-down-and-think.

[5] A Rossi, TR Vanacker and S Vismara, 'Equity Crowdfunding: New Evidence from US and UK Markets' (2021) 1 *Review of Corporate Finance* 407.

alone, IBCF grew by 201 per cent. Almost 95 per cent of the funded deals were eligible for the EIS or the SEIS schemes.[6]

The two largest IBCF platforms, Crowdcube and Seedrs, almost dominate the UK's IBCF market. In 2021, Crowdcube facilitated 234 announced funding rounds, amounting to £198 million in investments into UK companies. Seedrs facilitated 272 deals, amounting to £126 million in the same year.[7] IBCF platforms such as Seedrs and Crowdcube have been raising significant amounts of funds for small businesses in the UK. Between 2021 and 2023, the IBCF was involved in 19 per cent of smaller business equity deals. It symbolises IBCF platforms' growing importance as an alternative to traditional financing manes in the UK.[8] Crowdcube and Seedrs attempted to expand by merging into one large private equity platform in October 2020. The merge attempt was investigated by the Competition and Markets Authority (CMA) for potential anticompetitive effects. The merge was eventually terminated in 2021.[9]

7.2. Information Disclosure and the Unique Agency Problem of IBCF

While IBCF provides a transformative and accessible financing tool for startups, its unique structure and reliance on a large, diverse pool of non-professional investors introduce distinct challenges. One of these is the issue of its unique agency problem, which results in information asymmetry, which prompts robust regulatory oversight and effective information disclosure mechanisms.

The unique agency problem of IBCF is caused by the very nature of the IBCF market: the existence of a large number of inexperienced financial consumers. One of the distinctive characteristics of IBCF is that, unlike traditional sources of finance, firms are funded by drawing on comparatively small contributions from large numbers of financial consumers without the facilitation of traditional financial intermediaries.[10] This unique feature of IBCF results in a highly diverse group of financial consumers. Single investment objectives or a group of investment objectives,[11] such as those held by institutional investors in traditional securities markets, do not normally exist in crowdfunding investments.

This brings several problems. The existence of a large number of diversified minority shareholders/financial consumers exacerbates shareholder apathy and can trigger collective action problems. The heterogeneous preferences of the diversified investor group further deepen agency conflict between the financial consumers (the shareholders) and

[6] FCA, 'A Review of the Regulatory Regime for Crowdfunding and the Promotion of Non-readily Realisable Securities by other Media' (2015), www.fca.org.uk/publication/thematic-reviews/crowdfunding-review.pdf.

[7] British Business Bank and Beauhurst, 'Small Business Equity Tracker 2024' (2024), www.british-business-bank.co.uk/about/research-and-publications/small-business-equity-tracker-2024.

[8] ibid.

[9] ibid.

[10] E Mollick, 'The Dynamics of Crowdfunding: An Exploratory Study' (2014) 29 *Journal of Business Venturing* 1.

[11] ibid.

the promoters of startup firms. Without traditional intermediaries that are subject to comprehensive financial supervision, agency problems may become worse due to a lack of sound regulation on due diligence of the promoters of the entrepreneurial firms.[12]

The lack of traditional intermediaries means direct contact between the financial consumers and the promoters; ultimately, the financial consumers, with no specialisation in financial investment and limited access to information on 'the industry, past performance of the entrepreneur and many other pieces of value-relevant information',[13] is investing directly in entrepreneurial firms. Those entrepreneurial firms often rely significantly on intellectual property or unique business models, and are therefore likely to be reluctant to comply with disclosure requirements because of concerns about potential business ideas being 'stolen' as a result of exposure to the 'wider audience' of the 'crowd'. Hence, information asymmetry deepens.[14]

7.3. Financial Consumer Protection Through Information Disclosure

Unlike the product and labour markets, information stands at the centre of the securities market. Information failure is the main form of securities market failure. Most barriers to a well-functioning securities market are directly or indirectly related to information asymmetry, which, therefore, attracts government intervention.

First, given the complexity of financial instruments and transactions, it is essential for an investor, in particular, a consumer financial investor, to have a comparatively high level of financial skill and knowledge so that they can interpret the relevant information prior to any purchase or disposal of a financial product. This requirement is, nevertheless, difficult to fulfil because it is commonly accepted that non-professional economic players act according to principles of 'bounded rationality', which restricts their ability to understand, remember and manage information.[15] The disadvantageous position of consumer financial investors becomes even more obvious when compared with the ability of those who enjoy an information advantage and occupy a privileged position in the market. In the context of this chapter, the crowdfunding platform or the investees have an information advantage over the investors. Second, it is arguable that information is costly to both the producers and consumers of information, which limits their incentives to acquire and provide information.[16]

Public intervention in financial markets is also inspired by the assumption that public goods,[17] such as publicly available information in the financial market, are

[12] One in five companies involved in IBCF in the UK between 2011 and 2013 have become insolvent. E Dunkley, 'Crowdfunding Rides to The Rescue of Many SMEs' *Financial Times* (9 February 2016).

[13] Schwienbacher and Larralde (n 1) 10.

[14] ibid.

[15] H Simon, *Models of Bounded Rationality* (MIT Press, 1997) 291.

[16] Some argue that, in a broad sense, perfect information is largely equated with zero information cost: L Philips, *The Economics of Imperfect Information* (Cambridge University Press, 1988) 23.

[17] J Stiglitz, 'The Role of the State in Financial Markets' (1993) 7 *The World Bank Economic Review* 19; J Stiglitz, 'Knowledge as A Global Public Good' in I Kaul, I Grunberg and M Stern (eds), *Global Public Goods: International Cooperation in the 21st Century* (Oxford University Press, 1999) 308, 308–26.

generally under-supplied even in competitive markets. The public benefits from public goods are universally provided by their suppliers. However, private suppliers of public goods have limited incentive to supply for two reasons. First, it is difficult to exclude those who have not paid for such goods, ie, free-riders, because it is either impossible or too costly to do so. As a result, suppliers are discouraged from providing these services. Second, suppliers are attracted to businesses offering low investment but high returns, while some public services require a considerable proportion of sunk costs with relatively fixed returns. As a result, public goods such as publicly available information in the financial market are undersupplied.[18]

Given the importance of information in financial markets and the problem of information asymmetry, the regulation of information disclosure is one of the most crucial parts of investor protection policy aiming to rectify imperfect information, overcome the insufficient supply of public goods and achieve the optimum quality of information.[19] Information asymmetry and lack of regulation may be abused by fraudsters, resulting in unwanted adverse selection[20] in the IBCF sector. Consumer investors in the non-professional investment market have been protected by information disclosure regulations over the years.[21]

Information disclosure is key for the IBCF platforms; because of the high level of information asymmetry accelerated by its unique agency problem and the lack of sound accounting and corporate governance mechanisms that are commonly in place in traditional securities markets, the financial consumers face a much higher degree of risk.[22] Disclosure mechanisms, such as disclosure of financial risks and transparency in fee structures during financial promotion, are essential in mitigating the heightened risks posed by the unique agency problem of IBCF platforms.

7.4. IBCF: Disruptive Technology and the Realignment of Regulations

Christensen argues that technological innovations impact performance trajectories in distinct ways. Sustaining technologies focus on gradual improvements, enhancing features that existing customers already value. These technologies maintain or slightly advance performance standards within familiar markets. In contrast, disruptive technologies offer a different set of features that mainstream customers may not initially value. Often, these innovations underperform in key areas considered important by established customers. As a result, mainstream users are typically reluctant to adopt disruptive products for familiar tasks. Initially, disruptive technologies find their place in

[18] ibid.

[19] ibid.

[20] The classic 'lemons' problem reveals adverse selection resulting from misevaluation caused by information asymmetry. A Agrawal, C Catalini and A Goldfarb, 'Some Simple Economics of Crowdfunding' in J Lerner and S Stern (eds), *Innovation Policy and The Economy* (MIT Press, 2014).

[21] D Bugeja, *Reforming Corporate Retail Investor Protection: Regulating to Avert Mis-Selling* (Hart Publishing, 2019) 3–12; N Moloney, *How to Protect Investors* (Cambridge University Press, 2010) ch 1.

[22] Agrawal, Catalini and Goldfarb (n 20).

new markets or novel applications. Over time, they often enable the creation of entirely new market spaces.[23] The IBCF falls in the description of disruptive technologies.

Twigg-Flesner employed the notion of disruption in the context of law. Judging by Twigg-Flesner's four-step model, the FCA's rule on the protection of the IBCF financial consumers appears to be akin to a re-alignment of law rather than a higher level of disruption where a new derogation in law is permitted and targeted laws can potentially be seen as the better solution beyond their intended target.[24]

7.5. FCA Regulations Re-aligned to Protect IBCF Financial Consumers

In the UK, the IBCF is regulated under the FSMA. Firms operating IBCFs must be authorised by the FCA. The FCA monitors the IBCF platforms' compliance with financial promotions, investor suitability and disclosure obligations, ensuring market integrity and investor protection. The FCA outlines specific expectations for platforms engaging in IBCF. Under the FCA's integrated framework, which encompasses supervision, policy development and competition oversight, the responsibility for monitoring the activities of the IBCF platforms lies with the Consumer Investments Directorate.[25]

Research by the FCA revealed that many financial consumers underestimate the risks of high-risk online financial products. Forty-five per cent of new self-directed financial consumers were unaware they could lose money. This research highlights the urgent need for enhancing IBCF transparency and improving investor education. Those are key to ensuring individuals understand the potential dangers of high-risk investment products.[26]

The re-alignment of FCA financial promotion disclosure rules for IBCF financial consumer protection has largely fallen on the restriction on financial promotion of IBCF platforms and limiting the participation to investors who have the ability to understand the risks involved and can bear those risks.

The FCA requires IBCF platforms to promote 'non-readily realisable security'[27] only to retail clients who

> confirm that, in relation to the investment promoted, they would receive regulated investment advice or investment management services from an authorised person or are venture capital contacts or corporate finance contacts; or are certified or self-certify as sophisticated investors; or are certified as high net worth investors; or certify that they will not invest more than 10 per cent of their net investible financial assets in unlisted equity and debt securities.[28]

[23] JL Bower and CM Christensen, 'Disruptive Technologies: Catching the Wave' (1995) 73 *Harvard Business Review* 45.

[24] C Twigg-Flesner, 'The Potential of the COVID-19 Crisis to Cause Legal "Disruption" to Contracts and Contract Law' in E Hondius et al (eds), *Coronavirus and the Law in Europe* (Intersentia, 2021).

[25] FCA, 'FCA Expectations for Investment-based Crowdfunding Platforms' (15 January 2024).

[26] FCA (n 4); BritainThinks, 'Understanding Self-Directed Investors: A Summary Report of Research Conducted for the Financial Conduct Authority' (March 2021) 5.

[27] This term applies to securities that are not 'readily realisable securities', 'packaged products' or 'non-mainstream pooled investments'. See FCA (n 2).

[28] In line with the rules in COBS 10.

Where advice is not provided, the IBCF platforms would apply an appropriateness test[29] prior to sending retail clients direct offer financial promotions for those securities.[30]

A financial promotion is defined in Section 21 of the FSMA 2000 as 'an invitation or inducement to engage in investment activity, communicated by a person in the course of business'.[31] Only firms authorised by the FCA can issue a financial promotion in the UK. Financial promotions are a means through which financial information, including risks, rewards and product specifics, are communicated to potential financial consumers. Financial promotions require the disclosure of important information to help financial consumers make informed decisions.

According to the FCA Policy Statement PS22/10, financial promotions of high-risk investments must adhere to strict disclosure rules to ensure that communications with potential investors are fair, clear and not misleading. These requirements align with broader transparency and accountability principles set out in the FCA Handbook.[32]

In 2014, the FCA conducted a review of the financial promotion of IBCF and the IBCF websites. It engaged with firms' senior management, monitored the IBCF websites and reviewed monthly management information of the platforms. This supervision by the FCA was to ensure that investments were limited to suitable customers and that financial promotions were 'clear, fair, and not misleading'[33] regarding the nature and performance of investments and the potential exit opportunities for investors, eg claims that shares offered on a platform were identical to those held by venture capitalists needed to be verified, as when venture capitalists profit from successful investments while crowdfunding financial consumers experience equity dilution, reducing their share of profits. This supervision led to various regulatory actions primarily aimed at protecting financial consumers.[34]

The review revealed issues in most of the firms examined. They included, but were not limited to, lack of balance, with benefits highlighted prominently while risks were understated, incomplete, omitted, or selectively presented information, which created a potentially misleading or overly optimistic impression of the investment and downplaying important details, such as risk warnings. For instance, some platforms diminished risk warnings by emphasising that no capital had been lost or by making these warnings less prominent than performance claims.

Following the review, the FCA contacted all relevant IBCF firms and instructed them to make necessary changes to their websites. These changes were required to ensure compliance with FCA rules and to make promotions fair, clear and not misleading. All firms responded promptly and implemented the required changes.[35]

[29] In line with the rules in COBS 10.
[30] FCA (n 2).
[31] FSMA 2000, s 21.
[32] FCA, 'PS22/10: Strengthening Our Financial Promotion Rules for High-risk Investments and Firms Approving Financial Promotions' (2022), www.fca.org.uk/publications/policy-statements/ps22-10-strengthening-our-financial-promotion-rules-high-risk-investments-firms-approving-financial-promotions.
[33] FCA (n 2).
[34] ibid.
[35] ibid.

In the 2016 FCA Interim Feedback to the Call for Input to the Post-Implementation Review of the FCA's Crowdfunding Rule, concerns about transparency and fairness in investment platforms were raised. It was questioned whether platforms provide sufficient information for financial consumers and analysts to properly evaluate investment opportunities. Some raised concerns about conflicts of interest arising where investors, including occasions where platform employees were given more favourable investment terms than outsider financial consumers. It was specifically noted that some platforms allow owners or directors to invest alongside or ahead of other investors.[36] The FCA agreed to take account of the feedback in day-to-day supervision and the work on the post-implementation review. This work on the post-implementation review seeking to address those concerns is reflected in the 2021 FCA Portfolio Strategy Letter[37] and the 2022 FCA Policy Statement 22/10.[38]

In the 2021 FCA Portfolio Strategy Letter: Investment-Based Crowdfunding, the FCA stressed that it is essential that customers are made aware of the risks associated with the investments being promoted, as well as the risks arising from their categorisation by the firm. Before any investment decisions are made, information about the customer's knowledge and experience must be collected, an appropriate financial consumer classification must be assigned, and the suitability of the investment opportunity must be assessed. The nature and risks of the investment products being offered should be carefully considered, and accurate and relevant information must be disclosed to ensure customers can make informed decisions. Additionally, records of financial consumer classifications and key data used in the assessment process must be maintained.

The Portfolio Strategy Letter requires the level of analysis and due diligence conducted on funding recipients to be clearly communicated to potential financial consumers. This clarity enables financial consumers to evaluate whether further research is necessary before making an investment decision. Furthermore, awareness of potential conflicts of interest must be maintained. Such conflicts may occur between businesses raising funds and financial consumers providing investments, or between the IBCF firm's interests and those of its clients. Proper management of these conflicts is required to ensure fairness and maintain financial consumer trust. Firms are expected to treat customers on both sides of the investment fairly.[39]

In August 2022, the FCA released PS22/10, titled 'Strengthening Our Financial Promotion Rules'. This document introduced new obligations for firms promoting high-risk investments (HRIs), which includes IBCF, to retail clients.[40] The first set of rules, which mandated risk warnings on financial promotions, came into effect on 1 December 2022. The remaining rules were implemented on 1 February 2023. The interventions in this Policy Statement are to prevent harm to consumers from investing in high-risk investments that do not match their risk tolerance.[41]

[36] FCA, 'FS16/13 Interim feedback to the call for input to the post-implementation review of the FCA's crowdfundingrules'(2016)29,www.fca.org.uk/publications/feedback-statements/fs16-13-interim-feedback-post-implementation-review-crowdfunding-rules.

[37] FCA, 'Portfolio strategy letter: investment-based crowdfunding' (July 2021).

[38] FCA (n 32).

[39] FCA (n 37) 2.

[40] FCA, 'FCA 22/33: Financial Promotions and High-Risk Investments Instrument 2022' (2022).

[41] FCA (n 32).

In December 2022, the FCA conducted a review of risk warnings issued and revealed that compliance levels fell significantly short of expectations.[42] A consequent, more detailed examination of how firms implemented the remaining rules that came into effect on 1 February 2023 was conducted.[43]

According to the new obligations for firms promoting HRIs, including IBCF, from 1 December 2022, new Conduct of Business Sourcebook (COBS) rules regarding direct offer financial promotions and promotions of non-readily realisable securities and peer-to-peer (P2P) agreements would apply. COBS 4.7 is dedicated to rules on direct offer financial promotions and promotions of non-readily realisable securities and P2P agreements.

COBS 4.7.-1AUK is relevant to a firm communicating a direct offer of financial promotion in relation to its Markets in Financial Instruments Directive (MiFID), equivalent third country or optional exemption business. IBCF firms are required to disclose the following information referred to in Articles 47 to 50 of the MiFID Org Regulation as is relevant to that offer or invitation to a client, including the firm and its services for clients and potential clients (including information on communications, conflicts of interest and authorised status), financial instruments, safeguarding of client financial instruments or client funds, and costs and associated charges. COBS 4.7.1R is relevant to a firm communicating a direct offer financial promotion that does not relate to its MiFID, equivalent third country or optional exemption business. Under COBS 4.7.1R, a firm must ensure that a direct offer financial promotion that is addressed to, or disseminated in such a way that it is likely to be received by, a retail client contains the information referred to in the rules on information disclosure as is relevant to that offer or invitation; and additional appropriate information about the relevant business and relevant investments so that the client is reasonably able to understand the nature and risks of the relevant business and relevant investments, and consequently to take investment decisions on an informed basis. Information disclosure must include information about a firm and its services, information concerning the safeguarding of designated investments belonging to clients and client money, information about costs and associated charges, and a description of the nature and risks of designated investments. It must also disclose any additional appropriate information about the relevant business and relevant investments so that the client could understand the nature and risks of the relevant business and relevant investments to make informed decisions.[44]

7.6. Balancing between Information Disclosure and Compliance Costs

Agency problems in IBCF arise primarily from the diversity and inexperience of financial consumers, coupled with the absence of traditional financial intermediaries.

[42] These findings were published in the financial promotions quarterly data for Q1 2023. See FCA, 'Financial Promotions Quarterly Data 2023 Q1' (2023), www.fca.org.uk/data/financial-promotions-quarterly-data-2023-q1.

[43] FCA, 'Financial Promotions for High-risk Investments' (2024), www.fca.org.uk/publications/multi-firm-reviews/financial-promotions-high-risk-investments.

[44] See COBS 4.7.

Regulatory measures, such as stricter financial promotion rules, aim to address these problems by enhancing transparency and accountability. However, these measures come at a cost – both financially and strategically – for entrepreneurs and platforms. This raises an important question: should regulators strike a balance between ensuring transparency and mitigating the burdens placed on innovators and businesses, and how?

Disclosure requirements come with compliance costs and risks of intellectual property rights infringement and business idea theft for entrepreneurs. Policymakers will need to balance between information disclosure and compliance costs and risks to intellectual assets and business secrets. An equalitarian approach should be avoided, and the particular characteristics of crowdfunding must be taken into consideration in legislation and policymaking, along with a recognition that irrational behaviour[45] may not necessarily result in loss. However, it may damage the 'diversity, independence and decentralisation' of the 'crowd' and consequently reduce the 'crowd's wisdom'.[46]

In the context of IBCF, primary concerns for entrepreneurs include both economic costs related to ensuring compliance with mandatory disclosure requirements and the potential risks of intellectual property rights infringement and business idea theft. The latter probably presents the more fundamental concern, as most entrepreneurs rely heavily on innovation. Imitation by competitors could represent fatal damage to a new firm, especially during the initial fundraising process.[47] Moreover, being overly transparent could be detrimental to entrepreneurs since it may cause them to lose bargaining power when negotiating with manufacturers and investors.[48] Last but not least, information disclosure requirements requesting directors to disclose their innovations in a public IBCF platform could also impose further costs related to managing a large number of diverse and inexperienced funders.[49] Entrepreneurs will, therefore, have to constantly bear in mind the trade-off between an increase in liquidity and capital, the costs of compliance, and the potential risk of intellectual property and business idea theft.

In the UK, although there has been discussion on the cost–benefit analysis of IBCF platforms in the FCA consultations, most notably Consultation Paper 22/2 and the Policy Paper 22/10. The potential risks of intellectual property rights infringement, business idea theft and the potential loss of bargaining power of the entrepreneurs were not taken into account.

In its Consultation Paper 22/2, the FCA set the goal of balancing between ensuring that its reforms effectively influence consumer behaviour whilst having regard to the costs to firms. At the same time, the FCA said it respected the regulatory principle

[45] A Moritz, J Block and E Lutz, 'Investor Communication in Equity-Based Crowdfunding: A Qualitative Empirical Study' (2015) *Qualitative Research in Financial Markets* 309.

[46] Surowiecki argues that the diversity, independence and decentralisation of the 'crowd' has contributed to the 'crowd's ability to be wise'. J Surowiecki, *The Wisdom of Crowds: Why the Many are Smarter than the Few* (Abacus, 2005).

[47] Agrawal, Catalini and Goldfarb (n 20).

[48] E Markowitz, 'When Kickstarter investors want their money back' (2013), www.inc.com/eric-markowitz/when-kickstarter-investors-want-their-money-back.html.

[49] Agrawal, Catalini and Goldfarb (n 20).

that consumers were responsible for their own decisions. The FCA, however, encouraged and supported firms to exceed current requirements in the consultation paper.[50]

In the Policy Paper 22/10 following the consultation, the FCA revealed that among respondents who disagreed with the proposal, the most frequently cited concern was the practical difficulty and high costs of implementation. These respondents argued that firms might not have access to a customer's name early in the consumer journey. Additionally, they noted that firms cannot control technical problems, eg whether consumers use software that blocks pop-ups. Some respondents suggested that the FCA cost–benefit analysis should have included an assessment of the broader impact on UK capital market competitiveness. This includes potential effects on small and medium-sized enterprise financing in IBCF platforms.

The FCA explained that it would not be reasonably practicable to estimate the ongoing costs related to decreased revenues or increased financing expenses for affected firms and issuers. This is primarily because the FCA cannot predict the extent to which investment in high-risk financial products would decline as a result of the proposals with existing data. Consequently, it remained uncertain how much revenue might decrease, or financing costs might rise for the impacted entities. The FCA, however, concluded that it believed the benefits of these measures to outweigh the associated costs. Over time, the targeted amendments to financial promotion rules would contribute to long-term market growth and improved competitiveness. The FCA expected the targeted amendments would only marginally reduce implementation costs without significantly altering the overall balance between costs and benefits.

Current FCA regulation does not reflect the potential risk of exposing sensitive business ideas and intellectual property for entrepreneurs during the fundraising process. Those risks could make the entrepreneurs vulnerable to exploitation or misappropriation. Further re-alignment of rules from the FCA on confidentiality for both investors and platforms could potentially reduce these risks. It could also help entrepreneurs retain a fair degree of negotiating power when following the transparency requirements. By reconsidering the balance between information disclosure and compliance costs, the FCA can create a more balanced environment that supports investor confidence while protecting entrepreneurial innovation and intellectual property.

7.7. Concluding Remarks

In conclusion, the rapid growth of IBCF has improved access to finance for startups through disruptive technology in the UK, providing investment opportunities for financial consumers. However, this growth introduces risks, including information asymmetry and unique agency issues, primarily driven by diverse shareholding and the absence of traditional financial intermediaries. Therefore, the growth of IBCF in the UK has required a careful regulatory response from the FCA.

[50] FCA, 'CP22/2: Strengthening Our Financial Promotion Rules for High Risk Investments, including Cryptoassets' (2022), www.fca.org.uk/publications/policy-statements/ps22-10-strengthening-our-financial-promotion-rules-high-risk-investments-firms-approving-financial-promotions.

The FCA has re-aligned its regulations by refining financial promotion standards to enhance transparency to protect financial consumers. Nevertheless, striking a balance remains challenging. Excessive compliance costs could deter participation, while insufficient oversight may leave vulnerabilities unaddressed. More could perhaps be done to protect confidential business information and foster trust in the IBCF market.

The FCA is realigning its regulatory strategies to align with ongoing technological and market developments. A dynamic and forward-looking regulatory framework is essential. It must address current risks while anticipating future challenges in the IBCF sector. By achieving this balance, the FCA can create an environment where both innovation and financial consumer protection thrive, ensuring the long-term sustainable development of the UK IBCF market.

PART IV

Future Directions in Digital Consumer Law

8

The Quest for Protection of Vulnerable Consumers in Digital Financial Technologies

ANDREA MIGLIONICO*

8.1. Introduction

The rapid advancement of fintech (eg, open banking, peer-to-peer lending, online payments) has exploited the potential of affordable and broad access to services for market participants while, in parallel, increasing the use of algorithmic systems for automating decision-making processes.[1] The promise to expedite product delivery and reduce transaction costs has been lauded in various quarters,[2] yet sophisticated software may provide inaccurate outcomes which do not take account of relevant factors of disadvantaged customers while privileging certain categories of users (eg, white men, wealthy educated people, the elderly).[3] Machine learning analysis may contain biased methodologies and datasets inherent because of human error which are apt to amplify unfair practices, such as the marginalisation and exclusion of customers with protected characteristics (age, disability, race, religion, gender, sexual orientation, pregnancy and maternity), and lead to the redlining of applicants belonging to vulnerable groups.[4]

* The author is grateful to the reviewers for their constructive comments on earlier drafts.

[1] See the Report of the World Economic Forum, 'Forging New Pathways: The next evolution of innovation in Financial Services' (September 2020), www.weforum.org/publications/forging-new-pathways-the-next-evolution-of-innovation-in-financial-services; see also T Adrian and T Mancini-Griffoli, 'The Rise of Payment and Contracting Platforms' IMF Fintech Notes No 2023/005 (June 2023) 7–8, www.imf.org/en/Publications/fintech-notes/Issues/2023/06/16/The-Rise-of-Payment-and-Contracting-Platforms-534794; R Brownsword, 'Law, authority, and respect: three waves of technological disruption' (2022) 14 *Law, Innovation and Technology* 5, 23–24.

[2] I Mnohoghitnei et al, 'Embracing the Promise of Fintech' (2019) Q1 Bank of England Quarterly Bulletin 4–5; DW Arner, J Barberis and RP Buckley, 'The Evolution of FinTech: A New Post-Crisis Paradigm' (2015) 47 *Georgetown Journal of International Law* 1271; E Avgouleas and A Kiayias, 'The Promise of Blockchain Technology for Global Securities and Derivatives Markets: The New Financial Ecosystem and the 'Holy Grail' of Systemic Risk Containment' (2019) 20 *European Business Organization Law Review* 81, 102–03.

[3] S Mills, S Costa and CR Sunstein, 'AI, Behavioural Science, and Consumer Welfare' (2023) 46 *Journal of Consumer Policy* 387.

[4] L Sain Jones and GP Maynard, Jr, 'Unfulfilled Promises of the Fintech Revolution' (2023) 111 *California Law Review* 801, 837–38; A Chander, 'The Racist Algorithm?' (2017) 115 *Michigan Law Review* 1023, 1036–37.

Comparative performance analysis through quantitative metrics (eg, accuracy and fairness score) can detect areas where biases may affect outcomes of machine learning.[5] However, Wachter et al noted that 'these fairness metrics address technical bias, but not the underlying cause of inequality such as social bias'.[6] AI algorithms are generally classified as: deterministic, producing the same output from the same input determined by initial conditions, regardless of any elements of randomness (eg, linear regression and decision trees);[7] and adaptive, which is a complex machine learning algorithm that involves representation levels of sample data through large neural networks with multiple layers.[8]

Algorithms collect, analyse and process relevant data through algorithmic models which perform various tasks such as the assessment of the price and quality of products, customers' preferences and purchases.[9] A growing debate about the data-gathering and the dataset used to embed inputs into algorithms raises questions about the transparency and accuracy of outcomes for consumers.[10] Automated systems are powered by algorithms reliant on mathematical modelling, which execute decisions on instructed narratives.[11] They are programmed by gathering data which profile the characteristics of consumers (eg, religion, education, income) through software-based decision-making processes so as to provide the full range of services. However, they are often criticised for providing biased and inconsistent information about consumers' past behaviour and purchasing decisions.[12]

The dataset of algorithms contains several variables (eg, location of residence, social status, credit score) which are considered in sensitive decisions and may affect the final outcome. Empirical studies noted that algorithms may contain flawed methodologies inherent because of human inaccuracy which may replicate discriminatory practices (eg, price discrimination, biased assessment).[13] As observed, 'algorithmic biases do not materialise spontaneously: they reflect existing human biases, societal inequalities and genuine group differences'.[14] Further, discriminatory algorithms may reinforce existing

[5] M-Y Chan and S-M Wong, 'A Comparative Analysis to Evaluate Bias and Fairness Across Large Language Models with Benchmarks' OSF Preprints (29 March 2024) 3, doi.org/10.31219/osf.io/mc762.

[6] S Wachter, B Mittelstadt and C Russell, 'Bias Preservation in Machine Learning: The Legality of Fairness Metrics under EU Non-Discrimination Law' (2021) 123 *West Virginia Law Review* 735.

[7] A deterministic algorithm is constructed in such a way that it always performs a set of precisely defined steps in order to find a solution. For example, decision tree models can consistently replicate results with the same dataset and configuration which consistently validates findings and conducts comparative studies.

[8] This machine learning programming technology works with large datasets and gets high-level interactive features from the raw data. See S Gill et al, 'Transformative effects of IoT, Blockchain and Artificial Intelligence on cloud computing: Evolution, vision, trends and open challenges' (2019) 8 *Internet of Things* 100118.

[9] G Wagner and H Eidenmüller, 'Down by Algorithms: Siphoning Rents, Exploiting Biases, and Shaping Preferences: Regulating the Dark Side of Personalized Transactions' (2019) 86 *The University of Chicago Law Review* 581, 585–86; S Vijayakumar, 'Algorithmic Decision-Making' (2017) *Harvard Political Review*, harvard-politics.com/algorithmic-decision-making.

[10] C Coglianese and A Lai, 'Algorithm vs. algorithm' (2022) 71 *Duke Law Journal* 1281, 1306–07; DR Desai and JA Kroll, 'Trust but Verify: A Guide to Algorithms and the Law' (2017) 31 *Harvard Journal of Law & Technology* 1, 7–8.

[11] J Soh, 'The executive's guide to getting AI wrong' (2022) 9 *Asian Management Insights (Singapore Management University)* 79.

[12] C Rudin and J Radin, 'Why Are We Using Black Box Models in AI When We Don't Need To? A Lesson From An Explainable AI Competition' (2019) *Harvard Data Science Review* 1.2, hdsr.mitpress.mit.edu/pub/f9kuryi8/release/8.

[13] E Black et al, 'Less Discriminatory Algorithms' (2024) 113 *Georgetown Law Journal* 53.

[14] A Kelly-Lyth, 'Challenging Biased Hiring Algorithms' (2021) 41 *Oxford Journal of Legal Studies* 908.

societal biases which are embedded in predictive models to select applicants, assess the creditworthiness of individuals and screen consumers' choices. The training datasets instruct algorithms to generate accurate decisions although the transparency of a machine learning analysis raises concerns for the predictability and consistency of the decision-making process as the software designer decides what the output of the system will be and whether it will include reasons for its conclusions.[15] This raises criticisms of biased results that are designed (intentionally or in self-interested ignorance) to exploit protected attributes.[16]

The European Law Institute (ELI) Report suggested that

> the functionality and reliability of any given AI system heavily depend on the system's computing power, programming of the initial algorithm, including appropriate determination of the algorithm's objectives, the training data, and any 'self-learning' capacity coded into the algorithm.

However, the limitations of AI tools lie in the complex, sophisticated software which are based on backward-looking data and statistical methods.[17] Further, the ELI defines an AI system as a machine-based system that incorporates three main factors: use of data or domain-specific expert knowledge in development; creation of new know-how during operation; and formal indeterminacy of output.[18] This classification reflects a flexible approach which identifies a three-factor framework of functioning and application of a machine-based system interacting with the algorithmic systems and IT systems.

A range of new applications, often based on the transaction data made available through open banking, offer support for savings and decisions; along with programs making automated investment decisions and 'robo-advisors' proffering investment advice. For example, active investment funds are increasingly using machine learning and other technology-based decision-making in their portfolio allocations alongside management judgements.[19] Further, technology-supported asset classes are emerging, including loan-based crowdfunding and cryptoassets.

This chapter argues that the use of algorithmic systems for automating decision-making processes inflates consumer vulnerability. It posits that the exploitation of digital technologies in financial services exacerbates the dependence of vulnerable consumers on artificial intelligence (AI) algorithms. The current regulatory framework has made little progress on how to counter self-interested outcomes designed to perpetuate unfair commercial practices with regard to minority groups (ie individuals with mental

[15] M Zalnieriute, L Bennett Moses and G Williams, 'The Rule of Law and Automation of Government Decision-Making' (2019) 82 *Modern Law Review* 425, 440. See also B Mittelstadt, S Wachter and C Russell, 'To protect science, we must use LLMs as zero-shot translators' (2023) 7 *Nature Human Behaviour* 1830.

[16] C Reed, *AI Fairness and Beyond. Law, Regulation, and Technology* (Hart Publishing, 2024) 111–12.

[17] European Law Institute, 'EU Consumer Law and Automated Decision-Making (ADM): Is EU Consumer Law Ready for ADM?' Interim Report of the European Law Institute (ELI Project on Guiding Principles and Model Rules on Algorithmic Contracts) (2022) 9.

[18] See 'Guidelines on the Application of the Definition of an AI System in the AI Act: ELI Proposal for a Three-Factor Approach' Response of the ELI to the EU Commission's Consultation (2024), www.europeanlaw-institute.eu/fileadmin/user_upload/p_eli/Publications/ELI_Response_on_the_definition_of_an_AI_System.pdf.

[19] Technology underpins the growth of comparison sites and their use as an alternative to advice from brokers or the media in making saving and investment decisions, and is increasingly used in both passive and active investment vehicles. Automated market making and trade execution maintain the net asset value of exchange traded funds (ETFs) against their benchmark and the index tracking of passive mutual funds.

health issues, ethnicity, low-income households and disabled people). Consumers are exposed to 'black box' techniques of automated systems (technical barriers to scrutinise the internal decision-making process of algorithms),[20] which may lead to negative externalities such as marginalisation of certain classes of users.[21] The United Nations Convention on the Rights of Persons with Disabilities[22] urged for rapid implementation of digital, media and information literacy programmes to address the digital divide and support equal access to technology systems.[23] However, the impact of automated systems on vulnerable consumers poses challenges for regulators to calibrate risks of discriminatory practices.[24]

The chapter is structured as follows. Section 8.2 discusses consumer protection in digital financial technologies, arguing that harmful algorithmic systems reveal dependence and reliance on automated processes. On this view, it is contended that algorithmic systems can undermine an individual's liberty to think and act rationally, reducing a person's cognition and decision-making capacity.[25] This section considers Fineman's vulnerability theory[26] along with the paternalistic view (libertarian paternalism)[27] to explore whether regulators provide adequate resilience assets (eg, social protection networks) to mitigate the reliance of consumers on AI systems and ensure fairness in the digital environment.[28] The vulnerability theory can promote unduly paternalistic laws and policies which limit individuals' autonomy. Further, the universal state of vulnerability and dependency, and the state's corresponding responsibility for enhancing resilience across populations, need to lead to paternalism which is not a suitable public policy response to the individuals' vulnerabilities.[29] Further, the paternalistic view may fail to reduce disadvantage conditions deriving from information asymmetries in digital transactions which affect consumers when making informed decisions.[30] The concept of vulnerability is defined here as category-based in relation to the algorithmic harms (eg, manipulative or biased operations in AI tools such as risk scoring, deepfakes

[20] Sandra Wachter, Brent Mittelstadt and Chris Russell, 'Counterfactual Explanations without Opening the Black Box: Automated Decisions and the GDPR' (2018) 31(2) *Harvard Journal of Law & Technology* 842. The lack of transparency in black-box algorithms is further elaborated in Maayan Perel and Niva Elkin-Koren, 'Black Box Tinkering: Beyond Disclosure in Algorithmic Enforcement' (2017) 69(1) *Florida Law Review* 182.

[21] Sandra Wachter, 'The Theory of Artificial Immutability: Protecting Algorithmic Groups Under Anti-Discrimination Law' (2022) 97(2) *Tulane Law Review* 149, 152–53.

[22] United Nations Convention on the Rights of Persons with Disabilities (12 December 2006).

[23] See 'New and emerging technologies need urgent oversight and robust transparency: UN experts' (2 June 2023), https://www.ohchr.org/en/press-releases/2023/06/new-and-emerging-technologies-need-urgent-oversight-and-robust-transparency.

[24] See https://www.ungeneva.org/en/news-media/meeting-summary/2022/03/le-conseil-des-droits-de-lhomme-dialogue-avec-les-rapporteurs.

[25] Karen Yeung, 'Hypernudge': Big Data as a mode of regulation by design' (2017) 20(1) *Information, Communication & Society* 118, 129.

[26] Martha Albertson Fineman, 'The Vulnerable Subject: Anchoring Equality in the Human Condition' (2008) 20(1) *Yale Journal of Law & Feminism* 1.

[27] Cass R. Sunstein, 'The Ethics of Nudging' (2015) 32(2) *Yale Journal on Regulation* 413.

[28] WK Viscusi, 'Nudges Versus Financial Incentives' in CR Sunstein and LA Reisch (eds), *Research Handbook on Nudges and Society* (Edward Elgar 2023) 189–90.

[29] NA Kohn, 'Vulnerability Theory and the Role of Government' (2014) 26 *Yale Journal of Law and Feminism* 14.

[30] BEUC, 'EU Consumer Protection 2.0. Protecting fairness and consumer choice in a digital economy' Position Paper (2022) 3, www.beuc.eu/sites/default/files/publications/beuc-x-2022-015_protecting_fairness_and_consumer_choice_in_a_digital_economy.pdf.

and generative AI) rather than Fineman's universal propensity for vulnerability. This characterisation points to the psychological impairment of the individual's autonomy to make independent choices.[31] The discussion is complemented with an analysis of the equitable doctrine of unconscionable bargain which originates from a situation of disadvantage where one party is normally in a weaker bargaining position.[32] This doctrine requires a degree of exploitation or manifest unfairness in the bargains which merit special concern because of inequitable relationships between parties.[33]

Section 8.3 examines the regulatory framework at the UK level with a particular focus on the Equality Act 2010 (EA 2010) which needs appropriate reforms as vulnerable groups are more exposed to discriminatory practices in digital technologies, such as unfair predictions based on algorithmic profiling. It contends that disadvantaged individuals may be ignored by biased data employed in computer software which replicates past inaccurate information about certain attributes of those categories of consumers (eg, postal code, buying behaviour, browsing products).[34] Algorithms may lead to inadvertent discrimination regarding these attributes given the potential for bias and inaccuracy of outcomes.[35]

Section 8.4 discusses the Financial Conduct Authority (FCA)'s consumer duty rules[36] and the implementation of a principles-based regime which can offer a solution to the exploitation of consumers' vulnerability due to the increasing use of algorithmic decision-making systems in financial services. Finally, section 8.5 provides conclusive remarks on the innovative and disruptive effects of digital financial technologies on vulnerable consumers.

8.2. Transparency and Fairness in the Algorithmic Systems

The use of algorithmic systems to assist human assessment in digital transactions shows 'herding effects' in the decision-making process.[37] Users tend to entrust algorithmic recommendations to make choices, although this behaviour shows an imbalance of positions between transactional parties. This conduct can impair the freedom to form an independent assessment about the merits of the transaction; it can create an excessive disadvantage for the weaker party because of unfamiliarity with sophisticated AI

[31] S Lu, 'Regulating Algorithmic Harms' University of Michigan, Law & Economics Working Papers 277 (2024) 4–5, repository.law.umich.edu/law_econ_current/277. The author argues that algorithmic harms exacerbate inequality through AI-generated content that disproportionately discriminates against minorities.

[32] N Enonchong, 'The modern English doctrine of unconscionability' (2018) 34 *Journal of Contract Law* 211.

[33] S Valentine Shiffrin, 'Paternalism, Unconscionability Doctrine, and Accommodation' (2000) 29 *Philosophy & Public Affairs* 213, 249. The author contends that 'paternalism [is a behaviour] that can occur through [an action] or omission, even a non-freedom-diminishing omission'.

[34] J Tomlinson, J Maxwell and A Welsh, 'Discrimination in digital immigration status' (2022) 42 *Legal Studies* 315, 320–21.

[35] F Pasquale, *The Black Box Society: The Secret Algorithms That Control Money and Information* (Harvard University Press, 2015) 107.

[36] See www.fca.org.uk/publications/policy-statements/ps22-9-new-consumer-duty.

[37] H Bollaert, F Lopez-de-Silanes and A Schwienbacher, 'Fintech and access to finance' (2021) 68 *Journal of Corporate Finance* 8.

algorithms.[38] Algorithmic systems inflate information asymmetry between consumers and businesses, which raises concerns about the transparency and discriminatory practices of algorithms.[39] As noted, 'the more dependent a consumer is on algorithms, the less informed the consumer will become in making choices related to products and services'.[40] Algorithmic systems can also affect fairness in the protection of consumers throughout their relationships with traders: for example, AI elaborates insights extracted from an individual's activities to understand their personal needs and vulnerabilities which can inflate conditions of disadvantage.[41]

Consumers may be obfuscated and therefore less aware of alternative choices because businesses attempt to hide unfair practices regarding the quality and price of a product.[42] Further, consumers may find it difficult to understand complex information made available through algorithmic processes, which complicates the assessment of product attributes and affects individual preferences.[43]

AI algorithms channel information supplied by service providers employing addictive design features to increase engagement and steer users towards harmful content to accommodate firms' profits rather than pursuing consumers' preferences.[44] The veracity of their recommendations is questioned with respect to the genuine content provided in the advertisement and marketing activities which are mostly oriented to the interests of big tech companies.[45] This shows an imbalance between the interest of consumers to access transparent information and the interest of technological applications to profit from their services.[46] As a result, algorithmic systems may influence individuals to adopt decisions they would not otherwise make; in particular, AI may influence the behaviours of individuals and the ability to make informed, rational, and meaningful decisions.[47]

AI in the provision of banking services includes robo-advising, algorithmic credit scoring, payment processing, investment management and wealth advising. Specifically, financial technologies emerged in loan-based crowdfunding such as peer-to-peer lending (P2P) and cryptoassets for investment (eg, cryptocurrencies and tokens).[48]

[38] A Cherednychenko, 'Conceptualising unconscionability in the context of risky financial transactions: how to converge public and private law approaches?' in M Kenny, J Devenney and L Fox O'Mahony (eds), *Unconscionability in European Private Financial Transactions: Protecting the Vulnerable* (Cambridge University Press, 2010) 248–49.

[39] J Kleinberg et al, 'Discrimination in the Age of Algorithms' (2018) 10 *Journal of Legal Analysis* 113, 163.

[40] TY Ebrahim, 'Algorithms in Business, Merchant-Consumer Interactions, & Regulation' (2021) 123 *West Virginia Law Review* 885.

[41] P Siciliani, C Riefa and H Gamper, *Consumer Theories of Harm: An Economic Approach to Consumer Enforcement and Policy Making* (Hart Publishing 2019) 22.

[42] KN Johnson, 'Automating the Risk of Bias' (2019) 87 *George Washington Law Review* 1242.

[43] Desai and Kroll (n 10) 1; R Van Loo, 'Consumer Agents' (1 January 2025) 27–28, ssrn.com/abstract=5199350.

[44] E Mik, 'The Algorithmic Exploitation of Consumers' in LA DiMatteo, C Poncibò and G Howells (eds), *The Cambridge Handbook of AI and Consumer Law. Comparative Perspectives* (Cambridge University Press 2024) 176.

[45] C Riefa and L Clausen, 'Towards Fairness in Digital Influencers' Marketing Practices' (2019) 8 *Journal of European Consumer and Market Law* 64, 72–73.

[46] O Lynskey, 'Regulating 'Platform Power' (2017) LSE Law, Society and Economy Working Papers no 1, 9–10, ssrn.com/abstract=2921021.

[47] Lu (n 31); Yeung (n 25); L Herrine, 'What Is Consumer Protection for?' (2022) 34 *Loyola Consumer Law Review* 25.

[48] Cryptoassets are digital assets which are recorded in databases called distributed ledgers and hosted on a network of different computers. See HJ Allen, *Driverless Finance. Fintech's Impact on Financial Stability* (Oxford University Press, 2022) 89.

P2P lending allocates financial resources to market participants without the involvement of traditional intermediaries (banks). Similar to P2P lending is the technique of crowdfunding, which gathers funds for a business project from multiple individuals operating through online portals. P2P platforms quickly assess the creditworthiness of borrowers using a variety of factors such as gender, age, level of education, income and employment, which can reveal inaccurate information about the credit history of applicants.[49] The regulation of platforms articulated in the EU Digital Services Act (DSA)[50] introduced obligations for content moderation processes and risk management of services. Platforms are required to make 'reasonable efforts' to verify the reliability of the information submitted although they do not hold a duty of disclosure after the information has been obtained, unless it is requested by public authorities in relevant procedural processes.[51] The legislation focuses on intermediary service providers, introducing liability exemptions which raise concerns about the limited scope for consumers to challenge investigations or other activities aimed at detecting, identifying and removing illegal content.[52] The DSA does not limit the discretion of platforms to decide what legal content can be prohibited by providers,[53] and effective remedies for misleading information or unsafe products are not well conceived, leaving unanswered questions of consumer protection with respect to enforcement mechanisms for individual users.[54]

The automated investment solutions pose both old and new challenges. The old challenges, which arise with all savings and investment products marketed to retail customers, question whether customers are making properly informed decisions with appropriate advice and whether they are not investing in unsuitable products. The new challenges arise from the oversight of automated systems and emergent phenomena. These include the use of comparison sites and potentially adverse consumer impact, eg behavioural pricing, based on how people search online and drive to pure price rather than price- and quality-based decisions.[55]

The appropriateness of recommendations emerges from robo-advisors that offer relatively low-cost personal investment advice.[56] Robo-advisors are automated financial advisory services for asset management with minimum human involvement and a more

[49] The P2P lending platforms act as information intermediaries bridging the gap of information asymmetries between investors and borrowers. See L Lu, *Global Fintech Revolution. Practice, Policy, and Regulation* (Oxford University Press, 2024) 179.

[50] Regulation (EU) 2022/2065 of the European Parliament and of the Council of 19 October 2022 on a Single Market For Digital Services and amending Directive 2000/31/EC.

[51] C Cauffman and C Goanta, 'A New Order: The Digital Services Act and Consumer Protection' (2021) 12 *European Journal of Risk Regulation* 758, 761.

[52] H Schulte-Nölke, 'The EU Digital Services Act and EU Consumer Law' in A De Franceschi and R Schulze (eds), *Harmonizing Digital Contract Law* (Nomos/Hart, 2023) 705–06.

[53] M Husovec, 'Rising above Liability: The Digital Services Act as a Blueprint for the Second Generation of Global Internet Rules' (2023) 38 *Berkeley Technology Law Journal* 883, 901.

[54] C Busch and V Mak, 'Putting the Digital Services Act in Context: Bridging the Gap Between EU Consumer Law and Platform Regulation' (2021) 10 *Journal of European Consumer and Market Law* 109. It is noted that 'the DSA also takes no clear position on the question whether marketplace operators can be held liable under product liability rules for damages caused by defective goods sold by third-party sellers via the online marketplace' (at 111).

[55] A Datta, MC Tschantz and A Datta, 'Automated Experiments on Ad Privacy Settings. A Tale of Opacity, Choice, and Discrimination' (2015) 1 *Proceedings on Privacy Enhancing Technologies* 92.

[56] An example is Nutmeg; see www.nutmeg.com. For a commentary see H Vieira, '"WealthTech": The challenges facing the wealth management industry' LSE Business Review (16 June 2017), blogs.lse.ac.uk/businessreview/2017/06/16/wealthtech-the-challenges-facing-the-wealth-management-industry.

efficient process of investment consultancy. Looking specifically at automated advice and wealth management, the robo-advisors provide speed and lower-cost investment services, matching consumers' preferences and products' assessments (eg, saving plans and pension management). They collect information supplied by the consumers and operate through algorithms.[57] The service is fast and less costly, and potentially superior to advice from human advisers, although it does not automatically preserve customers from faulty advice.[58] The key issue is obtaining an independent assessment of the quality of this automated advice. However, investor protection concerns arise from the expansion of P2P lending markets and other forms of platform-based investment.[59] In P2P lending platforms, investors participate directly in lending by acquiring a participatory ownership share in loans made to a diversified range, typically of more than 200 individual borrowers without recourse to banks or other loan intermediaries, and their returns depend directly on loan performance.[60] A variety of methods can be used to match investors and borrowers, raising questions of whether retail investors are inadequately informed and protected.[61]

8.2.1. The Role of Online Financial Platforms

Online financial platforms show scarce incentives to protect consumers because they are more concerned with monetising revenue with third-party service providers when acting as sales intermediaries and advertising media.[62] This behaviour reflects an imbalance in the power of algorithmic systems, which can create an unfair advantage and exploitation of vulnerability.[63] The superior bargaining power dictated by one party alters the reasonableness of the relationship, which amounts to substantive unfairness in the information provided to consumers.[64] It is argued that the

[57] C Carney, 'Robo-Advisers and the Suitability Requirement: How They Fit in the Regulatory Framework' (2018) 2018 *Columbia Business Law Review* 586, 614–15.

[58] M Zalnieriute, L Bennett Moses and G Williams, 'The Rule of Law and Automation of Government Decision-Making' (2019) 82 *Modern Law Review* 446.

[59] D Chen, A Kavuri and A Milne, 'Growing Pains: The Changing Regulation of Alternative Lending Platforms' in R Rau, R Wardrop and L Zingales (eds), *The Palgrave Handbook of Technological Finance* (Palgrave-MacMillian, 2021) 441. Alternative forms of platform-based service providers in the borrowing side of financial intermediation include P2P, marketplace, loan-based crowdfunding and balance-sheet lending, which are the new technology-based types of investment platforms. Others include donation-based, reward-based and equity-based crowdfunding. For an overview see I Jenik, T Lyman and A Nava, 'Crowdfunding and Financial Inclusion' World Bank CGAP Working Paper (March 2017) 5.

[60] R Lenz, 'Peer-to-Peer Lending: Opportunities and Risks' (2016) 7 *European Journal of Risk Regulation* 688, 689–90.

[61] A Milne and P Parboteeah, 'The Business Models and Economics of Peer-to-Peer Lending' CEPS, ECRI Research Report No 17 (2016), www.ceps.eu/ceps-publications/business-models-and-economics-peer-peer-lending. See also O Havrylchyk, 'Regulatory framework for the loan-based crowdfunding platforms') OECD Economics Department Working Papers No. 1513 (2018) 13, www.oecd-ilibrary.org/content/paper/24ad924a-en.

[62] On this point see BEUC, 'Ensuring Consumer Protection in the Platform Economy' Position Paper (2018), www.beuc.eu/position-papers/ensuring-consumer-protection-platform-economy; A Fletcher et al, 'Consumer Protection for Online Markets and Large Digital Platforms' (2023) 40 *Yale Journal on Regulation* 910.

[63] *Royal Bank of Scotland v Etridge (No 2)* [2001] UKHL 44, [2001] 4 All ER 449. For an overview see R Stone and J Devenney, *The Modern Law of Contract*, 14th edn (Routledge, 2022) 368–69.

[64] J Gardner, 'Being Conscious of Unconscionability in Modern Times: Heller v Uber Technologies' (2021) 84 *Modern Law Review* 874, 882–83.

market power of big tech companies exhibits the appetite to manipulate customers' perception of inclusiveness in digital services.[65] Further, it can be observed that the increasing market power of large tech companies shaped a society of technocrats in which agents are rational but subject to manipulation that hinders their freedom of choice.[66]

Automated platforms stand in a dominant bargaining position which requires special responsibilities toward those over whom they display power or who are particularly dependent on them.[67] The role of AI systems in mediating personalised recommendations to consumers has implications for the selection and delivery of products.[68] The techniques used in online advertisements to solicit customers to choose a product affect the process of control and decision control, making the individual's judgement meaningless.[69] For example, the commercial practice of algorithmic price personalisation inflates forms of discrimination between consumers on protected characteristics by profiling them through the collection of their personal information for the sole purpose of maximising suppliers' profit.[70]

Promises of pricing algorithms have been lauded for allowing e-commerce firms to adapt prices to market conditions quickly and at relatively competitive levels, as shown by large online retailers (eg, Amazon and eBay), which employ a dynamic pricing algorithm for their products.[71] However, these pricing strategies leverage a firm's ability to use algorithms mounting concerns about their implications on consumer outcomes. The UK Competition and Markets Authority (CMA) evidenced that dynamic pricing techniques across a range of sectors (eg, air travel, passenger rail, Ticketmaster, ticket resale, ride hailing and hotels), where a business adjusts its prices according to changing market conditions, are susceptible to producing a risk of consumer harm.[72] This may be inflated by the use of AI and automated tools which can affect consumers' trust in markets, and their ability to get good deals. The CMA reported that 'dynamic pricing can lead to poorer outcomes in certain circumstances, such as when consumers are confused or concerned because prices change rapidly and they are unsure why'.[73]

Dynamic pricing often reflects 'reservation' or 'locking-in' strategies during the purchasing process, where prices are based on factors beyond demand and supply

[65] IH-Y Chiu and D Mantzari, 'Regulating Fintech and BigTech: Reconciling the Objectives of Financial Regulation and Promoting Competition' in K Stylianou, M Iacovides and B Lundqvist (eds), *Fintech Competition: Law, Policy, and Market Organisation* (Hart Publishing 2023) 268–70.

[66] D Markovits, 'Consumer Protection, Behavioral Economics & Democracy', Keynote speech delivered at the International Association of Consumer Law (IACL) Conference, Rudolf Steiner Haus, Hamburg (20 July 2023).

[67] J Cartwright, *Unequal Bargaining. Study of Vitiating Factors in the Formation of Contracts* (Clarendon Press 1991) 197–98.

[68] JM Paterson, 'Misleading AI: Regulatory Strategies for Algorithmic Transparency in Technologies Augmenting Consumer Decision-Making' (2022) 34 *Loyola Consumer Law Review* (Symposium Issue) 572.

[69] D Ariely, 'Controlling the Information Flow: Effects on Consumers' Decision Making and Preferences' (2000) 27 *Journal of Consumer Research* 234.

[70] P Chapdelaine, 'Algorithmic Price Personalization and the Limits of Anti-Discrimination Law' (2024) 69 *McGill Law Journal* 489.

[71] A MacKay and SN Weinstein, 'Dynamic Pricing Algorithms, Consumer Harm, and Regulatory Response' (2022) 100 *Washington University Law Review* 111, 114.

[72] CMA, 'Letter to government from CMA Chair and CEO' (4 September 2024), www.gov.uk/government/publications/letter-to-government-from-cma-chair-and-ceo.

[73] CMA, 'Dynamic pricing' Policy paper (20 June 2025), www.gov.uk/government/publications/dynamic-pricing-project-update/update-dynamic-pricing.

conditions, such as competitors' prices. Most concerns regard the lack of understanding of how prices might vary according to the time of purchase and the rationale for price fluctuations; vulnerable consumers are particularly exposed to disadvantage conditions of inaccurate and misleading pricing information which prevent them from making good choices.[74]

Regulators should mitigate circumstances where users' activities are driven by the perception that they are independently making choices in their best interest while they are unconsciously unaware of the risks around those decisions.[75] This can result in unfair commercial practices such as fake reviews and drip pricing if they are likely to cause the 'average consumer' to take a 'transactional decision' they would not have otherwise taken.[76] Consumers may be particularly vulnerable to aggressive and misleading commercial practices apt to distort relevant information in providing services or products crucial for the decision-making process.[77] The need to ensure a fair balance between the transactional parties questions the enforcement mechanisms to correct this inequality of positions.[78] A measure of legal protection for vulnerable consumers (eg, illness, ignorance, inexperience, impaired faculties, financial need or other circumstances) could be found in the unconscionability and inequality of bargaining power although this doctrine is, in practice, very rarely used by courts in England and Wales.[79]

The doctrine of unconscionability originates from the transactional imbalance and relational inequality between parties.[80] In the digital context, the relationship cannot be considered to be at arm's length due to the position of algorithm-driven platforms over the weaker party. Digital financial platforms tend to exploit consumers' profiles and behaviour,[81] which can lead to conditions of dependence as a result of unconscionable bargaining perpetrated on vulnerable individuals.[82] One difficulty with the unconscionable bargain doctrine is that it would not apply to platform situations which involve a trilateral relationship with buyers and sellers. As noted, 'unconscionability would require it to focus more on the nature of the contract itself rather than the events

[74] CMA, 'Tips for businesses using dynamic pricing' Guidance (20 June 2025), www.gov.uk/government/publications/dynamic-pricing-tips-for-businesses/tips-for-businesses-using-dynamic-pricing.

[75] C Baker and CK Odinet, 'The Gamification of Banking' (2025) 2025 *University of Illinois Law Review* 101, 138.

[76] CMA, 'The CMA's approach to direct consumer protection' Guidance (April 2025), www.gov.uk/government/publications/the-cmas-approach-to-direct-consumer-protection.

[77] CMA, 'Unfair commercial practices' Guidance on the protection from unfair trading provisions in the Digital Markets, Competition and Consumers Act 2024 (4 April 2025), www.gov.uk/government/publications/unfair-commercial-practices-cma207.

[78] CMA, 'Direct consumer enforcement rules' Rules on the direct consumer enforcement regime set out in the Direct Markets, Competition and Consumers Act 2024 (4 April 2025); 'Direct consumer enforcement guidance' Guidance on the direct consumer enforcement regime set out in the Digital Markets, Competition and Consumers Act 2024 (14 March 2025), www.gov.uk/government/publications/direct-consumer-enforcement-guidance-cma200.

[79] L Fox O'Mahony and J Devenney, 'The Elderly, Their Homes and the Unconscionable Bargain Doctrine' in M Dixon (ed), *Modern Studies in Property Law*, Vol 5 (Bloomsbury Publishing 2009) 285. See also the case of *Adare Finance DAC v Yellowstone Capital Management SA* [2020] EWHC 2760 (Comm).

[80] R Bigwood, 'Undue Influence: Impaired Consent or Wicked Exploitation' (1996) 16 *Oxford Journal of Legal Studies* 503, 508–09.

[81] R Bigwood, *Exploitative Contracts* (Oxford University Press, 2003) 243–44.

[82] D Capper, 'Protection of the vulnerable in financial transactions – what the common law vitiating factors can do for you' in M Kenny, J Devenney and L Fox O'Mahony (eds), *Unconscionability in European Private Financial Transactions. Protecting the Vulnerable* (Cambridge University Press, 2010) 166–67.

that led to it being formed'.[83] The concept of unconscionability in contracts is generally used as a corrective tool in cases where vulnerable individuals seek protection from the harmful consequences of their exploited decisions.[84] Specifically, the scope of an unconscionable bargain is to promote an individual's welfare against restrictions on liberty and autonomy: however, this paternalist characterisation has been subject to criticisms, in particular on the effects of paternalism in mitigating the impact of unequal bargains.[85]

The rationale behind such characterisation is the protection of legitimate interests to prevent inequitable relationships. Shiffrin argued that

> the unconscionability doctrine is two-sided: one is both refusing to assist (accommodate) the exploitative behaviour of one party, and, in (welcome) effect, although not necessarily in intention, one is bailing out the disadvantaged, exploited party and saving her from the costs of a harsh contract.[86]

In online transactions, the unconscionability doctrine could be considered in ways that refrain digital providers from exploiting their unequal bargaining power and unfair behaviours against vulnerable users.[87] However, the unconscionable bargain doctrine showed uncertainty due to different approaches evident in case law where the interpretation of its applicability in contractual relationships has been the conundrum of judicial decisions.[88]

In *Jones v Morgan*, the court held that 'the unconscionable bargain doctrine cannot be successfully invoked unless one of the parties to the contract has exploited the other in a "morally culpable" or "morally reprehensible" manner which falls into the realms of "special disadvantage"'.[89] This case echoed the interpretation of the unconscionable bargain doctrine given by the High Court in *Alec Lobb (Garages) Ltd and others v Total Oil Great Britain Ltd*, which identified the characteristics of a bargain on the ground of unconscionability as follows: (i) that one party was at a serious disadvantage to the other, 'whether through poverty or ignorance or lack of advice or otherwise', so that circumstances existed of which unfair advantage could be taken; (ii) that the weakness of the one party had been exploited by the other in some morally culpable manner; and (iii) that the resulting transaction has been, not merely hard and improvident, but overreaching and oppressive.[90] In *Multiservice Bookbinding Ltd v Marden*, it was held that a bargain cannot be unconscionable unless 'one of the parties has imposed the objectionable terms in a morally reprehensible manner; that is to say, in a manner which affects his conscience'.[91] This line of authority suggests that unconscionable conduct makes contracts voidable, and avoiding the contract is a self-help remedy although the party

[83] R Stone and J Devenney, *The Modern Law of Contract*, 15th edn (Routledge, 2025) 416.
[84] *Williams v Walker-Thomas Furniture Co* 350 F.2d 445 (DC Cir 1965); *A&M Produce Co v FMC Corp* 186 Cal Rptr 114 (Cal Ct App 1982). See also MJ Trebilcock, 'The Doctrine of Inequality of Bargaining Power' in AT Kronman and RA Posner (eds), *The Economics of Contract Law* (Little, Brown & Company, 1979) 80–81.
[85] M Chen-Wishart, 'Unconscionable Bargains: What are the Courts Doing?' (University of Otago, New Zealand, 1987) 39.
[86] Shiffrin (n 33) 249.
[87] S Saintier, 'Defects of Consent in English Law: Protecting the Bargain?' in L DiMatteo and M Hogg (eds), *Comparative Contract Law: British and American Perspectives* (Oxford University Press 2016) 129–30.
[88] J Devenney, 'A pack of unruly dogs: unconscionable bargains, lawful act (economic) duress and clogs on the equity of redemption' (2002) *Journal of Business Law* 539, 540.
[89] *Jones v Morgan* [2001] EWCA Civ 995 [33].
[90] *Alec Lobb Garages Ltd v Total Oil Great Britain Ltd* [1983] 1 WLR 87 [94]–[95].
[91] *Multiservice Bookbinding Ltd v Marden* [1979] Ch 84 [110].

can resort to court if it is disputed. As a result, a contract can be rescinded for unconscionable conduct without needing to identify an existing relationship of influence or dependency between the parties.[92]

Digital contracts with big tech companies (eg, Meta, Uber, YouTube, Google) expose consumers to the dominant position of automated platforms.[93] For example, Amazon is a marketplace platform that employs machine learning algorithms to provide personalised product recommendations based on users' previous browsing and purchasing behaviour.[94] Most cases among US common law courts have considered the doctrine of unconscionability in a review of contracts of adhesion to protect consumers against unfair contracting practices.[95] Standardised forms of digital agreements are generally affected by several factors which can impair the correct formation of consensus: unequal bargaining power; lack of express consent before collecting personal data; clauses which are difficult to understand; and unequal enforcement of terms among unequally situated parties.[96] The unconscionable bargain doctrine makes the whole contract unenforceable and can be considered to restrain the superior position of digital platforms.[97] The Consumer Rights Act 2015 (CRA 2015) unfair terms regulation would apply in relation to individual terms.[98] CRA 2015, s 62 introduces a test of 'fairness' to regulate the requirement for contract terms and notices to be fair. The provision states that 'a term is unfair if, contrary to the requirement of good faith, it causes a significant imbalance in the parties' rights and obligations under the contract to the detriment of the consumer'.[99] The CRA 2015 sets fairness standards in circumstances where terms must be transparent and prominent, in particular when the assessment of the price cannot be considered for fairness.[100] However, the transparency and prominence rules do not clarify the information regime for categories of prices and charges in contracts, showing limits in relation to informed decision-making and consumer protection.[101]

[92] N Andrews, A Tettenborn and G Virgo, *Contractual Duties: Performance, Breach, Termination and Remedies*, 4th edn (Sweet & Maxwell 2023) ch2, s VII.

[93] BE Boliek, 'Upgrading Unconscionability: A Common Law Ally for a Digital World' (2021) 81 *Maryland Law Review* 46.

[94] O Budzinski, S Gaenssle and N Lindstädt-Dreusicke, 'Data (r)evolution: the economics of algorithmic search and recommender services' in S Baumann (ed), *Handbook on Digital Business Ecosystems* (Edward Elgar, 2022) 350–51.

[95] The doctrine of unconscionability has been applied to protect consumers from onerous terms and the discriminatory application of digital contracts. See the case *Technologies Inc v Heller* 2020 SCC 16. See also AR Salazar, 'Unconscionability, Smart Contracts, and Blockchain Technology: Are Consumers Really Protected against Power Abuses in the Digital Economy?' (2021) 9 *International Journal on Consumer Law and Practice* 74, 77–78; S Blount, 'Unconscionability in online business to consumer contracts' (2021) 2 *ANU Journal of Law and Technology* 5, which examines circumstances where courts invalidated online standard form contracts for unconscionability. The cases *Comb v PayPal* 18 F Supp 2d 1165 (ND Cal, 2002) and *Shroyer v New Cingular Wireless Services Inc* 98 F 3d 976 (9th Cir, 2007) show the attitude of the US courts to set aside contracts in their entirety for procedural unconscionability.

[96] ibid 49.

[97] Enonchong (n 32) 246.

[98] See www.legislation.gov.uk/ukpga/2015/15/contents.

[99] CRA 2015, s 62(4).

[100] For commentary see P Giliker, 'The Consumer Rights Act 2015 – a bastion of European consumer rights?' (2017) 37 *Legal Studies* 78, 96–97.

[101] C Willett, 'Control of Price Related Terms in Standard Form Contracts in the UK: Regulating Prices and Charges in the UK: Information Versus Substance, General Clauses Versus Rules Developed by Regulators'

8.2.2. Digital Consumer Vulnerability

Digital market conditions determine features in which certain individuals are more susceptible to harm than other individuals that belong to a more 'average' category.[102] However, the concept of average consumer is debated, and a commonly accepted definition is missing in the regulatory framework. Article 5 of the EU Unfair Terms Directive requires 'plain intelligible language' in the case of written contracts in considering the needs of the 'average consumer'.[103] An 'average consumer' is considered a rational actor who formulates preferences and makes choices based on publicly available information supplied in the markets.[104] However, the notion of the 'average consumer' is disputed given contrasting court decisions on the degree of consumer protection and the concept of 'reasonable' that the average consumer should be expected to be.[105] Rationality and transparency of decisions represent the main hurdles for consumers to access online products because of unfamiliarity and lack of understanding with sophisticated computational software.[106] These challenges encompass vulnerabilities which are inherent in the social conditions of individuals and arise from psychologically harmful circumstances such as dependence on technological innovations.[107] An interesting view on the treatment of groups of vulnerable consumers is found in the Unfair Commercial Practices Directive (UCPD),[108] which provides a definition of the circumstances of vulnerability for certain categories of individuals. Article 5.3 of the UCPD sets out the vulnerable consumer standard in commercial practices which are likely to materially distort the economic behaviour only of a clearly identifiable group of consumers because of their mental or physical infirmity, age or credulity in a way which the trader could reasonably be expected to foresee. These practices should be assessed from the perspective of the average member of that group. The UCPD focuses on the impact of aggressive commercial practices on consumer vulnerability, identifying static factors for determining whether a particular action is harmful only to that group of consumers. An analysis

in YM Atamer and P Pichonnaz (eds), *Control of Price Related Terms in Standard Form Contracts* (Springer Nature Switzerland AG, 2020) 723.

[102] N Helberger et al, 'EU Consumer Protection 2.0. Structural asymmetries in digital consumer markets' BEUC Report (March 2021) 5–6; R Calo, 'Digital Market Manipulation' (2014) 82 *George Washington Law Review* 995, 1003.

[103] Council Directive 93/13/EEC of 5 April 1993 on Unfair Terms in Consumer Contracts [1993] OJ L 95/29.

[104] V Mak, 'Standards of Protection: In Search of the "Average Consumer" of EU Law in the Proposal for a Consumer Rights Directive' (2011) 19 *European Review of Private Law* 25; R Incardona and C Poncibò, 'The average consumer, the unfair commercial practices directive, and the cognitive revolution' (2007) 30 *Journal of Consumer Policy* 21; CR Sunstein, 'Social Norms and Social Roles' (1996) 96 *Columbia Law Review* 903, 946–47.

[105] See the case C-646/22 *Compass Banca SpA v Autorità Garante della Concorrenza e del Mercato (AGCM)*, ruled by the CJEU on 14 November 2024. For a commentary see the blog posted by JA (Joasia) Luzak, 'European "consumer" notion: Continued broad application in 2024' (7 January 2025), recent-ecl.blogspot.com/2025/01/european-consumer-notion-continued.html?m=0.

[106] F Galli, *Algorithmic Marketing and EU Law on Unfair Commercial Practices* (Springer Nature Switzerland AG, 2022) 181–82.

[107] BS Turner, *Vulnerability and Human Rights* (The Pennsylvania State University Press, 2006) 25–26.

[108] Directive 2005/29/EC of the European Parliament and of the Council of 11 May 2005 concerning unfair business-to-consumer commercial practices in the internal market and amending Council Directive 84/450/EEC, Directives 97/7/EC, 98/27/EC and 2002/65/EC of the European Parliament and of the Council and Regulation (EC) No 2006/2004 of the European Parliament and of the Council.

of the text suggests that the provision encompasses the 'average' vulnerable standard and the concept of a class-based approach to vulnerability, which is limited to specific personal circumstances and it does not reflect other conditions of impairment.[109] The members of these groups of vulnerable consumers are regarded as uniform, and there is limited scope to consider dynamic and flexible circumstances such as relational or situational factors (context-based external factors, eg, losing a job or going through a divorce) which may change the state of vulnerability.

The concept of vulnerability has been elaborated in the 'United Nations Department of Economic and Social Affairs 2003 Report on the World Social Situation', which recognised that the vulnerable nature 'exists at all levels and dimensions of society and forms an integral part of the human condition, affecting both individuals and society as a whole', and it is 'a state of high exposure to certain risks and uncertainties, in combination with a reduced ability to protect or defend oneself against those risks and uncertainties and cope with their negative consequences'.[110]

The OECD policy reports and recommendations defined consumer vulnerability as disadvantaged classes of groups because of 'socio-demographic characteristics, behavioural characteristics, personal situation, or market environment', which are detrimental attributes for protected categories.[111] In the doctrinal debate, Fineman argues that vulnerability refers to a perpetual state of human experiences which relate to dependence on societal factors associated with physical or cognitive needs.[112] Elements of vulnerable conditions, whether social or medical, contribute to impediments that can be manifested in barriers to accessing environments because of different impairments (eg, disability, injury or illness). Fineman's universal propensity for vulnerability reflects conditions of inequalities in contingent or material life circumstances such as disparity of treatment, disadvantaged position, and economic and social dependence.

The vulnerability theory can promote unduly paternalistic laws and policies which limits individuals' autonomy. Further, the universal state of vulnerability and dependency, and the state's corresponding responsibility for enhancing resilience across populations, need not lead to paternalism which is not a suitable public policy response to the individuals' vulnerabilities.[113] This chapter advocates that to some degree the digital environment makes all consumers vulnerable to the complex, sophisticated AI algorithms of automated platforms. Consumers are more exposed to the data-driven commercial practices and need an additional layer of protection. As Helberger et al noted, 'digital vulnerability describes a universal state of defencelessness and

[109] E Kaprou, 'The current legal definition of vulnerable consumers in the UCPD: benefits and limitations of a focus on personal attributes' in C Riefa and S Saintier (eds), *Vulnerable Consumers and the Law: Consumer Protection and Access to Justice* (Routledge, 2020) 52–53.

[110] United Nations Department of Economic and Social Affairs, 'Report on the World Social Situation. Social Vulnerability: Sources and Challenges' (New York, 2003) 8.

[111] OECD, 'Consumer Vulnerability in the Digital Age' OECD Digital Economy Papers No 355 (June 2023) 15.

[112] M Albertson Fineman, 'Vulnerability and Social Justice' (2019) 53 *Valparaiso University Law Review* 358. Vulnerability and dependency are universal and inherent to the human condition, and governments need to ensure that all people have equal access to the societal institutions that distribute resources.

[113] NA Kohn, 'Vulnerability Theory and the Role of Government' (2014) 26 *Yale Journal of Law and Feminism* 14.

susceptibility to (the exploitation of) power imbalances that are the result of increasing automation of commerce, datafied consumer–seller relations, and the very architecture of digital marketplaces'.[114] On this view, the UCPD Guidance adopted by the EU Commission has made substantive progress by considering unfair and aggressive commercial practices in the digital environment, which focus on circumstances of vulnerability for consumers susceptible to sophisticated marketing and advertising media techniques.[115]

Circumstances of financial vulnerability can be exploited in algorithmic systems used in credit arrangements such as crowdfunding, P2P lending and bank-to-consumer lending, which can implicate discriminatory, exclusionary and predatory practices in the credit market (eg, over indebtedness).[116] Riefa observed that 'in a digital environment all consumers are in fact vulnerable and thus, we ought to expect vulnerability to be the norm rather than the exception'.[117] Digital financial technologies show a promising perception of affordable and accessible services; however, they can affect the capacity of consumers to make autonomous choices.[118]

Post-Brexit, the regulatory framework of digital contracts appears fragmented as it seems UK legislation is lacking vision on how to adapt to the EU policy strategy on the digital single market.[119] Specifically, the directive on contracts for the supply of digital content and digital services to consumers (DCSD)[120] showed divergences from the CRA 2015 in terms of the definition of 'digital content' (which includes cloud computing and social media services), 'price' (where the consumer pays or undertakes to pay a price, and provides or undertakes to provide personal data to the trader) and the 'burden of proof' (the presumption of conformity at the time of supply is on the trader provided it becomes apparent within one year of supply). On this view, Giliker observed that 'in balancing consumer and business interests, the EU and the UK have made different policy judgements'.[121] Further, the remedial framework of the CRA 2015 and DCSD differs in the procedure for termination, inflating uncertainty in contract law and consumer protection rights as the UK appears to be at risk of being left behind the EU.[122]

[114] Helberger et al (n 102) 5.

[115] Guidance on the interpretation and application of Directive 2005/29/EC of the European Parliament and of the Council concerning unfair business-to-consumer commercial practices in the internal market C/2021/9320. For commentary see E Kaprou, 'Aggressive commercial practices 2.0: Is the UCPD fit for the digital age?' (2023) 12 *Journal of European Consumer and Market Law* 76.

[116] K Johnson, F Pasquale and J Chapman, 'Artificial Intelligence, Machine Learning, and Bias in Finance: Toward Responsible Innovation' (2019) 88 *Fordham Law Review* 504.

[117] C Riefa, 'Protecting Vulnerable Consumers in the Digital Single Market' (2022) 33 *European Business Law Review* 609.

[118] B Clough, 'Disability and Vulnerability: Challenging the Capacity/Incapacity Binary' (2017) 16 *Social Policy & Society* 469, 476–77.

[119] See www.europarl.europa.eu/factsheets/en/sheet/43/the-ubiquitous-digital-single-market.

[120] Directive (EU) 2019/770 of the European Parliament and of the Council of 20 May 2019 on certain aspects concerning contracts for the supply of digital content and digital services.

[121] P Giliker, 'Examining English contract law in the light of Brexit – an end to the European dream?' in R Merkin and J Devenney (eds), *Essays in Memory of Professor Jill Poole* (Routledge, 2019) 28; P Giliker, 'Legislating on Contracts for the Supply of Digital Content and Services: An EU/UK/Irish Divide?' (2021) 2 *Journal of Business Law* 152. It is observed that the CRA 2015 does not extend to contracts where the consumer provides or undertakes to provide personal data to the trader and no specific provision is made for digital services.

[122] J Devenney, 'Brexit, Consumer Law and Legal Pluralism: the Case for an Optional Instrument on Core Consumer Law' (2025) *Journal of Business Law* (forthcoming).

Automated platforms display gatekeeping functions in determining the terms and access to credit facilities (eg, creditworthiness assessments), which influence the welfare of vulnerable groups in managing payments and finance.[123] Further, automated platforms display an unconscientious bargaining power over vulnerable consumers which arises from the superior (dominant) position in the transactions.[124] It is a form of passive acceptance of exploitative relationships in which the limited knowledge and relative inexperience of consumers in using automated systems can result in biased outcomes.[125] Digital financial platforms should mitigate these circumstances by providing accurate information on marketing and pricing, which should help consumers make accurate choices.[126] The crux of the matter is the transparency of algorithmic processing of consumer information, which may reflect wrong human assessments and past biased decisions.[127]

The algorithms analyse aggregated data and produce outcomes although an algorithm's decision does not reflect a consumer's optimal choice as the decisional parameters are different for each user's preference.[128] As noted, 'the 'intelligence' of a machine learning algorithm is oriented to outcomes, not process; a "smart" algorithm is designed to reach consistently accurate results on a chosen task, even if the algorithm does not "think" like a person'.[129] Consumers are often influenced by marketing information which inflates the perception of operating in perfect conditions of product allocation. Algorithms elaborate information relevant to consumers' profiles but can reveal situations of disadvantage which raises concerns about the genuine assessment of data.[130]

Consumers can be undermined from making good decisions because of the level of sophistication in the digital environment which creates obstacles to access information, advice and market price.[131] Further, exploitation of attributes can result in situations of indirect psychological harm,[132] which is a form of 'disability' created by the environment of financial technology that makes vulnerable consumers disabled. This form of disability is intended to be different from an actual cognitive impairment that is created biologically in the individual. Psychological harm inflates disparities of treatment for consumers where the more powerful party in the transaction (ie, the digital platform) exercises discretionary control over resources on which the more vulnerable are reliant, and cannot obtain elsewhere or where people are unable to protect themselves or their

[123] S Kourabas and CY Tsang, 'Big Techs and Global Financial Regulation: Intersection, Challenges, and Solutions' (2024) 40 *Banking and Finance Law Review* 173.

[124] RW Clark, *Inequality of Bargaining Power* (Carswell, 1987) 63–64.

[125] J Devenney and A Chandler, 'Unconscionability and the taxonomy of undue influence' (2007) 8 *Journal of Business Law* 569.

[126] *Lloyd's Bank Ltd v Bundy* [1975] QB 326. See also M Moore, 'Why Does Lord Denning's Lead Balloon Intrigue Us Still? The Prospects of Finding a Unifying Principle for Duress, Undue Influence and Unconscionability' (2018) 134 *Law Quarterly Review* 257, 263–64.

[127] R Van Loo and N Aggarwal, 'Amazon's Pricing Paradox' (2023) 37 *Harvard Journal of Law & Technology* 1.

[128] M Clegg et al, 'Unveiling the Mind of the Machine' (2024) 51 *Journal of Consumer Research* 343–344.

[129] Johnson, Pasquale and Chapman (n 116) 508.

[130] MS Gal and N Elkin-Koren, 'Algorithmic Consumers' (2017) 30 *Harvard Journal of Law & Technology* 315.

[131] O Lynskey, 'The Power of Providence: The Role of Platforms in Leveraging the Legibility of Users to Accentuate Inequality' in M Moore and D Tambini (eds), *Digital Dominance: The Power of Google, Amazon, Facebook, and Apple* (Oxford University Press, 2018) 188–89.

[132] RE Goodin, *Protecting the Vulnerable: A Reanalysis of Our Social Responsibilities* (University of Chicago Press, 1985) 109–10.

interests.[133] AI algorithms are not capable of reproducing human cognition and emotion which are essential to evaluate the personal attributes of consumers; their outputs are based on parameters which refer to backward-looking historical data. The employment of algorithms to make decisions on those attributes (ie, social relations and social interactions) questions the fairness of algorithmic predictions.[134] Decision-making processes require human thinking which cannot be automated: algorithmic systems may reproduce existing biases because they do not hold human judgement for evaluating the accuracy of information.[135]

8.2.3. Algorithmic Decision-Making Systems in Financial Services

The dependence on algorithmic systems weakens the awareness of consumers' actions and the cognitive capacity to make autonomous choices.[136] Automated tools are increasingly used in financial institutions with loan and insurance origination, substantially lowering costs and offering potential improvements in risk measurement and management.[137] For example, banks and credit reference agencies use machine learning systems such as linear regression, logistic regression and decision trees, to cluster groups of people and calculate credit scores.[138] This data-driven approach based on predictions can expedite transactions although algorithmic credit scoring poses the question of credit fairness as it may inflate biases towards specific personal characteristics such as race, gender, marital status or sexual orientation.[139] Financial technologies can exacerbate discriminatory outcomes in automated credit assessment where the decisional parameters and proxies of algorithms do not reflect the accurate status of customers.[140] However, discrimination is only one type of vulnerability, and vulnerability goes beyond discrimination.

Cases of discriminatory outcomes deriving from biased algorithms employed to assess customers' creditworthiness can be found in the credit market sector,[141] life insurance

[133] AW Wood, 'Exploitation' (1995) 12 *Social Philosophy and Policy* 143–44.

[134] O Lobel, *The Equality Machine: Harnessing Digital Technology for a Brighter, More Inclusive Future* (PublicAffairs, 2022) 47–48.

[135] P De Filippi and A Wright, *Blockchain and the Law. The Rule of Code* (Harvard University Press, 2018) 147.

[136] MS Gal, 'Algorithmic Challenges to Autonomous Choice' (2018) 25 *Michigan Technology Law Review* 76.

[137] K Langenbucher, 'Consumer credit in the age of AI: Beyond anti-discrimination law' SAFE Working Paper No 369 (2022) 36–37, doi.org/10.2139/ssrn.4298261.

[138] H Sargeant, 'Algorithmic decision-making in financial services: economic and normative outcomes in consumer credit' (2023) 3 *AI and Ethics* 1304–05.

[139] M Hurley and J Adebayo, 'Credit Scoring in the Era of Big Data' (2016) 18 *Yale Journal of Law and Technology* 167–68.

[140] IN Cofone, 'Algorithmic Discrimination Is an Information Problem' (2019) 70 *Hastings Law Journal* 1389, 1394, documenting how 'automated decision-making not only mirrors existing biases, but it has the potential to amplify them' (1398).

[141] Firms employ algorithmic decision-making processes to assess whether to grant individual consumers credit and provide credit-scoring to applicants. Algorithmic systems are trained on data which reflect proxies that contain general information about protected characteristics. As it has been argued, 'a dataset that does not contain explicit data about people's sexual orientation can still give information about people's sexual orientation'. See F Zuiderveen Borgesius, 'Discrimination, artificial intelligence, and

policies[142] and algorithmic credit scoring,[143] which demonstrate that automated systems tend to replicate wrong human decisions and inaccurate training data (target variables and class labels).[144] Discrimination and predatory practices in credit access raise concerns about the socio-legal implications of algorithmic systems for vulnerable consumers.[145] Specifically, discriminatory practices against poor consumers are found in the creditors' refusal to grant credit to all those living in a particular area whatever the merits of an individual applicant because of a disproportionate number of defaulters from the area.[146] The decision of credit denial reflects patterns of discrimination recorded in the source data; however, discriminatory profiles and classifications in credit approval can also reflect practices of redlining related to factors of race, gender and other protected characteristics.[147] Credit scoring predicts the probability of a person repaying any credit advanced; it is a tool for making credit decisions based on the personal attributes of the debtor, either matching them statistically to the profile of others who have repaid or examining the borrower's behaviour with existing indebtedness.[148]

Algorithmic credit scoring systems may impair creditworthiness in decision-making processes.[149] They employ data which contains patterns on customers' sensitive information and provide a judgement about the creditworthiness of certain individuals based on parameters which, if biased, can translate into discriminatory predictions.[150] Lenders use this set of information to support their assessment which is elaborated through machine learning models predictive of the borrower's behaviour.[151] The use of algorithms in consumer credit underwriting reveals conditions of unequal access to the lending market.[152]

An interesting example is the mis-selling scandal of UK payment protection insurance (PPI)[153] against loss of income that would prevent repayment, sold alongside

algorithmic decision-making' (Council of Europe, Directorate General of Democracy, 2018) 13, rm.coe.int/discrimination-artificial-intelligence-and-algorithmic-decision-making/1680925d73.

[142] K Powell, 'Black Men Deserve To Live Long' Vibe (30 October 2023), www.vibe.com/features/editorial/black-men-deserve-1234807713.

[143] L Rice and D Swesnik, 'Discriminatory effects of credit scoring on communities of color' (2013) 46 *Suffolk University Law Review* 966.

[144] H Cossette-Lefebvre and J Maclure, 'AI's fairness problem: understanding wrongful discrimination in the context of automated decision-making' (2023) 3 *AI and Ethics* 1255, 1265–66.

[145] ABuccella, '"AI for all" is a matter of social justice' (2023) 3 *AI and Ethics* 1150.

[146] R Bartlett et al, 'Consumer-Lending Discrimination in the FinTech Era' NBER Working Paper No 25943 (June 2019) 2–3, www.nber.org/papers/w25943.

[147] D Pedreschi et al, 'The Discovery of Discrimination' in B Custerset al (eds) *Discrimination and Privacy in the Information Society. Data Mining and Profiling in Large Databases* (Springer Verlag, Berlin 2013) 92.

[148] C Scott and J Black, *Cranston's Consumers and the Law*, 3rd edn (Cambridge University Press, 2000) 242–43. See also FCA, 'Consumer credit – high-cost short-term credit lending data' (2019), www.fca.org.uk/data/consumer-credit-high-cost-short-term-credit-lending-data-jan-2019.

[149] For example, before granting a mortgage, a bank may consider the credit score of the borrower, with additional meaningful intervention carried out by humans before any decision is applied to an individual.

[150] BK Hassani, 'Societal bias reinforcement through machine learning: a credit scoring perspective' (2021) 1 *AI and Ethics* 239.

[151] S Kumar Trivedi, 'A study on credit scoring modeling with different feature selection and machine learning approaches' (2020) 63 *Technology and Society* 1.

[152] J Jia-Xi Wu, 'Algorithmic Fairness in Consumer Credit Underwriting: Towards a Harm-Based Framework for AI Fair Lending' (2024) 21 *Berkeley Business Law Journal* 88.

[153] The problems of PPI and the response to the consumer complaints about PPI are described in FSA, 'The assessment and redress of Payment Protection Insurance complaints, Feedback on CP/09 and further consultation' (March 2010), www.fca.org.uk/publication/consultation/cp10_06.pdf. The Appendix 3 'Open letter' lists 15 common failings in the sale of PPI, including pressurised selling, failure to notify about the cooling-off

mortgage and consumer credit products. PPI morphed from an add-on customer service to becoming a substantial source of returns in addition to and often substantially exceeding the profits earned from the underlying credit products themselves, underpinned by the sale of overpriced or unnecessary insurance.[154]

PPI mis-selling was driven by the use of simplistic gross revenue metrics, the difference between payment received for the PPI and the costs to the institution of providing it (usually through sale to a third-party insurer), without any assessment of the appropriateness of the sales margins. The profits taken from PPI relied excessively on the perspective of *caveat emptor* (always a comforting thought for a firm making embarrassingly high returns), without taking any serious account of the financial understanding or situation of customers, and whether the margins were appropriate for such simple products with few barriers to the entry of competing providers. PPI was more egregious because customers were often sold a service that they not only did not need, but for which there was little transparency on costs and alternative providers with whom they could compare costs and quality.

With modern information technology, regulators can now expect management to compute and monitor the margins charged on individual products and services, and, where these are large, require firms to understand themselves the underlying commercial drivers. Large margins can be justified, even in a competitive environment where other providers can freely offer competing products and services as compensation for risk, or as a return for providing an additional premium quality. The regulatory expectation should be that margins are reviewed to establish they are not a consequence of mispricing or other unfair treatment. What is required is a broader dialogue between regulators and individual firms, and also between regulators and the industry as a whole on using technology to develop appropriate systems and processes to achieve desired commercial and regulatory outcomes.

Financial technologies changed how discrimination manifests itself in financial services which proliferate in biased algorithms.[155] Technological solutions may fail to ensure equal conditions and 'to reckon with both the complexity of the issues they purport to solve and their impacts on people excluded from the technological development process'.[156] This questions whether the law can act as a corrective measure to discriminatory practices and algorithmic opacity.[157]

period, not adequately describing the product, not clarifying if it was offering financial advice, where offering financial advice, not taking reasonable care to establish the suitability of the product, inadequate price disclosure, selling policies where the total costs exceeded the benefits of the policy, and hiding costs within the original loan. The FCA in 'Payment protection insurance explained' (22 August 2020), www.fca.org.uk/ppi/ppi-explained, summarises the outcome after the passing of the 2019 final deadline for customer compensation claims: 'As many as 64 million PPI policies have been sold in the UK, mostly between 1990 and 2010, some as far back as the 1970s. But we found that PPI was often mis-sold. More than £33bn has already been paid back to people who complained about the sale of PPI.'

[154] The PPI mis-selling scandal showed the failure of firms to comply with the prudential sourcebook and regulatory rules such as suitability, know your customer and best advice. See J Black and R Nobles, 'Personal Pensions Misselling: The Causes and Lessons of Regulatory Failure' (1998) 61 *Modern Law Review* 789, 792. It is argued that 'the pensions episode indicates that general rules are subject to limits inherent in the interpretive context in which they operate' (819).

[155] A Morse and K Pence, 'Technological innovation and discrimination in household finance' (February 2020) NBER Working Paper 26739, www.nber.org/papers/w26739.

[156] HJ Allen, 'Fintech and Techno-Solutionism' (2 January 2024) 6, ssrn.com/abstract=4686469.

[157] V Eubanks, *Digital Dead End: Fighting for Social Justice in the Information Age* (MIT Press 2011) 47–48.

8.3. Vulnerable Consumer Protection in the UK Equality Act 2010

Consumer vulnerability can be exploited in the form of direct and indirect discrimination in financial services, raising concerns about whether the EA 2010 would be applicable as an effective regulatory response. Protected characteristics are defined in EA 2010, section 4, which identifies categories of individuals in need of greater attention because of discriminatory behaviour based on the grounds of such characteristics.[158] Specifically, the EA 2010 provides a general degree of protection for vulnerable people preventing forms of discrimination and inequality against those individuals. However, the regulatory framework is largely centred on grounds-based categories of discrimination rather than identified disadvantaged groups, which does not reflect the variety and complexity of human experience and identity with the result of excluding socio-economic status as a legally protected characteristic.[159] The listed protected characteristics are defined by specific categorisation of objectives rather than pointed at the changing social construction of identity. This regulatory approach inevitably leaves out socio-economic conditions of groups and individual identities which are not considered in their relational, contingent and multidimensional lived experience. A shift towards social inclusion which encompasses recognition and disadvantage would favour a more comprehensive view of the grounds-based system of the EA 2010.[160]

The legislation is largely standardised across domains including employment, provision of services, and education. The Act regulates discriminatory practices which directly or indirectly treat an individual less favourably than another without the protected characteristic; it also addresses unfair treatment against members of the protected groups. The test of less favourable treatment is subject only to a defence of an 'objective justification' for that treatment; however, this regulatory approach does not capture potential discriminatory outcomes of algorithmic decision-making systems (eg, biased machine learning process), which combine multiple characteristics based on proxies for those attributes.[161]

Algorithms that use parameters which include personal attributes such as gender and race or their proxies such as geographic location for race, if not updated and calibrated accurately, can lead to biased outcomes. Gender bias in algorithms can be found in the loan approval decisions where the procedure can use a training dataset that presents unfair disadvantages against female applicants (eg, higher rejection rates without relevant reasons) in comparison with male applicants.[162] For example, a woman on unpaid maternity leave can be exposed to systemic bias in the mortgage application. The risk assessment of banks involves automated processes on personalised finance to classify the creditworthiness of individual applicants. The employment of algorithmic systems to make predictions based

[158] See www.legislation.gov.uk/ukpga/2010/15/contents.

[159] K Malleson, 'Equality Law and the Protected Characteristics' (2018) 81 *Modern Law Review* 598, 602.

[160] L Vickers, 'The Expanded Public Sector Duty: Age, Religion and Sexual Orientation' (2011) 11 *International Journal of Discrimination and the Law* 43, 54.

[161] Reed (n 16) 70–71.

[162] N Kordzadeh and M Ghasemaghaei, 'Algorithmic bias: review, synthesis, and future research directions' (2022) 31 *European Journal of Information Systems* 390.

on proxies such as the likelihood to fail the payment of a loan can reveal discriminatory effects. In this case, the woman cannot get a mortgage without returning to work, which raises the following question: Do you give a mortgage to a woman who built up enough savings to fund unpaid maternity leave, or do you incite a woman with a professional network of ideal mortgage customers to expose systemic bias against working mothers? This suggests that a personalised mortgage application process implies disparities in the assessment of lending decisions; the position of a woman on unpaid maternity leave exhibits circumstances of vulnerability in the credit context which are exploited in the use of algorithmic systems for lending decisions.

As a result, the algorithmic system may consider gender as a relevant factor for assessing the creditworthiness of candidates. This refers to proxy discrimination which manifests where an inherently discriminatory criterion is directly embedded into the algorithm and poses legal challenges under UK discrimination law as the deployment of automated decision-making systems reveals increasing forms of discriminatory biases.[163] This would be a case of direct discrimination, as the algorithmic system would take a protected characteristic such as sex as a proxy for a non-protected characteristic such as income. For example, when an automated credit-scoring system classifies women with a lower credit score because the training dataset (with which the system was trained) included only women with lower income compared to men. EA 2010, section 13 regulates forms of direct discrimination, and section 14 is applicable if more than one protected characteristic is used as a proxy.

Among the regulated protected grounds, the EA 2010 provides that it is unlawful to discriminate based on age unless the practice is covered by an exception from the ban and a legitimate reason can be shown for the differential treatment ('objective justification'). Unlawful discrimination on grounds of protected characteristics which involves the commission of a statutory tort under the EA 2010 renders the agreement unenforceable as the performance is contrary to public policy.[164] An unlawful act or conduct to discriminate does not invalidate the contract, but the discriminatory terms contrary to statute are unenforceable.[165] In *Hounga v Allen*, the Supreme Court held that unlawful discrimination is a statutory tort although the application of the defence of illegality to claims in tort is highly problematic.[166] An interesting case of potential unlawful discrimination is observed in the online platform design choices which profile users by race, religion or country of birth through a search interface.[167]

The prohibition on age discrimination is designed to ensure that the law prohibits only harmful treatment that results in genuinely unfair discrimination because of age. It does not outlaw the many instances of different treatments that are justifiable or beneficial.[168]

[163] J Adams-Prassl, R Binns and A Kelly-Lyth, 'Directly Discriminatory Algorithms' (2023) 86 *Modern Law Review* 174.

[164] The rationale for the unenforceability refers to the 'public policy' to prohibit certain types of conduct or behaviour which discriminates the performance of the contract. See C MacMillan, 'Contracts and Equality: The Dangers of Non-disclosure Agreements in English Law' (2022) 18 *European Review of Contract Law* 151.

[165] Terms in contracts, collective agreements or rules of undertakings are unenforceable or void if they result in unlawful discrimination, harassment or victimisation.

[166] [2014] UKSC 47 [24].

[167] J Meers, 'Discrimination at the Interface: The Equality Act 2010 and Platform Interface Design' (2024) 87 *Modern Law Review* 640, 655.

[168] See www.gov.uk/guidance/equality-act-2010-guidance#equalities-act-2010-legislation.

The Act offers protection against discrimination based upon the concepts of protected characteristics and prohibited conduct, which leaves the court to investigate whether there is a causal link between the two categories. As a result, 'the prohibited conduct only becomes prohibited if it is, in some sense, connected to a protected characteristic'.[169] EA 2010, section 5 addresses the protected characteristic of age, which means a person belonging to a particular age group. An age group includes people of the same age and people of a range of ages. Where people fall in the same age group they share the protected characteristic of age. The English courts have shown reluctance to offer rigorous scrutiny when evaluating whether age-differential treatment is objectively justified under anti-discrimination law. Landmark decisions have affirmed that age discrimination must be understood as different from other forms of discrimination, such as race or sex discrimination, creating in this way a lower category of discriminatory actions.[170]

The Act prohibits age discrimination in goods and services, although there is an exception for providing financial services such as bank accounts, loans, insurance, credit cards, warranties, mortgages and investments. Financial businesses can continue to use age as a factor in designing, pricing and offering their products. However, where businesses carry out a risk assessment to provide a financial service the exception will only apply if the assessment, in so far as it involves a consideration of the person's age, is done by reference to information which is both relevant to the assessment of risk and from a source on which it is reasonable to rely.[171]

Age is one of the protected characteristics covered by the EA 2010, the others being disability, gender reassignment, marriage and civil partnership, pregnancy and maternity, race, religion or belief, sex, and sexual orientation. EA 2010, section 10 provides that religion or belief (including any philosophical belief) are protected characteristics. Discrimination on the grounds of sexual orientation, gender reassignment (EA 2010, section 7) and religious belief or political opinion was considered a form of direct discriminatory practice in a few court decisions.[172] Interestingly, the legislation protects disability as a 'physical or mental impairment'; EA 2010, section 6 refers to a disabled person on the protected ground of disability, which includes various formulations of impairment as evidenced in several significant cases.[173]

[169] T Hervey and P Rostant, "All About That Bass'? Is non-ideal-weight discrimination unlawful in the UK?' (2016) 79 *Modern Law Review* 248, 281.

[170] *R (on the application of British Medical Association) v HM Treasury* [2024] EWCA Civ 355; *Seldon v Clarkson Wright & Jakes* [2012] UKSC 16, [2012] 3 All ER 130; *Lockwood v Department of Work and Pensions & Another* [2013] EWCA Civ 1195, [2014] 1 All ER 250; *R v Secretary of State for Work and Pensions, ex p Carson and Reynolds* [2005] UKHL 37, [2006] 1 AC 173. See also S Goosey, 'Is age discrimination a less serious form of discrimination?' (2019) 39 *Legal Studies* 533.

[171] The law allows financial providers to offer products to certain age groups, but it does not permit providers to make assumptions about individuals because of their age. See Financial Ombudsman Service, 'Just a number? Age, complaints and the ombudsman' (November 2015), www.financial-ombudsman.org.uk/files/1762/age-insight-briefing-2015.pdf.

[172] *Lee v Ashers Baking Company Ltd* [2018] UKSC 49; *Forstater v CGD Europe* [2022] ICR 1; *Sutcliffe v Secretary of State for Education* [2024] 1878 EWHC (Admin); *Legge v Environment Agency* [2024] 3 WLUK 609.

[173] *Dolan v Prestwick Aircraft Management Ltd* [2024] 9 WLUK 507; *University of Bristol v Abrahart* [2024] EWHC 299 (KB); *X v Governors of a School* [2015] UKUT 7 (AAC). The English courts also pointed to EA 2010, s 15, which regulates forms of discrimination arising from disability. See *South Gloucestershire Council v Hundal* [2024] EAT 140; *Leicester City Council v Gibbin* [2024] EAT 138; *Nightingale v Bromford Housing Association Ltd* [2024] EWHC 136 (KB).

The EA 2010 is, to a very limited extent, capable of addressing discriminatory practices in algorithmic lending decisions, and algorithmic bias manifested in the automated credit scoring process. The legislation affords legal safeguards to individuals affected by poor assessments and redlining behaviours, but limited protection is recognised for vulnerable consumers against indirect discriminatory practices in algorithmic decision-making systems (eg, gaps in a credit record which may be due to health issues).[174] The protected attributes relate to the workplace and wider society although non-discrimination provisions do not address circumstances where vulnerability arises from unfair practices in digital technologies, leaving unregulated situations where disadvantaged conditions can be the result of harmful decisions of algorithmic systems.[175]

A closer analysis of the EA 2010 suggests that the legislation regulates forms of discrimination perpetuated in the financial sector, making it applicable to financial services in general, such as insurance providers (eg, insurance contracts and policies),[176] pension schemes[177] and lending activities.[178] EA 2010, section 119 sets out the available remedies for discriminatory practices which differ on the ground of the distinction between direct and indirect discrimination.[179] Specifically, the provision refers to an action for reparation, a petition for a judicial review, and an award for damages, which may include compensation for injured feelings (whether or not it includes compensation on any other basis).[180] In *Billy Graham Evangelistic Association v Scottish Event Campus Ltd*, the court held that 'the structure of section 119 in relation to remedies is such as to encourage compliance by considering damages only after other remedies have been considered'.[181]

EA 2010, section 29 provides that a service provider must not discriminate against a person requiring the service (eg, banking services are subject to the provisions of the Act).[182] However, it could not be effective in protecting digital vulnerable consumers: there is a pressing need to reform the Act to capture discriminatory automated

[174] J Graham, 'Risk of discrimination in AI systems. Evaluating the effectiveness of current legal safeguards in tackling algorithmic discrimination' in A Lui and N Ryder (eds), *FinTech, Artificial Intelligence and the Law. Regulation and Crime Prevention* (Routledge, 2021) 222–23.

[175] O Bar-Gill, CR Sunstein and I Talgam-Cohen, 'Algorithmic Harm in Consumer Markets' (2023) 15 *Journal of Legal Analysis* 1, 22–23.

[176] *Royal London Mutual Insurance Society Ltd, Re* [2018] EWHC 2215 (Ch).

[177] *Lloyds Banking Group Pensions Trustees Ltd v Lloyds Bank Plc* [2020] EWHC 3135 (Ch).

[178] *Green v Southern Pacific Mortgage Ltd* [2018] EWCA Civ 854.

[179] Proof of direct discrimination generally results in an award of financial compensation, whereas the remedy for indirect discrimination might be an order to cease to use the apparently neutral rule or practice. On this point see H Collins and TKhaitan (eds), *Foundations of Indirect Discrimination Law* (Hart Publishing, 2018) 23.

[180] The main remedies available are damages (including compensation for injuries to feelings), an injunction and a declaration. According to s 124(4)(5), where the case is based on indirect discrimination and the respondent proves that they did not intend to treat the claimant unfavourably, then the court or tribunal must look at the other remedies available before awarding damages. For commentary see M Butler, *Equality and Anti-Discrimination Law: The Equality Act 2010 and other anti-discrimination protections* (Spiramus Press, 2016) ch 9.

[181] 2022 SLT (Sh Ct) 219 [285].

[182] The EA 2010 requires service providers to make reasonable adjustments for individuals on protected grounds. EA 2010, s 20 provides that where a service puts a disabled person at a substantial disadvantage in relation to a relevant matter in comparison with persons who are not disabled, a provider of that service must take such steps as are reasonable to avoid the disadvantage.

decision-making processes against individuals with protected characteristics. Specifically, the Act should regulate circumstances of vulnerability arising from deceptive, manipulative and biased decisions of algorithmic systems.[183] Ongoing reform to the EA 2010 aims to implement policy measures that replace obsolete rules with a view to affording adequate protection for vulnerable consumers.[184]

8.3.1. The Remedy for Breach of EA 2010

EA 2010, section 142 ('Unenforceable terms')[185] establishes the remedy for breach of legislation in circumstances where terms of contracts discriminate against a person or would otherwise lead to conduct prohibited by the Act unenforceable in that respect. Specifically, section 142(1) provides that a 'term of a contract is unenforceable against a person in so far as it constitutes, promotes or provides for treatment of that or another person that is of a description prohibited by this Act'. This provision interplays with common law illegality doctrine, which refers to contracts contrary to public policy where performance involves the breach of a statute, making a contractual term unenforceable.[186] The doctrine focuses on the state's protection of its citizens rather than ensuring justice between the parties: it aims to protect the integrity of the legal system as a public interest when a contract is affected by illegality.[187]

In *Patel v Mirza*, the Supreme Court clarified the illegality rule according to the following criteria: (1) to consider the underlying purpose of the prohibition which has been transgressed and whether that purpose will be enhanced by denial of the claim;[188] (2) to consider any other relevant public policy on which the denial of the claim may have an impact; and (3) to consider whether denial of the claim would be a proportionate response to the illegality, bearing in mind that punishment is a matter for the criminal courts.[189] An instructive case is *Jivraj v Hashwani*, where the Supreme Court reversed the decision held by the Court of Appeal that a provision in an agreement that arbitrators were to be appointed from a particular ethnic community was void.[190] Specifically, the Supreme Court questioned whether a particular religion or

[183] J Atkinson, 'Automated management, digital discrimination, and the Equality Act 2010' (2020) 159 *Employment Law Bulletin* 3, 4–5.

[184] The Equality Act 2010 (Amendment) Regulations 2023, www.legislation.gov.uk/uksi/2023/1425/contents/made.

[185] See www.legislation.gov.uk/ukpga/2010/15/section/142. EA 2010, Pt 10 deals with discriminatory provisions of contracts and other agreements. Terms which provide for conduct prohibited by the Act are unenforceable, as are agreements to exclude any provision of the Act. In relation to disability, there is a provision which makes the terms of certain 'non-contractual' agreements unenforceable, specifically those relating to the provision of employment services and group insurance arrangements.

[186] A Burrows, 'A New Dawn for the Law of Illegality' Oxford Legal Studies Research Paper No 42/2017 (2017), ssrn.com/abstract=2979425; A Burrows, 'Illegality after Patel v Mirza' (2017) 70 *Current Legal Problems* 55.

[187] A Burrows, 'Illegality as a Defence in Contract' Oxford Legal Studies Research Paper No 15/2016 (2016), ssrn.com/abstract=2758797.

[188] The first criterion includes the prevention under the EA 2010 of direct and indirect discrimination on the basis of protected characteristics.

[189] [2016] UKSC 42 [120].

[190] [2011] UKSC 40, [2011] 1 WLR 1872.

belief was a legitimate and justified requirement of an occupation, concluding that a stipulation that an arbitrator be of a given religion could be relevant, given the breadth of the discretion given to the parties and the arbitrator to structure the arbitration process.[191] As noted, 'even if the discrimination is unintentional, it may well be that the policy of not allowing the legal process to be used in a way that undermines its integrity would lead a court to refuse to enforce such an agreement'.[192] The approach used by the courts is that the application of the illegality defence can be justified on the basis of the public policy concerns to protect the integrity of the legal system that underlie the defence.

The explanatory notes of the EA 2010 state that 'a person who would have been disadvantaged by any such term will still be able to rely on it so as to obtain any benefit to which it entitles him'.[193] For example, an agreement that contains a term that implies a requirement that the contractual party should only negotiate with people of certain ethnicities, which is unlawful direct discrimination related to race, could not be enforced by the counterparty. If the party complied with the discriminatory term, a person discriminated against under it could make a claim against the party for unlawful discrimination under other provisions in the Act.

The available remedies include damages, an injunction, quashing orders, a declaration of rights and responsibilities, interests on damages and costs. The Act provides a remedy for the person to whom the causing, instruction or inducement is addressed; and the person who is subjected to the discrimination, harassment or victimisation if it is carried out provided that they experience a detriment as a result. The EA 2010 also provides that compensation for discrimination may include injury to feelings, and takes into consideration the vulnerability of the claimant, the degree of distress, the seriousness of the treatment and how long it persisted as well as the manner in which the defendant dealt with the complaint.[194]

The body responsible for enforcing the EA 2010 is the Commission for Equality and Human Rights (EHRC) which applies equality law to financial services providers, including banks, insurance companies, building societies, credit card companies, loan companies, hire purchase companies and credit unions.[195] The EHRC makes clear that all relevant activities carried out by 'service providers', including public sector financial service providers, are subject to the EA 2010.[196] The EHRC raised concerns about the disparity of access to digital service providers for older and disabled people, who find difficulties operating through electronic devices being a category, particularly at risk of

[191] [2016] UKSC 42 [59]–[61].
[192] Stone and Devenney (n 83) 430.
[193] See www.legislation.gov.uk/ukpga/2010/15/notes/division/3/10/1.
[194] Awards for injury to feelings under Pt 3 of the Act are typically lower than under Pt 5 as a result of the relationship that exists with one's employer as opposed to a service provider.
[195] See www.equalityhumanrights.com/guidance/business/guidance-businesses/equality-law-banks-and-other-financial-services-providers?return-url=https%3A%2F%2Fwww.equalityhumanrights.com%2Fsearch%3Fkeys%3Dpublic%2Bsector%2Bfinancial%2Bservice%2Bproviders%2B%26f%255B0%255D%3Dcontent_type%253Aguidance_article.
[196] Chs 3 and 11 ('Services and Public Functions') of the Code of Practice (2011), www.equalityhumanrights.com/equality/equality-act-2010/codes-practice/services-public-functions-and-associations-code-0#document-download.

digital exclusion.[197] The Services, Public Functions and Associations Statutory Code of Practice (Equality Act 2010 Code of Practice)[198] provides a catalogue of legal obligations which guide the courts and tribunals as evidence in legal proceedings brought under the Act.

The Report recommended that the use of AI technologies does not result in undesirable outcomes against groups with protected characteristics.[199] The Code of Practice refers to 'website services' provided by 'information society service providers' when delivering information or entertainment to the public, although a specific provision on digital financial service providers is missing in the formulation of the Act.[200] This may pose challenges for the EHRC because the EA 2010 does not provide specific regulatory protections which address discriminatory practices in algorithmic decision-making processes.[201] A broader interpretation of service providers in EA 2010, section 29 seems to include online platforms and 'online' service providers, capturing de facto most companies operating in the 'platform economy' – from e-commerce websites and user-generated content-sharing platforms to social media companies.[202]

8.3.2. Consumer Vulnerability in the UK Digital Markets, Competition and Consumers Act 2024

The UK's Digital Markets, Competition and Consumers Act 2024 (DMCCA 2024)[203] aims to address economies of scale and the increasing market power of digital platforms, which may lead to biased prices and poor outcomes for consumers. The DMCCA 2024 responds to the need to reduce anticompetitive practices in digital markets as well as prohibit harmful behaviour of big tech companies. The legislation gives extensive statutory duties to the Competition and Markets Authority to strengthen enforcement mechanisms and consumer protection law.[204] One of the key concerns is the outcomes that consumers in vulnerable circumstances receive, and whether they are as good as the outcomes of other consumers. Undesirable outcomes are designed to increase the exclusion of minority groups. The legislation identifies characteristics of vulnerability, such as age, physical or mental health and credulity,

[197] EHRC, 'Strategic plan 2022–25', 15, www.equalityhumanrights.com/sites/default/files/2022/about-us-strategic-plan-2022-2025.pdf.

[198] See 'Equality Act 2010 Statutory Code of Practice Services, public functions and associations' (2011) www.equalityhumanrights.com/sites/default/files/servicescode_0.pdf. The Code covers discrimination in services and public functions as set out in EA 2010, Pt 3and discrimination by associations. It explains the steps that service providers should take to ensure that they do not discriminate against service users.

[199] ibid 16.

[200] ibid ch 3, 152–53. See also EHRC, 'Code of practice for services, public functions and associations: consultation 2025', www.equalityhumanrights.com/equality/equality-act-2010/codes-practice/code-practice-services-public-functions-and-associations.

[201] Centre for Data Ethics and Innovation, 'Review into bias in algorithmic decision-making' (November 2020) 109.

[202] Meers (n 167) 644–45.

[203] See www.legislation.gov.uk/ukpga/2024/13/contents/enacted.

[204] S Whitfield, I Hodgskiss and A Westley, 'The UK's new competition regime for digital markets: to remedy a gap in the CMA's toolkit' (2023) 22 *Competition Law Journal* 63, 64.

although it is not very clear whether the concept of 'mental health' replaces the concept of 'mental infirmity' used in the UCPD, which introduces a degree of flexibility when it comes to mental health conditions.

The DMCCA 2024 sets out some of the circumstances when a group of consumers may be vulnerable to commercial practices, or products relating to commercial practices. For example, aggressive practices focus on the exploitation of bargaining power in the consumer relationship which significantly limits the consumer's ability to make an informed decision.[205] However, the legislation does not clarify whether the vulnerability results from manipulative or unfair practices of the digital platforms.[206] Specifically, the Act does not mention digital vulnerability as a result of cognitive impairment (eg, mental health), which may exploit disadvantaged conditions of unserved or underserved individuals. The Explanatory Guidance does not make clear if the concept of 'mental health' replaces the category of 'mental infirmity'; further, it is not clear how mental health can apply as a legal standard for commercial practices.

The DMCCA 2024 expands the concept of consumer vulnerability to economic disadvantage aspects, which should reflect a detrimental relationship rather than personal characteristics. For example, the legislation includes external causes of vulnerability relevant for detriment such as going through a divorce or losing a job. Further, the Act seems to be removing the vulnerable consumer test that only applies where the practice is likely to distort the economic behaviour of the vulnerable group.[207] Instead, it adopts a new vulnerable test where financial circumstances can be taken into account as a factor in vulnerability. Therefore, the DMCCA 2024 develops the category of protected characteristics including mental health and 'circumstances they are in' as causes of vulnerability which may lead to a reclassification of those protected attributes.

8.4. The FCA's Consumer Duty Rule

The FCA regulatory principles adopted a flexible approach to consumer protection for vulnerable groups harmed by algorithmic systems.[208] The FCA introduced a consumer duty rule which consists of an outcomes-based regime underpinned by cross-cutting rules and guidance.[209] The duty established an obligation for a firm to act with the target to deliver good outcomes for retail customers (Principle 12 of the FCA's Principles for Businesses).[210] The consumer duty requires firms to evaluate

[205] DMCCA, 2024 s 228.

[206] DMCCA 2024, s 247. See P Cartwright, 'The Vulnerable Consumer and The Digitals Markets, Competition and Consumers Bill in the UK' (2023) 12 *Journal of European Consumer and Market Law* 173, 174–75.

[207] P Cartwright, 'Understanding and Protecting Vulnerable Financial Consumers' (2015) 38 *Journal of Consumer Policy* 119, 127–28.

[208] BoE, PRA and FCA, 'Artificial Intelligence and Machine Learning' Discussion Paper no 5 (2022), www.bankofengland.co.uk/prudential-regulation/publication/2022/october/artificial-intelligence.

[209] See www.fca.org.uk/firms/consumer-duty.

[210] Principle 12 replaced Principle 6 of the FCA's Principles for Businesses, which states: 'A firm must pay due regard to the interests of its customers and treat them fairly'. See www.handbook.fca.org.uk/handbook/PRIN.pdf.

their products, services and processes with a view to protecting retail customers in business relationships. Its purpose is to set higher expectations for the standard of care that firms afford to customers to ensure they meet the needs of vulnerable individuals.[211]

The FCA defines a vulnerable consumer as 'someone who, due to their personal circumstances, is especially susceptible to detriment, particularly when a firm is not acting with appropriate levels of care'.[212] Identifiable vulnerable 'groups' based on personal attributes are elderly consumers, who may experience difficulties remaining connected with financial services, customers with physical or mental health disabilities, and disadvantaged individuals exposed to unfair treatment in banking and financial services (eg, under-representation of women).[213] Further, the FCA considers causes of vulnerability economic factors such as life events (eg, job loss, divorce, over-indebtedness and bereavement) which can deteriorate the conditions of individuals when interacting with financial services.[214]

The duty rule makes explicit reference to the need for firms to provide an additional level of care to ensure they meet the needs of vulnerable customers. It applies to a firm's retail market business and covers the regulated activities of a firm in a distribution chain which involves a retail customer. Specifically, the FCA expects retail customers with characteristics of vulnerability to benefit from the overall improvements in outcomes as the consumer duty can offer a solution to discriminatory practices perpetuated in the use of algorithmic decision-making in financial services. For example, the consumer duty rules can pose a remedy against undesirable lending practices in the credit markets, and deter predatory lenders from imposing oppressive terms in credit arrangements.

The FCA's rule can establish an additional duty for firms not to discriminate against customers' profiles in the use of algorithmic systems such as automated credit-scoring; this duty can translate into a mandatory obligation for financial providers to avoid circumstances of vulnerability exploited in harmful predatory business behaviour. The consumer duty makes firms responsible for addressing biases or practices that impede consumers from achieving good outcomes (financial services providers need to ensure that the algorithmic systems employed to support their credit and pricing decisions do not lead to discriminatory outcomes). In parallel, firms need to identify situations where groups of individuals with protected characteristics may be exposed to disadvantaged conditions. Firms should be able to detect any outcomes which represent a potentially unfair or unequal treatment against retail consumers and which are not aligned with their obligations under the EA 2010. As stated, the duty rule requires firms to provide

[211] See www.fca.org.uk/firms/consumer-duty.

[212] FCA, 'Consumer Vulnerability' Occasional Paper No 8 (February 2015) 20, https://www.fca.org.uk/publication/occasional-papers/occasional-paper-8.pdf.

[213] FCA, 'Guidance for firms on the fair treatment of vulnerable customers' FG21/1 Finalised guidance (February 2021) 11–12, www.fca.org.uk/publication/finalised-guidance/fg21-1.pdf.

[214] According to the FCA (n 212), specific risk factors which contribute to identifying vulnerable groups are long-term/significant illness; carers; older people (over 65); low basic skills (people who struggle with literacy and/or numeracy, with or without a formally diagnosed learning difficulty; job loss/unemployment; bereavement).

an additional layer of protection in vulnerable circumstances which raises the standard of care for all consumers.[215]

The FCA provides that

> while firms should empower customers to make choices for themselves, customers remain ultimately responsible for their decisions and actions. Firms must nevertheless understand and take account of behavioural biases, and the impact characteristics of vulnerability can have on consumer needs and decisions.[216]

However, it is not clear if the consumer duty would reduce unfair and detrimental practices (eg, exploitation of consumers with protected characteristics)[217] in digital financial transactions. Fair treatment of customers is a prominent concern in the employment of digital technologies, which prompts questions about oversight and transparency.[218] The FCA recognised the need to address unfair practices in automated decision-making processes through binding measures with particular attention to the fair treatment of vulnerable customers.[219] The 'treating customers fairly' approach deals with potential harm arising from algorithmic systems, although the main innovations seem to lie in the characteristics of vulnerabilities which comprise resilience and capability.[220]

The consumer duty makes explicit reference to vulnerable consumers, but the FCA leaves firms large discretion to assess circumstances of vulnerability based on the protected characteristics regulated in the EA 2010.[221] It also requires firms 'to deliver good outcomes for retail clients', which should align with the reasonable expectations of customers. Neither the 'consumer duty' nor the 'treating customers fairly policy' mitigates conditions of vulnerability exacerbated by digital technologies. To address this problem, the duty rule requires firms to monitor the results of automated systems that customers receive and address their potential harm to vulnerable users. However, the successful implementation of this outcomes-based approach mostly depends on a close collaboration with supervisory authorities that should comply with the risk-based approach to monitoring algorithmic processing.[222]

[215] See www.fca.org.uk/publications/good-and-poor-practice/consumer-duty-implementation-good-practice-and-areas-improvement.

[216] FCA, 'A new Consumer Duty. Feedback to CP21/36 and final rules' Policy Statement PS22/9 (July 2022) 40, www.fca.org.uk/publication/policy/ps22-9.pdf. See also FCA, 'Final non-Handbook Guidance for firms on the Consumer Duty' FG22/5 (July 2022) 35, www.fca.org.uk/publication/finalised-guidance/fg22-5.pdf. It is pointed out that 'where a firm is planning to alter or withdraw a product or service, they should consider whether it could lead to foreseeable harm for their customers or a specific group of customers (such as customers with characteristics of vulnerability) and take steps to mitigate the impact of the potential harm'.

[217] S Brown, 'Un-boxing vulnerability in protection of the credit consumer' (2019) 7 *Journal of Business Law* 511, 524–25.

[218] T Zarsky, 'The Trouble with Algorithmic Decisions: An Analytic Road Map to Examine Efficiency and Fairness in Automated and Opaque Decision Making' (2016) 41 *Science, Technology, & Human Values* 118, 122–23.

[219] FCA, 'Guidance for firms on the fair treatment of vulnerable customers' (February 2021), www.fca.org.uk/publication/finalised-guidance/fg21-1.pdf.

[220] See www.fca.org.uk/firms/fair-treatment-customers.

[221] FCA, 'Consumer Duty: The next steps' (6 December 2023), webinars.fca.org.uk/consumer-duty-the-next-steps/room.

[222] UK Government, 'Establishing a pro-innovation approach to regulating AI' Policy Paper (2022), www.gov.uk/government/publications/establishing-a-pro-innovation-approach-to-regulating-ai/establishing-a-pro-innovation-approach-to-regulating-ai-policy-statement.

8.5. Concluding Remarks

The rapid development of digital financial technologies has raised issues and new legal questions that are unlikely to be resolved within existing laws, and the unconscionable bargain doctrine seems unlikely to be of much assistance. The employment of automated systems in commercial transactions poses challenges for regulators and public authorities; the existing approach of the law is inadequate to address the 'disruption' of unfair commercial practices by digital traders in their dealings with consumers. This chapter has examined consumer vulnerability in light of the increasing use of algorithmic decision-making processes in financial services, suggesting that the FCA's consumer duty can offer a response to this problem.

The broad adoption of algorithmic applications exacerbates conditions of disadvantage with respect to the sophisticated AI algorithms embedded in automated applications.[223] The algorithmic codes formulate a series of statements which profile the behaviour and routine habits of consumers. However, algorithms may contain opaque parameters which are apt to amplify undesirable decisions against disadvantaged customers. Despite the innovative and lauding promises of digital technologies, the employment of algorithmic systems in financial services raises concerns for unexpected outcomes which are detrimental for consumer protection.

AI innovations expedite transactions, reduce costs and improve the quality of products through automated platforms, but customers are exposed to algorithmic harms because of the technical complexity inherent in the algorithmic processes. Consumers are often targeted by harmful AI innovations which collect individuals' personal data (for example, from websites) without express consent, and disclose it to the public. Reliance on AI algorithms turns to dependence, questioning how the regulatory framework should respond to ensure fairness and accuracy of outputs. Discriminatory algorithmic models lead to disruptive decisions for vulnerable customers; the law should prevent harmful automated processes by implementing the FCA's 'consumer duty', which can be a deterrent to biased algorithmic decision-making in financial services. It is an innovative regulatory tool to monitor the performance of firms in reducing unintended outcomes that cause harm and risks to vulnerable consumers.

The ongoing debate about the reform of the EA 2010 highlights the lack of adequate protection to address inequality and unfairness in biased algorithms. The FCA regulatory principles and the consumer duty rule can provide a solution to the exploitation of protected attributes in the use of algorithmic decision-making systems. The persuasive role of fintech platforms tends to create asymmetry of relationships between the transactional parties which exploit positions of disadvantage.[224] Therefore, the use of automated decision-making processes has determined a diminishing of resilience assets (eg, individual autonomy and independence) while, at the same time, inflating

[223] N Helberger et al, 'Choice Architectures in the Digital Economy: Towards a New Understanding of Digital Vulnerability' (2022) 45 *Journal of Consumer Policy* 175, 176.

[224] C Ondersma, 'A Human Rights Approach to Consumer Credit' (2015) 90 *Tulane Law Review* 417–18.

circumstances of financial vulnerability.[225] On this view, AI algorithms show limitations in reducing risks of harm deriving from the impact of discriminatory outcomes in automated systems. Algorithmic procedures create an imbalance of positions between digital platforms and users resulting in an unconscionable bargaining power against vulnerable individuals, which reflects the conditions of online consumers: 'What are you hiding? Is it this is what you see, but if that's all you see, well then you don't see me, you can't see me.'[226]

[225] MM Naeser Seldal and EK Nyhus, 'Financial Vulnerability, Financial Literacy, and the Use of Digital Payment Technologies' (2022) 45 *Journal of Consumer Policy* 281, 300.
[226] I Holland, *The Man without a Face* (JP Lippincott, 1972) 136.

9

Cryptocurrencies and Consumer Protection: *Caveat Emptor*

HENRY HILLMAN AND THOMAS BURGESS

9.1. Introduction

Cryptocurrencies have attracted a wide range of interest; inevitably, that has included criminals seeking to benefit from the new technology and extract money from victims. The functioning of cryptocurrencies is still poorly understood across the general population,[1] and the world of cryptocurrencies uses novel terminology, which at times is simply alternative terminology to the world of traditional finance.[2] The speed, novelty and limited regulation of cryptocurrencies[3] leaves United Kingdom (UK)-based consumers particularly vulnerable to fraud. This chapter will assess the advantages and disadvantages for consumers buying cryptocurrencies before assessing common frauds. It then moves on to explore recent regulatory reform, as well as the role of 'good Samaritans', which are individuals or groups within the crypto community who attempt to protect or educate consumers in the absence of formal safeguards. Ultimately, the chapter argues that despite innovation in financial technology, consumers remain poorly protected and increasingly exposed to harm from fraudsters operating both within and around the cryptocurrency space. Therefore, despite the huge progress in consumer protection in the past half a century, buyers of cryptocurrencies are to follow the age-old principle of *caveat emptor*; let the buyer beware. This raises broader concerns about how rapid technological innovation can create new forms of consumer harm in the absence of adequate oversight or protective infrastructure.

[1] T Johnson, '5 Common Misconceptions Regarding Cryptocurrency' techspective (28 March 2025), techspective.net/2025/03/28/5-common-misconceptions-regarding-cryptocurrency; 'The 5 Biggest Misconceptions About Crypto' How-To-Geek (9 May 2022), www.howtogeek.com/799924/the-5-biggest-misconceptions-about-crypto.

[2] Cointree, 'A-Z of Cryptocurrency Terminology & Vocabulary', www.howtogeek.com/799924/the-5-biggest-misconceptions-about-crypto; M Martin, 'Crypto Glossary: Terms and Definitions for Beginners' tastycrypto (5 September 2024), www.tastycrypto.com/basics/crypto-glossary.

[3] FCA, 'FCA research reveals increase in cryptoasset ownership' (17 June 2021), www.fca.org.uk/news/press-releases/fca-research-reveals-increase-cryptoasset-ownership.

9.2. Identifying Cryptocurrencies

The term 'cryptocurrency' refers to a decentralised virtual currency which operates based on a combination of cryptography and blockchain technology.[4] A blockchain is a distributed digital ledger that records transactions across a network in a transparent and tamper-resistant manner.[5] Decentralisation allows cryptocurrencies to function differently to fiat currency systems where financial institutions keep track of deposits into customers' accounts and in turn withdrawals from their accounts, and central banks manage the wider monetary system. Cryptocurrencies are typically launched by their developers in proposals known as white papers, which detail the technical and conceptual foundations of a cryptocurrency project, such as the purpose of the cryptocurrency, the technology behind it, and how it aims to solve specific problems.[6] However, this is not a mandatory requirement. After the release of a white paper, if enough of a community is founded, the ongoing development of the software is commonly developed via open-source edits proposed by users and adopted based on community acceptance. Since the emergence of the first widely known cryptocurrency,[7] Bitcoin, in 2008,[8] the sector has developed rapidly, to include nearly 10,000 cryptocurrencies.[9] Competing cryptocurrencies utilise blockchain and cryptographic technology in varying ways, offering features such as faster transaction speeds or enhanced privacy. These differences can significantly influence consumer choices. For example, a consumer may prioritise speed for everyday transactions, while another may seek out privacy-focused coins to limit the traceability of their financial activity.

Cryptocurrencies utilise cryptographic techniques to conceal the sender and receiver's identities. Southall and Taylor[10] trace public-key cryptography, used by Bitcoin and many other currencies, back to proposals made by Chaum in the early 1980s. Chaum proposed sending private messages with a dual key system;[11] messages were encrypted and sent using a public key, the message could only be unencrypted using a private key. He later suggested this technique could enable anonymous digital payments,[12] a concept that, while enhancing user privacy, also creates challenges for consumer protection, such as the difficulty of tracing fraudulent transactions or recovering lost funds.

Blockchain, or distributed ledger technology, in conjunction with cryptographic messaging, facilitates the existence of cryptocurrencies. A blockchain is an immutable

[4] T. Burgess, 'A multi-jurisdictional perspective: To what extent can cryptocurrency be regulated? And if so, who should regulate cryptocurrency?' (2024) *Journal of Economic Criminology* 5.

[5] ibid.

[6] Whitebit, 'What is a White Paper in Crypto, and Why is it Important?' Whitebit Blog (28 November 2023), blog.whitebit.com/en/what-is-a-white-paper-in-crypto.

[7] Though widely considered the first cryptocurrency, the original paper proposing Bitcoin references previous proposals for web-based money such as: W Dai, 'b-money' (1998), www.weidai.com/bmoney.txt.

[8] S Nakamoto, 'Bitcoin: A Peer-to-Peer Electronic Cash System' (31 October 2008), www.nakamotoinstitute.org/static/docs/bitcoin.pdf.

[9] 9,824 cryptocurrencies are listed on prominent price tracking site CoinMarketCap: 'All Cryptocurrencies', www.coinmarketcap.com/all/views/all.

[10] E Southall and M Taylor, 'Bitcoins' (2013) 19 *Computer and Telecommunications Law Review* 177, 177.

[11] D Chaum, 'Untraceable Electronic Mail, Return Addresses and Digital Pseudonyms' (1981) 24 *Communications of the ACM* 84.

[12] D Chaum, 'Blind Signatures for Untraceable Payments' in D Chaum. RL Rivest and AT Sherman (ed), *Advances in Cryptology*, Session III (Springer US, 1982) 199–203.

ledger formed into a series of connected entries known as blocks. Each block updates the ledger with the latest transactions in the network and a cryptocurrency's blockchain is usually publicly available.[13] Härdle et al observe that blockchains may vary in implementation, but share common features, most notably that the structure is distributed rather than centralised.[14] While it is true that the technology surrounding cryptocurrencies can increase the security of the user, this requires a significant level of understanding on behalf of the user. Where the user has a lesser understanding, the risk of fraud is increased as victims may not understand the thing that they believe they are purchasing.

A user requires a wallet to transact with cryptocurrency. Three broad categories of wallet can be identified: hardware, software and custodian wallets.[15] A user is free to switch between the types of wallets, providing they have the requisite hardware or software for their new wallet. A cryptocurrency wallet may also be described as 'hot' or 'cold', which refers to whether they can be disconnected from the internet. 'Cold' storage refers to storing cryptocurrency offline.[16] Hardware wallets are physical devices,[17] which are used to store a user's private key. As Houy et al note, hardware wallets are the only wallets truly able to be called 'cold' in that a user can store their cryptocurrency offline.[18] Software wallets are applications that do not require a separate dedicated physical device; they can be installed on a compatible device, such as a computer or smartphone. While software wallets provide similar functionality to hardware wallets, they are less secure as the device they are installed on is usually connected to the internet; they are therefore categorised as 'hot' wallets.[19] Custodian wallets are the least technically involved option for a user to hold, send and receive cryptocurrencies. A custodian wallet operates in a similar fashion to a bank account in that transactions and security are facilitated by the wallet provider. Custodian wallets do not require the user to acquire any specific hardware and they can be accessed via any device which can connect to and browse the internet. As custodian wallets are software wallets, and are hosted by service providers, they are not compatible with offline storage and are considered 'hot' wallets. Custodian wallets are the only wallets that face regulation in the over-200 jurisdictions that have committed to the Financial Action Task Force's (FATF) Recommendations.[20] The FATF, an international body dedicated to combating money laundering and terrorist financing, sets global guidelines for regulating virtual asset activities, primarily through the designation of virtual asset service providers (VASPs). These providers include exchanges and custodial wallet services, which must comply

[13] As demonstrated by: Blockchain, 'Block Explorer: Bitcoin' www.blockchain.com/explorer; 'Block Explorer: Ethereum' www.blockchain.com/explorer?currency=ETH; and 'Block Explorer: Bitcoin Cash' www.blockchain.com/explorer?currency=BCH Blockchain.

[14] WK Härdle, HR Campbell and RCG Reule, 'Understanding Cryptocurrencies' (2020) 18 *Journal of Financial Econometrics* 181, 183.

[15] S Houy, P Schmid and A Bartel, 'Security Aspects of Cryptocurrency Wallets – A Systematic Literature Review' (2024) 56 *ACM Computing Surveys* Article 4, 4:5.

[16] ibid.

[17] See examples: BitBox, 'BitBox02', www.bitbox.swiss/bitbox02; Coldcard, 'Coldcard Mk4', www.coldcard.com; and Trezor, 'Compare Trezor Hardware Wallets', www.trezor.io/compare.

[18] Houy, Schmid and Bartel (n 15) 4:4.

[19] ibid.

[20] Financial Action Task Force, 'Countries', www.fatf-gafi.org/en/countries.html.

with anti-money laundering (AML) and counter-terrorist financing (CTF) obligations, such as customer due diligence and transaction monitoring.

However, this regulatory framework focuses on service providers rather than individual users. Therefore, while custodian wallet providers are required to implement stringent compliance measures, end-users holding cryptocurrencies in such wallets do not face direct regulatory obligations. This regulatory gap means that although service providers operate under supervision designed to reduce illicit activity, consumers themselves remain largely unregulated and therefore continue to face significant risks, including exposure to fraud and financial loss without the safety net of direct consumer protection measures.

9.3. Cryptocurrency Market and Geography

Cryptocurrencies are not difficult to produce. Many operate using very similar codes and processes; the well-known cryptocurrency Dogecoin was created as a joke to demonstrate that anyone can make a cryptocurrency. Lacking formality and existing within internet culture, a significant portion of the cryptocurrency space is tied to humour and meme culture, as evidenced by the popularity of Dogecoin, which takes its name from the Doge meme.[21] Identifying the number of cryptocurrencies in existence is difficult as many are created and lie dormant due to lack of adoption; just over 10,000 were estimated to exist in 2024,[22] but that estimate will be inaccurate by the time of publication. Each cryptocurrency highlights how it is different from competitors, typically making claims regarding their transaction speeds, such as Ripple,[23] or differentiating themselves based on the way in which their blockchain operates, such as Ether, which runs on the Ethereum blockchain.[24]

The Ethereum blockchain is also used by cryptocurrencies which are described as 'tokens'; these are cryptocurrencies which do not have their own proprietary blockchains, but operate on a pre-existing blockchain, most commonly Ethereum. Ethereum blockchain functions differently to that of Bitcoin as it allows users to run what it calls 'smart contracts', which are simple programs based on 'if = then =' logic. Blockchain smart contracts allowed for the development of non-fungible tokens (NFTs), as the ownership of these tokens can be tracked via the Ethereum blockchain.[25] NFTs and other rapidly created digital tokens can expose consumers to significant fraud risks. These assets are often marketed with hype but little transparency, leading uninformed buyers to believe they are purchasing something with stable or intrinsic value, such as ownership of digital art or exclusive rights, when in fact they are acquiring nothing more than a speculative or even worthless token. The lack of clear regulation, coupled

[21] A debate on the topic of memes would be getting away from the subject of this text; Doge generally refers to humours text in broken English, mimicking the supposed thoughts of a dog, accompanying an image of a Shiba Inu dog.

[22] Statista, 'Number of cryptocurrencies worldwide', www.statista.com/statistics/863917/number-crypto-coins-tokens.

[23] Ripple, 'XRP', www.ripple.com/xrp.

[24] Ethereum.org, 'What is Ethereum' (updated 16 April 2025), www.ethereum.org/en/what-is-ethereum.

[25] Ethereum.org, 'Non-Fungible Tokens (NFT)' (updated 16 April 2025), www.ethereum.org/en/nft.

with complex or misleading language used in promotions, leaves consumers vulnerable to misrepresentation, inflated pricing, and outright scams.

Being native to the internet, cryptocurrencies permeate physical borders, which makes determining geographical distribution difficult. Estimates based on the location of the recipients of transactions place North America as the most popular region for cryptocurrency, with the UK included in Central, Northern and Western Europe as the third most common area for transactions.[26] Within Europe, the UK receives significantly more cryptocurrency than any other country,[27] and globally the UK receives the third most cryptocurrency, behind the United States (US) and India.[28] The level of activity within the UK alongside the novel complexities of cryptocurrencies justifies an examination of the vulnerability of UK consumers.

Bitcoin, and other cryptocurrencies, are exchanged globally and are referred to in similar terms as money, such as the term 'currency' within cryptocurrency, the term 'cash' in Bitcoin Cash, and the symbol used in Bitcoin's logo being akin to a monetary symbol. Cryptocurrencies are also exchanged for traditional fiat currencies, at times for significant sums, most notably Bitcoin, which has a record of $106,000 per bitcoin in December 2024.[29] This widespread use of financial language and the high market value of cryptocurrencies contribute to the perception of legitimacy, yet this masks the uncertain and often elusive status of the consumer within the crypto ecosystem.

9.4. The Elusive Consumer

Consumers are poorly defined in English law, typically identified through characteristics they do *not* possess. The Consumer Rights Act 2015 (CRA 2015) defines a consumer as 'any natural person acting for purposes outside his trade, business or profession'.[30] An individual engaging with cryptocurrencies will generally be considered a consumer if they are acting for personal purposes, rather than as part of a business activity, regardless of their level of knowledge, experience or financial resources. This position was upheld in *Payward Inc v Chechetkin*[31] and *Ang v Reliantco Investments Ltd*,[32] where the courts confirmed that wealth or sophistication does not negate consumer status; the decisive factor is whether the individual is acting outside the scope of a professional or commercial activity. Furthermore, consumer status is also significant in determining jurisdiction. Both *Payward* and *Ang* reaffirmed that, under UK and EU rules, where a party qualifies as a consumer, jurisdiction will typically lie with the courts of the consumer's domicile.

[26] Chainalysis, 'The 2023 Geography of Cryptocurrency Report' (October 2023), www.chainalysis.com/wp-content/uploads/2024/06/the-2023-geography-of-cryptocurrency-report-release.pdf.

[27] ibid 30.

[28] ibid 10 (USA) and 50 (India).

[29] Statista, 'Bitcoin (BTC) price per day' (27 August 2024), www.statista.com/statistics/326707/bitcoin-price-index.

[30] CRA 2015, s 2(3).

[31] [2023] EWHC 1780 (Comm).

[32] [2019] EWHC 879 (Comm).

While it is relatively clear who will be a consumer user of cryptocurrencies, identifying and protecting them in a landscape littered with privacy and anonymity is challenging. Cryptocurrency proponents commonly extol the freedom and privacy that cryptocurrencies provide,[33] eschewing traditional finance and embracing a more counterculture position. Bitcoin developed in the wake of the sub-prime mortgage crisis and ensuing credit-crunch.[34] Those seeking to survey and better understand cryptocurrency consumers have reported difficulties in obtaining and retaining participants in their studies.[35] The FCA noted that participants are difficult to identify.[36] Reasons cited were the private nature of cryptocurrency trading, and that individuals were uncomfortable discussing finances. This was especially so where they had made a loss, leading to a notable number of dropouts.[37] The anonymity and decentralisation inherent in cryptocurrency systems make it difficult to identify or reach individual consumers. Due to this limited transparency, it becomes harder for regulators, online platforms and even people who are trying to help to detect scams early, to notify users, offer refunds or otherwise act before the fraud is perpetrated.

9.5. Common Traits in Cryptocurrency Consumers

The FCA determined that there are three factors that may be fuelling cryptocurrency investment: a weakened trust in mainstream media; looking for the next shortcut; and acting on recommendations.[38] The report found trust in the media to be a contributing factor to cryptocurrency investment, citing the Edelman Trust that only 32 per cent of the population trust the media, with the figure dropping to 23 per cent in young people.[39] Ofcom noted increasing reliance on alternative sources for news in 2017, with 47 per cent of adults getting news mainly from social media posts.[40] The figure is more profound in 16–24-year-olds where 69 per cent of respondents said they got their news mostly from social media.[41] Reliance on non-traditional news sources links to the third factor identified by the Revealing Reality report: acting on recommendations.

[33] 'Ethics of Cryptocurrency: A Sword of Freedom or Double-Edged Risk?' Analytics Insight, White Paper (13 Feb 2025), www.analyticsinsight.net/white-papers/ethics-of-cryptocurrency-a-sword-of-freedom-or-double-edged-risk; T Zhang, 'Privacy Evaluation of Blockchain Based Privacy Cryptocurrencies: A Comparative Analysis of Dash, Monero, Verge, Zcash, and Grin' (2023) 8 *IEEE Transactions on Sustainable Computing* 574.

[34] H Song Shin, 'BIS Speech: The great crypto crisis is upon us' (16 December 2022), www.bis.org/speeches/sp221216.htm.

[35] YouGov, 'Cryptoassets consumer research 2024 (Wave 5) On behalf of the Financial Conduct Authority' (Version 2, March 2025), www.fca.org.uk/publication/research-notes/cryptoasset-consumer-research-2024-wave-5.pdf.

[36] Revealing Reality, on behalf of the FCA, 'How and Why Consumers Buy Cryptocurrencies' (March 2019), www.revealingreality.co.uk/wp-content/uploads/2019/04/RR_FCA-cryptoassets.pdf.

[37] ibid 7.

[38] ibid 47.

[39] Edelman, '2018 Edelman Trust Barometer' (2018), www.edelman.co.uk/research/edelman-trust-barometer-2018-uk-findings.

[40] Ofcom, 'The Changing World of News: Qualitative Research' (2018), www.ofcom.org.uk/siteassets/resources/documents/research-and-data/tv-radio-and-on-demand-research/tv-research/news/news-consumption-2018/the-changing-world-of-news.pdf?v=323322.

[41] ibid.

Revealing Reality found that 'respondents' engagement with cryptoassets was often prompted by the advice of surprisingly few but inordinately influential recommendations'.[42] Relying on a single influential source could easily expose individuals to biased opinions and leave them vulnerable to fraud.

Further fraud risks are present in common traits of cryptocurrency consumers that they are seeking to 'get rich quick' and 'get ahead'.[43] Acting with haste is known to aid fraudsters, as individuals will be too focused on the gains and not consider the risks.[44] This is compounded by respondents hoping to use cryptocurrencies to 'make money for minimal effort, seeking what they saw as the "smart" way or the "shortcut"'.[45] A lack of trust in mainstream media and a desire to get rich quickly is a dangerous mix as it leaves individuals relying on the advice of unverifiable sources to make significant financial investments.[46]

The FCA has followed up on the initial research in four of the past five years, observing increases in the general public's awareness of cryptocurrencies year-on-year. In 2024, it was stated that 93 per cent of adults were aware of cryptocurrencies, which was an increase from 91 per cent in 2022.[47] The FCA's research also found approximately 12 per cent of UK adults, equating to around seven million individuals, own cryptoassets, an increase from four per cent in 2021.[48] Of those that had bought cryptocurrencies, 20 per cent of cryptoasset users stated that being 'influenced by friends and family' was the main reason for purchase, six per cent of cryptoasset users reported using long-term savings to invest, while 14 per cent utilised credit cards or overdrafts.[49] However, only 58 per cent of cryptoasset users believe they have a good understanding of how cryptoassets and the underlying technology work, an increase from 47 per cent in 2022.[50] The FCA's research further reveals that 27 per cent of cryptoasset users indicated they would be more likely to invest if the market were regulated, with 25 per cent expressing a preference for regulation that includes financial protection in the event of losses.[51] This underscores the critical role of regulatory frameworks in fostering consumer confidence and participation in the cryptoasset market.

Cryptocurrencies can be challenging, or even off-putting for new and prospective users, due to their perceived complexity and unfamiliar concepts when compared to

[42] Revealing Reality, on behalf of the FCA (n 36).

[43] ibid.

[44] 'Fraud Strategy: stopping scams and protecting the public (accessible)' Policy Paper (updated 1 June 2023), www.gov.uk/government/publications/fraud-strategy/fraud-strategy-stopping-scams-and-protecting-the-public.

[45] ibid.

[46] JE Fisch and JS Seligman, 'Trust, financial literacy, and financial market participation' (2022O) 21 *Journal of Pension Economics and Finance* 634.

[47] FCA, 'Research Note: Cryptoasset Consumer Research 2024' (2 May 2025), www.fca.org.uk/publications/research/research-note-cryptoassets-consumer-research-2024.

[48] ibid.

[49] ibid.

[50] M Bartlam et al, 'FCA Research finds increased Cryptoasset Ownership but Declining Consumer Understanding' (2021), www.dlapiperintelligence.com/investmentrules/blog/articles/2021/fca-research-finds-increased-cryptoasset-ownership-but-declining-consumer-understanding.html.

[51] FCA, 'Research Note: Cryptoasset Consumer Research 2024' (2 May 2025), www.fca.org.uk/publications/research/research-note-cryptoassets-consumer-research-2024.

traditional finance. The FCA found that almost half of UK cryptocurrency purchasers did not believe they had a good understanding of how cryptocurrencies work.[52] As custodian wallets are the most accessible type of wallet, they can be an ideal starting point, especially for users lacking the understanding or confidence to engage with the intricacies of cryptography. The FCA concluded that most cryptocurrency users used an online exchange to purchase cryptocurrencies,[53] with the majority using Coinbase, which offers a custodian wallet service.[54] The concentration of users within custodian wallet providers has positives and negatives. Operating in the ecosystems of established service providers means regulation, and even some protective measures can be applied; Coinbase has been proactive in the past, blocking users from sending cryptocurrency to a known scam address.[55] A drawback is that large entities have been at the centre of hacks and scandals, such as Mt Gox[56] and FTX,[57] which can cause users to lose all of their (uninsured) holdings. Custodian wallet users still need to enter the correct address details, and transactions cannot be undone, so they will not be protected from administrative errors as they might be in traditional banking, and user safeguards are also absent.[58] Consumers in cryptocurrencies remain largely unprotected, and reliant on their service providers.

9.5.1. Consumer Motivations for Buying Cryptocurrencies

The principal motivation for purchasing cryptocurrency appears to be speculation, having seen the rises and falls in the value of Bitcoin. The notion of being able to get rich through cryptocurrencies is propelled by success stories.[59] New cryptocurrencies may be advertised based on their return on investment, which is also driven through examples of successes. The token NXT had a return of 1,265,555 per cent, but this is distorted by the values of money involved. NXT tokens were sold at $0.0000168 during the initial offering and traded at $0.213 when success was reported.[60] In August 2024, NXT traded at $0.0008431, so an original investor could still sell at a profit.[61] Regardless of the per coin values, a small investment in NXT accompanied by a well-timed sale could have

[52] FCA, 'Research Note: Cryptoassets Consumer Research 2023 (Wave 4)' (8 June 2023) 43, www.fca.org.uk/publication/research-notes/research-note-cryptoasset-consumer-research-2023-wave4.pdf.

[53] ibid Chart 21.

[54] ibid Chart 22.

[55] BBC News, 'Twitter hack: Exchange "blocked 1,000 Bitcoin transactions"' (21 July 2020), www.bbc.co.uk/news/technology-53485170.

[56] BBC News, 'Top Bitcoin exchange MtGox goes offline' (25 February 2014), www.bbc.co.uk/news/technology-26333661.

[57] BBC News, 'The fall of the FTX "King of Crypto" Sam Bankman-Fried' (13 December 2022), www.bbc.co.uk/news/technology-63612489.

[58] See example here: BBC News, '"I was careful and followed instructions closely, but still lost my crypto"' (21 April 2025), www.bbc.co.uk/news/articles/c93gydxj8n7o.

[59] See examples: R Frank, 'Bitcoin rally helps create more than 84,000 new crypto millionaires in a year' CNBC (27 August 2024), www.cnbc.com/2024/08/27/bitcoin-rally-new-crypto-billionaires.html; and Cointree, '12 Bitcoin Success Stories: Meet Bitcoin Millionaires', www.cointree.com/learn/bitcoin-success-stories.

[60] Cointelegraph, 'Top ICOs with the Biggest ROI' (11 September 2018), web.archive.org/web/20180911081733/https://cointelegraph.com/ico-101/top-10-icos-with-the-biggest-roi.

[61] Coin Market Cap, 'Nxt', www.coinmarketcap.com/currencies/nxt.

yielded astronomical profits, and this can be enough evidence for some individuals to invest in new cryptocurrencies.

Cryptocurrencies are a highly liquid asset. Cryptocurrency markets are open 24 hours a day and not restricted by the trading hours of stock exchanges. High liquidity is appealing for buyers as cryptocurrency values can swing wildly. For instance, between 2020 and 2025, Bitcoin's price movements have been significantly more volatile than the 2017–2018 period. In 2021, Bitcoin reached an all-time high of $64,800 on April 14, before experiencing a sharp decline to $30,000 by 19 May, marking a 53 per cent drop in just over a month.[62] The market rebounded in late 2021, with Bitcoin reaching a new peak of $69,202 on 5 March 2024, before correcting to around $62,300.[63] More recently, in 2025, Bitcoin surpassed the $100,000 mark for the first time, driven by factors such as increased institutional adoption and the approval of Bitcoin ETFs in the US.[64] Cryptocurrency trading is volatile and fast-moving, which creates the potential to make huge profits.

Smaller, lower-value cryptocurrencies are often referred to as 'altcoins'. Despite the comparatively low values of altcoins, an individual who buys a large amount of an altcoin could still make considerable profits if it increases in value. Altcoins' affordability, and the hope they will increase in value, helps fuel the 'get rich quick' appeal of cryptocurrencies identified by the FCA.

The open access of cryptocurrencies means investors who may not have access to the financial sector can take part in the market. Individuals can purchase small quantities of cryptocurrency, compared to the larger sums usually required when investing in traditional financial markets. Information surrounding a cryptocurrency can be viewed on relevant platforms and does not require the services of a financial advisor; therefore, an individual can invest in cryptocurrencies with little-to-no fees.

A final appeal to consider surrounding cryptocurrencies is their novelty, technological advancement, and generally fresher, less formal reputation. This quality is difficult to quantify, but many people can see what they choose to see in cryptocurrencies. Cryptocurrencies have a counterculture nature, a lack of formal rules, and an appeal to a more youthful demographic that may be unable or unwilling to engage with the established financial system. Depending on their levels of understanding, cryptocurrency users may not identify as consumers; they may believe they are informed enough or consider cryptocurrency trading as their profession.

9.5.2. Consumer Vulnerabilities when Buying Cryptocurrencies

Consumers buying cryptocurrencies face numerous risks, some of which mirror the appeals for investing, including volatility, lack of regulation and the prevalence of scams.

[62] H Ma, 'Volatility Dynamics Analysis of Bitcoin (BTC-USD) and MicroStrategy (MSTR)' (2024) *Advances in Economics, Management and Political Sciences* 145, 190–99.

[63] ibid.

[64] B Jafar, 'As bitcoin breaches $100k, bankers who quit tradfi for crypto feel vindicated' Financial News (10 December 2024), www.fnlondon.com/articles/bitcoin-at-100-000-tradfi-talents-crypto-move-has-paid-off-90637c6b.

While the volatility in values can be appealing for those seeking to make money, more commonly the value of altcoins remains low or drops below the original purchase price. Using a popular listing website and ordering the 'top 100' cryptocurrencies by price, only Bitcoin is valued at more than $3,000, and then including Bitcoin, only five coins have values over $1,000, and one other is worth over $500. The fall-away in values is steep from there: from number 12 on the list the value is below $100; and from number 25, values are below $10 a coin.[65] The value per coin is not indicative of the value of an individual's holdings. An indication of the volatility in cryptocurrency markets is that a prominent market data site provided a 'fear and greed' index to assess the current behaviour of the market.

Cryptocurrency activity remains largely unregulated. The UK amended the Money Laundering, Terrorist Financing and Transfer of Funds (Information on the Payer) Regulations 2017 (MLR 2017),[66] in accordance with the European Union's Fifth Anti-Money Laundering Directive.[67] The FCA is now responsible for AML/CTF regulation of cryptocurrency service providers, which includes cryptocurrency exchanges that trade fiat currency for cryptocurrency,[68] or between cryptocurrencies,[69] or provide custodian wallet services.[70] Such regulation will be unlikely to protect consumers, as fraudsters may operate through exchanges, or simply create dummy websites that they direct their victims to.

Even with the potential workarounds, the legislation is only valuable if it is utilised by the FCA. However, the FCA's implementation of the regulation was lacklustre; only four entries were registered in January 2021, rising to six by June 2021, 29 by the end of 2021, and only reaching 51 by April 2025.[71] Questions might be raised as to the integrity of the approved register, as three of the four original entries are registered at the same address and two of those entries lack a registered telephone number. Based on the state of both the register and the temporary register, the dedication of the FCA to regulating cryptocurrency service providers appears limited. Similarly to the maintenance of the register, the use of enforcement is needed, yet, to date, the FCA has only imposed one enforcement action, in July 2024,[72] and issued a warning that related to Binance.[73]

[65] Correct as of 3 April 2025 using Coin Market Cap, 'Today's Cryptocurrency Prices by Market Cap', www.coinmarketcap.com/ accessed 30 April 2025.

[66] Money Laundering, Terrorist Financing and Transfer of Funds (Information on the Payer) Regulations 2017, SI 2017 No 692 amended by The Money Laundering and Terrorist Financing (Amendment) Regulations 2019, SI 2019 No 1511.

[67] Council Directive 2018/843/EU of 30 May 2018 amending Directive (EU) 2015/849 on the prevention of the use of the financial system for the purposes of money laundering or terrorist financing and amending Directives 2009/138/EC and 2013/36/EU (Text with EEA relevance) [2018] OJ L 156/43.

[68] Money Laundering, Terrorist Financing and Transfer of Funds (Information on the Payer) Regulations 2017, SI 2017 No 692, reg 14A(1)(a).

[69] ibid reg 14A(1)(b).

[70] ibid reg 14A(2).

[71] FCA, 'Registered Cryptoasset firms' (last updated 1 April 2025), register.fca.org.uk/s/search?predefined=CA.

[72] FCA, 'FCA takes first enforcement action against firm enabling cryptoasset trading' (25 July 2024), www.fca.org.uk/news/press-releases/fca-first-enforcement-action-against-firm-enabling-cryptoasset-trading.

[73] FCA, 'Consumer warning on Binance Markets Limited and the Binance Group' (26 June 2021), www.fca.org.uk/news/news-stories/consumer-warning-binance-markets-limited-and-binance-group.

The volatility of cryptocurrency trading, alongside the limited regulation and the low levels of understanding in the general population regarding cryptocurrencies, means that scams are a real risk, with several common models being used. Generally, consumers will be most vulnerable to scams as they are likely to be least informed; this vulnerability is increased in cryptocurrency consumers based on the common traits identified in them.

9.6. Common Scams

The development of the internet has made fraud easier to commit as online interactions lack nuances such as body language and voice inflection, and technological advancements enhance the armoury of the criminal. Once a potential victim is lured in, fraudsters can control what they see, and the information presented to the victim. Several common types of cryptocurrency frauds have developed, which will appear familiar to anyone with experience of wider fraud as many are akin to existing schemes repackaged in a cryptocurrency format. The scams below are known in terms used within the cryptocurrency, but can often be contrasted to a pre-existing fraud.

9.6.1. Initial Coin Offerings

An initial coin offering (ICO) is a mechanism to launch a cryptocurrency by selling the newly created cryptocurrency rather than waiting for the mining process to produce a larger enough circulating supply. ICOs are usually accompanied by a white paper which sets out the goals of the project for which funding is sought. ICOs get compared to crowdfunding and initial product offerings (IPOs). An ICO is akin to crowdfunding in that they are pitched to the public. A key difference is that an ICO lacks a product in return for the investment; in an ICO the benefit for the investor is the potential increase in the value of the cryptocurrency. Backing an ICO in the hope of selling the cryptocurrency for profit, differentiates ICOs from crowdfunding campaigns, making them more comparable to an IPO. However, while shares give investors a level of ownership of the company, an ICO does not. This fundamental difference means and ICO and IPO are far apart; one gives an ownership stake in a company and the right to a share in profits through dividends, whereas the other simply gives early access to a cryptocurrency.

The eventual goal for a newly created cryptocurrency is for it to be accepted on cryptocurrency exchanges, which will increase the level of awareness of the cryptocurrency and potentially increase its value while supporting the project attached to the cryptocurrency. ICOs have fallen in popularity, due to the high levels of risk and because of the development of initial exchange offerings (IEOs) in their place.

Countless ICO scams exist, including Bitconnect, PlusToken, and PlexCoin. In a typical ICO scam, Bitconnect promised massive returns on Bitcoin investments, which were akin to a pyramid scheme as early investors would benefit from chains of referrals.[74]

[74] K Sedgwick, 'Cracks Appear as Critics Label Bitconnect a Ponzi Scheme' Bitcoin.com (9 November 2017), news.bitcoin.com/cracks-appear-critics-label-bitconnect-ponzi-scheme.

The ICO market lost credibility within the cryptocurrency sector, and spoof ICOs were created which clearly outlined their nefarious aims in a response to the many scam ICOs that existed.[75] Ponzicoin outwardly projected its 'scam' status, claiming never to have actually taken any money, but instead highlight the issue of scams.[76] Other open scams still took money, such as Useless Ethereum Token, which stated that users would be giving 'some random person on the internet money'.[77] Even the US Securities and Exchange Commission created its own fictitious ICO in an effort to educate consumers on the risks.[78]

In 2018, the *Wall Street Journal* identified 'red flags' in 271 out of 1,450 ICOs.[79] This included 121 ICOs not disclosing any employees' names, 111 copying sections from other white papers verbatim, and five using stock images to create fictitious boards of executives. The issue of scams has been eased through IEOs replacing ICOs. IEOs are vetted by a cryptocurrency exchange, and the exchange risks its reputation on the project which increases levels of trust.

There are clear links to be drawn between ICOs and both Ponzi schemes and boiler room scams, with victims investing on the promise of unrealistic returns, only for the organisers of the scheme to disappear. The cryptocurrency sector refers to such schemes as 'exit scamming'[80] in keeping with a trend for using different terminology to the traditional financial sector.[81] These common scams may appear obvious to many, and experienced individuals are unlikely to be duped, but they are not the target. Greedy or naïve individuals are much easier victims for financial scammers, and based the 2018 FCA report, these traits are common in cryptocurrency investors.

9.6.2. Rug Pulls

A rug pull is a scam that lures in victims on false pretences. Once they have committed by investing, the 'rug' is pulled from under their feet, leaving them with a worthless asset. The precise nature of the rug pull will vary, but the schemes may appear complex and be large scale, such as OneCoin in which real-world in-person conventions were held, or more opportunistic and comparably small, such as Squid Token, which took

[75] O Solon, 'Bitcoin, titcoin, ponzicoin: jokes and scams fuel a cryptocurrency gold rush' *The Guardian* (2 February 2018), www.theguardian.com/technology/2018/feb/02/bitcoin-bananacoin-prodeum-cryptocurrencies.

[76] Ponzicoin, 'Our Incredible Journey', www.ponzicoin.co/home.html.

[77] Useless Ethereum Token, 'The world's first 100% honest Ethereum ICO', web.archive.org/web/20210312115558/https://uetoken.com.

[78] Securities and Exchange Commission, 'The SEC Has an Opportunity You Won't Want to Miss: Act Now!' (16 May 2018), www.sec.gov/news/press-release/2018-88.

[79] S Shifflett and C Jones, 'Buyer Beware: Hundreds of Bitcoin Wannabes Show Hallmarks of Fraud' *The Wall Street Journal* (17 May 2018), www.wsj.com/articles/buyer-beware-hundreds-of-bitcoin-wannabes-show-hallmarks-of-fraud-1526573115.

[80] J Gjorgjev, 'What are crypto exit scams, and how to protect against them?' Cointelegraph (8 April 2024), www.cointelegraph.com/news/how-to-protect-against-crypto-exit-scams.

[81] G Hou, 'Cryptocurrency money laundering and exit scams: Cases, regulatory responses and issues' in S Corbet (ed), *Understanding cryptocurrency fraud: The challenges and headwinds to regulate digital currencies* (De Gruyter, 2022) 83–96.

advantage of the popularity of the Netflix show, *Squid Games*, but had no connection to it. Typically, rug pulls are committed by the developer of the fraudulent cryptocurrency, in contrast to 'pump and dump' scams which are usually committed by individuals not connected to the cryptocurrency utilised for the scam.

An example of a rug pull can be seen in liquidity stealing. This type of scheme can be more like a traditional fraud with a cryptocurrency front; the aim is to recruit as many investors as possible before absconding with the money. A prominent example is OneCoin. OneCoin was not a cryptocurrency, but an investment fraud presenting itself as a cryptocurrency. Although there was never a blockchain or other characteristics of a cryptocurrency, it is synonymous with cryptocurrency scams. Fronted by Ruja Ignatova, OneCoin was a pyramid scheme – commonly known to be scams – but advertised itself as a multi-level marketing model currency. It is not known how much money the scheme made, $4bn is widely suggested,[82] but it could be as high as $15bn.[83] Using multi-level marketing within cryptocurrencies is not exclusive to OneCoin. During the ICO boom, offerings, such as Bitconnect, incentivised early investors by offering money for referring the scheme to others. The exit for the perpetrator of a liquidity stealing scam is to abscond with their victims' money. In the case of Ruja Ignatova, as of August 2024, she remains on the run.[84]

Not all rug pulls involve pyramid schemes. Some rely on coding the fraudulent coin through a process known as a 'limited sell order'. A limited sell order may exist in a contract, restricting how and when a buyer may sell something, but this must be agreed between the parties. In a cryptocurrency scam a limited sell order can render a coin or token worthless as it may stop the buyer ever being able to sell. This was the case with Squid Token, which only allowed victims to buy the cryptocurrency, and not sell it afterwards.[85] The scam made use of the record-breaking Netflix show, Squid Game and demonstrates the opportunistic nature of some fraudsters, taking advantage of youthful and potentially inexperienced cryptocurrency users. As found by the FCA in 2018, this is a large demographic within the cryptocurrency sector.

9.6.3. Pump and Dump

Perhaps the most informal of terms, and unfortunately euphemistic, a pump and dump scam has a simple premise: buy a large holding of a low-priced cryptocurrency and aggressively advertise it to drive up demand and with it, price (pumping), then at a chosen point, sell the holdings and leave the market (dumping). In traditional finance, this type of scam is known as a boiler room scam.[86] Boiler room scams

[82] J Redman, 'Onecoin Websites Suspended as the $4 Billion Ponzi Crumbles' Bitcoin.com (4 December 2019), news.bitcoin.com/multiple-onecoin-websites-suspended-as-the-4-billion-dollar-ponzi-crumbles.

[83] BBC News, 'Cryptoqueen: How this Woman Scammed the World, then Vanished' (24 November 2019), www.bbc.co.uk/news/stories-50435014.

[84] Federal Bureau of Investigation, 'RUJA IGNATOVA', www.fbi.gov/wanted/topten/ruja-ignatova.

[85] BBC News, 'Squid Game crypto token collapses in apparent scam' (2 November 2021), www.bbc.co.uk/news/business-59129466.

[86] FCA, 'Share, bond and boiler room scams' (last updated 20 March 2023), www.fca.org.uk/consumers/share-bond-and-boiler-room-scams.

get their name from the tightly packed telecoms offices they were perpetrated from, which is not how a cryptocurrency pump and dump will be conducted. Where boiler room scams focused on calling up victims, pump and dump scams try to have their chosen cryptocurrency promoted by influencers or pushed on relevant cryptocurrency websites. False claims are made about the profitability of the cryptocurrency to build a groundswell that increases the price. Instead of using 'boiler rooms' the activity is conducted through private chat groups. Similarities can be drawn between pump and dump schemes and ICOs, although in a pump and dump the scheme is not typically executed by the developers of the cryptocurrency – the chosen cryptocurrency is just a vehicle for the fraud.[87]

9.6.4. Romance Scams and Pig Butchery

While many cryptocurrency scams are designed to attract and defraud as many people as possible as quickly as possible, a romance scam or pig butchery scam is a longer fraud with more personal aspects. The premise of the scam is akin to the previous frauds, in that the victim is ultimately lured by unrealistically high returns, but their confidence or commitment in the scheme is secured either on the promise of romance or based on previous profits.

In a romance scam the victim is targeted with messages from what appears to be a desirable person. The scammer then builds up a rapport with the victim, using flattery and highly emotive messages. The scam may then take two main routes: if the victim is persuaded to send personal images, they may be blackmailed into sending the fraudster money; alternatively, the fraudster will use the emotional attachment formed by the victim to extract money for various false purposes.[88] Cryptocurrency payments limit the traceability of the transactions.

Pig butchery scams run on a similar premise of gaining the victim's trust, but play on a different emotion: greed. A victim is contacted regarding cryptocurrency investment, and scammer will try to build a rapport, telling the victim how much money they make in cryptocurrency trading. The victim is directed to a trading platform showing apparently live markets to view the investment they could make; this is a false site, with the fraudster controlling what the victim sees. Where a romance scam will likely have a longer social engineering phase, to build up a relationship, a pig butchering scam has a longer extraction phase; the victim is invited to make smaller investments and will be shown their investments gaining high returns. They may even be sent some returns to further support the fraud and increase confidence. The aim of a pig butchering scam is to secure the maximum investment from the victim, the 'fattening' stage increasing the confidence of the victim so they believe they are making the 'too good to be true' profits, which entices them to make a much larger investment on the expectation of the same

[87] Chainalysis, 'Crime: Pump and Dump' (1 February 2024), www.chainalysis.com/blog/crypto-crime-2024-pump-and-dump.

[88] Action Fraud, 'Romance Fraud', www.actionfraud.police.uk/a-z-of-fraud/dating-fraud.

percentage increase.[89] Once the fraudster has extracted as much money as possible from the victim, they will stop communicating with them. Due to being relatively novel, and with the press coverage surrounding them, cryptocurrencies are suited to pig butchery scams. Fraudsters can play on the interest of the victim and the speed of the markets to create pressure on the victim to invest.

Pig butchering and romance scams require more social engineering than other cryptocurrency scams, but the amounts of money extracted per victim will be higher; typically, victims in the wider-reaching scams will only invest smaller amounts. A pig butchering scam may also use similar lures to a romance scam in the messaging phase, especially for heterosexual male victims.[90]

9.7. UK Response to the Development of Cryptocurrencies

The UK has implemented the Fifth Anti-Money Laundering Directive and, since 10 January 2020, the FCA is responsible for AML/CTF regulation of cryptocurrency service providers that exchange fiat currency for cryptocurrency, exchange one cryptocurrency for another, or provide custodian wallet services.[91] The approach of the UK has been slower than other jurisdictions. It was required to extend AML/CTF regulation to cover cryptocurrencies in order to comply with the 5th Anti-Money Laundering Directive of the EU,[92] and it took five years after the initial consultation to apply any regulation to cryptocurrencies,[93] and nearly 11 years after Block Zero was mined.

The position of the FCA in relation to cryptocurrencies is one of caution. It has not demanded regulation and has taken time to utilise its regulatory powers against cryptocurrency service providers. The protection of consumers is limited; the public is warned against investing on the risk of losing their money. The FCA makes it clear that the Financial Services Compensation Scheme does not apply to cryptocurrencies and that the services of the Financial Ombudsman will not be available if things go wrong. The FCA updated its investment advice pages to specifically address cryptocurrencies in 2023.[94] The advice, and pages in general, now use more informal terminology, akin to the language used in the cryptocurrency sector, which may make it more accessible to cryptocurrency consumers. There are clear warnings and issues to be aware of, and it stresses the need for consumers to take time to think about the investment before they

[89] Avon and Somerset Police, 'Pig Butchering Scams', www.avonandsomerset.police.uk/media/32961926/pig-butchering-scams.pdf.

[90] BBC News, '"Pig butchering" scammers target BBC reporter' (5 August 2024), www.bbc.co.uk/news/videos/ckdgdkrd2n2o.

[91] Money Laundering, Terrorist Financing and Transfer of Funds (Information on the Payer) Regulations 2017, SI 2017 No 692, reg 14A.

[92] Council Directive 2018/843/EU of 30 May 2018 amending Directive (EU) 2015/849 on the prevention of the use of the financial system for the purposes of money laundering or terrorist financing and amending Directives 2009/138/EC and 2013/36/EU (Text with EEA relevance) [2018] OJ L 156/43.

[93] GOV.uk, 'Digital currencies: call for information', www.gov.uk/government/consultations/digital-currencies-call-for-information/digital-currencies-call-for-information.

[94] FCA, 'InvestSmart Crypto: The basics' (March 2023), www.fca.org.uk/investsmart/crypto-basics.

spend their money. While these warnings are clear on the relevant pages of the FCA's website, it is highly unlikely that vulnerable individuals will see these warnings. As the FCA's commissioned research has found, prevalent characteristics in cryptocurrency buyers includes a rejection of mainstream news sources, which will likely include the FCA website.

At present, cryptocurrencies are only regulated for AML/CTF purposes. There are no official accreditation schemes to assure the public regarding the cryptocurrency they are purchasing. Introducing such schemes poses challenges, given the characteristics of cryptocurrency buyers, who may be unlikely to verify the credibility of these certifications. The decentralised and pseudonymous nature of cryptocurrencies complicates the establishment of standardised accreditation processes. Additionally, the global nature of cryptocurrencies means that regulatory standards vary significantly across jurisdictions, making universal accreditation schemes difficult to implement.[95] Furthermore, it is difficult to see how an accreditation scheme would assist, given the characteristics of those buying cryptocurrencies meaning they are unlikely to check it. Regulation is set to change in 2025, as the Financial Services and Markets Act 2000 (FSMA) is to be amended to include 'qualifying' cryptocurrencies and stablecoins as specific investments, which will bring such assets into the regulated perimeter.[96] If enacted, this will increase the protection of consumers as they will qualify for the same safeguards as consumers within the traditional financial system, including having adequate consumer redress schemes. Qualifying cryptocurrencies must be 'fungible' and 'transferable'.[97]

While the relevant compensation or redress schemes do not currently apply, Sinclair and Taylor note that in relation to ICOs, investors could have recourse through the CRA 2015, which repealed and replaced the previous acts and consolidated and updated consumer protection laws.[98] In the context of ICOs, investors may have recourse through the CRA 2015 if they believe that the terms of the investment are unfair. However, pursuing such claims can be challenging. As Sinclair and Taylor note, identifying a relevant party against whom to take action may be difficult, and the process could incur significant costs, including the need for specialist investigators to trace the cryptocurrency and legal representation. Specialist cryptocurrency investigators exist, but will be more focused on high-value cases than consumer losses, unless a class action can be organised. Even if the lost funds can be traced, it is not possible to freeze the assets or reappropriate them without also tracking down the perpetrators of the scam, which is likely to be complicated.

[95] NS Uzougbo, CG Ikegwu, and AO Adewusi, 'Enhancing consumer protection in cryptocurrency transactions: Legal strategies and policy recommendations' (2024) 12 *International Journal of Science and Research Archive* 520.

[96] GOV.uk, 'Policy paper: Regulatory regime for cryptoassets (regulated activities) – Draft SI and Policy Note' (30 April 2025), www.gov.uk/government/publications/regulatory-regime-for-cryptoassets-regulated-activities-draft-si-and-policy-note.

[97] The Financial Services and Markets Act 2000 (Regulated Activities and Miscellaneous Provisions) (Cryptoassets) Order 2025 (30 April 2025), reg 88F, assets.publishing.service.gov.uk/media/680f6387faff81833fcae94b/0302425_draft_RAO_SI.pdf.

[98] P Sinclair and A Taylor, 'The English law rights of investors in Initial Coin Offerings' (2018) 4 *Journal of International Banking & Financial Law* 214.

The ByBit hack, which resulted in a loss of $1.5bn in cryptocurrency, demonstrated that even with almost every known cryptocurrency investigator on the case, experienced criminals can still cash out their proceeds.[99] In this case, North Korea was the suspected origin of the hackers and the destination for the funds. A consumer will have the law on their side in nearly all cases, but the odds remain stacked against them due to the practicalities of taking legal action and the available resources of most consumers. Moreover, the effectiveness of the CRA 2015 in providing consumer protection in the cryptocurrency sector is limited by the decentralised nature of cryptocurrencies and the pseudonymous identities of many participants. These characteristics complicate the enforcement of consumer rights and the identification of responsible parties. Therefore, while the CRA 2015 offers a legal framework for challenging unfair terms, its application in the cryptocurrency market may be constrained by these inherent challenges.

9.8. Consumer Protection Through Good Samaritans

While formal consumer protection is not in place in the UK, buyers can take steps to protect themselves, with some websites operating in a 'Good Samaritan' style, allowing prospective buyers to check a cryptocurrency before they buy it. The benefit of these sites is that they can reduce the number of victims that a scam affects, and participants within cryptocurrency circles may be more likely to check these than government authorities' websites.[100] While the Good Samaritans of the internet are welcome and appear to be trying to give sound advice to market participants, the lack of cohesion and order to the cryptocurrency sector is present in these sites too. There is no clear leader in the space, so to check for a scam a consumer will need to refer to multiple websites and forums. There are Reddit threads that can be a useful source of information, but they are reliant on moderators filtering out bad actors, and the most popular 'CryptoScam'[101] thread only has 68,000 followers. Websites that are dedicated to checking for scams do exist, and more established sites will rank the threat levels they identify. However, the administrators of these sites risk suffering from fatigue as the role will not draw income. One such site was for sale in 2024.[102]

Established cryptocurrency service providers could also step up their levels of protection which would help them attract more custom. Large service providers such as Coinbase have intervened in the past, but this does not appear to be a regular occurrence. Achieving higher levels of protection is not straightforward, as insurance schemes for cryptocurrencies are not realistic given the volatility in their values, but implementing checks, automated warnings, or address checkers would be a useful starting point.

[99] BBC News, 'North Korean hackers cash out hundreds of millions from $1.5bn ByBit hack' (10 March 2025), www.bbc.co.uk/news/articles/c2kgndwwd7lo.

[100] M Bartoletti et al, 'Cryptocurrency Scams: Analysis and Perspectives' (2021) 9 *IEEE Access* 148353, www.researchgate.net/publication/355689506_Cryptocurrency_Scams_Analysis_and_Perspectives.

[101] Reddit, 'r/CryptoScams', www.reddit.com/r/CryptoScams.

[102] Isthisascam, 'isthisascam', web.archive.org/web/20240806203321/https://isthiscoinascam.com.

Establishing a cooperation between regulators and service providers could instigate better consumer protection, but such regulation is currently lacking.

9.9. Conclusions

Consumer protection in the cryptocurrency sector remains fragmented, inconsistent and inadequate. The legislators and regulators are reluctant to act, either through a lack of understanding or appreciation of cryptocurrencies, or through a belief that the issue is not one that warrants attention. While FCA research suggests that most retail investors risk only what they can afford to lose, this generalisation obscures the significant individual harms experienced by a minority, often those most vulnerable to deception.

The investigative barriers to pursuing cryptocurrency fraud are substantial; as the fraudsters frequently operate outside UK jurisdiction, their identities concealed by pseudonymity and anonymising technologies. Tracking and seizing cryptoassets often requires significant technical expertise and cross-border cooperation. At the same time, characteristics specific to cryptocurrency consumers, such as mistrust of mainstream institutions, reliance on informal online communities, and exposure to hype-based decision-making, heighten their exposure to fraud. While this does not suggest fault on the part of victims, it demands a more nuanced regulatory and educational response.

Importantly, many scams are not technologically novel, but recycled frauds repackaged in crypto form. This 'innovation veneer' obscures long-standing manipulation tactics. Adding to the confusion is the linguistic and cultural divide between the traditional financial sector and cryptocurrency communities. Divergent terminology such as 'exit scamming' instead of misappropriation, or the informal use of 'white papers' in place of regulated prospectuses, contributes to misunderstandings and weakens consumer defences.

A public education based on these faults must be a cornerstone of any reform strategy. Additionally, any information campaigns should employ terminology familiar to both crypto insiders and traditional retail investors, while also including collaboration with respected figures from within cryptocurrency communities, especially with those already engaged in Good Samaritan-style initiatives, as this could enhance credibility and reach. These peer-led efforts, while currently informal and unregulated, show promise in warning consumers about scams more effectively than official channels.

Most importantly, predicting future directions in cryptocurrencies is difficult due to its still nascent state. Consumers appear to be engaging with cryptocurrencies and, from the research that has been undertaken, most consumers are using established and relatively well-known service providers which can offer them a complete service for purchasing and managing their holdings. Given the preference of many consumers for this approach, two avenues for consumer protection could be envisaged: one led by the service providers themselves, and the other led by regulators. If service providers were to consider implementing more consumer protection to grow the appeal of their offering, this could spark healthy competition. Offering a smoother and more confident customer experience is not unlike what can be seen in the retail sector where companies may differentiate themselves by going beyond minimum standards through their returns policy, for example. In the UK, proposed legislative reform means a regulation-led development will see consumer protection measures mandated upon all providers, which should be more consistent than voluntary schemes, but difficult to enforce. Regulation also risks creating a combative attitude in the regulated sector and attempts to only meet the minimum standards required. The analysis undertaken by the FCA suggests that while a growing number of consumers are buying cryptocurrencies, they do not appear to be risking more money than they can afford to lose. This also correlates with the advice that the FCA provide on its webpages.

Ultimately, the sector continues to operate under conditions akin to *caveat emptor*, with consumers navigating high-risk environments using partial knowledge and limited safeguards. As both adoption and sophistication of scams grow, the current state of crypto consumer protection is unsustainable. A hybrid approach, combining statutory regulation, voluntary best practices, and culturally attuned educational strategies, is not only desirable, but essential.

10

Digital Assistants and Consumer Law – Disruption or Innovation?

CHRISTIAN TWIGG-FLESNER

10.1. Introduction

There can be little doubt that the arrival of consumer-facing applications based on the fruits of decades of artificial intelligence (AI) research[1] has the potential for disruptive effects[2] in many areas.[3] The seemingly impressive performance of recent generative AI (GenAI) models has led to widespread claims that large-scale automation is imminent.[4] Yet, as investments in GenAI, in particular, have reached eye-watering amounts,[5] there is also a growing recognition that GenAI technology has inherent imperfections that would limit its usefulness.[6] Nevertheless, the search for new applications based on GenAI technology has pointed to various use-cases, including the possibility of developing consumer-focused 'AI agents'[7] that can automate various processes, including making contracts for a consumer.[8] In essence, these applications would automate some of the stages a consumer would usually follow in deciding whether to make a purchase. Crucially, this could be the final step taken by a consumer to conclude a legally binding contract, the placing of the order (assuming that such

[1] A Narayanan and S Kapoor, *AI Snake Oil* (Princeton University Press, 2024) 165.

[2] In the sense used by CM Christensen. See *The Innovator's Dilemma – When New Technology Causes Great Firms to fail* (Harvard Business Review Press, 1997); also CM Christensen, ME Raynor and R McDonald, 'What is Disruptive Innovation?' (2015) 93 *Harvard Business Review* 44.

[3] See eg, A Singla et al, *The state of AI – How organizations are rewiring to capture value* (McKinsey Global Publishing, 2025).

[4] *cf* T Coshow et al, *Top Strategic Technology Trends for 2025: Agentic AI* (Gartner, October 2024).

[5] See eg, B Kindig, 'AI spending to exceed a quarter of a trillion next year' *Forbes* (14 November 2024), www.forbes.com/sites/bethkindig/2024/11/14/ai-spending-to-exceed-a-quarter-trillion-next-year.

[6] M Mitchell, 'Artificial intelligence learns to reason' (2025) 387 *Science*, www.science.org/doi/10.1126/science.adw5211; M Nezhurina et al, 'Alice in Wonderland: Simple Tasks Showing Complete Reasoning Breakdown in State-Of-the-Art Large Language Models', doi.org/10.48550/arXiv.2406.02061; G Marcus and E Davis, *Rebooting AI* (Vintage Books, 2019).

[7] The term 'agent' in this context should not be confused with the specific legal notion of 'agent' and 'agency', but rather be understood in its technological sense. There are many different types of AI agents. *cf* S Kapoor et al, 'AI Agents that matter' (2024) arXiv:2407.01502.

[8] eg, E Griffith, 'AI isn't magic, but can it be "agentic"?' *New York Times* (6 September 2024); R Waters, 'Move over copilots: meet the next generation of AI-powered assistants' *Financial Times* (22 September 2024).

applications would operate in the online environment only).[9] Thus, for instance, instead of having to place a weekly groceries order, an application could work out what a consumer might need in any given week, based on a variety of parameters, and automatically place an order. One might expect to see a variety of different applications emerge over time, with different degrees of automation and complexity, and likely with a variety of different designations; indeed, there are already several terms in use that all describe this kind of application, including 'digital agent', 'AI agent',[10] 'agentic system', 'electronic agent',[11] 'digital delegate'[12] or 'custobot'.[13] In this paper, such applications will be referred to as 'digital assistants', adopting the terminology of the European Law Institute's (ELI) *Guiding Principles and Model Rules on Digital Assistants for Consumer Contracts* (DACC), on which more below.

As there is now a reasonable prospect that some digital assistant applications might become available for consumer use, the question this contribution seeks to ask whether, and to what extent, their arrival would affect UK consumer law.[14] Answering this has multiple aspects: first, fundamentally, it will be necessary to analyse what this development would mean for the nature of consumer transacting, particular its impact on consumer autonomy; secondly, if such analysis reveals that there is a need to introduce new legal rules, or modify existing rules, to capture any new features brought about by the use of digital assistants by consumers (or contract automation generally); thirdly, there is a deeper question as to whether the fundamental assumptions underpinning consumer law are at least open for re-examination, eg, the assumption that consumers are informationally disadvantaged.[15]

Furthermore, if new legal rules are required or at least desirable to deal with the consumer protection aspects of digital assistants, then thought will need to given as to the shape such rules might take. It will be argued below that the recent ELI DACC model rules are innovative and that they provide a template for developing UK consumer law. The DACC are a good example of how innovation not only produces technological advances but also provides an opportunity for innovation in shaping consumer law. One of the key advantages of consumer law is that it is inherently instrumentalist in its pursuit of specific regulatory objectives[16] to ensure adequate consumer protection. This provides a fertile ground for developing innovative legal solutions for novel challenges created by technological developments, rather than

[9] *cf* the Electronic Commerce (EC Directive) Regulations 2002 (SI 2002 No 2013), regs 11–12.

[10] *cf* N Kolt, 'Governing AI Agents' (2025) 100 *Notre Dame Law Review* (forthcoming).

[11] AJ Bellia, 'Contracting with Electronic Agents' (2001) 50 *Emory Law Journal* 1047. This is also the term used in C Wendehorst, 'Principles for AI in Contracting (Version 3.0)' in V Sagaert and J Vananroye (eds), *Privaatrecht plenis coloribus. Liber Amicorum Mathias Storme* (Kluwer, 2024); for an earlier version, see (2024) 13 *Journal of European Consumer and Markets Law* 43.

[12] C Twigg-Flesner, 'Consumers, Digital Delegates, Contract Formation and Consumer Law' in L Di Matteo, G Howells and M Hogg, *AI and Consumers* (Cambridge University Press, 2024).

[13] D Scheibenreif and M Raskino, *When machines become customers*, 2nd edn (Gartner, 2023).

[14] A note on the use of the term 'UK consumer law' in this chapter: it is used here to refer to consumer law in England, Wales and Scotland. Northern Ireland has slightly different rules under the arrangements with the EU. It is therefore not used entirely correctly, but is a more convenient shorthand than 'British consumer law', and preferable to 'English, Welsh and Scottish consumer law'.

[15] *cf* C Busch, 'Consumer Law for AI Agents' (2025) *German Law Journal* 000.

[16] *cf* EL Rubin, 'From Coherence to Effectiveness' in B van Gestel, H-W Micklitz and EL Rubin (eds) *Rethinking Legal Scholarship* (Cambridge University Press, 2017).

attempting to shoehorn AI-driven automation into existing legal frameworks based on active human involvement. Indeed, as will be discussed later, the role of the human consumer as an active decision-taker would change, with the consumer (mostly) taken out of the decision-making process.

10.2. Impact of Digital Assistants on Consumer Law

The intense focus on the possible application of current AI technologies has culminated in identifying potential new consumer-focused applications of these technologies.[17] There are already long-standing concerns within consumer law and policy debates over algorithmic manipulation,[18] and these concerns will not only continue but probably be exacerbated by the arrival of digital agents. It has already been established that all consumers are in a heightened position of vulnerability in the digital environment,[19] making this an important postulate for consumer law. Manipulation by algorithms and so-called dark patterns is already a major concern.[20]

There are more benign effects of this development. It has also reinvigorated the potential for contract automation,[21] ie, the substitution of a technology-based process for human decision-making regarding the conclusion of contracts. The possibility of such a development in the consumer context demands a discussion of the potential impact of contract automation, particularly through digital assistants, on consumer law.

Fundamentally, it is important to avoid the fallacy that there is an incontrovertible link between technological development and legal 'disruption'.[22] Not every (disruptive) technological development necessarily demands new laws, even where the impact on the business landscape is substantial.[23] Conversely, it is no less important to avoid the fallacy that existing legal rules are always adequate to cover the challenges arising from applications of new technologies. Instead, it is essential to identify what is different about a technological development and its applications in order to identify whether this has resulted in new challenges that need to be tackled, and whether any solutions that

[17] See eg, J Devenney and G Howells, 'Developing product liability networks for AI systems in the medical context' (2025) 76 *Northern Ireland Legal Quarterly* 118.

[18] See eg, E Mik, 'Algorithmic Exploitation of Consumers' in L Di Matteo, G Howells and M Hogg, *AI and Consumers* (Cambridge University Press, 2024); M Herbosch, 'Fraud by generative AI chatbots: On the thin line between deception and negligence' (2024) *Computer Law & Security Review* 52.

[19] N Helberger et al, 'Choice Architecture in the Digital Economy: Towards a New Understanding of Digital Vulnerability' (2022) 45 *Journal of Consumer Policy* 175.

[20] eg, S Spencer, 'The Problem of Online Manipulation' (2020) *University of Illinois Law Review* 959; M Leiser, 'Psychological Patterns and Article 5 of the AI Act: AI-Powered Deceptive Design in the System Architecture and the User Interface' (2024) 1 *Journal of AI law and Regulation* 5.

[21] The idea of automating the contracting process is neither new, nor has it escaped the attention of law-makers (see eg, Art 12 of the UN Convention on the Use of Electronic Communications for International Contracts). It had already received a boost in the context of blockchain-based smart contracts: E Mik, 'Deconstructing Smart Contracts' in N Kim and S-A Elvy (eds), *The Cambridge Handbook of Emerging Issues at the Intersection of Commercial Law and Technology* (Cambridge University Press, 2025).

[22] *cf* the notion of 'legal disruption' used in C Twigg-Flesner, 'The Potential of the COVID-19 Crisis to Cause Legal "Disruption" to Contracts and Contract Law' in E Hondius et al (eds), *Coronavirus and the Law in Europe*, (Intersentia, 2021).

[23] *cf* Christensen, Raynor and McDonald (n 2).

are identified are beyond the scope of current laws.[24] Where some changes to existing laws are required, it might be said that this is already disruptive to the law,[25] although true *legal* disruption might only result from changes made to the law to address the challenges posed by new technology applications which lead to a more comprehensive recalibration of an area of law.[26]

Thus, an inquiry into whether the arrival of digital assistants would necessitate changes to consumer law needs to start by identifying what might be different once digital assistants are used by consumers for their contracting activities, particularly when compared with the way consumers conclude contracts now. This will serve to distil the challenges that would need to be addressed in consumer law. Existing consumer law can be tested against these findings to identify where there are gaps; in this regard, the two fallacies noted above must be heeded.

10.2.1. What are the Key Challenges?

First, digital assistants are one potential application that could be utilised for contract automation, based on algorithmic technologies, particularly AI algorithms. It is difficult to provide a definition of AI that would capture all its permutations. The Organisation for Economic Co-operation and Development (OECD) offers this definition of an AI system:

> [A] machine-based system that, for explicit or implicit objectives, infers, from the input it receives, how to generate outputs such as predictions, content, recommendations, or decisions that can influence physical or virtual environments. Different AI systems vary in their levels of autonomy and adaptiveness after deployment.[27]

At the heart of such systems are computer algorithms, of which there is a wide variety,[28] most significantly deep-learning algorithms trained on very large datasets (whether text or image data). Deep learning algorithms are trained before being made available for use (eg, through creating applications that incorporate the technology), but, depending on the design of the algorithm, can continue to fine-tune the way in which outputs are made in light of data added during deployment (ie, the period of active operation of the relevant application).[29] For instance, an AI system might acquire information about a consumer that would progressively establish a detailed digital profile of that consumer. In this regard, such algorithms differ from symbolic,

[24] See eg, C Twigg-Flesner and G Howells, 'Adapting Consumer Law to New Technologies' in R Brownsword and L DiMatteo (eds), *The Cambridge Handbook of the Governance of Technology* (Cambridge University Press, 2025).

[25] R Brownsword, 'Law Disrupted, Law Re-Imagined, Law Re-Invented' (2019) *Technology and Regulation* 10.

[26] C Twigg-Flesner, 'The Potential of the COVID-19 Crisis to Cause Legal "Disruption" to Contracts and Contract Law' in E Hondius et al (eds), *Coronavirus and the Law in Europe* (Intersentia, 2021) 1107–08.

[27] OECD, *Recommendation of the Council on Artificial Intelligence*, lit I, first indent, legalinstruments.oecd.org/en/instruments/OECD-LEGAL-0449.

[28] See eg, P Dimingos, *The Master Algorithm* (Penguin, 2015), who discusses many common types of algorithms.

[29] See eg, M Mitchell, *Artificial Intelligence – A Guide for thinking humans* (Penguin Books, 2019) ch 2; S Russel and P Norvig, *Artificial Intelligence – A modern approach* (Pearson, 2022) chs 19–23.

or deterministic, systems,[30] which are essentially rule-based and provide outputs that are predictable and verifiable. Each of these approaches has its own merits and drawbacks, and efforts are underway to develop a hybrid approach combining elements of both, so-called 'neuro-symbolic' AI.[31]

Digital assistants could be based on different types of algorithms, or combinations thereof, although one might expect digital assistants with more complex and varied capabilities to be based on some form of deep-learning technology which allows for some level of adaptiveness. This entails that the way in which such digital assistants make their decisions might, at least for some aspects, vary and alter over time in light of the data the digital assistant encounters and processes once deployed. One novelty arising from the technology itself would therefore be its adaptiveness and the degree of unpredictability about the decisions a digital assistant would make.

Secondly, the extent to which digital assistants could automate a consumer's actions for concluding a contract needs to be considered. This will vary depending on the design of each digital assistant,[32] including the extent to which such applications will operate autonomously, ie, without the consumer's intervention in the steps leading up to concluding a contract. Some digital assistants might be limited to assisting consumers with searching for products they are interested in (as is already the case with the digital voice assistants in widespread use). Others might be a little more advanced and act as a type of recommender system, whether on request by the consumer or on its own motion. With both search and recommender assistants, any decision on whether to conclude a contract would be with the consumer, as it is now, although there would be some prior narrowing-down of the choices available.[33]

However, many digital assistants might do more and take the necessary steps to conclude a contract for the consumer. A narrow digital assistant might only conclude contracts for one identified product to be sourced from one supplier (eg, toner cartridges for a printer, or coffee pods for a coffee maker). Others might source the best deal for one product from one of several possible suppliers. More capable digital assistants might select a variety of items to be supplied by a named supplier (eg, a weekly groceries order from the consumer's preferred supermarket). The most advanced might be capable of concluding contracts for a variety of goods and services with any supplier of those good or services, based on criteria set by a consumer. All of these permutations have in common that they would remove a consumer from active involvement in the decision-making loop leading to the conclusion of a particular contract. Instead, that decision would be made by the digital assistant. This would prompt the question whether a consumer would still be bound by the contract which has been concluded in this way, and the implications of deciding that the consumer is or is not bound. The fact that the human consumer has been taken out of the decision-making process seems to mark a key difference from the paradigm of consumer law that consumer contracts are

[30] See Mitchell (n 29) ch.1.

[31] See research in progress under the auspices of the Alan Turing Institute, *Neuro-symbolic AI – Integrating deep learning and symbolic structures*, www.turing.ac.uk/research/interest-groups/neuro-symbolic-ai.

[32] For a summary of the various permutations, see eg, R Brownsword, 'Autonomy, delegation, and responsibility: agents in autonomic computing environments' in M Hildebrandt and A Rouvroy (eds), *Law, Human Agency and Autonomic Computing* (Routledge, 2011) 73.

[33] *cf* N Blickstein Shcory and S Gal, 'Voice Shoppers' (2022) 88 *Brooklyn Law Review* 111.

concluded through the active decision by a consumer, and that such a decision should be free and informed and not result from misinformation or manipulation.[34] Instead, there might be greater concern about the manipulation of digital assistants and the resulting detriment this could cause for consumers.

Thirdly, a digital assistant could be designed to draw on a wide range of data sources and therefore base its decisions on a much wider range of data than a consumer would. Furthermore, a digital assistant might not be affected in the same way by the behavioural-cognitive limitations of the consumer's decision-making process; in particular, a digital assistant might be capable of processing much more information in a more balanced manner, without the heuristics, or shortcuts, human consumers typically use.[35] Obviously, it is far from clear whether there will be digital assistants that will be capable of doing this, nor whether this will become a feature of most digital assistants. Indeed, concerns over the reliability and robustness of current deep-learning technology would suggest that digital assistants would also be far from perfect in the way they would consider information.[36] Indeed, a digital assistant might become a target for manipulation itself due to the weaknesses of the AI system incorporated into the digital assistant, eg, through hidden prompts that manipulate the way in which the algorithm processes data to take a decision.[37]

But if such capabilities were to become widespread, and digital assistants were widely adopted by consumers, it might undermine a key assumption on which much of consumer law is based: the need to redress the informational imbalance of consumers.[38] As things stand with the technology, however, this is not likely to become an immediate issue that would trigger a recalibration of the assumptions on which consumer law is based.[39]

In summary, the two dominant novelties of digital assistants, therefore, are likely to be: first, the adaptive nature of the algorithms at the core of digital assistants; and, secondly, the removal of the human consumer from the decision-making process leading up to the conclusion of a contract. With regard to the associated legal challenges, these two novelties are connected rather than distinct, ie, some of the questions arising from taking the human consumer out of the decision-making process are shaped by the adaptive nature of the algorithms on which digital assistants are built. The most significant question is whether contracts concluded by a digital assistant bind a consumer and whether there are instances when a decision taken by a digital assistant does not, or should not, result in a consumer being bound.

[34] For this, the information requirements eg, under the Consumer Contracts (Information, Cancellation and Additional Charges) Regulations 2013 (S.I 2013 No 3134) or the prohibitions of unfair commercial practices under DMCCA 2024, ss 225–28, are key provisions.

[35] Busch (n 15).

[36] ID Raji et al, 'The fallacy of AI functionality' (2022) *FAccT* 959; ST Piantadosi and F Hill, 'Meaning without reference in large language models' (2022) arXiv:2208.02957v2; L Rosenberg, 'The Manipulation Problem: Conversational AI as a Threat to Epistemic Agency' (2023) arXiv:2306.11748v1.

[37] For an instance reported in the press, see N Evershed, 'ChatGPT search tool vulnerable to manipulation and deception, tests show' *The Guardian* (24 December 2024). See also R Van Loo, 'Digital Market Perfection' (2019) 117 *Michigan Law Review* 815.

[38] I Ramsay, 'Framework for Regulation of the Consumer Market Place' (1985) 8 *Journal of Consumer Policy* 353; O Seizov, AJ Wulf and J Luzak, 'The Transparent Trap: a multidisciplinary perspective on the design of transparent online disclosures in the EU' (2019) 42 *Journal of Consumer Policy* 149; C Busch, 'The Future of Pre-Contractual Information Duties: From Behavioural Insights to Big Data' in C Twigg-Flesner (ed), *Research Handbook on EU Consumer Law* (Elgar, 2016).

[39] *cf* N Kolt, 'Predicting Consumer Contracts' (2022) 37 *Berkley Technology Law Journal* 71.

10.2.2. Attribution of Digital Assistant's Actions

The question of whether a consumer should be (legally) bound by the decisions of a digital assistant concerns the attribution of the actions of a digital assistant, ie, whether the actions of a digital assistant should be attributed to the consumer, and whether there should be limits to this attribution. Of course, this is not a new question as such; the possibility of using software to automate the conclusion of a contract and questions of attribution have been debated extensively in the scholarly literature.[40] Whilst there is general agreement in the literature that there should be attribution to the person whose actions are automated through an algorithm, the legal routes by which this result is obtained vary, often in order to identify limits to this attribution in case the algorithm has taken an 'unexpected' decision.

For most lawyers, the instinctive starting point is to search for an answer in existing legal rules, rather than develop a solution first before considering how this would translate into law. Considering existing law is fine if this is done with the intention of assessing its fitness for new circumstances rather than limited to finding a way of applying existing laws to new challenges. It is helpful to recall Brownsword's distinction between a 'coherentist' and 'regulatory-instrumentalist' mindset as reflecting these two approaches: a coherentist mindset is concerned with finding solutions in existing law, whereas a regulatory-instrumentalist is primarily concerned about law that is fit for purpose.[41] 'Fitness for purpose' essentially means that the law properly addresses the new challenges arising from applications of new technologies.

Much of academic scholarship thus far has approached the attribution question with a coherentist mindset. For instance, one recurring suggestion is that an answer can be found by applying the law of agency because a digital assistant would appear to fulfil an intermediary role comparable to an agent in the legal sense.[42] There is a superficial attractiveness in that agency law addresses the legal effects of an intermediary's actions that were authorised by their principal; in a similar way, a digital assistant has been 'authorised' by a consumer to automatically conclude contracts for the consumer. Furthermore, agency law also covers instances where an agent has acted beyond its authority, or where the agent's actions conflict with the interests of the principal. This could help solve the tricky question of what might be done with 'unexpected contracts' resulting from the adaptive nature of the AI technology driving the digital assistant, which might be viewed as akin to a lack of authority. However, a crucial difference is that an agent in the context of agency law should have the resources to compensate their principal where acts beyond their authority result in losses, but a digital assistant would have no such resources.[43] This alone would mean that applying agency law directly is not a good solution; however, agency law could still provide useful pointers for addressing questions

[40] For an early discussion, see T Allen and R Widdison, 'Can computers make contracts?' (1996) 9 *Harvard Journal of Law & Technology* 26. See also C Markou, *Consumer Protection, Automated Shopping Platforms and EU Law* (Routledge, 2019) and E Mik, 'From Automation to Autonomy: some non-existent problems in Contract Law' (2020) 36 *Journal of Contract Law* 205.

[41] He has also referred to this as 'Law 1.0' and 'Law 2.0', respectively: see R Brownsword, *Law 3.0: Rules, Regulation and Technology* (Routledge, 2020).

[42] eg, S Chopra and L White, 'Artificial Agents and the Contracting Problem: A solution via an agency analysis' (2009) *University of Illinois Journal of Law, Technology and Policy* 363.

[43] *cf* Markou (n 40) 181.

of attribution and 'unexpected contracts' by analogy[44] and with modifications.[45] A less challenging approach is to identify how the use of a digital assistant by a contracting party would relate to the elements of contract formation, including the objective expression of that party's intention to be legally bound.[46] Choosing to deploy a digital assistant indicates, objectively, that the party intends to be bound by the contracts concluded through the digital assistant,[47] based on any parameters that might have been set by that party and taking account of the digital assistant's functionalities.[48] A more straightforward approach still is simply to regard a digital assistant a 'tool' used for concluding contracts,[49] notwithstanding their inherent unpredictability resulting from their adaptiveness.[50] In short, '[AI algorithms] are tools and the output of their operations must be attributed to those who operate them.'[51] In English law, there is support for treating systems that automate the conclusion of a contract as tools, rather than as something distinct from the contracting party that has automated its actions. This was accepted in the case of mechanical ticket machines over 50 years ago,[52] and later adopted in the context of a deterministic (or symbolic) software algorithm.[53] One might expect that, if a court were asked to consider contract automation through an adaptive AI algorithm, the same conclusion would be reached. Approaching the question of attribution from a coherentist angle leads to the conclusion that the actions of a digital assistant would be attributed to the consumer; however, there is an advantage of clarity in putting this position beyond the vagaries of doctrines not designed for this situation by adopting a clear rule that leads to the same result. Doing so would not only have the advantage of clarity and legal certainty, but also make it easier to find a solution in respect of any limitations to attribution, which would start from such an attribution rule.

10.2.3. Setting Limits to Attribution

Whilst attribution of a digital assistant's actions to a consumer should therefore be uncontroversial, it will be more difficult to set limits to this attribution, ie, will there be instances where a contract concluded through the actions of a digital assistant should nevertheless not be attributed to a consumer and therefore not binding? This is the 'unexpected contract' situation, ie, a contract which is not merely unwanted by the consumer

[44] *cf* Lauren Henry Scholz, 'Algorithmic Contracts' (2017) 20 *Stanford Technology Law Review* 128, 165.

[45] Kolt (n 10).

[46] *Smith v Hughes* (1871) LR 6 QB 597; *RTS Flexible Systems v Molkerei Alois Muller (UK Production)* [2010] UKSC 14.

[47] eg, V Ooi, 'Contracts formed by software: an approach from the law of mistake' (2022) *Journal of Business Law* 97.

[48] Mik (n 40); Mik, 'Much ado about artificial intelligence: or the automation of contract formation' (2022) 30 *International Journal of Law and Information Technology* 484.

[49] On AI as a tool more generally, see A Narayan and S Kapoor, 'AI as normal technology', /knightcolumbia.org/content/ai-as-normal-technology.

[50] Markou (n 40) 176.

[51] Mik (n 40) 229.

[52] *cf Thornton v Shoe Lane Parking* [1971] 2 QB 163, where Lord Denning offered an explanation of how contracting with a ticket machine would work. The other members of the panel, Megaw LJ and Sir Gordon Wilmer, declined to express a view.

[53] *R (ex p Software Solutions Partners Ltd) v HMCE* [2007] EWHC 971 (Admin), an administrative law decision regarding a challenge to tax rules rather than a contract law case.

even though it is within the range of contracts the consumer should have expected,[54] but a contract resulting from a change in the way the digital assistant processes data to take a decision which has resulted in contracts that were beyond what might have been expected by the consumer. Contract lawyers might be quick to appeal to what is generally called 'unilateral mistake'. In English law, this notion applies to a mistake made by one party, but not the other (who may or may not be aware of the first party's mistake). For instance, a consumer might argue that an order placed by a digital assistant for something a consumer would never purchase, or an order for a very high price, was placed mistakenly and that the consumer should not be bound. However, in English contract law, the actions of the parties and their intentions are determined objectively, and if, objectively, it appears that the parties have reached an agreement, then there is a binding contract.[55] In the absence of a misrepresentation, even the knowledge of the other party that the first party was mistaken will not usually mean that a contract is set aside, except where the mistake was one as to the terms of the contract.[56] However, where a party has made a mistake as to the terms of the contract,[57] and the other party knew, or at least ought to have known,[58] about this, there is no contract.[59] The difficulty for succeeding with a unilateral mistake claim where the actions of the digital assistant are the source of the mistake is that the digital assistant will have operated within its programming, including any adaptive features, even if the consumer might not have expected the digital assistant to place the order under challenge.[60] Mistake is therefore unlikely to be of much help to consumers in these circumstances.[61]

One might instead consider the parallel with unauthorised acts by an agent referred to above for a potential solution, albeit one that would require analogous development to fit the particularities of contracting through digital assistants: if the action was 'unexpected' it might be treated as unauthorised. On that basis, there would be no attribution to a consumer, and thus no contract. However, agency law recognises that there can be situations that make it appear that an agent has greater authority than the agent actually has, and a third party can still hold the principal liable under the purported contract. In English law, this arises from a representation by a principal that an agent did have the requisite authority on which the third party relied,[62] although such 'apparent authority' is difficult to establish where the transaction would not be in the commercial interests of the principal.[63] If one attempted to draw an analogy for the case of digital assistants, it would broadly suggest

[54] On this distinction, see also M Giancaspro, '"I, Contract": evaluating the Mistake Doctrine's Application Where Autonomous Smart Contracts Make "Bad" Decisions' (2022) 45 *Campbell Law Review* 53, 85.

[55] *Smith v Hughes* (1871) LR 6 QB 57.

[56] ibid.

[57] But not a different matter surrounding the contracting process: *Quoine Pte Ltd v B2C2 Ltd* [2020] SGCA(I) 02 (Singapore).

[58] *Hartog v Colin & Shields* [1939] 3 All ER 566; *Chwee Kin Keong v Digilandmall.com Pte Ltd* [2005] 1 SLR 502 (Singapore).

[59] *Centrovincial Estates plc v Merchant Investor Assurance Company Ltd* [1983] Com LR 158.

[60] Giancaspro (n 54).

[61] This may be different in other jurisdictions where mistake doctrines are broader: M Herbosch, 'Contracting with artificial intelligence' (2023) 87 *Rabel Journal for Comparative and International Private Law* 672.

[62] *Freeman & Lockyer (a Firm) v Buckhurst Park Properties (Mangal) Ltd* [1964] 2 QB 480; *First Energy (UK) Ltd v Hungarian International Bank Ltd* [1993] 2 Lloyds Rep 194.

[63] *Criterion Properties plc v Stratford UK Properties LLC* [2004] UKHL 28.

that a contract concluded through the digital assistant would appear to be authorised to any third party unless that party was aware of any limitations, particularly if the contract would not seem to be in the consumer's (economic) interests.[64] However, it seems difficult to gauge what might be in the consumer's interests, considerably more so than what might be in the commercial interest of a business, so simply reasoning by analogy would not get very far. In the absence of any clear evidence that there has been a breakdown in the functionality of the digital assistant or external interference, it would probably be difficult to escape treating any unexpected actions as part of a digital assistant's "apparent authority", and in most instances, a consumer would be bound by the digital assistant's actions. As a consequence, consumer would be considerably exposed to the risk of being bound by 'unexpected' contracts and the resulting financial cost. One could argue that this outcome is inherent to digital assistants and that this is something that would have to be accepted by consumers. However, were this to result in many instances of consumers suffering financial losses, there would undoubtedly be a need for intervention. Something would need to be done to delineate the limits of attribution.

This is a major challenge awaiting consumer law that, and a clear legal test will be needed to identify where the limits of attribution will be. An appropriate balance will need to be struck between enabling the automation of transactions concluded through digital assistants whilst recognising the inherent uncertainty about how a digital assistant will perform on the one hand, and the need for a limit to the attribution where the digital assistant has acted beyond what could have been expected to ensure consumers have some protection when contracting through digital assistants.

There is no obvious solution for this, and one could explore a number of tests for defining the boundaries. A good starting point for such a test might be Lord Mance's observations in his dissenting judgment in the well-known Singaporean case of *Quoine v B2C2*.[65] In essence, he argued that the deployment of AI algorithms has inherent risks (of unexpected actions)[66] which are assumed by the party deploying an algorithm. However, he further argued that there must be limits to this (tacit) assumption of risk. He proposed a test which would consider whether an honest and reasonable person with knowledge of the relevant circumstances would regard the contract as beyond what might have been expected.[67] On the facts of the case, this was a serious breakdown in the system, so he would have concluded (had the majority not taken a different view for other reasons) that the contract in *Quoine* was not binding. Irrespective of Mance's precise formulation of his test, which was elaborated in the context of Singapore's doctrine of equitable mistake, the wider point that a person deploying an algorithm to automate their role in the conclusion of contracts assumes the risk that its actions may be unwanted or even unexpected, but that there should be a limit to that risk assumption. That limit would need to be carefully set out in consumer law for consumer contracts and would likely require a lower threshold than in commercial situations, because consumers are less equipped to assess and manage the additional risks that contracting through a digital assistant would involve.

[64] By analogy with *Criterion Properties plc v Stratford UK Properties LLC* (ibid).

[65] *Quoine Pte Ltd v B2C2 Ltd* [2020] SGCA(I) 02.

[66] At [193].

[67] At [198].

10.2.4. Taking the Consumer Out of the Decision-Making Process

The implications of taking the human consumer out of the decision-making process are wider than the question of attribution, however. In particular, it raises questions over whether the potential benefits that automation might bring and the potential for new business models to establish should be controlled in some way to ensure that opting to utilise a digital assistant for contract automation does not mean that a consumer is effectively surrendering all control to the digital assistant. It is essential that there is some balance between the purpose of a digital assistant to automate the contracting process and the implications of taking the human consumer out of the decision-making process. Whilst it is beyond dispute that humans are not perfect decision-makers because of well-known behavioural constraints, humans still make decisions – as consumers, humans decide whether to conclude a contract, even if this means paying over the odds or ending up with a product that underperforms or is not what the consumer expected. Indeed, much of consumer law seeks to ensure that consumers at least have the opportunity to make better decisions, and that redress is available for instances when things have gone wrong.

Automation would change the human consumer's role as the decision-maker, although one might counter-argue that the consumer has merely made their decision at an earlier point: rather than deciding whether to go ahead with a contract at the relevant moment in the formation process, the consumer has effectively made the decision to be bound by all the contracts concluded through the digital assistant. This would mean that the crucial decision-making point is no longer whether to place an order or make a purchase, but rather the decision to let the digital assistant take care of these matters.[68] On this view, if any additional consumer law rules are needed, they should be targeted at the decision to deploy a digital assistant rather than the automated decision-making process. But it would be wrong to see these as mutually exclusive points of attack; rather, both the decision to deploy a digital assistant and the effects of actions taken by a digital assistant need to be fully addressed in consumer law.

However, the adaptiveness of the algorithms on which a digital assistant is based will invariably leave some degree of uncertainty as to what sort of contracts the digital assistant might conclude. It would be undesirable to leave consumers irretrievably exposed to the algorithmic whims of a digital assistant and the resulting financial consequences of the digital assistant's actions. Much of this could be addressed by ensuring that a digital assistant is given clear parameters within which to perform its functions. This would enable a consumer to determine in advance what sort of contracts a digital assistant should conclude automatically. It would still leave open the possibility that the occasional contract might be undesirable for the consumer, so some additional ability to intervene before a contract is concluded, even if only by having the opportunity to stop the automated process, would be helpful. Furthermore, a consumer should retain the freedom to disable, or suspend, their digital assistant to stop it from arranging contracts altogether.[69]

[68] Busch (n 15).

[69] The ELI DACC model rules cover all these aspects. See also Twigg-Flesner (n 12) for a discussion of these options.

The arrival of digital assistants therefore raises several matters that would need to be covered by consumer law to ensure that there is no gap in consumer protection when digital assistants are used for contracting. At the very least, the implications of taking the human consumer out of the decision-making process, particular the final step to be taken by a consumer towards the conclusion of a contract, would need to be addressed. Whilst the fact that a contract was concluded using an algorithmic process of itself might not trouble the law too much, the consequences of not having a human consumer in that process demand that robust consumer protection is in place. The importance of this has already been recognised, notably by ELI, which adopted the DACC in April 2025. The remainder of this contribution will focus on the DACC themselves as well as the case for adoption by the UK to prepare its consumer law for digital assistants in consumer contracting.

10.3. The ELI DACC Model Rules

The potential for widespread contract automation offered by AI algorithms has been the focus of two significant initiatives, both primarily concerned with general, or commercial, contract law: UNCITRAL's *Model Law on Automated Contracting* 2024 (MLAC), and Christiane Wendehorst's *Principles for AI in Contracting* (PAIC). Neither specifically considered consumer contracts, but that gap has been filled by the work of ELI, which adopted the DACC in April 2025.[70]

The DACC provide a set of model rules totalling 25 Articles with detailed explanatory comments spread across five chapters that address a variety of matters to enable and support the use of digital assistants specifically for consumer contracts. They are not intended as an exhaustive model law, but instead provide additional rules for the use of digital assistants for consumer contracts which could be integrated into existing laws on consumer contracts. Nevertheless, unlike UNCITRAL's MLAC, which provides the essential rules to enable automated contracting, the DACC offer a detailed set of model rules that could be adopted as they are, or with modifications to align with existing consumer law rules, where required. It is important to note that the DACC were deliberately not written for the EU context and should therefore appeal to non-EU jurisdictions (including the UK), too.

Within the DACC, a distinction is made between two different contracts, both of which are likely to be relevant to the use of digital assistants by consumers. First, there is the contract for the supply of the digital assistant to the consumer, which is how a digital assistant would be supplied to a consumer. This could happen in different ways: a digital assistant might be offered as a standalone application to be downloaded onto a consumer's smartphone or other device; alternatively, it could be integrated into a physical product (eg, in a 'smart fridge'); or it could be an integrated feature of a website. Such contracts will in many jurisdictions – including the UK – be treated as contracts for

[70] The present author was the lead co-reporter for the project alongside fellow co-reporters, Christoph Busch, Marie Jull Sørensen, and Teresa Rodríguez De Las Heras Ballell; they were supported by a project team and ELI's advisory bodies.

the supply of digital content, software or a digital service;[71] in the case of an integrated digital assistant, ie, smart goods, such a contract might be treated instead as one for the supply of goods,[72] but there are some additional matters not typically covered by the rules applicable to such contracts which had to be addressed in the DACC, including specific information requirements regarding digital assistant and their functionalities (Article 11 DACC), the contractual impact of deactivation (Article 13 DACC; see below); and provisions on conformity and liability (Articles 14 and 16 DACC). Secondly, there is the contract between a consumer and third-party businesses concluded through the digital assistant, referred to as an 'algorithmic contract' in the DACC. This is dealt with in chapter 4 DACC and addresses a number of key matters regarding this contract, many of which are discussed below.

The DACC are underpinned by eight guiding principles which were first developed in an interim report focusing on the immediate steps that could be taken to adapt EU consumer law to the use of digital assistants by consumers.[73] These guiding principles were subsequently refined further and are the basis of many of the model rules in the DACC. Together, they seek to provide the basis for a set of model rules that balance the need for effective consumer protection with the desire to enable innovation. Thus, guiding principle 2 confirms that consumer law applies to contracts concluded through a digital assistant, reinforced by Article 18 DACC, which states that 'consumer law applies to any contract concluded between a consumer and a business' whether or not either party has used a digital assistant for their 'contractual relations'.[74] This ensures that existing consumer laws extend to situations where contracts are concluded through digital assistants. It also underlines that, fundamentally, there is no reason to treat contracts concluded through a digital assistant as different from other contracts as far as the application of consumer law is concerned. Furthermore, Article 17 DACC stresses that contracts concluded through a digital assistant cannot be denied validity merely because a digital assistant was used.

Guiding principle 2 and Article 18 are supplemented by provisions such as Article 21 DACC on the compliance with obligations to provide information, a common feature of consumer law. This article allows a business to comply with a legal obligation to provide information to a consumer by making this information available to the consumer's digital assistant on condition that the digital assistant has the functionality to store or transmit information so it is also available to the consumer, and the business knows about this functionality.

[71] Directive (EU) 2019/770 of the European Parliament and of the Council of 20 May 2019 on certain aspects concerning contracts for the supply of digital content and digital services.

[72] See CRA 2015, s 16; *cf* Arts 2(5)(b) and 3(3) of Directive (EU) 2019/771 of the European Parliament and of the Council of 20 May 2019 on certain aspects concerning contracts for the sale of goods, amending Regulation (EU) 2017/2394 and Directive 2009/22/EC, and repealing Directive 1999/44/EC [2019] OJ L 136/28.

[73] European Law Institute, *EU Consumer Law and Automated Decision-Making (ADM): Is EU Consumer Law ready for ADM?* (December 2023), www.europeanlawinstitute.eu/projects-publications/current-projects/current-projects/eli-guiding-principles-and-model-rules-on-algorithmic-contracts.

[74] 'Contractual relations' is a shorthand used in the DACC to cover 'the pre-contractual and post-contractual actions for, and conclusion, performance, withdrawal from, avoidance or termination of a contract' (Art 2(1) DACC). Individual digital assistants might only be capable of dealing with some of these aspects, and the DACC will apply, for example, to a digital assistant used for contract conclusion only.

Article 21 DACC is one of many articles which reflect the objective of the DACC both to enable the use of digital assistants and ensuring a high level of consumer protection. Thus, at a general level, guiding principle 4 states that 'There should be no barriers to the use of digital assistants, and transactions arranged through a digital assistant should be legally effective.' This feeds through into several model rules, especially Article 3 DACC. Article 3(1) DACC grants consumers the right to use a digital assistant for contractual relations with a business, with paragraphs (2) and (3) precluding the use of contract terms or online interface design in such a way that consumers would not be able to use a digital assistant.[75] Article 3(4) DACC emphasises that a consumer must not be *required* by a business to use a digital assistant though – and where a digital assistant is an integrated feature of a product, the main functionality of the product must not be affected by the consumer's decision not to use that digital assistant.[76] This provision preserves the freedom of consumers to remain 'in the loop' and not be forced to accept automation at all, or to disable this functionality if the consumer is unhappy with its performance.

Article 3(4) DACC also reflects a further key guiding principle: principle 7 requires that a consumer must be able to remain in control of a digital assistant, and this control can be exercised through setting parameters, through the ability to prevent the (automated) conclusion of a contract, and through the deactivation of the digital assistant. Not being required to use a digital assistant is one aspect of remaining in control, but guiding principle 7 is more ambitious, as it also stresses the importance of parameters as well as the ability to prevent the conclusion of contract and to allow for the deactivation of the digital assistant. This is fleshed out in several articles: Article 5 DACC focuses on the selection and modification of the parameters within which a digital assistant should perform its functions,[77] as well as the ability to review the consumer's user profile where that is used by the digital assistant as part of its decision-making process. Article 6 DACC deals with the possibility of preventing the conclusion of a contract either by requiring express confirmation by the consumer or by offering the consumer the opportunity to prevent the conclusion of the contract.[78] Finally, Articles 7 (and 13 DACC) deal with the temporary or permanent suspension of a digital assistant.[79]

This leads to one of the distinctive and innovative features of the DACC: the extensive use of design requirements for digital assistants. Article 5–7 DACC are all part of chapter 2, which sets out several design requirements which all digital assistants intended to be used by consumers for their contractual relations must satisfy before they are supplied to consumers.[80] Compliance with the design requirements is required

[75] Art 3(5) DACC excludes the application of paras (2) and (3) to micro and small enterprises.

[76] There may be legitimate ground recognised in the applicable consumer law for not allowing a consumer to use a digital assistant, and this is recognised in Art 3(5) DACC.

[77] See Art 5(1) DACC, setting out a non-exhaustive list of relevant parameter; note also Art 5(5) DACC on an initial start-up review of all the parameters.

[78] See Art 6(2)(a)–(b) DACC. For some transactions, a consumer can opt out of either (Art 6(3)), and different requirements can be set for different transactions (Art 6(4)). A consumer who fails to 'object' in the time-window is bound by the resulting contract: Art 24 DACC.

[79] Art 13 DACC focuses on the contractual consequences under the contract for the supply of the digital assistant.

[80] Art 4(1) DACC.

for a digital assistant to be in conformity with the contract,[81] ie, in UK terminology, of 'satisfactory quality'.[82] In addition to the requirements in Articles 5–7 DACC, there are additional requirements regarding the functionality of a digital assistant: a technical feature that allows disclosure of a digital assistant;[83] the requirement that a digital assistant must be designed and operated in a way that does not manipulate or otherwise affect the ability of a consumer to make free and informed decisions;[84] and a requirement to provide some degree of documentation of decision-making.[85]

The use of detailed design requirements was a deliberate choice made by ELI to ensure a greater degree of *ex ante* controls over the use of digital assistants for contracting to give effect, in particular, to the objective enshrined in guiding principle 7 that a consumer must be able to remain in control of their digital assistant. This clearly does not mean that a consumer has to be continuously involved or monitor the actions of their digital assistant, as this would largely undermine any benefit of automation; rather, it requires that a consumer has the opportunity to intervene both before and during deployment.

The expression of these guardrails in the form of design requirements rather than additional consumer rights was chosen because it would likely be largely ineffective to rely solely on *ex post* enforcement of consumer rights, whether in individual or collective actions or through regulatory enforcement, because this would only happen after problems have arisen. The purpose of the design requirements is to reduce the number of potential problems. In one sense, chapter 2 DACC is a form of product-specific regulation which is already familiar from the field of product safety, and a legal obligation that technological processes are designed to comply with particular legal objectives is also known eg, from Article 25 (UK) GDPR on 'Data Protection by design and default'. The difference between the DACC design requirements and other approaches is the detail stipulated for the various design requirements. It fits into the idea of 'regulation by design'[86] as specific design features are mandated by the articles in chapter 2.[87] It was inspired by concept of 'technological management' developed by Roger Brownsword in his writings on the relationship between law and technology.[88] In essence, this concept entails that technology can be used to channel behaviours by enabling or restricting particular conduct and that technological means can be used to implement particular regulatory objectives. The DACC model rules have integrated technology into the 'regulatory toolbox' for consumer contracts made through digital assistants, and use the technology to achieve the objective of keeping the consumer in control and therefore in an enabling, or even empowering, rather than a restricting function. The DACC recognise that in the digital context, applications of new

[81] Arts 4(2) and 14(a) DACC.

[82] *cf* CRA 2015, s 34.

[83] Art 8 DACC.

[84] Art 9 DACC.

[85] Art 10 DACC.

[86] 'Regulation by design' can go beyond this, of course: see K Prifti, 'The theory of "regulation by design": towards a pragmatist reconstruction' (2024) *Technology and Regulation* 152.

[87] *cf* R Leenes and F Lucivero, 'Laws on Robots, Laws by Robots, Laws in Robots: Regulating Robot Behaviour by Design' (2014) 6 *Law, Innovation and Technology* 193, 201–02.

[88] E.g., R Brownsword, "Law Disrupted, Law Re-imagined, Law Re-invented" (2019) *Technology and Regulation* 10–30 [https://doi.org/10.26116/techreg.2019.002].

technologies should not only be a target for regulation, but can also be harnessed to give effect to particular regulatory objectives. The integration of design requirements with legal rules remains important, and in the DACC, several design requirements are linked with model rules providing individual consumer rights, including the contractual quality requirement and associated remedies,[89] or the contractual implications of suspending a digital assistant.[90]

Several of the features mandated by the design requirements in chapter 2 DACC are also important when dealing with the issue of attribution of a digital assistant's actions and any limitations thereto. It was noted above that any limitations to the attribution of the actions of a digital assistant are best approached as a matter of risk allocation, with the risk of unexpected contracts distributed appropriately between all the affected parties. The starting point has to be that a person who chooses to deploy a digital assistant is deemed to have accepted the risks that flow from this choice, and this is also the case in the DACC. Guiding principle 1 states that 'the actions of a digital assistant are attributed to the person using it', fleshed out in Article 22(1) DACC which provides that 'a person who uses a digital assistant for contractual relations is bound by the actions taken by the digital assistant and all the actions of the digital assistant are attributed to that person'. This applies to both consumers and businesses utilising digital assistants for their contractual relations. However, the design requirements, particularly those in Articles 5–7 and 9 DACC, provide important risk management features that enable consumers to manage this risk through the setting of parameters, the ability to intervene to prevent the conclusion of a contract, and to suspend a digital assistant. Furthermore, the risk of being bound by the actions of a digital assistant, allocated to a consumer through Article 22(1), is not unlimited; according to Article 22(2) DACC, actions of a digital assistant which 'deviate from those which could reasonably be expected by the consumer' have no legal effect, nor are they attributed to the consumer. In such a situation, the risk of a 'failed' transaction falls on the business in that a contract seemingly concluded is rendered ineffective by Article 22(2) DACC. Article 22(3) DACC specifies factors which are included in determining, on an objective basis, what a consumer might reasonably be entitled to expect: information about the adaptive capability of the digital assistant and whether its operation was inconsistent with such information; whether a consumer could not reasonably have expected that the action in question would be taken;[91] and whether the action was the result of external factors including loss of access or errors in third-party data or cybersecurity breaches. It is clear that this will require a case-by-case analysis, usually when a consumer seeks to challenge a particular contract. It is important to bear in mind that Article 22(2) DACC is not the consumer's first line of defence: as well as the *ex ante* controls already explained, many legal systems, including the UK, provide for a right of withdrawal after a contract has been made which would allow a consumer to escape such a contract in any case.

[89] Arts 4(2), 14(a) and 16 DACC.

[90] Art 13 DACC.

[91] The comments to Art 22(2) DACC give as an illustrative example a digital assistant that was asked by a consumer to play a song by their favourite artist; once the song ends, the digital assistant offers to play another song. The consumer's positive response results in the digital assistant concluding a subscription contract with a streaming service. This was not an action expected in the circumstances.

However, where such a right is not, or no longer, available, Article 22(2) DACC provides an important further protection for consumers.[92]

In order to limit the risk exposure of businesses in such circumstances, Article 25 DACC, the only Article in chapter 5, holds the supplier of the digital assistant liable to a business for any losses that business has suffered because of Article 22(2) DACC. Article 25 DACC is limited to making available the right to compensation, although the precise conditions for awarding compensation would be for the applicable law, which would also determine the type of losses that are recoverable as well as whether some losses would be too remote to be recoverable. This is an important provision, because it provides a route for recourse outside a contractual relationship; it is also challenging insofar as it concerns pure economic losses not arising from personal injury or damage. However, in the context of the DACC, this provision is important because it ensures that the risks arising from the use of digital assistants by consumers are distributed appropriately; without this provision, businesses affected by the actions of the consumer's digital assistant would be exposed to the risk of loss arising from contracts caught by Article 22(2) DACC.

In addition, there are several important protections for consumers. Article 12 DACC, which applies in respect of the contract for the supply of a digital assistant, addresses potential conflicts of interest between the interests of a consumer with those of other persons in the operation of the digital assistant. This might arise, eg, where an online marketplace platform provides a digital assistant to automate contracts on the platform; here, the consumer's interests might conflict with those of the businesses selling via the platform. Where the conflict exists at the time of contracting, this must be disclosed and explained before the consumer concludes the contract for the supply of the digital assistant.[93] Where this only arises after conclusion of that contract, the supplier must notify the consumer without delay, at which point the consumer has a period of 14 days during which to cancel the contract without penalty.[94] A failure to disclose a conflict of interest allows a consumer to terminate the contract for the supply of the digital assistant without penalty, once the consumer has become aware of the conflict.[95] Here, the DACC have taken a balanced approach between consumer protection in cases of conflicts of interest and the need to avoid stifling innovative business models. However, the comments to the Article stress that this position should be reviewed if evidence of consumer detriment in such instances emerges.

Furthermore, it is recognised that the use of digital assistants creates new risks of manipulation of consumers.[96] It was already noted that Article 9 DACC mandates that consumers must not be manipulated in any way by their digital assistant. This might

[92] Businesses are not granted a similar right under the DACC, but Art 22(4) DACC recognises that a business may wish to protect itself through an appropriate contract term in case the business's digital assistant has concluded an 'unexpected contract'. Such a term would only be effective under that sub-paragraph insofar as it deals with actions which are 'so unexpected that a reasonable person would concluded that there has been a serious failure in the operation of the digital assistant'. This is a higher threshold than in Art 22(2) DACC, but this is acceptable because a business is generally more capable of managing its risk exposure than a consumer.

[93] Art 12(1)–(3) DACC.

[94] Art 12(4) DACC.

[95] Art 12(5) DACC.

[96] M Herbosch, 'Fraud by generative AI chatbots: On the thin line between deception and negligence' (2024) *Computer Law & Security Review* 52.

include the way in which the digital assistant's user interface is designed, or the way information is provided. Article 9 DACC complements other rules prohibiting manipulation that might already be in existence, such as the rules prohibiting unfair commercial practices in UK law.[97] In addition, Article 23 DACC prohibits attempts to manipulate digital assistants themselves. This states that 'a business must not use the structure, design, function or manner of operation of their online interface in a way that is likely to materially distort or impair the ability of a digital assistant to perform its functions'. This provision recognises that instead of trying to manipulate a consumer directly, an unscrupulous business might attempt to manipulate a digital assistant instead, whether through prompt injections hidden in text not visible to a human eye.

Overall, the DACC offer a comprehensive set of Model Rules, designed to interact with existing consumer laws by offering essential additions to both enable the use of digital assistants and maintaining strong consumer protection. The DACC are innovative in their approach, not least in combining detailed resign requirements with other types of legal rules. They are driven by the objective of ensuring consumer protection as digital assistant become available and have not shied away from innovative approaches in that pursuit rather than being constrained by existing consumer law. They offer an important model for legislators around the globe.

10.4. Digital Assistants for Consumer Contracts in UK Consumer Law

The potential arrival of digital assistants for consumer contracts (and it must be stressed that it is still a potential development at the time of writing, optimistic media reports notwithstanding) invariably leads to the question of whether UK consumer law is ready for their arrival, and, if not, what steps might need to be taken to get it 'digital assistant – ready'. Building on the preceding section, it will be suggested below that there is a case to take action now, and, if that case were accepted, a strong argument for reforming UK consumer law on the basis of the DACC.

An initial question is whether there is any need to do anything, at least at this point. Whilst instances of automating consumer contracting have been around for some time, there is, as yet, no sign of reliable digital assistants becoming available. This is significant, because the lack of widespread uptake of digital assistants means that there are, as yet, no instances of concrete consumer problems or detriment regarding contract automation. However, this could change rapidly as efforts to monetise progress in AI development ramp up, although it is also possible that such developments might take longer.

This invariably weakens the case for action now – the lack of identified real-world problems might make it premature for legislation to be adopted. Indeed, it is a well-known problem to time regulatory and legislative reactions to technological developments to make sure this happens at the right point in time, ie, neither too soon nor too late. Usually, law and regulation are behind technological developments and need to keep

[97] Originally contained in the Consumer Protection from Unfair Trading Regulations 2008, they are now found in DMCCA 2024, Pt 4, Ch 1.

up to minimise the gulf between where technological developments and their applications are heading and the scope of the relevant laws and regulations.[98] This problem is often referred to as the 'pacing problem'.[99] The conundrum lawmakers and regulators face is that acting too rapidly could mean that whatever steps are taken are insufficient, over-inclusive or ultimately fail to hit their target,[100] but waiting for too long means that any efforts to intervene might be ineffective.[101] However, this is not an absolute rule; sometimes, a particular development can be anticipated without it having materialised yet or concrete problems having emerged. In such a case, getting ahead of the game by introducing appropriate laws and/or regulatory measures to provide a framework to channel such a development is worth attempting.[102]

Are digital assistants a candidate for early intervention? One might argue that contract automation has been discussed for such a long time in the academic literature, but few instances of actual problems have reached the courts or the attention of lawmakers, so perhaps there is no need to do anything, at least for now. Action would only be required once evidence of consumer detriment or harm were to emerge. On the other hand, the technologies supporting contract automation have advanced considerably, particularly in their agility and adaptability in light of data-driven algorithms, and what might have sounded fanciful two decades ago now could soon be on the cusp of becoming reality. Furthermore, the fact that there has been such a long-running academic discourse means that the potential challenges and ways of responding have been rehearsed thoroughly. Digital contract automation through adaptive technologies has been long anticipated, with the implications for consumer contracts a more recent contribution to the scholarly debates. This would therefore seem to be a case for acting now, rather than waiting for concrete problems to materialise as digital assistants are rolled out to consumers. Admittedly, there is still a lot of uncertainty about the kinds of digital assistants that might emerge, but with early trials underway, the process should start sooner rather than later.

Assuming that it would be right to act sooner rather than later, the next question is how UK consumer law could be adapted to digital assistants. To answer this question, some general observations about the current state of consumer law need to be made.[103] In the UK, consumer law is primarily legislation-based through a combination of primary[104] and secondary legislation.[105] Many provisions had their origins in European Union (EU) consumer law as it was on 31 January 2020, the date on which the UK withdrew from the

[98] MJ Copps, 'Disruptive TechnologyDisruptive Regulation' (2005) *Michigan State Law Review* 309.

[99] eg, GE Marchant, BR Allenby and JR Herket (eds), *The growing gap between emerging technologies and legal-ethical oversight – the Pacing Problem* (Springer, 2011).

[100] *cf* L Bennett Moses, 'Recurring Dilemmas: The Law's Race to Keep up with Technological Change' (2007) *University of Illinois Journal of Law, Technology and Policy* 239.

[101] R Hagemann, J Huddleston Skees and A Thierer, 'Soft law for hard problems: the governance of emerging technologies in an uncertain future' (2018) 17 *Colorado Technology Law Journal* 37, esp 55–79.

[102] Twigg-Flesner and Howells (n 24).

[103] These have been discussed elsewhere recently in more depth: see C Twigg-Flesner, 'United Kingdom: An incomplete transformation of Consumer Law' in H-W Micklitz and C Twigg-Flesner, *The Transformation of Consumer Law and Policy in Europe* (Hart, 2023).

[104] Such as the CRA 2015 or Parts 3 and 4 DMCCA 2024.

[105] eg, the Consumer Contracts (Information, Cancellation and Additional Charges) Regulations 2013 (SI 2013 No 3134).

EU. Any legislation which had been adopted by the EU before that date but was not due to be implemented and applied until after that date does not form part of UK law, including the 2019 directives on digital content and digital services,[106] and consumer sales[107] as well as the so-called 'Omnibus Directive' which amended existing legislation in respect of several digital economy issues.[108] Similarly, the EU's digital law measures adopted in recent years also do not form part of UK law, nor is there the same extent of equivalent domestic legislation.[109]

The Consumer Rights Act 2015 (CRA 2015) provides some consumer protection in respect of the supply of digital content,[110] primarily with regard to quality and fitness for purpose of digital content and associated remedies, as well related provisions. However, the legislation is already showing its age and would benefit from reform, not least to address matters which were not addressed sufficiently in 2015. These include rules on the availability of updates and upgrades of digital content, and the respective obligations and rights of consumers and traders, as well as better treatment of goods relying on digital content for their functionality (so-called 'smart goods'[111]). Thus, with regard to updates ('modifications'), CRA 2015, section 40 is limited to requiring 'modified' digital content to still fulfil the various conformity requirements as to digital content in sections 34–36, as well as permitting the addition or improvement of features as long as the digital content continues to comply with its contractual description and other relevant information given to the consumer. Unlike EU law,[112] it does not mandate the availability of updates, nor the duration for which such updates should be available. This gap also affects 'smart goods', which, additionally, raise the question of whether consumers should have any rights when such goods become unusable due to outdated digital content or as a result of an update. Indeed, smart goods are not sufficiently tackled in the CRA 2015, other than through CRA 2015, section 16, which deems a problem in the digital content element of such goods to be a problem with the goods themselves, allowing a consumer to rely on the remedies provided for a non-conformity of goods rather than digital content.[113]

Any matters not addressed in primary and secondary legislation remain, for the present discussion, a matter for the common law of contract. For consumer contracts, the common law remains relevant for several important aspects, including the fundamental

[106] Directive (EU) 2019/770 of the European Parliament and of the Council of 20 May 2019 on certain aspects concerning contracts for the supply of digital content and digital services [2019] OJ L 136/1.

[107] Directive (EU) 2019/771 of the European Parliament and of the Council of 20 May 2019 on certain aspects concerning contracts for the sale of goods, amending Regulation (EU) 2017/2394 and Directive 2009/22/EC, and repealing Directive 1999/44/EC [2019] OJ L 136/28.

[108] Directive (EU) 2019/2161 of the European Parliament and of the Council of 27 November 2019 amending Council Directive 93/13/EEC and Directives 98/6/EC, 2005/29/EC and 2011/83/EU of the European Parliament and of the Council as regards the better enforcement and modernisation of Union consumer protection rules [2019] OJ L328/7.

[109] Although elements of the DMCCA 2024, as well as the Online Safety Act 2023 address some of the issues covered in EU digital law.

[110] See Pt 1, Ch 3.

[111] The Product Security and Telecommunications Infrastructure Act 2022, ss 4–6 refers to such goods as 'connectable products'.

[112] *cf* Art 8(2)–(3) and Art 19 of Directive (EU) 2019/770.

[113] For a more detailed discussion of the CRA 2015, see C Twigg-Flesner and D Ndolo, *Atiyah and Adams' Sale of Goods*, 15th edn (Pearson, 2025) ch 19.

question of when and whether a contract was concluded between consumer or trader. The common law also deals with any other aspect of that contract not regulated through primary or secondary legislation. Some aspects are covered by both the common law and legislation; several of the so-called vitiating factors (misrepresentation, undue influence and duress) overlap with the regulation of unfair commercial practices.[114]

All of this has resulted in a somewhat unhappy hybrid regulation of consumer contracts, not least because the underpinning principles, or values, of the common law of contract and consumer law are different.[115] Whilst consumer law might have started as a corrective to the generally applicable law, the breadth of consumer law has resulted in some tension between both.[116] Thus, Brownsword has noted that 'the regulation of consumer transactions has nothing to do with contract law',[117] and, on the flip-side, Beale has pointed out that 'English contract law is … in effect designed for big business'.[118] Although Brownsword would regard both the common law and consumer legislation as part of the 'regulatory repertoire'[119] for consumer contracts, the density of consumer law would suggest that the role of the common of law contract should be confined as much as possible, and, ideally, phased out altogether.[120] This would be a different project altogether and go beyond upgrading UK consumer law for digital assistants.

All this is important for shaping the approach which UK consumer law should adopt when responding to the potential arrival of digital assistants. For some matters, the common law of contract might offer solutions already, eg, with regard to the basic question of attribution of the actions of a digital assistant, but the many consumer protection aspects discussed above would require specific legislative action. However, rather than relying on what might already be possible with existing legal rules, it would be preferable to ensure that consumer law is truly fit for purpose and provides a clear and sufficiently certain legal environment for contract automation through digital assistants. Rather than having to start with a clean sheet, the UK should take advantage of the work carried out by ELI already and consider developing legislation based on the DACC Model rules so as to get ahead of the curve, rather than waiting for consumer problems to emerge first (which, as explained earlier, might be too late to address those problems).

The ELI's DACC provide a detailed set of model rules, and these should, at the very least, be a starting point for UK consumer law, because the DACC, whilst influenced by EU-derived consumer law, are jurisdiction-neutral and not solely designed to improve the EU's consumer *acquis*. Some aspects of the DACC would slot relatively easy into existing UK legislation; for instance, the provisions regarding a contract for the supply

[114] *cf* DMCCA 2024, ss 225–28.

[115] C Willett, 'Re-theorising Consumer Law' (2018) 77 *Cambridge Law Journal* 179.

[116] *cf* Twigg-Flesner (n 103); for a more optimistic view see J Paterson and E Bant, 'Contract and the Challenge of Consumer Protection Legislation' in TT Arvind and J Steele, *Contract Law and the Legislature* (Hart Publishing, 2020).

[117] R Brownsword, 'Regulating Transactions: Good Faith and Fair Dealing' in G Howells and R Schulze (eds), *Modernising and Harmonising Consumer Contract Law* (Sellier, 2009) 88.

[118] H Beale, 'The Impact of the Decisions of the European Courts on English Contract Law: The Limits of Voluntary Harmonization' (2010) 18 *European Review of Private Law* 501, 526.

[119] Brownsword (n 117) 98–99.

[120] Twigg-Flesner (n 103).

of a digital assistant in chapter 3 could be added to the CRA 2015, Part 1, Chapter 2 on contracts for the supply of digital content. Some of this would require the insertion of additional sections, eg, provisions that would adopt Article 11 DACC (information requirements), Article 12 DACC (disclosure of conflicts of interest) and Article 13 DACC (deactivation of a digital assistant). Article 14 DACC could be included within section 34 on satisfactory quality, whereas Article 16 DACC would already be covered by section 42(6)–(7) regarding damages claims for non-conformities of digital content.

However, it would equally be possible to enact either separate legislation on digital assistants, or to insert a separate chapter into either the CRA 2015 or the Digital Markets, Competition and Consumers Act 2024 (DMCCA 2024). It would, in any case, be necessary to go beyond amending existing statutory provisions to adopt chapter 4 DACC on 'algorithmic contracts', ie, contracts concluded through the use of a digital assistant. Although Article 17 DACC on the legal recognition of such contracts would likely be part of domestic law already,[121] the other provisions, particularly on disclosure (Article 19 DACC), information (Articles 20–21 DACC), attribution (Article 22 DACC) and manipulation of digital assistants (Article 23 DACC) would require new provisions.

For instance, as discussed above, the attribution rule in Article 22(1) DACC would almost certainly already be found in the common law, a clear statutory rule would put this beyond any doubt. Furthermore, the limitations of the common law treatment of unilateral mistake would make it essential that the limits to attribution in the case of unexpected contracts is also included in consumer legislation. The wording of Article 22(2) DACC might then be adjusted in UK law to consider what a *reasonable* consumer might have expected, rather than what a consumer's reasonable expectations were (a small but important drafting clarification).

Furthermore, there are the design requirements in chapter 2 DACC which are closely linked to the other provisions in the DACC. The most straightforward way of adopting these would be through statutory rules on design requirements.[122] Alternatively, a technical standard for digital assistants incorporating the design requirements could be adopted and compliance with this mandate in legislation. This would have the advantage of making it easier to modify such a standard, should it become necessary.

On balance, the adoption of separate legislation on digital assistants, or at least of a separate chapter in existing legislation, should be preferred over targeted amendments. This would avoid fragmentation of the rules on digital assistant that might otherwise result from the insertion of supplementary provisions one some matters (eg, on the contract for the supply of a digital assistant, as well as adding to Part 1 of the CRA 2015. additions would also be need to Part 2 on unfair terms to adopt Article 3(2) DACC and Article 22(4) DACC).

[121] *cf* the fact that Art 9(1) of the E-Commerce Directive (Directive 2000/31/EC of the European Parliament and of the Council of 8 June 2000 on certain legal aspects of information society services, in particular electronic commerce [2000] OJ L 178/1) on the legal recognition of contracts concluded by electronic means was not expressly implemented in the Electronic Commerce (EC Directive) Regulations 2002 (SI 2002 No 2013).

[122] Although there is UK legislation in the form of the Product Regulation and Metrology Act 2025 that provides for the adoption of regulations setting out product requirements and might have lent itself to the adoption of regulations on digital assistant design requirements, the power to enact such regulations appears to be limited to tangible products only.

In short, as this chapter has demonstrated, the ELI DACC offer a set of model rules that could, at the very least, be a starting point for developing UK consumer law to ensure that consumers will be adequately protected once digital assistants hit the market and to ensure that there is clarity regarding the conditions within which such a market might grow. Some action would be needed as current UK consumer law is not sufficient to address all the challenges that have already been identified.

10.5. Conclusions

This chapter has made a case for anticipatory action to prepare consumer law for the emergence of digital assistants for consumer contracting. It would be anticipatory insofar as digital assistants of this type have yet to become widely available, but it was argued that the fact that there is at least a reasonable prospect that this might happen, and that early action might be needed to ensure consumer protection is extended to this development and that this development is channelled early both to provide guidance to creators and suppliers of such digital assistants as well as to provide clarity for business as to the implications of contract automation through digital assistants.

It also demonstrates the impact of technological developments on issues that have been discussed for a long time. The potential for contract automation is not new and has been discussed for some time in the scholarly literature as well as having been used in practice. However, the advances in AI technologies and the opportunities for developing applications this offers have given fresh impetus to this, but also raising concerns for consumer protection. Consumer law has all too frequently been developed only once significant consumer detriment has occurred, but the pace of technological development and the difficulty of harnessing applications once they have been deployed widely demands earlier interventions. Although there is still some uncertainty as to whether the current state-of-the-art in AI can provide a sufficiently robust technology for digital assistants, the potential is there, and with the implications of contract automation by any technological means already well-rehearsed, steps to prepare consumer law for this development should be taken now. The ELI DACC model rules provide a comprehensive set of balanced rules that offer the potential for a legal framework that protects consumers whilst promoting innovation. Enhancing UK consumer law would not only ensure that UK consumer law can be brought up-to-date in light of advances in digital technologies, but get ready for what may yet be to come.

PART V

Future Directions in Other Areas of Consumer Law

11

The (Servitised) Circular Economy: Are Consumers Truly Empowered?

MONICA VESSIO AND SÉVERINE SAINTIER

11.1. Introduction

The circular economy has become synonymous with sustainability and, as such, is often posited as the main tool to bolster the drive to net zero by 2050.[1] A multidimensional concept, it is made up of different facets and there has been no shortage of multidisciplinary literature gathering the essence of what a circular and sustainable supply chain should look like.[2] Somewhat uncontroversially, the broad principles of a circular supply chain are to eliminate waste, circulate products and materials, and regenerate nature. The circular economy is a disruptive concept in that it challenges the traditional linear take-make-dispose[3] method, questioning the notion that materials, products and resources have an end-of-life, by showing these can have a longer life than conventionally accepted. Resources can be harnessed and looped back into the system delivering a feedstock for future products and materials by adopting innovative business models and strategies aligned with circular values such as re-use, repair, refurbish, remanufacture or recycle.[4]

[1] Research Briefing, 'The UK's Plans and Progress to Reach Net Zero by 2050' (12 August 2025); see also n 18 below. Ellen MacArthur Foundation (one of the early proponents of a circular economy), *Towards the Circular Economy, Economic and Business Rationale for an Accelerated Transition*, EMF Report, www.ellenmacarthurfoundation.org; M Geissdoerfer et al, 'The Circular Economy – A New Sustainability Paradigm? (2017) 143 *Journal of Cleaner Production* 757. The idea is not entirely new since 'before the 18th century European industrialisation, there were inherent indigenous concepts of circularity'. F Lesniewska and K Steenmans, *Circular Economy and the Law Bringing Justice into the Frame* (Routledge, 2023) 4.

[2] United National Environment Programme, www.unep.org/explore-topics/green-economy/what-we-do/environment-and-trade-hub; J Kirchherr et al, 'Conceptualizing the Circular Economy (Revisited): An Analysis of 221 Definitions' (2023) 194 *Resources, Conservation & Recycling Journal* 1.

[3] An economic model described as 'a traditional open-ended economy model developed with no built-in tendency to recycle, which is reflected by treating the environment as a waste reservoir'; B Su et al, 'A Review of the Circular Economy in China: Moving from Rhetoric to Implementation' (2013) 42 *Journal of Cleaner Production* 215.

[4] Not all these started as circular initiatives, but they are all aligned with circular values. Circular economy was traditionally represented by the four loops: product-life extension, re-use, remanufacturing and recycling; K Salonitis and P Stavropoulos, 'On the Integration of the CAx Systems Towards Sustainable Production' (2013) 9 *Procedia CIRP* 115; Ellen MacArthur Foundation, *Towards the Circular Economy Vol 2: Opportunities for the Consumer Goods Sector* (2013).

Seen both as 'a necessity and an economic opportunity',[5] many companies all over the world have adopted circular economy-aligned principles to prevent value leakage and to capture value in their supply chains.[6] Although the original underlying conceptual idea of the circular economy is to help with waste reduction,[7] it is far more than simply creating a recycling economy. The goal is to keep products in use at their highest value for as long as possible.[8] This has been said to motivate manufacturers to design products to lengthen their utility lifespan as much as possible, and in some cases has led businesses to promote a servitisation model-based supply chain, where the service rather than the product is 'sold' to the customer.

Servitisation models (the term 'subscription model'[9] is also used in this chapter) promoted as circular supply chain business models,[10] appear, at first blush, a win-win for all. The suppliers, in theory, make less product, less energy is consumed in the production process, and consumers have a better-quality product to use, products remain in use (serviced and maintained) for longer periods, and suppliers make more money.[11] However, we posit that the reality is different: whereas suppliers are benefiting financially,[12] the advantages for consumers (and plausibly the environment) are less clear. In practice, consumers are placed on continual payment schemes and effectively dispossessed of the opportunity to own the products. By 'continual' or 'perpetual' payment cycles, we do not mean a binding payment schedule (contracts that never end); rather, we intend to highlight the necessity of having to continue to lease in such cases, and therefore continue to make payments because the consumer never gains ownership. Although consumers (as citizens) have a role to play in helping to achieve sustainable consumption, their protection must remain a priority amidst sustainability considerations.[13]

[5] RM Ballardini, J Kaisto and J Similä, 'Developing Novel Concepts in Private Law to Foster the Circular Economy' (2021) *Journal of Cleaner Production* 1.

[6] MAK Rizvi et al, 'Designing Through Value Co-creation: A Study of Actors, Practices and Possibilities' 2019 IEEE International Conference on Industrial Engineering and Engineering Management (December 2019) 571; A Urbinati, D Chiaroni, and V Chiesa, 'Towards a New Taxonomy of Circular Economy Business Models' (2017) 168 *Journal of Cleaner Production* 487.

[7] The UK generated 27.7m tonnes in 2021, an increase of 2.4% from 2020. England is responsible for the vast majority, generating 23.1m tonnes (84% of the UK total) in 2021: www.gov.uk/government/statistics/uk-waste-data/uk-statistics-on-waste. The EU contributed 2.2b tonnes of waste each year. 'Sustainable Waste Management: What the EU is Doing' (6 April 2018), www.europarl.europa.eu/topics/en/article/20180328STO00751/sustainable-waste-management-what-the-eu-is-doing.

[8] European Commission, *Closing the Loop – an EU Action Plan for the Circular Economy*, 2-12-2015, COM(2015) 614 final; Urbinati, Chiaroni and Chiesa (n 6).

[9] In fact, we use the terms 'subscription' and 'servitisation' interchangeably. However, the concept is distilled in section 11.3 below).

[10] See for example CA González Chávez et al, 'Towards Sustainable Servitization: A Literature Review of Methods and Frameworks' (2021) 104 *Procedia CIRP* 283.

[11] R Wise and P Baumgartner, 'Go Downstream: The New Profit Imperative in Manufacturing' (1999) *Harvard Business Review* 89. M Wang et al, 'The Economics of Circular Supply Chains: Transformative Implications for Businesses and Stakeholders' (2005) 513 *Journal of Cleaner Production*; LA Guardiola, A Meca and J Timmer, 'Cooperation and Profit Allocation in Distribution Chains' (2007) 44 *Science Direct Decision Support Systems* 17.

[12] JL Heskett et al, 'Putting the Service-Profit Chain to Work' (1994) 72 *Harvard Business Review* 164.

[13] R Krantz, 'A New Vision of Sustainable Consumption' (2010) 14 *Journal of Industrial Ecology* 7, 8; V Mak and E Terryn, 'CE and Consumer Protection: the Consumer as a Citizen and the Limits of Empowerment through Consumer Law' (2020) 43 *Journal of Consumer Policy* 227.

The main theme of this chapter is the analysis of the servitisation model from a consumer protection perspective. Of particular focus is gaining insight as to whether and to what extent a servitised supply chain would have on consumers. This understanding is important, from a regulatory perspective, to ensure that the law continues to meet the needs of consumers in a rapidly changing society. The discussion is situated within the broader context of the pursuit of a sustainable society, which necessitates a whole system approach, considering the issues in a threefold manner – environmental preservation, economic prosperity and social equity – in order to achieve balance, much like a tripod (section 11.2). The discussion critically considers how servitisation is posited as a process that enables a circular economy (we show this is an assumption and unsubstantiated)[14] when the general reasons for the development of servitisation as a model have been identified primarily as economic (profit), user needs (utility/profit) and competition (profit again).[15] We propose that the former perspective is a one-sided view (section 11.3). This is particularly clear when considering the types of problems that consumers face in the context of a product-as-a-service supply chain. Because servitisation has not been proven to be environmentally 'better' than the sales model (we show it does not make a difference in the rate of re-use), greenwashing also forms an integral part of the discussion. While there have been legislative movements to thwart greenwashing practises in both the European Union (EU) and the United Kingdom (UK) recently, these do not provide answers to the additional complications that emanate from a servitised environment identified in this chapter. While our focus is on UK and EU law, the theoretical underpinnings extend across jurisdictional boundaries. Left unchecked, a subscription economy leads to several issues, which include: (i) discrepancy in quality for subscription products; (ii) the erosion of consumer choice between buying and leasing; and (iii) price distortions which can lead to consumer disenfranchisement. We link price distortions, that may arise between what we refer to as 'for-leasing' models (servitised) and 'for-sale' models, and consumer disenfranchisement, through loss of ownership and ability to leverage assets. Further, we posit that ownership is tied with dignity, hence that an unregulated subscription economy that disables consumers from owning private property may lead to loss of dignity. We consider this discourse in light of the existing regulatory framework, and the new Digital Markets, Competition and Consumers Act 2024 (DMCCA 2024)[16] which, despite a move in the right direction, does not fully address these additional complications specific to servitisation (section 11.4). Finally, we make recommendations as to how the above three issues may be ameliorated (section 11.5).

[14] See for example, RM Ballardini, J Kaisto and J Similä, 'Developing Novel Concepts in Private Law to Foster the Circular Economy' (2021) *Journal of Cleaner Production* 279, 283 and contra, H Corvellec and HI Stål, 'Evidencing the Waste Effect of Product-Service Systems (PSSs)' (2017) *Journal of Cleaner Production* 1422.

[15] The categorisation is from R Rabetino, M Kohtamäki and H Gebauer, 'Strategy Map of Servitization' (2017) *International Journal of Production Economics* 144, 192). Hojnik refers to 'locking-out competitors': J Hojnik, 'Servitisation, IOT and Circular Economy: Need for Regulatory Intervention at EU level?' in B Keirsbilck et al (eds), *Servitization and Circular Economy: Economic and Legal Challenge* (Intersentia, 2023) 35.

[16] The Act came into force in May 2024 and provides for the regulation of competition in digital markets, amends the Competition Act 1998 and the Enterprise Act 2002, and makes other provisions about competition law and consumer rights protection.

11.2. Circular Economy as a Whole-System Approach

The prevailing linear take-make-dispose consumptive line has a well-known adverse impact on natural resources.[17] In maximising the economic and environmental value of resources, the underlying idea of the circular economy is that businesses will contribute towards improving sustainable development and increased business resilience. Although supported in broad terms at policy level, with ambitious targets set across the world to achieve a climate neutral economy,[18] the implementation of a 'fully circular economy' remains limited and far from mainstream[19] – unsurprisingly given the complexities associated with the task.

Viewed, however, as a 'societal transition in which the circulation of materials eventually contributes to economic, environmental and societal benefits',[20] the circular economy has the potential to encapsulate a whole system approach. With the ability to aim for a tripartite equilibrium – encompassing environmental preservation, economic prosperity and social equity – it is important to recognise the conflicting yet interconnected nature of these goals. Achieving such tripod stability requires reconciling these aims through systemic change. This paradigm shift should also be supported by a strong legal and political framework.[21] More importantly, these changes must foster a truly integrated and holistic approach. Stahel effectively captures this interconnectedness:

> Sustainability depends on several interrelated systems. Each is essential for the survival of humans on Earth. This means that priorities cannot be argued over, nor can there be speculation about which of these systems humankind can afford to lose first. In fact, humans cannot risk losing ground in any of these areas.[22]

In other words, in a whole system environment, all components must be considered together as they are interrelated and each affect the other, whether positively or

[17] W McDonough and M Braungart, *Cradle to Cradle Remaking the Way We Make Things* (New Point Press, 2002); T Jackson, *Prosperity Without Growth Economics for a Finite Planet* (Routledge, 2009); JR Ehrenfeld and AJ Hoffman, *Flourishing: A Frank Conversation about Sustainability* (Standford University Press, 2013).

[18] The EU has set targets to have a climate-neutral circular economy by 2050: European Commission, *A New Circular Economy Action Plan for a Cleaner and More Competitive Europe*, COM(2020) 98 final 2. For a critical review of some of these legislations, see Lesniewska and Steenmans (n 1) ch 2. At the international level, see UN Economist Network, 'New Economics for Sustainable Development: Circular Economy', www.un.org/sites/un2.un.org/files/circular_economy_14_march.pdf.

[19] E Mateo, T Turumen and J Atlaranta, 'Demand-Pull Instrument to Support the Circular Economy: a Global Perspective' (2022) 2 *Journal of Environmental Law and Policy* 103.

[20] A Reichel et al, *Circular Economy in Europe: Developing the Knowledge's base European Environmental Agency Report* (2016) 2; L Alaerts et al, 'Towards a More Direct Policy Feedback in Circular Economy Monitoring via a Societal Needs Perspective' (2019) 5, both cited by C Lavigne and S Rousseau, 'Trust and Consumers' Attitudes Towards Product-Service Systems Comparing Flanders and the Netherlands' in B Keirsbilck et al (eds), *Servitization and Circular Economy: Economic and Legal Challenge* (Intersentia, 2023) 31.

[21] J Hojnik, 'Ecological Modernization through Servitization: EU Regulatory Support for Sustainable Product Service Systems' (2018) 27 *Review of European Community & International Environmental Law* 166.

[22] WR Stahel, 'The Functional Economy: Cultural and Organizational Change' in DJ Richards (ed), *The Industrial Green Game: Implications for Environmental Design and Management* (National Academies Press, 1997) 91.

negatively. A balanced discourse is necessary, 'not only to benefit current generations but also future generations'.[23] From a policy landscape perspective, new measures of prosperity must be considered and such measures must go beyond the conventional measures of gross domestic product (GDP)[24] and national competitiveness, 'to bring long-term thinking and systems inter-linkages to the forefront of policy decisions'.[25] Production (supply) must be linked with consumption (demand).[26] This transactional dynamic must also be supported through protective measures, protecting consumers (socio-economically) and protecting the environment. Like any integrated system, an imbalance in one part will create problems in other parts. Thus, consumption and production, must develop in tandem within this ecosystem.

The servitisation model has been proffered as a useful tool to circularise the supply chain and reach this coherent whole.[27] However, this much promised 'ecological modernisation'[28] is not the panacea originally contemplated. Any tool promoting sustainability must not only consider all relevant stakeholders, but must first and foremost be sustainable. In the next section we consider whether servitisation, not originally developed as a sustainability business model[29] but now selling itself as such, provides the requisite balance or whether more needs to be done to protect consumers.

11.3. Servitisation: An Unbalanced Business Model

Servitisation, product-as-a-service models or product-service-systems, as they are often referred to in non-legal literature,[30] are not a new phenomenon; since the 1980s manufacturers have been moving their business models from only selling products

[23] The quote is an adaptation of Lesniewska and Steenmans (n 1) 135, with reference to social equity.

[24] It is essential to recognise that GDP, the common measure of economic growth, was not designed to assess citizens' well-being. Instead, GDP primarily reflects a nation's production capacity and economic output. A Kapoor and B Debroy, 'GDP Is Not a Measure of Human Well-Being' (2019) *Harvard Business Review*.

[25] Krantz (n 13) 8. The French were already looking at such diversified measures in 2009; see the Report of the Commission on the Measurement of Economic Performance and Social Progress, 2009. However, recent movements have also occurred in the UK, for example the Office for National Statistics (ONS) has been working on measuring well-being beyond GDP, considering dimensions like the environment, society and personal well-being. By doing so, it provides a more holistic view of how a country is doing beyond purely economic measures. ONS, 'Measuring Wellbeing and Going "Beyond GDP"' National Statistical (9 May 2024), blog.ons.gov.uk/2024/05/09/measuring-wellbeing-and-going-beyond-gdp.

[26] Both sides must be sustainable: Mak and Terryn (n 13). Referring to a sustainable consumption policy landscape, Krantz (n 13) states it as 'a complex network of systems inter-linkages, difficult trade-offs, and powerful feed-back loops within the political, business, and natural environments'.

[27] K Hedvall et al, 'Enabling a Circular Economy Through Green Service Strategies' in L Witell (ed, *Service Innovation and Management Future of Business and Finance* (Springer, 2025); J Han, A Heshmati and M Rashidghalam, 'Circular Economy Business Models with a Focus on Servitization' (2020) 12 *Sustainability* 8799.

[28] Hojnik (n 21) 166.

[29] E Manzini, C Vezzoli and G Clark, 'Product-Service Systems. Using an Existing Concept as a New Approach to Sustainability' (2001) 1 *Journal of Design Research* 27.

[30] For a study on what these systems involve see, 'What is Product-Service Systems (PSS) – A Review on PSS Research and Relevant Policies' IGES Kansai Research Centre Discussion Paper KRC-2006-No.1E (2006).

to providing combinations of products and services.[31] Known by other names[32] and iterations,[33] servitisation[34] can be broadly classified into two groups. The first is ownership transfer with enhanced services, where ownership of the product is transferred to the consumer through a sale and additional services are provided such as repair and maintenance.[35] The second is service-only transactions, where ownership of the product remains with the trader or manufacturer, and only the service associated with the product is transferred to the consumer. Examples include letting out machines or leasing of cars.[36] In this chapter we focus on the service-only transaction, premised on the idea of people accessing rather than owning what they use.[37] In other words, establishing long-term leasing relationships with consumers,[38] where businesses retain ownership and do not sell products. Moving away from traditional ownership in private property, the process shifts from 'product-focused markets to function-focused markets'.[39]

Given that the main drivers for such a system are financial,[40] doubts as to whether servitisation really lives up to its green credentials are raised.[41] As a concept, servitisation's link with sustainability is not always very clear, with the overall peril of 'same-but-circular business models'.[42] The subscription model, driven by businesses, has given rise to an imbalanced system which is neither sustainable, nor protects consumers. The shortcomings of the servitisation (for-leasing) model are threefold.

[31] Li et al, 'Exploring Product–Service Systems in the Digital Era: a Socio-Technical Systems Perspective' (2019) *The Total Quality Management Journal* 897, 913.

[32] Other terms are also used, for example, 'tertiarisation' and 'service infusion': Hojnik (n 21).

[33] The main iteration used in the academic literature is product service system (PSS). As remarked, there are differences between servitisation and PSS, and yet the terms are used interchangeably to indicate the same concept. H Schlamuylders, 'Movable Servitisation – Contractual liability in the B2C relationship' in B Keirsblick et al (eds), *Servitisation and Circular Economy: Economic and Legal Challenges* (Intersentia, 2023) 137.

[34] First coined over 30 years ago by S Vandermerwe and J Rada, 'Servitization of Business: Adding Value by Adding Services' (1988) 6 *European Management Journal* 314. See also H Lightfoot, TS Baines and P Smart, 'The Servitisation of Manufacturing: A Systematic Literature Review of Interdependent Trends' (2013) 33 *International Journal of Operations & Production Management* 1408.

[35] J Hojnik, 'The Servitization of Industry: EU Law Implications and Challenges' (2016) 53 *Common Market Law Review* 1575, 1606. See also Manzini, Vezzoli and Clark (n 29) 30, who state: 'In essence the right of product ownership is shifted from a client to the producer or service provider'.

[36] ibid.

[37] F Bostoen and W Devroe, 'From Sales to Subscription in the Car Sector: Competition Law Implications and the Refusal to Sell to Consumers' (2018) 39 *European Competition Law Review* 411, 412.

[38] A Neely, 'Making the Shift to Services' (2014) *Institute for Manufacturing Review* 12, 13.

[39] Lavigne and Rousseau (n 20) 15–32, 15. See S Chaudhari et al, 'Paradoxes and Coping Mechanisms in the Servitisation Journey' (2022) *Industrial Marketing Management* 323.

[40] Refer to nn 11 and 12. This has been more recently corroborated by the OC&C WRAP Report which underscores that product longevity and repairability are not merely environmental imperatives but commercially advantageous strategies. By reducing returns and warranty claims, enhancing brand equity and facilitating ongoing customer interaction through repair services, upgrades and resale programmes, such approaches create measurable economic value. In parallel, the Report also highlights how rental and product-as-a-service models allow firms to capture additional value throughout the product lifecycle ('Are Businesses Leaving Money on the Table?' (2025)).

[41] For a non-exhaustive list, see Hojnik (n 21) esp para 3, 164 and its associated references (esp fns 14, 43, 44 and 48). Bostoen and Devroe (n 37) highlight the ability of the model to circumvent competition rules and to have negative impact on consumer choices (over repairs especially), which has sustainable implications. On the paradoxes of implementing a true subscription model, see Chaudary et al (n 39).

[42] Steenmans and Lesniewska (n 1) 73.

First, it is not clear that such subscription models are 'greener' or environmentally better. Businesses involved in selling prioritise the cost-effectiveness of manufacturing, with the point of sale representing the final income from that customer, at least in the short term. On the contrary, choosing for-leasing models enables businesses to maintain an ongoing relationship with the consumer, ensuring a continuous stream of income over time. The latter model, however, does not necessarily equate to less energy consumption or less waste creation. Let us compare vehicles sales with vehicle leasing as an example. Say eight million individuals need to travel from points A to Z a certain number of times a year; the question arises: do leased vehicles (owned by large corporations) contribute less to carbon emissions than privately owned vehicles, both constantly moving from points A to Z? We answer in the negative for obvious reasons. Another example, remaining within the transport context, are services that connect passengers with drivers through a mobile app service, Uber for instance. What are the long-term carbon footprints of vehicles driven continuously for eight hours a day[43] compared to vehicles used, for instance, only one to two hours a day?[44] Considering all variables, including energy consumption, in-production, usage, maintenance, and the additional driving required for vehicles to reach different customers, the necessary data is currently lacking to substantiate claims that seem to be driven more by stakeholder opportunism than concrete evidence.[45] A form of greenwashing, really, discussed in section 11.4.1 below.

Secondly, the current corporate approach – that of goods subscription, designed to prompt consistent leasing – is not a far departure from the paradigm of the industrial revolution, where planned obsolescence was the norm, designed to prompt frequent replacements.[46] Both models are underpinned by the same incentive – profit. The for-leasing business models appear rather uncomplicated: entice consumers to continue leasing to establish an enduring state of dependency.[47] This leads to the second issue, created by subscription economies; that of irresponsible consumptive choices, referred to as the 'rebound effect'.[48] Let us consider, for instance, the choice between owning one or two washing machines throughout a lifetime or continually leasing various (each time newer or better) models from the manufacturer.[49] This type of 'advantage' is advertised to consumers[50] designed to prompt frequent 'upgrade'. This model may

[43] Limit of hours an Uber driver can take per day.

[44] The average UK driver drives 7,500 miles per year (www.britanniacarleasing.co.uk/news/annual-uk-car-milage), whilst the average UK Uber driver drives 5,000 miles per month, which is 60,000 miles per year (www.nimblefins.co.uk/business-insurance/courier-insurance-uk/uber-pay).

[45] '[M]ore work including research … needs to be done': Manzini, Vezzoli and Clark (n 29) 38.

[46] Planned obsolescence emerged as early as the 1920s, when the Phoebus cartel allegedly conspired to limit lightbulb lifespans to 1,000 hours. By the 1930s, amid the Great Depression, it was even proposed as public policy – Bernard London (an American real estate broker known for his 1932 paper, 'Ending the Depression Through Planned Obsolescence') advocated legislation to enforce product expiry as a means of reviving consumption and industry.

[47] The knowledge that products represent only a small part of the total value creation, and the main part of total value creation stems from services is by no means new. This is sometimes referred to in the literature as the 'value proposition' – see R Oliva, and R Kallenberg, 'Managing the Transition from Products to Services' (2003) 14 *International Journal of Service Industry Management* 160 – or 'service contribution' – see H Gebauer and T Friedli, 'Behavioral Implications of the Transition Process from Products to Services (2005) 20 *Journal of Business and Industrial Marketing* 70.

[48] Manzini, Vezzoli and Clark (n 29) 36.

[49] Already an available option: www.laundry365.co.uk.

[50] youraverageguystyle.com/lifestyle/the-benefits-of-leasing-a-car-for-fashionable-guys.

create less responsible user behaviour[51] and in turn has greater environmental impact.[52] A lessee, obliged to continuously make payment, will naturally desire the latest model on the market, aligning with market-driven consumer attitudes and playing into the profit-oriented corporate mindset.[53] Influencing and/or directing the issue of consumer behaviour and consumption patterns when presented with subscription models is beyond the scope of this chapter. We nevertheless submit that from an environmental perspective, the net effect would likely be worse in a servitised environment than in a for-sale one, due to extra production required to satiate, what is ultimately 'created' consumer desires.

Finally, we identify the imbalance that is created by producing 'better' goods (more durable) to withstand repeated cycles of use, for the subscription model,[54] and lesser quality products when made for sale. In the conventional linear economy supply chain, corporations primarily focus on selling large quantities to maximise profit,[55] manufacturers for the most part build products with cost-efficiency in mind, often sacrificing durability. In contrast, where products are built for leasing, the emphasis shifts towards creating durable, long-lasting products and parts. The overarching idea of a subscription economy is to maintain a product in optimal working condition for as long as possible

[51] For example, see A Tucker, 'Product Services for a Resource-Efficient and Circular Economy – a Review' (2015) 97 *Journal of Cleaner Production* 76; A Annarelli, C Battistella and F Nonino, 'Product Service System: a Conceptual Framework from a Systematic Review' (2016) 139 *Journal of Cleaner Production* 1011; L Hüer et al, 'Impacts of Product-Service Systems on Sustainability – A Structured Literature Review' (2018) 73 *Procedia CIRP* 228. Rifkin posits that what consumers are chasing when they buy luxury is not physical comfort, but access to a way of life: J Rifkin, *The Age of Access: How the Shift from Ownership to Access is Transforming Capitalism* (Penguin, 2000). According to J Rosenblum, 'Age of Success: How the Shift from Ownership to Access is Transforming Capitalism' (2000) 32 *Washington Monthly*, Rifkin argues that, unchecked, 'these trends lead to a world where the cultural sphere is strip-mined for experiences. Commercialized networks of access then process these experiences and deliver them to captive consumers, whom companies have spent years profiling and prodding. The results, in Rifkin's mind: millennia-old cultures destroyed and the emergence of a society where empathy and compassion find themselves deadened because sanitized, commercial, paid-for experiences have replaced human interactions'.

[52] K Intlekofer, B Bras and M Ferguson, 'Energy Implications of Product Leasing' (2010) 44 *Environmental Science and Technology Journal* 4409; VV Agrawal et al, 'Is Leasing Greener than Selling?' (2012) 58 *Management Sciences Journal* 523.

[53] '[T]he new status of the user (leaser not owner) could cause irresponsible consumption': R Allais and J Gobert, 'A Multidisciplinary Method for Sustainability Assessment of PSS: Challenges and Developments' (2015) 15 *Journal of Manufacturing and Science and Technology* 56, 63.

[54] F Tietze and EG Hansen, 'To Own or to Use? How Product Service Systems Facilitate Eco-Innovation Behavior' (Academy of Management Conference, Orlando, April 2013). See also, AW Thompson et al, 'Benefits of a Product Service System Approach for Long-life Products: The Case of Light Tubes' in T Sakao, T Larsson and M Lindahl (eds), *Proceedings of the 2nd CIRP IPS2 Conference 2010 Linkoping* 13–14 April, 83–89. This study came about through a partnership between the researchers and Aura Light International AB, a company that produces long-life fluorescent light-tubes. See also the claims by the World Economic Forum, 'What is Servitization, and How Can it Help Save the Planet?', www.weforum.org/agenda/2020/11/what-is-servitization-and-how-can-it-help-save-the-planet (20 November 2020).

[55] The mass production model has led to the emergence of practices like fast fashion and planned obsolescence, and other strategies which compromise product quality while simultaneously boosting production. C Sabel and J Zeitlin, 'Historical Alternatives to Mass Production: Politics, Markets and Technology in Nineteenth Century Industrialization' (1985) 108 *Past and Present* 133; CR Duguay, S Landry and F Pasin, 'From Mass Production to Flexible/Agile Production' (1997) 17 *International Journal of Operations and Production Management* 1183; V Dinges et al, 'The Future of Servitization: Technologies that will Make a Difference' (Cambridge Service Alliance, University of Cambridge, 2015); C Raddats et al, 'Motivations for Servitization: the Impact of Product Complexity' (2016) 36 *International Journal of Operations and Production Management* 572.

so that the product can serve as a leased good for as long as possible, or be modular in design so as to facilitate refurbishment or remanufacture once returned from being leased. While production of goods built for longevity, durability and modularity are environmentally sound concepts, the system under which this type of product is created raises questions of equity. Is the message that consumer-owned products should be less durable/modular (sustainable) while those offered by corporations promoting leasing solutions (robed as circular) are built to have sustainable features? If the answer is in the affirmative then the message portrayed is that with for-sale products, manufacturers can/must/are free to build less modular, less durable less 'green' products; whereas if producing for-leasing products, these are built with durability, modularity and longevity design goals, though not necessarily for sustainability reasons. Either way, this dichotomy creates dependent consumers: one set forced to continuously purchase, the other set to continuously lease. Additionally, the end-product used has been referred to as the tip of the material iceberg, as the product itself only contains a small percentage of the raw materials involved in making and delivering the good.[56] Leasing models can be environmentally worse despite the remarketing of products.[57]

It is clear that for a supply chain to be truly sustainable, it should *not* matter how products are consumed. Products should be manufactured for longevity, durability and modularity irrespective of which supply loop they enter, whether for-sale or for-leasing models. Companies like Le Creuset and Zippo, for example, offer products with lifetime guarantees and warranties and repair services, regardless of the products' age.[58] Their product model is founded on quality, durability and longevity.

The sustainable future of production lies in creating items built to last a lifetime, to be modular and non-toxic so that not only will they last longer, but when they are at end-of-life they can enter recycling or remanufacturing cycles seamlessly. This should not be the standard that only leased goods are held to, but *all* goods. This aspect is non-negotiable; it forms the first (environmental) leg of the tripod. To some extent this concern has been ameliorated, in the EU, by the Ecodesign for Sustainable Products Regulation ('Ecodesign Regulation'),[59] which came into force on 18 July 2024, which establishes a framework for setting ecodesign requirements for sustainable products and aims to enhance the durability, reusability, upgradability and recyclability of products.[60] However, it seems that the UK has been less proactive. Whilst it does have the Ecodesign for Energy-Related Products and Energy Information Regulations 2021 (which came into force on 1 July 2021), which by setting specific ecodesign requirements, aim to

[56] McDonough and Braungart (n 18). Studies have confirmed this by looking at the entire energy expenditure of the production process; see, for example, Corvellec and Stål (n 15) 1422.

[57] Agrawal et al (n 51) 529.

[58] www.zippo.co.uk/pages/order-faq.

[59] Regulation (EU) 2024/1781 of the European Parliament and of the Council of 13 June 2024 establishing a framework for the setting of ecodesign requirements for sustainable products, amending Directive (EU) 2020/1828 and Regulation (EU) 2023/1542 and repealing Directive 2009/125/EC. See of particular relevance the products aspects as defined in Art 5 as read with Annex I.

[60] Regulation (EU) 2024/1781 has affected Directive (EU) 2019/771 (20 May 2019 on Certain Aspects Concerning Contracts for the Sale of Goods) which defined durability. The updated definition emphasises not only the lifespan of a product, but also its ability to maintain functionality and performance over time, including with regular use and maintenance. This change aims to ensure that products are designed to last longer and remain functional.

improve the energy efficiency and environmental performance of energy-related products, these regulations cover only electrical appliances. It seems that the UK missed the opportunity to take the same steps as the EU in relation to regulating against obsolescence and for durability, modularity and longevity for all products when passing the DMCCA 2024 into force. Furthermore, whilst the Consumer Rights Act 2015 (CRA 2015)[61] (for consumption) and the Sale of Goods Act 1979[62] (for production) include durability of goods as an aspect of quality of goods (implied terms in contracts of sale), neither statute recognises the durability of goods as an important concept for achieving more sustainable consumption patterns and a circular economy. Regulation must therefore be realigned to ensure that products are manufactured with quality, durability, modularity and longevity as requisite characteristics (environmental). Recommendations to this effect are proposed in section 11.5.

11.4. Protecting all Consumers in their (Consumptive) Choices

The dominant driving force of the pursuit of profit behind servitisation business models, put forward as having circular or sustainable impact, whilst serving to gain corporate social responsibility accolades, is regrettable not only for the general quest for a more sustainable society, but also for consumers' social and economic agency. The aim of this section is to unpack what is intended here, for consumers and consumer law. To do so opens the door for some initial (and tentative) suggestions as to a way forward (section 11.5).

Servitisation, as a concept is often portrayed as being 'consumer oriented'[63] by providing 'easier access, convenience and flexibility'.[64] However, consumers 'can only play a part if sustainable choices are actually available'.[65] This creates a problem for consumers who actively choose to engage with such models because of their green credentials.[66] The fact that such business models are not per se conservational[67] is something that consumers must be protected against.

Furthermore, and although consumers have an important role to play in the quest for environmental sustainability, the idea that the subscription economy moves the consumer from a passive to an active one, thereby rendering the traditional view of the consumer as a 'vulnerable and susceptible consumer' to being 'diminished, at least at a conceptual level', is too simplistic.[68] Indeed, servitisation raises a more pernicious

[61] s 9(3)e.

[62] s 14* (2B).

[63] Hojnik (n 16) 33.

[64] F Bostoen, L Van Acker and W Devroe, 'Servitisation and Competition Law' in B Keirsbilck et al (eds), *Servitization and Circular Economy: Economic and Legal Challenge* (Intersentia, 2023) 69.

[65] Mak and Terryn (n 13) 229.

[66] The concept of the consumer citizen originated in S McGregor, 'Consumer Citizenship: A Pathway to Sustainable Development' keynote speech at the International Conference on Developing Consumer Citizenship (Hamar, Norway, April 2002) 2, 5. For discussion on the green consumer, see Mak and Terryn (n 14) 228.

[67] Hojnik (n 16) 41.

[68] ibid 57.

risk – loss of empowerment – which is equally applicable to all consumers, not just the vulnerable. The two aspects are considered below in turn.

11.4.1. Greenwashing and the Latest Legislative Attempts to Combat the Practice

Greenwashing – the practice of conveying a false impression or providing misleading information about how a company's products are environmentally friendly – is a form of marketing spin whereby companies claim to be more sustainable than they actually are.

The legislative consumer landscape is not an empty slate when it comes to tackling greenwashing. Both the EU and more recently the UK have taken steps to circumvent greenwashing practises.

At European level, the European Commission, in order to strengthen the impact of the Unfair Commercial Practices Directive (UCPD) 2005[69] with regards misleading environmental claims (and therefore better protect the green consumer), revised the guidance on the application of the Directive,[70] by amendment, with Directive 2024/825 ('Empowering Consumers Directive (ECD) 2024').[71] The EU has emphasised the importance of the ability of consumers to be able to make informed purchasing decisions and thus contribute to more sustainable consumption patterns,[72] placing the duty on traders to furnish clear, pertinent and dependable information, and specifically regulate consumer law to combat unfair commercial practices that would deceive consumers and hinder their ability to make sustainable consumption decisions.[73] These practices include those linked to the premature obsolescence of goods, deceptive environmental assertions, misleading details about product or trader social attributes, and sustainability labels that lack transparency and credibility (greenwashing).[74]

The ECD 2024 emphasises that consumers must be empowered to make well-informed decisions, thereby driving demand and the availability of sustainable goods. To achieve this, consumers should not be deceived regarding products' environmental or social attributes, as well as circularity characteristics (such as durability, reparability or recyclability). Thus, to the list of the main characteristics of a product in

[69] Directive 2005/29/EC of the European Parliament and of the Council of 11 May 2005 concerning unfair business-to-consumer commercial practices in the internal market and amending Council Directive 84/450/EEC, Directives 97/7/EC, 98/27/EC and 2002/65/EC of the European Parliament and of the Council and Regulation (EC) No 2006/2004 of the European Parliament and of the Council ('Unfair Commercial Practices Directive').

[70] An update also occurred in 2016: European Commission 2016, ec.europa.eu/info/sites/info/files/factsheet environmental claimsnon-food_2015 en.pdf). For a brief discussion see also Mak and Terryn (n 13) 231.

[71] Directive (EU) 2024/825 of 28 February 2024 on Empowering Consumers for the Green Transition (EU) 2024/825 of the European Parliament and of the Council of 28 February 2024 amending Directives 2005/29/EC and 2011/83/EU as regards empowering consumers for the green transition through better protection against unfair practices and through better information. Member States must incorporate the Directive into their national laws by 27 March 2026, with enforcement beginning on 27 September 2026.

[72] Directive (EU) 2024/825 Preamble.

[73] ibid.

[74] ibid.

respect of which traders' practices can be considered misleading, the amendments to the UCPD 2005 will add environmental and social characteristics as well as circularity aspects.[75] Through environmental and climate-related claims, traders create the impression that consumers contribute to a low-carbon economy by purchasing their products. To ensure the fairness and credibility of such claims the UCPD has been amended to prohibit such claims, where the claims are not supported by clear, objective, publicly available and verifiable commitments and targets given by the trader and set out in a detailed and realistic implementation plan that shows how those commitments and targets will be achieved and that allocates resources to that end. The claims should also be verified by a third-party expert, who should be independent from the trader, free from any conflicts of interest, with experience and competence in environmental issues, and who should be able to monitor the progress of the trader regularly with regard to the commitments and targets, including the milestones for achieving them.[76]

It is not within the purview of this chapter to discuss the ECD 2024 amendments in detail, only to indicate, in the overview provided above, the elevated awareness of the EU to greenwashing dangers, with an especial link to sustainability and circularity claims. Following Brexit, ECD 2024 does not affect the UK, but it is nevertheless relevant as a potential guide for the UK's continued commitment to taking the necessary steps to a transition to a more sustainable society and a more circular economy.[77]

In 2023 the UK addressed the issue of greenwashing with respect to financial products with the Sustainability Labelling and Disclosure of Sustainability-Related Financial Information Instrument,[78] and in 2024 it passed the DMCCA 2024, which impacts the Consumer Protection from Unfair Trading Regulations 2008 (UCPR 2008), the domestic incorporation[79] of the UCPD 2005. The UCPR 2008 aimed to protect consumers from misleading actions[80] or omissions[81] that could influence their purchasing decisions, decisions that they would not have taken had they been aware of the correct information.[82] While these regulations could have gone a long way to protecting consumers against unfair practices, and some specific blacklisted practices could have had particular relevance with reference to environmental claims,[83] such practices were

[75] ibid Art 1(2)(a).

[76] ibid Art 1(2)(b).

[77] Policy Paper Circular Economy Package Policy Statement (30 July 2020), www.gov.uk/government/publications/circular-economy-package-policy-statement/circular-economy-package-policy-statement. More recently, the UK Government announced the first UN-backed centre for circular economy in February 2024: www.gov.uk/government/news/uk-to-establish-worlds-first-un-backed-centre-for-circular-economy-research.

[78] This instrument prohibits exaggerated, misleading or unsubstantiated claims about environmental, social and governance (ESG) credentials of investment products. The measures are aimed at protecting consumers and enhancing trust in sustainable investment products inter alia by applying greenwashing rules to FCA-regulated firms. www.handbook.fca.org.uk/instrument/2023/FCA_2023_39.pdf.

[79] Incorporated into domestic law on 26 May 2008.

[80] reg 5.

[81] reg 6.

[82] UCPR 2008, reg 5. For the European aspect refer to Guidance on the Interpretation and Application of Directive 2005/29/EC Concerning Unfair Business-to-Consumer Commercial Practices in the Internal Market; see also Mak and Terryn (n 14) 231.

[83] UCPR 2008, reg 3(4)(d), Sch 1: where a trader claims to be a signatory to a code of conduct when they are not (s 1) or that a code of conduct or a product has an endorsement which it does not have (ss 3, 4), or where a trader displays a trust, quality or equivalent mark without having obtained the necessary authorisation (s 2). See also, Mak and Terryn (n 13) 231.

not covered directly by the regulations and greenwashing of the servitisation model was not investigated.[84]

The DMCCA 2024 does, however, address misleading marketing practices. The Act strengthens the enforcement of consumer protection laws, giving the Competition and Markets Authority (CMA) the power to directly impose fines on companies that make misleading claims.[85] The DMCCA does not explicitly reference environmental issues, but presumably the relevant sections would include claims based on the lack of sustainability, eco-friendliness or environmentally beneficial products or services are. A person guilty of an unfair commercial practice[86] can on a summary conviction in England and Wales be fined, and in Scotland or Northern Ireland can be subjected to a fine not exceeding the statutory maximum. A person may also, on conviction on indictment, be liable to imprisonment for a term not exceeding two years or to a fine (or both).[87] This, together with the power of the Secretary of State under the Act, to amend the list of automatically prohibited practices,[88] highlights a broader effort to address deceptive marketing practices and ensure that consumers receive accurate information regarding the (sustainability) of products and services. However, the regime seems to have been transposed from the UCPR 2008, which means similar issues will arise in the application of these sections. Furthermore, the sections appear to place the onus on the consumer to prove that but for the sustainability/environmental claims they would not have purchased the products, a fairly tricky burden to overcome.

Although welcome steps, what the DMCCA 2024 and the Sustainability Labelling and Disclosure of Sustainability-Related Financial Information Instrument do not consider are the maligned issues of the possible price distortions that may be created by subscription models. The sub-quality 'for-sale goods' that may be produced alongside the better quality 'for-leasing goods' are also not addressed by these instruments. The question is whether the UK has any legislative tools to ameliorate these two issues. One proposal would be to adapt or interpret the CRA 2015 (as well as the Sale of Goods Act from the production, business-to-business aspect) to introduce sustainable obligations. Another is to interpret the DMCCA 2024 in such as way so as to include within the understanding of unfair commercial practices some of the more nefarious consequences of servitisation. The template is therefore present and the disrupting element can be accommodated by the existing template. These and further suggestions are explored in section 11.5 below.

The issues raised above are of a transactional nature and therefore do not go to the economic agency of the consumer. Although crucial in supporting the role of consumers in the development of a sustainable consumption, we turn to more a disturbing

[84] The definition of 'product' in the Regulations covers both goods and services (reg 2), it does not, however, address the issues specific to servitisation that have been raised in this chapter.

[85] Contained in ss 225–240 ensconced within the applicable Pt 4, Ch 1.

[86] A commercial practice is unfair if it is likely to cause the average consumer to take a transactional decision that they would not have otherwise taken, as a result of the practice involving a misleading action or omission an aggressive practice; a contravention of the requirements of professional diligence; it omits material information from an invitation to purchase, or it is listed in Sch 20, see DMCCA 2024, s 225(4).

[87] s 297 as read with DMCCA 2024, s 240.

[88] DMCCA 2024, s 242, which also grants the Secretary of State power to add, remove or amend a description of commercial practice to the list in Sch 20.

consequence that may arise from a subscription environment on all consumers – the loss of empowerment – addressing the socio-economic aspects.

11.4.2. The Disenfranchised Consumer

Servitisation, motivated by profit, lacking environmental concern but guised under the mantle of sustainability, if left unchecked will not only deplete consumer choice but will lead to market price distortions, at the centre of which is a move away from consumer ownership and towards a perpetual leasing environment. Such paradigm shifts in property ownership affect two broad aspects. The first is that ownership is connected to financial empowerment. Take an average consumer who owns a car and a house. She can leverage assets by selling them and replacing them with smaller and cheaper assets (cashflow) or she can use those assets as security to gain access to finance (loan). Either option can provide access to capital. A leased asset cannot (see sections 11.4.2.1 and 11.4.2.2). The second is that ownership, the right to own and the capacity to own are closely linked to the human rights discourse, particularly dignity, which is linked to empowerment (11.4.2.3).

11.4.2.1. Loss of Right to Ownership

Servitisation models can function solely as financial instruments.[89] As business strategies focused on increasing productivity became insufficient for maintaining competitiveness,[90] companies shifted from offering only physical products to providing integrated solutions to boost market share.[91] Despite the various iterations of the servitisation model, they all fundamentally emphasise a transition from selling products to offering services, altering property rights.[92] This shift can jeopardise consumer ownership rights, significantly consolidating financial power of large corporations.[93]

This is because, ultimately, owning a product might become prohibitively expensive, reducing consumers' purchasing power to a more restricted leasing capability. Take Apple, for instance, a company that not only designs its products, but also develops the accompanying software.[94] Apple maintains control over every aspect of the production

[89] C Vezzoli et al, *Product-Service System Design for Sustainability* (Routledge, 2014).

[90] JL Heskett, WE Sasser, and LA Schlesinger, *The Service Profit Chain*, (Free Press, 2007); O Kallenberg and R Kallenberg, 'Managing the Transition from Products to Services' (2003) 14 *International Journal of Service Industry Management* 160.

[91] ibid.

[92] H Schlachmuylders, 'Movable Servitization – Contractual Liability in the B2C Relationship' in B Keirsbilck et al (eds), *Servitization and Circular Economy: Economic and Legal Challenge* (Intersentia, 2023) 137 citing S Fisher et al, *Leasing Society, report requested by the European Parliament's Committee on Environment, Public Health and Food Safety* (2012) 12.

[93] Thomas points out the normative problems that would come if there is a move towards a leasing economy, as it 'presupposes a party with a more powerful ownership interest, above that of the lessee', and makes the point that the circular economy will entail '*enhancement* of direct ownership, in the hands of a limited number of initiators'. S Thomas, 'Legal Considerations for a Circular Economy' in T Tudor and C Dutra (eds), *Routledge Handbook of Waste, Resources and the Circular Economy* (Routledge, 2020) 181.

[94] The concept of using Apple as an illustration originated from Dustin Benton, Head of Energy and Resources at The Green Alliance. Benton, however, employed this example to signify a vertically integrated

and service phases, enabling it to reclaim used products, refurbish them, and market them as new or refurbished.[95] However, a significant concern emerges in a scenario where a corporation, like Apple, shifts from selling products to leasing or exclusively providing services while retaining ownership. In such cases, end-users would be required to return the product at the end of the lease term, regardless of their preferences, or (if contractually provisioned by the corporation) renew their lease arrangement. This would effectively force them into a new leasing arrangement (whether for the old product or a new one), creating a perpetual subscription cycle that makes consumers dependent[96] and undermines their agency and autonomy.[97]

This dependency is serious since it shows that servitisation models, if unchecked, could have a wider societal impact rendering all consumers vulnerable. This is important in terms of social equity, the last leg of the tripod.

If caution is not practiced, the purchase price of a simple washing machine, for example, might become unmanageable, even to the average consumer. On an individual basis, this raises issues of consumer over-indebtedness 'due to the numerous subscriptions to services contracts'.[98] Beyond this, this could lead to what can be termed the 'Airbnb Effect'. This term originates from the impact Airbnb has had on the property market. Airbnb vacation rentals have become a lucrative investment, with vacation home purchases surpassing the growth of existing-home sales by 44 per cent from 2019 to 2020.[99] High returns and the possibility of having vacation homes financed make the investment attractive. However, a significant portion of the revenue is concentrated in the hands of a small number of landlords.[100] As a result, the short-term rental industry contributes to a shortage of housing, causing rent prices to rise sharply. The theory behind the Airbnb Effect is that when long-term rentals suitable for residents and families are converted into short-term rentals for visitors, the already limited housing supply decreases. Large corporations and real estate investment firms are also expanding their short-term rental portfolios.[101]

Here, we are imagining a slightly different version of the Airbnb Effect, in that rather than shortage of goods, a subscription economy can lead to a concentration of owners. The impact this would have on all consumers and society is clear.[102] The

corporation. This designation arises from the fact that Apple retains control over all three crucial components: product sales, design and development of the product. Consequently, it has the capacity to retrieve the product, refurbish it, install new software, and, according to Benton's argument, market the product as if it were brand new. See www.youtube.com/watch?v=YUkuURhrn1E.

[95] Provided Apple adheres to jurisdiction-specific regulations with regard to these different phases, legislatively there is nothing prohibiting this model from being implemented.

[96] Hojnik refers to consumers has becoming 'locked-in' by these business models. She also points out that the dependency is further facilitated by the endless 'upgrades' (Hojnik (n 15) 35).

[97] www.theguardian.com/money/2009/jun/21/computer-leasing-deal.

[98] D Voinot, 'Servitization in Real Estate and Insolvency Risk' in B Keirsbilck et al (eds), *Servitization and Circular Economy: Economic and Legal Challenge* (Intersentia, 2023) 214.

[99] travelnoire.com/the-airbnb-effect-on-an-already-high-cost-shrinking-housing-market.

[100] Voinot (n 97).

[101] ibid. Some regulations have been attempted both in the UK and in the EU, but do not appear to address any price distortion or property unavailability issues: www.gov.uk/government/news/short-term-lets-rules-to-protect-communities-and-keep-homes-available; www.europarl.europa.eu/doceo/document/A-9-2023-0270_EN.html.

[102] On this point, see M Roarke and Fox O'Mahony, 'Real Property Transactions in the Network Society' (2023) 46 *Journal of Consumer Policy* 445.

Airbnb Effect transforming into the 'Bosch Effect' or the 'BMW Effect,' and so on. What initially seemed like a noble idea can be co-opted by large corporations to the detriment of consumers. Assets, even an old but functional washing machine, are valuable, and it is better to have access to one than to lack it due to the inability to meet monthly payments, often burdened with various add-ons like insurance, service fees and credit fees for deferred payments.

Not only vulnerable consumers are exposed to risk in this situation, but the average consumer will face the same outcome. They will be encountering identical market prices and face the same market model pressures. The Airbnb Effect will not be consumer-selective.

11.4.2.2. Leveraging Assets

To be recognised as a person under private law entails the ability to own property and to have legal rights and responsibilities.[103] Thus, a person is an individual (consumer) who possesses the ability to hold property rights.[104]

Sohm, in the following quote, demonstrates, quite powerfully, how private property does not only exist in the interest of the individual, but is the bedrock of our modern societies:[105]

> Private property is the foundation upon which every free, self-contained individuality is built up. To realise such an individuality in oneself is the aim of every human being; to bring forth individualities is the destination of the history of mankind. Every nation depends on its free men for the supply of that force which advances and uplifts the national life, carrying the whole community along with it. Private property helps to create the atmosphere in which liberty thrives, and without liberty it is impossible for the individual members of a community to put forth to the full their moral, intellectual, and material powers, and impossible, consequently for the community as a whole to bring its development to a triumphant issue. Private property does not exist solely in the interests of the individual; it is the strong rock upon which life and the welfare of the whole nation are firmly founded.

Modern society is made up of the welfare of the individual who must be financially empowered to utilise their full moral, intellectual (social) and material prowess (economic). The initial stage involves creating a society where individuals can meet their social needs, including education and employment. Simultaneously, the economic aspect is crucial for developing financial skills, enabling them to contribute to the greater good.[106]

Given the recognised importance of the economic role of consumers in the economy, and wider society, the focus on property is not only logical but also crucial, and its protection advantages consumers. Leveraging private property or other high-value asset to build capital is a strategic approach that can enhance consumers' financial position. Owning an immovable property, for example, which appreciates in value over time, would allow consumers to benefit from the increased equity; furthermore,

[103] R Sohm, *The Institutes* (tr J Crawford Ledlie), 3rd edn (Clarendon Press, 1901) Book 1, section 30.
[104] ibid.
[105] ibid.
[106] A Smith, *An Enquiry into the Nature and Cause of the Wealth of Nations* (E Cannon ed) (Metheun, 1961) 475.

properties can be used to create rental income. Homeowners can also borrow against the equity in their property. This equity can be used for various purposes, such as home improvements, education expenses, or debt consolidation. This power to leverage can be translated to immovables; vehicle for example can be sold for cash flow exigencies, goods can be rented or sold and used as security to access finance. Property also gives access to credit, which has played a crucial role in the development of 'the consumer society'.[107]

The servitisation model upsets the current focus on property and is not without risk in terms of over-indebtedness with the potential to recreate what has been referred to as to as 'an "economy of indebtedness"'.[108] If the consumer is priced out of owning private property (AirBnB Effect), the power of the consumer to self-finance (or access finance) will be dismantled. This is an unfair and unreasonable position to place consumers in. It is thus the role of the regulator to step in and framework the servitised environment to protect the consumer. In this regard we suggest legislative safeguarding of pricing models of for-sale products in that they should be on par with for-leasing models, providing consumers with an equitable selection. A perpetual subscription economy, left unchecked, could price out the ownership model (render it too expensive to own) and return humans to a feudalistic template. Rifkin's call to re-distance the cultural sphere from the commercial and to fight against a world where access is always negotiable and controlled by a small group of multinational corporations[109] is therefore echoed.

11.4.2.3. Ownership and Dignity

As the principles of a circular economy reshape the patterns of socio-materiality – the way materials and human activities interact within society – questions are raised about how these fundamental needs, like access to goods, are met and governed. Regulations and economic models impact the consumptive aspects of consumers' lives, and as the need to transition to a more circular trading environment becomes more evident, the way consumers can acquire and use resources needs to be placed under scrutiny and safeguarded.

The importance of property and ownership is at the centre of commercial transactional discourses.[110] If the circular economy empowers market leaders to shape the way consumers consume goods, and corporations retain the power of ownership, this will place consumers on a proverbial wheel of perpetual leasing. The transition from a linear economy to a fully circular one should not ignore these socio-economic aspects.

The depletion of choice due to, inter alia, distorted pricing is connected to the decline of autonomy, which, in turn, is tied to human dignity. Upholding and safeguarding choice contributes to human sovereignty. The control over decisions regarding which assets to buy, lease, or sell forms an intricate amalgamation of impulses that, collectively,

[107] Voinot (n 97) 214.

[108] Voinot (n 97), citing R Libchaber, *Le Rôle des Perceptions en Droit: Dette et Endettement au XXième Siècle in Mélanges en L'Honneur de Philippe Théry* (Dalloz, 2022).

[109] Rifkin, taken from Rosenblum, *Age of Success*.

[110] Thomas (n 93) 184.

define the essence of humanity.[111] Without these freedoms, human dignity may deteriorate, leading individuals to become mere automatons following a predetermined order.[112] Brownsword captures it succinctly:[113]

> [H]uman dignity as empowerment has its own version of the triple bottom line, namely: that one's capacity for making one's own choices should be recognised; that the choices one freely makes should be respected; and that the need for a supportive context for autonomous decision-making (and action) should be appreciated and acted upon. Human rights then translate these underlying demands into entitlements that are due to each human as of right – and the fundamental rights, … is to make one's own choices and have those choices realised and respected.

In as much as an economic model works to adversely interfere or erode the capacity for autonomous action, there is a prima facie violation of human dignity.[114] Article 17 of the Universal Declaration of Human Rights 1948 states that 'everyone has the right to own property alone as well as in association with others and no one shall be arbitrarily deprived of his property'. The Declaration also states in Article 1 that 'all human beings are born free and equal in dignity and rights', while the Preamble recognises that the inherent dignity and the equal and inalienable rights of all members of the human family as 'the foundation of freedom, justice and peace in the world'. The same pronouncement is made in the International Covenant on Economic, Social and Cultural Rights 1966 and the Civil and Political Rights 1966. Brownsword argues that these declarations are the essential ingredients that ground human dignity as empowerment. He encapsulates the fundamental importance of dignity:[115]

> [T]he injunction to respect human dignity is much more than a demand that we commonly make in contexts where we detect demeaning or degrading treatment … it is the infrastructure on which the entire superstructure of human rights is constructed.

It is with these ideas in mind that when hearing the phrase 'you will own nothing, and you will be happy', promoted by the World Economic Forum,[116] raises concerns that such commandment is little more than a call for wealth concentration. A harbinger of an economic system that disregards free choice in favour of corporate agendas. Agendas that lack proven alignment with green objectives.

The notion that private property is integral to human dignity and consumer agency – empowerment through equitable choices – demands robust protection through

[111] Hegel, in what is referred to as the personality of property theory, propounds that freewill is externalised through property and must be developed by acquiring external things. GWF Hegel, *Elements of the Philosophy of Right* (AW Wood eds) (Cambridge University Press, 1991).

[112] Authors' views formed from reading various texts. F Fukuyama, *Our Posthuman Future* (Farrar, Straus and Giroux, 2002); R Brownsword, 'What the World Needs Now: Techno-regulation, Human Rights and Human Dignity' in R Brownsword (ed), *Global Governance and the Quest for Justice* (Hart Publishing, 2004); C Fried, 'Privacy' (1968) 77 *Yale Law Journal* 475.

[113] Brownsword (ibid) 211.

[114] ibid.

[115] ibid 211.

[116] See video at www.facebook.com/worldeconomicforum/videos/8-predictions-for-the-world-in-2030/10153920524981479/?locale=en_GB; www.weforum.org/agenda/2016/11/shopping-i-can-t-really-remember-what-that-is. The World Economic Forum is a voluntary international organisation for public-private co-operation. It is not managed by elected individuals.

comprehensive regulation. It is imperative that regulatory frameworks not only safeguard the rights of individuals to own and control property, but also address the nuanced and extensive implications that arise from the pervasive adoption of contemporary economic models. These models, while fostering innovation and economic growth, often lead to subtle yet profound consequences that can undermine the very principles of dignity and agency they are meant to uphold. Therefore, regulation must be crafted to ensure that the opportunities for private property ownership are objectively protected, and that the potential for exploitation and disenfranchisement is minimised. By doing so, we can uphold the fundamental values of human dignity and consumer empowerment in an increasingly complex and interconnected economic landscape.

We have outlined specific problems above; below we make some tentative recommendations.

11.5. Recommendations

Given the interrelated nature of a whole system approach and the need to balance conflicting interests between producers and consumers, arriving at a catch-all solution is not straightforward. Furthermore, considering the diverse range of services offered within the context of a servitised environment, a one-size-fits-all solution will not be suitable. However, left unaddressed, the problems identified in this chapter could have significant negative impacts. At legislative level, it would require regulators to examine the effects of the servitisation model, not only from its alleged but seemingly unfounded green claims but more importantly from the effects that such business models could have on consumer agency. Though not directly aimed at servitised transactions, both the UK and EU have taken steps towards ameliorating greenwashing concerns through the relevant sections of the UK's DMCCA 2024 and the EU's ECD 2024. However, shortcomings have been identified, such as the lack of direct mention of environmental 'greenwashing' claims, though this could be assuaged through interpretative application of the Act.

Evidentiary burdens should not be on consumers. The burden of proof should be on manufacturer or sellers in issues relating to environmental claims. This approach can help balance the power dynamics between consumers and corporations by implementing a legal presumption that any environmental claim made by a company is misleading unless proven otherwise. This would require the company to provide evidence supporting their sustainability claims, rather than the consumer having to prove they are false. At first blush this may seem onerous on companies however, it is not, for the simple reason that if a company is alleging something then they should only do so on the basis of fact in which event the company should have this information readily available – in fact, so readily available that provision of such information to the consumer should thwart any considerations of legal action by the consumer.[117]

[117] See, for example, Consumer and Markets Authority, *Guidance Complying with Consumer Law when making Environmental Claims in the Fashion Retail Sector* (18 September 2024).

Private property, as has been shown in this chapter, has long been linked to financial autonomy (cash flow, income, leveraging) and dignity of the person. To allow businesses to erode the power of ownership, slowly and systematically, from the consumer and replace it with regular subscription instalments would decouple consumers from financial autonomy. This should not be sacrificed in the name of pseudo-sustainability, as cutting off one of the tripod legs would cause it to topple.

The DMCCA 2024 has introduced a new regulated subscription regime. However, the problematics of price distortions and financial disenfranchisement have not been addressed, despite the opportunity to do so.

Part 4, Chapter 1 DMCCA 2024 regulates 'subscription contracts'. It defines these as contracts between traders and consumers for the supply of goods, services or digital content on an automatically recurring basis, in exchange for payment by the consumer, which are not excluded contracts.[118] The section on subscription contracts goes to the usual protection that consumers have been traditionally granted, relating to information and cooling-off rights. Following the UCPR 2008, Chapter 1 DMCCA deals with aggressive practices that are unfair.[119] Practices are aggressive when they involve harassment, coercion or undue influence, none of which address the issue of price distortions and disempowerment of consumers, which also leave consumers vulnerable and without protection.

Our first suggestion to tackle such gaps is therefore aimed at prevention of price distortion. Regulation should balance the difference between a sale business model and a servitisation business model price warp for the same or similar products. Under the DMCCA 2024 this could be seen as an unfair 'commercial practice' that appreciably impairs the ability of the average consumer to make an informed decision. In other words, if the way the servitised model is priced materially distorts the economic behaviour of the average consumer with regard that product in relation to a sale product, this could be deemed as an unfair practice and contrary to the general prohibition of unfair commercial practice.[120] The reading of the sections listed under Prohibited Commercial Practices, must be interpreted in light of the overarching prohibition contained in section 225, which directs that a commercial practice is unfair if it is likely to cause the average consumer to take a transactional decision they would not have taken if not as a result of a practice that is a misleading action, omission, an aggressive practice or a contravention of the requirements of professional diligence.

Furthermore, and as a more proactive solution, would be the inclusion in Schedule 20 DMCCA of dissuasive pricing as an unfair commercial practice.[121] In other words, any pricing models that are aimed at convincing a consumer to opt for servitised models rather than for-sale transactions, especially in light of the fact that never owning would in the long-run cost the consumer more. In addition, the courts might need to acknowledge that pricing structures of servitisation models could significantly influence consumer choice, and adjust their interpretation accordingly. The understanding

[118] DMCCA 2024, s 254. Excluded contracts are contracts relating to the supply of essential services such as heat, water, gas, electricity and sewerage. These may be amended by the Secretary of State (s 225 as read with Sch 22).

[119] DMCCA 2024, s 228.

[120] DMCCA 2024, s 225.

[121] DMCCA 2024, s 242 gives powers to the Secretary of State to amend Sch 20.

of the pricing models should be simplified in such a way as to be comprehensible to any ordinary consumer. These should be displayed and made readily available to consumers, and include long-term consequences of the opportunity loss. A drive to educate consumers in this regard should be initiated.

The second set of recommendations we propose are to ensure 'like-for-like' product manufacturing standards. Durability was discussed in this chapter as an example; however, the circular economy encompasses much more than making durable products. To lower the energy footprint and reduce the use of virgin materials, concepts such as longevity, modularity and ease of decoupling goods for refurbishment, recycling and remanufacturing are characteristics that need to be built into the product at design stage. These considerations should not be designed only into products whose future is a leasing lifecycle, but *all* products. Adaptation through interpretative efforts by the courts of the rights contained in the CRA 2015 could be a solution. Alternatively, a direct amendment could be made. For example, when considering the satisfactory quality element implied into the business-to-consumer contract by the CRA 2015, the quality of goods includes their state and condition, and the following aspects (among others) of the quality of goods: fitness for all the purposes for which goods of that kind are usually supplied; appearance and finish; freedom from minor defects; and safety and durability.[122] In order to add environmental and social characteristics as well as circularity aspects to the element of satisfactory quality, additional characteristics could include requirements of longevity (different to durability), modularity of products,[123] percentage use of non-virgin (recycled) materials and other sustainable qualities.[124] This would have the advantage of embedding those in the existing framework, allowing for existing remedies to apply. This shows the robust nature of the CRA 2015. The discussion opens up more questions, for example, whether these inclusions would be in line with the existing rights under the CRA 2015, such as the lack of possibility to exclude them. The same can – and must – be given the interlinked nature of the supply chain, applied to the implied terms in the Sale of Goods Acts 1979. To effect a transition toward a more sustainable and circular trading and consumption environment, substantial and courageous action is imperative. If the changes brought by the DMCCA 2024 are a sign of things to come, this is somewhat encouraging.

11.6. Conclusion

Within the framework of the circular economy, the subscription economy is frequently lauded as a remedy for environmental challenges associated with production. However,

[122] CRA 2015, s 9(3).

[123] This is a sophisticated requirement that would likely need to be linked to standardisation instruments.

[124] Beheshti made similar suggestions in the context of the Sale of Goods Act 1979. He explored to what extent a manufacturer, in the context of a private sales agreement, is liable for failing to comply with the guiding principles of circular economy in the process of designing and producing goods. R Beheshti 'The Circular Economy and the Implied Terms of Contract in English Sales Law' (2021) 13 *Journal of Property, Planning and Environmental Law* 31. K Kryla-Cudna, 'Sales Contracts and the Circular Economy' (2020) *European Review of Private Law* 1207, although tackling the problem from a slightly different angle (her paper examines the remedies of repair and replacement in refurbished rather than new goods), is also an exploration of adapting current statute to more circular principles.

this is not always the case. This chapter has illustrated the potentially disruptive impact of servitisation-based supply chains on consumers, particularly concerning their rights and levels of protection. Consumers who choose such models should be assured that their decisions genuinely contribute to the transition towards more sustainable trading and consumption practices, while also ensuring their socio-economic protection. This has significant implications for consumer law, as it has been demonstrated that additional protection is required on a broader scale. Consumers in a servitised business environment face the risk of disenfranchisement. Private property has been equated with both the right to dignity and the right to economic freedom, both of which are essential for the consumer as an individual and enable the consumer to thrive. Through individual prosperity, consumers naturally contribute to societal and economic welfare. This is not only crucial for consumers as a collective, but also has profound implications for consumer law as a discipline. By disenfranchising consumers, we jeopardise the economic role that consumers play in society.

The shift towards a subscription-based model has not been demonstrated to yield environmental benefits; rather, it has led to adverse effects across three critical dimensions: environmental, societal, and economic. While efforts to combat greenwashing are being implemented through practical initiatives, the potential marginalisation of consumers due to price distortions, the need to protect the rights of private property ownership, and the unfairness arising from the disparity in production quality between for-sale and for-leasing goods has not been adequately addressed. Consequently, regulation must intervene, potentially through the realignment of existing consumer legislation: expanding the scope of the DMCCA 2024 to include practices that may lead to price distortion under unfair practices, or alternatively, broadening Schedule 20 DMCCA to encompass such practices; amending or expanding the understanding of the implied terms of satisfactory quality in both the CRA 2015 and the Sale of Goods Act 1979 to include environmental qualities such as durability, longevity and modularity. Adapting regulation is important to prevent the concentration of control within a small niche of multinationals, thereby preventing consumer disenfranchisement, through loss of ownership opportunity. This realignment of consumer law is essential to ensure the continued protection of all consumers, regardless of their vulnerabilities.

12

The 'Missing Link': Direct Enforcement, Monetary Penalties and Consumer Protection in the Digital Markets, Competition and Consumers Act 2024

PETER CARTWRIGHT

12.1. Introduction

There is little doubt that the effective public enforcement of consumer law plays a central role in ensuring that consumer protection regimes achieve their objectives. In the United Kingdom (UK), the principal general enforcers of consumer law are the Competition and Markets Authority (CMA) and local authority trading standards services ('Trading Standards'). The CMA and Trading Standards operate alongside a range of specialist sector enforcers such as the Civil Aviation Authority, Financial Conduct Authority (FCA) and Information Commissioner. Although there have been changes to the powers available to consumer protection enforcers in recent years, their principal tools have been in place for decades.[1] The weaknesses with these powers have been well documented and were major drivers for the creation of the Digital Markets, Competition and Consumers Act 2024 (DMCCA 2024). The DMCCA 2024 is a substantial and wide-ranging piece of legislation, covering competition law (in particular relating to digital markets) as well as consumer protection. Among its provisions, the Act makes significant changes to the enforcement of consumer protection law, including allowing the CMA to take direct action and impose monetary penalties on traders for the first time.

This chapter considers some of the significant changes that the DMCCA 2024 introduces to the enforcement of consumer protection law. It begins by introducing the principal enforcers and explaining how they have utilised the instruments at their disposal to date. It then sets out some of the main limitations of criminal and civil enforcement. Next, the chapter outlines the chief changes introduced by the Act with particular focus on the direct enforcement powers made available to the CMA. The chapter assesses these powers critically. It considers the extent to which they represent

[1] A major change to civil enforcement came with the creation of enhanced consumer measures as a result of the CRA 2015. This is discussed below.

a genuine innovation in enforcement, address the weaknesses established in the existing regime and better align with the objectives of consumer protection.

12.2. Consumer Protection Enforcers and their Powers

In the UK, most consumer protection enforcement has traditionally been undertaken by Trading Standards rather than the CMA (and its predecessor, the Office of Fair Trading). Nevertheless, those enforcers share many powers. In 2012 the Government emphasised that the CMA should take care not to duplicate the work of Trading Standards. Instead, it argued that the CMA should use its consumer enforcement powers as remedies 'in markets where competition is not working appropriately due to practices and market conditions which make it difficult for consumers to exercise choice'.[2] The CMA has explained its role in enforcement by identifying the situations where it may be more appropriate for it, rather than Trading Standards, to take action.[3] The first is where breaches of the law point towards systemic failures in a market, whether geographically or by sector. The second is where changing the behaviour of a single business would be likely to set a precedent or have other market-wide implications. The third is where there is the opportunity to set important legal precedent. The final situation is where CMA perceives that there is a strong need for deterrence or to secure compensation for consumers.[4] The CMA is therefore concerned primarily with conduct that has the most far-reaching implications.[5] Overall, the CMA has said that it aims to: 'ensure that its interventions deliver high impact results, for example, by changing market behaviour, clarifying laws or providing the necessary level of deterrence to those who might otherwise flout their legal obligations'.[6]

Both the CMA and Trading Standards enforce a range of consumer protection legislation. The most significant and far-reaching substantive consumer laws in the UK are found in Consumer Rights Act 2015 (CRA 2015) and (now) the DMCCA 2024. As well as much else, the latter replaces many of the provisions previously included in the Enterprise Act 2002 (EA 2002) and the Consumer Protection from Unfair Trading Regulations 2008. The most significant formal powers that enforcers have had are criminal enforcement (prosecution) and civil enforcement (in particular the obtaining of enforcement notices), and these powers remain available, albeit in amended forms.

To assess the significance of the changes introduced by the DMCCA 2024, it is helpful to consider the principal weaknesses of the criminal and civil enforcement regimes that the changes impact. These weaknesses demonstrate the need for some degree of disruption to the established order and, in particular, a need to better-align enforcement powers with the aims of consumer protection.

[2] BEIS, 'Empowering and Protecting Consumers: Government response to the consultation on institutional reform' (April 2012) para 6.42.

[3] CMA, *Consumer Protection: Guidance on the CMA's approach to use of its consumer powers* CMA7 (March 2014) para 3.9.

[4] ibid. These points were reaffirmed in CMA, *Consumer Protection: Enforcement Guidance* CMA58 (17 August 2016) para 3.11.

[5] See also the comments in CMA, *Annual Plan 2024/25*, 14 March 2024, para 1.3.

[6] CMA (n 4) para 3.10.

12.3. Criminal Enforcement and its Limitations

The UK has commonly placed strict liability criminal offences in its consumer protection law and the DMCCA 2024 continues this tradition.[7] For example, it allows traders to be prosecuted for engaging in misleading and aggressive commercial practices.[8] Even though enforcement of these criminal offences will commonly be informal (as described below), thus allowing for a degree of flexibility and discretion, there remain objections to using the criminal law to protect consumers.[9] These objections may be ideological and/or practical.

12.3.1. Ideological Concerns

Some commentators have questioned the extent to which areas such as consumer protection are appropriate subjects for the criminal law, particularly where strict liability is imposed.[10] In attempting to identify what he called 'a Principled Core of Criminal Law', Ashworth suggested that criminal law should only be used to censure 'substantial wrongdoing'.[11] He saw the label of criminality as implying that the relevant conduct deserves significant censure and that the label should not be attached where this is lacking. Similar concerns were raised by Macrory. Like Ashworth, he concluded that conviction should, wherever possible, reflect the seriousness of the wrongdoing, in terms of both culpability and harm.[12]

Given that consumer protection offences will sometimes involve little harm/threat of harm, and do not typically require the prosecution to prove fault in the form of *mens rea*, it might be argued that they may fail in these regards. The label of criminality involves a stigma.[13] Where the circumstances do not deserve that stigma, a conviction may be a disproportionate outcome.[14]

One response to these concerns is to argue that consumer protection offences are 'regulatory offences' and so 'not criminal in any real sense'.[15] If it is widely accepted that there is a category of offences that are not *really* criminal, it could be argued that we need worry little about using that label. Scott, for example, suggests that strict criminal liability could be viewed as simply reflecting 'the plural nature of contemporary criminal law, and of the emergence of a class of "regulatory crime" capable of being distinguished from the more stigmatising "real crime"'.[16] Nevertheless, it is unclear that the public would recognise this distinction.

[7] See generally P Cartwright, *Consumer Protection and the Criminal Law* (Cambridge University Press, 2001).

[8] s 237.

[9] Cartwright (n 7) ch 3.

[10] The term 'strict liability' is used here to encompass offences that do not require proof of *mens rea*.

[11] A Ashworth, 'Is the Criminal law a Lost Cause?' (2000) 116 *LQR* 225.

[12] R Macrory, *Regulatory Justice: Sanctioning in a post-Hampton World* (Cabinet Office, 2006).

[13] ibid para 1.28.

[14] ibid.

[15] *Sherras v De Rutzen* [1895] 1 QB 918 (DC).

[16] C Scott, 'Enforcing Consumer Protection Laws' in G Howells et al, *Handbook of Research on International Consumer Law* (Edward Elgar 2020) 537, 550.

Writing in the 1960s, Ball and Friedman emphasised the extent to which the label of criminality had a symbolic meaning for the public, and concluded that 'businessmen abhor the idea of being branded a criminal'.[17] Furthermore, the actual impact of conviction is unpredictable with some impacts, in particular those that result from adverse publicity, being especially difficult to predict and quantify.[18] This leads us to consider practical concerns.

12.3.2. Practical Concerns

While these ideological concerns are pertinent, perhaps the main objections to prosecuting traders under the criminal law are practical. In particular, it seems questionable whether prosecution significantly helps to achieve the principal aims of consumer protection.

First, it is widely accepted that that one of main aims of using prosecution is to deter. Wells argued that the majority of corporate crime is deterrent-based in that 'the purpose of instituting sanctions has been to discourage violations and encourage good practice'.[19] From this perspective, prosecution might appear inadequate. It is frequently argued that deterrence is most likely to be achieved where traders conclude that the probability of being apprehended, convicted and sanctioned, combined with the downside of conviction (in particular the level of sanction imposed) outweighs the perceived benefits of contravention.[20] Gobert and Punch reflected this approach, arguing that companies are 'the prime example of the rational cost benefit calculators which those who champion deterrence theory had in mind'.[21]

There are shortcomings to this model of 'optimal deterrence'. In the 1990 White Paper *Crime, Justice and Protecting the Public*, the Government argued that 'it is unrealistic to construct sentencing arrangements on the assumptions that most offenders will weigh up the evidence in advance and base their conduct on rational calculation'.[22] Despite its limitations, it seems reasonable to assume that profit-maximising traders may be influenced by their perceptions of: (a) the probability of being sanctioned; and (b) the penalty they may receive if they are. Viewed from this perspective, it is easy to see why regulatory offences may not operate as a compelling deterrent. A reasonably well-informed trader may recognise that the vast majority of contraventions do not lead to prosecution, that some of those that do will not lead to conviction, and that many of those which do lead to conviction are likely to result in a relatively low formal sanction.[23] While it is true that the impact of conviction on a trader extends beyond any

[17] H Ball and L Friedman 'Use of Criminal Sanctions in the Enforcement of Economic Legislation: a Sociologial View' (1965) 17 *Stanford Law Review* 197, 216–17.

[18] See JC Coffee Jr. '"No Soul to damn no Body to kick" An Unscandalized Inquiry into the Problem of Corporate Punishment' (1981) 79 *Michigan Law Review* 386.

[19] C Wells, *Corporations and Criminal Responsibility*, 2nd edn (Oxford University Press, 2001) 31.

[20] See eg G Becker, 'Crime and Punishment: as Economic Approach' (1968) *Journal of Political Economy* 169; A Ogus, *Regulation: Legal Form and Economic Theory* (Clarendon Press, 1994). This is considered in more detail below.

[21] J Gobert and M Punch, *Rethinking Corporate Crime* (LexisNexis, 2003) 219.

[22] (1990) Cm 965 para 2.8.

[23] A Ogus, 'Better Regulation – Better Enforcement' in S Weatherill (ed), *Better Regulation* (Hart Publishing, 2007) 111.

formal sanction, it is doubtful that the risk of prosecution achieves effective deterrence. In making the case for the DMCCA 2024, the Government concluded that 'there is little deterrence for traders who breach consumer protection law'.[24]

12.3.3. Criminal Enforcement and Compliance Strategies

It is important to remember that, from an instrumental perspective, consumer protection offences are not designed only to deter and are not only enforced through prosecution. In some respects, it might be more appropriate to view them through the lens of encouraging and incentivising compliance. While prosecution remains an option, enforcers will commonly enforce the criminal law through what might be termed 'compliance strategies'.[25] A compliance strategy has as its aim securing conformity with the law 'by means of ensuring compliance or by taking action to prevent potential law violation without the necessity to detect, process and penalise violations'.[26] This contrasts with a deterrence strategy, the aim of which is

> to secure conformity with the law by detecting violation, determining who is responsible for the violation, and penalising violations to deter violations in the future, either by those who are punished or by those who might do so were violations not penalised.[27]

Gunningham describes these strategies as 'polar extremes, hypothetical constructs unlikely to be found anywhere in their pure form'.[28] It is true that, while a wealth of literature has emphasised the extent to which a focus on compliance provides the starting point, this does not mean that formal action will not follow where it is thought appropriate.[29] Nevertheless, informal compliance mechanisms still loom large in the enforcement of consumer law. The Institute for Government has recently recognised this, describing how in the exercise of its consumer protection powers, the CMA 'normally attempts to address breaches through mediation.'[30]

There are different explanations for why enforcers so frequently adopt this compliance-focused approach. One is that it allows for the more efficient allocation of resources. It has been suggested that Trading Standards might typically spend one day investigating a contravention, two days issuing informal cautions, four issuing formal cautions and perhaps 10 preparing prosecutions.[31] In the words of Ayres and Braithwaite, 'punishment

[24] Department for Business and Trade, 'Strengthening Consumer enforcement and dispute resolution: policy summary briefing', www.gov.uk/government/publications/digital-markets-competition-and-consumers-bill-supporting-documentation/strengthening-consumer-enforcement-and-dispute-resolution-policy-summary-briefing#:~:text=7.,protection%20breaches%20like%20mis%2Dselling.

[25] AJ Reiss, 'Selecting Strategies of Social Control over Organisational Life' in K Hawkins and J Thomas (eds), *Enforcing Regulation* (Kluwer Nijhoff, 1984) 23–24.

[26] ibid 23.

[27] ibid 22–23.

[28] N Gunningham, 'Strategising compliance and enforcement: responsive regulation and beyond' in C Parker and V Lehman Nielsen, *Explaining Compliance: Business Responses to Regulation* (Edward Elgar, 2011) 199, 201.

[29] I Ayres and J Braithwaite, *Responsive Regulation* (Oxford University Press, 1992).

[30] Institute for Government, *Competition and Markets Authority*, www.instituteforgovernment.org.uk/explainer/competition-and-markets-authority.

[31] Ogus (n 23) 112.

is expensive, persuasion is cheap'.[32] It may also be that enforcers see informal action as producing less resentment on the part of traders.[33] This is particularly important given that transgressions are not always intentional. In many cases, prosecution might appear a disproportionate and counterproductive response, even where contravention is clear. Finally, the law may, to some extent, demand that enforcers avoid prosecution as a first step. The CMA follows the *Principles of Good Regulation*, and these require it to see that its enforcement actions are: proportionate; consistent; targeted; transparent and accountable.[34] Too frequent a recourse to prosecution could be inconsistent with this.

The use of compliance strategies has important implications for the operation of the criminal law. On the one hand, it may reduce some of the ideological objections by ensuring that prosecution is a last resort and only used where all the facts justify it. On the other, it may reduce the (already) limited deterrent effect of the criminal law by signaling that prosecution is unlikely. There is good reason to doubt that the criminal law, enforced in these ways, achieves the objectives of consumer protection.

12.4. Civil Enforcement and its Limitations

The concerns with the use of criminal sanctions outlined above would be less troubling were civil enforcement to have filled the gaps appropriately. Unfortunately, the weaknesses of the civil enforcement regime have long been apparent.

Part 8 EA 2002 allowed enforcers to obtain undertakings from, and seek enforcement orders against, traders for breach of a wide range of consumer protection laws. Since Part 8 was reformed by the CRA 2015, enforcers have been able to attach 'enhanced consumer measures' (ECMs) to undertakings, and courts have been empowered to attach them to undertakings and orders.[35] There are three types of ECM, which are referred to as redress measures, compliance measures and choice measures. In short, redress measures are focused on offering redress (including compensation) to consumers, compliance measures are intended to prevent or reduce the risk of occurrence or repetition of the conduct in question, and choice measures are intended enable consumers to choose more effectively between traders. These reforms brought clear benefits for enforcers.[36]

Nevertheless, shortcomings remained. In 2019, Lord Tyrie, then Chair of the CMA, wrote to the Secretary of State for Business, Energy and Industrial Strategy to complain that the CMA's consumer protection powers were 'unfit for its current purpose'.[37] He identified three main weaknesses. The first was that the CMA had no power to order that unfair practices stop; its only option was to pursue traders through the courts. He contrasted that

[32] Ayres and Braithwaite (n 29) 19.

[33] ibid 20.

[34] Legislative and Regulatory Reform Act 2006, s 21 and the *Regulators Code*.

[35] See P Cartwright, 'Redress, Compliance and Choice: Enhanced Consumer Measures and the Retreat from Punishment in the Consumer Rights Act 2015' (2016) 75 *CLJ* 271.

[36] ibid.

[37] Rt Hon Lord Tyrie, Letter to the Secretary of State (21 February 2019), www.gov.uk/government/publications/letter-from-andrew-tyrie-to-the-secretary-of-state-for-business-energy-and-industrial-strategy#:~:text=Andrew%20Tyrie%2C%20Chair%20of%20the,protection%20regimes%20of%20the%20CMA.

with the powers available to the authority under competition law where it would determine whether the law had been broken and impose fines on the trader responsible. The second was that where the CMA successfully pursued civil action, no fines could be imposed upon the trader for the contravention of the law. Finally, he noted that where the CMA obtained undertakings from a trader instead of taking it to court, it could not impose fines on a trader who failed to comply with the undertaking. Tyrie's conclusion was that where firms were prepared to risk breaking the law any deterrence would be very limited and that there would frequently be 'no business case for compliance'.[38] The Penrose Report, which was set up to examine how the UK's approach to competition and consumer issues could be improved, identified similar problems.[39] It described the civil enforcement regime as slow, bureaucratic and weak, and argued that it 'allows firms to carry on ripping off consumers for years while their lawyers slow everything down to a crawl in the courts'.[40] Citizens Advice has also argued forcefully that current timelines 'allow harms to persist for unjustifiably long periods and increase incentives for firms to drag investigations out'.[41]

These shortcomings allowed traders to drag out proceedings with little adverse consequence. Just how long civil enforcement could take is illustrated by the timeline associated with CMA action against secondary ticketing sites including Viagogo.[42] In 2015, four secondary ticketing platforms formally agreed with the CMA to give improved information to buyers about the tickets listed on their sites. After the CMA decided that further action was necessary, three of the platforms agreed in April 2018 to amend their practices. The fourth did not, and in November 2018 the court made an enforcement order under Part 8 which required the platform to change its practices. In March 2019, the CMA warned the platform that its practices were still not fully compliant with the order. In July 2019, the court declared that not all of the platform's practices were compliant. It was only in September 2019 that the CMA suspended its preparations for contempt of court proceedings with the platform finally having addressed the CMA's remaining outstanding concerns. This was almost four years after the initial formal agreements were made.

The Government recognised some of these weaknesses, as was evident from its Green Paper, *Modernising Consumer Markets*.[43] However, it set out a far fuller and more comprehensive response in its 2021 White Paper, *Reforming Competition and Consumer Policy* which, ultimately, led to the DMCCA 2024.[44]

12.5. Reforming Competition and Consumer Policy

The White Paper identified weaknesses in enforcement, highlighting in particular procedural difficulties for enforcers and weak sanctions for breaching the law. It was clear that the system needed re-alignment in several ways. First, there was a need for

[38] ibid 20.
[39] J Penrose, 'Power to the People' (February 2021).
[40] ibid para 2.2.
[41] Citizens Advice, 'Reforming Competition and Consumer Policy: Response' (undated) 17.
[42] BEIS, *Reforming Competition and Consumer Policy* CP 488 (July 2021) Fig 12.
[43] BEIS, *Modernising Consumer Markets: Consumer Green Paper* (April 2018).
[44] *Reforming Competition and Consumer Policy* CP 488 (July 2021).

re-alignment with best practice, drawing on experiences in other jurisdictions. It was notable, for example, that the UK was the only G7 state without civil penalties for common breaches of consumer protection such as unfair trading.[45] Second, there was a need for realignment with powers relating to the enforcement of competition law, the benefits of which a number of commentators had emphasised. Finally, and perhaps most crucially, there was a need for re-alignment with the key objectives of consumer protection enforcement. While proposing that some tweaks be made to the existing system, it also championed a more fundamental shift, suggesting that:[46]

> An administrative enforcement regime where the CMA can control the timetable for investigations and conclude cases faster would bring infringements to an end sooner and secure redress for consumers more promptly. It would also be more efficient and could free up resources for better enforcement outcomes.

It further concluded that:[47]

> With stronger powers, including fines for frustrating enforcement procedures or breaking the law which can be deployed without a series of lengthy court actions, the CMA could shorten enforcement by many months or years, stopping harm to consumers far sooner.

Not everyone was enamoured with the proposals, with the British Retail Consortium labelling the proposed new direct enforcement powers 'draconian'.[48] However, the majority of respondents were supportive.[49] Which?, for example, said 'we would expect the proposed powers to significantly increase the efficiency and effectiveness of the CMA's enforcement actions' and suggested that 'the ability to be a more active regulator, and the stronger deterrent effect of administrative powers, should be significantly more effective in influencing business behaviour and supporting compliance'.[50] The resulting legislation was the DMCCA 2024.

12.6. The Digital Markets Competition and Consumers Act

The DMCCA 2024 received Royal Assent on 24 May 2024. Part 3 of the Act deals with enforcement of consumer law. When it comes to investigating what the DMCCA 2024 says about enforcement, a distinction needs to be drawn between changes to court-based procedures (in Chapter 3), and the introduction of a direct (administrative) enforcement regime (in Chapter 4). The procedures are outlined below, with a focus on

[45] OECD, 'Best practices for Consumer Policy: Report on the effectiveness of enforcement regimes' (20 December 2006).

[46] ibid para 3.18.

[47] ibid para 3.14.

[48] British Retail Consortium, 'BEIS Consultation on Competition and Consumer Protection Comments from the BRC' (September/October 2021).

[49] Consultation responses are available at www.gov.uk/government/consultations/reforming-competition-and-consumer-policy#:~:text=The%20government%20response%20to%20this,competitive%20strategy%20for%20the%20CMA.

[50] Which?, 'Consultation Response: Reforming Competition and Consumer Policy' (15 March 2023) 39.

the latter. Before examining those, it is helpful to say something briefly about relevant infringements which are dealt with in Chapter 2.

12.6.1. Chapter 2: Relevant Infringements

Chapter 2 DMCCA 2024 explains the types of infringement in respect of which action can be taken under Chapters 3 and 4. Relevant infringements are those commercial practices which: harm the collective interests of consumers; meet the UK connection condition; and meet the specified prohibition condition.[51] To be a commercial practice that meets the UK connection condition, the trader must have a place of business in the UK or carry on business in the UK, and/or the commercial practice must occur in the carrying on of activities by the trader that are 'by any means directed to consumers' in the UK.[52] Where the activities are by any means directed to consumers in the UK, it does not matter whether those activities are carried on in the UK or elsewhere.[53] To meet the specified prohibition condition for Chapter 3 (the court-based regime), the commercial practice must be: in breach of an enactment listed in Part 1 of Schedule 15 (to the extent specified) or in breach of an obligation or rule of law listed in Part 2 of that Schedule.[54] To meet the specified prohibition condition for Chapter 4, the commercial practice must be in breach of an enactment listed in Schedule 16 (to the extent specified).[55]

There are a number of points to note here. First, Part 8 EA 2002 initially introduced a court-based enforcement regime for the two categories of infringements (community infringements and infringements of laws of UK origin) that existed at the time of its enactment. Part 8 was amended several times, resulting in there being two categories of infringement, which were named domestic infringements (laws of UK origin) and Schedule 13 infringements (laws of Community origin). Part 3 DMCCA 2024 replaces Part 8 and aligns the two, providing for the single category of infringement outlined above. The change to a UK connection condition should make it easier for enforcers to target traders outside the UK.

12.6.2. Chapter 3: The Court-Based Regime

Chapter 3 of Part 3 DMCCA 2024 gives courts the power to make consumer protection orders and to accept undertakings as an alternative to making those orders. It largely represents an evolution of the powers contained in Part 8 EA 2002 rather than a major innovation. For example, section 151 replaces the two categories of public enforcer found in Part 8 with one category of public designated enforcer. Under section 153 a public designated enforcer (including the CMA and Trading Standards) can apply for an enforcement

[51] s 148(1).
[52] s 149(1).
[53] s 149(2). For detailed discussion see Digital Markets Competition and Consumers Bill Explanatory Notes HCB294-EN ('Explanatory Notes') paras 911–19.
[54] s 150(1).
[55] s 150(2).

order against a trader.[56] There are requirements to consult which are only suspended if the CMA thinks that an application for an order should be made without delay.[57] The policy intent of consultation is, as was the case under Part 8, 'to provide an opportunity to stop or prevent the relevant infringement without the need for court action'.[58]

The process of consultation in the seeking of orders is, as the Chartered Trading Standards Institute has pointed out, 'a vital tool in its own right' as it is a process that can bring compliance.[59] For example, a trader might be willing to bring itself into compliance having recognised that it has made an error. Enforcers are also able to accept undertakings from traders as part of this process. Under section 163(1), where an enforcer could make an application under section 153 for an enforcement order or interim enforcement order, it may instead accept an undertaking. The CMA describes an undertaking as

> a voluntary commitment from a person relating to their conduct which is intended to resolve the CMA's concerns, without requiring the admission that there has been an infringement or the payment of a monetary penalty as part of the resolution.[60]

The White Paper viewed them as very valuable enforcement tools, arguing that 'given voluntarily [they] are usually a quicker way to secure compliance with consumer protection law and redress for injured parties' and that they 'can also circumvent full investigation and court procedures, which can last for a long time and be expensive for enforcers and businesses alike'.[61] Under section 164(1) an undertaking under section 163(2) may include a requirement to take such enhanced consumer measures as the enforcer accepting the undertaking considers just and reasonable.

Under section 156, the court may make an enforcement order against, or accept an undertaking from, a trader where it considers that they have engaged in, are engaging in, or are likely to engage in, a relevant infringing practice. The court can also include such enhanced consumer measures as it considers to be just, reasonable and proportionate in an enforcement order or undertaking.[62]

In many ways, these powers reflect those that they replace. However, a significant innovation is in the ability of the court to require payment of a monetary penalty. Where a public designated enforcer applies for an enforcement order or interim enforcement order they may, under section 153(4), include an application for the payment of a monetary penalty. Section 153(5) makes clear that this can only be made in respect of a practice that the trader has engaged or is engaging in (rather than one that the enforcer considers they are likely to engage in). Section 158(2) provides that an enforcement order may include a requirement for a monetary penalty. This (or a notice accompanying service

[56] The Act generally uses the terms 'person' and 'respondent' depending on the precise context. The Explanatory Notes to the Bill (n 53) generally use 'enforcement subject' (in particular to include both the infringer and an accessory). This chapter uses the term 'trader' for simplicity.

[57] s 155(5).

[58] Explanatory Notes (n 53) para 945.

[59] Chartered Trading Standards Institute, 'Reforming Competition and Consumer Policy' Consultation Response (October 2021) 18.

[60] CMA Direct Enforcement Guidance: CMA200con (14 March 2025) para 4.3 Trading standards are also able to accept undertakings.

[61] *Reforming Competition and Consumer Policy* (n 44) para 3.49.

[62] s 157. This largely states and updates EA 2002, s 219B.

of it) must set out the 'monetary penalty information'.[63] The penalty must be for a fixed amount not exceeding £300,000 or, if higher, 10 per cent of the value of the turnover (if any) of the trader.[64]

There are also powers relating to further proceedings. Under section 166, where the court makes 'a consumer protection order' or accepts an undertaking, an enforcer can apply to the same court regarding a failure to comply with the order or undertaking.[65] If the court finds that an undertaking is not being complied with, it may make a consumer protection order and/or make an order to require the trader to pay a monetary penalty.[66] Under section 167, where an enforcer has accepted an undertaking, it can apply to the court in respect of a failure to comply with the undertaking. If the court finds that the undertaking is not being complied with, it can make a consumer protection order and/or make an order requiring the trader to pay a monetary penalty.[67] The requirement to pay a monetary penalty can only be imposed if the court is satisfied that the failure in question is without reasonable excuse.[68]

Section 168 provides that where a monetary penalty is imposed under section 166 or section 167, the amount of the penalty must be: a fixed amount; an amount calculated by reference to a daily rate; or a combination of the two.[69] The penalty must not exceed: (a) in the case of a fixed amount, £150,000 or, if higher, of the total value of the turnover (if any) of the trader; (b) in the case of an amount calculated by reference to a daily rate, for each day £15,000 or, if higher, five per cent of the total value of the daily turnover (if any) of the trader; and (c) in the case of a combination, such fixed amount and such amount per day.[70] In addition to any right of appeal on a point of law, traders liable to pay a monetary penalty by virtue of an order under section 166(5)(b) or section 167(4)(b) are entitled to appeal against the decision to impose the penalty or the nature or amount of the penalty.[71] This broad right of is appeal 'on the merits'.[72] The importance of monetary penalties is discussed in detail below.

12.6.3. Chapter 4: The Direct Enforcement Regime

With the important exception of the provisions on monetary penalties, Chapter 3 DMCCA 2024 largely represents an updated version of Part 8. By contrast, the 'administrative model' of enforcement which is found in Chapter 4 represents a major innovation.

Chapter 4 gives powers to the CMA to decide whether breaches of consumer law have taken place and to impose directions and monetary penalties on businesses without the need to go to court. In Parliament, Kevin Hollinrake (when Minister of State

[63] See s 203 and explanation below.
[64] s 158(5).
[65] s 166(3).
[66] s 166(5)(a)–(b).
[67] s 167(4)(a)–(b).
[68] s 167(5).
[69] s 168(2).
[70] s 168(3).
[71] ss 166(8)(a)–(b) and 167(8)(a)–(b) respectively.
[72] Explanatory Notes (n 53) para 1013.

for Enterprise, Markets and Small Business) argued that these powers would enable the CMA 'to act faster and take on more consumer cases on behalf of the public, resulting in a further estimated direct benefit to consumers of tens, or potentially hundreds, of millions of pounds'.[73] Under the new regime the CMA can issue a range of notices (set out below). The DMCCA 2024 also makes provision for the imposition of monetary penalties in a number of scenarios. These are considered below.

Section 180 gives the CMA the power to investigate suspected infringements which then triggers the use of direct enforcement powers. If the CMA has reasonable grounds to suspect that an 'infringing practice' has occurred, is occurring or is likely to occur, it can investigate the trader. Under section 180(3), the CMA may publish a notice of investigation, and it has recently stated that 'Unless there are exceptional circumstances, the CMA would expect to continue its established practice of announcing the investigation and identifying the parties under investigation at this stage'.[74] By informing other traders and consumers of the alleged infringement this might encourage them to provide relevant information. The CMA may (indeed, is likely to) use its compulsory powers to gather information from those under investigation and/or third parties.[75] It may also discuss obtaining undertakings or settlement at this stage, depending on all the facts.[76]

12.6.3.1. Provisional Infringement Notices

After it has begun an investigation, the CMA may give a provisional infringement notice (PIN) to the trader under DMCCA 2024, section 181. As their name implies, PINs reflect the CMA's provisional view pending the outcome of a full investigation.[77] They are designed primarily to ensure that the trader can understand the case against them and has an appropriate opportunity to make representations. Section 181(4) states that the PIN must set out certain details, including the grounds on which it is given, directions which specify what the trader needs to do to bring themselves into compliance, and the process by which the trader can make representations to the CMA. In some cases the directions referred to in section 181(4) will include the taking of enhanced consumer measures. Where this is the case, the PIN must make this clear and include details of those measures to be taken. Where the CMA is considering imposing a monetary penalty, the PIN must state this, set out the proposed amount of the penalty, and set out any further factors which it considers may justify both the imposition and the amount of the proposed penalty.[78]

12.6.3.2. Final Infringement Notices

There is no obligation on traders to submit representations on the PIN. If they choose not to, the CMA can proceed with the case and decide whether or not to give a final

[73] *Hansard* HC Vol 741, col 104 (20 November 2023).
[74] Guidance (n 60) para 2.5.
[75] ibid para 2.11.
[76] ibid para 2.12.
[77] Explanatory Notes (n 53) para 1071.
[78] s 81(8).

infringement notice (FIN) to the relevant party under DMCCA 2024, section 182. In making this decision, the CMA must have regard to whether the trader has previously given an undertaking (whether under Chapter 3 or 4 DMCCA 2024 or Part 8 EA 2002) or been subject to a court order.

The FIN must specify certain details. These include: the CMA's finding of facts; other factors which justify it issuing the notice; in the event that a penalty is imposed, the penalty notice information contained in section 203, and the trader's rights to appeal.[79] A FIN may require the trader to comply with such directions as the CMA considers appropriate to secure compliance with the requirements of the PIN, including directions to take such ECMs as the CMA considers just and reasonable, and to pay a monetary penalty.[80] However, the CMA can only impose a monetary penalty if it is satisfied that the trader has engaged in or is engaging in an infringing practice.[81] The maximum penalty is a fixed amount not exceeding £300,000 or, if higher, 10 per cent of the total value of the turnover (if any) of the trader.[82]

The trader may also be required to publish the FIN (in full or in part) and/or a corrective statement in a form and manner which the CMA considers appropriate to eliminate any continued effects of the infringement.[83] This might be appropriate, for example, to inform consumers where the subject has engaged in misleading advertising.[84] The CMA has recently confirmed that when a FIN is given, the CMA will typically issue a press announcement, make an announcement on the Regulatory News Service and publish details of the decision on the CMA's website.[85]

12.6.3.3. Online Interface Notices

Section 184 DMCCA 2024 empowers the CMA to give an online interface notice (OIN).[86] As well as traders in the UK who the CMA is satisfied have engaged in, are engaging or are likely to engage in practices that constitutes relevant infringements, OINs can be given to third parties subject to a jurisdictional test. Where the third party is outside the UK they must be a UK national, an individual who is habitually resident in the UK, a firm established in the UK, or a person who 'carries on business in the UK or by any means directs activities in the course of carrying on a business to consumers in the UK'.[87] Section 184(4) sets out what an OIN can require a person to do. These actions are: removing content from or modifying content on an online interface; displaying or restricting access to an online interface; displaying a warning to consumers accessing an online interface; and deleting a fully qualified domain name and taking any steps

[79] s 182(7).
[80] s 182(4).
[81] s 182(5).
[82] s 182(6).
[83] s 198(8)–(9).
[84] Explanatory Notes (n 53) para 1082.
[85] Guidance (n 60) para 2.80.
[86] The term 'online interface' is defined by s 184(10). The Explanatory Notes (n 53) make clear that it includes websites and apps (para 1090).
[87] s 184(3).

necessary to facilitate the registration of that domain name by the CMA. OINs must set out the grounds on which they are given and state that the respondent has the right to appeal against the notice (as well as the main details of that right).[88]

A detailed account of OINs is beyond this work, and it is important to note that they are an instrument of last resort; they can only be given to a person if the CMA is satisfied that:[89]

(a) There are no other available means under section 162 or another provision of this chapter of bringing about the cessation or prohibition of the infringement which, by themselves, would be wholly effective, and
(b) It is necessary for the directions contained in the notice to be given to avoid the risk of serious harm to the collective interests of consumers.

12.6.3.4. Undertakings and Directions

The ability to accept undertakings has long been an important tool in the CMA's armoury and they remain important in Chapters 3 and 4 DMCCA 2024. As discussed above, undertakings can be given to the court or to the enforcer. The CMA can accept an undertaking where it has started an investigation (which is continuing) and has not given a final infringement notice or online interface notice in relation to the matter being investigated.[90] Undertakings can be offered at any time during an investigation and the CMA has discretion to accept them unless and until a FIN has been issued. The strengths of the ability to accept undertakings are considered above. One of the main weaknesses identified with the civil enforcement regime under the EA 2002 related to the lack of sanction for breaches of undertakings. CMA now has powers to directly enforce compliance with undertakings.[91]

12.6.3.5. Provisional Breach of Undertakings Enforcement Notice

The CMA can give a provisional breach of undertakings notice where it has accepted an undertaking and has reasonable grounds to believe that the trader has failed to comply with one or more of its terms.[92] The notice must specify why the CMA believes the terms to have been breached and set out the CMA's proposed directions to ensure compliance.[93] The trader must also be given the opportunity to make representations. If the CMA is proposing to impose a monetary penalty, it must also state this fact, the amount of the penalty, and any further factors that the CMA considers would justify the imposition of the penalty.[94]

[88] s 184(6).
[89] s 184(5).
[90] s 185.
[91] The powers related to the provision of false or misleading information and non-compliance with information notices which are beyond the scope of this chapter.
[92] s 188(1).
[93] s 188(3).
[94] s 188(6).

12.6.3.6. Final Breach of Undertakings Enforcement Notice

Where the CMA has given the trader a provisional breach of undertakings notice, the deadline for making representations has passed, and the CMA is satisfied that the trader has failed to comply with one or more of the terms of the undertaking, it may issue a final breach of undertakings enforcement notice.[95] The notice would need to set out the reasons for the CMA's conclusions, specify any actions to be taken by the trader and, if a penalty is imposed, specify the monetary penalty information.[96] In terms of monetary penalties, the CMA could impose a fixed amount, daily amount, or combination of the two. In the case of a fixed amount, the penalty must not exceed £150,000 or, if higher five per cent of the total value of turnover. In the case of a daily rate, it must not exceed £15,000 or, if higher, five per cent of the total value of daily turnover. Where the CMA is satisfied that the trader has failed to comply with one or more terms of the undertaking, it can only require payment of a monetary penalty where it is satisfied that the failure is without reasonable excuse.[97]

12.6.3.7. Provisional Breach of Directions Enforcement Notice

Where the CMA gives direction in a final infringement notice, online interface notice or final breach of undertakings enforcement notice, it is classified as an 'enforcement direction'.[98] Where the CMA gives an enforcement direction and has reasonable grounds to believe that the trader has failed to comply with the direction without reasonable excuse, it can issue a provisional breach of directions enforcement notice.[99] The CMA would specify the reasons for issuing the notice, its proposed directions to achieve compliance with the direction, and details of the representation process.[100] If the CMA was considering imposing a monetary penalty it would also have to give details of that.[101]

12.6.3.8. Final Breach of Directions Enforcement Notice

Where the CMA has given a provisional breach of directions enforcement notice in respect of suspected failure to comply with an enforcement direction, the deadline to make representations has expired, and the CMA is satisfied that the trader has failed to comply with the relevant enforcement direction without reasonable excuse, it may issue a final breach of directions enforcement notice.[102] This will set out the reasons for the notice, and specify the monetary penalty information.[103] The CMA may impose a fixed amount, daily amount, or combination of the two. Any fixed amount must not exceed

[95] s 189(2).
[96] s 189(5).
[97] s 189(4).
[98] s 191(6).
[99] s 191(2).
[100] s 191(3).
[101] s 191(5).
[102] s 192(2).
[103] s 192(4).

£150,000 or, if higher, five per cent of turnover. Any daily rate penalty must not exceed £15,000 or, if higher, five per cent of the total value of daily turnover.[104]

When something is 'without reasonable excuse' in the provisions above will, according to the CMA, be considered objectively on a case-by-case basis.[105] CMA will consider factors such as whether 'a significant and genuinely unforeseeable or unusual event beyond the party's control has caused the failure'.[106]

12.6.3.9. Power of the Court to Enforce Directions

The CMA can apply to the court for an enforcement order if it believes that a trader has failed to comply with an enforcement direction, or a direction given in a final breach of directions enforcement notice.[107] The section may be described as providing a 'backstop power' for the CMA to enforce compliance with directions by applying to the court for an order.[108] The Explanatory Notes recognise that while CMA-imposed penalties will generally incentivise compliance: 'there may be cases where this prospect is potentially ineffective or insufficient and the prospect of a court order (which would result in contempt proceedings if breached) would act as an appropriately stringent sanction'.[109]

12.6.3.10. Appeals

A trader to whom a 'relevant notice' (including a final infringement notice, final breach of undertakings notice and final breach of directions enforcement notice) is given may appeal to the court against the decision to impose a monetary penalty, the nature or amount of the penalty, and the giving of directions.[110] The following are all grounds for appeal in relation to monetary penalties: the decision to impose a monetary penalty was based on an error of fact; the decision was wrong in law; the amount of the penalty is unreasonable; or the decision was unreasonable or wrong for any other reason.[111]

These provisions, which allow appeals on the merits, mean that the court is able to inquire into the correctness of the CMA's findings of fact (and analysis of and conclusions drawn from those facts), interpretation of the law and exercise of discretion.[112] The Explanatory Notes state that: 'The policy intent is that a court conducting an appeal on the merits under this section should interfere only if it concludes that the decision is wrong in a material respect'.[113] The CMA had accepted that an appeal route needed to be built into the new process and while it argued that the appropriate standard would

[104] s 193(3)–4).
[105] Guidance (n 60) para 7.47.
[106] ibid.
[107] s 194(2).
[108] Explanatory Notes (n 53) para 1136.
[109] ibid para 1138.
[110] s 202(1).
[111] s 202(2). s 202(3) provides near identical reasons for challenging directions.
[112] Explanatory Notes (n 53) para 1173.
[113] ibid para 1177 citing *T-Mobile v Ofcom* [2008] EWCA Civ 1373.

be one of judicial review, it has said that it 'understands that there may be calls for a full merits standard where financial penalties are imposable'.[114] It will be interesting to see the extent to which the ability to appeal is used. Given the potentially high monetary penalties involved and the broad grounds for appeal, it seems likely that traders will contest the CMA's decisions relatively frequently.

12.7. The DMCCA 2024, Monetary Penalties and Effective Enforcement

The DMCCA 2024 makes important changes to the enforcement regime, as the discussion above demonstrates. A key question is whether these changes are likely to amount to a significant improvement in outcomes. While this is difficult to predict with confidence at such an early stage, it is possible to reflect on the changes and draw some conclusions.

Andrew Tyrie's letter to the Secretary of State argued that the first weakness of enforcement was that the CMA had no power to order that unfair practices stop. Tyrie contrasted the powers that the CMA had in relation to consumer protection unfavourably with its powers relating to competition. He argued that the CMA needed the powers to be able to decide whether consumer protection law had been broken, declare that it had been broken, direct traders to stop the infringement, and impose fines.[115] He further suggested that where there were urgent cases, the CMA should be able to order that 'practices it suspects may be harming consumers' are stopped on an interim basis.[116] Again, this would be in line with the CMA's powers regarding breaches of competition law. This concern is addressed by the introduction of direct enforcement powers. The CMA can now serve infringement notices on traders, backed up by monetary penalties. Court-based powers remain under Chapter 3, and the CMA has stated that retaining these powers (along with the ability to prosecute) 'will help the CMA to continue co-operating and co-ordinating effectively' with other enforcers such as Trading Standards.[117] However, the ability for the CMA to serve notices rather than rely on the courts to stop unfair practices is a major advance, giving it far more control over the process.

It is in relation to the second and third weaknesses identified by Tyrie that the importance of monetary penalties is particularly apparent. The second weakness was that where the CMA successfully pursued civil action (for example, under Part 8) no fines could be imposed upon the trader for the contravention of the law. When the CRA introduced ECMs, there was some debate as to whether it was possible to use civil enforcement powers under Part 8 and prosecution in combination.[118] It was argued at the time that consumer protection would be compromised if this were not

[114] CMA, 'Reforming Competition and Consumer Policy' CMA 149con (4 October 2021) para 2.162.
[115] Tyrie letter (n 37) 21.
[116] ibid.
[117] BEIS, *Reforming competition and consumer policy: government response* CP 656 (April 2022).
[118] Department for Business Innovation and Skills, *Civil Enforcement Remedies* (November 2012) para 1.8, assets.publishing.service.gov.uk/media/5a79bf73e5274a684690bd08/12-1193-civil-enforcement-remedies-consultation-on-extending.pdf.

possible.[119] The Government's Guidance subsequently made clear that while in most cases ECMs would be an alternative to criminal prosecution, 'there may be cases where the offences are serious enough to warrant them being used in conjunction with criminal prosecution'.[120] Nonetheless, civil enforcement typically remained an alternative to prosecution and, as Tyrie observed, where civil enforcement was pursued, financial penalties were not imposed for the breach in question. The DMCCA 2024 now gives powers to impose monetary penalties to both the courts and to the CMA. This appears to be a major step forward, particularly from the perspective of deterrence. Finally, Tyrie pointed out that where the CMA obtained undertakings from a trader instead of taking it to court, it could not impose fines on a trader who failed to comply with the undertaking. Under the DMCCA 2024, the CMA can issue a final breach of undertakings enforcement notice which may specify directions to achieve compliance, a monetary penalty, or both. This should make it easier to enforce undertakings.

Before the DMCCA 2024, a key limitation was the absence of any 'sanction' or 'penalty' (in the sense that those terms are commonly understood) within the civil enforcement regime. ECMs could produce desirable outcomes, but were really penalties, still less punishments. They have consequences, and so might plausibly deter misconduct, but they do not censure misconduct in the way that other sanctions do. The most striking instrument in the new enforcement toolkit of the CMA is the ability to impose monetary penalties. The need for enforcers to be able to impose such penalties has been discussed for decades and there has been general agreement that their absence was a major omission in the area of consumer protection (and beyond). For example, they were a key tool proposed by the Macrory Report, which led to the passing of the Regulatory Enforcement and Sanctions Act 2008. Part 3 of that Act sets out a range of civil sanctions that can be used as an alternative to prosecution. Unlike a host of other enforcers, consumer protection authorities were unable to apply for sanctioning powers under that Act.

A 'Civil Sanctions Pilot' was established in 2010 to investigate whether the power to impose monetary penalties might be extended to consumer protection enforcers.[121] In its 2012 Paper, *Civil Enforcement Remedies* the Department for Business, Innovation and Skills (BIS) decided that the creation of ECMs was preferable and despite calls for monetary penalties to be introduced, the idea was dropped.[122] However, calls for such powers did not go away. For example, in 2019, Which? published a policy report in which it called for the CMA to 'have powers to issue administrative fines that are sufficiently high to ensure deterrent and punitive impact, without having to resort to the courts'.[123] Other commentators have made similar pleas.[124] The remainder of this chapter will consider the extent to which the most significant of the new powers, monetary penalties, are likely to achieve some key aims.

[119] Cartwright (n 35).

[120] Department for Business Innovation and Skills, *Enhanced Consumer Measures – Guidance for Enforcers of Consumer Law* (May 2015) 5.

[121] Department for Business Innovation and Skills, *Civil Sanctions Pilot* (March 2010), assets.publishing.service.gov.uk/media/5a79d87940f0b66d161ae8e5/10-706-civil-sanctions-pilot.pdf.

[122] Department for Business Innovation and Skills (n 118).

[123] Which?, 'Creating a successful enforcement system for UK consumers' Policy Report (February 2019) 17.

[124] See eg Tyrie letter (n 37); Penrose (n 39); OECD (n 45).

12.7.1. Monetary Penalties and Deterrence

This chapter has emphasised the extent to which deterrence is a key objective of enforcing consumer protection law. Deterrence is a clear example of a consequentialist theory of penalties.[125] The point of imposing the penalty is to have a consequence; to change behaviour. Deterrence can be individual (sanctioning someone to discourage them from acting in the same or a similar way in future) or general (sanctioning someone to discourage others acting in the same or similar way to the person being sanctioned).

The economic model of 'optimal deterrence' was mentioned above. It has been argued that, in its simplified version, utility maximising traders (sometimes referred to in this context as 'amoral calculators') will comply with the law where $pD>U$.[126] This is where p represents the perceived probability of apprehension and conviction, D represents the perceived costs incurred as a result of apprehension and conviction, and U represents the perceived benefits resulting from violation.[127] These assumptions may form the basis of an enforcement strategy, with enforcers able to increase the deterrent effect of their actions by raising the values of p and D.

There is a clear logic to the idea of optimal deterrence. Where a rational trader is endeavouring to maximise profit, they will be incentivised to consider whether a particular course of action is beneficial. A cost–benefit calculation is made and action taken accordingly. Of course, not all traders will be motivated solely by profit. On the contrary, it is hoped that most would take other matters into account when deciding how to act and that many will seek to comply with the law as a matter of principle.[128] Nevertheless, Ramsay has argued that optimal deterrence may have particular resonance when applied to traders: 'Since corporate activity is normally undertaken to reap some economic benefit, corporate decision-makers choose courses of action based on a calculation of potential costs and benefits'.[129]

While there are limitations to this model, it is surely the case that any deterrent effect will be low where traders believe that enforcement action is extremely unlikely. An account of regulatory offences by Ogus estimated that criminal prosecutions accounted for just 0.05 per cent of reported contraventions.[130] There are various explanations for the paucity of prosecutions, but their resource intensive nature is surely one factor.

Furthermore, any deterrent effect that persists will be compromised where traders conclude that, even if enforcement action is successfully pursued, the adverse impact is small. Formal penalties imposed following contravention have frequently been criticised as low across many sectors.[131] Back in 2010 Ipsos MORI undertook some work

[125] P Cartwright, 'Credible Deterrence and Consumer Protection: Lessons for the Financial Conduct Authority' in N Ryder, U Turksen and S Hassler (eds), *Fighting Financial Crime in the Global Economic Crisis* (Routledge, 2015) 29, 38.

[126] The language of 'amoral calculators' is associated with R Kagan and J Scholz, 'The "Criminology and the Corporation" and Regulatory Enforcement Strategies' in K Hawkins and J Thomas (eds), *Enforcing Regulation* (Kluwer, 1984).

[127] See Becker (n 20); Ogus (n 20); Cartwright (n 7).

[128] Ayres and Braithwaite (n 29) 19.

[129] I Ramsay, 'Developments in the Law: Corporate Crime' (1978–79) 92 *Harvard Law Review* 1227, 1231.

[130] Ogus (n 23) 111.

[131] Macrory (n 12) para 1.23.

for the Office of Fair Trading (the forerunner of the CMA) on 'Drivers of Compliance and Non-Compliance in Consumer Law'.[132] Alongside market pressures, the research identified limited understanding of consumer law and the limited deterrent effect from consumer protection law and its enforcement as the main drivers of non-compliance. While it found little understanding on the part of traders about the likely level of fines, it identified a general perception that action was unlikely and penalties were low.[133] This seems unsurprising and reflects other findings. Ogus suggests that the principal reason for the paucity of enforcement action is the high cost of enforcement. He found that in a typical consumer protection case, trading standards would devote one 'officer day' to investigation, two on issuing informal cautions, four on formal cautions and 10 preparing prosecutions. Prosecution would also involve five days of senior management time with legal costs on top.[134]

For the provisions in the DMCCA 2024 to operate successfully as a deterrent it is important that any perception of enforcement action being unlikely and penalties being low is changed. There is reason to be optimistic here. For a start, the move to an administrative model gives the enforcer far more control over these matters. As Ogus observed: 'if … [monetary] penalties can readily be imposed without a formal hearing and without satisfying the evidential threshold required in criminal justice cases, then p will be substantially increased'.[135] Furthermore, monetary penalties are likely to increase D significantly. As noted above, before the DMCCA 2024 there were no fines under the Part 8 regime for contravention of the law, nor for non-compliance with an undertaking. While there have been examples of significant fines being imposed following prosecution for consumer protection offences, these are rare.[136] Under the DMCCA 2024 penalties are potentially much more substantial.

It is difficult to assess whether penalties have been set at the optimal level to secure effective deterrence. As explained above, maximum penalties vary depending upon the breach in question. For example, the maximum penalty in a FIN is a fixed amount not exceeding £300,000 or, if higher, 10 per cent of the total value of the turnover (if any) of the trader.[137] In the case of a final breach of undertakings or directions enforcement notice the CMA may impose a fixed amount, daily amount, or combination of the two. Any fixed amount must not exceed £150,000 or, if higher, five per cent of turnover. Any daily rate penalty must not exceed £15,000 or, if higher, five per cent of the total value of daily turnover.[138] The actual level of penalty imposed will depend on a number of matters. In relation to monetary penalties for breaches of substantive consumer law, the CMA has set out in Guidance the approach it proposes to take and it is helpful to ponder the CMA's intended approach.[139] This approach involves five steps.

[132] OFT, *Drivers of Compliance and Non-compliance with Consumer Law* (report by Ipsos MORI) OFT 1225a (May 2010) para 1.9.
[133] ibid.
[134] Ogus (n 23) 112.
[135] ibid 113.
[136] Macrory (n 12) table 1.3.
[137] s 182(6).
[138] s 193(3).
[139] CMA (n 74).

Step one involves calculating the starting point by having regard to the seriousness of the infringement and the relevant turnover.[140] Assessing seriousness involves considering the level of harm (or risk of harm) from the infringement and the culpability of the party. In terms of level of harm, category one infringements would be those that have the overall effect of causing major economic or non-economic harm to consumers, or which would be lower (category two) cases were escalating factors not present. Examples of escalating factors include infringements that have a particular impact on vulnerable consumers and infringements which involve the use of physical force or financial coercion. When it comes to determining the level of culpability, relevant factors will include whether the conduct was intentional or accidental and whether the trader's operations regularly involve the infringing practice.

Step two refers to an adjustment for deterrence and to take account of the size of the party.[141] For example, the CMA states that 'It may be necessary to impose a higher penalty on a larger party than a smaller one involved in similar conduct in order to have a sufficient deterrent effect'.[142] Step three involves an adjustment for aggravating or mitigating factors.[143] For example, an aggravating factor might be continuing the infringement after having received a warning from an enforcer, while a mitigating factor might be having paid redress to affected consumers before the trader has received a PIN.

Step four concerns an adjustment to ensure that a penalty is proportionate (and within the statutory maximum).[144] The CMA states that it will have regard to all the relevant circumstances when assessing if a penalty is proportionate. In its words: 'The overall assessment should appropriately reflect the seriousness of the infringement and the need sufficiently to deter both the party and others from similar breaches'.[145] As a final step, the CMA may apply a discount of the penalty of up to 40 per cent where the party has settled.[146]

The penalties available, and the CMA's proposals on how they would be used, suggest that there is scope for effective, credible deterrence under the DMCCA 2024. A perusal of the factors that are likely to impact the level of penalty demonstrates that the CMA is mindful of the need to ensure that the penalty reflects matters such as the size, culpability and attitude of the trader. All these are relevant to deterrence. Furthermore, section 205 delegates power to the Secretary of State to make regulations which amend the maximum amount for non-turnover-based penalties. The Guidance makes clear that this is designed to offset the erosion in the real value of the maximum penalties and 'to achieve the intended policy outcome of effective deterrence of non-compliance in a proportionate manner'.[147]

It was noted above that it is not enough to increase penalties, nor to increase the frequency of enforcement action for deterrence. Insofar as traders are amoral calculators,

[140] Guidance (n 60) para 7.21.
[141] ibid para 7.27.
[142] ibid para 7.28.
[143] ibid para 7.32.
[144] ibid para 7.35.
[145] ibid para 7.39.
[146] ibid para 7.41.
[147] Explanatory Notes (n 53) para 1186.

their actions will be based on the *perception* of these matters. The FCA (and its predecessor the Financial Services Authority; FSA) recognised this with its policy of pursuing 'credible deterrence' and its strategy of making its policy highly visible. In the words of the FSA's then Chief Executive, 'To achieve credible deterrence, wrongdoers must not only realise that they face a real and tangible risk of being held to account, but must also expect to face meaningful sanctions'.[148] For deterrence to be achieved, it is important both that the CMA uses its new powers and clearly communicates the fact that it is doing so.[149]

12.7.2. Monetary Penalties and Compliance

The language of deterrence appears most appropriate when dealing with 'amoral calculators'. Despite their inevitable pursuit of profit many traders will not fit this description. Kagan and Scholz distinguished between amoral calculators, political citizens and the organisationally incompetent recognising that those with different motivations might be treated differently.[150] Contraventions of consumer protection law are frequently careless or accidental and/or based on errors of understanding rather than deliberate. This was evidenced by research for the OFT (the predecessor of the CMA), which found that a key driver of non-compliance was not malign intent, but limited understanding of obligations.[151]

It was noted above that it is one thing to back up norms with criminal sanctions and another to prosecute in individual cases where those norms are infringed. While the CMA has been given a host of new powers, it is expected that they will not be deployed as a matter of course; compliance strategies will remain extremely important. It is important, for example, that the CMA considers the attitudes of traders in its decisions about what action, if any, to take. In championing their 'tit for tat' approach to enforcement, Ayres and Braithwaite made a strong case for basing enforcement decisions on the revealed attitudes of the regulated.[152] Hodges has argued that this reflects the reality of enforcement, with a clear move away from what he terms 'authoritarian repression' to 'reliance on treating most businesses as responsible and motivated to comply with the rules, and who can be expected to amend their behaviour through guidance, assistance and support'.[153] It is clear that the CMA is aware of these arguments. While there is no need for an intention to break the law for a monetary penalty to be applied, it is clear that the existence of deliberation, and the regularity of breaches and the extent to which a trader has ignored advice are all factors that the CMA will take into account. These are discussed explicitly in the context of how culpable conduct is for the purpose of assessing a monetary penalty.[154]

[148] FSA, 'Enforcement Annual Performance Account 2012-13' (undated) 5.
[149] Cartwright (n 125).
[150] Kagan and Scholz (n 126).
[151] OFT, *Factors Affecting Compliance with Consumer Law and the Deterrent Effect of Consumer Enforcement* (OFT 1228) (June 2010).
[152] Ayres and Braithwaite (n 29) 19–20.
[153] C Hodges, *Law and Corporate Behaviour* (Hart, 2015) 179.
[154] Guidance (n 60).

However, they will also be relevant to the decision as to whether formal enforcement action should be taken in the first place.[155]

From an instrumental perspective, monetary penalties should help to ensure deterrence for those traders for whom a focus on deterrence makes sense: those who take informed decisions to break the law. Penalties are less of an issue where a contravention is unintentional, perhaps resulting from carelessness or ignorance. When it comes to securing compliance, it is particularly important to remember that tools other than monetary penalties will be particularly important. At one end of the scale informal action may suffice. Where more formal action is appropriate we have seen that the CMA has a range of options. For example, a FIN may require the trader to comply with such directions as the CMA considers appropriate to secure compliance with the requirements of a PIN, including directions to take such ECMs as the CMA considers just and reasonable. One form of ECM is 'compliance measures', which are 'intended to prevent or reduce the risk of the occurrence or repetition of the infringing conduct'. This 'may include measures imposed for the purpose of improving compliance with consumer law more generally'.[156]

However, it is important still to have penalties available to deploy in some cases where contraventions are not deliberate. In particular, traders need to be incentivised to take care. All traders can be expected to devote appropriate attention and resources to their activities, and the availability of substantial sanctions may play a role in securing that. While tools other than monetary penalties may be more obviously targeted at securing compliance, the availability of penalties will increase the probability of those tools achieving a satisfactory outcome.

12.7.3. Monetary Penalties and Symbolism

The discussion above has focused on the role of the CMA's new powers (and in particular monetary penalties) in deterring misconduct and achieving compliance. It can be argued that the principal aims of enforcement are in this way instrumental. This accords with the interpretation of such penalties as consequentialist.[157]

However, there are also non-consequentialist theories of sanctioning (typically referred to as theories of punishment, although I am using the term 'sanctioning' as it is more commonly used in context of regulation). These reflect the idea that it is legitimate to impose a penalty on a trader, not to ensure deterrence or improve compliance, but because they deserve it. Non-consequentialist theories, which are sometimes labelled 'retributive justice' include just deserts theories.[158] Just deserts is founded upon the notion that penalties should reflect the severity of the wrongdoing in which the trader has engaged and be fair, determinate and proportionate. A key aim of the penalty is to reflect the nature of the conduct to which it relates.

155 CMA (n 4).
156 Guidance (n 60) para 5.13.
157 Cartwright (n 125) 38.
158 See generally RA Duff and D Garland, *A Reader on Punishment* (Oxford University Press, 1994).

Non-consequentialist theories such as just deserts are generally discussed in the context of the criminal law. In that context, a particularly important issue is that of fair labelling. In its consultation paper, *Criminal Liability in Regulatory Contexts*, the Law Commission argued that:[159]

> The criminal law should only be employed to deal with wrongdoers who deserve the stigma associated with criminal conviction because they have engaged in seriously reprehensible conduct. It should not be used as the primary means of promoting regulatory objectives.

One possible strength of monetary penalties over fines that result from prosecution is that monetary penalties do not involve labelling the trader as a criminal. Although contravention of consumer protection law which leads to the imposition of a monetary penalty will typically involve the commission of a criminal offence, the imposition of a monetary penalty is a civil matter. Where breaches of consumer protection law do not involve seriously reprehensible conduct, it might be argued to be more appropriate to impose monetary penalties than fines.

On the basis of these arguments it might seem logical to argue that prosecution should be reserved for those cases where the conduct is seriously reprehensible and civil action used in cases that fall short of that. In its response to the consultation on the White Paper, the Government stated that alongside the new powers, the CMA 'will retain the ability to use criminal enforcement options via the criminal courts *for the most serious breaches of consumer law*' [my italics].[160] However, there are weaknesses to this logic. One obvious weakness is that monetary penalties are likely to be significantly higher than fines. To the extent that the formal penalty should reflect the wrongdoing, monetary penalties appear more suited to being imposed for the most severe transgressions. A second weakness is that it seems doubtful that the public would appreciate the distinction between a (civil) monetary penalty and a (criminal) fine. Indeed, it seems likely that many members of the public will assume that conduct attracting a high monetary penalty will be more reprehensible than that attracting a lower fine. It is important to keep the possibility of prosecution, however, particularly where a custodial sentence may be appropriate. Furthermore, conduct that leads to the imposition of a very high monetary penalty is likely to be deserving of a significant level of stigma. The concerns may in practice be more apparent than real.

12.8. Conclusions

The DMCCA 2024 has introduced a range of new enforcement powers which are relevant both to the courts and to enforcers, including the CMA. While many of the new provisions represent an evolution of existing powers, the direct enforcement powers given to the CMA under Chapter 4 are particularly innovative in the context of the UK. Of those direct enforcement powers, the ability of the CMA to impose monetary

[159] Law Commission, *Criminal Liability in Regulatory Contexts* Consultation Paper 195 (2010) para 1.28.

[160] Department of Business, Energy and Industrial Strategy 'Reforming Competition and Consumer Policy: Government Response to Consultation' CP656 (April 2022) 79.

penalties is especially striking. Writing in anticipation of the powers being implemented, CMA argued that:[161]

> [T]he introduction of a new administrative enforcement model will transform the impact of the consumer enforcement action we take – empowering us to decide when consumer law has been broken, rather than having to take each case to court, and giving us the ability to directly impose significant financial penalties.

It is too early to be able to assess with confidence what impact these new powers will have. However, by identifying some of the main aims of consumer protection enforcement, and assessing the extent to which the new powers align with those, there are strong grounds for optimism. Whether viewed through the lens of deterrence or compliance, the direct enforcement powers appear well placed to deliver the principal objectives that the enforcement of consumer law seeks to achieve. The power to impose monetary penalties alongside other tools gives the CMA an important additional lever. It is not clear how commonly penalties will be imposed and it may be that the power will be used sparingly as part of a responsive enforcement strategy. In this way, it may be helpful to have that power in the background while enforcers use other tools (including more established tools such an ECMs) in a responsive manner.[162] However, to the extent that the new regime is to achieve optimal deterrence, it will be necessary to signal that monetary penalties will be imposed whenever appropriate. It appears that the CMA may finally have the enforcement toolkit it has long needed.

[161] CMA, *Annual Plan 24/25* 14 March 2024, para 6.25.
[162] Ayres and Braithwaite (n 29).

13

The Potential for the Expansion of the UK Collective Actions Regime at the Competition Appeal Tribunal to Consumer Claims

ARIEL FLAVIAN*

13.1. Introduction

Consumer redress is notoriously difficult. One main obstacle is the individual nature of redress. One of the innovations in the last 10 to 15 years has been the introduction of collective actions processes alongside a development of alternative dispute resolution (ADR) processes. Collective redress mechanisms play a crucial role in ensuring access to justice for consumers because the nature of consumer claims is that they tend to be low-value and yet affect many individuals. Without bundling claims into one action, the cost of pursuing individual claims is normally higher than the expected personal damages. Thus, consumers would often shy away from bringing any forms of action and suffer the burden of the detriment.

Collective and group action procedures are therefore required to provide expeditious, effective and proportionate resolution of complex multi-party litigation. In the UK, there are three options available to consumers to obtain collective redress: group litigation orders; representative actions; and, in addition, the Competition Act 1998 was amended by Schedule 8 of the Consumer Rights Act 2015 (CRA 2015) with provisions for collective actions in front of the Competition Appeal Tribunal (CAT) (albeit limited to competition law). This chapter largely focuses on the latter. While the first two mechanisms can service consumer claims, the third is not currently able to, and this chapter reflects on the potential for the CAT procedure to address the needs of consumers. This is largely because the group litigation orders and the representative actions have not to date been procedure with sufficient flexibility to allow for large-scale adoption, thus

* With thanks to Professor Christine Riefa for her assistance in shaping earlier drafts of this chapter and her useful insights.

leaving the needs of consumers in the UK somewhat neglected when it comes to obtaining collective redress.

This chapter starts with a brief overview of the limitations of the collective redress mechanisms in place in the UK. It then moves to dissect the mechanics of collective actions at the CAT for competition claims exploring its genesis and main characteristics. The chapter reflects on the potential of the CAT procedure to bring about improvements to consumer welfare, and whether it could also be envisaged as a viable avenue for redress for consumer law infringements. It concludes that while still in development and, in many respects, still an imperfect procedure, the use of collective actions at the CAT could provide consumers with much needed relief for large-scale, small-value consumer law infringements alongside offering much-needed market corrections through findings of competition law infringements.

13.2. Limitations of Current Collective Regimes in the UK to Service the Needs of Consumers

The first mechanism is a group litigation order (GLO) under the Civil Procedure Rules 1998 (CPR) 19.21[1] introduced in the wake of the Woolf Reforms.[2] As this procedure requires each individual member of the class to bring its own individual action, it is not very suitable to cater for mass actions of small claims. The English GLO merely serves as a case management umbrella under which a conglomeration of individual actions is managed.[3] Besides, the 'opt in' nature of the GLO is an impediment to the procedure[4] as consumers need to actively join proceedings. As a result, there have been only 123 cases brought under the GLO procedure[5] since its inception in the CPR from 2 May 2000.[6] Nevertheless, it has included some noteworthy cases,[7] including

[1] GLOs were introduced in the UK to give effect to The Right Honourable the Lord Woolf, Master of the Rolls, 'Access to Justice Final Report to the Lord Chancellor on the civil justice system in England and Wales' (July 1996) ('Woolf Report'), which recommended that new procedures dealing with multi-party claims needed to be introduced. According to CPR 19.21, a 'Group Litigation Order … means an order made under rule 19.22 to provide for the case management of claims which give rise to common or related issues of fact or law (the "GLO issues")'.

[2] A 1995 report by the Law Society was followed by a full chapter in the Woolf Report (n 1). Lord Woolf observed that group action procedures were necessary, since they provide expeditious, effective and proportionate methods for resolving complex multi-party litigation. In 2000, the Civil Procedure Rules 1998 came into force introducing r 19(3) dealing with group litigation.

[3] R Mulheron, 'Reform of Collective Redress in England and Wales: A Perspective of Need' Civil Justice Council (2008). See also CPR PD 19B – Group Litigation. See also N Andrews, 'Multi–Party Proceedings in England: Representative and Group Actions' (2001) 11 *Duke Journal of Comparative and International Law* 249.

[4] Mulheron (n 3).

[5] For a full list, see www.gov.uk/government/publications/group-litigation-orders/list-of-group-litigation-orders. ('GLO list').

[6] Civil Procedure (Amendment) Rules 2000 (SI 2000 No 221) r 9.

[7] It is also the procedure used for the Post Office litigation, www.gov.uk/government/publications/group-litigation-orders/list-of-group-litigation-orders#the-post-office-group-litigation.

the emission cases against Volkswagen,[8] BMW,[9] Nissan,[10] Jaguar and many other car manufacturers.[11]

The second collective procedure in England is the representative action under CPR 19.8.[12] This rule adopted the old mechanism of representative actions,[13] allowing such actions only in cases in which individuals hold the 'same interest' in the claim.[14] In claim for damages, the courts' strict adherence to the 'same interest' requirement led to a standstill. The UK Supreme Court recently held in *Lloyds v Google*,[15] in the context of alleged breach of the Data Protection Act 1988, that the requirement of having the same interest in the action could not be met in actions for damages which require individual assessment. In cases such as these, CPR 19.8 cannot therefore be a vehicle to bring collective claims which are not unified in their nature and require individual evidence.

However, the Lloyd's case did not shut the door completely for declaratory actions or actions which arise from the same factual set of evidence with similar amounts of damages. Indeed, not long after the decision, an attempt to use the representative action was successful in *Commission Recovery v Marks and Clerks LLP*.[16] In this case, the High Court held that a claim regarding secret commissions, notwithstanding that the members of the action had different claims and remedies, may still fulfil the 'same interest test' since there was no conflict of interest between the members of the class, or any prejudice to the class.[17] This decision was recently affirmed by the Supreme Court.[18] However, even after this decision the representative action under CPR 19.8 continues to have limited utility in bringing collective redress and therefore still suffers from a rather limited ability for consumers to vindicate their rights. Indeed, classes of consumers tend to be disparate compared to the common interest the claimants shared in *Commission Recovery* where they had been clients of the law firm offering patent renewal services.

The third option is the collective procedure for breach of competition law in the Competition Act 1998, as amended by Schedule 8 CRA 2015. It enables consumers to bring collective actions in front of the CAT and be awarded damages for the harm caused by anti-competitive behaviours. There lies one of its most significant limitations as it does not yet cater for consumer law infringements despite being introduced in consumer legislation. Instead, it is focused on protecting consumers that have suffered the effects of anti-competitive behaviours. Yet, the regime may be worthy of notice by

[8] See orders 105 and 120 GLO list.

[9] See order 115 GLO list.

[10] See order 114 GLO list.

[11] See order 113 GLO list. Also see orders 117–123. For more on those actions in the UK and other jurisdictions, see F di Rattalma (ed), *The Dieselgate, a Legal Perspective* (Springer, 2017).

[12] The procedure was originally under Art 19.6 CPR, but was renumbered without major alteration in the Civil Procedure (Amendment) Rules 2023.

[13] Originally adopted from RSC Ord 15 r 12 (1).

[14] CPR 19.8; see n 12.

[15] [2021] UKSC 50.

[16] [2024] EWCA Civ 9.

[17] On the other hand, in *Prismall v Google* [2023] EWHC 1169 (KB) a representative claim under CPR 19.8 was struck out at first instance, and this was approved by the Court of Appeal on 11 December 2024. See *Prismall v Google* [2024] EWCA Civ 1516.

[18] www.globallegalpost.com/news/uk-supreme-court-refuses-marks-clerk-permission-to-appeal-in-secret-commissions-case-638501501.

consumer lawyers as it could act as a blueprint for a viable mechanism enabling more effective private redress in the future.

13.3. Potential of the Collective Action Regime in Front of the CAT to Respond to Consumer Needs for Redress

The procedure, even with its current limitation in scope, has great value for consumers. This is because, while it is not yet a procedure to be used to effect redress for infringement to consumer law in the UK, it is clear that by offering consumers a unique opportunity to obtain redress for infringement of competition law, it could act as a deterrent and encourage businesses to behave fairly. Indeed, the regime has the potential to already indirectly reshape consumer protection, for a number of connected reasons. First, it allows consumers to claim for harm suffered and alter the behaviour of firms who, so far, could simply await individual claims or only punctual public enforcement interventions in the competition law sphere. This could, in turn, stimulate healthier competition and foster consumer welfare. Second, it may well re-invigorate the consumer–competition law relationship leading to better outcomes for consumers. In the past, competition law was always branded as the protector of consumers without offering them a seat at the table. It now can enable them to drive competition law enforcement and multiply interventions on the market, making competition law more effective.

In an ideal world, the CMA might have pursued all anti-competitive behaviours, but in reality, it is only able to focus on a small number of them each year. In any event, the CMA is unable to recover damages for the harm suffered by consumers and hence, while an anti-competitive behaviour may be stopped and a fine be imposed, consumers are left out of pocket all the same. The collective action regime ensures that consumers can recover their loss from the company/companies that caused it. Consumers are empowered to do this, either following a finding by the CMA of an infringement of competition law (so-called follow-on actions) or by mounting their own cases (stand-alone actions).[19] To date, most cases have been stand-alone.

13.4. The Genesis of the Collective Action Regime at the CAT

Despite being nearly 10 years old, the CRA 2015 regime for collective actions is still in its infancy, following a slow and protracted start. The first two cases, *Gibson*[20] and *Merricks*[21] were not initially certified by the CAT. However, whilst the Gibson case was later withdrawn,

[19] Under CRA 2015, s 81.

[20] *Dorothy Gibson v Pride Mobility Products Limited* [2017] CAT 9.

[21] *1266/7/7/16 Walter Hugh Merricks CBE v Mastercard Incorporated and Others* (Competition Appeal Tribunal, 8 September 2016).

Mr Merricks took his case to the Court of Appeal.[22] The Court of Appeal found that the case should be returned to the CAT for a re-hearing on certification issues with some instructions on the tests that should be applied to the certification procedure.[23] The main difference between the Court of Appeal's approach and the first instance decision was the level of evidence that should be provided in order to obtain certification.

In July 2017, the Tribunal had rejected the application mainly because the expert evidence did not convince the CAT that the excessive interchange fees Mastercard had applied to traders had been passed on to the consumers and because there was not sufficient information to support a 'top-down' calculation of damages. The Court of Appeal took a different view. It required that the expert methodology concerning the pass-on issue be 'capable' of assessing the level of pass-on, and that the representative can demonstrate the calculation at trial. The Court of Appeal approach required a lower threshold for granting a collective proceedings order (CPO). The Court of Appeal took the view that, at the certification stage, it is enough to show that 'the claim has a real prospect of success'.[24] This decision was subject to an appeal to the Supreme Court which eventually dismissed the appeal by Mastercard in December 2020.[25] The case was only then remitted to the CAT for the CPO application to be determined in accordance with the proper tests provided in the appellate judgments. It was therefore only in March 2021 that the CAT decided to grant certification to Mr Merricks,[26] five years after the case was first submitted to the Tribunal. Merricks was the first case to be certified since the new regime was introduced in the CRA 2015. The unfortunate result of those prolonged proceedings was that all other collective redress cases pending at the CAT were stayed until March 2021.

Since 2021 however, collective actions in front of the CAT have multiplied and the rate at which new cases are coming forward is gathering pace. There are, at the time of writing, over 40 cases live for consideration by the CAT. More are in preparation and have not yet been filed. Thirteen cases have already been certified. The amount of damages being claimed in these certified claims is in excess of £22.5 billion.[27] If awarded, those damages will be distributed to the consumers affected as well as used to pay the lawyers involved and litigation funders and insurers recouping their risky investments. If, after distribution, any money is left, the regime in the UK allows for a payment to be made to a designated charity in opt-out cases,[28] but may also revert to the defendants in settlements,[29] as it seems the case in *Justin Gutmann v First MTR South Western Trains Limited and Another*.[30]

[22] The decision of the CAT was criticised in Rachael Mulheron, 'Revisiting the Class Action Certification Matrix in *Merricks V Mastercard Inc*' (2019) 30 *King's Law Journal* 396, DOI: 10.1080/09615768.2019.1656392.

[23] For a detailed analysis of the Court of Appeal approach to certification, Rachael Mulheron (n 22).

[24] *Merricks v Mastercard* [2019] EWCA Civ 674.

[25] *Mastercard v Merricks* [2020] UKSC 51, www.supremecourt.uk/cases/uksc-2019-0118.html.

[26] Walter Hugh Merricks CBE v Mastercard Incorporated and Others [2021] CAT 28.

[27] N Stopford, '£1.3 billion BT compensation trial ends and billions more could be owed to UK consumers' Consumer Voice (22 March 2024), consumervoice.uk/legal/bt-compensation-trial-ends-and-billions-more-could-be-owed-to-uk-consumers.

[28] Competition Appeal Tribunal Rules 2015 (SI 2015 No 1648), r 93 (6).

[29] ibid r 94(9)(g). In fact, the CAT has recently approved the reversion of the unclaimed damages to the defendants in the second settlement approved in the UK in *Justin Gutmann v First MTR Southwestern Trains Limited and Another* [2024] CAT 32.

[30] *Gutmann* (n 29).

In this case, the CAT was aware that the take-up rates for class members may be low (approximately only 10 per cent due to the nature of the class composed of train passengers) and the low amount of personal damages. Yet, it approved the settlement with the revision of the unclaimed damages to the defendant, albeit reluctantly, and without any award of damages to a charity. The Competition Appeal Tribunal explained:

> There could have been a balance going to charity. It has not been proposed here. In the submissions of the parties, with some exaggeration, it was asserted it would not be appropriate for any unclaimed balance to go to charity. We do not accept that. It may be appropriate, but it may not be necessary. We cannot require parties to pay anything to charity.[31]

13.5. Key Features of the Collective Actions at the CAT

Collective proceedings in competition law are conducted under the Competition Act 1998, section 47B. The collective actions at the CAT follow the rules contained in Competition Appeal Tribunal Rules 2015 and a more detailed guidance is offered by the Competition Appeal Tribunal Guide to the proceedings 2015.[32] However, the rules are still relatively new and, in many respects, untested. The CAT has, for example, dealt with new issues, for the first time, such as the extent of disclosure,[33] the suitability of funding arrangements,[34] settlements,[35] etc. This has meant that several cases have progressed more slowly while the Court of Appeal had to ponder procedural and substantive law points. Meanwhile, the body of rules and details grows at a steady pace. For example, the list of practice directions[36] coming to serve as a useful reference point are helping to develop a clearer procedural system which will likely help parties save time. For example, the practice direction on confidentiality rings now crystalises the position the CAT has adopted over several cases.[37]

13.5.1. Class Representation

The class of consumers who have been harmed by anti-competitive conduct has to be represented by a class representative. Class representatives are not required to have a particular set of qualification or prior experience. A person who proposes to be the

[31] See ibid [120].

[32] www.catribunal.org.uk/sites/cat/files/2017-12/guide_to_proceedings_2015.pdf.

[33] *UK Trucks Claim Limited v Stellantis NV and Ors; Road Haulage Association Limited v Man SE and Ors* [2022] CAT 25 [223]. See also the discussion about disclosure at:*Mark McLaren Class Representative Limited v MOL (Europe Africa Limited) and Ors* [2022] CAT 10 [169].

[34] *BT Group PLC v Le Patourel* [2022] EWCA Civ 593 [77].

[35] *Gutmann* (n 29).

[36] www.catribunal.org.uk/index.php/rules-and-guidance.

[37] www.catribunal.org.uk/sites/cat/files/2024-01/Practice%20Direction%20DISCLOSURE%20-%20MANAGEMENT%20OF%20CONFIDENTIAL%20INFORMATION%20%204%20Jan%202024_2.pdf. See for example in relation to the duty of an employee to return a laptop which contains confidential materials: *David Courtney Boyle v Govia Thameslink Railway Limited & Others* [2024] CAT 26.

representative (PCR) may commence collective redress proceedings only if the Tribunal makes a CPO.[38] To obtain a CPO, two conditions need to be satisfied: the authorisation condition and the eligibility condition.

The authorisation condition focuses on the proposed class representative. The requirements for authorisation of a class representative are set out in section 47B(5) and (8) of the Competition Act 1998. A class representative can be authorised whether or not, it is a member of the class,[39] but 'only if the Tribunal considers that it is just and reasonable for that person to act as a representative in those proceedings' (section 47(8)(a)–(b)).

The rules around certification of the class representative are further detailed in section 78 of the Competition Appeal Tribunal Rules 2015. Specific rules are laid out under Part 5 of the Rules. In considering what would be just and reasonable for the applicant to act as a class representative, the tribunal takes several factors into account, which comprises whether the person:

- will fairly and adequately represent the interests of the class members (which may include the ability of an individual to manage the litigation and/or the nature of a pre-existing body managing the litigation);
- is the most suitable (and this will be particularly relevant in case of a carriage dispute where two or more class representatives are proposed);
- can pay the defendant's recoverable costs (if they were ordered to do so) and would be able to cover any undertaking as to damages required by the Tribunal on an interim injunction.

Another requirement taken into account is whether or not the class representativ has prepared a plan to bring proceedings forward. This includes three main requirements: (i) a method for bringing the proceedings on behalf of represented persons and for notifying represented persons of the progress of the proceedings; (ii) a procedure for governance and consultation which takes into account the size and nature of the class; and (iii) any estimate of and details of arrangements as to costs, fees or disbursements which the Tribunal orders that the proposed class representative shall provide.[40]

Of course, this is on top of assessing if the competition law claim itself is suitable for being litigated in front of the CAT (the eligibility condition). The requirements of eligibility for a CPO are set in Rule 79 of the CAT Rules and provides that the court should be satisfied that the claims: (a) are brought on behalf of an identifiable class of persons; (b) raise common issues; and (c) are suitable to be brought in collective proceedings.

In deciding whether in opt-out proceedings the class consists of identifiable class of persons the court has to be satisfied that there are means to determine who are the class members. With regards to opt in proceedings the court may examine the communality of the claims. The overall requirement from the class representative is

[38] Competition Act 1998, s 47B(4).

[39] In *Gutmann v Apple* [2023] CAT 67 the argument that Justin Gutmann could not act as a class member since he was not an owner of an iPhone and hence not member of the class was rejected by the CAT.

[40] r 78(3)(c).

to show that the claim is suitable for collective procedure. Therefore, where the CAT finds that the representative fails to present sound methodology the application may be denied.[41]

In addition, the PCR has to show that the claims are suitable for an aggregate award of damages. After the decision in the Supreme Court in *Mastercard Inc v Merricks*[42] it is enough for the PCR to present a methodology which offers a realistic prospect of establishing loss on a class-wide basis. The UK Supreme Court adopted the commonality test which was set in the Canadian *Pro Sys* case.[43] In *Pro Sys*, Rothstein J stated at [118] that:

> [T]he expert methodology must be sufficiently credible or plausible to establish some basis in fact for the commonality requirement. This means that the methodology must offer a realistic prospect of establishing loss on a class wide basis so that, if the overcharge is eventually established at the trial of the common issues, there is a means by which to demonstrate that it is common to the class (i.e. that passing on has occurred). The methodology cannot be purely theoretical or hypothetical but must be grounded in the facts of the particular case in question. There must be some evidence of the availability of the data to which the methodology is to be applied.

Indeed, once the requirements for certification were set by the Supreme Court in the *Mastercard* case at a lower standard from that which was envisaged at the first instance, other cases passed the barriers quite swiftly and met both the eligibility and the suitability requirements. The *Pro-Sys* test presents a 'low threshold': establishing 'some basis in fact' for the satisfaction of the 'common issues requirement' requires '*only a minimum evidentiary basis and [is] not an onerous [test]*'.[44]

In *Mark McLaren Class Representative Limited v MOL (Europe Africa) Ltd*, the court explained that the Tribunal must satisfy itself that the methodology is bound to work, or will work on the balance of probabilities, whatever the evidential challenges. The Tribunal is not conducting a mini-trial at the certification stage. The Tribunal's role is not to determine the best methodology available, but to assess the one put forward by the PCR.[45] Having said this, in the carriage dispute (see below) between *Hunter* and *Hammond*,[46] the Tribunal decided on the claim to proceed in fact based on the best out of the two economists methodologies put in front of it.[47]

13.5.2. Carriage Disputes

When two class representatives are attempting to represent the class, the Tribunal has the power to decide which of the proposed claimants will represent the class. These disputes are known as carriage disputes. Where the parties do not reach an agreement on the question of the class representation, the Tribunal may issue an amalgamation

[41] *Commercial and Interregional Card Claims I Limited v Mastercard; Commercial and Interregional Card Claims II Limited v Mastercard; Commercial and Interregional Card Claims I Limited v Visa*; and *Commercial and Interregional Card Claims II Limited v Visa* [2023] CAT 38.

[42] *Mastercard v Merricks* (n 25).

[43] *Pro-Sys Consultants Ltd v Microsoft Corpn* [2013] SCC 57 [118].

[44] *Mastercard v Merricks* (n 25).

[45] [2022] CAT 10 [107].

[46] *Julie Hunter v Amazon.com, Inc and others* [2024] CAT 8.

[47] [2024] CAT 8 [36].

order to consolidate the two claims. The CAT will also welcome agreement between the parties on carriage disputes and may amalgamate two claims to one action where the parties reach an agreement which is regarded as reasonable.[48] Otherwise, the President provided that:

> Where a carriage dispute is resolved by agreement between those persons having conduct of rival applications for certification, this Tribunal will be slow to second guess that agreement …[49]

The CAT indicated in a number of judgments that the main factor to look at is the benefit of the class members,[50] including scrutinising arguments and methodology.[51] The CAT, to date, has given little weight to the question which of the two claims was filed first.[52] The current approach seems to be that a decision on carriage disputes should be made in the earliest stages of the case before certification in order to save expenses from the parties and not to complicate and cause delay to the decision on certification which with a roll up hearing on carriage and certification.[53]

13.5.3. Opt-In and Opt-Out Claims

Under Rule 79 of the CAT Rules, the court is required to consider whether the collective proceedings should be 'opt-in' or 'opt-out'.[54] It allows claimants to be included in the class on an opt-out basis, meaning that all are included unless they do not wish to join. Opt-in can also be ordered in particular cases but, so far, opt-out has been the mechanism of choice by claimants. The rule provides that in determining whether the claim should proceed on opt-in or opt-out proceedings the Tribunal may take into account additional considerations including the strength of the claims and the practicability of the proceedings which are in front of the court to be brought as opt-in collective proceedings, having regard to all the circumstances, including the estimated amount of damages that individual class members may recover.[55]

With regard to the strength of the case, in *Evans v Barclays Bank PLC & Ors*[56] the Court of Appeal agreed with the rationale put forward by the CAT that stronger cases

[48] *Charles Arthur v Alphabet Inc & Others* and *Claudio Pollack v Alphabet Inc and Others* – Consolidation order [2023] CAT 65.

[49] *Charles Arthur/Claudio Pollack* Consolidation order [2023] CAT 65, Reasons [4].

[50] Section 6.32 of the guide provides that: 'The third factor relevant to the assessment of the proposed class representative applies where more than one applicant is seeking approval to act as the class representative for opt-out proceedings in respect of the same or overlapping claims. In such a scenario, the Tribunal will consider who would be the most suitable representative: Rule 78(2)(c). The Tribunal will seek to arrive at a decision which is in the best interests of all class members and is fair to the defendants. The factors that are likely to be relevant to this assessment include: the proposed class definition and scope of the claims; the quality of the litigation plan referred to above; and the experience of the lawyers of the competing proposed class representatives.'

[51] *UK Trucks Claim Limited* (n 33) [144]. See also *Julie Hunter v Amazon.com and Robert Hammond v Amazon.com* [2024] CAT 8.

[52] *Evans v Barclays Bank PLC & Ors* [2023] EWCA Civ 876 [138].

[53] See *Hunter and Hammond* (n 51) [29].

[54] Where group members who are not domiciled in the UK wish to join the proceedings they may do so only on opt-in basis as provided in r 80-1A(h)(iii).

[55] See r 79(3) and sections 6.38 and 6.39 of the guide.

[56] [2023] EWCA Civ 876.

may be considered as better qualified for opt-out proceedings. However, the Court of Appeal was of the opinion that the examination of the strength of the case at the certification stage may be premature because the court does not make a definitive determination of the prospects of a case at the CPO application stage. With regards to practicability the Court of Appeal mentioned that 'it is now clear from case law that where there would be no proceedings save on opt-out terms, that is a powerful factor in favour of a claim being certified as opt-out'.[57]

It seems that the main idea behind this test is that where the claims are based on substantial personal damages there are grounds to believe that the group members will not remain apathic to their rights and therefore will be ready to come forward and take part in the legal proceedings. On the other hand, where the class consists of a large number of members, with small amount of damages, it should give rise to an opt-out action.[58] The Court of Appeal in *Evans* mentioned that where there are multiple class members and the amount of their personal damage is low it is not practicable to expect that an opt-in action will succeed. Furthermore, the court was of the opinion that it is a strong argument to allow an action on an opt-out basis where there would be no proceedings if an opt-in action will go ahead.[59]

Another factor which should be taken into account is the availability of funding. Therefore, if it seems that an opt-in claim will lead to very few sign-ups, the result is the that funders will be reluctant to fund the case and the action will fail.

The mere fact that the class may involve both small-claim-holders as well as business claimants with high value claims should not lead to certification of the claim in both opt-in and opt-out basis. Therefore, the CAT refused to order a mix opt-out and opt-in procedure on the grounds that it is not practical.[60]

13.5.4. Damages

The regime allows for the class to recover damages, although unlike in the United States (US) the Tribunal cannot order punitive damages. The amounts claimed so far are fetching high sums, although it is not yet clear if claimants will be able to make their case and recover the amounts claimed. Many of the cases are in the early stages and far from trial. But there are early indications that the system can bear fruit, for example with *Justin Gutmann v First MTR Southwestern Trains Limited and Another*.[61] Under this settlement Stagecoach South Western Trains Limited has undertaken to pay the sum of £25 million to class members who submit a claim for compensation. The class members are divided into three pots and their eligibility depends on the evidence which they provide to support their claim.[62] Merricks has also announced that it has reached a settlement

[57] ibid [123].
[58] See for example the decision of the Court of Appeal in *Justin Le Patourel v BT Group PLC* [2022] EWCA Civ 593.
[59] *Le Patourel* [2022] EWCA Civ 593 [82].
[60] *Mark McLaren Class Representative Limited v MOL (Europe Africa) Ltd and Others* [2022] CAT 10 [162]–[167].
[61] See n 29.
[62] The details of the settlement are published at www.boundaryfares.com/Home/SettlementFAQs.

with Mastercard, for a figure of around £200 million, to present to the CAT in 2025,[63] sparking public disagreement with the claim's own funders who regard the offer as too low.[64] However, there is also a possible danger that the minutiae of economic quantification of damages, which was a key obstacle in the *Merricks* claim, may seriously derail the hopes held in this enforcement mechanism. If cases cannot conclude, providing, notably, funders, with the right type of returns, it is possible that the procedure could be neglected in future years.

13.5.5. Litigation Funding

Litigation is indeed a very central issue to the success of the procedure. It is one also considered at certification stage where it is a prerequisite that the PCR has sufficient funding for the proceedings.[65] The CAT looks at the PCR funding as part of the requirement to examine whether the PCR would act fairly and adequately in the interests of the class members.[66] Collective redress cases are very expensive partly because they require expert evidence and are being governed by 'the loser pays' principle. As a result, funding is also linked to expensive insurance premiums to guard against orders for cost issued against the PCR. Those are normally funded by the litigation funder as part of the pot of money advanced to the PCR. The CAT examines the litigation funding agreements (LFA) and in some cases required changes in the LFA, where the CAT felt the level of return or conditions of funding warranted calling out at the certification stage,[67] although it had so far stuck to the premise that fuller scrutiny of the LFA should take place at settlement or at judgement stage.

Funding agreements were originally mainly structured in such a way that funders would be paid out of the damages received in the case. However, the Supreme Court recently held that litigation funders provide claims management services.[68] Therefore LFAs, which award the funder a percentage of the damages or settlement sums, should be considered damages-based agreements (DBA).[69] Those are prohibited in opt-out collective proceedings at the CAT by the Competition Act 1998, section 47C(8).[70] Following the decision in *Paccar*, the funding agreement used by class representative and proposed class representative were rendered unenforceable overnight resulting in uncertainty in the litigation funding market. To ensure perennity of the collective action regime, the then Conservative Government intervened to safeguard the rights of litigation funders for remuneration by proposing the amendment of the Courts and Legal Services Act 1990 (CLSA 1990),

[63] www.reuters.com/business/finance/mastercard-reaches-agreement-principle-settle-mass-uk-fees-case-2024-12-03.

[64] www.lawgazette.co.uk/news/funder-to-challenge-premature-mastercard-case-settlement/5121721.article.

[65] Tribunal's Guide to Proceedings 2015, para 6.33.

[66] 1408/7/7/21 *Elizabeth Helen Coll v Alphabet Inc and Others* [2022] CAT 39 [24].

[67] This was for example the case in *Liza Lovdahl Gormsen v Meta* [2024] CAT 11.

[68] As defined in the Financial Services and Management Act 2000, s419, as litigation funding includes the provision of financial services or assistance under s 419A(2)(a).

[69] *Paccar Inc and Ors v Road Haulage Association Limited* [2023] UKSC 28.

[70] The Courts and Legal Services Act 1990, s 58AA defines DBAs.

section 58AA.[71] A draft bill[72] was put forward. However, in the wake of the announcement of a general election in May 2024, the bill was lost due to lack of parliamentary time before the dissolution of Parliament. This is greatly impacting the availability of third-party funding[73] and posing a non-negligeable threat to the viability of collective actions in the UK.[74] The new Government did not revive the bill when it came to power. However, reforms are being considered with the launch of a consultation coinciding with the release of an interim report by the Civil Justice Council.[75]

Meanwhile, a number of cases have the potential to be derailed on funding points and a number are being heard by the Court of Appeal. This is the case in *Justin Gutmann v Apple* following a CAT decision on the provisions of the litigation funding agreement,[76] notably regarding the enforceability of a clause in the LFA which enables the funder to be paid ahead of the class. It is also the case of *Kent v Apple* and *Alex Neill v Sony* where defendants are arguing that the new LFA structures based on a multiplier of the funder's investment is still a DBA within the meaning of CLSA 1990, section 58AA and therefore unenforceable in opt-out collective actions.[77]

13.6. CAT Collective Actions as a Tool Shaping Consumer Markets and Enforcement?

The collective action procedure already has the ability to reshape consumer outcomes via the application of competition law rules. Even if not applying consumer law, the market correction offered by the more widespread application of competition law will undoubtably benefit consumers. However, there may also be some merit in questioning the possibility of expanding the collective procedure to consumer law infringements. This would for example enable consumers wronged by an unfair practice to obtain redress for the harm as a group. If expanded to consumer law infringements, alongside

[71] The bill proposed to change the definition of a DBA to provide that an agreement to the extent that it is a litigation funding agreement is not a DBA. The bill also provided for having retroactive effect: the amendments were to be treated as always having had an effect (s 58(3)). Note that the fix to litigation funding was first proposed to be included in the draft Digital Markets, Competition and Consumers Bill (cl 126), but was later carved out to be included in this stand-alone instrument.

[72] Litigation Funding Agreements (Enforceability) Bill introduced to the House of Lords 19 March 2024 (HL Bill 56), bills.parliament.uk/bills/3702/publications, and the explanatory notes: bills.parliament.uk/publications/54764/documents/4594.

[73] www.law.com/international-edition/2024/05/29/litigation-funders-disappointed-as-key-bill-dropped-ahead-of-election/?slreturn=20241118-44930.

[74] See for example the comments made during parliamentary debates on the DMCCA 2024 by Lord Sandhurst, who noted the words of Lady Neville-Rolfe during the Committee on the Consumer Rights Bill: 'there is a need for claimants to have the option of accessing third-party funding so as to allow those who do not have a large reserve of funds or those who cannot persuade a law firm to act pro bono to be able to bring a collective action case in order to ensure redress for consumers. Blocking access to such funding would result in a collective actions regime that is less effective', and adding 'Restricting finance could also create a regime which was only accessible to large businesses. This would weaken private enforcement in competition law, which is of course not the Government's wish or intention [Official Report, 3/11/14; col. GC583.].'

[75] www.judiciary.uk/wp-content/uploads/2024/10/CJC-Review-of-Litigation-Funding-Interim-Report.pdf.

[76] *Gutmann v Apple* [2024] CAT 22 on permission to appeal; *Gutmann v Apple* [2024] CAT 18 for the ruling on funding.

[77] *Alex Neill Class Representative Limited v Sony Interactive Entertainment Europe Limited* [2023] CAT 73; *D. Rachael Kent v Apple Inc & Apple Distribution International Ltd* [2024] CAT 5; *Gutmann v Apple* [2024] CAT 22.

competition law infringements, the CAT procedure could offer some viable remedies for consumers who would not otherwise pursue consumer law infringements under the current collective regimes available to them, or even individually. This could be a particularly useful addition because public enforcement continues to be limited, in spite of the Digital Markets, Competition and Consumers Act 2024 (DMCCA 2024) augmenting the CMA's ability to intervene, notably through administrative means.[78]

13.6.1. Enlarging CAT Remit to Consumer Law Claims via Legislative Means

In the preparatory phase for the DMCCA 2024, responses to the government consultation flagged the lack of access to justice for consumers, and supported collective redress as a means to improve it.[79] Some responses laid out some of the advantages of an 'enlarged' collective action process in the UK to offer consumers who are victims of unfair practices notably could find a remedy.[80] The inclusion of collective actions was considered on two occasions in the process of adoption of the DMCCA 2024.

An amendment 114 to clause 225 was introduced at the Committee stage and proposed by Seema Malhotra.[81] Clause 225 stated that consumer rights to redress may be provided for in future secondary legislation. The amendment proposed required the Secretary of State to prepare a report on the merits of introducing a consumer right to individual and collective redress through secondary legislation (as is the case in EU Member States[82]) within 12 months of the DMCCA 2024 being passed. Notably the amendment was defeated because the minister pointed out that the responses to the consultation and proposals for reforms had been mixed on the issue of collective redress. Some concerns were raised about the unintended consequences of creating a 'claims culture' alongside the possible disincentives to consumer groups bringing these types of proceedings.[83] The minister gave assurances that the evidence would be kept under review and the amendment was withdrawn.[84]

A second amendment was introduced by Rt Hon Sir Robert Buckland MP in November 2023. The amendment was to insert a new clause that would have brought consumer law collective claims within the remit of the CAT.[85] It proposed to add to

[78] DMCCA 2024, Pt 3.

[79] See, for example, Legal Services Board, 'Reforming competition and consumer policy. Legal Services Board response to BEIS consultation' (September 2021) 3, also mentioning the potential need for the regulation of funding.

[80] See, for example, response to the consultation from Professor Christine Riefa; individual 9 (on behalf of individuals who have filed collective claims with the CAT), www.gov.uk/government/consultations/reforming-competition-and-consumer-policy.

[81] Page 152 line 33.

[82] This model would give consumer bodies the right to represent consumers in collective action proceedings which is the model in operation in the EU. It differs from the model in operation in the UK in front of the CAT, where consumer bodies alongside individuals or pre-existing bodies can put forward a case.

[83] L Conway,' Digital Markets, Competition and Consumers Bill 2022-23: Consumers: Progress of the Bill', Research Briefing, House of Commons Library, CPB 9845 (7 September 2023) 33.

[84] ibid 34.

[85] Amendment proposed by Rt Hon Sir Robert Buckland MP, at [NC26], p 20, publications.parliament.uk/pa/bills/cbill/58-04/0003/amend/digitalmarkets_rm_rep_1115.pdf.

the clause concerning proceedings before the Tribunal, allowing claims for damages in respect of infringements of the provisions of Part 4 of the DMCCA Bill. This amendment had not been added to the version of the bill that was passed to the Lords.[86]

Yet, during the Parliamentary debate on the Bill (5 December 2023), at second reading stage in the Lords, some members of the House of Lords spoke in favour of collective action for consumer claims.[87] Notably one of the reasons for suggesting an enlargement of the procedure to consumer law was the risk that individuals would find it difficult to finance proceedings and hence would not act. Lord Etherton flagged that the knowledge of the likelihood of the difficulties faced by consumers harmed by the same breach to bring cases would act as a 'disincentive for those who are subject to conduct requirements and pro-competition intervention to comply with their obligations'.[88] Lord Etherton also made the case for borrowing where appropriate from the regime in place in competition law for breaches of consumer law.[89]

The DMCCA Bill was passed on 22 May 2024 without containing provisions to align collective redress in consumer law cases to competition law. However, the process of its adoption certainly showed that the issue was a live one and that it had gathered some robust interest, albeit not sufficient to get it over the line and included in this reform. This is somewhat regrettable as the absence of a well formulated regime to assist consumers in obtaining collective justice on a broader scale hinders access to justice in the UK. Particularly, in a landscape where individual consumer claims do not qualify for legal aid and access to justice for consumers is channelled through to an ADR system well known for being clunky and largely ineffective.[90] New reforms in ADR systems contained in the DMCCA 2024 may provide some relief for individual disputes, but would still not be suitable for collective actions. This is also particularly concerning in light of the Supreme Court's reluctance to find creative ways to assist consumers acting together, notably in *Lloyds v Google*.[91]

13.6.2. Enlarging CAT Remit via Judicial Intervention

All may not be lost for consumers. The CAT handed down few judgments that seemed to promote the interests of consumers albeit only numerous claims only reached to the final stages.[92]

[86] www.leighday.co.uk/news/blog/2024-blogs/latest-developments-for-group-legal-claims-in-england-wales-could-lead-to-stronger-consumer-protection-and-greater-access-to-justice.

[87] Rt Hon Lord Etherton KC highlighting the need for a mechanism enabling consumers to make collective redress claims where multiple parties have been harmed by the same breach. Other peers spoke in favour of such a regime and its possible borrowing from the competition law regime where appropriate. See Lord Etherton, *Hansard* Vol 834 (5 December 2023) at [5:58], hansard.parliament.uk/Lords/2023-12-05/debates/8A9A99FB-CD4C-4591-B357-02A1FA287FCB/DigitalMarketsCompetitionAndConsumersBill. See also Lord Fox, Baroness Kidron (CB), who mentioned her concern shared with Lord Fox concerning the unmet need for collective action, Lord Sandhurst (focusing on funding) and Lord Clement Jones (LD).

[88] ibid.

[89] ibid.

[90] Reforms were put forward in the DMCCA 2024.

[91] [2021] UKSC 50.

[92] See, for example, *Liza Lovdahl Gormsen v Meta Platforms, Inc and Others* [2024] CAT 11 where the applicant was invited to substantially re-work her CPO application and given months to make the required changes; see also in the Buy Box case carriage dispute the case of *Julie Hunter* [2024] CAT 8, whose application has been put in reserve despite losing the carriage dispute.

In addition, the type of claims that have been presented to the CAT have widened in scope,[93] maybe paving the way for consumer claims in the future. This includes the *Gutmann*[94] boundary fare case where the claim centred around lack of transparency about the way in which fares were charged, effectively leading to double-charging of consumers. Gutmann's most recent case against Apple[95] concerns a claim that is in part centred on the provision of substandard products or falling short of advertised expectations of consumers, concepts that may be more familiar to consumer lawyers than competition ones. The claimant, however, was anxious to emphasise that the claim was not a defective product claim, but rather a case of an abuse of dominant position arising from a lack of transparency relating to a product defect.[96]

There are other examples flagged as evidence of a broadening of the claims being heard by the CAT, notably with the recent certification of data-related claims in the case of *Liza Lovdahl Gormsen v Meta Platforms, Inc and Others*[97] in stark contrast with the approach taken in the UK Supreme Court case of *Lloyd v Google*[98] and the cases brought by Carolyn Roberts against a number of water companies. In *Roberts*, the claims are essentially environmental claims with a competition infringement hook. The claims centre around the fact that water companies understated the number of pollution incidents occurring out of their sewage service to qualify for higher revenue against performance indicators, therefore misleading the regulator in the process. The water companies benefited from a higher revenue cap and thus made more money from consumers than if they had reported the actual number of incidents.

13.7. Conclusion

Despite many teething issues, the CAT has showed an ability in negotiating new problem areas and in carving out a regime that is likely to have a positive effect, extending to consumers much needed protection, albeit indirectly, by ensuring markets work more optimally for them.

Inevitably, however, many of its findings are being tested in the Court of Appeal. It thus will take time for a clearer procedural pathway to emerge, and many bumps and setbacks are to be expected. In particular, what seems critical is the settlement of the uncertainty around funding because without it no claims can be brought forward.

As a procedure, the collective action regime in front of the CAT seems to offer advantages for consumer claims that may make it a better suited procedure that the other regimes currently available. While the legislator did not harness the DMCCA 2024 to expand on this promising regime and offer consumers access to the CAT for

[93] www.pinsentmasons.com/out-law/analysis/data-case-shows-cat-claims-are-broadening.
[94] [2021] CAT 31 [101].
[95] *Justin Gutmann v Apple Inc and others* [2023] CAT 67.
[96] [2023] CAT 67 [15].
[97] [2024] CAT 11.
[98] www.pinsentmasons.com/out-law/analysis/lloyd-v-google-supreme-court-representative-action.

collective redress in consumer infringements, it is clear that there was some appetite for it and that the issue of collective redress for consumers is a live one. The CAT itself has showed it ability to cast a net slightly wider than perhaps originally intended, making steps into what may be seen as more traditional consumer protection issues. This may pave the way for further reforms to open the gates for collective redress of consumer infringements when the legislator is finally ready to do so.

14

Re-aligning Consumer Law with the Convention on the Rights of Persons with Disabilities: A Human Rights-Based Approach to Consumer Contracting

BENJAMIN CLUBBS COLDRON

14.1. Introduction

In this chapter the human rights obligations of state parties and private entities, designed to ensure that consumer transactions are accessible to all, and more specifically persons with mental disabilities, are scrutinised. Consistent with this collection's emphasis on disruption, innovation and re-alignment, the rise of digital platforms and data-driven marketing is described as a form of disruption to traditional consumer law assumptions. Surveillance capitalism (a term for how corporations mine and commodify personal data as raw material for profit) is seen as a force that has reshaped markets and undermined the concept of the rational consumer to an even greater extent than previous critiques have described.[1] Modern corporate practices have even given rise to what some commentators call 'futilitarian' economics and this arguably reduces all consumer capabilities to rationally engage in consumer markets, but also impacts people with mental disabilities in ways that might be seen as discriminatory. These trends call for legal innovation and re-alignment: consumer law must evolve and re-align with human rights and universal design principles to conform to requirements of the United Nations (UN) Convention on the Rights of Persons with Disabilities (CRPD).

Section 14.2 outlines the context of consumer transactions under neoliberal ideology. We examine how economic assumptions undermine traditional models of rational choice to an ever greater extent. For example, many online platforms (increasingly integral to the daily lives of millions of people) have progressively become less user-friendly as providers prioritise profits over growth – a phenomenon dubbed 'enshittification'.[2]

[1] S Zuboff, *The Age of Surveillance Capitalism* (2023) *Social Theory Re-Wired* 203.

[2] C Doctorow, '"Enshittification" Is Coming for Absolutely Everything' *Financial Times* (8 February 2024), www.ft.com/content/6fb1602d-a08b-4a8c-bac0-047b7d64aba5; see also J Ryan, 'The Coming Enshittification of AI: Will AI Follow Internet Search and E-Commerce Down the Path of Enshittification, or Can We Finally Have Nice Things?' (2024) 1 *The Journal of Business and Artificial Intelligence* 2.

Similarly, poor customer service in telecom and internet markets, inaccessible financial products and exploitative subscription traps have made rational economic decisions especially difficult for consumers. This trend toward maximising consumer confusion and futility has been memorably called futilitarian economics. Even absent the worst of these practices, many businesses and employees engage differently with consumers who have mental or cognitive disabilities, exploiting their vulnerabilities or simply cutting off access to goods and services for fear that contracts will be unenforceable if the consumer has issues with mental capacity (rather than accommodating such impairments). One example of this might be online gambling companies identifying and targeting those with gambling addiction and other mental health challenges at times of greatest vulnerability.[3] In addition to these difficulties in pre-contractual processes, consumers with mental disabilities often face extra barriers after contracting – for example, problems paying bills or resolving malfunctions.

Consumer protections typically do not shield against all poor choices, but they do offer enhanced safeguards for the vulnerable. The ideal 'average' consumer is expected in law to shop around for the best deal, and inefficient providers should exit or improve. But in the current digital environment (dominated by large social media platforms, the Internet of Things, monopolistic marketplaces, algorithmic targeting, and dark patterns) the assumption of a self-regulating market of rational consumers is strained to the breaking point. Various international efforts have recognised consumer protection as a fundamental right (in some national constitutions) and as a body of law which can be used to apply human rights principles. The CRPD affirms that full participation and inclusion of persons with disabilities in consumer markets is a vital aspect of implementing all sorts of rights in practice. In this light, consumer law is fundamentally intertwined with the realisation of disability rights.

For persons with psychosocial or cognitive disabilities – that is, disabilities arising from mental health conditions or affecting cognitive functions – unique legal and practical challenges arise. Disabled persons in the UK and worldwide frequently face high barriers to exercising consumer rights. For instance, a recent UK parliamentary report emphasised that disabled people 'should not have to look for alternatives or settle for less' when accessing goods and services, noting that market forces have failed to improve the persistently poor accessibility of private-sector offerings.[4] Such findings underscore the need to re-align consumer law with disability equality through universal design. Only by updating rules and practices can the rights of disabled consumers be fully realised. Section 14.3 sets out the obligations the CRPD places on state parties (including the UK) regarding participation of persons with disabilities in consumer markets. State parties must take proactive steps to ensure that private sector services meet accessibility obligations. We show how the CRPD's equal recognition principle mandates supported decision-making and reasonable accommodation in transactions. It is this body of law that consumer rights and protections must compliment. Section 14.4 then introduces

[3] Digital Advisory Panel, 'Advice on the Impact of Online Platforms on Gambling-Related Harm' Gambling Commission UK (September '), www.gamblingcommission.gov.uk/licensees-and-businesses/guide/digital-advisory-panel-advice-on-the-impact-of-online-platforms-on-gambling.

[4] Women & Equalities Commission, House of Commons, *Accessibility of Products and Services to Disabled People: Fourth Report of Session 2023–24*, HC 183 (2024), committees.parliament.uk/publications/43831/documents/217608/default.

reform recommendations for consumer law, policy and practice to better uphold the rights of persons with disabilities in contracting for consumer goods and services.

14.2. Futilitarian Economics and the Irrational Consumer

In an age of surveillance capitalism (the data-driven business model of tech firms[5]), Zuboff argues that companies unilaterally claim private human experience as free raw material for translation into behavioural data. This is then analysed and packaged as prediction products sold to businesses with a commercial interest in knowing what we will do in the present and in the future. Within this system consumer transactions remain framed by a neoliberal ideology that assumes individuals will freely engage in contracts to maximise their welfare.[6] Self-interested and rational consumers, in this view, form the 'invisible hand' of the market, promoting efficiency and innovation for society. Under ideal market conditions, freedom to contract should allow people to escape bad deals: if a credit, water or energy contract fails to deliver, the rational consumer will simply terminate it and switch providers. One such assumption is that individual citizens will freely engage in contractual relationships to maximise their own welfare. Self-interested and rational consumers, within this framework, will promote innovation and efficiency. The sum of individual self-interested transactions will in theory have benefits for the individual and for society in general.[7]

In so-called 'ideal market conditions', freedom to contract allows individuals to protect themselves from undesirable transactions. It is through consumption that quality of life is supposed to be maintained and improved, and state redistribution is seen as inefficient and providing inappropriate incentives.[8] Current economic theory seems to imply that irrational citizens undermine the self regulation of economic systems through market forces; irrational and even misguided consumer choice undermines efficiency and is bad for society. When seen in this way, irrational consumption is a problem that should be fixed through treatment in mental health, psychological and psychiatric institutions or through exclusion.

It is not unusual for irrational consumption habits (problem gambling,[9] alcohol addictions,[10] eating disorders,[11] compulsive buying, etc[12]) or the rejection of

[5] Zuboff (n 1).

[6] F Etro, 'Product Selection in Online Marketplaces' (2021) 30 *Journal of Economics & Management Strategy* 614.

[7] J Narveson, 'The "Invisible Hand"' in AE Singer (ed), *Business Ethics and Strategy: Volumes I and II* (Routledge, 2018) 125.

[8] J McMahon, 'Behavioral Economics as Neoliberalism: Producing and Governing Homo Economicus' (2015) 14 *Contemporary Political Theory* 137; Y Varoufakis, *Foundations of Economics: A Beginner's Companion* (Routledge 2002) 30–93.

[9] V-P Pöysti and M Majamäki, 'Cultural Understandings of the Pathways Leading to Problem Gambling: Medical Disorder or Failure of Self-Regulation?' (2013) 21 *Addiction Research & Theory* 70.

[10] C May, 'Pathology, Identity and the Social Construction of Alcohol Dependence' (2001) 35 *Sociology* 385.

[11] AE Atchison and HF Zickgraf, 'Orthorexia Nervosa and Eating Disorder Behaviors: A Systematic Review of the Literature' (2022) 177 *Appetite* 106134.

[12] M Crowe, 'Constructing Normality: A Discourse Analysis of the DSM-IV' (2000) 7 *Journal of Psychiatric and Mental Health Nursing* 69; AL Briney, *An Examination of the Nature of a Problematic Consumer Behavior:*

worker/consumer roles in the capitalist system[13] to be medicalised as symptoms of mental disorder.[14] Such symptoms can justify detention for treatment or diagnosis under the Mental Health Act 2007 in the UK and thus the deprivation of rights to liberty and autonomy. Under the European Court of Human Rights this is accepted so long as the individual is 'shown to be of "unsound mind"… [and] the persistence of such a disorder [is established]'.[15] It should be noted that making the removal of rights dependent on disability is inconsistent with the CRPD, which states in Article 14(1) that 'the existence of a disability shall in no case justify a deprivation of liberty'.

Disability under the CRPD is defined as an interaction between persons with impairments and external barriers that hinder their full and effective participation in society on an equal basis with others. The Convention recognises that disability is not just about physical or mental impairments, but arises from the way society is organised and the barriers it creates. Article 1 specifically defines people with disability as those with long-term physical, mental, intellectual or sensory impairments which, in interactions with various barriers, hinder their full and effective participation in society on an equal basis with others. Mental disability is not separately defined in the CRPD, but it falls under the broader category of 'mental or intellectual impairments'. This includes various cognitive, psychological and intellectual conditions that affect an individual's functioning. The Convention emphasises that persons with mental disabilities have the same rights as others and requires states to eliminate discrimination and provide appropriate support to enable their full inclusion and participation.[16]

The literature on behavioural economics provides tools for identifying and understanding various irrational tendencies in human behaviour that do not depend on the existence of a disability.[17] Key themes include bounded rationality,[18] limited self-control[19] and the impact of cognitive biases on consumer choices.[20] Researchers explore phenomena such as loss aversion, anchoring and hyperbolic discounting to explain why

Compulsive Purchasing as a Learned Adaptive Response, Addiction, and Personality Disorder. PhD dissertation, University of North Texas, Department of Marketing, August 1989; A Dahal and A Fertig, 'An Econometric Assessment of the Effect of Mental Illness on Household Spending Behavior' (2013) 37 *Journal of Economic Psychology* 18; S Naik and D Ram, 'Abuse and Health Consumer Behavior in Women with Mental Illness in Remission' (2015) 30 *European Psychiatry (Supplement 1)* 1, doi.org/10.1016/S0924-9338(15)31407-3; DG Alcoforado, FVS Melo and RG Alcoforado, 'Depression and Consumption Habits: A Cross-Cultural Study' (2022) *Journal of Consumer Marketing*, doi.org/10.1108/JCM-02-2021-4421; A Müller, JE Mitchell and M de Zwaan, 'Compulsive Buying' (2015) 24 *The American Journal on Addictions* 132.

[13] M Holmqvist, 'Medicalization of Unemployment: Individualizing Social Issues as Personal Problems in the Swedish Welfare State' (2009) 23 *Work, Employment and Society* 405; S Ramon, 'Neoliberalism and Its Implications for Mental Health in the UK' (2008) 31 *International Journal of Law and Psychiatry* 116.

[14] McMahon (n 8).

[15] *Winterwerp v Netherlands*, App No 6301/73, ECtHR (24 October 1979) para 39.

[16] P Bartlett, 'The United Nations Convention on the Rights of Persons with Disabilities and the Future of Mental Health Law' (2009) 8 *Psychiatry* 496, 496–98.

[17] LA Reisch and M Zhao, 'Behavioural Economics, Consumer Behaviour and Consumer Policy: State of the Art' (2017) 1 *Behavioural Public Policy* 190. For an interesting hybrid of behavioural economic and social theory see also AS Hayes, 'The Behavioral Economics of Pierre Bourdieu' (2020) 38 *Sociological Theory* 16, doi.org/10.1177/0735275120902170.

[18] S DellaVigna, 'Psychology and Economics: Evidence from the Field' (2009) 47 *Journal of Economic Literature* 315.

[19] RH Thaler, *Misbehaving: The Making of Behavioral Economics* (WW Norton & Co, 2015).

[20] D Kahneman, *Thinking, Fast and Slow* (Macmillan, 2011).

consumers make seemingly irrational decisions.[21] The self-interested, rational consumer appears to be a myth, and irrationality can be induced to some extent by context and environment. Algorithmic manipulation of consumers in the digital environment has the capabilities to do this to a wide range of consumers.[22]

Despite the evidence that citizens do not behave in ways that are conducive to ideal market conditions, the logic of consumer law is still tied to the idea of the rational agent. This framing perhaps moderates demand for greater legal protections and obligations placed on companies to deal fairly with consumers. If a consumer freely enters a contract for credit, water or power, and the service does not arrive or meet reasonable expectations, the rational, self-interested consumer will in theory terminate the contract. However, it is clear in sectors like energy retail that the 'incentive for consumers to engage with choices they face … is low, with available evidence suggesting that a significant proportion of consumers have never materially engaged with their choice of energy tariffs'.[23]

So called 'enshittification' of online platforms (seen as integral to the daily lives of many – particularly those who are more social isolated due to disability[24]), chronically poor customer services in telecom and internet markets, inaccessible financial services and exploitative subscription traps appear to be expressly designed to ensure that rational economic decisions are more difficult for consumers to make.[25] This trend towards maximising irrationality and engendering a sense of futility in enforcing consumer rights has been described as 'futilitarian' economics.[26] Recent reports from disability rights organisations show the use of algorithmic price-fixing has seen disabled consumers identified as being in greater need of particular goods and services and consequently receiving higher prices.[27]

'Futilitarian economics' is not a recognised term in mainstream economic literature or philosophy, but refers to business practices and models that, consciously or inadvertently, embrace practices that lead to futility in consumers, thus avoiding accountability. Those designing digital architectures and consumer support in confusing, misleading and obtuse ways, or dark patterns that create, target and exploit contextual vulnerabilities in pre-contractual processes, are creating consumer experiences that maximise futility.[28] These types of practices prioritise short-term gains without considering reputation and consumer loyalty. In the absence of empirical data we still might infer that

[21] ibid endnote 10.

[22] N Helberger et al, 'Consumer Protection 2.0: Structural Asymmetries in Digital Consumer Markets', BEUC Report (2021), www.beuc.eu/publications/beuc-x-2021-018_eu_consumer_protection.0_0.pdf.

[23] Department for Energy Security & Net Zero, 'Delivering a Better Energy Retail Market: A Vision for the Future and Package of Targeted Reforms' (2023), www.gov.uk/government/publications/delivering-a-better-energy-retail-market/delivering-a-better-energy-retail-market-a-vision-for-the-future-and-package-of-targeted-reforms-html.

[24] European Disability Forum, 'Council Must Agree to Accessible Digital Services for Persons with Disabilities' (20 April 2022), www.edf-feph.org/council-must-agree-to-accessible-digital-services-for-persons-with-disabilities.

[25] Doctorow (n 2).

[26] N Vallelly, *Futilitarianism: Neoliberalism and the Production of Uselessness* (Goldsmiths Press/MIT Press, 2021).

[27] Tech Policy Press, 'Priced Out: How Surveillance Pricing Leaves People with Disabilities at Risk', www.techpolicy.press/priced-out-how-surveillance-pricing-leaves-people-with-disabilities-at-risk.

[28] See n 16.

those symptoms of mental illness like depression or anxiety might be impacted more by such practices.

Even where services are not designed in such a way, businesses and employees might be reluctant to engage with those with mental disabilities due to legitimate concerns about invading a consumer's privacy or discrimination if they ask disability-related questions or suggest extra assistance or support.[29] Consumers with mental disabilities may also encounter barriers to resolving problems with their product after the contract is made, such as issues with paying bills or if the product malfunctions or is substandard.

Protections do not go so far as to safeguard the unwise or reckless, but do offer enhanced protections to the 'vulnerable'. The average consumer should seek to compare multiple alternative providers and choose the most desirable. The undesirable provider should eventually go out of business or improve. Consumers, it is assumed will seek out efficient and beneficial contractual relationships.[30] While perfect conditions obviously do not exist in any market, in the age of very large social media platforms, the Internet of Things, monopolistic digital marketplaces and artificial intelligence (AI)-augmented targeting and dark patterns, even moderate assumptions about self-regulating consumer markets and rational customers are being tested to the extremes.[31] The rise of so called 'illiberal democracies' and populist and authoritarian interference with markets (see President Trump's trade war[32]) appears to coincide with these assumptions being tested to their limits.

Various attempts have been made in international law to 'recognise consumer protection at the fundamental rights level' and consumer rights are now included in numerous national constitutions as welfare state rights.[33] The Unfair Commercial Practices Directive 2005/29/EC (UCPD) was adopted to harmonise consumer protection across the European Union (EU) by banning misleading and aggressive commercial practices in business-to-consumer transactions. Central to the Directive is the concept of the 'average consumer' who is reasonably well informed, observant and circumspect. Practices that are likely to materially distort the economic behaviour of such a consumer and breach standards of professional diligence are prohibited. However, the Directive also introduces a critical modification of this standard by recognising the existence of 'particularly vulnerable' consumers. Article 5(3) provides that a commercial practice may be considered unfair if it would distort the economic behaviour of a clearly identifiable group of consumers who are particularly susceptible due to their age, credulity, or physical or mental infirmity, and where the trader could reasonably be expected to foresee that effect. In such cases, the benchmark becomes not the hypothetical average consumer, but the

[29] Y Maker et al, 'Improving Access and Support for Consumers with Cognitive Disabilities: A Guide for Retailers' (University of Tasmania, 2019), hdl.handle.net/102.100.100/502831.

[30] Varoufakis (n 8) 43–117.

[31] G Noto La Diega, *Internet of Things and the Law* (Routledge, 2022).

[32] T Fetzer and C Schwarz, *Tariffs and Politics: Evidence from Trump's Trade Wars* (2021) 131 *Econmics. Journal* 1717.

[33] I Benöhr and H-W Micklitz, 'Consumer Protection and Human Rights' in G Howells, I Ramsay and T Wilhelmsson (eds), *Handbook of Research on International Consumer Law*, 2nd edn (Edward Elgar Publishing, 2018) 16.

average member of the affected group, ie the average person with bipolar disorder or autism.[34]

In its interpretive guidance, the European Commission clarifies that this category of particularly vulnerable consumers includes both cognitive and psychosocial disabilities, confirming that practices which exploit the specific limitations of consumers with mental impairments may be unlawful even if those same practices would not mislead or coerce others.[35] This development is significant in positioning persons with mental disabilities not merely as beneficiaries of benevolent legal protection, but as rights-holders entitled to equitable treatment in consumer markets.

Yet, despite its progressive framing, scholars have noted the UCPD's limitations. The vulnerability category remains tied to a paternalistic logic, in which mental disability is viewed as a fixed characteristic requiring protection rather than a socially and contextually constructed status requiring accommodation. Moreover, the Directive does not impose proactive duties of accessibility or reasonable accommodation on traders. It instead operates retrospectively, assessing whether harm was caused and whether it could have been foreseen by the trader in question. This framing of mental disability in terms of exceptional vulnerability must be considered in light of the CRPD's alternative approach, which emphasises autonomy, legal capacity and equal participation.

Recent legislative reforms in the UK have further developed the law on consumer vulnerability. The Digital Markets, Competition and Consumers Act 2024 (DMCCA 2024) transposes and updates the substance of the UCPD into primary domestic law. In doing so, it expands the legal definition of vulnerability in a way that more closely aligns with contemporary understandings of consumer harm and the relational model of disability.[36] Under DMCCA 2024, section 247, a commercial practice is considered unfair if it materially distorts or is likely to materially distort the economic behaviour of a group of consumers who are particularly vulnerable due to their mental or physical health, age, credulity or the circumstances in which they find themselves, and if the trader could reasonably be expected to foresee this vulnerability.[37]

Notably, this formulation includes 'mental health' as a freestanding cause of vulnerability, explicitly recognising the impact of mental disabilities, and introduces 'circumstances' as an open category encompassing situational vulnerabilities, such as bereavement, unemployment or financial crisis, that may affect any consumer at a given time. The vulnerability test now extends beyond static or inherent characteristics, and encompasses dynamic, relational and contextual factors. This means that mental disability is no longer treated solely as a fixed and individualised condition, but is understood in relation to the consumer's environment and particular transactional context.

This evolution in the legal framing of consumer vulnerability represents a significant shift. It aligns with the CRPD's rejection of the medical model of disability

[34] European Parliament and Council, *Directive 2005/29/EC on Unfair Commercial Practices* [2005] OJ L 149/22.

[35] European Commission, *Guidance on the implementation/application of Directive 2005/29/EC on Unfair Commercial Practices*, SWD(2016) 163 final.

[36] The relational model of disability views disability as arising from the interaction between an individual's impairment and the social, environmental and institutional barriers they face, rather than from the impairment alone.

[37] DMCCA 2024, Pt 4 (esp ss 245–47).

and its endorsement of the social model, which locates disability in the interaction between individual impairments and external barriers. The DMCCA's recognition of situational and mental health-related vulnerabilities potentially allows for more sensitive and inclusive regulatory enforcement, as well as greater awareness on the part of traders and service providers. However, while the law now acknowledges a broader spectrum of consumer vulnerability, it continues to rely on retrospective assessment and does not impose affirmative duties on businesses to ensure accessibility or to make reasonable accommodations for persons with mental disabilities in the contracting process.

For persons with mental disabilities, this represents both an opportunity and a limitation. On one hand, the broader scope of protection offered by the DMCCA 2024 strengthens the legal foundation for challenging commercial practices that exploit cognitive or psychosocial impairments. It offers regulators and courts a more flexible and nuanced basis on which to assess unfairness, including in relation to digital dark patterns, manipulative sales tactics or inaccessible consumer interfaces. On the other hand, the law stops short of guaranteeing the positive supports that may be necessary for disabled consumers to exercise their autonomy in the market on an equal basis with others. It does not, for instance, impose obligations to provide information in accessible formats, to allow for supported decision-making processes, or to design consumer pathways that scaffold understanding and deliberation.[38]

The full and effective social participation and inclusion of persons with disabilities is a guiding principle of the CRPD. In this context, consumer law appears to be fundamentally intertwined with the implementation and realisation of human rights generally and in relation to disability rights in particular. For persons with mental disabilities involving challenges with mental health and emotional well-being, and cognitive disabilities involving challenges with memory, attention, perception, problem-solving and language (henceforth 'mental disabilities'[39]), unique legal and practical challenges arise. Persons with disabilities around the world, including in the UK, frequently face high barriers to exercising their rights as consumers.

14.3. Disability Rights and Consumer Law, Policy and Practice

14.3.1. The Convention on the Rights of Persons with Disabilities

The CRPD came into force for the UK on 3 May 2009.[40] On 5 January 2011, the EU also ratified the CRPD. The CRPD drafting process was unusual in that it was negotiated and adopted relatively quickly, and had unprecedented levels of involvement from persons

[38] European Disability Forum, *Disability and Consumer Protection: A Human Rights Approach* (2023).

[39] This is sometimes termed 'psycho-social disabilities'. See M Price, 'Defining Mental Disability' in Lennard J. Davis (ed), *The Disability Studies Reader*, 4th edn (Routledge, 2013) 292, 292–99.

[40] Bartlett (n 16) 496–98.

with disabilities and their representative organisations in its drafting.[41] The emphasis on co-production and political inclusion of persons directly affected by the prospective rights and obligations is an expression of the principles embodied in the Convention itself, which moves away from a beneficent paternalism towards a more liberal framing of disability rights modelled on other civil rights movements. The CRPD affirmed the application of universal human rights to persons with disabilities and specified the obligations of states parties to ensure that human rights protections extended to persons with disabilities without discrimination.[42]

The CRPD defines disability as a condition that arises 'from the interaction between persons with impairments and attitudinal and environmental barriers that hinders their full and effective participation in society on an equal basis with others'.[43] This reflects and extends the 'social model' of disability that was developed by members of the disability rights movement in the 1980s and 1990s.[44] The social model was proposed as a corrective to the traditional 'medical' or 'individual' models, expressed in consumer law as an emphasis on inherent vulnerabilities, that have long dominated policy and practice.[45] This traditional model views disability as an inherent characteristic to be medically remedied or ameliorated. Inequalities that persons with disabilities suffer are then framed as tragic inevitabilities. Exclusion of disabled persons from society is regarded as an individual problem and the reasons for exclusion are located within the individual.[46]

The social model, as formulated in the CRPD, rejects the traditional medical model of disability and conceptualises it as a social construct.[47] This means acknowledging that, while individuals may experience a physical, mental, intellectual or sensory impairment that affects their appearance or functioning, people are only 'disabled' to the extent that society creates barriers to their ability to live an independent life, and to participate and be fully included in society on an equal basis with others.[48] Capability is therefore contextually dependent. This perspective repositions impairment as an element of human diversity to be recognised and provide a justification for strong positive obligations on state signatories to 'reasonably accommodate' by ensuring that social, economic and physical environments are inclusive.[49]

[41] R Kayess and P French, 'Out of Darkness into Light? Introducing the Convention on the Rights of Persons with Disabilities' (2008) 8 *Human Rights Literature Review* 1, 3–4; T Degener, 'Disability in a Human Rights Context' (2016) 5 *Laws* 35.

[42] UN, 'Committee Negotiating Convention on Rights of Disabled Persons Concludes Current Session on Persons with Disabilities', Press Release SOC/4680 (12 August 2005), www.un.org/press/en/2005/soc4680.doc.htm.

[43] Convention on the Rights of Persons with Disabilities, Preamble, para (e), 13 December 2006, 2515 UNTS 3.

[44] Degener (n 41).

[45] M Oliver, 'The Individual and Social Models of Disability', paper presented at the Joint Workshop of the Living Options Group and the Research Unit of the Royal College of Physicians on People with Established Locomotor Disabilities in Hospitals (23 July 1990).

[46] See (n 13) 36–37.

[47] M Oliver, 'The Social Model in Action: If I Had a Hammer' in C Barnes and G Mercer (eds), *Implementing the Social Model of Disability: Theory and Research* (Disability Press, 2004) 18.

[48] T Shakespeare, 'The Social Relations of Care' in G Lewis, S Gewirtz and J Clarke (eds), *Rethinking Social Policy* (Open University, 2000) 52.

[49] See n 13.

The CRPD enshrines the social model of disability in international human rights law and obliges the UK as a signatory to focus their efforts on the social causes of disability that produce and perpetuate exclusion. One such factor is the way consumer transactions are designed and regulated. The CRPD definition of disability, in foregrounding the social response and dismissing underlying impairment, is potentially radical with potential implications for millions of people worldwide. However, implementation has been lacking and realisation dependent on both recognition and redistribution.[50] Realignment is necessary for consumer law to ensure these principles are better upheld.

Recent research found notable discrepancies in the challenges faced by disabled individuals in comparison to their non-disabled counterparts when it comes to accessing products and services.[51] A recent report from the UN Committee on the Rights of Persons with Disabilities cited a significant proportion of disabled people surveyed (41.6 per cent) reporting difficulty accessing products like groceries, medicine and clothes, whereas only 15.8 per cent of non-disabled individuals encountered similar challenges. Accessing services posed greater difficulty for disabled individuals (51.5 per cent) compared to non-disabled individuals (25.2 per cent), encompassing areas such as banks, restaurants, hairdressers, sports facilities and cinemas. Among disabled individuals, those aged 75 and above reported the most difficulties accessing products (53.9 per cent), highlighting age-related disparities associated with digital illiteracy and other barriers. Disabled individuals of all age groups reported more challenges in accessing services compared to their non-disabled counterparts, with the highest disparity again observed in the 75 and over age group (58.8 per cent of disabled individuals compared to 22.1 per cent of non-disabled individuals). Disabled individuals faced more difficulty accessing medicine and financial services, with a 15 per cent and 10.7 per cent difference, respectively, compared to non-disabled individuals. The statistics also reveal that disabled individuals were more likely to identify barriers to accessing products and services, with difficulty using transport being the most significant difference (22.9 per cent for disabled individuals compared to 6.1 per cent for non-disabled individuals).[52] Online services might ameliorate some of these difficulties but also introduce new challenges as the power imbalance between consumer and company become more extreme.

The Committee on the Rights of Persons with Disabilities ('the Committee') has highlighted a range of disability human rights concerns in the UK, including issues related to accessibility, independent living, inclusive education, employment discrimination and

[50] N Fraser, 'From Redistribution to Recognition? Dilemmas of Justice in a "PostSocialist" Age' (1995) *New Left Review* 68.

[51] Office for National Statistics, 'Disabled People's Access to Products and Services, Great Britain: February to March 2022' in J Foubert et al (eds), *Data and Analysis from Census 2021* (2022), www.ons.gov.uk/peoplepopulationandcommunity/healthandsocialcare/disability/articles/disabledpeoplesaccesstoproductsandservicesgreatbritain/februarytomarch2022; A Leahy and D Ferri, 'Barriers to Cultural Participation by People with Disabilities in Europe: A Study across 28 Countries' (2023) 39 *Disability & Society* 2465, doi.org/10.1080/09687599.2023.2222898; Tech Policy Press, 'Priced Out: How Surveillance Pricing Leaves People with Disabilities at Risk', www.techpolicy.press/priced-out-how-surveillance-pricing-leaves-people-with-disabilities-at-risk.

[52] See n 48.

mental health stigmas.[53] The recommendations emphasise the importance of recognising and enforcing the right of disabled people to live independently, be included in the community and choose their living arrangements. Additionally, the UN call for social security policies that protect the income of disabled people and their families, accounting for the extra costs associated with disability. It appears from the recent attempt by the UK Government to reduce access to personal independence payments that policy is going in the opposite direction.

Accessibility of pre-contractual information for persons with disabilities have been discussed as a route to greater compliance with the CRPD in EU consumer law. However, approaches based on mere transparency have their limits even in relation to 'rational' consumers.[54] The significance of Article 12 (regarding equal recognition before the law) has been considered in relation to EU consumer law by Casarosa, who concluded that the legislation in force at the EU level does not always consider the needs of people with disabilities, but rather the more general category of 'vulnerable groups'.[55] Implications of Article 12 CRPD for English contract law in relation to contractual capacity have been explored to an extent by Varney, who concluded that incapacity and disability must never be conceptually equated. The contractual incapacity defence should not rely on the production of evidence of medical conditions, but focus instead on whether the circumstances of the transaction created a form of credulity.[56]

It is arguable that Article 29 CRPD (the right to participate in political and public life on an equal basis with others) is also engaged. From asserting a political identity by using particular products or services, to boycott and buycott campaigns, political gesture through consumer choice is relatively common.[57] Political consumerism involves individuals utilising their personal consumption choices to signify endorsement for political causes, encompassing areas like environmental preservation, fair trade and ethical treatment of both humans and animals.[58] Although these activities have a political *animus*, the target of consumer campaigns is often not governments. Rather, the primary targets

[53] CRPD, 'Progress on Disability Rights in the United Kingdom: 2023' (2023), www.equalityhumanrights.com/our-work/our-human-rights-work/monitoring-and-promoting-un-treaties/crpd/progress-disability-rights?return-url=https%3A%2F%2Fwww.equalityhumanrights.com%2Fsearch%3Fkeys%3Dprogress%2Bdisability%2Brights.

[54] L Waddington, 'Reading a Duty to Provide Accessible Pre-Contractual Information for Consumers with Disabilities into EU Consumer Protection Law' (2022) 45 *Journal of Consumer Policy* 307.

[55] F Casarosa, 'The Rights of People with Disabilities in EU Consumer Law' in D Ferri and A Broderick (eds), *Research Handbook on EU Disability Law* (Edward Elgar Publishing, 2020) ch 19, 343–58, doi.org/10.4337/9781788976428.00027.

[56] E Varney, 'Redefining Contractual Capacity? The UN Convention on the Rights of Persons with Disabilities and the Incapacity Defence in English Contract Law' (2017) 37 *Legal Studies* 493, 493–519, doi.org/10.1111/lest.12166.

[57] A McClimens and M Hyde, 'Intellectual Disability, Consumerism and Identity: To Have and Have Not?' (2012) 16 *Journal of Intellectual Disabilities* 135, doi.org/10.1177/1744629512445844; JP Elman, '"Find Your Fit": Wearable Technology and the Cultural Politics of Disability' (2018) 20 *New Media & Society* 3760.

[58] WL Bennett, 'The UnCivic Culture: Communication, Identity, and the Rise of Lifestyle Politics' (1998) 31 *PS: Political Sci. & Pol.* 741; M Hooghe and S Goubin, 'The Democratic Potential of Political Consumerism: The Effect of Visibility Bias and Social Stratification; (2020) *International Political Science Review* 1, doi.org/10.1177/0192512120962131.

might be large corporations as consumers seek to shape business practices and assert their political values.[59]

In light of the increasing use of consumer action as an expression of political opinion, there is an argument to be made that the right to political inclusion could also find meaningful engagement through realignment of consumer law.

14.3.2. Consumer Law as an Expression of Disability Rights

Consumer transactions are an integral part of daily life, including everything from purchasing food at the local supermarket, to signing up for a hire purchase agreement for a car or entering a subscription contract for Amazon Prime, to signing up for a mortgage to buy your first house. The ability to contract for basic or essential services is also an important foundation for social, economic and political inclusion. For instance, living independently and being included in the community (Article 19 CRPD) will only be possible for many citizens if they can connect utilities to their homes, access mobile, landline and internet services and arrange payment for those services though their bank accounts.[60]

There has long been debate over the relationship between consumer protections and human rights.[61] Many human rights[62] can only be realised through the introduction of consumer protection measures including rights to quality goods and services, to training and information, health protection, safety, protection of economic interests and to compensation for damages.[63] Many of these rights are reaffirmed in the CRPD. For example, Articles 4 and 5 CRPD require states party to recognise that 'all persons are equal before and under the law'[64] and to prohibit and eliminate discrimination on the basis of disability 'by any person, organisation or private enterprise'.[65] Article 5 also requires that reasonable accommodation be provided to persons with disabilities.[66] This means that necessary and appropriate modification and adjustments should be made (not imposing a disproportionate or undue burden), where needed to ensure that persons with disabilities can enjoy or exercise their rights and fundamental freedoms on an equal basis with others.[67] The freedom to contract is one such fundamental freedom.

[59] M Bostrom, 'Rejecting and Embracing Brands in Political Consumerism?' in M Bostrom, M Micheletti and P Oosterveer (eds), *The Oxford Handbook of Political Consumerism* 205, 205–25 (Oxford University Press, 2019).

[60] Y Maker et al, 'Supporting People with Decision-Making Impairments: Choice, Control and Consumer Transactions' (2017) 24 *Journal of Law & Medicine* 756, 758.

[61] I Benöhr and Hans W Micklitz, 'Consumer Protection and Human Rights' in Geraint Howells et al (eds), *Handbook of Research on International Consumer Law* First Edition (Edward Elgar, 2010) 18.

[62] eg International Covenant on Economic, Social and Cultural Rights, opened for signature 16 December 1966, 993 UNTS 3 (entered into force 3 January 1976).

[63] S Deutch, 'Are Consumer Rights Human Rights?' (1994) 32 *Osgoode Hall Law Journal* 537, 562.

[64] Convention on the Rights of Persons with Disabilities (n 43) Art 5(1).

[65] ibid Arts 4(1)(e), 5(2).

[66] ibid Art 5(3).

[67] ibid Art 2.

The CRPD imposes on state parties obligations to ensure that persons with disabilities are not discriminated against in their dealings with private entities, including companies providing goods and services. Article 9 CRPD addresses accessibility and obliges state parties to take measures to ensure that persons with disabilities have access, on an equal basis with others, to transportation, information and communications and other facilities and services open or provided to the public.[68] In the case of *Nyusti v Hungary*,[69] the Committee elaborated on the extent of the obligation of state parties to ensure that private companies avoid discrimination and ensure accessibility.[70] In that case, which concerned the accessibility of banking services for blind or visually impaired persons, the Committee recommended that the Hungarian Government create a legislative framework targeting private financial institutions with concrete, enforceable and time-bound benchmarks for monitoring and assessing the gradual modification and adjustment of previously inaccessible banking services, into accessible ones.[71] This case illustrates that state parties must take proactive steps to ensure that private sector services meet accessibility obligations, thereby protecting the rights of persons with disabilities in consumer contexts and reinforcing the state's duty to eliminate discrimination across all sectors.

Other articles of the CRPD imply the need to protect and empower persons with disabilities when they act as consumers. As noted above, Article 19 describes the right to live independently and be included in the community.[72] It requires states party to ensure that persons with disabilities have choice over their place of residence, access to a range of in-home, residential and other community support services, including personal assistance necessary to support living and inclusion in the community through equal access to mainstream services and facilities. According to the Committee, this also means that services such as the internet must be 'available, universally accessible, acceptable and adaptable for all persons with disabilities within the community'.[73] Article 21 affirms that the rights of freedom of expression and opinion, and to access information, are held by all persons with disabilities.[74] It requires that information intended for the public be made available in accessible formats, for example, and imposes an obligation on states parties to urge and encourage private service providers to do so in accessible and usable formats.[75] It is unclear what this might entail, but it is clear that many of the basic rights and freedoms contained in the CRPD will not be achievable if consumers with disabilities are not adequately informed in accessible ways of their rights and obligations. It is a necessary pre-condition.

Consumer law provides various practical means by which state parties can urge and encourage and even require companies to reasonably accommodate persons with various disabilities, which we will discuss in the next section.

[68] ibid Art 9.

[69] Committee on the Rights of Persons with Disabilities, Communication No 1/2010: *Szilvia Nyusti and Péter Takács v Hungary*, CRPD/C/9/D/1/2010 (21 June 2013).

[70] ibid.

[71] ibid para 10(2)(a). See O Lewis, 'Nyusti and Takács v Hungary: Decision of the UN Committee on the Rights of Persons with Disabilities' (2013) 4 *European Human Rights Law Review* 418.

[72] Committee on the Rights of Persons with Disabilities (n 69) Art 19.

[73] Committee on the Rights of Persons with Disabilities, General Comment No 5 (2017) on Living Independently and Being Included in the Community, UN Doc CRPD/C/GC/5, 32 (27 October 2017).

[74] Convention on the Rights of Persons with Disabilities (n 43) Art 21.

[75] ibid Art 21(a), (c).

14.3.3. Consumer Contracting for Persons with Mental Disabilities

As individuals, we function not only as economic agents (ie consumers), but also as political and social beings. Even within the contractual realm, where our actions may seem motivated by economic self-interest, we persist as social and political actors, guided by values such as fairness, non-discrimination and human dignity.[76] Hence, we should not view our economic environment as a separate sphere where human rights principles become less relevant. In contractual relations, we cultivate our economic identity, driven by principles like individual autonomy and the sanctity of contract. Here, we expect the freedom to select our contracting parties and terms, recognising the binding nature of our agreements once choices are made.[77] As long as our free will remains unimpeded by factors like unfair commercial practices, incapacity or undue influence, we can willingly engage in imbalanced transactions, bound by the agreements we voluntarily enter.[78]

There are compelling arguments however, for voiding or otherwise interfering in, contracts, under specific circumstances, particularly when egregious imbalances of power exist in the contracting process and this might result in disproportionate harm to the weaker party. Such determinations are shaped by considerations of public policy and social values, with a focus on equitable principles aimed at safeguarding consumer autonomy.[79]

Despite the UK's ratification of the CRPD in 2009, it is not integrated into domestic law and would offer limited direct assistance in domestic courts. In the case of *R (on the application of NM) v Islington LBC*,[80] Sales J acknowledges that the CRPD is an 'unincorporated international treaty' and does not hold direct authority in English law. Similarly, in *R (on the application of MA) v Secretary of State for Work and Pensions*,[81] Laws LJ advises exercising caution regarding the use of unincorporated international conventions. However, even though the CRPD is not formally integrated into domestic law, its significance as a ratified instrument by the UK cannot be ignored. As highlighted by Carnwath LJ in *AH v West London Mental Health Trust*,[82] by ratifying a Convention, a state commits to aligning its laws with the norms and values upheld by the Convention whenever possible. The acknowledgment of universal legal capacity in the CRPD and its emphasis on principles like the protection of human dignity raise important questions about the incapacity defence in contract law. While the defence may be deemed consistent with the CRPD if it applies universally and refrains from equating incapacity with disability, neither the Convention nor

[76] Y Maker et al, 'Ensuring Equality for Persons with Cognitive Disabilities in Consumer Contracting: An International Human Rights Law Perspective' (2018) 19 *Melbourne Journal of International Law* 178.

[77] P Benson, *Justice in Transactions: A Theory of Contract Law* (Belknap Press, 2019). 62.

[78] ibid 185.

[79] A Dhanda, 'Constructing a New Human Rights Lexicon: Convention on the Rights of Persons with Disabilities' (2008) 5 *International Journal on Human Rights* 43, 49.

[80] *R (on the application of NM) v Islington LBC* [2008] EWHC 2876 (Admin), [2009] 1 WLR 2554.

[81] *R (on the application of MA) v Secretary of State for Work and Pensions* [2013] EWCA Civ 50, [2013] 1 WLR 1602.

[82] *AH v West London Mental Health Trust* [2011] UKUT 74 (AAC) [15]–[16].

the Committee offer specific guidance on defining or delineating the scope of the incapacity defence.

In England equitable doctrines that mandate interference in the sanctity of contract include situations where one party (A) lacks the mental capacity to comprehend the transaction, and the other party (B) is aware or should have been aware of this incapacity.[83] Contracts entered into by A under B's undue influence, where a significant relationship of influence exists, and the resulting transaction demands an explanation, also fall within this purview.[84] Additionally, contracts in which B knowingly exploits A's vulnerability, leading to a disadvantageous transaction for A, could be deemed justifiable grounds for voiding.[85] Consumer law in the UK, and in the EU more generally, also interferes in the contracting process by, for instance, inserting contractual terms into consumer contracts.[86] These examples underscore the importance of protecting individuals from unfair power imbalances in contractual relationships and are in some cases an expression of human rights principles.

Questions regarding A's contractual capacity are determined in the UK by reference to the Mental Capacity Act 2005 (MCA 2005) for contracts for necessary goods and services, or the common law for all other contracts.[87] These tests adopt a time- and issue-specific approach to assess whether A had the mental capacity to enter into a particular contract. Under the MCA 2005, a person lacks capacity if, at the time of entering into the contract, he or she was unable to make a decision because of an impairment of, or a disturbance in the functioning of the mind or brain. Under the common law the prevalent approach, outlined in *Moulton v Camroux*[88] and reinforced in *Imperial Loan v Stone*,[89] is that contracts are voidable if the individual can prove both that mental capacity to understand the transaction was lacking, and that the other party knew of such incapacity.[90] According to *Dunhill v Burgin*,[91] such knowledge can also include constructive knowledge, although Lady Hale's arguments have been criticised by some academic commentators, who question the basis and scope of such an extension.[92] Making contracts voidable on the basis of a company's knowledge of mental incapacity might have the practical effect that companies will avoid contracting with such persons if they can. This will mean people with mental disabilities are more likely to be excluded from participation in this crucial area of life. Rather, mechanisms should be put in place to support people to maximise their capacity in this area and reassure companies that they can have confidence and security in contracting with people with mental disabilities.

[83] *Imperial Loan v Stone*, [1892] 1 QB 599 (CA); *Hart v O'Connor* [1985] AC 1000 (HL); *Dunhill v Burgin* [2014] UKSC 18.

[84] *Royal Bank of Scotland Plc v Etridge (No 2)* [2001] UKHL 44.

[85] *Fry vLane*, (1888) 40 Ch D 312.

[86] C Twigg-Flesner, 'The Implementation of the Unfair Contract Terms Directive in the United Kingdom' (2007) *Contemporary Issues in Law* 235.

[87] E Varney, 'Redefining Contractual Capacity? The UN Convention on the Rights of Persons with Disabilities and the Incapacity Defence in English Contract Law' (2017) 37 *Legal Studies* 493.

[88] *Moulton v Camroux* (1848) 2 Exch 487, 501.

[89] *Imperial Loan v Stone* [1892] 1 QB 599.

[90] ibid [601].

[91] *Dunhill v Burgin* [2014] UKSC 18.

[92] HG Beale et al (eds), *Chitty on Contracts*, 32rd edn (Sweet & Maxwell, 2015).

In the UK there is some guidance in place for supported, or substitute, decision-making in relation to consumer choices for people who lack the capabilities to engage in such transactions as well as more general measures, such as personal independence payments, are designed with such support in mind that might be considered. Companies are under an obligation to provide relevant information in accessible formats to people with disabilities, but in many cases, this appears to be insufficient to provide people with mental disabilities the necessary scaffolding to make informed decisions. Even those without such disabilities can often be led astray by misleading or manipulative practices.

The MCA 2005 does provide guidance for mental health professionals to support decision-making, including consumer transactions, for people under their care, but this is dependent on time and resources and is largely discretionary. If an individual is identified as lacking capacity to make a decision, any action taken, or decision made on their behalf, must be in their best interests. This includes considering their past and present wishes, feelings, beliefs and values. So a person who in the past has expressed interest in a particular hobby and who is trying to subscribe to an online service related to that hobby, but who appears to lack mental capacity to achieve this end, might be supported by a mental health nurse to enter their bank details and click 'agree' on the terms and conditions of use if this is seen as a reasonable use of resources.

When applying the MCA 2005, practitioners should prefer the 'least restrictive' option in terms of their rights and freedoms. In addition, advance decisions and lasting powers of attorney (LPA) mean that individuals can make advance decisions or create LPAs, designating someone to make decisions on their behalf if they lose capacity. This can include decisions related to financial matters, such as applying for a loan or mortgage.

Provision of such support is likely to be inconsistent. For many, support will not routinely be available from social care or health services unless they are institutionalised and, even then, may depend on factors such as staffing levels and professional culture. Family and friends may step into this gap and there may also be a guardianship order so a nominated person can make a replacement decision in the case of persons with more profound and long-term cognitive impairments, but this is likely to vary significantly in quality and availability too.

People with mental disabilities, when engaging in consumer transactions, are often not supported to engage with the contracting process directly.[93] If problems arise, the impairment will be seen as a reason to allow contracts to be voided, but it is not clear that this protective and beneficent measure is compatible with the principles of the CRPD in absence of systematic and universal support mechanisms. On the one hand, the ability to enter into contracts at all may be called into question and this could amount to discrimination based on failure to recognise people as equal under the law. In other cases, they may claim that the contract should be void as they lacked the mental capacity to enter into it in the first instance or their vulnerability should have been identified, triggering a duty to safeguard or accommodate. Consumer protections and rights must deal with these issues directly in line with the CRPD.

[93] Citizens Advice, 'Beyond Good Practice Guides: Improving Support with Essential Services for People with Mental Health Problems' (2018), www.citizensadvice.org.uk/Global/CitizensAdvice/Consumer%20publications/Beyond%20good%20practice%20guides.pdf.

Previous research has shown that people with mental health problems are likely to benefit from both financial and non-financial support in consumer interactions. Overall, the literature indicates that, in many areas, providers still do not offer effective protection and support for people with mental health problems.[94] In addition, the UK Government has raised thresholds for people with disabilities accessing out-of-work benefit payments and attacked the legitimacy of their claims for additional resources due to increases in flexible work.[95] According to some charitie,s an estimated 370,000 people with disabilities and chronic health conditions will be ineligible for incapacity benefits, worth an extra £5,000 a year, and forced to look for work under planned reforms unveiled by the chancellor in the 2023 autumn statement.[96] In 2025 a major Labour Party rebellion against its own government was the only thing that stopped personal independence payments being severely curtailed, which would have plunged many people into situations where they could not pay for or access the supports they need to live independently. These policies would have subjected people with disabilities to a reduction in both financial and non-financial support, undermineing their ability to conduct consumer transactions on an equal basis with others, to be recognised as equal participants in political and civic life, and to be treated as equal under the law.[97]

A significant number of consumers with disabilities are unaware that they are entitled to receive assistance with essential services directly from service providers. Despite the apparent efforts of companies to inform people in accessible ways, evidence suggests that customer awareness of available support is practically non-existent.[98] Many providers communicate information about support through letters or bills, but a considerable portion of people experiencing mental health challenges find it difficult to open, read or understand such communications.

Even well-executed promotional campaigns to inform consumers of their apparent entitlements face limitations. When individuals are aware that support is available, they encounter difficulties accessing it independently. Reports indicate that rigid evidence requirements and complex processes in customer support exacerbate these challenges.[99] The support provided across sectors has been described as patchy, inconsistent and unreliable.[100] While water sector support systems are generally well designed and delivered, the overall effectiveness of support for individuals with mental health problems is lacking in the energy, telecoms and financial service sectors. This is despite regulatory

[94] Money & Mental Health Policy Institute, 'Regulating for People: A Report on How Regulators Can Better Support Customers with Mental Health Problems' (2020), www.moneyandmentalhealth.org/publications/regulators-report.

[95] F Ryan, 'Disabled People Forced to Work from Home or Risk Losing Benefits' *The Guardian* (21 November 2023), www.theguardian.com/uk-news/2023/nov/21/disabled-people-work-from-home-laura-trott-benefits.

[96] P Crerar, 'Thousands on Disability Benefits to Lose £5,000 a Year' *The Guardian* (22 November 2023), www.theguardian.com/society/2023/nov/22/thousands-on-disability-benefits-to-lose-extra-5000-a-year-in-autumn-statement.

[97] HM Treasury, 'Autumn Statement 2023' (2023), www.gov.uk/government/publications/autumn-statement-2023.

[98] See n 8; and C Rogers and B McCay, 'Beyond Good Practice Guides: Improving Support with Essential Services for People with Mental Health Problems' Citizens Advice 14 (2018), www.citizensadvice.org.uk/Global/CitizensAdvice/Consumer%20publications/Beyond%20good%20practice%20guides.pdf.

[99] ibid 21–23.

[100] ibid 24.

bodies such as the Financial Conduct Authority (FCA) producing various policies and guidance.[101]

If support in essential services is inadequate, then in sectors seen as non-essential, it is likely to be non-existent. In consumer markets products such as smart wearables, connected cars and smart homes can be important support systems which can ameliorate the lack of capabilities resulting from various mental disabilities. In these markets, all consumers are already arguably rendered more vulnerable (in the sense of induced credulity) due to the ways in which digital architectures and datafication make the power imbalance between producers, service providers and consumers more acute.[102]

14.3.4. Equal Recognition as the Bedrock of Consumer Rights

Article 12 CRPD 'reaffirm[s] that persons with disabilities have the right to recognition everywhere as persons before the law'.[103] It also requires that persons with disabilities enjoy legal capacity on an equal basis with others in all aspects of life.[104] This places an obligation on state parties to provide access to the support that persons with disabilities may require in exercising their legal (including contractual) capacity.[105] The Committee has made it clear that legal capacity is not the same as mental capacity.[106] It defines mental capacity as 'the decision-making skills of a person, which naturally vary from one person to another and may be different for a given person depending on many factors, including environmental and social factors'.[107]

The Committee has stated that, 'Under article 12 of the Convention, perceived or actual deficits in mental capacity must not be used as justification for denying legal capacity'.[108] Article 12 is a direct challenge to the legal personhood of persons with disabilities being voidable in law.[109] It can no longer be assumed that an actual or perceived mental incapacity means that a person should not have legal capacity to make their own decisions.[110] This is a challenge to the MCA 2005 regime of substitute decision-making where guardians or mental health professionals assume the right to act in the 'best interests' of people who are considered unable to make their own

[101] FCA, CONC 2.10 Mental Capacity Guidance, FCA Handbook (4 January 2014), www.handbook.fca.org.uk/handbook/CONC/2/10.html#:~:text=Where%20a%20firm%20reasonably%20suspects,reasonable%20steps%20without%20success%20to.

[102] B Clubbs Coldron et al, 'Conceptualising Cyborg Vulnerability: Reassessing Fundamental Principles of Consumer Policy in the Internet of Things' (unpublished manuscript, under review for *Journal of Consumer Policy*, 2024).

[103] Convention on the Rights of Persons with Disabilities (n 43) Art 12(1).

[104] ibid Art 12(2).

[105] ibid Art 12(2)–(3).

[106] CRPD, General Comment No 1, UN Doc CRPD/C/GC/1, 13 (2014).

[107] ibid.

[108] ibid.

[109] See E Flynn & A Arstein-Kerslake, 'Legislating Personhood: Realising the Right to Support in Exercising Legal Capacity' (2014) 10 *International Journal of Law in Context* 81; B McSherry, 'Legal Capacity Under the Convention on the Rights of Persons with Disabilities' (2012) 20 *Journal of Law & Medicine* 22, 24.

[110] CRPD (n 106) 14–15.

decisions.[111] Supported decision-making is now the mandated approach in international law.[112]

Article 12 also specifies that states parties must provide safeguards to prevent abuse in relation to this right, including ensuring that, 'measures relating to the exercise of legal capacity respect the rights, will and preferences of the person'.[113] Finally, it explains that persons with disabilities have equal rights to 'own and inherit property, to control their own financial affairs and to have equal access to bank loans, mortgages and other forms of financial credit'.[114]

In the context of consumer transactions, Article 12 means that persons with even profound cognitive disabilities must have the legal capacity to contract recognised on an equal basis with others. This requires that the basis for limitations on an individual's legal capacity to contract are non-discriminatory in both purpose and effect – in line with the definition of discrimination in Article 2 CRPD. Where the state limits an individual's legal capacity to contract, it must do so on an equal basis for people with and without mental disabilities. Thus, supportive measures must not be disproportionately applied in practice to those with disabilities and should not be dependent on evidence of impairment. One way to do this would be to ensure either universal or personalised inclusivity is baked into the design of goods and services, allowing all consumers to benefit from the enhance protections that might be designed to protect those with greater needs (so called universal design).

Laws that limit an individual's legal capacity to contract vary by jurisdiction and are often found in multiple areas of the law.[115] For example, substituted decision-making laws – such as trusteeship, guardianship, conservatorship and interdiction – can deny an individual subjected to them the right to contract.[116] Some companies may refuse to deal with certain customers based on their perceived mental incapacity rather than support and accommodate them, and this may also fall foul of the CRPD if states have not put in place measures to avoid this practice.

These laws may be viewed by the Committee as a denial of legal capacity to contract whether or not they were designed to protect the very consumers purportedly discriminated against. The CRPD prioritises the principle of equality and non-discrimination over and above the principles of paternalism and beneficence, and it is unclear whether in practice this will be experienced as a benefit or not. As we have seen, common law rules of equity can invalidate a contract where the

[111] ibid 27–28.

[112] L Francis, 'Supported Decision-Making: The CRPD, Non-Discrimination, and Strategies for Recognizing Persons' Choices About Their Good' (2021) 1 *Journal of Philosophy of Disability* 57,doi.org/10.5840/jpd20211198.

[113] Convention on the Rights of Persons with Disabilities (n 43) Art 12(4).

[114] ibid Art.12(5).

[115] See, eg, CRPD, Concluding Observations on the Initial Periodic Report of Hungary, 8th Sess, UN Doc CRPD/C/HUN/CO/1 (22 October 2012) 26; CRPD, Concluding Observations on the Initial Periodic Report of Argentina, 8th Sess., UN Doc CRPD/C/ARG/CO/1 (8 October 2012) 19–20, 31–32; CRPD, Concluding Observations on the Initial Report of Lithuania, 15th Sess, UN Doc CRPD/C/LTU/CO/1 (11 May 2016) 25–26.

[116] See, eg, CRPD, Concluding Observations on the Initial Report of Ethiopia, 16th Sess, UN Doc CRPD/C/ETH/CO/1 (4 November 2016) 25–26; CRPD, Concluding Observations on the Initial Report of Mauritius, 14th Sess, UN Doc CRPD/C/MUS/CO/1 (30 September 2015) 21–22; CRPD, Concluding Observations on the Initial Report of the Republic of Korea, 12th Sess, UN Doc CRPD/C/KOR/CO/1 (29 October 2014) 47–48.

contract was entered into under circumstances that are said to vitiate consent, such as through undue influence, duress, misrepresentation or unconscionable conduct.[117] The purpose of these laws is to prevent unfair contracting practices and to protect individuals who are viewed as vulnerable from exploitation or abuse. This is a laudable aim. What some disability rights activists argue is that they have the effect of denying the legal capacity of the contracting parties and create a deterrent to companies in dealing with seemingly 'irrational' consumers.[118] In practice the law will not recognise the exercise of legal capacity to enter into these kinds of contracts because if it judges that consent is not valid or has been vitiated. Mental disability plays a significant role in a finding that consent was lacking.[119]

This occurs, for example, where persons with cognitive disabilities are disproportionately placed under trusteeship or guardianship and lose their legal capacity to contract with a substitute decision-maker appointed on a blanket basis. It also happens where a person is assumed to lack capacity to contract or to be vulnerable to undue influence simply because they have a cognitive disability or mental illness.

Aside from contracts being voidable on the basis of mental incapacity, mental health law is also prima facie inconsistent with the CRPD as interpreted by the Committee, because decisions that an individual is considered incapable of making can still be made by a substitute decision-maker under the MCA 2015 or overruled under other parts of the law. This is a system that allows for substitute decision-making triggered by the identification of impairment. Systematic determinants of incapability are individualised through medical evidence in the judicial process.

The MCA 2015 test defines lack of capacity as being unable to make a decision due to a disturbance in mind or brain, aligning with the common law test that requires proof of insanity at the time of contracting. The level of understanding needed for contract validity varies with the transaction's nature, and the MCA test is broadly consistent with common law principles. It is obviously arguable that protecting the interests of those lacking capacity necessitates substitute decision-making, but questions arise regarding the extent to which this protection in practice aligns with principles of consumer autonomy and dignity. A more universal interpretation of contractual capacity under common law, considering economic and social factors rather than medical diagnosis, could be a way of avoiding interventions being targeted based on a person's disability or impairment.

While the MCA 2105 requires the individual's wishes, feelings, values and preferences to be taken into account in how decisions are taken by the substitute, objective factors may also be considered and may take precedence over the subjective factors related to the individual's choice. Disabled people are the targets of the policy and legal capacity is rarely considered relevant in cases where disability status is not established.[120] On the basis of the Committee's guidance these laws would likely be viewed as discriminatory in law and in practice.

[117] JM Paterson and G Brody, '"Safety Net" Consumer Protection: Using Prohibitions on Unfair and Unconscionable Conduct to Respond to Predatory Business Models' (2015) 38 *Journal of Consumer Policy* 331.

[118] Bartlett (n 16).

[119] ibid.

[120] P Bartlett, 'At the Interface Between Paradigms: English Mental Capacity Law and the CRPD' (2020) 11 *Frontiers in Psychiatry* 570735.

International human rights law recognises the concept of progressive realisation, acknowledging that the full realisation of certain rights, especially economic, social and cultural rights, may take time and depend on available resources. In exceptional circumstances – for example, where individuals with disabilities pose a danger to themselves or others – some human rights may be temporarily derogated from, but only to the extent strictly required by the exigencies of the situation. Certain rights, like the right to life and freedom from torture, cannot be derogated from under any circumstances. The right to social inclusion and the right to legal capacity under the CRPD should not be prioritised over the people's basic welfare. Any emergency measures taken must be proportionate to the threat or situation. Governments are expected to justify such measures and demonstrate their necessity and proportionality so blanket measures that do not take into account individual circumstances will rarely be justified.

Realising the aims of Article 12 CRPD requires more empirical research into the types of support that persons with mental disabilities would like when entering into consumer transactions. It also requires a collaboration between industry, persons with disabilities and policymakers to ensure that appropriate supports are made available. Finally, it requires a review of the rules around contractual capacity and legislative intervention to de-link disability from the voiding of a contract; consumer protection law and consumer rights might be enhanced to consider the specific obligations of companies dealing with 'irrational consumers'. Other areas such as guardianship and substituted decision-making laws might be reformed to require supportive decision-making. This last issue would require more monitoring, perhaps through the Care Quality Commission and its equivalents. These are baseline requirements of Article 12.

In the next section I introduce recommendations that could resolve some of these inconsistencies with the CRPD and provide reasonable accommodations for persons with mental disabilities.

14.4. Reasonable Accommodation of the Irrational Consumer in the context of essential services

Article 12, paragraph 3 CRPD requires that states parties provide access to support for the exercise of legal capacity. 'Supported decision-making' gives primacy to a person's will and preferences, and ensures that their rights are respected. Support for exercising legal capacity can take the form of support with voting, support when interacting with the justice system, and support to enter contracts and financial transactions. Different levels of support may be necessary depending on a person's circumstances, including the nature of the disability and the social barriers he or she is subject to. These can range from informal support (accessible information, accessible buildings, and 'circles of support' involving trusted family members and friends in decision-making) to more formal support arrangements (such as formal 'representation agreements' and supported decision-making personnel). In the context of consumer transactions, supported decision-making could be facilitated by: having one or more support persons throughout the transacting process; designing consumer pathways crafting contracts that are easy to understand; providing additional information or opportunities for queries or amendments; and providing extra time for people to process the information. This would signify a major re-alignment of consumer law and would require care in implementation to take into account various unintended consequences.

Processes that differentiate between individuals based on disability or impairment are potentially discriminatory under the CRPD. Such practices often rely on unfounded assumptions about the decision-making capabilities of people with mental disabilities. Assessments of decision-making ability may falsely assume the ability to accurately assess the inner workings of a person's mind. In practice, individuals may vary in their capacity for consumer decision-making, and focusing on impairment can perpetuate stigma and undermine autonomy. Additionally, this focus diverts attention from the systemic barriers faced by people with mental disabilities.

An expanded concept of vulnerability might help increase support and inclusion for people with mental disabilities whilst avoiding some of these basic pitfalls. Helberger et al, for example, argue that rather than a definition of vulnerability in law tied to inherent characteristics, more relational and even universal vulnerabilities should be recognised as warranting greater protection. They outline a concept of digital vulnerability that captures this greater emphasis on the relational, architectural and privacy-related nature of vulnerability and manipulation thereof.[121]

Service providers must be encouraged to work towards improving access to suitable and appropriate services for all consumers, including consumers with disabilities. A *sui generis* right to reasonable accommodation with contractual capacity in consumer transactions may be a possible solution. This is a burden on providers of goods and services and must be proportionate to avoid undue impact on small and medium sized businesses.

Making the focus of such a right contextual and relational potentially avoids discriminatory targeting of persons with mental disabilities by companies seeking to avoid transactions that might be voided, or by courts in depriving people of their freedom of contract.

Expanding on approaches to accommodating digital and cyborg vulnerabilities (ie those resulting in dependency on technologies integrated into our bodies and environments in ways that foster dependency)[122] and the work of Maker et al, we can see that reasonable accommodations for irrational consumer behaviour more broadly should be standard practice.[123] Making goods and services more accessible for everyone would ensure greater inclusion for those with mental disabilities, allowing them to make consumer choices. These choices are often made before the consumer enters a contract, in the pre-sale or pre-contract process.[124] Obligations to enhance pre-sales and precontractual processes, as well as processes for getting assistance or dealing with problems with a service, should be made adaptable to common types of irrationality not just those dependent on mental impairment.

[121] N Helberger et al, 'Digital Fairness for Consumers' (BEUC The European Consumer Organisation, 2024), www.beuc.eu/sites/default/files/publications/BEUC-X-2024-032_Digital_fairness_for_consumers_Report.pdf.032_Digital_fairness_for_consumers_Report.pdf.

[122] Clubbs Coldron et al (n 102).

[123] Yvette Maker et al, 'From Safety Nets to Support Networks: Beyond "Vulnerability" in Protection for Consumers with Cognitive Disabilities' (2018) 41 *University of New South Wales Law Journal* 818, search.informit.org/doi/10.3316/informit.913287843790474.

[124] ibid.

The current consumer rights and protections for those who need support with contracting and associated decision-making seem to start from the opposite end in that it is primarily focused on mechanisms to set aside contracts (or apply lower thresholds for identifying unfair practices) for those classified as vulnerable. Voiding contracts is common where there are concerns about a lack of informed consent.[125] While this legal mechanism may be an important protection against predatory and exploitative behaviour, the current law and policy potentially has the effect of discouraging social inclusion and equal access to goods and services for consumers with mental disabilities. In practice it also appears to violate the principles of the CRPD.

The realisation of the rights to equal recognition before the law, as outlined in Article 12 CRPD, can be more effectively facilitated through the implementation of universal supports for consumers rather than a piecemeal approach which treats persons with disabilities as vulnerable and particularly irrational, and in some cases excludes them entirely. To this end, regulators, perhaps operating within the framework of UK Regulators Network (a group of economic regulators collaborating on cross-sector issues), the Consumer Forum (a platform for coordination among consumer advocacy bodies) and the Disability Unit (a government body responsible for disability policy and promoting inclusion across departments) should establish minimum standards of support applicable across all essential services which would reasonably accommodate irrational consumer behaviours. Reasonable attempts should made to scaffold decisions, based on discharging a duty of care to ensure informed consent in the pre-contractual phase. Providers of goods and services should not withdraw offers based on assessments of mental incapacity.

The absence of clear standards for dealing with mentally disabled consumers poses uncertainty for suppliers in meeting their obligations and for regulators to enforce. Consumers need various goods and services to accommodate their needs consistently, so that they can switch suppliers to find the best deals and uphold the logic of the invisible hand of the market. In designing and implementing legislative solutions, such as a *sui generis* right to reasonable accommodation with contractual capacity, adequate representation from people with mental disabilities (perhaps through the Disability Unit[126] or Consumer Forum[127] in the UK) and under the guidance of a dedicated minister, could play a pivotal role in identifying and implementing minimum standards of reasonable accommodation of irrational consumers. Specifically, individuals grappling with mental distress of various kinds might reasonably expect access to well-trained, specialised customer support, repairs for faulty equipment without excessive paperwork or evidential hurdles, protection against premature disconnection where payment issues arise, and resolution of arrears or debts in-house.

Providers across sectors such as broadband, mobile and current accounts might be required to adopt systematic, market-wide mechanisms akin to priority service registers.

[125] ibid.

[126] Disability Unit, Equality Hub & Mims Davies MP, 'New Disability Action Plan to Make UK Most Accessible Place in the World' press release (5 February 2024), www.gov.uk/government/news/new-disability-action-plan-to-make-uk-most-accessible-place-in-the-world.

[127] Department for Business and Trade and Department for Business, Energy & Industrial Strategy, 'Modernising Consumer Markets: Green Paper' (11 April 2018), www.gov.uk/government/consultations/consumer-green-paper-modernising-consumer-markets.

These registers could record and address the unique needs of particular consumers, ensuring a seamless transition between providers without the need for re-registration. The use of the register could be monitored so that personal data is used in accordance with GDPR standards and is not abused to exclude or discriminate. Furthermore, it is imperative that providers offer multiple communication channels through which customers can request additional support. Restricting access to a single medium might discourage individuals with mental disabilities from seeking the assistance they require. Consumers should have the freedom to choose the form of communication that best suits them.

Additional support should not be restricted on the basis of demonstrable disability and should be based on individual needs. Evidence requirements to access higher levels of support should only be present if companies can demonstrate they are necessary and proportionate, and this should be monitored. This should encourage universal design. Simplicity and consistency in evidence requirements for accessing support are also paramount. Individuals with mental disabilities, as well as people going through bereavement or experiencing anxiety or depression, should all be eligible for support with essential services which reasonably accommodate their needs. These support mechanisms should be prominent and clear in application forms and promotional materials. Lastly, mental disabilities should not provide justification for voiding contracts where this would not be in the best interests of the individual or against their wishes (whether expressed in advance or otherwise). To achieve this, new case law would have to be developed by bringing relevant text cases, or the implementation of the CRPD right to legal capacity should be spelled out in new legislation. This approach might ensure a fairer and more accessible system that better aligns with the principles of equality and recognition before the law.

Ensuring the meaningful participation of individuals with profound cognitive disabilities in consumer contracting is a complex task that necessitates adherence to the principles outlined in CRPD Articles 12 and 5. To begin with, providing information in accessible formats is a pre-requisite and bare minimum. However, as with average consumers, information is rarely enough to shift the balance of power in consumer transactions. For those with cognitive disabilities, offering personalised communication support is also crucial as it recognises that individuals may require assistance to scaffold their contractual capacity, make informed decisions and to communicate those decisions. This might come from government provisions such as personal independence payments, social workers or mental health practitioners rather than companies themselves,

Legal representation through guardianship or replacement decision-making should be approached cautiously. While it can be a valuable support mechanism for some, it must align with the individual's will and preferences, ensuring that it respects and enhances, rather than restricts, legal capacity. Replacing a persons expressed wishes in favour of a beneficent assessment of best interests (often more convenient for caregivers) should be considered inconsistent with the rights of the consumer and the citizen. Inclusive contract design and delivery – there is a difference between terms and conditions being delivered audibly through a smart speaker and a lengthy document emailed to the consumer – are key in allowing individuals to express their own interests, ensuring that contractual information is comprehensible and delivered in an accessible and appropriate medium. It should be emphasised, however, that remedying information asymmetries is not an effective way of protecting consumers, and emphasising these obligations over more interventionist approaches can often be a cop-out for law and policymakers.

Encouraging advance planning and decision-making in cases where impairments fluctuate is consistent with supported decision-making principles, but in the realm of consumer contracting poses challenges. It is not feasible to consider all the choices for products and services that might be relevant nor anticipating needs and market offerings. Advanced decision making allows individuals to express their preferences when they have the capabilities to do so, promoting autonomy while recognising that decision-making abilities may vary over time, but many with profound cognitive impairments may not have much fluctuation in capabilities. Consumer profiling may assist with determining preferences where advanced planning is not possible, or has not been undertaken in relation to a specific product or service, but depends on data on previous decision-making and, even if this were present, could ultimately be experienced as disempowering. Determining preferences based on consumer profiles has server limits and is vulnerable to manipulation by companies locking vulnerable consumers into repetitive consumer habits. In cases of profound and enduring cognitive impairments, ensuring a high level of personal and customer support which are equipped to assist individuals appears the only way to align practice with the principles of accessibility and non-discrimination. The legal and political question then arises as to the reasonableness or such accommodations when such high levels of resource are required, and the benefits in terms of empowerment are debatable.

Where scaffolded decision-making is achieved and persons with cognitive disabilities enter into contracts, both parties must have reasonable certainty that the terms will be honoured. Flexibility on the part of companies might be necessary in terms of enforcement against those with mental disability. Legal capacity should not be arbitrarily restricted based on cognitive abilities even if voiding a contract might be beneficial for a person with mental disabilities. Training initiatives in companies and for people who support decision-making contribute to creating an inclusive environment, fostering awareness about the rights and needs of individuals with cognitive disabilities. Regulatory safeguards such as unfair commercial practices and unfair contractual terms legislation, if implemented in ways that recognise the contextual vulnerabilities of individuals (as opposed to being dependent on inherent vulnerabilities), might also reinforce the CRPD's objectives, ensuring legal capacity is not denied based solely on cognitive abilities.

Collaborating with advocacy groups in developing law, policy and practice is way of making the process more inclusive, ensuring that the voices of individuals with mental disabilities are considered in decision-making processes that directly impact them. This collaborative effort serves as a bridge between policymakers, service providers and the advocacy community, fostering an environment that respects the rights and autonomy of individuals. Examining regulatory safeguards, such as unfair commercial practices and contractual terms legislation, is also essential. These safeguards should specifically address the rights and protections of individuals with the full spectrum of mental disabilities in consumer transactions, including guidelines for businesses and legal frameworks that recognise and respect their rights.

The provision of support for individuals with cognitive disabilities is often constrained by limited resources and workforce availability. While human rights, including those outlined in the CRPD, are considered fundamental and universal, their realisation may be hindered by legal limitations, competing rights and practical concerns. In determining the extent of support, the principle of proportionality is key, ensuring that any restrictions imposed are necessary to achieve a legitimate aim and are balanced against individual rights and broader societal interests. If limitations are deemed necessary, they should be implemented in the least restrictive manner possible. This may involve leveraging contributions from private companies or establishing voluntary levies to fund support services, with a focus on minimising interference with individuals' enjoyment of their rights.

The amalgamation of these recommendations seeks to strike a balance between the necessity of support mechanisms and the imperative to uphold the legal capacity of individuals with mental disabilities. By adhering to the principles of Article 12 UNCRPD, these recommendations collectively contribute to building an inclusive framework that respects the dignity and autonomy of every individual in consumer contracting processes.

14.5. From Futilitarianism to Inclusive Legal Design

Our current consumer markets, informed as they are by neoliberal ideology and a futilitarian logic in consumer relations, disproportionately impact vulnerable consumers, particularly those with mental disabilities. These practices exploit or ignore the needs of those whose cognitive, emotional or psychological functioning does not meet widespread expectations of autonomy and rational self-interest. In failing to accommodate divergent decision-making capacities, consumer markets too often create exclusion and disadvantage under the guise of neutrality and choice. But recent legal developments present a new opportunity to challenge this trajectory and re-imagine a more inclusive and resilient consumer law regime.

The DMCCA 2024 represents a moment of legal innovation that carries the potential to disrupt the longstanding assumptions underpinning the average consumer standard in UK consumer law. Through its revised vulnerability test, which explicitly includes mental health and situational distress, the Act moves away from a static view of 'inherent' vulnerability and towards a more contextual and relational understanding of consumer harm. The formal recognition that a commercial practice may be unfair if it exploits a group vulnerable due to mental health or life circumstances (such as bereavement or financial hardship) offers the basis for more expansive regulatory intervention. The explicit legislative recognition of 'mental health' as a trigger for regulatory protection is, if not transformative, then certainly evolutionary, bridging the CRPD's rights-based model and the pragmatic tools of consumer protection. It marks a moment of legal re-alignment away from a strictly paternalistic framework and towards one that, at least in principle, acknowledges the need for accessibility, support and accommodation in consumer processes. Resources are needed to properly implement these changes and realise the benefits for consumers with disabilities.

The challenge is no longer simply to prohibit unfair practices in hindsight, but to encourage the design of systems that anticipate and scaffold diverse consumer capabilities from the outset. Designing products, services and digital architectures with inclusivity in mind is no longer merely a matter of corporate ethics or social responsibility. It is fast becoming a legal imperative and a practical design challenge. Platforms and providers that implement accessibility by design (eg plain-language options, user-directed content filters, multiple modes of communication, and support for assisted decision-making) are not only safeguarding themselves against liability, but also broadening their appeal across user demographics. Universal design, in this sense, becomes both a tool for compliance and a strategy for growth and enhanced reputation.

Accommodating cognitive diversity through design has the potential to produce spill-over benefits for all consumers. Features originally developed to assist persons with mental disabilities such as simplified user interfaces, clear consent prompts, or opt-out reminders, frequently enhance usability for broader user groups, including the elderly, those in crisis or users with low digital literacy. By centring the needs of the so-called 'irrational consumer', market participants may actually arrive at more rational systems overall. Such innovations demonstrate that vulnerability is not a marginal concern, but a universal condition that may emerge in any consumer given the right circumstances.

Incorporating inclusive design principles into consumer transaction thus contributes to a regulatory model that aligns with both economic and human rights rationales. As the CRPD makes clear, the right to participate in economic and social life on an equal basis requires that supports be provided, not simply that discrimination be avoided. Re-aligning consumer protections with Article 12's vision of legal capacity means that consumers with mental disabilities must be actively supported in decision-making processes, not merely protected from unfair influence after harm has occurred. This reframing challenges the law to adopt not only protective but also enabling functions, such that persons with mental disabilities can navigate consumer environments with autonomy and confidence.

Viewed through the lens of the broader themes of disruption, innovation and re-alignment, the legal and institutional responses to the consumer harms outlined must be understood as both a critique of existing models and a constructive intervention. Digitalisation has disrupted long-standing assumptions of consumer rationality and autonomy. Surveillance capitalism and data-driven targeting, combined with algorithmic personalisation and dark pattern design, have created transactional environments that actively undermine deliberative consumer choice. As this chapter has argued, persons with mental disabilities are often on the frontline of these harms, not because of their impairments, but because of the systemic failure of consumer law to accommodate them.

To move from symbolic inclusion to substantive equality, the legal framework must be integrated with principles of inclusive and universal design, robust accessibility obligations and a commitment to co-produced standards that reflect the lived experiences of consumers with mental disabilities. Innovation in legal doctrine must be matched by innovation in design, practice and institutional culture. Without such co-ordinated re-alignment, the risk remains that the promise of consumer equality for persons with mental disabilities will be left unrealised. The futilitarian economy will persist, repackaged in the language of choice, engagement and consumer empowerment, while continuing to exclude those who do not conform to its idealised subjects. To challenge this, a shift in both legal reasoning and design thinking is required. Reasonable accommodation of cognitive and emotional diversity must be put at the centre of regulatory and commercial practice. In doing so, consumer law would not only better fulfil its human rights obligations under the CRPD, but also become a more inclusive, adaptive and future-facing field, responsive to the challenges and disruptions of the digital age for all consumers.

INDEX

A
A v National Blood Authority 46
accountability
  investment-based crowdfunding 137
  Principles of Good Regulation 250
addictive behaviour
  addictive interfaces 55, 150
  sellers targeting 288, 289
advertising
  mass advertising 9
  misleading 257
  online financial platforms 153
Advertising Standards Authority 10
agency
  digital assistants 203–204
agentic systems *See* **digital assistant for consumer contract**
Airbnb Effect 237–238, 239
Alec Lobb v Total Oil 155
algorithmic systems *See also* **digital assistant for consumer contract; digital financial technologies**
  algorithmic price-fixing 291
  deep-learning 200–201, 202
  manipulation 199, 202, 218, 291
  Quoine v B2C2 206
  smart algorithms 160
  targeting via 288
  unpredictable decision-making 200, 203–206, 207
All-Party Parliamentary Group for Consumer Affairs and Trading Standards 31
All-Party Parliamentary Group on Insurance and Financial Services 29, 35–36, 39
altcoins 185, 186
alternative dispute resolution (ADR) 271, 284
Ang v Reliantco Investments Ltd 181
arbitration, codification 8
artificial intelligence *See also* **digital assistant for consumer contract**
  adaptiveness/deep-learning 200–205, 207, 215
  consumer targeting 292
  consumer-focused applications 199
  definition of AI system 200
  financial services 150–151
  law's pacing problem 215, 219
  product liability 58, 60
  product safety 57, 60
  regulation 198–199
Ashworth, A 247
Association of British Insurers 22, 23, 28, 30, 31, 32–33, 36
Atiyah, P 8
Australia
  Insurance Contracts Act 1984 25, 37
Awrey, D et al 124
Ayres, I and Braithwaite, J 249–250, 266

B
Ball, H and Friedman, L 248
bankarisation 8–9
Bates v PO Ltd 95, 96, 97
Beale, H 21, 26, 27, 38, 217
Beeby, S 34
Bellingham, H 34
Bentham, J 8
Billy Graham Evangelistic Association v Scottish Event Campus 167
Birds, J 19
Black, J 127
blockchain technology
  cryptocurrencies 178–179, 180
  distributed structure 179
  meaning 178–179
Borrie, G 10, 12, 13, 31, 36
Borrie, G and Diamond, AL
  The Consumer, Society and the Law 4–5, 7, 10–11, 15, 16
Boston Scientific v AOK Sachsen-Anhalt Gesundheitskasse 46
Bradgate, R et al 121
brands 8
Brexit
  assimilated EU law 52, 77, 79, 83
  competition 50

consumer law, impact on 44–47
Digital Markets, Competition and Consumers Act 2024 54–56, 63
economic impact 61–62
EU Competition and Markets Authority 48
EU Consumer Protection Cooperation Regulations 48–49, 64
EU Digital Content and Services Directive 59–60, 67–68
EU General Product Safety Regulation 57–58
EU Product Liability Directive 58–59
EU Representative Actions Directive 57
EU-derived subordinate legislation 50–52
European Union (Future Relationship) Act 2020 49
European Union (Withdrawal) Act 2018 47, 51, 54
European Union (Withdrawal Agreement) Act 2020 54
EU–UK Trade and Co-Operation Agreement 49–50, 64
future re-alignment with EU 43, 44, 58, 62, 63–65
Irish, UK divide 68–69, 72, 77–86
Northern Ireland 53–54
Northern Ireland Protocol 54
post-Brexit changes to EU law 67, 69–70
post-Brexit consumer law vision 43, 60, 65
promised bonfire of EU regulations 43, 47–49, 65
Retained EU Law (Revocation and Reform) Act 2023 51–52
Retained EU Law (Revocation and Reform) Bill 2022 43, 50–51
Stormont Brake 54
Windsor Framework 53, 54

Bristol Bus Boycott 5–6
British Empire 5
British Insurance Association 23, 24
British Insurance Law Association 21, 22
Brown, G 32
Brownsword, R 38, 203, 211, 217, 240
Burton J 46
business idea theft
investment-based crowdfunding 134, 140
business-to-business transactions 6–7
good faith principle 123
business-to-consumer transactions 6–7
financial markets and services 121, 123
good faith principle 123
professional diligence 123

C

Calleary, D 70
Carnwath LJ 300
Carr, K 36
Carter v Boehm 18
Casarosa, F 297
case law
assimilated EU case law 51
English case law in Ireland 68
***caveat emptor* principle** 7, 163
cryptocurrency fraud 177, 195
Chalmers, M 8
Chambers of Commerce 7–8
Chandelor v Lopus 7
Chaum, D 178
Cherednychenko, OO 83
Chicago School of Economics 11
Christiensen, CM 135
circular economy
benefits to supplier 224, 229–230, 236
burden of proof 241
concept, generally 223–225
consumer choice 225, 229–230, 232–233, 236–241, 242
consumer dependent 237
consumer disenfranchisement 224, 225, 236–241, 242–243, 244
consumer protection 223–225, 232–244
Consumer Rights Act 232, 235, 243, 244
continual payment schemes 224
disruptive concept, as 223, 244
DMCCA 225, 232, 234–235, 241–242, 244
economic prosperity 225, 226–227, 244
economy of indebtedness 239
environmental benefit 224, 225, 226–227, 229, 230–232, 233–236, 241, 243–244
environmental claims 241
EU Circular Economy Plan 63, 231–232, 233–234
EU regulation 231–234, 241
function-focused market 228
greenwashing 225, 229, 233–236, 241, 244
leasing 224, 228, 229–232, 235–237, 239
ownership 224, 225, 228, 236–241, 242, 244
perpetual subscription cycle 224, 236, 237, 239–240
price distortion 225, 235, 236, 237–239, 242, 244
product quality 229–232, 235, 236, 243, 244

profit-orientated mindset 224, 229–232, 236, 239
re-use rates 225, 230, 231, 243
rebound effect 229–230
regulation 231–232, 234–244
Sale of Goods Act 1979 232, 235, 243, 244
service-only transactions 228
servitisation (product-as-a-service) 224–225, 227–232, 239
shortcomings 227–232, 241
social equity 225, 226, 237, 244
supply and demand 227
transparency 233
unfair commercial practices 234–235, 242–243
whole-system approach 226–227

Civil Aviation Authority 245
Civil Procedure Rules 1998 272, 273
Clarke, M 36
Clarke, R 83
codification 8
coercion
DMCCA provisions 55–56
coherentism 38, 203–204
Cole, D 21
Collins, H 96, 97, 98
Commission Recovery v Marks and Clerks LLP 273
Commonwealth 5
compensation *See also* **consumer redress, collective actions**
CMA enforcement 246
enhanced consumer measures 250, 262
competition
Appeal Tribunal, collective actions 271–272, 273–286
benefits of trade 62–63
consumer protection and 125, 128–129
consumer redress *See* consumer redress, collective actions
DMCCA provisions 54
energy supply 105
enforcement of standards 246
EU–UK Trade and Co-Operation Agreement 50
financial markets and services 111–112, 114, 115, 119, 125, 128–129
freedom not to contract 105
infringements 274
Competition Act 1998 271, 273, 276
Competition and Markets Authority (CMA)
appeals 260–261
Brexit, impact of 48–49
civil actions 251, 261–262
court consumer protection orders 252, 253–255
court enforcement orders 260
criminal prosecutions 250–251, 262
direct enforcement 245, 252, 255–261, 268–269
DMCCA, powers under 128, 170, 235, 249–269
enforcement powers 128, 170, 245, 246, 249–269, 274
FCA, alignment with 128
final breach of directions notice 259–260
final breach of undertakings notice 259, 262, 264
final infringement notices 256–257, 264
mediation, addressing breaches through 249
monetary penalties 245, 254–269, 274
online interface notices 257–258
provisional breach of directions notice 259
provisional breach of undertakings notice 258
provisional infringement notices 256
public designated enforcer, as 253–254
third parties, enforcement against 257–258
undertaking by trader 254, 258–259
consumer
algorithmic manipulation 199, 202, 218, 291
autonomy 103–105, 125, 159, 161, 198, 199, 201–202, 207–208, 210, 236–241, 242, 300, 311, 312
circular economy *See* circular economy
compensation, CMA enforcement 246
contextualised view of 91–92
contract *See* consumer contract
cryptocurrency consumers 181–187
definition 72, 73, 181
digital assistants *See* digital assistant for consumer contract
disabled *See* disability
disenfranchisement 225, 236–241, 242, 244
domicile 181
jurisdiction over, determining 181
manipulative sales tactics 294
profiling 311
reasonable expectation of 120, 121, 122, 125–126, 218
resilience 103, 105, 106
self-regulation 288, 289, 292
status, case law 181
consumer choice
circular economy 225, 229–230, 232–233, 236–241, 242
contractual capacity 301–302
digital financial technologies 55–56, 153, 159

DMCCA provisions 55–56
enhanced consumer measures 250
financial markets and services 55–56, 129, 153
freedom to contract 8, 105, 289, 298, 300, 308
neoliberal ideology 105, 287
political gesture through 297–298
Consumer Council 10
consumer credit
algorithmic credit scoring 150, 151, 160, 161, 162, 164–165, 167
digital financial technologies 159
FCA regulation 113, 115, 117
Consumer Duty
aim 119, 123, 124
breach 126–127
business-to-consumer relationships 121, 123
consumer empowerment 125, 129, 173
consumer interest prioritised 223–224
consumer protection 124–130
consumer responsibility 119, 122, 125
consumer support 119
consumer understanding 119
Duty champions 124
enforcement 120, 126
fair trade practices 121, 124, 173
firms 118, 119, 122, 124
fitness for purpose requirement 119
foreseeable harm 120
FOS, complaints to 120
good faith principle 120, 121, 122–124, 125–126, 128, 129
good outcomes, responsibility to deliver 118, 119, 121, 122, 127, 171
interpretation, problems of 127
introduction and purpose 111, 112–113, 117, 118–119
outcomes 119–120, 121
potential consumers 121
price and value outcome 119, 120, 129
Principle 119, 120
product liability 124
products and services 119
reasonable expectation of customers 120, 121, 122, 125–126
retail customers 119, 120
risk-based approach to compliance 127
rules 119–120, 149, 171–173
SMEs as retail customers 119, 123
unregulated activity, application to 119
vulnerable consumers 119–120, 125, 129, 149, 171–173, 174
consumer insurance
application forms 37
Association of British Insurers 22, 23, 28, 30, 31, 32–33, 36
British Insurance Association 23, 24
British Insurance Law Association 21, 22
Carter v Boehm 18
deliberate or reckless non-disclosure 25, 30
disclosure rule 17–25
inadvertent non-disclosure 25, 30
innocent non-disclosure 20, 25
Insurance Ombudsman Bureau 20–21, 22
intermediary, position of 30
Lambert v Co-operative Insurance 18
Marine Insurance Act 1906 18, 25, 26, 34, 38, 39
materiality test 19
Pan Atlantic v Pine Top 18
proportionality principle 20, 23–24, 25, 30
questions, insurers obliged to ask 37
reform *See* consumer insurance reform
utmost good faith 18
Consumer Insurance (Disclosure and Representations) Act 2012 *See also* **consumer insurance reform**
Bill 31–37
'burden neutral' 35
developmental stages 17–40
disclosure rule before the Act 17–21
empirical evidence backing Bill 24–25
length 39
purpose 17
reforms introduced by 37
Royal Assent 37
Special Public Bill Committee 36
consumer insurance reform *See also* **Consumer Insurance (Disclosure and Representations) Act 2012**
action group 32, 36
All-Party Parliamentary Groups 29, 31, 35–36, 39
approaches to 38–40
attempted 19–21
Australia, Insurance Contracts Act 1984 25
Bill 29–30, 31–37
building consensus for 30
EU draft directive 23–24
FOS survey 24–25
industry support for 28, 30
industry-initiated 20
Law Commission Consultation Paper 27–28, 30
Law Commission reports 17, 21–27, 38

lobbying for 28–29, 39–40
media publicity 35, 39
National Consumer Council report 19
opposition to 28, 30, 31, 32–33, 36
political support for 31–32, 33–35, 39
scoping study 25–27

consumer law
accidental contraventions 266
approaches to reform 38–40
assimilated EU law 52, 77, 79, 83
Brexit *See* Brexit
business-to-consumer relationships 121, 123
commercial practices 253; *See also* unfair commercial practices
complexity 44–45
compliance, incentivising 249–250
consumers as collective 124
contract law and 14, 216–217
criminal law as key tool 45
digital assistants for consumer contracts 199–201, 209, 214–219
disability rights 287–314
drivers of compliance 263–264
enforcement *See* enforcement 45
EU, transposition to UK 44–47
EU-derived subordinate legislation 50–52
human rights-based approach 287–314
instrumentalisation 87, 198–199
insurance *See* consumer insurance
pacing problem 215, 219
post-Brexit vision 43, 60, 65
Retained EU Law (Revocation and Reform) Act 2023 50–52
roots 16
scholarship, genesis 4–6, 9–16
social history 3–16
UK, generally 5, 45

consumer protection
aggressive commercial practices 247, 292
breach *See* enforcement
Brexit *See* Brexit
categorical protection 87, 93
circular economy 223–225, 232–244
competition and 125, 128–129
compliance, incentivising 249–250
consumers as collective 124
criminal law 246, 247–250
cross-border digital markets 48–49, 54–56
cryptocurrencies 177, 184, 192–195
digital assistants for consumer contracts 208–219
disabled consumers *See* disability
energy supply 87–89, 91, 93, 96–107
enforcement *See* enforcement
enhanced consumer measures 250, 257, 262
essential services, access to 87–89, 303–304
EU–UK Trade and Co-Operation Agreement 49–50, 64
financial markets and services 111, 112, 113, 114, 115, 117, 122–130, 173
good faith principle and 125–126
human right, as 288, 292, 298–299
investment-based crowdfunding 131, 134–139
misleading commercial practices 152–156, 247, 292
Molony Report 9–10, 11
redress *See* consumer redress, collective actions
scholarship, development 13–15
strict liability 247
transactional element, focus on 87, 88, 90, 95–96, 105
vulnerable consumers *See* consumer vulnerability

Consumer Protection Act 1987 45, 46

Consumer Protection (Amendment) Regulations 2014 44

Consumer Protection from Unfair Trading Regulations 234–235, 246

consumer redress, collective actions
carriage disputes 278–279
class members 280–281
class representatives 276–279
collective actions orders 275, 277–278
commonality test 278
Competition Appeal Tribunal 271–272, 273–286
damages 275–276, 280–281
distribution of damages 275–276, 281
eligibility condition 277–278
enforcement 250, 265, 282–286
EU Representative Actions Directive 57
Evans v Barclays Bank 279–280
funding CAT litigation 280, 281–282
genesis 274–275
group litigation orders 271, 272–273
Gutmann v Apple 282, 285
Gutmann v First MTR South Western Trains 275–276, 280, 282, 285
Kent v Apple 282
limitations 272–273, 274
Lovdahl Gormsen v Meta Platforms 285
Mastercard Inc v Merricks 275, 278, 280–281
Merricks v Mastercard Inc 275, 280–281
Neill v Sony 282

opt-in proceedings 277, 279–280
opt-out proceedings 277, 279–280, 281
Paccar v Road Haulage Association 281
potential to reshape consumer markets 282–286
Pro Sys 278
representative actions 271, 273
Roberts 285
settlements 280–281
threshold 275, 278

Consumer Rights Act 2015
circular economy, regulation 232, 235, 243, 244
collective actions regime 271, 273, 274–275
conformity provisions 74, 75, 76, 84
cryptocurrencies 192–193
definition of consumer 72, 181
definition of trader 73
digital content 59, 75, 82–83, 84, 159, 216
digital services 59, 72, 75, 82–83
duty of care 119
enforcement powers 246, 250
enhanced consumer measures 250, 257, 262, 269
EU Directives compared 82–83
generally 3, 15–16, 44, 45, 216
Irish Consumer Rights Act compared 68, 71–77
modifications 216, 218
prominence rule 156
remedies 74–75
section 64 45
smart goods 75, 216
transparence rule 156
unfair terms regime 45, 123, 156

consumer support
confusing or inaccessible interfaces 291, 294, 313
Consumer Duty 119
disabled consumers 291, 294, 310–312, 313
universal design principle 287, 288, 305, 310, 313

consumer vulnerability *See also* **disability**
addicted consumers 288, 289–290
automated decision-making 145, 160–163, 164–175, 197–206
autonomy and vulnerability 103–105, 125, 159, 161, 311, 312
biased data 146–147, 148, 149, 160, 161, 162, 164–165, 167, 174
capacity/disability 55, 100, 170–171, 172, 287–314
caveat emptor principle 163
circumstances, based on 55
class-based approach 158, 162
consumer protection 91, 96–107, 292
cryptocurrencies 177, 179, 180–181, 183, 185–195
current view of vulnerable consumers 90, 102–103, 106
definition 101–102, 157–159, 172, 293
dependency/harm 102, 105
digital assistants *See* digital assistant for consumer contract
digital vulnerability 85, 145–175, 308
discrimination 145–146, 147–148, 149, 150, 153, 161–162, 164–175
DMCCA provisions 170–171, 293–294, 312
energy justice concept 91–95, 99, 102, 103, 106–107
energy poverty 87–88, 99
energy supply 87–88, 99, 100, 101–104, 106
entrenched 101–102, 103
Equality Act 2010 149, 164–170, 174
equality principle 288, 304–307
essential services, access to 87–89, 92, 98–99, 100–104, 106–107, 303–304
EU Unfair Commercial Practices Directive 157–158, 159, 292–293
excluded consumers 102
FCA Consumer Duty 119–120, 125, 129, 149, 171–173, 174
financial markets and services 17, 117, 119–120, 125, 129, 145–148, 157–175
Fineman's vulnerability theory 101, 102, 148, 149, 158
fluctuating 102
identifying 101
inequality and intervention 100–104, 105, 107
information asymmetry 87, 133–135, 139–141, 149, 150, 160–161, 174, 202, 310–311
less favourable treatment 164
libertarian paternalism 148, 158
marginalisation and exclusion 145
OECD definition 158
power asymmetry 9, 85, 101, 152–156, 159, 174, 296, 310
PPI mis-selling scandal 162–163
predatory practices 159, 162, 172
protected characteristics 145, 153, 162, 164–174

relational contract theory 90–99, 106
servitisation model and 232–233
social 87–88, 89, 99, 293–294, 295–296
systemic 89, 94
test for 293, 312
transactional 87–88, 89, 106
UN recognition of vulnerability 158
unconscionable bargain doctrine 149, 154–156
vulnerability to product 55

consumerism
advent 8
advertising 9
bankarisation 8–9
depersonalisation 8

Consumers' Association 22, 24

contract
agent's unauthorised acts 205–206
algorithmic 209, 218
automation 197–206
business relationships 96
Collins' paradigm 96
common aim 97–99, 106
common law 216–217, 218
consumer law 14, 216–217
contractual capacity 297, 300–314
depersonalised transactions 8
digital assistants *See* digital assistant for consumer contract
energy supply *See* energy supply
essential services, for *See* essential services
freedom of 8, 105, 289, 298, 300
implied terms 96, 98, 106, 107
lack of informed consent 309
length 98
mechanical ticket machines 204
opt-out option 104–105
pay-off for both parties 98
performance obligations 98–99
power imbalance 296, 300, 301, 310
relational contract theory 90–99, 106, 123, 126
smart contracts 180
social purpose 97–98
unconscionable bargain doctrine 149, 154–156
undue influence, entered under 55–56, 217, 300, 301
unfair terms *See* unfair terms
unilateral mistakes 205
universal service obligations 97, 98
vitiating factors 217
voidable 300–302, 304, 306, 307, 308–311
vulnerable consumers *See* consumer vulnerability

Cranston, R 15, 16
Consumers and the Law 11–12
Legal Foundations of the Welfare State 12

credit scoring
algorithmic 150, 151, 160, 161, 162, 164–165, 167

***Crime, Justice and Protecting the Public* White Paper** 248

criminal law
enforcement via 246, 247–251, 262
tool in consumer law 45

cross-border digital markets
consumer protection 48–49, 54–56
EU Consumer Protection Cooperation Regulations 48–49, 64

Crothers, B 32

crowdfunding *See also* **investment-based crowdfunding**
digital technologies 147, 150, 151, 159
open access 185

cryptocurrency
administrative errors 184
altcoins 185, 186
Bitcoin 178, 182, 184, 185, 186
blockchain technology 178–179, 180
boiler room scams 189–190
ByBit hack 193
caveat emptor principle 177, 195
Coinbase 184, 193
concealment of sender and receiver's identities 178, 182, 192
consumer motivations 182–185, 192
consumer protection 177, 184, 192–195
Consumer Rights Act 2015 192–193
consumer vulnerability 177, 179, 180–181, 183, 185–195
cryptography 178–179
customer due diligence 180
decentralised nature 178, 192–193
digital financial technologies 150
Dogecoin 180
dummy websites 188
Ethereum blockchain 180
exit scamming 188, 194
FATF guidelines 179–180
FCA advice 191–192, 195
founding 178
fraud 177, 179, 180–181, 185–195
FSMA amendments 192
geographical distribution 181

global nature 192, 194
Good Samaritans 177, 193–194
hackers 193
initial coin offerings 187–188, 192
investigation, barriers to 194
liquidity 185
marketing 180–181
meaning 178–180
money laundering 179–180, 186, 191, 192
number in existence 180
NXT 184–185
OneCoin 188–189
open-source edits 178
pig butchery scams 190–191
price volatility 185, 187
privacy offered by 178, 182, 192
production 180
public-key cryptography 178
pump and dump scams 189–190
purchasing 184
red flags 188
regulation 179–180, 182, 183, 185, 186–187, 191–193, 195
regulatory gap 180
romance scams 190–191
rug pull scams 188–189
sector growth 178
service providers 179–180, 186, 193–194
smart contracts 180
software development 178
stablecoins 192
storage 179
terminology 177, 188, 191, 194
terrorist financing 179–180, 186, 191, 192
tokens 180
transactions 179–180, 184
transparency 180, 182
UK regulation 177, 186–187, 191–193, 195
virtual asset service providers 179–180
wallets 179–180, 184, 186, 191
white papers 178, 194

custobots *See* **digital assistant for consumer contract**

cybersecurity
product liability 58

D

dark patterns 199, 288, 291, 292, 294
data-driven marketing 287
data protection regulation 211
deep-learning systems 200–201, 202
deregulation
law and economics movement 11
deterrence
amoral calculators 263, 265–266
credible 265–266
enforcement as deterrent 246, 248–249, 263–269
Di Lorenzo, V 126–127
Diamond, AL 10, 13, 14
digital assistant
supply to consumer, contract for 208–209, 217–218
digital assistant for consumer contract
adaptiveness/deep-learning 200–205, 207, 212, 215
agency 203–204
agent's unauthorised acts 205–206
algorithmic contracts 209, 218
algorithmic manipulation 199, 202, 218
attribution of actions by 203–206, 212, 218
business, loss suffered by 213
choosing to deploy 204, 212
conformity 209
consumer autonomy 198, 199, 201–202, 207–208, 210
consumer law 199–201, 209, 214–219
consumer protection 208–219
consumer vulnerability 199
contract automation 197–206
contract binding, whether 202, 203–207
control 210
dark patterns 199
deactivation 209, 210, 218
design requirements 210–211, 212
development 197
disclosure of interest 218
ELI model rules 198–199, 208–214, 217–219
impact on consumer law 199–201
information to consumer 209, 212, 218
integrated digital assistants 208, 209, 216
liability 209, 213
PAIC 208
potential for fraud 199
recommender assistants 201
right of withdrawal 212–213
role 197–198
satisfactory quality 211
search assistants 201
third-party business, contract with 209
tool, treatment as 204
UK consumer law 208, 214–219

UNCITRAL Model Law 208
unilateral mistake claims 205
unpredictable decision-making 200, 203–206, 207

digital content
conformity provisions 74, 75, 76, 84
Consumer Rights Act 2015 59, 75, 82–83, 84, 159, 216
EU Digital Content and Services Directive 59–60, 67–68, 69–70, 72, 75–77, 159
Irish Consumer Rights Act 2022 72, 75–82
meaning 59, 159
personal data, supply in return for 69, 76, 84
smart goods 208–209, 216

digital financial technologies
addictive interfaces 55, 150
algorithmic/automated decision-making 145–147, 148, 149–152, 160–175
average consumer, meaning 157
banking services 150, 151, 159
behavioural pricing 152, 153
biased data 146–147, 148, 149, 150–152, 160, 161, 162, 164–165, 167, 174
comparison sites 152
consumer autonomy 159, 161
consumer credit 159
credit scoring 150, 151, 160, 161, 162, 167
crowdfunding 147, 150, 151, 159; *See also* investment-based crowdfunding
cryptoassets *See* cryptocurrency
data-gathering and processing 146–147, 149–152, 156, 161–162, 174
deepfakes 148–149
digital assistants *See* digital assistant for consumer contract 218
disadvantage, algorithmic systems creating 150–156, 174–175
discriminatory practices 145–146, 147–148, 149, 150, 159, 161–162, 164–175
DMCCA provisions 170–171
drip pricing 154
dynamic pricing 153–154
EU Digital Market strategy 159
EU Digital Services Act 151
EU Unfair Commercial Practices Directive 157–158, 159
EU Unfair Terms Directive 157
fairness 148, 149–152, 154, 156, 167, 173, 174
fake and misleading online reviews 56, 69, 78–82, 85, 154
FCA Consumer Duty 149, 171–174
freedom of choice 55–56, 153, 159
generally 129
generative AI 149
herding effects 149
human error 145, 146, 160, 162
information asymmetry 149, 150, 160–161
information verification 151
innovative and disruptive effects 149
insurance providers 167
investment advice 147, 150–152, 156
limitations of AI tools 147, 148–149, 175
locking-in strategies 153–154
machine learning analysis 145–147, 156, 160, 161, 164, 165
marginalisation and exclusion 145, 148
misleading commercial practices 152–156, 247, 292
online advertising 153, 160
online platforms 152–156, 160
peer-to-peer lending 139, 145, 150–151, 152, 159
pension management 152, 167
performance analysis 146
portfolio allocation 147
power imbalance 152–156, 159
predatory practices 159, 162, 172
pricing 152, 153–154, 160
rapid expansion 145
risk scoring 148–149, 164–165
robo-advising 150, 151–152
savings plans 152
standardised forms of agreement 156
technology-supported asset classes 147
training datasets 147, 162, 164, 165
transparency 146, 147, 149–152, 156, 157, 160, 173
unconscionable bargain doctrine 149, 154–156
unfair terms 156, 173
vulnerable consumers 145–149, 157–175
wealth advice and management 150–151

digital markets
behavioural pricing 152, 153
comparison sites 152
cross-border consumer protection 48–49
digital vulnerability 85
digitalisation generally 67–68, 83, 84–85
EU Consumer Protection Cooperation Regulations 48–49
EU Digital Market strategy 82, 83, 159
EU Omnibus Directive 67–68, 69–70, 72, 77–82

EU Sale of Goods Directive 67–68, 69–70, 216
EU–UK Trade and Co-Operation Agreement 50, 64
fake and misleading online reviews 56, 69, 78–82, 85, 154
Financial Conduct Authority 129
financial technologies *See* digital financial technologies
Irish Consumer Rights Act 2022 72, 75–82
monopolistic 288, 292
personal data, supply in return for 69, 76, 84
transparency 52, 56, 69
unfair terms 52

Digital Markets, Competition and Consumers Act 2024
addictive interfaces 55
ADR system 284
aim 170
circular economy, regulation 225, 232, 234–235, 241–242, 244
circumstances, vulnerability based on 55
CMA powers 128, 170, 245, 246, 249–269
coercion, harassment or undue influence 55–56
commercial practices 253
court consumer protection orders 252, 253–255
digital assistants 218
direct enforcement 245, 252, 255–261
drip pricing 54–55
enforcement powers 85, 245, 246, 247, 252–269
EU law compared 79–82, 85–86
fake and misleading online reviews 56, 69, 78–82, 85
freedom of choice 55–56
generally 54–56, 63, 68, 85–86
infringements 253, 261
Irish Consumer Rights Act compared 68, 79–82
monetary penalties 245, 254–269
professional diligence principle 123
Royal Assent 252
subscription traps 56, 288
transparency 56
unfair commercial practices 121, 293–294
vulnerability test 293, 312
vulnerability to product 55
vulnerable consumer protection 170–171, 293–294, 312

digital platforms *See* **online platforms**

digital services
Consumer Rights Act 2015 59, 72, 75, 82–83, 84–85
definition 76
EU Digital Content and Services Directive 59–60, 67–68, 69–70, 75–77, 216
EU Digital Services Act 151
Irish Consumer Rights Act 2022 75–82
meaning 59
personal data, supply in return for 69, 76, 84
Product Regulation and Metrology Act 2025 63–64
UK regulation 84–86

Director General of Fair Trading v First National Bank 126

disability *See also* **consumer vulnerability**
addiction 288, 289–290
consumer law and disability rights 288–314
consumer profiling 311
consumer vulnerability 55, 170–171, 172, 287–288, 291–292, 293–294, 308
contractual capacity 297, 300–314
definition 290, 295, 296
digital vulnerability 85, 145–175, 308
DMCCA provisions 293–294, 312
equal recognition principle 288, 304–307, 309, 310, 313
essential services contracts 303–304, 307–312
EU consumer law 297
futilitarian economics 287–294, 312–314
human rights in the UK 296–297
irrational consumption habits 289–291
Mental Capacity Act 301, 302, 304–305, 306
Nyusti v Hungary 299
pre-contractual information 297, 308, 310–311
progressive realisation of rights 307
social model of 293–294, 295–296
substitute decision-makers 302, 306–307, 310–311
supported decision-making 302–305, 307–312, 313
UN CRPD 148, 287, 293, 294–302, 304–314
universal design principle 287, 288, 305, 310, 313
voidable contracts 300–302, 304, 306, 307, 308–311

discrimination
behavioural pricing 152, 153
Billy Graham Evangelistic Association v Scottish Event Campus 167

digital financial technologies 145–146, 147–148, 149, 150, 153, 159, 161–162, 164–170, 174
direct and indirect 167
disability, against *See* disability
Equality Act 2010 149, 164–170, 174
Hounga v Allen 165
insurance providers 167
lending activities 167
less favourable treatment 164
mental health conditions 55, 170–171, 172
pension schemes 152, 167
protected characteristics 145, 153, 162, 164–173
remedies 167, 168–170
vulnerable consumer protection 149, 150, 164–175

dispute resolution
merchant class 8, 9
unequal bargaining power 9

disruption, forms of
circular economy 223, 244
investment-based crowdfunding 135–136
technologies 199, 287, 313

Dobbin, J 32
Doherty, J 86
Douglas-Home, A 5
drip pricing 54–55, 154
Dunhill v Burgin 301
duress, contract law 217

duty of care
Consumer Rights Act 2015 119

E

e-commerce *See* **digital markets**
Ecodesign for Energy-Related Products and Energy Information Regulations 2021 63, 231–232
electronic agent *See* **digital assistant for consumer contract**
Electronic Money Regulations 2011 119

emerging technology
product liability 60

energy supply
allocation, system governing 101
autonomy and vulnerability 103–105
business commodity, as 100
changing suppliers 98
competitive market 105
consumer protection 91, 96–107
consumer resilience 104, 105, 106
contract, generally 90–99
contract length 98
contract performance obligations 98–99
contract renewal 98
contractual relations 91, 98, 104–105, 106
decentralisation and democratisation 94–95, 103–104
dependence 105
distribution 100–104
energy justice concept 91–95, 99, 102, 103, 106–107
energy poverty 87–88, 99
energy transition impacting 88, 90, 91, 99, 103–104, 105, 106
freedom of contract 105
fundamental social significance 90–91, 95–96, 97–98, 100, 106
global nature of markets 93
hierarchical and exclusive systems 93–94
inequality and intervention 91, 99, 100–104, 105, 106, 107
market engagement 104–105
monopolies 105
Norweb v Dixon 91
power asymmetry 101, 102
pricing 101, 102, 105
private sector 90–91, 100
public policy 95, 98–99, 100
relational contract theory 90–99, 106
state role 100
universal service obligations 97, 98
vulnerable consumers 87–88, 99, 100–104, 106–107
whole-system approach 92–94, 106

enforcement
accidental consumer law contraventions 266
amoral calculators 263, 265–266
appeals 260–261
civil 246, 250–251, 252, 261–262
clarifying laws 246
CMA powers 128, 170, 245, 246, 249–269, 274
commercial practices 253
compensation 246, 250
competition standards 246
compliance, incentivising 249–250
consumer law, generally 245
consumer redress measures 250, 265, 271–286
Consumer Rights Act powers 246, 250
cost-benefit calculation 248, 263–264
costs of enforcement 249–250, 264
court consumer protection orders 252, 253–255
court enforcement orders 260
criminal prosecution 246, 247–251, 262

culpability, determining 265, 266
deterrent, as 246, 248–249, 263–269
direct 245, 252, 255–261, 268–269
DMCCA powers 85, 245, 246, 247, 252–269
DMCCA relevant infringements 253, 261
enforcement notices 246
enhanced consumer measures 250, 257, 262, 269
final breach of directions notice 259–260
final breach of undertakings notice 259, 262, 264
final infringement notices 256–257, 264
interim orders 254
length of procedure 251–252, 254
Macrory Report 262
mediation 249
misleading advertising 257
monetary penalties 245, 254–269, 274
online interface notices 257–258
Penrose Report 251
precedent with market-wide implications 246
Principles of Good Regulation 250
proportionality principle 265
provisional breach of directions notice 259
provisional breach of undertakings notice 258
provisional infringement notices 256
public designated enforcers 253–254
publication of infringement notices 257
Reforming Competition and Consumer Policy White Paper 251–252, 254
Regulatory Enforcement and Sanctions Act 262
sector enforcers 245
seriousness of infringement 265
strict liability 247
systemic market failures, where 246
third parties, against 257–258
Trading Standards 245, 246, 249, 253–254, 261, 264
undertaking by trader 254, 258–259
unfair trading 252
weaknesses of system 245, 246–252, 261
enhanced consumer measures (ECMs) 250, 257, 262, 269
enshittification 287, 291
Enterprise Act 2002 246, 250
Enterprise Investment Scheme 132
environmental protection
circular economy *See* circular economy
greenwashing 225, 229, 233–236, 241, 244
Equality Act 2010
Code of Practice 170
enforcement 169–170
injury to feelings 169
Jivraj v Hashwani 168–169
less favourable treatment 164
online platforms/service providers 170, 174
Patel v Mirza 168
prohibited conduct 166
remedy for breach 167, 168–170
vulnerable consumer protection 149, 164–170, 174
essential services *See also* **energy supply**
business commodity, as 100
changing suppliers 98
common aim of contract for 97–99
consumer protection 91, 96–107
consumer resilience 104, 105, 106
contract length 98
contract performance obligations 98–99
contract renewal 98
dependence 105
disabled consumers 303–304, 307–312
disconnection 98
freedom of contract 105, 308
inequality and intervention 100–104, 105, 106, 107
monopolies 105
private sector 100
public policy 95, 98–99, 100
relational contract theory 90–99, 106
social purpose 97–98, 100
universal service obligations 97, 98
vulnerable consumers 87–89, 92, 99, 100–104, 106–107, 303–304
Etherton, Lord 284
European Law Institute (ELI)
digital assistant model rules 198–199, 208–214, 217–219
European Union
Anti-Money Laundering Directive 186, 191
Brexit *See* Brexit
catalyst for legal change 3
Circular Economy Plan 63
Competition and Markets Authority 48
Consumer Protection Cooperation Regulations 48–49, 64
Digital Content and Services Directive 59–60, 67–68, 69–70, 72, 75–77, 82–83, 159, 216
Digital Market strategy 82, 83, 159
Digital Services Act 151
draft insurance directive 23–24

Ecodesign Regulation 231–232
Empowering Consumers Directive 233–234, 241
EU-derived subordinate legislation 50–52
EU–UK Trade and Co-Operation Agreement 49–50, 64
future re-alignment with 43, 44, 58, 62, 63–65
General Product Safety Regulation 57–58
greenwashing, regulation 233–235
impact of EU consumer law 44–47
law, transposition to UK law 44–47
Markets in Financial Instruments Directive 139
maximum harmonisation directives 83
Modernisation Directive 56
New Deal for Consumers 67
Omnibus Directive 67–68, 69–70, 72, 77–83, 216
Online Dispute Resolution Regulation 47
Product Liability Directive 45–47, 58–59
RAPEX 64
Renewable Energy Directive 94
Representative Actions Directive 57
Sale of Goods Directive 67–68, 69–70, 71, 72, 73, 77, 82–83, 216
UK, assimilated EU law 52, 77, 79, 83
UK consumer law, divergence 83
Unfair Commercial Practices Directive 45, 54–56, 78–79, 83, 157–158, 159, 233–234, 292–293
Unfair Contract Terms Directive 45, 51–52, 71, 77, 83

European Union (Future Relationship) Act 2020 49
European Union (Withdrawal) Act 2018 47, 51, 54
European Union (Withdrawal Agreement) Act 2020 54
Evans, J 36
Evans v Barclays Bank 279–280

F

fake and misleading online reviews
Digital Markets, Competition and Consumers Act 56, 69, 78–82
EU Omnibus Directive 78–80
generally 78, 85, 154
Irish Consumer Rights Act 78–82
Farrand, J 20–21
feminism 6
Ferran, E 112, 115
finance
availability 8–9
credit facilities 9
digital technologies *See* digital financial technologies
hire purchase 9
investment-based crowdfunding *See* investment-based crowdfunding
Financial Action Task Force
cryptocurrency guidelines 179–180
Financial Conduct Authority (FCA) 245
breach of FCA rules 116, 126–127
CMA, alignment with 128
common law principles, incorporation 112
competition objective 111–112, 114, 115, 125, 128–129
consumer choice 129
consumer credit regulation 113, 115, 117
Consumer Duty *See* Consumer Duty
consumer empowerment 117, 125, 129, 173
consumer protection objective 111, 112, 113, 114, 115, 117, 122–130
consumer vulnerability 117, 119–120, 125, 129, 171–173, 174
creation and operational framework 113
cryptocurrency regulation 186, 191–192
digital market 129
disclosure obligations 136–141
discretion 115
enforcement measures 116
financial promotion rules 138–139, 140
Handbook 115, 119, 137
High Level Principles 111, 115, 116, 121, 122, 127, 129, 171
integrity objective 111, 114, 126
international competitiveness and growth objective 111, 114
investment-based crowdfunding regulation *See* investment-based crowdfunding
objectives 111–112, 113–115, 128, 129
Occasional Papers 116
policy 113, 116–118, 129
powers 111, 116
Principles of Good Regulation 250
proportionate approach 115, 117, 129, 250
regulatory/supervisory framework 113, 115–116
research and reform areas 117
risk analysis by 114, 120, 122
risk warning rules 139
role 111–112, 114–116
rules of conduct, issue 111, 115–116
Senior Managers and Certification Regime 117, 122, 127, 129
SMEs as retail customers 119, 123
statutory mandate 113
strategic objective 111, 114, 129

thematic review 116
Treating Customers Fairly Initiative 116, 122, 127
financial markets and services
AI in provision 150–151
algorithmic systems *See* digital financial technologies
automated decision-making 145–147, 148, 149–152, 160–163
breach of Consumer Duty 126–127
breach of FCA rules 116, 126–127
commission payments 112
common law principles, incorporation 112
competition 111–112, 114, 115, 119, 125, 128–129
consumer behavioural factors, consideration 116
consumer capability 114, 117, 129
consumer care 114
consumer choice 129
consumer credit 113, 115, 117
Consumer Duty *See* Consumer Duty
consumer empowerment 117, 125, 129, 173
consumer motivation 116
consumer protection 111, 112, 113, 114, 115, 117, 122–130
consumer responsibility 112, 113, 119, 122, 125
consumer support 119
consumer understanding 119
consumer vulnerability 17, 119–120, 125, 145–148, 157–175
crowdfunding *See* investment-based crowdfunding
cryptoassets *See* cryptocurrency
digital *See* digital financial technologies
discrimination 145–146, 147–148, 149, 150, 153, 159, 161–162, 164–170
duty of care 218–219
dynamic pricing 153–154
ease of market entry 114
Electronic Money Regulations 119
fair trade practices, Consumer Duty 121
FCA *See* Financial Conduct Authority
fitness for purpose requirement 119
foreseeable harm 120
freedom of choice 55–56, 153
good faith principle 112, 120, 121, 122–124, 125–126, 128, 129
good outcomes, responsibility to deliver 118, 119, 121, 122, 127, 171
harmful innovations or products 112, 117–118
High Level Principles 111, 115, 116, 121, 122, 127, 129
information and advice 114, 147
initial public offerings 132
innovation 114
locking-in strategies 153–154
marginalisation and exclusion from 145
misleading commercial practices 152–156, 292
non-professional economic players 134
online 118
Payment Services Regulations 119
potential consumers 121
price and value 119, 120, 129
private suppliers of public goods 135
public intervention 134–135
reasonable expectation of customers 120, 121, 122, 125–126
regulation generally 111–112
risk analysis 114, 120, 122, 164–165
rules of conduct 111, 115–116
SMEs as retail customers 119, 123
unconscionable bargain doctrine 149, 154–156
unregulated activity 119
wealth advice and management 150
Financial Ombudsman Service (FOS) 22, 24–25, 38
complaints to 120
cryptocurrencies not covered 191
Financial Services Authority (FSA) 22, 23, 38
Financial Services Compensation Scheme
cryptocurrencies not covered 191
Financial Services and Markets Act 2000 111, 113, 136
cryptocurrencies 192
Financial Services and Markets Act 2023 111
Fineman, M
vulnerability theory 101, 102, 148, 149, 158
fintech *See* **digital financial technologies**
Fraser J 95, 96, 97
fraud
algorithmic manipulation 199, 202, 218
cryptocurrency fraud 177, 179, 180–181, 185–195
dark currencies 199
digital assistants 199
Freedom of Information Act 2000 23, 93
Friedan, B
The Feminist Mystique 6
fulfilment services provider 58
futilitarian economics 287–294, 312–314
meaning 291

G
Gardiner v Gray 7
Gilad, S 127
Giliker, P 159
Girobank 9
Gobert, J and Punch, M 248
good faith principle
business-to-business contracts 123
commercial relationships 123
consumer insurance 18
consumer protection 125–126
financial services 112, 120, 121, 122–124, 125–126, 128, 129
relational contracts 123, 126
unfair commercial practices 45
unfair contract terms 123
Yam Seng v ITC Ltd 126
Green Prosperity Plan 62
greenwashing 49
circular economy 225, 229, 233–236, 241, 244
transparency 233–234
group litigation order 271, 272–273
Gunningham, N 249
Gutmann v Apple 282, 285
Gutmann v First MTR South Western Trains 275–276, 280, 285

H
Hale LJ 301
harassment
DMCCA provisions 55–56
Härdle, WK et al 179
Harman, H 31–32
Harris, M 20, 21
Harvey, BW 12–13, 15, 16
Helberger, N et al 85, 158–159, 308
Henes, J 24
Hertzell, D 27, 36
hire purchase 9, 10
Hirst, P 94
Hoban, M 34
Hodges, C 266
Hodgson, Lord 36, 37
Hollinrake, K 255–256
Hong Kong
consumer insurance law 37
Hounga v Allen 165
Houy, S et al 179
Howells, G 14, 15
human rights
consumer protection as 288, 292, 298–299
progressive realisation 307
re-aligning consumer law with 287–314
UN CRPD 148, 293
Hunt, R 20–21

I
Ignatova, R 189
Imperial Loan v Stone 301
implied terms
contracts 96, 98, 106, 107
Irish Consumer Rights Act 73, 77
incorporation rules
transparency 52
individualism/collectivism balance 4, 15
Industrial Revolution 7, 12
information asymmetry
consumer vulnerability 87, 133–135, 139–141, 149, 150, 160–161, 174
digital assistants for consumer contracts 202
digital financial technologies 149, 150, 160–161
investment-based crowdfunding 133–135, 138, 139–141
lack of informed consent 309
Information Commissioner 245
insurance
business, non-disclosure rule 26, 27
consumer *See* consumer insurance
Insurance Ombudsman Bureau (IOB) 20–21, 22
intellectual property
investment-based crowdfunding 140
International Covenant on Civil and Political Rights 240
International Covenant on Economic, Social and Cultural Rights 240
international trade, development 7
internet
addictive interfaces 55, 150
cryptocurrencies *See* cryptocurrency
digital assistants *See* digital assistant for consumer contract
Good Samaritans 177, 193–194
hackers 193
investment-based crowdfunding *See* investment-based crowdfunding
internet of things 57, 58
consumer vulnerability 288, 292
investment advice
algorithmic systems 150–152
investment-based crowdfunding *See also* **digital financial technologies**
accessibility as financing option 132–133, 141
accountability 137, 140

agency problem 131, 133–134, 139–141
algorithmic systems 150
appropriateness test 137
assessment process 138
authorisation 136, 137
business secrets/intellectual property 134, 140
communications with potential investors 137
conflicts of interest 138
consumer protection 131, 134–139
cost–benefit analysis 140–141
costs of compliance 139–141, 142
definition 132
digital platforms 132–133
disclosure obligations 133–135, 136–141
disruptive nature 135–136
equity dilution 137
fairness 138
FCA Portfolio Strategy Letter 138
FCA regulation 131, 132, 136–142
financial promotions 136–137, 138–139, 140
information asymmetry 133, 134–135, 138, 139–141
intellectual property rights infringement 134, 140
investor education 136
non-professional economic players 134
non-readily realisable security 136
recipients, analysis/due diligence 138
records of assessment process 138
regulatory challenges 131
risk warnings 136, 138–141
startup firms 132, 141
transparency 131, 136, 137, 138, 140, 142

Ireland
Brexit and 53–54, 68–69, 72
Consumer Credit Act 1995 71
consumer law 14, 37
Consumer Protection Act 2007 71, 78, 79
Consumer Rights Act *See* Irish Consumer Rights Act 2022
English case law 68
English law and 68
Northern Ireland Protocol 54
Sale of Goods and Supply of Services Act 1980 70
UK consumer law, divergence 68, 71–82, 83

Irish Consumer Rights Act 2022
background 70–72
complexity 77
conformity provisions 73–75, 76, 84
contract termination 77
definitions tied to EU standard 72–75
digital supply and services 72, 75–77
EU Omnibus Directive 72, 77–82
fake online reviews 78–82
goods with digital elements 77
implied terms 73, 77
limitation period 77
remedies 74–75, 76–77
UK consumer law compared 68, 71–82, 83
withholding payment 77

irrational consumer *See* **disability**

J

Jivraj v Hashwani 168–169
Johnson, B 50
Jones v Bright 7
Jones v Morgan 155

K

Kagan, R and Scholz, J 266
Kelly, C 83
Kent v Apple 282

L

labelling
EU–UK Trade and Co-Operation Agreement 50
Labour movement 5
Labour Party 12
laissez-faire ideology 7
Lambert v Co-operative Insurance 18
law and economics movement 11, 13
law reform
achieving 38–40
coherentism 38, 203–204
regulatory interventionism 38, 39, 203
Laws LJ 300
Lawton LJ 18
leasing
circular economy schemes 224, 228, 229–232, 235–237, 239
Leggatt LJ 95, 96, 98, 128
legislation
developmental stages 17–40
liability
A v National Blood Authority 46
artificial intelligence 58, 60
Boston Scientific v AOK Sachsen-Anhalt Gesundheitskasse 46
civil 246, 250–251
consumer protection, strict liability 247
criminal 246, 247–250

cybersecurity 58
defect, interpretation 46–47
digital assistant for consumer contract 209, 213
emerging technology 60
EU Product Liability Directive 45–47, 58–59
fulfilment services providers 58
internet of things 58
legitimate expectations 46
long-stop limitation period 58
online platforms 58
software 58, 59, 60
libertarian paternalism 148, 158
Lloyds v Google 273, 284, 285
Longmore LJ 36
Lovdahl Gormsen v Meta Platforms 285
Lowe, R and Woodroffe, G 13–15, 16

M
Macmillan, H 5
MacNeil, I 95
Macrory, D 247
Macrory Report 262
McVicar, I 32
Major, J 15
Maker, Y et al 308
Mance LJ 206
Marine Insurance Act 1906 18, 25, 26, 34, 38, 39
market
digital *See* digital markets
impersonalisation 8
political interference 292
surveillance, EU–UK Agreement 50
marking
EU CE marking 63
EU–UK Trade and Co-Operation Agreement 50
Mastercard Inc v Merricks 275, 278
May, T 63
medicinal products
EU–UK Trade and Co-Operation Agreement 50
mental capacity *See* **disability**
Mental Capacity Act 2005 301, 302, 304–305, 306
mercantile law 3, 6–9
Merchandise Marks Act 1887 10
merchant class 7–9
mergers and amalgamations 8
Merkin, R 25, 37
Merricks v Mastercard Inc 275
Micklitz, H-W 3
Micklitz, H-W and Twigg-Flesner, C 67–68
misrepresentation
contract law 217
mobile roaming services
EU–UK Trade and Co-Operation Agreement 50
***Modernising Consumer Markets* Green Paper** 251
Molony Report 9–10, 11
money laundering
cryptocurrencies 179–180, 186, 191, 192
EU Directive 186, 191
Money Laundering, Terrorist Financing and Transfer of Funds (Information on the Payer) Regulations 2017 186, 191, 192
monopolistic markets 105, 288, 292
Moreno-Lax, V and Vavoula, N 103
Moulton v Camroux 301
Multiservice Bookbinding Ltd v Marden 155

N
National Consumer Council 24
National Federation of Consumer Groups 10, 24
National Health Service 5
Neill v Sony 282
neoliberal ideology 11–12, 287, 289, 312
consumer choice 105, 287
energy market 100, 107
New Zealand
Contracts of Insurance Act 2024 37
Newby LJ 29–30
Norweb v Dixon 91
Nyusti v Hungary 299

O
Office of Fair Trading v Abbey National Plc 45
Ogus, A 263, 264
online dispute resolution
EU Regulation 47
online platforms
data-driven marketing 287
data-gathering and processing 69, 76, 84, 146–147, 149–152, 156, 161–162, 174
digital financial technologies 152–156
enshittification 287, 291
investment-based crowdfunding 132–133
online interface notices 257–258
power imbalance 152–156, 159, 296, 300
product liability 58
product safety 58
surveillance capitalism 287, 289, 313

Organisation for Economic Co-operation and Development (OECD)
consumer vulnerability, definition 158
ownership
dignity and empowerment 225, 236–241, 242, 244
servitisation model 224, 225, 228, 236–241, 244
Universal Declaration of Human Rights 240

P
Paccar v Road Haulage Association 281
Pan Atlantic v Pine Top 18
Patel v Mirza 168
payment processing
algorithmic 150
payment protection insurance (PPI)
mis-selling 162–163
Payment Services Regulations 2017 119
Payward Inc v Chechetkin 181
peer-to-peer lending
digital technologies 139, 145, 150–151, 152, 159
Penrose Report 251
Perpetuities and Accumulations Act 2009 29
postal services
EU–UK Agreement 50
Powell, E 6, 12
predatory practices
digital financial technologies 159, 162, 172
price indication
EU Omnibus Directive 69
pricing
algorithmic price-fixing 291
behavioural pricing 152, 153
digital financial platforms 152, 153–154, 160
drip pricing 54–55, 154
dynamic pricing 153–154
energy supply 101, 102, 105
product liability *See* **liability**
Product Regulation and Metrology Act 2025 58, 59, 63–64
product safety
artificial intelligence 57, 60
data protection by design and default 211
EU General Product Safety Regulation 57–58
EU–UK Trade and Co-Operation Agreement 50, 64
fulfilment services providers 58
internet of things 57
online platforms 58
Product Regulation and Metrology Act 2025 58, 59, 63–64
Product Safety Review 58, 59
software 58, 60
product-service-systems *See* **circular economy**
professional diligence principle
EU law 45

Q
Quoine v B2C2 206

R
Race Relations Act 1968 6
Ramsay, I 3, 4, 15, 125, 263
Rapid Exchange of Information System (RAPEX) 64
recycling *See* **circular economy**
Rees-Mogg, J 50
***Reforming Competition and Consumer Policy* White Paper** 251–252, 254
regional specialisation 7
Regulatory Enforcement and Sanctions Act 2008 262
regulatory interventionism 38, 39, 203
Reich, N 99
relational contract theory 90–99, 106
good faith principle 123, 126
representative action
Commission Recovery v Marks and Clerks LLP 273
declaratory actions 273
EU Directive 57
generally 271, 273
Lloyds v Google 273, 284, 285
same interest 273
Restrictive Trade Practices Act 1956 10
Retained EU Law (Revocation and Reform) Act 2023 51–52
Retained EU Law (Revocation and Reform) Bill 2022 43, 50–51
Riefa, C 14, 159
Rifkin, J 239
Robbins Report 6, 12
Roethe, T 3, 4, 15
Rothstein J 278
Rozenberg, J 33

S
Saintier, S 129
Sale of Goods Act 1893 8, 10, 14–15, 68, 70
Sale of Goods Act 1979 13, 14, 45
circular economy, regulation 232, 235, 243, 244

Sales J 300
Sanders, D 37
Sassoon, Lord 36
Scott, C 247
Seed Enterprise Investment Scheme 132
seller, bargaining power 9, 85, 101, 174
servitisation model *See* **circular economy**
Shiffrin, SV 155
Siciliani, P, Riefa, C and Gamper, H 121
Sinclair, P and Taylor, A 192
Singapore
consumer insurance law 37
Slade, L 20
smart goods
Consumer Rights Act 2015 75, 216
EU 2019 Directives 69–70
integrated digital assistants 208–209, 216
regulatory gap 75, 216
Smith J 43
software
product liability 58, 59, 60
product safety 58, 60
Sohm, R 238
Southall, E and Taylor, M 178
stablecoins 192
Stahel, WR 226
standardisation 7, 8
Starling, N 33
Stormont Brake 54
subscription model *See* **circular economy**
subscription trap 56, 288
surveillance capitalism 287, 289, 313
Sustainability Labelling and Disclosure of Sustainability-Related Financial Information Instrument 234, 235
sustainability *See* **circular economy**

T
terrorist financing, cryptocurrencies 179–180, 186, 191, 192
Thatcher, M 4, 11, 15
Third Parties (Rights Against Insurers) Act 2010 29
token, cryptocurrency 180
Toulson, R 21
trader, definition 72–73
Trading Standards
consumer law enforcement 245, 246, 261, 264
public designated enforcer, as 253–254
Trading Standards Institute (TSI) 31, 37
transparency
common law incorporation rules 52
Consumer Rights Act 2015 156
cryptocurrencies 180, 182
digital financial technologies 146, 147, 149–152, 156, 157, 160, 173
digital markets 52, 56, 69
greenwashing 233–234
Gutmann v First MTR South Western Trains 285
investment-based crowdfunding 131, 136, 137, 138, 140, 142
PPI mis-selling scandal 163
pre-contractual information 297, 308, 309
Principles of Good Regulation 250
unfair contract terms 51–52, 156
transport networks 7
Trump, D 292
Twigg-Flesner, C 122, 136
Tyrie, Lord 250–251, 261

U
UNCITRAL
Model Law on Automated Contracting 208
unconscionable bargain doctrine 149, 154–156
Alec Lobb v Total Oil 155
Jones v Morgan 155
Multiservice Bookbinding Ltd v Marden 155
undue influence
contract law 55–56, 217, 300, 301
Digital Markets, Competition and Consumers Act 2024 55–56
unfair commercial practices
circular economy 234–235, 242–243
consumer redress *See* consumer redress, collective actions
digital technologies 167, 173, 174
DMCCA provisions 121, 293–294
duress 217
EU Directive 45, 54–56, 78–79, 83, 157–158, 159, 233, 292–293
EU Omnibus Directive 69, 77–82
generally 300
good faith 45, 123
greenwashing 233, 234–235
misrepresentation 217
power imbalance 296, 300, 301, 310
private rights of redress 44
professional diligence 45, 123
UK connection 253
undue influence 55–56, 217, 300, 301
vulnerable consumer standard 157–158, 173
Unfair Contract Terms Act 1977 44
unfair terms
common law incorporation rules 52
Consumer Rights Act 2015 45, 123

digital markets 52
Director General of Fair Trading v First National Bank Plc 126
EU Omnibus Directive 69
EU Unfair Terms Directive 45, 51–52, 83, 157
prominence rule 156
sham negotiations 44
transparency 51–52, 156
Unfair Terms in Consumer Contracts Regulations 1999 44

unfair trading, penalty regime 252

United Nations Convention on the Rights of Persons with Disabilities (CRPD) 148, 287, 293, 294–300
definition of disability 290, 295, 296
equal recognition principle 288, 304–307, 309, 310, 313
re-aligning consumer law with 287–314
social model of disability 293–294, 295–296
state obligations 288, 295–296, 298–299, 305
UK law 300

Universal Declaration of Human Rights 240

universal design principle 287, 288, 305, 310, 313

V

Varney, E 297

venture capitalism 137

Vicary-Smith, P 32

virtual asset service providers (VASPs) 179–180

vulnerable consumers *See* **consumer vulnerability**

W

Wachter, S et al 146

Weatherall, S 14, 15

weights and measures standardisation 7

welfare state 5, 12

Wells, C 248

Wendehorst, C 208

Whittle, J 36, 37

Willett, C 14

Wilson, H 5, 11

Windsor Framework 53, 54

World Economic Forum 240

Worsfold, D 29

Y

Yam Seng v ITC Ltd 95, 96, 126, 128

www.ingramcontent.com/pod-product-compliance
Ingram Content Group UK Ltd.
Pitfield, Milton Keynes, MK11 3LW, UK
UKHW020237290926
15470UKWH00002B/582

9 781509 975556